AF361264

THE BYZANTINE PLATONISTS, 284–1453

THE BYZANTINE PLATONISTS, 284–1453

Edited by Frederick Lauritzen
and Sarah Klitenic Wear

FRANCISCAN UNIVERSITY PRESS

Franciscan University Press
1235 University Boulevard
Steubenville, OH 43952
740-283-3771

Distributed by:
The Catholic University of America Press
c/o HFS
P.O. Box 50370
Baltimore, MD 21211
800-537-5487

Library of Congress Cataloging-in-Publication Data
available from the Library of Congress

ISBN 978-1-7366561-0-5

Cover Image: Bibliothèque Nationale de France, Paris, Par. Gr. 1242
(Theological works of John VI Kantakuzenos) f. 92 v, Transfiguration,
1370–1375.
Printed in the United States of America.

Contents

Foreword

In the splendid hall of the Alexandrian pictorial cycle, located in the seat of the Scuola Grande di San Marco, Giovanni Bellini's painting can be found. The painting depicts San Marco (the saint of Venice) preaching in Alexandria of Egypt. The scene is depicted in a large square with a vast and strange building in the background: San Marco preaches in front of the mythical Alexandrian library. There are no doubts regarding the topic of our patron saint's proclamations in that setting, at that moment and to that public (pagans at the time but represented as Muslims in Bellini's painting). There is no place for doubt since the enormous painting is preceded, on one side, by a smaller canvas that shows San Marco in the act of healing the shoemaker Aniano's hand, and it is followed on the other side by a work in which our patron saint is performing the baptism of the miraculous, that is, the healing of the soul.

The thematic line of the virtues is even more impressive. It was conceived by the Dominican Francesco Colonna, according to the Thomistic doctrine, and it was executed toward the end of the fifteenth century on the astonishing facade of our Scuola, impressing even Leonardo da Vinci. The iconography of the theological and cardinal virtues represents spiritual and corporal charity works, from which the most significant work, *La porta di Cristo* (*The Gate of Christ*), is the personification of Charity. Therefore it is not in giving or doing that we remain in virtue, but in being.

This original fifteenth-century setting demonstrates how Venice was, many centuries later, still Byzantine and Platonic both fundamentally and in its production of culture and civilization, welcoming the truth about the existence of the soul, the inseparable metaphysical and physical reality of an individual, and the tendency to mediate between the human and the divine (characteristic of Greek culture and a deep manifestation of Platonism). It is understood as the Christian encounter between transcendence and man, which is a reason for spirituality to renounce its strength—expression of an omnipotent who gives up his immense power in order to have a relationship of love with all that is human.

As contemporary thinkers also believe, in this reality it is possible to find the whole history and understanding of protection and care of individuals in their fragility as a subject of suffering, sickness, and poverty. This concept represents an authentic treasure of the nontotalitarian origins of Europe, that is, an alternative to violence.

This is preserved as a precious possession for both present and future in the Scuola Grande di San Marco, which became a perpetual moral model at the center of the Mediterranean since the fifteenth century and was a source of rediscovery of the authentic European origins.

These experiences explain our significant interest in developing studies about the work of Plato and the Byzantine Neoplatonists. Promoted with courteous support from the Franciscan University of Steubenville (Ohio), this volume proposes to shed light on those historical Greek and Byzantine lines of thought that unified, in both conjecture and practice, the spiritual and corporal human dimensions that are already indivisible in themselves.

This reality represents a precious teaching for the contemporary world, which is already starting to disregard metaphysics and is marked by a sad and progressive process of secularization of Christianity. It is an essential teaching that is also helpful for health systems, health workers, and public authorities that are currently often convinced of their superiority over—if not their complete control of—immanent reality, with no more predictable limits for any scientific activity. This is precisely the effect of the increasingly disseminated misfortune that goes with every statement about the existence of the soul and its immortality. There is no cure without the soul, however. Unfortunately, this relativism is so widespread that it has even conquered many Christian and ecclesial circles that, in the climate of the COVID-19 pandemic, seem to confuse even physical and spiritual health.

We are fortunate enough within our Venetian historical and monumental sphere to receive a strong and stable call upon knowledge and the doctrine of truth through the post-Tridentine allegorical system that still exists in the Dominican Library (Biblioteca domenicana Ss. Giovanni e Paolo). This library played an exceptional role regarding Western cultures before the frequent removals and spoliation by Napoleon. It was a place of preservation and study of valuable Greek and Latin codices since the fourteenth century, and then it held the manuscripts donated by Fra Gioacchino Torriano in the fifteenth century.

This crossroads of civilization is closely related to us since it continues to offer the idea of an order we are called to adopt but reject the very existence of. Many visitors and enthusiasts look at our works of art with astonishment and bewilderment; they do not know how to interpret them and can no longer read them, and unfortunately, even if they did understand them, they would refuse their meaning. It is the West denying and fighting itself, falling into a demise of its own making. What we are also doing with this publication belongs therefore to a cultural emergency and to an equal duty of testimony of undeniable values and real knowledge.

Mario Po'
Cultural Center and Museum of Scuola Grande di San Marco
Venice

Preface and Acknowledgments

The papers collected here were—for the most part—given over the course of two pleasant autumn days, October 3 and 4, 2019, at an event generously hosted by the Scuola Grande di San Marco in Venice. This volume is the first in a series of volumes derived from conferences hosted on the topic of Platonism in Byzantium.

This volume takes a cross-section of Platonists authors—Christian and non-Christian—from early through late Byzantium. The essays have been organized chronologically by author, beginning with Plotinus and ending with the Latin reception of Byzantium Platonism in the West. The arrangement of chapters, however, gives rise to a number of topics seen throughout the volume. The doctrine of the soul, issues regarding the One/God, as well as Trinity within a hierarchical universe permeate these scientific essays. Moreover, use of authority by authors is also an important issue that arises: this includes the reception of authors such as Plato and the Platonists, and how Plato coheres with Scripture as authority used by Christian authors.

In "The Personhood of the One," Lloyd P. Gerson discusses Plotinus's account of the personhood of the One, the first principle of all. Plotinus's One was a challenge to Trinitarianism because Trinitarianism necessarily involved the interaction of the person that God is with other persons. For Christians, God's providence and response to prayer create an interaction; for Plotinus, however, God's simplicity prevents interpersonal activity. Although Platonist hymns and prayers use the interactive element of personhood for the multitude of deities, Plotinus believed in the existence of gods and allowed for their interaction with us. The Neoplatonic tradition withholds personal attributes from the absolutely simple first principle of all.

Carl O'Brien's "The Platonism behind Basil's Trinitarian Theology" discusses how Basil's Trinitarian theology underwent chronological development—something Basil himself considers a journey to perfection—although it can still be regarded as a coherent whole. While Basil does not adopt the Platonic metaphysical structure, he assimilates aspects of Greek thought into his biblical exegesis. O'Brien discusses this referring to Basil's theory of time, his views concerning the knowability of God, and his adoption of a metaphysics of light. In his teachings on time, his primary interest is to show that there is not temporal priority of the Father over the Son. As with the Platonists, Basil argues that God is only knowable in a certain sense; ordinary language and ordinary concepts (such as "Fatherhood") can be applied to God if they are "purified." Knowledge of God does not entail knowledge of his essence. Finally, Basil uses the image of light to describe the relationship between lower entities and the first principle.

In "Platonism and Gregory of Nyssa," Mark Edwards argues that while Gregory evokes the style and words of Plato, he does so as an inheritor of parts of the Platonic tradition rather than as a wholesale follower of Plato. While Gregory, as with all Christians, bears a certain debt to Plato's doctrine of the soul, in his *De Anima*, Gregory shows that the Christian view of the Resurrection is incompatible with Plato's teachings. Edwards compares Gregory on these views with the teachings of Origen.

Sarah Klitenic Wear in "Language of Interaction in Cyril's Trinitarian Theology and Proclus's Theory of the Henads" discusses the connection between Cyril's description of how the Father, Son, and Holy Spirit interact with how Proclus describes the relationship among henads in the realm of the One. Namely, Cyril describes the Father, Son, and Holy Spirit existing in an unmixed unity. The Son contains all the traits of the Father; everything that the Father possesses Christ also possesses. Likewise, for Proclus, there is a mutual unity of the henads so that all are in all—everything that can be said of one henad can be said of all. Distinction occurs between the members of the Trinity and between the henads in their mode, particularly in their mode with respect to participation. Christ's being fully reveals the properties of the Father to us—that is, the Son's mode of being manifests the characteristics of the Father to us. Proclus's henads, likewise, are unified aspects of God. Internally, they exist in an unmixed unity. Every god exists wholly in every other god. Differentiation exists in the form of peculiarity (*idiotēs*) for supra-essential entities.

In "Proclus and the Tripartite Soul in Plato's *Republic*," John F. Finamore shows how Proclus discusses the relationship between the three elements and the grades of virtues in such a way that continues the teachings of Porphyry and Iamblichus on this topic. Finamore looks at Treatise 7 of his *Republic* commentary, Porphyry's "On the Powers of the Soul," and Iamblichus's *De Anima*. Based on a study of the *Republic* commentary, Finamore finds that for Proclus the soul had a different relationship to the virtues when it was embodied and when it was freed from the body. The four virtues belonged to all three elements of the soul when the soul was embodied; at this stage, all three parts of the soul must work together, resulting in a unified soul. When the soul was freed from the body, however, virtue belonged to the rational element alone.

Marilena Vlad's "Damascius: New Insights in the Platonic Tradition" looks at Damascius's hypotheses on the one in his *Commentary on the Parmenides*. Here Damascius says that the One is and the One is not—for Damascius, the One is not unsurpassable because it stands below the ineffable. She shows how this teaching allows the sensible world to appear as a consequence of the intelligible world; it is an intelligible possibility. Unlike his predecessor Iamblichus, Damascius proposes the ineffable as first principle and traces its presence down to the level of the sensible world. Vlad explains that every level projects something of the first principle. The sensible world, as a world of appearance, contains the ineffable. But anything identifiable in reality already has an aspect of unreality, of appearance, as a non-effable symbol.

Ilaria Ramelli in "'Pagan' and Christian Platonism in Dionysius: The Double-Reference Scheme and Its Meaning" says that Dionysius uses a double-reference scheme alluding to the "pagan" Platonic and the Christian traditions at the same time. Like Origen, Dionysius references Plato and Scripture together, using Platonic concepts and terminology as they apply to Christian ideas or vice versa. As examples of this double-reference scheme, Ramelli looks at the works attributed to Dionysius's master (which can refer to both Origen and Proclus); the notion of *apokatastasis* and reversion; and love, *agape*, and *eros*.

"Body and Soul in Dionysius the Areopagite," by Filip Ivanović, presents Dionysius's theory of the body and soul relationship. As with Proclus, Dionysius denies that the body is intrinsically evil. Moreover, Dionysius rejects any separation of the body from the soul. Rather, Dionysius turns to the example of the Incarnation of Christ. While the human person experiences passions and desires, the example of Christ who harmonized body and soul shows us that an individual can make right decisions and live a good life.

Dionysios Skliris's "'Chalcedonian Participation': St. Maximus the Confessor's Christian Neoplatonism" explores the relationship between transcendence and participation in the thought of Maximus the Confessor. He shows how one can have participation in the divine, despite the divine's utter transcendence above sensible reality; this concept, moreover, affects Maximus's Trinitarian theology, cosmology, soteriology, spirituality, and theory of evil. Skliris shows how Maximus describes participation using language of Energeia, since the participation of beings in God is considered as tantamount to God being active and operating in them. Finally, participation takes place in the *ecclesia* as the mystical body of Christ.

In "Plato's *Parmenides* in Seventh-Century Constantinople: George of Pisidia's *Hexameron*, 1639–93," Frederick Lauritzen shows that the *Hexameron* of George of Pisidia (a poem about nature, creation, and the One) follows closely the notions present in the *Parmenides* on the question of parts and wholes, place and movement. Based on a reading of this poem, it seems that George of Pisidia understands the first hypothesis of the *Parmenides* to comprise six categories: (1) wholes/parts, (2) place, (3) movement, (4) definition, (5) time, and (6) knowability, the first three of which George expounds upon. Moreover, as with the other later Neoplatonists, George of Pisidia holds that there is a plurality (in a manner of speaking) within the unity of the divine first principle. Based on this and other evidence in the *Hexameron*, it appears that George of Pisidia was aware of debates surrounding the first hypothesis of the *Parmenides*.

George Diamantopoulos's chapter, "The Cardinal Virtues in the Works of Nicetas Stethatos," organizes the cardinal virtues in Stethatos's *De Anima* treatise. From such an examination, Diamantopoulos shows that Stethatos interprets the cardinal virtues in light of Neoplatonic doctrines. Stethatos provides a mystical explanation for the virtues; that is, he connects the virtues with the second stage of contemplation of nature, after purification, as a condition of mystical theology. Through this connection, man is called not only to be virtuous, but also to represent in himself an intelligible world secretly united with the Triadic God. This world includes also an intelligible paradise, which the virtues nourish.

Denis Walter's "John Italos on *Authypostaton* and *Authyparkton* in *Quaestio* 7 and His Processing of Psellos's *Phil. min.* I, Op. 7" examines John Italos's understanding of the classical pair of terms *authypostaton* and *aut-*

hyparkton. For this purpose, the tradition will first be briefly discussed, and then, through an examination of Op. 7 of the *Philosophica minora* I of his teacher Psellos, similarities and differences in content will be worked out. Both Psellos and Italos use the pair of terms in a similar way. Psellos's more differentiated discussion shows that *on* as well as *ousiai,* to which primarily *eidê,* as well as *noes* and *psychai* but also *sômata* (in a reduced way) belong, are each called *authypostaton* or *authyparkton.* The graduality of the terms is justified by the distance of these "entities" from God. John Italos not only follows the structure of the Psellian text in several aspects, but also shows a content-related proximity to his teacher.

Christian Förstel's chapter, "Nikephoros Choumnos and Platonism" describes how Choumnos accepts some of the Platonic doctrines when they are compatible with Christianity. Even when he rejects some of these views, however, he argues within a Platonist framework. For instance, Choumnos rejects the doctrine of the undescended soul, but he argues against it by demonstrating how this theory is contradictory to the role Plotinus assigns to the soul in the sensible world. In addition to citing Plotinus to argue on behalf of the preexisting soul, he also quotes Plato's *Republic* and *Phaedo.* In particular, Choumnos appears to have read Plotinus on the desire of the soul, *Enn.* IV.3.14. Moreover, Choumnos also cites Aristotle as he challenges the radical separation between intelligible and sensible worlds and between the soul and body.

In "'It Will Overcome Its Own Nature': The Topic of Self-Reversion of the Intellect in *Logos on Saint Peter of Athos* by St. Gregory Palamas and in *Ennead* V.3," Timur Shchukin reads a passage in the earliest work of Gregory Palamas, *Logos on Saint Peter of Athos.* Here Palamas describes the process of self-knowledge of the ascetic: his mind first turns to itself, freed from all sensual and passionate, and then goes beyond its own nature to contemplate God and connect with him. Shchukin connects Palamas on this topic with *Enn.* V, 3. Palamas appears to agree with Plotinus on contemplative return in some aspects but disagrees with him on key points and argues that the result of self-conversion of the intellect is not acquisition of natural boundaries, as Plotinus insists, but overcoming them in an endless striving to God. Shchukin points out that Gregory Palamas argued with the humanist thinkers who were under the influence of Plotinus, in particular, with Nicephorus Gregoras.

According to Denis J.-J. Robichaud in "Cardinal Bessarion and the *Corpus Dionysiacum:* Platonic Love between East and West," Bessarion was part of the first phase of critical studies of the *Corpus Dionysiacum* in the Latin West. In a move that preserved the apostolic identity of Ps.-Dionysius, Bessarion identified Ps.-Dionysius's teachings as Platonic, but not Neoplatonic. For instance, Bessarion integrates the Platonic views of *eros* with the Christian tradition, looking particularly at *DN* IV, of interest to Bessarion because of its use of Plato's *Symposium*. In his comments on these passages, Bessarion demonstrates that Ps.-Dionysius is citing the *Symposium* verbatim. Based upon his Christianized understanding of Platonic eros that stems from his interpretation of Ps.-Dionysius on the topic, Bessarion offers a reading unique for his time.

Stephen Gersh discusses the relationship between George Gemisthos Pletho and Marsilio Ficino in "Marsilio Ficino's Debt to George Gemistos Pletho: Recollection and Appropriation." While there is evidence from Ficino himself that Pletho supplied the inspiration for the foundation of the Florentine Academy, there are few references to Pletho among Ficino's writings prior to the 1490s. He discusses several factors that point to a shared philosophical purpose between the two thinkers: namely, their view on the immortality of the soul and the alignment of both thinkers to Christian thinking, rather than the doctrines of Aristotle. Ficino, however, rejects Pletho's theory of the relation of determinism and freedom.

⸺

The editors would like to thank the Franciscan University of Steubenville Department of Classics for funding toward the 2019 conference in Venice. The editors warmly thank the director of the Scuola Grande di San Marco, Marcus Po, for hosting the conference that gave rise to this volume.

THE BYZANTINE PLATONISTS, 284–1453

CHAPTER 1 ‖ The Personhood of the One

Lloyd P. Gerson

When early Christian philosophers and theologians sought to appropriate Greek philosophical wisdom for the purposes of articulating and advancing the Gospel, they early on had to face the fact that Greek conceptions of the first principle of all did not easily cohere with the God of Scripture. In particular, Trinitarian theology was not naturally expressed in the metaphysical terms that led to the positing of a first principle of all. Those many Christian views on this matter that eventually came to be rejected as heretical were in fact various attempts to articulate Scripture and a defensible metaphysics at the same time. In this essay, I focus mainly on Plotinus's account of the personhood of the One, the first principle of all. Even though Plotinus's successors did not accept without question everything that Plotinus said on this score, his reasons for placing the One at the apex of a metaphysical hierarchy served as a fundamental challenge to anyone adhering to some form of Trinitarianism.[1]

Regarding the personhood of God or the first principle of all, we may take for convenience the definition of personhood offered by the Christian philosopher and theologian Richard Swinburne:

[God is] a person without a body (i.e., a spirit) present everywhere, the creator and sustainer of the universe, a free agent, able to do everything (i.e., omnip-

1. See Van Riel, *Plato's Gods*, chap. 3, who argues that Christian Platonists followed Aristotle, not Plato, in conflating theology and metaphysics. Plato himself, as well as Plotinus, subordinates theology to metaphysics. The "race" of gods is worthy of a special study, but the gods are just parts of the universe, not its first principle or principles.

otent), knowing all things, perfectly good, a source of moral obligation, immutable, eternal, a necessary being, holy, and worthy of worship.[2]

Doubtless, each element of this definition may be submitted to scrutiny. Most striking about this definition, however, is that, suitably nuanced, it bears a reasonable resemblance to a definition of the One that we can derive from Plotinus's *Enneads.* And yet Plotinus will, at least by implication, reject the Christian account of the first principle of all. As I shall try to show, the reason for this is that the personhood of God, when derived from reflection on Scripture, necessarily involved the interaction of the person that God is with other persons. Such interaction requires rational beings employing their rationality interactively. Prayer and response to prayer constitute the most obvious example of this. But also God's providential care for individuals and the doctrine of atonement seem to require interpersonal activity.[3] And yet, for Plotinus, the necessary absolute simplicity of the first principle of all precludes all this, even though Plotinus does not seem to use personal pronouns for the One ironically.

First, let me briefly survey the relevant background. Plato says of the Idea of the Good in *Republic* that it is "happiest of that which is" (εὐδαιμονέστατον τοῦ ὄντος).[4] Plotinus does not directly refer to this passage. But it seems clear enough that he understood the principal characteristic of εὐδαιμονία to be self-sufficiency (αὐταρκεία).[5] And he does characterize the One in this way.[6] We should hesitate, though, to infer personhood directly from self-sufficiency. As we shall see presently, one of the most important features of personhood is the ability somehow or other to interact with other persons. To take a simple example, interaction is a requirement for contractual relations of any sort. One cannot interact with the dead or with imaginary persons or so-called future persons or with inanimate objects. It is necessary for there to be interaction—in the case of

---

2. See Swinburne, *Coherence of Theism,* 2. Swinburne adds, "that God is a person, yet one without a body, seems the most elementary claim of theism" (104). See Page, "Wherein Lies the Debate?," 297–317, who distinguishes the view that God is a person from the view, also of Christian provenance, that God is *not* a person because persons are all embodied. As Page rightly argues, the debate turns on whether the absolutely simple first principle of all can have personal attributes in any way comparable to those of embodied human beings.

3. E.g., Just. Dial. 1.4, who distinguishes pagan Greek philosophical reflection on God from Christian reflection on the basis that the former does not and the latter does recognize God as being provident for individuals as individuals.

4. See Pl. R. 526E4–5 Slings, referring to E2.

5. See, e.g., Plot. 1.4 [46], 4.23–24 Henry Schwyzer.

6. See Plot. 5.3 [49], 13.17; 5.4 [7], 1.12–14; 6.9 [9], 6.16–26 Henry Schwyzer.

contracts, agreement—for there to be a valid contract. For example, a covenant between God and the people of Israel. In addition, this interaction must be of a particular sort, since though we can interact with animals, they cannot enter into contracts with us. The interaction must be voluntary and rational. So, God could not enter into a covenant with the people of Israel unless he had a choice to do so or not. A contract is not valid if one part enters into it under threat of violence. By contrast, Aristotle's Unmoved Mover is self-sufficient.[7] Indeed, it is also said to have the best life ($\zeta\omega\acute{\eta}$), which no doubt implies self-sufficiency. But the personhood of the Unmoved Mover is far from clear at least if interaction with the universe is held to be a requirement for personhood. One might even suggest that Aristotle's "construction" of the "profile" of the Unmoved Mover is specifically intended to exempt it from all personal interaction. He does this precisely because such interaction would at least *impede* self-sufficiency.

The Stoics present a most interesting case for many reasons. In Cleanthes's *Hymn to Zeus*, interaction is unequivocally introduced right at the beginning of the poem.

> Most glorious of the immortals, called by many names, ever all-mighty
> Zeus, leader of nature, guiding everything with law,
> Hail! For it is right that all mortals should address you,
> Since all are descended from you and imitate your voice …

Zeus guides all things and is addressed by mortals in praise. The interaction is even more explicitly emphasized as the poem progresses.

> But Zeus, giver of all, you of the dark clouds, of the blazing thunderbolt
> Save men from their baneful inexperience
> And disperse it, father, far from their souls; grant that they may achieve
> The wisdom with which you confidently guide all with justice
> so that we may requite you with honor for the honor you give us
> praising your works continually, as is fitting
> for mortals …

This poem is especially enlightening precisely because of the assumption of demythologization behind it, not in spite of it. Zeus is not, for the Stoics, a person in the sense that Olympian deities were persons for those in the Homeric world; rather, "Zeus" is the name for the active principle in nature, the $\lambda\acute{o}\gamma o\varsigma$ that pervades all and is, at least philosophically speaking, equivalent to a universal law of physical necessity.

---

7. See Arist. *Metaph.* N 4, 1091b16–19 Ross.

The Stoics at least appear to meet the criterion of personhood for the first principle of all if that criterion is set in terms of interaction as above. And yet, when scores of critics of Stoicism in antiquity rejected the personhood of the Stoic god, they did so mainly for the reason that interaction with a necessary principle was grossly distortive of what the paradigm of personal interaction was taken to be. It is, of course, open to the Stoics to brush off this criticism with the observation that human interaction hardly provided the paradigm of personhood, especially within a Stoic metaphysical framework. That Zeus operates necessarily and therefore without deliberation and the possibility of alternative action does not disqualify Zeus from personhood, and even from prayer, except possibly petitionary prayer. One can easily imagine Stoic opponents—and these would include, latterly, Christian theologians—complaining that authentic interaction required that a person be able to act with regard to another person *because* of what that other person did. To return to our example of contract, voluntarily entering into a contract implies that you do so in response to, for example, what the other person is offering. And the possibility of rejecting the offer is taken to be real. But the Stoic Zeus is oblivious to petitionary prayer, which is for them perverse and the product of a delusion. So, should we say that the Stoic Zeus is not a person or the wrong kind of person?

The next bit of relevant background I want to adduce comes from the Middle Platonists. In chapter 10 of Alcinous's *Didaskalikos*, we find clearly stated the standard Middle Platonic conflation of the Idea of the Good in *Republic*, the Demiurge in *Timaeus*, and Aristotle's Unmoved Mover.[8] Apart from Plotinus, many assume that the conflation of the Unmoved Mover with the Demiurge is a rather crude exegetical error. I think Plotinus is right on this point, and I shall return to his reasoning in a moment. But here I wish to focus on the momentous conflation of the Idea of the Good and the Demiurge. I think it is in fact indisputable that Plato himself does not conflate the two, for at least two reasons, one textual and one philosophical. First, at *Timaeus* 48C2–6 (cf. 53D4–7), Timaeus clearly distinguishes an investigation into the first principle or principles of all from the present investigation, which includes, as the text has just said, the "works of reason," that is, what the Demiurge does and what he is.[9] The reason for

8. See Alcin. *Didasc.*10.3 Hermann and J. Dillon's commentary in *Alcinous*, 106–7.

9. We may add that at Pl. Tim. 29E Burnet, the Demiurge is said to be "good" (ἀγαθός), which seems all on its own to exclude the possibility that the Demiurge should be the Good itself, which can have no attributes that would undermine its absolute simplicity. At 10.4, Alcinous denies that God is good on the grounds that if he were, then he would participate in

setting aside the investigation into first principles is that it is too difficult for the present mode of exposition. Despite the contortions of Platonists in antiquity and Platonists of today, there is no basis in the text for maintaining that the Demiurge is the Idea of the Good. The philosophical reason is briefly that the Demiurge has a nature or οὐσία, and owing to its nature it is eternally contemplating all intelligible reality. For this reason, it hardly seems possible that the Demiurge should be equated with that which is "above" (ἐπέκεινα) οὐσια. No doubt, neither the one nor the other of these two reasons are dispositive for many. My point here, however, is that by thus conflating Good, Demiurge, and Unmoved Mover, Alcinous can help himself to a robust set of attributes for the first principle, seemingly more than enough to establish for it substantial personhood. So, we can presume that not only is the first principle of all good, but also that he is "ungrudging" (ἀφθόνος).[10] On the basis of his deliberation, he strives to make the cosmos as perfect as possible. He is unfailingly benevolent and provident, though admittedly it is not easy to see how his providence differs in any serious way from that of the Stoic Zeus. We might note in passing that one of the conceptual benefits of conflation is actually undercut by making the first principle the Demiurge. For the Demiurge is not omnipotent; he is constrained by "necessity" (ἀνάγκη). Thus any attempt to confront an array of problems, especially the problem of evil, from the Platonic perspective adopted by Alcinous, among others, is going to have to wrestle with, shall we say, constrained omnipotence. Paradoxically, this will lead to the enrichment of the concept of personhood for the first principle.

My next bit of background material comes from the fragments of Numenius's *On the Good*. I mention him in particular because he decisively rejects the general Middle Platonic conflation of the Idea of the Good and the Demiurge.[11] The chief conclusion that one arrives at upon reading this material is that Numenius is perfectly aware that the Good cannot be the Demiurge because these have incompatible metaphysical positions within the Platonic hierarchy. If the Demiurge is active in producing the cosmos,

---

goodness. But that is indeed precisely what *Timaeus* implies when it says that the Demiurge is good and then goes on to deny that the Demiurge is the first principle of all. And just to tie off the loose end here, in *Republic*, of which *Timaeus* is explicitly said to be a continuation, the Good is said to be the unhypothetical first principle of all. See Pl. *R.* 510B6–7; 511B5–6; 533A8–9, C7–D4 Slings.

10. See Pl. *Tim.* 29E1–2 Burnet. Arguably, the Idea of the Good is ungrudging, too, since it is eternally overflowing in its goodness. See Pl. *R.* 508B6–7 Slings. But its ungrudgingness is definitely not in response to anything. Nor is it the expression of choice.

11. See especially Numen. frs. 11–22 Des Places.

then the first principle of all must be "inactive" (ἀργός).[12] If the Demiurge has some sort of internal complexity owing to his intellect and to his contact with matter, then the first principle of all must be absolutely simple.[13] It is therefore unnecessary that the first principle take up a demiurgic task; rather, he should be considered to be the father of the Demiurge.[14] The relation between the first and the second is like that of the relation to the one who tills and the one who plants.[15] The first has prepared the way for the second and therefore has no contact with anything else. Yet the first is, too, an intellect, eternally contemplating intelligibles and so possessed of an "innate motion" (κίνησις σύμφυτος) owing to the "pouring out" (ἀναχεῖται) of which the entire order of the cosmos exists and its everlasting preservation is secured.[16] Numenius's idiosyncratic interpretation of Plato is most evident when he goes on to claim that the first, the Good, is the Demiurge of οὐσία, whereas the second is the Demiurge of becoming.[17] But the Good then has οὐσία inherent in it, and it is not exactly "beyond" οὐσία.[18] Nevertheless, it is "Being itself" (αὐτοόν).[19] Numenius is not unjustified in distinguishing the Good from οὐσία at the same time as he names it αὐτοόν. For though Plato puts the Good above οὐσία, he nevertheless says that it is "the brightest of that which is" (τοῦ ὄντος τὸ φανότατον) and the "best among things that are" (τοῦ ἀρίστου ἐν τοῖς οὖσι).[20] As we shall see, that οὐσία is "inherent" in the Good even though the Good as its principle is something that Plotinus will have his own distinctive way of expressing.[21]

Finally, I briefly mention Origen of Alexandria, who in his Περὶ Ἀρχῶν says that God is an *intellectualis natura simplex*, adding for emphasis that it

12. See Numen. fr. 12.10–14 Des Places.

13. See Numen. fr. 11.12–17 Des Places.

14. See Numen. fr. 12.2–4 Des Places.

15. See Numen. fr. 13.2–7 Des Places.

16. See Numen. fr. 15 Des Places. Curiously, the "innate motion" is evidently taken from the κίνησις νοῦ of Pl. *Lg.* 897C5–6 Burnet, where it certainly does not refer to the Good. The "pouring out" must be referring to the "overflowing" (ἐπίρυττον) of the Good (Pl. *R.* 508C6–7 Slings); Numen. fr. 17.2–3: πρῶτον νοῦν Des Places.

17. See Numen. fr. 16.2–5 Des Places.

18. See Numen. fr. 16.10 Des Places.

19. See Numen. fr. 17.4. See Krämer, *Der Ursprung der Geistmetaphysik*; Alex. Aphr., *In Metaph.* 125.15.

20. See Pl. *R.* 518C9, 532C6–7 Slings.

21. Simplicius's commentary on the *Enchiridion* of Epictetus, epilogue, expresses an interesting Platonizing version of the Stoic *Hymn to Zeus*, which might be fairly said to be a petitionary prayer. He urges the assistance of god in "removing the mist from the eyes of our souls" so that we may clearly know the human and the divine. It is difficult to know both whether or to what extent this is an appeal to grace of some sort and to whom the prayer is addressed.

must not be thought of as complex (*compositum esse non est putandum*).[22] God is the "mind" (*mens*) from which all intellectual being or mind exists. Origen, whose citations from Numenius show that he was familiar with his work, was perhaps encouraged by the consonance of Numenius's language with his own conception of God.[23] Origen was enough of a philosopher to intuit the exigencies of absolute simplicity in the first principle of all. He was also enough of a Christian theologian to want to endow the first principle of all with sufficient personhood to make the deliverances of Scripture compelling.

Plotinus's principal reason for maintaining that the first principle of all must be absolutely simple is that only that which is absolutely simple can be "self-explained" (αἴτιον ἑαυτοῦ).[24] And if there were nothing that is self-explained, then a vicious infinite regress of explanations arises, vicious because in that case there is no explanation for anything at all.[25] But absolute simplicity comes with a price. The One cannot be anything but itself; indeed, it cannot even be one, where "be one" is understood to be a predicative statement. In that case, how then can anything be derived from the One, or in terms stated above, how can it be the explanation for anything? The answer that Plotinus gives to this question is both a brilliant bit of Platonic exegesis and a monumental challenge *avant la lettre* to attempts to enrich the concept of personhood, so to speak, in order to meld the God of Scripture with the metaphysical posit of an absolutely simple first principle of all. Plotinus says that the One is "the power of all things" (δύναμις πάντων).[26] As I have argued elsewhere, this "power" is not to be equated with potency of any kind, not even active potency. It is more accurately understood as virtuality in precisely the sense in which Aquinas,

22. See Or. *Princ.* I , 1, 6, p. 221, 14–17. P. Koetschau, 1913. In Or. *Cels.* 7.38, p. 188, 11 Koeteschau, Origen says that God is "mind or superior to mind and essence" (νοῦν τοίνυν ἢ ἐπέκεινα νοῦ καὶ οὐσίας), adding that God is "simple" (ἁπλοῦν). The hesitancy perhaps indicates that "mind" and "simplicity" are not easily conjoined.

23. See Edwards, *Origen against Plato*, 52–53, who is somewhat skeptical of any dependence of Origen on Numenius in the former's conception of God. Numenius is, I believe, indicative of the Middle Platonic theology of the first principle that would have provided Origen with the metaphysical architecture of his own theology. My central claim is that prior to Plotinus, austerity in the deduction of the nature of the first principle was not deemed necessary—and certainly not desirable—by either pagan or Christian.

24. See Plot. 6.8 [39], 14.41 Henry Schwyzer.

25. I think that Duns Scotus's rejection of the idea that God is *causa sui* is in fact compatible with Plotinus's claim that the One is αἴτιον ἑαυτοῦ. See Scotus's *De principiis* III 33. What Scotus does is enrich the notion of necessity such that God alone has necessity *a se*.

26. See Plot. 5.1 [10], 7.9–10; 5. 3 [49], 15.31; 5. 4 [7], 2.38; 6. 9 [9], 5.36–37 Henry Schwyzer.

for example, says that God is *virtualiter* all things.[27] It is what Damascius later vividly expressed in the metaphor of "white" light being virtually all the colors of the spectrum. It might appear that if Aquinas and Plotinus agree that the first principle of all is virtually all things, then there need be no *philosophical* disagreement about the personhood of that principle. And yet Aquinas also holds that God is *eminenter* all things.[28] That is, God is the paradigm of all that he produces, which is of course all that there is. And, indeed, there is one place in which Plotinus does say that the One is "a sort of" (οἷον) paradigm.[29] But I interpret this as a qualified ("sort of") explication of virtuality, rather than a concession to eminence. For Intellect is the true paradigm of essence, and therefore Intellect, not the One, is eminently all things. If the One were really the paradigm of essence, then Intellect would be otiose. To this assertion one might reply, "yes, indeed." But without Intellect, the distinctiveness among all intelligibles or Forms would be obliterated; otherwise, the simplicity of the first principle would be compromised.

For our purposes, what this means is that the One is virtually Intellect and Being, but not eminently Intellect and Being. For this reason, the One is above νόησις; it does not think, certainly not in the way that thinking occurs (even theoretical thinking) in a person viewed as an agent of inter-activity. If the One were eminently all things, it would be plausible that it would be eminently an intellect. Indeed, the One is said to have κατανόησις or "grasping" of itself.[30] But this does not involve form or essence, even form paradigmatically, since the presence of form is just the reason for denying absolute simplicity.[31] The One is also said to have ὑπερνόησις or "super-grasping."[32] Since this seems to be a term invented by Plotinus and is *hapax* in the *Enneads*, it is difficult to understand what it indicates. But it presumably does not compromise the simplicity of the One. The One cannot have the cognition of form that persons seem to need to interact. To say that the One is or has an intellect is, like Origen, to say not merely that God is eminently what we have or are, but that he is eminently interactive with all beings and especially with rational beings. If the One is eminently

---

27. See *Summa contra Gentiles* II 15; *In De divinis nominibus* 631, 665, 770; *Summa theologiae* I 79, 2.c; *De veritate* XXIII 2, ad 3um. See my *Plotinus*, 22–41.

28. See *Summa theologiae* I 4, 2, c; *De potentia Dei* IX 7, ad 2um.

29. See Plot. 6.88 [39], 14.39 Henry Schwyzer.

30. See Plot. 5.44 [7], 2.17 Henry Schwyzer.

31. See Plot. 6.9 [9], 2.1–8 Henry Schwyzer, where Plotinus argues that Being is one-many and Being is identical with Intellect. If that is so, then Intellect cannot be the first principle of all.

32. See Plot. 6.8 [39], 16.32 Henry Schwyzer.

all things, it could be said to be eminently intellectual, but not such that that entails the possibility of interactivity.

I am aware of the danger of supposing that the gulf between the Plotinian One and the Christian God is greater than it in fact is. After all, we could perhaps take κατανόησις and ὑπερνόησις merely to indicate the unique and transcendent cognition that God has without any suggestion that this is meant to prohibit the sort of robust personhood that scripturally based metaphysics and theology requires. Indeed, one may go further and actually embrace eminence for a second principle and not for the first as in Augustine's identification of the second person of the Trinity with the locus of truth as per Scripture.[33] And yet this will not in the final analysis work. For Intellect really is inferior to the One, in the way that orthodox Christian theology denies that the second person of the Trinity is inferior to the first. Intellect is inferior to the One according to the only available criterion of a hierarchy of being; namely, relative simplicity.

The absolute simplicity of the One does not, perhaps surprisingly, prevent Plotinus from arguing that the One has βούλησις (will).[34] Plotinus approaches this conclusion starting from an analysis of what exactly it means for something to be "up to us" (ἐφ' ἡμῖν). The conclusion of this analysis is that we do what is up to us when we act to achieve the Good to which we are oriented. This is the real Good, not the merely apparent Good. When we act otherwise, we are acting, as Plato insists, unwillingly. Applying this analysis to the One, it can only act for the Good, there being nothing else in it which can determine it to act otherwise. So, it is eternally true that what the One does is "up to it."[35] What is up to it, since it is the Good itself, is activity. The Good is essentially diffusive of its goodness. The medieval tag *bonum est diffusivum sui* encapsulates well the essence of Platonism.

But that whatever the Good does is up to it does not mean, most emphatically, that it could have acted otherwise than as it acts. This peripatetic way of describing freedom is rejected by Plotinus because it implies deliberation, which is inimical to that which is absolutely simple.[36] But more

33. See Jn 14:6 (RSV).

34. See generally Plot. 6.8 [39] Henry Schwyzer and especially πᾶν ἄρα βούλησις ἦν καὶ οὐκ ἐν τὸ μὴ βουλόμενον (Plot. 21.14–15 Henry Schwyzer).

35. Plot. 6.8 [39], 13.10–11 Henry Schwyzer. Cf. Thomas Aquinas, *Summa theologiae* Ia, q. 59, a. 1; *Summa contra Gentiles* II 47; *De veritate* q. 23, a. 1. I think Aquinas's account of the divine will is essentially the same as Plotinus's. The differences between Plotinus and Aquinas, however, seem to me to revolve around the *content* or particular results of the divine will. In addition, Aquinas must insist that God possesses *electio*, which Plotinus's One does not.

36. See Plot. 6.8 [39], 21.3–4 Henry Schwyzer, where Plotinus emphatically rejects what

than that, it implies real alternatives. For the Good, however, which is virtually everything, and upon which the being of everything depends, there are no possible alternatives. Since all Being depends on the Good, what could be the alternative to all Being? In other words, possible worlds that are eternally possible but everlastingly unrealized do not comport with the Good as simple first principle.

With this conclusion, we can see from yet another perspective the contrast between the impersonal personhood of the One and the personhood of the God of Scripture.[37] All possible alternatives here below are contingencies, but no such alternative could be "up to" the Good. The Good or One could not have made it so that Oedipus did not kill his father and marry his mother. Nor could it have made it so that Moses saw the Promised Land. Presumably, it is an essential element of the personhood of the God of Scripture that he could have done this, even if, obviously, he did not. Plotinus's One/Good is literally nothing but its will, but it is impossible to ascribe voluntarism to it. The voluntarism of, for example, Peter Damian or Duns Scotus, is inconceivable for Plotinus. Apart from the tangled modal logic of necessity and contingency, the issue here is, I suspect, ultimately dependent on what are the requirements for personhood, even the supreme personhood of God. What becomes of interaction with God if God can only do what is up to him, where "what is up to him" represents the possible, but only because it is entailed by the actual: *ab esse ad posse*?

The contrast is equally evident in the difference between "the One is ἔρως" and "God is ἀγάπη."[38] The One is ἔρως for the same reason that it is the Good: its activity is self-directed because it is essentially other directed. I take it that ἀγάπη in *koinē* Greek is paradigmatically interactive. That is,

---

Alexander of Aphrodisias says in Alex. Aphr. *Fat.* 180.3, 26–27 and 196.13, 24–29, that freedom means being able to choose from among contraries (τὰ ἀντικείμενα). Choosing from among contraries requires deliberation, which requires the complexity of practical reasoning. There is no practical reasoning in Intellect; a fortiori, there is no practical reasoning in the One.

37. Frede, "Monotheism and Pagan Philosophy in Antiquity," 48, thinks it a "prejudice" to maintain that the God of Aristotle or the Stoics or Numenius or Plotinus is "impersonal" and not a "concrete person." I presume that by this Frede means that in all these cases the first principle is an intellect or at least intellectual in some sense. This seems to me to be insufficient to amount to personhood. See Hewitt, "God Is Not a Person," 281–96, who argues against the possibility of disembodied persons. This conclusion arises from the assumption that a person acts, if not interacts, and there can be no disembodied agents. But this seems to me to follow only from an unexamined naturalistic assumption about causal closure. I think Hewitt, 287–91, is right, though, in arguing that linguistic (inter)action between the disembodied and the embodied is highly problematic.

38. See Plot. 6.8 [39], 15.1–2 Henry Schwyzer; 1 Jn 4:8 (RSV).

only persons can have it. Plotinus's One is as giving as the God of Scripture —all that is possible is eventually realized—but this giving does not extend to the personal level, in the sense of the individual level. The One cannot and will not care for individuals or respond to their needs. I take it that it is practically the whole point of the Christian accounts of the first principle of all that this is not so.

The contrast I am making may be thought to be somewhat misleading since Plotinus himself implicitly recognizes the intelligibility of prayer. In trying to explain how the One produces Intellect, Plotinus says,

Let us speak of this matter, then, in the following manner, calling to god himself, not with spoken words, but by stretching our arms in prayer to him in our soul, in this way being able to pray alone to him who is alone.[39]

This invocation of God is not explicitly a petition, nor is it clear what sort of response is being elicited. Nevertheless, the very idea of prayer seems to base its intelligibility on a notion of interactive personhood that goes beyond what we have hitherto seen as following from the absolute simplicity of the first principle of all.

Let us consider briefly the context within which this prayer is made. Broadly speaking, what Plotinus is doing in V 1 and indeed throughout the *Enneads* is to "do" philosophy in the Platonic manner. For him, philosophy is necessary, although not sufficient, for the κάθαρσις that is reversion (ἐπιστροφή) to the Good.[40] The prayer here is, I suggest, a focusing of attention on the goal, which is self-recognition of one's true identity. The goodness of the One is eternally ubiquitous and unchanging. A prayer to the One is not a petition, but more like a mantra intended to encourage a hastening to the goal. Plotinus elsewhere compares the One to the Great King.[41] Indeed, prayers to such a king are no doubt petitionary. But the analogy between the One and the Great King must obviously be taken with all the qualifications required to compare the One with anything at all.

Although there is much prayer in Plotinus's successors that can be characterized as "attention-focusing," the theurgic prayers and hymns of Iamblichus and Proclus display an evident retroversion of Christian personalism reflected into a polytheistic framework. One can illustrate this almost at random from Proclus's hymns. Here is a passage from his hymn to the sun-god:

39. Plot. 5.1 [10], 6.8–12 . Cf. 4.9 [8], 4.6–7 Henry Schwyzer.
40. For philosophy as κάθαρσις see Pl., *Phd.* 67C5–D2, 69B5–C2 Burnet.
41. See Plot. 5.5 [32], 3.12–13 Henry Schwyzer.

> … receive my tearful supplication, pull me out of baneful
> defilement and keep me far from the punishing deities while mollifying
>   the fast eye of Justice that sees all.[42]

Although this and other hymns are not directed to the One, they do seem to adopt—most enthusiastically in the case of Proclus—the interactive element of personhood for the multitude of deities. But every personal attribute that Proclus's Christian opponents want to ascribe to God the entire Neoplatonic tradition wants to withhold from the absolutely simple first principle of all.

To relax the exigencies of absolute simplicity is to threaten the argument for a first principle of all. This is because the argument for a first principle of all is just the argument for the priority and necessity of an absolutely simple explanation for everything.[43] The principal philosophical, as opposed to cultural, complaint that Plotinus and his successors had against Christianity was that scriptural accounts of the first principle of all seemed to make of this principle a person capable of interactive relations with us.[44] Plotinus certainly did not disbelieve in the existence of gods or in the possibility of their interaction with us. But this was because he never thought to elide this "class" of beings with the first principle. The various iterations of Trinitarian theology, mostly formulated beyond Plotinus's lifetime, simply exacerbated the problem.

I think philosophers who want to defend a robust conception of divine personhood are right to insist that God's intellect is not like ours.[45] Nor is it incorrect to identify the activity of an "austere" intellect with a sort of providence much as the Stoics do. Nevertheless, God's putative ability to interact with human persons, at least, is derived from outside the argu-

42. See Procl. *H.* 1.36–38 (Vogt), translated by R. van den Berg in *Proclus' Hymns*, 142.

43. See Kretzmann and Stump, "Absolute Simplicity," 353–82, for an argument defending the absolute simplicity of God against charges that if God were absolutely simple, then as a necessary being, everything he produced would be necessary and not contingent. Plotinus deals with this problem in an entirely different way. We know that there are contingent beings. Therefore we know that it is necessary that contingent beings are possible. So, the One is the necessary cause of the being of the contingent. But the One did not *select* one contingent being from among a host of possible ones. Suffice to say, Plotinus's argument is not a defense of God's willing in a way that devolves to the particular even though the being of the particular depends ultimately on the One.

44. Philo of Alexandria provides a stellar example of the tension between a philosophical ascent to an absolutely simple and therefore impersonal first principle of all and a personal God of Scripture. Dionysius the Areopagite, especially in his *Divine Names*, provides the most explicit example of the importation of scriptural characterizations of God to the Platonic metaphysical framework.

45. See, e.g., Boys-Stones, *Platonist Philosophy*, 330–31.

mentative framework for positing an absolutely simple first principle. Just as Aquinas admitted that temporal creation was an article of faith because it could not be proved according to the light of reason alone, so the emphasis on God's interactive powers is, for Plotinus at any rate, an alien accretion to the body of Platonic thinking. The point is not just that absolute simplicity precludes interactive powers, it is that the introduction of interactive powers undercuts the argument for an absolutely simple first principle of all. No doubt, this is a benign result for those who believe that the human approach to God should be taken altogether outside of a philosophical or scientific framework.

Carl O'Brien

Introduction

Basil adopts two distinct positions toward Greek culture: an official position as Bishop of Caesarea, in which he criticizes Greek philosophy in spite of the debt which he owes to it, and a much more positive personal position expressed in correspondence with his own family. The official position is a negative one, which polarizes Greek philosophy against Christian "truth," illustrated by Basil's claim that the intense study of the philosophers has left them with the eyes of owls, blinded by the light of true wisdom (represented by Christianity), just as owls are blinded by the sun,[1] a claim made in the course of a homily. "And why is it necessary for us to make the effort to refute their [sc. the philosophers'] lies, since it is sufficient to contrast and compare their mutually contradictory books and as spectators to watch their war in great silence?"[2] Basil is naturally opposed to the typically Platonic view of the soul's transmigration: "Let us avoid the idle talk of the pompous philosophers who are not ashamed to make their own soul of

1. Bas. *Hex.* 8.7.34–39. The *Homilies on the Hexaemeron* are also significant regarding Basil's Platonism in the context of his interpretation of Genesis. Cf. O'Brien, "St Basil's Explanation of Creation," and idem, "Creation, Cosmogony and Cappadocian Cosmology."

2. Καὶ τί δεῖ πράγματα ἔχειν ἡμᾶς τὸ ψευδὲς αὐτῶν διελέγχοντας, οἷς ἐξαρκεῖ τὰς αὐτῶν ἐκείνων βίβλους ἀλλήλαις ἀντιπαραθέντας ἐν ἡσυχίᾳ πολλῇ θεατὰς αὐτῶν τοῦ πολέμου καθῆσθαι; (Bas. *Hex.* 3.8.37–41 Giet). Unless otherwise noted, translations are my own.

like form to the soul of a dog, saying that they have formerly themselves been women and shrubs and fish of the sea."[3] However, in *To the Young on Greek Literature,* a work intended for his nephews and therefore reflective of Basil's private position, he advocates that pagan literature is a useful subject of study for those who are too young to study the Scriptures. Indeed, he accepts that the style of Greek writing is more polished than that of the Bible, even if he presents scriptural clarity as a virtue:

εἴπερ μὴ ἑπόμεθα ταῖς παρ' ὑμῖν ἐκλογαῖς τῶν ῥημάτων, μηδὲ τὸ τῆς θέσεως αὐτῶν εὔρυθμον ἐπιτηδεύομεν. Οὐ γὰρ τορευταὶ λέξεων παρ' ἡμῖν· οὐδὲ τὸ εὔηχον τῶν φωνῶν, ἀλλὰ τὸ εὔσημον τῶν ὀνομάτων πανταχοῦ προτιμότερον. (Bas. *Hex.* 6.2. 24–28)

For we [Christians] do not follow your choice selection of words, nor do we take care to give them a well-ordered setting. For our diction is not polished nor are our tones euphonious, but everywhere the clarity of words enjoys the highest honor.

Basil's theological development was heavily formed by his reaction to the various heterodox positions that dominated the Church debates of his day and his quest to forge a unity out of the range of theological positions that he regarded as moderate. Additionally, Basil's Trinitarian theology underwent chronological development, although it can still be regarded as a coherent whole. (He himself regarded this development of his thought not in terms of change, but rather in terms of "being perfected," similar to the manner in which a seed grows):

ὅτι οὐδέποτε πεπλανημένας ἔσχον τὰς περὶ Θεοῦ ὑπολήψεις, ἢ ἑτέρως φρονῶν μετέμαθον ὕστερον. Ἀλλ' ἦν ἐκ παιδὸς ἔλαβον ἔννοιαν περὶ Θεοῦ ... ταύτην αὐξηθεῖσαν ἔσχον ἐν ἐμαυτῷ· οὐ γὰρ ἄλλα ἐξ ἄλλων μετέλαβον ἐν τῇ τοῦ λόγου συμπληρώσει, ἀλλὰ τὰς παραδοθείσας μοι παρ' αὐτῶν ἀρχὰς ἐτελείωσα. (Bas. *Ep.* 223.3. 34–40)

never did I hold errant notions concerning God, or having different opinions unlearn them subsequently, but the concept concerning God from my childhood ... this increased in strength have I held within me, for I did not take one view in exchange for another with the fulfilment of reason, but I brought to perfection the principles bestowed on me.

Basil's theology does not fit into a framework adopted from Platonic metaphysics. In this he differs from Origen, who posits a relationship be-

---

3. Φεῦγε φληνάφους τῶν σοβαρῶν φιλοσόφων, οἳ οὐκ αἰσχύνονται τὰς ἑαυτῶν ψυχὰς καὶ τὰς κυνείας ὁμοειδεῖς ἀλλήλαις τιθέμενοι· οἱ λέγοντες ἑαυτοὺς γεγενῆσθαί ποτε καὶ γυναῖκας καὶ θάμνους καὶ ἰχθύας θαλασσίους (Bas. *Hex.* 8.2.16–19 Giet).

tween the Father and the Son that is influenced by Platonic accounts of the relationship between a First God and secondary, demiurgic entities. For Origen, the Holy Spirit is removed from the framework of Greek philosophical interpretations, since, while he accepts that pagan thinkers have an imperfect knowledge of the Father and the Son, knowledge of the Holy Spirit is confined to Christians.[4] For Basil, such interpretations simply will not do. First, his interpretation of creation, as outlined in the *Hexaemeron*, is expressed in pastoral, rather than in philosophical, terms. Second, his polemical strategy often relies upon the criticism of Greek philosophy in his official position as bishop, even if this contrasts sharply with remarks made in a private capacity. Third, Basil has little use for the (Neo)platonic metaphysical structure of a hierarchy of hypostases, since it is a core feature of his Trinitarian theology that the Father and the Son are equal (at least in terms of substance), as is the case with his brother, Gregory of Nyssa, and in contrast to his opponent Eunomius or even Origen. That said, Basil frequently assimilates aspects of Greek thought into his biblical exegesis.[5] This is particularly observable in his development of a notion of time, his views concerning the knowability of God, and his adoption of a metaphysics of light.

Basil's Concept of Time

One area where Basil is heavily influenced by Platonism, even if he himself adopts a stridently anti-Platonic approach, is in relation to time. In *Adversus Eunomium*, an early work, Basil's approach is of particularly significance since it would subsequently influence Augustine's concept of time.[6] Although Plato does not explicitly define time as the movement of the heavenly bodies, some of his remarks in the *Timaeus* could certainly be interpreted in that way: "He [the Demiurge] intended to make a moving likeness of eternity and as he regulated the heaven, he made an eternal image of that eternity which remains in unity, moving in accordance with number, which we call time."[7] At *Ti.* 37E, Plato remarks that "For at that

4. Or. *Princ.* 1.3.1.18–21 Crouzel and Simonetti; Cf. O'Brien, "The Origin in Origen," 172–73. O'Brien, *Demiurge in Ancient Thought*, 247, 258–61, also examines the much more strongly Platonizing approach adopted by Origen to expound the relationship between the persons of the Trinity, which differs sharply from that adopted by Basil.

5. Cf. Hildebrand, *Trinitarian Theology of Basil of Caesarea*, 12.

6. Cf. Callahan, "Basil of Caesarea."

7. εἰκὼ δ' ἐπενόει κινητόν τινα αἰῶνος ποιῆσαι, καὶ διακοσμῶν ἅμα οὐρανὸν ποιεῖ μένοντος αἰῶνος ἐν ἑνὶ κατ' ἀριθμὸν ἰοῦσαν αἰώνιον εἰκόνα, τοῦτον ὃν δὴ χρόνον ὠνομάκαμεν (Pl. *Ti.* 37D Burnet).

time he contrived the days and nights and months and years to be put together and these did not exist before the heaven had come into being and these are all parts of time."[8] So, even if Plato only views particular parts of time as identical with the heavenly movements, rather than time as a whole, this position clearly has a Platonic provenance. Basil's attitude toward time provides a useful case study of his interaction with the Platonic tradition. First, Basil's interest in the nature of time is not, strictly speaking, a philosophical one (in the modern sense), but rather theological. He wishes to avoid the impression that there can be any (temporal) priority of the Father over the Son: according to the order and the prerogatives that come from time, it could be claimed that the Father is first and the Son second (1.19: PG 29, 556B). As an Arian, Eunomius's position is, of course, that the Father and Son are not consubstantial, and so he seizes upon the notion of temporal priority.

Second, given his priorities, Basil argues against Eunomius's position on time by appeal to Scripture. Although his response clearly shows knowledge of Greek philosophy, philosophical positions fade into the background in his argumentation, since Basil wishes to present Eunomius's position as an absurd one.[9] Though Basil presents his own doctrine of time, it is clear from *Adversus Eunomium* that the theological goal behind Basil's theorizing—combating Eunomius's Arianism—does not even require that Eunomius's Platonizing view of time is rejected; it simply forms part of Basil's rhetorical strategy to portray Eunomius as incompetent both in terms of his scriptural knowledge and philosophical methodology.

Eunomius's definition of time is cited by Basil as "a certain kind of movement of the stars," clearly meaning the sun, the moon, and the rest of the stars in which there is the power to move by themselves.[10] Basil makes two arguments. First, if one accepts the arguments of Eunomius (and Plato), there would be no time before the creation of the heavenly bodies. This is implied in Plato's account: "Time, then, came into existence together with the heaven in order that having been brought into existence together they might be dissolved together",[11] though Basil bases his response on the biblical account (Basil, *Eun.* 1.21). There would be no time before the

---

8. ἡμέρας γὰρ καὶ νύκτας καὶ μῆνας καὶ ἐνιαυτούς, οὐκ ὄντας πρὶν οὐρανὸν γενέσθαι, τότε ἅμα ἐκείνῳ συνισταμένῳ τὴν γένεσιν αὐτῶν μηχανᾶται· ταῦτα δὲ πάντα μέρη χρόνου (Pl. *Ti.* 37E Burnet).

9. DelCogliano, "Basil of Caesarea versus Eunomius of Cyzicus," 527.

10. Bas., *Eun.* 1.21.1–16: PG 29, 557C–560A Migne; cf. Eunomius, *apol.* 10.1–10.

11. Pl. *Ti.* 38B Burnet; cf. Pl. *Ti.* 37E Burnet.

fourth day. The second argument, criticizing the identification of planetary movement with time, a rejection of Plato's view in the *Timaeus*, also reflects Basil's characteristic appeal to Scripture:

Καὶ πάλιν, ὅτε ἐπολέμει τοῖς Γαβαωνίταις ὁ τοῦ Ναυῆ Ἰησοῦς, ἐπειδὴ ἀκίνητος ὁ ἥλιος ἔμεινε τῷ προστάγματι πεδηθεὶς, καὶ ἡ σελήνη κατὰ χώραν εἱστήκει, χρόνος οὐκ ἦν τὸ τηνικαῦτα; (Bas. *Eun.* 1.21.13–16: PG 29, 560A Migne)

And once again when Joshua, son of Nun, was battling the Gibeonites and the sun remained motionless, having been constrained by an ordinance and the moon was made to stand in its place (Joshua 10:12–13), was there time in these circumstances?

For Basil, while the movement of the planets takes place in time, this does not mean that it should be identified with time; Eunomius, "our great astronomer," as he is sarcastically referred to, has simply made a false inference, as Basil pointedly remarks:

Ὁ δὲ, ἐπειδὴ ἐν χρόνῳ οἱ ἀστέρες κινοῦνται, χρόνου αὐτοὺς εἶναι δημιουργοὺς ἀποφαίνεται. Οὐκοῦν κατὰ τὸν τοῦ σοφωτάτου λόγον, ἐπειδὴ καὶ κάνθαροι ἐν χρόνῳ κινοῦνται, ὁρισώμεθα τὸν χρόνον εἶναι ποιάν τινα κανθάρων κίνησι· οὐδὲν γὰρ τούτου τὸ παρ' αὐτοῦ λεχθὲν διαφέρει, πλὴν τῆς σεμνότητος τῶν ὀνομάτων. (Bas. *Eun.* 1.21.34–40: PG 29, 560C Migne)

But since the stars move in time, he proclaims that they are the craftsmen of time. Therefore, according to the reckoning of this most wise man, since dung-beetles also move in time, we should define time as a certain kind of movement of dung-beetles. For there is no difference from what he says apart from the solemnity of names.

Even when Basil agrees with Eunomius's position (regarding the concept of God as unbegotten), he is clear to attribute this to a knowledge common to all, just like a man who at the height of noon claims that the sun is the brightest of the heavenly bodies (*Eun.* 1.5.28–30: PG 29, 516A-B). In this way, although Basil refutes certain aspects of a Platonizing view, he undermines the extent to which a competent mastery of philosophical methodology can be attributed to Eunomius.

Basil portrays Eunomius's claim that day and night are only produced by the movement of the stars as a revelation that he does not even know what he is saying and an indication of the childishness of his thought. Basil, though, moves beyond criticism of Eunomius to present his own doctrine of time. Despite distancing himself from a specific Platonizing interpretation of Eunomius, Basil draws a dichotomy between time (in which the planetary movements take place) and eternity (which Basil associates with

God).[12] As DelCogliano has demonstrated, Basil's view of time is influenced by the Middle Platonist definition, which we find recorded at Alcinous, *Didaskalikos* 14.6.1–14: "for he made time as an extension of the cosmos' movement, as an image of eternity, which is the measure of the eternal cosmos' permanence."[13] If time is to be identified with a "certain kind of movement of the stars" (Χρόνον τοίνυν εἶναί φησι ποιάν τινα κίνησιν ἀστέρων, *Eun.* 1.21.4: PG 29, 557C Migne) and the stars are temporally later than God's unbegotten substance, then there is no temporality in the divine substance.[14] Basil himself defines time as "the extension corresponding to the formation of the cosmos" (Χρόνος δέ ἐστι τὸ συμπαρεκτεινόμενον τῇ συστάσει τοῦ κόσμου διάστημα, *Eun.* 1.21.28–30: PG 29, 560B Migne). It is a measurement of motion rather than motion itself. Since God created the cosmos, time is dependent upon God and not upon any created thing.

To be fair, one should note that Eunomius's position is also based upon an appeal to Scripture (*Prov.* 8:22), a fact that Basil himself acknowledges:

Οἱ δὲ πρὸς τὴν τοῦ Σολομῶντος καταφεύγουσι λέξιν· κἀκεῖθεν, ὥσπερ ἐξ ὁρμητηρίου τινός, τῆς πίστεως κατατρέχουσι. Διὰ γὰρ τὸ ἐκ προσώπου τῆς Σοφίας εἰρῆσθαι τὸ, "Κύριος ἔκτισέ με," ἐξεῖναι αὐτοῖς κτίσμα λέγειν τὸν Κύριον ὑπειλήφασιν. (Bas. *Eun.* 2.20.16–20: PG 29, 616A Migne)

And they [the "Eunomians"] have recourse to the text of Solomon and from it, as if from a military position, they inveigh against the faith. For on account of what is said in the person of Wisdom "Lord created me" (*Prov.* 8:22), they have assumed that it is allowable for them to call the Lord a creature.

Basil claims priority for his own interpretation of Scripture, since Eunomius's viewpoint is only mentioned once in Scripture (at *Prov.* 8:22; cf. Bas., *Eun.* 2.20.25–27 Migne). Furthermore, Eunomius adopts the incorrect approach to Scripture and is unable to uncover its hidden meaning (Bas., *Eun.* 2.20.27–31: PG 29, 616B Migne). In this sense, the manner in which Basil undermines Eunomius's competence in biblical exegesis parallels his representation of Eunomius's appeal to Platonic doctrine as an act of incompetence.

---

12. In this he is followed by Augustine in the *Confessiones*: cf. Callahan, "Basil of Caesarea," 454n41.

13. Καὶ γὰρ τὸν χρόνον ἐποίησε τῆς κινήσεως τοῦ κόσμου διάστημα, ὡς ἂν εἰκόνα τοῦ αἰῶνος, ὅς ἐστι μέτρον τοῦ αἰωνίου κόσμου τῆς μονῆς (Alcin, *didasc.* 14.6.4–6 Louis). Alcinous himself is also influenced in turn by Chrysippus.

14. Bas. *Eun.* 1.21.1–16: PG 29, 557C–560A Migne. Cf. DelCogliano, "Basil of Caesarea versus Eunomius of Cyzicus," 501–2.

Basil on Knowledge of God

Even if it is difficult to disentangle overt Platonism from the other strands that influence Basil's theology, he demonstrates similar concerns to the Platonists, particularly with regard to knowledge of God. The Platonic concern with the accuracy of applying language to higher metaphysical realities, going back to Plato's *Cratylus*, is illustrated by Basil's view that ordinary language and ordinary concepts (such as "Fatherhood") can be applied to God if they are "purified." Furthermore, Basil is concerned with how it is possible to have knowledge of God without knowledge of God's essence. However, Basil's concerns necessarily have a different orientation from those found in non-Christian Platonism, such as the manner in which he links knowledge of the divine with baptism. If knowledge of the Father is only possible through the Son, then it is by baptism that one attains knowledge of the Son by means of the Holy Spirit, summed up at 1 Corinthians 12:3: "No one can say Jesus is Lord except in the Holy Spirit."[15]

Πίστις δὲ καὶ βάπτισμα, δύο τρόποι τῆς σωτηρίας, συμφυεῖς ἀλλήλοις καὶ ἀδιαίρετοι. Πίστις μὲν γὰρ τελειοῦται διὰ βαπτίσματος, βάπτισμα δὲ θεμελιοῦται διὰ τῆς πίστεως ... Καὶ προάγει μὲν ἡ ὁμολογία πρὸς τὴν σωτηρίαν εἰσάγουσα· ἐπακολουθεῖ δὲ τὸ βάπτισμα ἐπισφραγίζον ἡμῶν τὴν συγκατάθεσιν. (Bas. *Spir.* 12.28.31–40 Pruche)

Faith and baptism, two methods of salvation, cohere to each other and are indivisible. For faith is made perfect by baptism and baptism is set on the foundation of belief ... Assent goes before and leads the way to salvation and baptism follows closely after, placing a seal upon our affirmation.

It is baptism that permits access to God by means of revealed names, thereby circumventing the problems which Plato had outlined in the *Cratylus* (*Eun.* 2.22: PG 29, 620C-D Migne; cf. *Eun.* 1.1.1–6: PG 29, 497A–500A Migne).[16] In this sense, while one can speak of a synthesis between Platonic and Christian thought in Basil, it is rather the case, as Hildebrand comments, that "he uses Greek ideas to express a Christian solution to the problems of ignorance."[17] Like the Father and Son, Basil stresses that the Holy Spirit is also "impenetrable in thought" (πρὸς θεωρίαν δυσέφικτον,

---

15. Trans. English Standard Version (ESV). Cf. Hildebrand, *Trinitarian Theology of Basil of Caesarea*, 176–78.

16. Cf. Radde-Gallwitz, *Basil of Caesarea, Gregory of Nyssa and the Transformation of Divine Simplicity*, 119.

17. Hildebrand, *Trinitarian Theology of Basil of Caesarea*, 175.

Spir. 22.53); this allows him to counter the denigration of the Holy Spirit advanced by his opponents by highlighting its separation from creation.

Basil's attack against Eunomius also adopts a broadly Platonic stance:

Ἓν μὲν οὐδέν ἐστιν ὄνομα ὃ πᾶσαν ἐξαρκεῖ τὴν τοῦ Θεοῦ φύσιν περιλαβὸν, ἱκανῶς ἐξαγγεῖλαι· πλείω δὲ καὶ ποικίλα κατ᾽ ἰδίαν ἕκαστον σημασίαν, ἀμυδρὰν μὲν παντελῶς καὶ μικροτάτην, ὡς πρὸς τὸ ὅλον, ἡμῖν γε μὴν ἐξαρκοῦσαν τὴν ἔννοιαν συναθροίζει. (Bas. *Eun.* 1.10.1–5: PG 29, 533C Migne)

There is no single name which suffices to encompass all of the nature of God and make it adequately known. But many manifold names, each with its own signification, gather together into one mass the conception which is absolutely faint and slight with regard to the whole and yet are sufficient for us.

Basil expresses a similar comment in his correspondence to Gregory of Nazianzus: "at that time when I wrote to you, who are most eloquent, I did not recognize that every theological utterance is inferior to the intention of the one uttering it" (*Ep.* 7.1.1–3).[18] This parallels the concerns expressed by Plato in the *Cratylus*. For example, four etymologies of the name Apollo are proposed, revealing the difficulty of human language to fully encompass the divine nature (*Cra.* 402E). Additionally, in Plato's examination of the distinction between human names such as Scamander and divine names such as Xanthos for the river god, drawn from Homer (*Iliad* XX.74; XXI.146), the human names are presented as less accurate designations (*Cra.* 391E). According to Basil, God receives a range of titles to account for the range of his activities (Bas., *Eun.* 1.7.15–17: PG 29, 525A Migne). Such Platonizing concerns are then deployed as a critique against Eunomius, who, Basil claims, conflates God's activities such as his demiurgy or his Providence with his substance (Bas. *Eun.* 1.8.22–24: PG 29, 528B Migne). Basil does not attribute this concept of God being beyond language to Platonism, but rather to the Jewish tradition: "the ancient piety of the Hebrews marked off the ineffable name of God with appropriate signs."[19]

The context here, though, is Christianized: Basil links the notion of God being beyond language and unnamable with the notion that God is beyond number and uncountable. This is a response to the claims made by the Pneumatomachians that his conception of the Holy Spirit amounted to worshipping three gods: "Either honor the Ineffable with silence or num-

---

18. Οὐδὲ τότε ἠγνόουν ὅτε ἐπέστελλον τῇ λογιότητί σου ὅτι πᾶσα θεολογικὴ φωνὴ ἐλάττων μέν ἐστι τῆς διανοίας τοῦ λέγοντος. Cf. Rousseau, *Basil of Caesarea*, 107.

19. ὡς ἡ παλαιὰ τῶν Ἑβραίων εὐλάβεια ἰδίοις σημείοις τὸ ἀνεκφώνητον ὄνομα τοῦ Θεοῦ διεχάρασσε (Bas. *Spir.* 18.44.14–15 Pruche).

ber sacred things piously."[20] According to Basil, the Father and the Son can be compared to the emperor and the image of the emperor, rather than two emperors (Bas. *Spir.* 18.45 Pruche: PG 32, 38C). In this, Basil differs sharply from the approach that we find in the Neopythagorean Numenius, who draws a distinction between the First, Second, and Third Gods. Basil must struggle with the notion of expressing God as simple, yet the range of theological terms applied to him would seem to indicate that he is composite.[21]

Clearly, Basil does not have a systematic approach toward his interaction with Platonism. Rather, as in his approach to time, he draws upon Platonizing elements in order to expose weaknesses inherent in Eunomius's theological position. Basil does not justify the claim that it is difficult to obtain knowledge of God by means of an appeal to Plato, but rather by an appeal to Scripture: "no one knows the Father except the Son" (Mt 11:27; Bas. *Eun.* 1.14.4–5: PG 29, 544A–B Migne). Again at Bas. *Eun.* 2.32.23–27: PG 29, 648B Migne:

ὥστε ἐκ μὲν τοῦ Πνεύματος τὴν τοῦ Μονογενοῦς δύναμιν θεωρεῖσθαι, ὁμοῦ δὲ καὶ τὴν οὐσίαν, ἐκ δὲ τοῦ Μονογενοῦς πάλιν τὴν τοῦ Πατρὸς δύναμίν τε καὶ οὐσίαν καταλαμβάνεσθαι·

So that the power and substance of the Only-Begotten would be contemplated on the basis of the Holy Spirit and again the Father's power and substance would be beheld on the basis of the Only-Begotten.

This general structure of an ascent toward a unitary First Principle is clearly reminiscent of Platonism, though Basil's understanding of the Son as the path to the Father is based on John 14:9: "Whoever has seen me has seen the Father."[22] Basil's point is that knowledge of the Father can only be obtained through the Son, and Eunomius fails to understand this by attempting to make the Son "alien to the Father" (ἀλλοτριῶν τοῦ Πατρὸς) by denying their consubstantiality, cutting off the route to Him (Bas. *Eun.* 1.18.16–18: PG 29, 553A Migne).

Basil's argument is that through his claim that the Father and Son are not consubstantial, Eunomius transgresses the injunction of John 5.23, "Whoever does not honor the Son does not honor the Father who sent him,"[23] while also creating a serious epistemological problem: we could

---

20. Ἡ γὰρ σιωπῇ τιμάσθω τὰ ἄρρητα, ἢ εὐσεβῶς ἀριθμείσθω τὰ ἄγια (Bas. *Spir.* 18.44.18–19 Pruche: PG 32, 37E–38A). Hildebrand, *Trinitarian Theology of Basil of Caesarea*, 97.

21. Bas. *Eun.* 2.29.23–36: PG 29, 640B–641A Migne.

22. Trans. ESV. Cf. Jn 12:45. For the notion of the Son as the image of the Father, see Col 1:15, and on Origen's use of this passage, see Hildebrand, *Trinitarian Theology of Basil of Caesarea*, 160.

23. Trans. ESV.

only know the Son who according to Eunomius is less than the Father, but we could not know the Father himself.[24] For Basil, there is an order in the relationship between Father and Son in terms of cause being prior to effect (Bas. *Eun.* 1.20.26–27: PG 29, 557B Migne), and indeed Basil sees this implicit in the title "Father" (Bas. *Eun.* 1.25.28–32: PG 29, 568C Migne), as he repeatedly emphasizes the term "Father" should not be interpreted in human or bodily terms (e.g., Bas. *Eun.* 2.22.45–48: PG 29, 621B Minge).

Since the Father is the Principle of the Son, the Father is greater than the Son in the sense that is meant in Christ's comment "The Father is greater than I," not in the sense that the substance of the Father differs from the Son, as Eunomius would have it (Bas. *Eun.* 1.25.34–35: PG 29, 568C Migne). Basil's position reveals that his theological argument concerning the generation of the Son does not really require refuting Eunomius's claims regarding time, since he does not see the Son as ever having being generated (so that the temporal argument is, in fact, moot). He cements this argument by means of a philological argument—reinterpreting Monogenes, which Eunomius takes to be "only begotten" to mean "begotten by one (parent)."[25] A similar line of argumentation is found at *Spir.* 6.14, where the relationship between Father and Son cannot be expressed in temporal terms in the same manner as it can in the case of things that have a beginning and an end: Basil again appeals to scriptural authority to undermine Eunomius's claim to the support of the saints for his position through an exegesis here of John's statement "in the beginning was the Word" (i.e., the Son).

Basil adopts the approach typical of Christian thinkers such as Origen (Or. *Princ.* I.3.1, where only the Christians have knowledge of the Holy Spirit) and Eusebius (at Eus. *P.e.* 1.6–8 Mras) in presenting competing theological views such as Jewish and Greek (including Platonic) thought, as well as opposing Christian views, as a less accurate understanding of God, in contrast to the particular vision they espouse:

Ἐπειδὴ καὶ Ἰουδαῖοι δοξάζειν τὸν Θεὸν οἴονται, καὶ Ἑλλήνων τις ἀκούσεται βουλομένων τι μέγα περὶ Θεοῦ λέγειν·ἀλλ' ὅμως οὐκ ἄν τις εἴποι μεγαλύνειν αὐτοὺς τὸν Θεὸν ἄνευ τῆς εἰς Χριστὸν πίστεως, δι' οὗ ἡ προσαγωγὴ τῆς γνώσεώς ἐστιν. (Bas. *Eun.* 1.26.37–41: PG 29, 569C Migne)

For the Jews suppose that they magnify God and some of the Greeks listen to anyone who says something great about God and nevertheless no one might say that they exalt God without belief in Christ, through whom there is the access to knowledge.

24. Hildebrand, *Trinitarian Theology of Basil of Caesarea*, 166, 171.
25. Anastos, "Basil's Κατὰ Εὐνομίου," 100–103.

For Basil, it is primarily belief in the Father and Son (sealed by baptism in the Father, Son, *and* Holy Spirit) that separates the Christians from "the mistake of the Greeks and the ignorance of the Jews."[26] This allows Basil to undermine Eunomius's position by presenting him not merely as an incompetent Christian exegete, but rather as not a Christian at all, by stressing the kern of the Christian faith as belief in an ungenerated Father and in an unbegotten Son (Bas. *Eun.* 2.22.30–32: PG 29, 620D–621A Migne). In actual fact, Basil is really engaging in a polemic not just against Eunomius and the Arians (who seem to be continuing Greek polytheism) but against other Christian groups such as the Sabellians (who like the Jews refuse to accept the divinity of the Son), rather than positioning himself against external opponents.[27] This representation of Christianity in terms of ethnic history, presenting it in opposition to Jewish and Greek thought, is typical of this period.[28] Clearly, this is a deliberate misrepresentation of Eunomius's position since he neither rejects the divinity of the Son nor advances a polytheistic agenda, but it suits Basil's agenda of rejecting the Platonizing elements of Eunomius's theology and his presentation of such Hellenizing elements as introduced without scriptural authority (and in direct opposition to the Christian tradition).

This interaction between Jewish, Christian, and Greek elements also entails a linguistic aspect, which can be seen behind Basil's attempt to develop both a vocabulary and a grammar of divinity in order to describe in precise Greek terms what is revealed in Scripture.[29] This is illustrated throughout the *De Spiritu Sancto* in Basil's concern with the correct use of prepositions to employ with each person of the Trinity to denote their interrelation with each other.[30] One of Basil's fundamental tenets is that the terms which are applied to Christ should be univocally applied to Christ, rather than applied only to one aspect of his nature.[31] Basil's strategy is to demonstrate that there are essential rules governing the appropriate application of language to God (and that Eunomius fails to follow these rules;

26. ἀπὸ τῆς Ἑλληνικῆς πλάνης καὶ τῆς Ἰουδαϊκῆς ἀγνωσίας (Bas. *Eun.* 2.22.15–16: PG 29, 620C Migne).

27. Cf. the *Adversus Eunomium* commentary of Sesboüé, Durand, and Doutreleau, vol. 1, 90n1, as well as Basil's explicit identification of the Jews with the Sabellians at *Homily* 24, 1: PG 31, 600b–c.

28. E.g., Eus., *P.e.* 1.6–8. Cf. O'Brien, "Middle Platonists and Pythagoreans."

29. Hildebrand, *Trinitarian Theology of Basil of Caesarea*, 41.

30. E.g., Bas. *Spir.* 5 and 29 Pruche, though this is the result of Basil responding to his opponents' adoption of the four Aristotelian causes, which he dismisses as an error resulting from closely studying the "heathen writers" (Bas. *Spir.* 5.5 Pruche).

31. Hildebrand, *Trinitarian Theology of Basil of Caesarea*, 42.

another reason why he does not offer a compelling theological vision). The only terms that should be applied to God are those derived from the Scriptures (Bas. *Eun.* 2.7: PG 29, 584B–585B Migne), and even in this case many terms are applied to the Son that do not have a reverential surface meaning and are only appropriate when their deeper significance is considered (Bas. *Eun.* 2.2.32–37: PG 29, 576C Migne). Eunomius is doubly undermined as someone who both lacks the necessary familiarity with Scripture to be an exegete (since Basil claims at Bas. *Eun.* 1.5.63–65: PG 29, 516A–517B Migne that the term *agennetos* is not applied to God by Scripture and at Bas. *Eun.* 2.2.36–37: PG 29, 576C Migne that there is no scriptural precedent for referring to the Son as a ποίημα) and furthermore is also ignorant of the correct methodological approach to Scripture in any case. Basil tries to position Eunomius as someone who despite his claims stands outside the tradition: "However, he claims to receive this name from the saints in order to include not only his contemporaries in his blasphemy, but also those who were saints long ago."[32] In this way, Basil represents Eunomius as displaying insufficient competence in both the Platonic and biblical traditions to offer a philosophically competent alternative interpretation of Scripture.

The Metaphysics of Light

Plato draws on the image of light to describe the relationship of lower entities to the First Principle (e.g., at Pl. *Rep.* VI 508B; VII 517C). In this "metaphysics of light" he is followed by Plotinus (e.g., Plot. *Enn.* IV 3 [27] 17.9–23). Basil too draws upon this imagery to describe the relationship between the Father and the Son with a particular stress on their consubstantiality:

εἰ δὲ οὕτω τις ἐκλαμβάνοι τὸ τῆς οὐσίας κοινόν, ὡς τὸν τοῦ εἶναι λόγον ἕνα καὶ τὸν αὐτὸν ἐπ᾽ ἀμφοῖν θεωρεῖσθαι, ὥστε καὶ εἰ καθ᾽ ὑπόθεσιν φῶς ὁ Πατὴρ τῷ ὑποκειμένῳ νοοῖτο, φῶς καὶ τὴν τοῦ Μονογενοῦς οὐσίαν ὁμολογεῖσθαι, καὶ ὄνπερ ἄν τις ἀποδῷ ἐπὶ τοῦ Πατρὸς τὸν τοῦ εἶναι λόγον, τὸν αὐτὸν τοῦτον καὶ τῷ Υἱῷ ἐφαρμόζειν· εἰ οὕτω τὸ κοινὸν τῆς οὐσίας λαμβάνοιτο, δεχόμεθα· καὶ ἡμέτερον εἶναι τὸ δόγμα φήσομεν. (Bas. *Eun.* 1.19.32–40: PG 29, 556A–B Migne)

And if someone might understand community of substance as contemplating the same account of substance of both the Father and the Son so that if the Father is conceived of as light with regards to his substance, so too should the substance

---

32. Καίτοι γε οὗτος παρ᾽ αὐτῶν εἰληφέναι τῶν ἁγίων τὸ ὄνομα τοῦτό φησιν, ἵνα ταῖς συκοφαντίαις μὴ μόνον τοὺς κατ᾽ αὐτὸν περιβάλῃ, ἀλλὰ καὶ τοὺς πάλαι ποτὲ γενομένους ἁγίους (Bas. *Eun.* 2.2.37–40: PG 29, 576C Migne).

of the Only-Begotten be agreed to be light and so too if someone should deliver an account of the Father, the same account should be applied to the Son. And if this is what is meant by community of substance, we accept it and we say that this is our doctrine.

Later in *De Spiritu Sancto*, Basil would express both the manner in which the Holy Spirit makes the Son knowable and its indivisibility from the godhead in terms of light:

οὐ μᾶλλόν γε, ἢ τῶν ὁρατῶν ἀποστήσεις τὸ φῶς. Ἀδύνατον γὰρ ἰδεῖν τὴν εἰκόνα τοῦ Θεοῦ τοῦ ἀοράτου, μὴ ἐν τῷ φωτισμῷ τοῦ Πνεύματος. Καὶ τὸν ἐνατενίζοντα τῇ εἰκόνι, ἀμήχανον τῆς εἰκόνος ἀποχωρίσαι τὸ φῶς. (Bas. *Spir.* 26.64,15–19 Pruche: PG 32, 53E–54B)

Light cannot be separated from that which is visible. It is impossible to see the image of the invisible God, unless by the light of the Spirit. And upon looking fixedly at the image, it is not possible to detach the light from the image.[33]

It is not simply the case that Basil draws upon the imagery of light. Rather, Basil's purpose for drawing on this imagery is to articulate both divine unity and plurality within the godhead. Since the context behind Plato's usage of the metaphysics of light is, in part, to convey the unity between the noetic and lower realms, we can identify here a Platonic feature in the background of Basil's thought. But while a metaphysics of light is firmly rooted in the Platonic tradition, the motivation for drawing upon light in this way can be traced to Eunomius's claim that light is not one, but divided by varying properties and Basil's need to shut down a line of argumentation that could be employed to support the claim that the Son is subordinate to the Father.[34]

For Basil, this "metaphysics of light" occurs against the background of articulating the Son's relationship to the Father in which context it influenced the text of the Nicene Creed.[35] It is reflected also in Athanasius's anti-Arian writings.[36] Basil's "metaphysics of light," then, is indebted to the Christian understanding of the Son as the Father's radiance (ἀπαύγασμα), based upon Hebrews 1.3: "The Son is the radiance of God's glory and the exact representation of his being, sustaining all things by his powerful word."[37] This is echoed in Basil's presentation of the Son as the Father's

33. This is an interpretation of Jn 4:24. Cf. Hildebrand, *Trinitarian Theology of Basil of Caesarea*, 186.

34. Eunomius, *apol.* apud Greg. Nyss., *Eun.* 3.19.46 (GNO 2:307.17–23).

35. Pelikan, "The 'Spiritual Sense' of Scripture," 341.

36. Ath., *Ar.* 1.7.25: PG 26: 64B; cf. the discussion at Pelikan, "'Spiritual Sense' of Scripture," 342.

37. Trans. ESV.

image and radiance.[38] The metaphysics of light is also availed of by Eunomius: Basil interprets his claim of light being in opposition to light to be an attempt to contrast the Son's substance with that of the Father (Bas. *Eun.* 2.26.1–18: PG 29, 632B–C Migne). For Eunomius, the metaphysics of light allows him to underline his claim to a hierarchy between Father and Son— the light of the Son is less bright than that of the Father, a claim that Basil disputes (Bas. *Eun.* 2.27.49–56: PG 29, 636B–C Migne).

Basil's stress on the notion of light (and its indivisibility) and the identification of light with both Father and Son illustrates his strategy of scriptural exegesis, combined with philosophical argument, to counter the claims of Eunomius that he regards as theologically unacceptable. In this case, the metaphysics of light, which had already been incorporated into the Christian tradition to counter the Arian position, is drawn upon by Basil to emphasize that the Father and the Son share the same *ousia*.

Basil's Response to Eunomius's Doctrines Concerning the Holy Spirit

Basil's attack on what he regards as Eunomius's blasphemies concerning the Son are closely related to his criticism of Eunomius's doctrine of the Holy Spirit. Since Eunomius views the Trinity in terms of a hierarchy of hypostases, he argues that just as the Son is the creature (*poiēma*) of the Father, the Holy Spirit is the created thing (*demiourgema*) of the Son (rather than belonging to both the Father and Son, which is Basil's position). Certain features of Basil's treatment of the Holy Spirit in the *Adversus Eunomium* indicate that pneumatology was not his primary concern. For example, Book III, in which Basil discusses the Holy Spirit, seems to have appeared subsequently to the other two books, which focus on the Son; at least if one takes seriously Basil's own comments at Bas. *Eun.* 2.34.7–9: PG 29, 652A Migne that he will take up the subject of the Holy Spirit in the future. Additionally, Book III, the book that primarily deals with the Holy Spirit, is significantly shorter than the first two books (which display a more complex argumentation),[39] while the third book contains only six arguments, the last of which is a textual analysis.

Basil even confesses ignorance of the nature of the Holy Spirit in the

---

38. Bas. *Eun.* 2.16.9–22: PG 29, 604B Migne; Bas. *Spir.* 7.16 Pruche: PG 32, 96A. Cf. Pelikan, "'Spiritual Sense' of Scripture," 341.

39. Cf. Anastos, "Basil's Κατὰ Εὐνομίου," 118. Of course, the Holy Spirit was subsequently the subject of a more elaborate treatment in *De Spiritu Sancto*.

earlier work. His defense of the Holy Spirit is tied to his defense of the status of the Son: Eunomius's argument is that the Father created the Son, whereas the Son (only) created the Holy Spirit and since the Holy Spirit, Eunomius claims, is lower in dignity than the Son, this is another reason why the Son should be regarded as less than the Father:

For he says, granted the Son is the creator of the Spirit —treat us propitiously Lord despite this idle chatter—and that this [Spirit] is not of such a kind to bestow any dignity upon his craftsman, on account of this the Son is not worthy to be compared with the Father, because the lowness of the beings he has created deprive him of equal honor of dignity.[40]

Basil's strategy for attacking this Platonizing hierarchy is again an appeal to Scripture: At John 17:20, Jesus prays that "all I have is yours and all you have is mine,"[41] demonstrating what became adopted as a fundamental theological principle that everything of the Son's is the Father's and there is nothing that belongs to the Father that does not also belong to the Son.[42] Furthermore, the Spirit is expressly declared to belong to both the Son (Rom 8:9)[43] and to the Father (1 Cor 2:12).[44] Additionally, Eunomius neglects both John 5:23 ("Whoever does not honor the Son does not honor the Father who sent him") and Luke 10:16 ("the one who rejects me rejects him who sent me").[45]

Though this appeal to the authority of Scripture may initially come across as something of a convenient substitute for philosophical argumentation, it is no doubt intended as a cogent countermeasure to Eunomius's claim that the Holy Spirit is third in rank and nature (after the Father and the Son), which itself does not rest heavily upon philosophical argumen-

---

40. Ἐπειδὴ γὰρ τοῦ Πνεύματος, φησί, ποιητὴς ὁ Υἱὸς (ἵλεως δὲ ἡμῖν, Κύριε, ἐπὶ τοῖς λαλουμένοις εἴης), τοῦτο δὲ τοιοῦτόν ἐστιν, ὡς μηδεμίαν σεμνότητα τῷ δημιουργήσαντι προστιθέναι, διὰ τοῦτο οὐδὲ συγκρίνεσθαι τῷ Πατρὶ ἄξιος, ἐκ τῆς ὧν ἐποίησεν εὐτελείας τὸ ὁμότιμον τῆς ἀξίας ἀφηρημένος (Bas. *Eun.* 2.33.31–36: PG 29, 649C Migne).

41. τὰ ἐμὰ πάντα σά ἐστιν καὶ τὰ σὰ ἐμά (Jn 17:10 Aland, Black, Martini, Metzger and Wikgren).

42. Anastos, "Basil's Κατὰ Εὐνομίου," 111, points out that this principle is applied to the activity of the Son.

43. εἰ δέ τις Πνεῦμα Χριστοῦ οὐκ ἔχει, οὗτος οὐκ ἔστιν αὐτοῦ (Rom 8:9 Aland, Black, Martini, Metzger and Wikgren). "Anyone who does not have the Spirit of Christ does not belong to him" (trans. ESV).

44. ἡμεῖς δὲ οὐ τὸ πνεῦμα τοῦ κόσμου ἐλάβομεν ἀλλὰ τὸ πνεῦμα τὸ ἐκ τοῦ Θεοῦ, ἵνα εἰδῶμεν τὰ ὑπὸ τοῦ Θεοῦ χαρισθέντα ἡμῖν. "Now we have received not the spirit of the world, but the spirit who is from God, that we might understand the things freely given us by God" (trans. ESV). Cf. the analysis of Anastos, "Basil's Κατὰ Εὐνομίου," 111–18.

45. Trans. ESV. Cf. Anastos, "Basil's Κατὰ Εὐνομίου," 91.

tation but is claimed by Eunomius as "the teaching of the saints,"[46] a point contested by Basil. Of course, for a Christian, Scripture plays a special role in establishing Trinitarian doctrine.[47] Yet Basil's methodology goes beyond relying upon an appeal to Scripture: rather, the appeals to Scripture are interconnected with his philosophical strategy. The scriptural arguments support the philosophical claim that even if the Son is regarded as the creator of the Holy Spirit, the Father is its ultimate cause. As the product of the Father, the Son occupies the second rank in relation to his cause, but this does not mean that the Son is second in nature, for they both have a single divinity in each of them.[48] Furthermore, the creation of the Holy Spirit should not be represented as an act that denigrates the dignity of the Son, for the Holy Spirit is also holy (*hagios*).[49] For Basil, the baptism that occurs in the name of the Holy Spirit is a confirmation of the Spirit's divinity.[50] This is illustrated by Matthew 28:19: "Go therefore and make disciples of all nations, baptizing them in the name of the Father and the Son and the Holy Spirit";[51] the Holy Spirit is inseparable from the Father and Son (Bas. *Spir.* 16), not just in baptism but also in worship (Bas. *Spir.* 25.64).

In outlining the relationship between the members of the Trinity (Bas. *Eun.* 3.6–7: PG 29, 668A–669D Migne), Basil counters Eunomius's claim that the Holy Spirit is a created thing (κτίσμα καὶ ποίημα, 3.6.4: PG 29, 668A) since it is neither without principle and unbegotten (ἄναρχος ... καὶ ἀγέννητος) like the Father or begotten (γέννημα) like the Son. Basil's argumentative strategy here is striking because it hinges on the admission of ignorance. The nature of the Holy Spirit is one of those things that remain hidden from us, yet it must rank above creation since as sanctifier and revealer it cannot share the same nature as that which it sanctifies and reveals (Bas. *Eun.* 3.6.29–31: PG 29, 668C Migne). In contrast to his previous line of argumentation, which favored a certain primacy of Scripture in develop-

---

46. Eun., *apol.* 25 (861) Vaggione; Basil, *Eun.* 3.1.16–17: PG 29, 653B. The "saints" are understood by Basil to refer to the Church Fathers.

47. This does not really require confirmation, but see, e.g., Ath. *Ep. Serap.* 2.8 (620) Savvidis.

48. φύσει δὲ οὐκέτι δεύτερος, διότι ἡ θεότης ἐν ἑκατέρῳ μία. "He is by no means second in nature, on account of the same divinity in each" (Bas. *Eun.* 3.1.34–35: PG 29, 656A Migne). Cf. Anastos, "Basil's Κατὰ Εὐνομίου," 112.

49. Καὶ ὥσπερ φύσει ἅγιος ὁ Πατὴρ, καὶ φύσει ἅγιος ὁ Υἱὸς, οὕτω φύσει ἅγιον καὶ τὸ Πνεῦμα τὸ τῆς ἀληθείας· διὸ καὶ ἐξαιρέτου καὶ ἰδιαζούσης τῆς τοῦ ἁγίου προσηγορίας ἠξίωται (Bas. *Eun.* 3.2.53–56: PG 29, 660C–D Migne). "And just as the Father is holy by nature and the Son is holy by nature, so too is the Spirit of truth holy by nature. On account of this, it is judged worthy of the remarkable and specific appellation of holy".

50. Cf. Basil's discussion at Bas. *Spir.* 10 Pruche.

51. Trans. ESV.

ing Trinitarian doctrine, Basil here places a strict limit. Eunomius claims scriptural authority for his assertion that the Holy Spirit is a κτίσμα at John 1:3 ("Through Him all things were made"),[52] for him the designation "all things" includes even the Holy Spirit (Bas. *Eun.* 3.7.32–34: PG 29, 669C Migne), though Basil makes it clear that he does not believe that we can simply feel free to apply Scripture to the Holy Spirit in this manner.

The restrained approach to scriptural interpretation found in the final chapter of *Adversus Eunomium* helps to shed light on Basil's approach. He employs Scripture in support of positions that he also defends by means of philosophical-theological arguments; this is illustrated by his reluctance to employ scriptural exegesis at the close of *Adversus Eunomium*, where it does not appear that he had yet adopted a closely thought out position to advance or defend.[53] (This view would seem to be reinforced by the subsequent composition of *De Spiritu Sancto*, when he had availed of the opportunity to develop a more detailed Pneumatology, though much of *De Spiritu Sancto* also concerns itself with refuting the attempted degradation of the Son in relation to the Father found in the writings of Basil's opponents.[54])

Conclusion

Eunomius's Trinitarian theology displays various Platonic or Platonizing features: a Platonic view of time; the understanding of the Father, Son, and Holy Spirit in terms of a hierarchy of hypostases; and an interest in the legitimacy of divine names. (The theme of divine names is found both in the Platonic tradition as well as in the Chaldaean Oracles, which themselves influenced several Neoplatonic texts.[55]) As a result, the most striking feature of Platonic influence to be found in Basil's theological thought is a reaction against the Platonic features of Eunomius's theology.

Basil conveys the impression of simply appealing to the authority of Scripture. Yet this is part of a sophisticated strategy both to undermine his opponents in order to further his own theological agenda and to support his developing attempts to form some sort of theological consensus

52. πάντα δι' αὐτοῦ ἐγένετο (Jn 1:3 Aland, Black, Martini, Metzger and Wikgren).

53. The Nicene definition focused more closely on the Son than on the Holy Spirit, since this was the more pressing problem in combating Arian thought; this also explains the prominence of clarifying doctrines concerning the Son (rather than the Holy Spirit) in Basil's response to Eunomius.

54. Bas. *Spir.* 5–8 Pruche.

55. Cf. Rist, "Basil's 'Neoplatonism,'" 185.

amongst the various heterodox groups in the Church of his day. A sophisticated understanding of Platonism underpins his formulation of several key concepts, such as time or knowledge of the divine, even if this is not overt. Given the position that Basil adopts toward Greek thought in his official capacity as Bishop of Caesarea, one would not expect it to be. The precise trigger for those formulations of Basil that betray a Platonic background is also not a response to Platonism per se, but rather to heterodox Christian opponents. Instead, what we find in Basil is an attempt to deal with theological problems, several of which had been much earlier identified by Platonism, and some of which are specifically Christian. Even when Basil attempts to resolve the issues raised by the Platonists, he does so within a specifically Christian context and with a Christian orientation, which encompasses and shapes his proposed solutions, even if these solutions are formulated against the backdrop of Platonic thought.

Mark Edwards

When we say of an ancient Christian writer that he is a Platonist, we mean, or ought to mean, one of two things: either that he treats Plato as an authority on matters of doctrine, or that he gives an axial place in his system of thought to tenets that are distinctively Platonic. The first of these claims could hardly be true of anyone whom the Church has come to reckon among its Doctors; it is manifestly not true of the subject of this essay, for Gregory mentions Plato only on seven occasions, four times to disparage him[1] and three times to insinuate that he, and not the Scriptures, is the true source of the teachings of Eunomius.[2] When we apply the second definition, we must insist upon the terms "axial" and "distinctive"; one is not a disciple of Plato simply because one repeats his etymology of the

1. Greg. Nyss. *Eun.* (*Gregorii Nysseni Opera* II, 322.9): to speak of God as Pantocrator, not father, is to speak like the Jews or Plato. Greg. Nyss. *Fat.* (GNO III.2.50.3): meaninglessness of fate illustrated by Plato's account of Herodicus's postponement of death by exercise at Pl. *R.* 406a Slings. Greg. Nyss. *Infant.* (GNO III.2.70.7): Plato wise enough to be silent on fate. Greg. Nyss. *Epistulae* VIII.2, GNO 33.84.13: a sophistical trope from the Platonic sanctum.

2. Greg. Nyss. *Eun.* (GNO I (II), 227): as Plato in the *Phaedrus* attributes motion and cessation to the soul, so Eunomius assumes that God may be idle, imaging that the exquisite diction of Plato will hide the barrenness of his thought from the unlearned. Greg. Nyss. *Eun.* GNO I (I), 344.13: Eunomius's theory of perfect correspondence between human speech and the real properties of God is indebted to the *Cratylus* of Plato. Greg. Nyss. *Eun.* GNO I (I), 344, 23: thinks it right to clothe dogma in the exquisite diction of Plato.

word *psuhkê*, while the dogma that the world has a temporal origin was incontrovertibly biblical, and would not have been called Platonic even by Christians who read the account of the genesis of the world in the *Timaeus* as literal history rather than myth.

It is evident that the style and the thoughts of Plato are more frequently evoked in Gregory's works than those of any other philosopher; yet this will not prove, as I argue in the first section of this essay, that he saw more than an affinity between doctrines that some held on Plato's authority and those that he himself held on the authority of the Church. Noting that a Christian is more likely to be indebted to Plato's teaching on the soul than to any other element in his system, I have tried in the second section to dispel some fallacies that continue to haunt academic study of this topic, especially in relation to Gregory's infamous predecessor Origen. In the third section I shall point out that in his *De Anima* Gregory firmly detaches himself—more firmly than Origen—from any Platonic beliefs that cannot be reconciled with the doctrine of resurrection. After discussing two unusual conjectures in other texts with regard to the origin of humanity, I shall conclude that Gregory's relation to Plato was always that of an interlocutor rather than a disciple. If this is a position that I have reached in other publications on Origen and Augustine, I can say by way of apology that, however banal it may seem, I have good evidence that it is seldom understood.

On Christianity and Platonism

Any of four reasons might be proposed for the presence of Platonic doctrines or allusions in the works of an educated theologian of the fourth century:

Platonic doctrines were part of the "inherited conglomerate," as modern Christians take for granted the discoveries of Copernicus, Newton, and Einstein, generally also accepting some form of Darwinism and egalitarian modes of social thinking that were unknown before the twentieth century.

Platonism was fashionable, and a Christian aspiring to fame might imitate its vocabulary, as some modern scholars align themselves with prevalent movements in literary theory or social philosophy to bring their work "up to date."

Plato was a classic, so reminiscences of his prose could play the same ornamental role in Christian discourse that biblical echoes used to play in the works of atheists.

The Christian author was conscious of an affinity in fundamental principles between biblical and Platonic thought, which encouraged him
to borrow Platonic expressions, and even concepts, where he felt that
doing so would elucidate biblical teachings, either for fellow believers
or for the unconverted.

Sympathetic readers of Gregory will obviously embrace (4), while al-
lowing that some phrases in his writings may have only the ornamental
value of (3). Platonism, after all, was widely perceived to be the one philosophy that taught:

some form of divine triadology (though probably not the consubstantiality of persons);
divine foreknowledge (at least once the ideas had been brought into the
intellect of the Demiurge);
the benign creation of the world (apparently "in" or "with" time);
a fall (though of individuals, not the mass);
a limited doctrine of providence (extending in Numenius even to individuals);
the immortality of the soul (though with transmigration rather than resurrection);
an afterlife of reward or punishment (admittedly temporary, but perhaps
not wholly bodiless); and
the ultimate goal of likeness to God (Pl. Thaet. 176b Burnet; Gn 1:26,
2 Pt 1:4).

Nevertheless, it is clear in every case that a Platonic metaphysic cannot
simply be imposed without qualification on credal or biblical tenets. Giulio
Maspero, for example, observes that when Logos functions as a name in
Platonism, it denotes not a personal being, let alone the transcendent Creator, but the rational principle of cohesion in the material cosmos. Again he
contrasts the passivity of Platonic *eros* (the desire of that which lacks beauty for the beautiful, which perishes when it has attained its object) with the
active and divine principle of love in Christian teaching, personified by one
who had "no beauty that we might know him." Much more characteristic
of Platonism is Gregory's use of the term *idea* to signify the essence of that
which is beautiful or good when abstracted from its material substrate; he
even modifies Platonic similes, likening matter to a mirror that does not
produce but reflects the idea of the good,[3] and exhorting us to bid farewell

---

3. Greg. Nyss. *Hom. Opif.* 12.11, p. 198 Sels.

to the matter that underlies the idea of beauty in order that we may behold the noetic beauty in which all other beautiful things participate.[4] For all that, we do not find, as in the *Timaeus*, that the ideas exist independently of the Demiurge, or even that they are necessary constituents of the demiurgic intellect, as in the *Enneads* of Plotinus. To Christians, the ideas or eternal forms can only be thoughts in the mind of God when this appellation denotes the first principle, whose thought is always the product of his will.

All this was as clear to Gregory as to Origen, who opposed the theory of self-subsistent ideas to his own surmise that the genera and species of all particulars, and even the discrete forms of those particulars, have existed eternally in the divine intellect (Or. Princ. 1.4.5). He does not define the first as a Platonic and the second as an Aristotelian theory, but assumes that one is implied and the other precluded by the scriptural affirmation that God created all things in wisdom. By contrast, or so he opined, the nature and provenance of the soul were matters on which he had license to speculate, since little had been handed down by Scripture or the Apostles except that the soul is a creature and that it survives death. In the ancient world, these questions fell into the province of physics rather than theology, and even the intransigent Tertullian, who never wasted a thought on any pagan view of God, can welcome voices from the schools into his *De Anima*, coupling scriptural testimonies with excerpts from physicians and philosophers who believed the soul to be a kind of body. By the fourth century, both the traducianism of Tertullian and the more elusive speculations of Origen were under suspicion of heresy; as Augustine pointed out to Jerome, however, the little that was excluded still left much to be ascertained. Thus it is in his dialogue on the soul that Gregory has to take a position not only against heretical Christians but also against unbelieving philosophers, who cannot be felled, as an Arius or an Apollinarius can, by weapons drawn wholly from the arsenal of Scripture.

Preparatory Observations

Since Gregory's desire to be less heretical than Origen has been construed as a rejection of Platonism, it is necessary to make some remarks on the scholarly handing of Origen's relation to this philosophy—remarks that are germane to any discussion of the relation between Christianity and philosophy in generally. Scholars who question the Platonism of Origen are

4. Greg. Nyss. *Virg.* at GNO VIII.1, 292, 13.

apt to be accused of a lack of nuance in their presentation of this philosophy. There is something of a paradox here, not only because the questioners are better known to academic students of Greek thought than their opponents, but also because the self-professed champions of the Platonism of Origen rarely succeed in ascribing to him any doctrine of the soul's fall that is even speciously Platonic. If we cite, as though it were Origen's Greek, the ancient charge that he held angels, humans, and demons to be intellects of the same nature, enclosed in bodies whose grossness is commensurate with the gravity of their sin in the incorporeal realm,[5] we shall not find clear support for it in his writings, and we shall find even less in the writings of the Platonists, for whom daemons are not fallen intellects but inhabit the rank assigned to them by nature between the human and the divine.

No Platonist can entirely dispense with a theory of transmigration, however, for they held the soul to be naturally immortal but also held that only a soul that is purged of its carnal appetites can subsist without a body. Yet almost all scholars agree that Origen found this position incongruous with the teaching of the Church—as indeed he was bound to do if he was not to disown the biblical promise of bodily resurrection. Again, no modern scholar contends that Origen held the proper abode of souls to be a realm of eternal forms; conversely, the doctrine of anamnesis or recollection cannot be subtracted from Plato's epistemology and therefore cannot be subtracted from his theory of transmigration, which he propounds, both in the *Phaedrus* and in the *Meno*, to account for the possibility of knowledge. For Origen, as for all Christians, revelation takes the place of recollection, and forms, if they exist at all, do so only as thoughts in the mind of God. That is the position of Philo the Jew,[6] but to ascribe it to Plato, Numenius, or Plotinus is to make them speak in a tongue that is not their own. Why, then, is it still so widely assumed that only those who are writing "confessionally"—that is, with a Lutheran preconception that all philosophy is alien to the Gospel—can contest the description of Origen as a Platonist?[7] One answer may be that, since a number of Platonizing theses were falsely attributed to Origen by his detractors, the proper interpretation of his thought is sometimes an exercise in correcting the errors of heresiologists; if such an

---

5. See below on *koros* at Or. *Princ.*, p. 96 Koetschau.

6. See Greg. Nyss. *Hom. Opif.* 16 Sels with Dillon, "Idea as Thoughts of God," 31–42.

7. See, e.g., Martens, "Response to Edwards," especially the opening pages. When I argue that passages preserved in the *Philokalia* by its rigidly orthodox editors must be susceptible of an orthodox reading, Martens assumes that I share the confessional interests that I have cited to establish a historical probability.

exercise is misinterpreted as an attempt to vindicate Origen's orthodoxy, it may appear that the freedom of historical inquiry has been circumscribed by theological interests. The reason most often stated, however—leaving us once again to wonder what in some quarters is understood by nuance—is that if one denies the Platonism of Origen, one denies him any commerce with pagan thought or literature, in clear defiance of his own pedagogic practice and the ostentatious erudition of his late tract *Against Celsus*.[8] To this is it surely sufficient to reply that the vast majority of philosophers in the ancient world were opponents of Platonism, and that the rigor and versatility of the Greek mind were seldom exhibited with such force as in the salvoes that were fired against the Academy from the Stoa and the Lyceum.

To say that ancient Christians were not Platonists is not to disparage Plato or to assert the incompatibility of philosophy with the Gospel; it is simply to say that, insofar as it was not merely a cult but a philosophy, Christianity formed a school by itself, guarding its first principles as jealously as the Stoics or the Peripatetics, but equally willing to take from its rivals whatever was consistent with these principles and useful for the completion of its own system. No school in late antiquity is hermetic, yet none is a hybrid: a Stoic may quote a precept from Epicurus without endorsing his equation of the Good with pleasure, and Platonists may acknowledge, with Aristotle, that divine goodness entails the eternity of the world without subscribing to his opinion that there is no incorporeal substance apart from God. The distinctive premise of Christian philosophy is the sufficiency of Scripture, and Origen therefore allotted to the Greek schools the ancillary role of providing tools for the exorcism of seeming contradictions or obscurities that cannot be removed by assiduous collation of biblical texts. No independent authority is attached to any Greek thinker in his writings; if citations from Plato preponderate over those from any other philosopher in his reply to Celsus, the reason is that Plato, being more commonly in agreement with the Scriptures than other thinkers, offers more material for their elucidation.

The Anthropology of the Afterlife

Gregory was, like Origen, a man of wide education in philosophy who believed in the inerrancy of the Scriptures. In Plato's view, which is shared by the modern academy, it is unworthy of a philosopher to rely on a single

8. See again Martens, "Embodiment, Heresy and the Hellenization of Christianity," 594–620, where he undertakes to refute me by advancing a number of theses that I hold against a thesis that I have repeatedly opposed.

book; Gregory's reply would perhaps be that it is unworthy of any mortal to put one's faith in a single teacher, unless one knows that teacher to be God. He himself made deft use of Aristotle's physical theories (which were not so well known to Origen) in his rebuttal of Eunomius;[9] the letter in which he distinguishes the *ousia* of God as the bearer of "catholic" predicates from the hypostases that are individuated by their own predicates may also have been inspired by Porphyry's reading of the *Categories* as a study of words insofar as they signify. An appreciative knowledge of Stoicism has also contributed to his prescriptions for the cultivation of Christian virtue.[10] To call him a Platonist, therefore, is to ignore much more than has been ignored when this label has been applied to Origen. The writing of his that most obviously courts this epithet is the *De Anima*, in which he takes as stringent a position as any Christian on the incorporeality of the soul. For this very reason, however, he is at all the more pains to prove that the true corollary of the natural immortality of the soul is not transmigration but resurrection: my soul is not, as Plato thinks, my whole self but that part of me whose survival must be posited to ensure that on the last day I can claim the regenerate body as my own.

Because he is combining exegesis with philosophy, he adopts the form of a dialogue, substituting his late sister Macrina for the prophetess Diotima, whom Socrates names as his mentor in the *Symposium*. Like Justin's imitation of the *Phaedrus* in the dialogue that results in his conversion form Platonism, the choice of medium may be a tacit satire on the bookishness of a school whose found had warned them the idolatry of the book. Be that as it may, Macrina proves herself to be more Platonic than the Platonists in her insistence on the incorporeality of the soul and on all that follows from this axiom. She explains away as metaphor the scene of the beggar reclining on Abraham's bosom in Luke's parable,[11] a text that had furnished Tertullian with one of his clearest proofs that the soul can occupy space and must therefore be a body. Yet deviations from Platonic doctrine are also evident at an early stage in the dialogue, most conspicuously in the definition of soul as "a generated substance, a living and intellectual substance, sufficing by itself to infuse into an organic and sensible body a vivifying power that

9. See Edwards, "Dunamis and the Christian Trinity in the Fourth Century," 105–22.

10. See the judicious observations of Boersma, *Embodiment and Virtue in Gregory of Nyssa*, 128–30.

11. See Greg. Nyss. *anim. et res* 8087, pp. 425–433 Ramelli. The gulf between the rich man and the beggar is the alienation from God and from one's own good that results from an evil life; the corporeal members are the scattered atoms that are not in fact reassembled in this intermediate state but only on the day of resurrection.

is able to comprehend the sensible."[12] This formula imitates the language of Aristotle and shares his presupposition that soul must be defined with reference to a body—a somewhat stronger precept than the Platonic observation that soul has a natural affinity for body.[13] Thus Gregory anticipates his conclusion that the destiny of the soul is to inhabit one body forever in perfect felicity—a conclusion that, as we shall see, he finds in no way incompatible with the dogmas that he and the Platonists hold in common.

 To defend the Christian doctrine of resurrection, he must refute the Platonic doctrine of transmigration, and a comparison between his method and Origen's is instructive. Origen addresses this subject only when some argument for transmigration is thrown in his way by a problematic text.[14] His policy is never to attempt a philosophic refutation but to stipulate, after gleaning from Scripture all that can be said in its favor, that theories of this kind are the preserve of Gnostic sects and no ἐκκλησιαστικὸς ἀνήρ (man of the church) will give them a hearing. In view of his own conjecture that God preferred Jacob to Esau (Or. Princ. 2.9.7) because of the latter's sins in a previous life, his critics can hardly be blamed for suspecting that he surreptitiously countenanced the heresy that he ostensibly deplored. Tertullian undertakes a more cogent rebuttal, often culling his arguments from pagan sources,[15] but he does not match the assiduity of Gregory, who makes it his object to prove that transmigration is inconsistent not only with reason and with Scripture but with the first principles of its own advocates. His case, directed chiefly against the Platonists who teach migration from human to animal bodies,[16] may be summarized as follows:[17]

12. Greg. Nyss. *anim. et res* 30, p. 364 Ramelli.

13. Alcin., *Didasc.* 25.6, Louis p. 34 Dillon.

14. He finds reasonable arguments for transmigration from human to human when discussing Jn 1:21 (is the Baptist Elijah?) but rejects them in the name of the Church (*Commentary on John* 1.11). More summarily (*Commentary on Romans* 7.8), he rejects the Basilidean claim that Rom 7:9 ("I was alive without the law ... sin revived") alludes to a period of incarceration in an animal body; at *First Principles* 1.8.4 (Latin) he rejects a possible argument from Lv 20:16, that if a beast who lies with a woman is to be killed, it must have a soul that is answerable for sin, and therefore rational.

15. See especially Tertullian *De Anima* 24 and 33 Waszink.

16. At Greg. Nyss. *anim. et res.*108, p. 436 Ramelli, Macrina expounds the doctrine of those outside our school, meaning evidently the Platonists. She divides them into those who entertain the baser opinion that human souls enter the bodies of brutes and those who admit only transmigration from human to human. She notes that the second (at least) assumes the number of souls to be immutable. The *Phaedrus* of Plato, literally interpreted, supports the first position; the second is attributed to Porphyry by Augustine, though modern scholars are divided as to his accuracy. See Johnson, "Astrology and the Will in Porphyry of Tyre," 186–201, esp. 192–96.

17. Greg. Nyss. *anim. et res.*109–20, pp. 459–73 Ramelli.

the soul is, as the Platonists concede, the stable element in our composition, but constant migration would rob it of its stability;

the theory has the absurd consequence that we cannot kill a snake or cut
a cluster of grapes without fearing to inflict an injury on our dead
relatives;

by sentencing erring souls to incarceration in animal bodies, the theory
entails that good and evil remain inextricably mixed;[18]

transmigration belies the theory of these same philosophers that matter is
the source of evil, for if embodiment is the consequence of primordial
sin, there must be evil in heaven;

the notion of a fall from heaven implies that we cannot be sure of our
permanent salvation;

the theory subjects the whole order of the world to chance by making
rational agents subject to antecedent causes; and

insofar as it grants a capacity for virtue to souls embodied (after their fall)
as rational creatures, the theory makes virtue a vice.

In rebuttal, Gregory urges the providence of God and the freedom of humans, once created as rational beings without any antecedent sin, to make
their choice between virtue and vice. He holds these tenets in common
with Origen (and with the main tradition of Christianity); he does not concede that Plato, in ascribing the choice of life to the free, if unrecollected,
decision of the soul before birth, is bringing within the power of the agent
even those factors that lie outside his control once he has been born. His
argument that the faculties of the soul mature with the body agrees with
Origen only in assigning a soul to the fetus (*First Principles* 1.7.1), but not in
assuming that soul to be already rational. (Porphyry, who stands between
them chronologically, argues in his *Ad Gaurum* that the fetus has an imaginative but not yet a rational soul.[19])

If then there is to be a resurrection of the body, as the Church teaches,
what will be the relation between this house for the soul and the osseous
tabernacle that it lays aside at the point of physical death? Origen had written that the *eidos* of the body is transferred to the soul: whether we follow
Methodius in taking this to mean *morphe* or surmise that some attempt is
being made to interpret Aristotle's definition of soul as the *eidos* of form
of an organic body, no material vehicle for the soul, in the common sense

18. Tertullian, *De Anima* 33.2 Waszink had already pointed out that the soul of a beast cannot repent of, or indeed remember, the sin for which it is undergoing punishment.

19. Porph. *Gaur.* 5, pp. 160–62 Brisson.

of the term "material," seems to be contemplated here. Yet Origen asserts more than once that no being except the persons of the Trinity can subsist without a body (Or. Princ. 3.6.4). For the most part, he also employs the words "corporeal" and "material" interchangeably, never questioning the reality in this world of the phenomena that we call material objects. He does, however, entertain the possibility that these objects are mere concretions of properties that do not require the substrate devoid of qualities to which Aristotle had given the name "prime matter."[20] If the *eidos* that is transferred from body to soul is a congeries of properties, it would be comparable to the scum of remembered sins and moral scars that the errant soul carries into the afterlife in Platonic speculations of this epoch. Because they held that the function of soul was to animate a body, it became increasingly common for philosophers of this school to equip it with a tenuous vehicle in the interludes between its escape from one gross body and its return to another. It has been argued that Origenists such as Didymus and Evagrius also allotted a subtle body to the soul both before and after its embodiment; whether or not they were reasoning independently of the philosophers, they certainly reasoned to a different end, for the body that they postulated was not a tabernacle but a temple to be occupied without fear of a second death. Gregory also disavows the Aristotelian concept of prime matter[21] but at the same shuns the idealism of Origen, defining matter instead as a composite of the elements rather than their substrate. The severance of soul and body is not, in his view, accompanied by any accretion of matter or its properties to the soul. There is no need of any such hybrid, for the soul, by virtue of its omnipresence—the logical consequence of its incorporeality—is able to maintain contact with every particle that constituted its body and therefore to bring them together on the last day. This theory that bodies are made up of discrete and irreplaceable atoms is clearly more Epicurean than Platonic, though Gregory may be aware of Pythagorean antecedents, and it was known to all that Epicureans believed the soul itself to be body, subject to posthumous dispersion. As always, it is more important to understand the tenor of Gregory's thought than its archaeology: he is yoking Platonic psychology to Epicurean physics not to enhance his reputation as a philosopher, but to vindicate a doctrine that was equally repugnant to the first principles of both schools.

20. Or. *Princ.* 4.4.7; cf. *Philokalia* 24.8.
21. See Marmodoro, "Gregory of Nyssa on the Creation of the World," 94–110.

A Problem of Protology

Gregory cannot accept the teaching of the *Phaedrus* that the proper abode of the soul is a supercelestial heaven undefiled by matter. Nevertheless, this dialogue, with its picturesque myth of the fall of souls, will spring at once to the mind of a modern reader who encounters the following passage in Gregory's *Commentary on the Song of Songs*:

Human nature when first created was winged, so that in its wings it might resemble God. (Greg. Nyss. Hom. in cant., GNO VI, 448.3)

The *Lexicon Gregorianum*[22] refers us to one of the more recondite passages in Origen's *First Principles* (2.9.1), which speaks of the defection from God, through *taedium laboris*, of certain intelligences or rational natures that were created in the beginning in sufficient number to adorn the world. This is one of two texts that are commonly cited to show that Origen did indeed hold the view ascribed to him by his Byzantine detractors, that all human souls were created as pure intellects at the foundation of the world and entered human bodies only as a consequence of *koros*, that is, of weariness of contemplating God.[23] I have argued elsewhere that this is a misreading, perhaps inspired by Philo's use of the same word to account for the descent of souls, or else by the Plotinian conceit that *nous* sinks down to the lower realm because it is sated to the point of drunkenness with contemplation.[24] Origen, for his part, makes satiety the cause of the soul's loss of virtue at Or. Princ. 1.3.8, but, as Peter Martens rightly observes,[25] he appears to be giving a reason not for its fall from heaven but for its apostasy in the present life. At 2.9.1, he may not be speaking of human souls, for while he certainly goes on to assert that all souls, however diverse their fortunes, were created in that *principium* or beginning which is Christ, the intelligences whose fall is described in 2.9.1 are the only ones for whom the phrase "in the beginning"[26] bears not only this theological sense but also its plain and natural meaning,

22. Ambrose, *De Isaac* is also cited but cannot be a source. See Fitzgerald, "Ambrose at the Well," 79–99, who dates *De Isaac* to 396.

23. See especially the texts assembled by Koetschau, *Origenes, Werke* 5, 96.

24. Edwards, *Origen against Plato*, 91–93.

25. Martens, "Embodiment, Heresy and the Hellenization of Christianity," n73. When he doubts, however, whether any scholar has cited *First Principles* 1.4.1 as evidence for the fall of preexistent souls into bodies, he overlooks Lampert, "Origen on Time," 657; Lauro, "Fall," 1001–10; Greggs, *Barth, Origen and Universal Salvation*, 55n4; Heine, *Origen*, 240n; Humphries, *Who Is Chosen?*, 15.

26. At Or. *Princ.* 2.9.1, the word for beginning is usually *initium*, not *principium*.

"at the time of the world's foundation." Most probably, then, these fallen beings are angels who joined the retinue of Satan and who therefore do have a plumage of some sort, as Origen remarks when contrasting this historic calamity with the imaginary shedding of the soul's wings in Plato's myth. Far from suggesting, however, that Gregory might have had this text in mind when he wrote that the archetype of humanity is winged, this exegesis shows it to be all but impossible that he would do so. Most obviously, there is no explicit mention of wings; insofar as they might be implicit in an account of the fall of angels, we have seen that Origen differentiates this from the Platonic fall of souls. If Gregory perceived the fall of angels to be the subject of this text, he would have held that it shed no light on the archetypal form of humanity; had he read it as a description of the fall of souls from a disembodied state, he would have deemed it heterodox. Whether or not he imputed this belief to Origen, he is as vehement as any of Origen's critics in denouncing the notion that one could grow weary of contemplating God. That would be possible only if God were a finite being—a tenet that can be attributed to Origen, not only because he identifies God with mind but also because, in the very passage that we are examining (Or. Princ. 2.9.1), he initiates the discussion by denying that even God could have created an infinite world.[27] There are intimations in Origen's later work that God is superior to mind, but not the explicit and repeated assertions of his infinity for which Gregory is renowned. In Gregory the conviction that the glory and power of God are inexhaustible entails that none of his creatures can experience satiety in beholding him; of his nine asseverations to this effect,[28] the three that occur in his *Life of Moses* are prompted by God's revelation of his hinder parts at Exodus 3:18, a text that Origen too had read as an exhortation to contemplate the Father from the sheltering rock of Christ.

We have still to explain why Gregory is prepared to adopt the metaphor of the winged soul in such works as his treatise *On Virginity*, where he exclaims that it is only on a heavenly wing that the soul can mount to heaven.[29] Elsewhere he declares that the wing is virtue. As though to dis-

---

27. As I point out in *Aristotle and Early Christian Thought*, his meaning is not that the power of God is finite—for God has the power to create a world of any magnitude—but that any world that God in fact creates must have certain dimensions, since there is logically no such thing as an actual infinity.

28. Greg. Nyss. *anim. et res.*96, p. 444 Ramelli; Greg. Nyss. *Hom. in eccl.* GNO V, 313.10; Greg. Nyss. *Hom. in cant.* GNO Vi, 366.14 and 425.15; Greg. Nyss. *V. Moys.* GNO VII.1, 114.19, 116.19–23 and 117.21; Greg. Nyss. *Beta.* GNO VII.2, 111.20; Greg. Nyss. *Instit.* GNO VII.2, 78.15.

29. Greg. Nyss. GNO VIII.1, 294.9 and 22; cf. 275.4.

claim any borrowing from Plato, however, he permits himself only one use of the noun *pterroruêsis*, in a combative summary of the opinions held by the "philosophers of the world" on the peregrinations of the soul.[30] The cognate verb *pterroruein*, however, is no longer on loan from the Greeks in the disquisition *On the Headings to the Psalms*, where it denotes the falling away of the disobedient soul from God.[31] In the same work Gregory says that the soul may be stirred to flight by shame, a dictum echoed in his treatise *On Perfection*.[32] References to the wings of the soul are more common in Gregory's book on the Psalms than in any of his other works, the majority being glosses on the Psalmist's prayer to escape on the wings of a dove from a world of sinners.[33] Plato too had said that to fly to God is to become like him (*Theaetetus* 176c), but only the Psalmist attributes wings to God himself when he prays that they may be extended for his protection (Pss 16 and 17:8). The Psalmist gives the older and purer version of a trope that has been abused by the philosophers of this world.

One for All

The notion of a winged archetype of humanity, therefore, is Gregory's improvisation on a biblical figure of speech. His argument for the universality of the inner man, however, is a solution to a difficulty raised by an important scriptural text. Having resolved at Genesis 1:26 to create man (*anthrôpos*) in his image and likeness, God proceeds to create man in his likeness, male and female. In the next chapter of Genesis, he fashions a male human being from the soil of paradise and only some verses later produces a female by the extraction of a rib. Gregory follows Origen, who in this case is at his most literal, by positing two creations, the first of the inner man and the second of the outer man, from whom we are all descended (thanks to the Fall) by biological reproduction. Whereas, however, Origen seems to assume the chronological priority of the inner man, Gregory accords to him only an ontological primacy, maintaining that body and soul are created together.[34] Waiving any question of the difference between the image and the likeness, he assumes that the inner man is characterized as male and female because he resembles God in exhibiting no differentiation

---

30. Greg. Nyss. *anim. et res.*117, p. 468 Ramelli; cf. Greg. Nyss. *anim. et res.*112, p. 462 Ramelli.
31. GNO V, 449.15.
32. Greg. Nyss. *Pss. Tit.* GNO V, 42.2; Greg. Nyss. *Perf.* GNO VIII.1, 213.22.
33. Greg. Nyss. *Pss. Tit.* GNO V, 52.5 and 145,2. Cf. Pss 54 and 55:7.
34. *De Anima* 121, p. 473 Ramelli.

of sex. Not only does he indeed have no peculiar attributes such as setting apart one outer man from another, but he also undergoes no individuation and is the selfsame entity in each of us:[35]

For first he says that God made man in the image of God, showing through these words, as the apostle says [Gal 3:28], that in such a one there is neither male nor female … The created man is given the generic name, not that of an individual, for by this generic use of the term which denotes the nature we are led to understand that, in the foreknowledge and power of God, the whole of humanity is comprehended in the original creation.

The unity of all human beings in Adam is implied by the fact that his name means man in Hebrew, and the physical solidarity that we enjoy through our descent from him is that which makes it possible, in Gregory's view, for the Word to redeem us by the simple assumption of the flesh. Yet Gregory is not speaking here of physical solidarity but of the universal presence of one incorporeal being, the inner man. He is not even proposing an analogy between the corporeal and the incorporeal, as Apollinarius does when he explains the genarchic unity of the Trinity by analogy with the biblical use of a man's name to embrace all his descendants. Nor is it pertinent to adduce the teaching of certain rabbis that the first human being, before the extraction of Eve, was a hermaphrodite, for this too is a theory regarding the outer man, and one to which Gregory himself did not subscribe.

Closer to this passage, both in phrasing and in philosophical import, is Porphyry's dictum in the *Isagoge* that all humans are one in the species, while conversely in the particulars the "common man" becomes many.[36] Porphyry was a student of the Platonists Longinus and Plotinus, but his *Isagoge* is an introduction to the logic of Aristotle, if not to his *Categories*. In his commentary on the latter work, Porphyry concludes that its subject is neither words alone nor the realities that they signify but "words insofar as they signify." I have argued elsewhere that Gregory adopts this supposition when he distinguishes the *ousia* in the Godhead from its hypostases, prescinding from any ontological question as to the identity of each person with the Godhead and limiting himself strictly to the logical task of distinguishing those attributes that are predicated commonly of the three persons from those which are predicated only of one.[37] It is probable that

<hr>

35. Greg. Nyss. *Hom. Opif.* 9 and 16, pp. 97 and 200 Seld.

36. Porph. *Intr.* 2.12 (6.21–23), p. 8 de Libera and Segonds. Against the Platonic reading of this passage, see Barnes, *Porphyry*, 136–38.

37. Edwards, "Porphyry and Cappadocian Logic," 61–74.

in the *Isagoge* too the common man is simply that which is signified by the term "man": he has no ontological status, or rather his status remains undefined. To say that he is one yet several in his instantiations is to say that all human beings participate equally in humanity, or in plain terms that all humans are equally human.

Gregory may be drawing on some such proposition when he declares in his letter to Ablabius that we ought not to employ the noun "man" in the plural. Although he has the usage of Scripture against him, he extends this prohibition in *Ad Graecos* to the horse and the ox (the two other tokens of the genus animal in Aristotle), and hence we must presume to every member of the category of substance.[38] All of which goes to show that Gregory's universal inner man cannot be derived from Porphyry, for he evidently regards the inner man as a real individual and not merely a logical species, ascribing his power to be present in each of us without division not to his status as a substance but to his unique preeminence as the image of God.

It was common in Christian thought to equate the outer man with the body and the inner man with the soul. It is thus no surprise that Gregory's concept of an inner man who is undividedly present in each of us should be strongly reminiscent of an argument in Plotinus that, if the soul is wholly present in every portion of the body that it animates, the soul of the all will be undividedly present in every part of the all, and hence every individuation of soul will be identical with this soul, and consequently with each other.[39] The last step follows only from the premise that if both A and B are identical with C, then A is identical with B—a commonsensical claim, no doubt, but one that both Plotinus and Gregory might have wished to qualify, as both are bound to maintain that each of us feels his own feelings, perceives his own percepts, and has his own soul to save. Nevertheless, they also agree that there is a sense, and not merely a logical sense, in which all human beings are one. Can we say therefore that Gregory is indebted to Plotinus? Certainly, he may have derived some hints from him toward the elucidation of the Scriptures, but even had he thought this a worthy object of philosophy, Plotinus could not have anticipated Gregory's deduction that the inner man, being only the image of God, is a creation out of nothing, any more than he could have understood how this incorporeal being could have been redeemed by the Incarnation of Christ.

38. Greg. Nyss. *Comm. Not.* GNO III.1, 29.14–20.
39. See above all Plot. 4.9.1 Henry Schwyzer.

Conclusion

In a previous paper I have argued that, while Gregory wrote his *Commentary on the Song of Songs* in conscious succession to Origen, he is richer in his evocation of Plato's vocabulary and imagery and (unlike Origen) closer to Plato than Paul in his anthropology.[40] In comparing their doctrines of the soul, I have reached the opposite conclusion: Gregory goes to conspicuous lengths to prove that he does not subscribe to any of the heresies that had been laid at Origen's door.[41] The reason for the difference is not far to seek, as his faith was on trial in one case and not in the other; but even as he parades his orthodoxy, he leaves no doubt that he is as much of a philosopher as his predecessor and conscious, as all good philosophers are, that one can profit by listening even to those who are not of one's own creed. Neither he nor Origen is a Platonist, and neither can we call either an anti-Platonist if we mean by this that their thought was shaped primarily by their opposition to Plato. Both were above all else loyal sons of the Church who sought out philosophy only with a view to defining, never with a view to transgressing, the bounds of filial piety; even as historians we must read them with this confessional proviso, for it was in their churchmanship that they found their own, and their only, way of being Greeks.

40. Edwards, "Origen and Gregory of Nyssa on the Song of Songs," 74–92.
41. See further Clark, *Origenist Controversy*.

CHAPTER 4 ‖ Language of Interaction in Cyril's Trinitarian Theology and Proclus's Theory of the Henads

Sarah Klitenic Wear

Introduction

In Proclus's *Commentary on Parmenides* 749.38 Steel on 129ab, Proclus addresses the aporia "The Unity of What is Different: how intelligible ideas can be united without being mixed" ἥνωται ἀσυγχύτως διακέκριται ἀδιαιρέτως. This aporia questions how distinct intelligible objects interpenetrate while retaining their own particularity (*idiotēs*); that is, they are not dissolved into a mixture. In this section of Proclus's *Commentary on the Parmenides*, Proclus show that the henads are united in the One while retaining their individual natures. That they retain their particular features is important, as it allows them to become principles of distinction; that is, as entities below them participate in henads, they create distinction throughout the universe. Proclus uses the terminology of ἀσύγχυτος and ἕνωσις to describe the interaction among henadic principles in the realm of the One.

Proclus's description of the interrelation of divine principles has a Christian analogue in fifth-century Alexandria. In Cyril of Alexandria's *Dialogues on the Trinity* and his *Commentary on the Gospel of John*, Cyril describes the three hypostases of the Father, Son, and Holy Spirit; these principles relate in a union without confusion. That is, they fully interact as they are united through *ousia*, and yet they also maintain distinction (*idiotēs*).[1] This terminology—or, rather, these three terms used together (*asynchytos, henosis,* and *idiotēs*)—describes the interaction of the three distinct principles within the Godhead that do not compromise its unity. Numerous studies[2] have linked Cyril's thought on relationship to Stoic language of relationship and mixture, as well as terminology found in Aristotle's *Categories* and commentaries on the *Categories,* including language of relationship in the *de corruptione.*[3] More specifically, scholars link the term *asynchytos* in Cyril to texts of Porphyry and Nemesius, where the soul inheres in the body "without confusion"; these proof texts scholars often trace as influential for Cyril's doctrine of the Incarnation.[4] Porphyry's *Sentence* 37 features a description of souls that are "present (*pareisin*) to each other without confusion (*ou sugkexumenai*), nor by making the universal a mere conglomeration; for they are not divided from one another by boundaries, nor again, are they blended with one another, even as the many items of knowledge are not blended into a single soul, and again, are not merely in the soul like bodies, maintaining a distinction of substance, but they are qualitatively distinct activities of the soul."[5]

Scholars have discussed the impact of this fragment on the thought of Cyril. Rist[6] doubts that Porphyry is the origin of the technical phrase *asynchytos henosis,* although the thought—if not the technical phrasing—certainly seems to appear in the passage above. Chase disputes Rist, citing *Ad Gaurum* 10, 5 as a source where a complete mixing does not indicate a destruction of individual parts.[7] While there may or may not be the

1. Cyril is credited with the formulation "union without confusion" that became doctrinal with the Chalcedonian Confession. It should be noted, however, that Basil also uses this technical terminology several times. Cf. Οὐ γὰρ ἵνα τὸ ἀλλότριον τῆς φύσεως εἰσαγάγῃ, ἀλλ' ἵνα ἀσύγχυτον Πατρὸς καὶ Υἱοῦ τὴν ἔννοιαν παραστήσῃ, οὕτω προήνεγκεν ὁ ἀπόστολος (Bas. *Spir.* 5.7.1.1 Pruche); θεωρουμένας τῇ οὐσίᾳ δέχοιτό τις εἶναι τὸ γεννητὸν καὶ τὸ ἀγέννητον, πρὸς τὴν τρανὴν καὶ ἀσύγχυτονΠατρὸς καὶ Υἱοῦ χειραγωγούσας ἔννοιαν (Bas. *Eun.* (book 5), vol. 29, p. 637.18 Pruche).

2. Torrance, *Christology after Chalcedon,* 59–74; Joachim, *Aristotle on Coming-to-Be and Passing-Away;* idem, "Aristotle's Conception of Chemical Combination," 72–86; Wolfson, *Philosophy of the Church Fathers,* 372–86.

3. Van Loon, *Dyophysite Christology of Cyril of Alexandria.*

4. Nemes. *Nat. Hum.* 3 [*PG* 40, 604A*ff.*]); Porph. *Sent.* 37 Brisson. The concept of mixture among a body or between two intelligibles in these texts has been discussed at length. For a review of secondary literature, especially on the question of whether Nemesius's discussion in Nemes. *Nat. Hum.* 38.14 and 42.16–17 Morani concerns Porphyry, see *On the Nature of Man* ed. Sharpless and van der Eijk, 78n372. See also Boulnois, "Patristique et historie des dogmes."

5. Dillon translation in Porphyrye, *Sentences* (ed. Brisson).

6. Rist, "Pseudo-Ammonius and the Soul/Body Problem," 402–15.

7. Chase, "La subsistence néoplanicienne de Porphyre."

precise terminology of *asynchytos henosis* in Porphyry, the concept certainly appears. It may be that this idea flourishes, so to speak—and becomes more elaborate—in mid-fifth-century Alexandria and Athens to describe the relationship among divine entities.[8]

While, ultimately, Cyril and Proclus hold views that rest on Porphyry's description of soul as intelligible principles interpenetrating without fusion, they both show a major expansion to the phenomena Porphyry describes. Cyril and Proclus describe divine principles within one divine entity or acting altogether as one divine entity; these principles unify while maintaining distinction. What, then, is the connection between Cyril and Proclus that they develop this theory of Porphyry's in the same direction?[9] It is difficult to trace a direct relationship between Cyril and Proclus, or even Syrianus, his closer contemporary, much less the Alexandrian and Athenian schools more broadly in the fifth century. It is unlikely that Proclus read Cyril, and neither Proclus nor Syrianus cites Cyril. Before Proclus became Syrianus's student in 431 in Athens, he spent some time studying philosophy with Olympiodorus the elder in Alexandria.[10] Little is known about Olympiodorus's school in Alexandria, but it is clear that the school of Hypatia before it in the 380s to 410s and the schools of the Hierocles, Ammonius, and Horapollon between the 430s and 520s had mixed populations of Christians and Hellenes.[11] There is the possibility, then, that the Porphyrian concept of intermingling among intelligibles becomes a topic of discussion in the mid-fifth century and that the idea spreads among Christian and Hellenic circles from Alexandria to Athens and back again. By examining Syrianus, Proclus, and Cyril on the topic, one gains insight into both the late Athenian Platonist concept of the henads, as well as Cyril's thoughts on the Trinity through a comparison of terms (*asynchytos*, "without confusion"), particularly when paired with *henosis* (union) and *idiotēs* (characteristic or property) and ideas. Such a comparison sheds light on Proclus's description of the way henads interrelate as modes of being in the Godhead and Cyril's understanding of the hypostatic unity of the Trinity.

8. Boulnois, "Patristique et historie des dogmes," 166–67, discusses Porphyry's *Sentence* 37 in light of Cyril's doctrine of the Incarnation.

9. Syrianus (fl. 432); Proclus (412–85); Cyril (375–444). Syrianus accepted Proclus as a student in 412, the same year Cyril was named bishop of Alexandria. Proclus's *Commentary on the Timaeus* was published in 437, just nine years after Cyril wrote his *Commentary on the Gospel of John*.

10. See Marin. *Procl.* 9 Masullo, where Proclus attends the philosophical school of Olympiodorus upon his second period of studying in Alexandria.

11. Dam. *Hist. Phil.*; Watts, "Doctrine, Anecdote, and Action."

Syrianus and Proclus on "Union without Confusion"

Syrianus discusses interpenetration among forms in the Intellect. Proclus seems to use some of his teacher's concepts as he develops his theory of relationship among henads. Proclus's theory of union without confusion among henads, however, is more extensive and depends upon the concepts of distinction and participation. In his *Commentary on the Metaphysics*, Syrianus uses the term *asynchytos* and its derivatives three times to describe the interaction among forms and to describe the interaction among the mathematicals.

In the first passage (p. 24, l. 12), Syrianus describes the interaction among the intellectual lives of stars as the content of the things seen; these are intellectual forms on the level of intellect. He says that those who are wise "contemplate in their unconfused unity (*asyngchyton henosin*), in their never-failing community and co-ordination (*syntaxin*) with intelligible substances."[12] In the second passage (p. 85, l. 21), Syrianus discusses the mathematicals. In this section, he says that it is not impossible for two solid bodies to come to be simultaneously, nor is it impossible for them to occupy the same place. Here he alludes to the Stoic concept that two solid bodies can occupy the same place through mutual interpenetration—he alters the Stoic view by saying that one of the two bodies must be immaterial. He then likens immaterial entities to light emitted by different lamps that extends throughout one room; these light rays interpenetrate each other without mixing and without internal division. As he progresses, it seems that he alludes to the irrational soul as one of the incorporeal entities. He says that the incorporeal entities spread and extend themselves along with bodies in all three dimensions. He adds that this is something that immaterial bodies that are dependent on souls are not prevented from doing, either.[13] Thus, in view of a discussion of Cyril's Trinitarian theology, what is significant here is Syrianus's insistence that entities can occupy one place when the discussion involves intelligibles.

In the third example (p. 119, 28; Syrian, *In Metaph.* 1179b33–35 Kroll), the forms are described as interpenetrating one another purely and with-

12. The lemma here is. οὐκ ἄστρα τε ἡγεῖσθαι εἶναι ὑπὲρ τοῦτον τὸν οὐρανὸν ἢ ἵνα συνηθέστερον εἴπω, τὰς νοερὰς τῶν ἄστρων ζωάς, ὧν τὴν ἀσύγχυτον ἔνωσιν καὶ τὴν ἀνέκλειπτον κοινωνίαν καὶ τὴν πρὸς τὰς νοητὰς οὐσίας σύνταξιν (Syrianus, *In Met.* 997b14–18 Kroll).

13. Dillon and O'Meara translation, p. 85: τοῖς φωσὶν ἐοικέναι τοῖς ἀπὸ διαφόρων λαμπάδων πεμπομένοις καὶ διὰ παντὸς τοῦ αὐτοῦ οἰκήματος κεχωρηκόσι καὶ δι' ἀλλήλων ἀσυγχύτως καὶ ἀδιαιρέτως πεφοιτηκόσι (Syrianus, *In Met.* Kroll).

out mingling: "Actually, as a general principle, the divine, intellectual forms might be said to be united with one another, and to interpenetrate one another purely and without mingling, but they would never be said to participate in one another in the way that secondary and lower natures participate in them."[14]

These forms—existing as unities in the realm of Intellect—provide unity and characteristics to entities below them. Proclus likewise describes the forms as "unconfused" in *Elements of Theology* (*ET*) 176, where "all intellectual forms are both implicit in each other and severally existent." He explains that the lack of confusion allows the forms to be participated in individually; this individuality is maintained in inferior principles precisely because it exists at the level of the form.[15] He adds, however, that the unity of the forms appears as "the undivided substance and unitary existence of the intelligence which embraces them." What appears next proves important for Cyril's understanding of the Trinity. In *Elements of Theology* 176, Proclus says:

On the other hand, the unity of the Forms is evidenced by the undivided substance and unitary existence (*ousia*) of the intelligence which embraces them. For things which have their being in a unitary principle devoid of parts, existing in one same mind without division (how should you divide that which is one and without parts?) must be together and mutually implicit, interpenetrating one another in their entirety without spatial intervention (*phoitōnta adiastatōs*).[16]

This is to say that the one undivided substance of Intellect embraces forms, just as one divine substance embraces the three hypostases of the Trinity, as we will see in the thought of Cyril. The key to Proclus's thought is that the distinctions of the *eidē* arise as each has its own nature—these separate

14. Dillon and O'Meara translation. ὅλως δὲ ἡνῶσθαι μὲν ἀλλήλοις καὶ χωρεῖν δι' ἀλλήλων καθαρῶς καὶ ἀσυγχύτως τὰ θεῖα εἴδη καὶ νοερὰ λέγοιτ' ἄν, μετέχειν δὲ καθάπερ αἱ δεύτεραι καὶ πολλοσταὶ φύσεις αὐτῶν μετέχουσιν οὐδαμῶς ἂν ἀλλήλων (Syrianus, *In Met.* Kroll).

15. δηλοῖ δὲ τὸ μὲν ἀσύγχυτον τῶν νοερῶν εἰδῶν ἡ τῶν ἑκάστου διακεκριμένως μετεχόντων ἰδιάζουσα μέθεξις. εἰ μὴ γὰρ τὰ μετεχόμενα διεκέκριτο καὶ ἦν χωρὶς ἀλλήλων, οὐδ' ἂν τὰ μετέχοντα αὐτῶν ἑκάστου μετεῖχε διακεκριμένως, ἀλλ' ἦν ἂν πολλῷ μᾶλλον ἐν τοῖς καταδεεστέροις ἀδιάκριτος σύγχυσις, χείροσιν οὖσι κατὰ τὴν τάξιν· πόθεν γὰρ ἂν ἐγίνετο διάκρισις, τῶν ὑφιστάντων αὐτὰ καὶ τελειούντων ἀδιακρίτων ὄντων καὶ συγκεχυμένων (Procl. *ET* 176 (10–16) Dodds).

16. Dodds translation. τὸ δὲ αὖ ἡνωμένον τῶν εἰδῶν ἡ τοῦ περιέχοντος ἀμερὴς ὑπόστασις τεκμηριοῦται καὶ ἡ ἐνοειδὴς οὐσία. τὰ γὰρ ἐν ἀμερεῖ καὶ ἐνοειδεῖ τὴν ὕπαρξιν ἔχοντα, ἐν τῷ αὐτῷ ἀμερίστως ὄντα (πῶς γὰρ ἂν μερίσαις τὸ ἀμερὲς καὶ τὸ ἕν;), ὁμοῦ ἐστι καὶ ἐν ἀλλήλοις, ὅλα δι' ὅλων φοιτῶντα ἀδιαστάτως (Procl. *ET* 176 Dodds). This is contrasted with soul in *ET* 197. While intellectual kinds exist in a unity, in soul they are distinguished and divided. "But if all are together in one being devoid of parts, they interpenetrate one another; and if they exist severally, they are on the other hand distinct and unconfused; so that each exists by itself and yet all in all."

natures allow for a distinct existence.[17] Genuine knowledge occurs when the forms exist in a communion within Intellect that maintains their distinction.[18] The concept of communion, moreover, is based on the active mutual partaking of the forms with each other. Thus the mutual interrelationship of forms with one another not only maintains the distinction, but also even allows for the distinction to exist—each form would not be itself, so to speak, unless it had the presence of the other forms within it.[19] Thus Proclus can proclaim about the form of Likeness that "Likeness, insofar as it is Likeness, participates in Unlikeness" (Procl. *In Parm.* 756.12–18, 23 Steel) Likeness's particularity is realized in relation to Unlikeness.

Compared to Syrianus, Proclus has a much more developed and extensive use of *asynchytos*. He uses the term when speaking of the relationship among forms (unities at the level of Intellect, the first emanation of the One) as well as henads (unities at the level of the One, the highest principle).[20] Proclus describes the "unmixed unity" of both forms and especially henads as intelligibles that interact but maintain their identity in slightly different ways. It may be of interest to see how he describes the union without confusion and in what way such a kind of union differs when he speaks about forms compared to his discussion of henads. In Proclus's universe, henads (also "gods") exist above the intelligible level of being and yet they interact with the world, unlike the supreme One.[21] Thus, unlike the One, which is unparticipable—that is, it is not affected by its production powers—the henads are participated substances (*ET* 116). Insofar as lower orders can partake in the goodness of the One, they do so through participation in the henads. Syrianus says that the second hypothesis of the *Parmenides* reveals a multiplicity of autonomous henads—each henad reveals a specific characteristic (*idiotēs*), one of the predicates attributed to the One—now specific of a divine order.[22] In *Elements of Theology* 133, Proclus describes henads as different modes of the unparticipated monadic One: "every God is a beneficent henad or a unifying goodness and has this mode of existence qua god." He adds that "for several heands … are distin-

---

17. Beierwaltes, "Nous: Unity in Difference," 234, cites Procl. *In. Prm.* 982.19*ff.* Steel.

18. Procl. *In Prm.* 754.9*ff.* Steel.

19. Beierwaltes, "Nous: Unity in Difference," 236.

20. On the differences between the forms and henads, see Chlup, *Proclus*, 114.

21. Mesyats, "Iamblichus's Exegesis of Parmenides' Hypotheses," 152, places the henads slightly below the One for Proclus but squarely within the One for Iamblichus. If this assessment is correct, perhaps it bears a closer resemblance to Christian teachings on the Trinity and the placement of the three hypostases within the Godhead.

22. Mesyats, "Iamblichus's Exegesis of Parmenides' Hypotheses," 154.

guished by their peculiar divine individuality (*idiotēs*)." That the henads are participated aspects of the Unparticipable One is key to understanding how they can be distinct while unified. Collectively, they exist as a unity (*ET* 113), and yet they maintain distinction. As Chlup explains, this unity in the midst of plurality makes sense depending on the viewpoint of the observer. In the realm of the One, the heands—as aspects of the One—are contained within the One and do not stand out as multiple entities.[23] From the perspective of lower orders, however, they appear multiple.

As a comparison between the forms and henads (particularly their interactions), it is helpful to examine Proclus's *Commentary on the Parmenides* 755, where Proclus describes the forms:

Consequently, we must not suppose that the Ideas (*eidē*) are altogether unmixed (*amikta*) and without community with one another, nor must we say on the other hand that each is all of them, as has been demonstrated. How, then and in what way are we to deal logically with the question? We must say that each of them is precisely what it is and preserves its specific nature (*idiotēta*) undefiled, but also partakes of the others without confusion (*asynchytōs*), not by becoming one of them, but by participating in the specific nature of that other and sharing its own nature (*idiotētos*) with it.[24]

Proclus describes the interaction among forms that exist at the level of Intellect in a passage similar to the quotation from Syrianus examined above. Here forms interact without confusion—they share in the nature of each other while maintaining their own nature.

And, again, this same sentiment is expressed in Proclus's *Commentary on the Republic* I 89.7–9:

"for although the divine genera are constantly united to one another, at the same time together with their unity they anticipate in themselves unconfused [*asynchyton*] distinctions."[25] Thus every single idea preserves its individuality; again, their mutual interpenetration helps preserve this individuality because one form is defined in contradistinction to the others (*ET* 176). That is, forms interpenetrate one another while maintaining differentiation. Proclus also describes the relationship among the henads

23. Chlup, *Proclus*, 114.

24. Morrow and Dillon translation: Οὐκ ἄρα ἄμικτα πάντη τὰ εἴδη θετέον καὶ ἀκοινώνητα ἀλλήλοις, ἀλλὰ μὴν οὐδὲ ἕκαστον τὰ πάντα ῥητέον, ὡς δέδεικται. Πῶς οὖν καὶ τίνα τρόπον περὶ αὐτοῦ διαλεκτέον; Ἕκαστον μὲν εἶναι ὅπερ ἐστὶ, σῶζον τὴν ἰδιότητα τὴν ἑαυτοῦ καθαρὰν, μετέχειν δὲ καὶ τῶν ἄλλων ἀσυγχύτως, οὐχ ὡς ἐκείνων γιγνόμενον, ἀλλ' ὡς τῆς ἰδιότητος τῆς ἐκείνου μεταλαμβάνον καὶ μεταδιδὸν ἐκείνῳ τῆς οἰκείας (Procl. *In Prm.* 755.5–14 Steel).

25. Trans. Chlup, *Proclus*, 115. ἀεὶ μὲν ἡνωμένων ἀλλήλοις τῶν θείων γενῶν, ὁμοῦ δὲ τὴν ἕνωσιν καὶ τὴν ἀσύγχυτον διάκρισιν ἐν ἑαυτοῖς προστησαμένων (Proclus, *In R.* Kroll).

in a similar way. The henads, unlike the forms, exist at the level of the One. These are the plurality of the gods existing in a unitary fashion; the henads are participated aspects of the unparticipated monadic One (*ET* 21). The henads thus exist in a unitary manner within the One, but when they act as cause, they exist in plurality from the perspective of lower hypostases. Radek Chlup explains this phenomenon with the analogy of a prism: "We can compare the One to light which contains all the colors, but is color-less in itself, only revealing its multicolored potentialities when it falls on the lower levels, refracts through them, and shows its colors in ways that correspond to the fitness of the recipients."[26] Thus the communion of the henads Proclus terms unity (*henosis*), and their distinction from one an-other he calls individuality (*idiotēs*).[27] Each henad is thus a member of a separate series, the members of which have the same essence.

Although the unitary aspect is fundamental to their internal activity, their individualization also defines the henads; it is this aspect, moreover, that is perhaps more pronounced than the forms as individualities. In his *Commentary on the Parmenides*, Proclus says (Procl. *In Parm.*, 1048.21–26 Steel):

And yet, in spite of this degree of unity in that realm, how marvelous and un-mixed is their purity, and the individuality of each of them is a much more per-fect thing than the otherness of the Forms, preserving as it does unmixed all the divine entities and their proper powers distinct.[28]

Because the henads exist at the level of the One, they are more unitary and distinct than the forms existing at the level of Intellect. At the level of the One, there is little difference between the One and the heands; rather, the cause of all things "has established the divine plurality around itself, having unified it with its own simplicity" (Procl., *Theol. Plat.* 3.3, 12.2–13.4 Saffrey Westerink) Individual henads, moreover, also exhibit an absolute lack of dependency or relationship to anything external to them. Instead, henads have an "individual particularity" (*idiotēs*)—this is the only characteristic that distinguishes one from the other.[29]

Proclus terms the relationship among henads as "a unity without con-

---

26. Chlup, *Proclus*, 114.

27. Procl. *ET* 118.1–3; 119.7; 133.5; 136.6; 145.1 Dodds; Chlup, *Proclus*, 115.

28. Trans. Morrow-Dillon. Ἀλλ' ὅμως καὶ ταύτης οὔσης ἐκεῖ τῆς ἐνώσεως, οὕτω θαυμαστή τίς ἐστι καὶ ἀμιγὴς αὐτῶν ἡ καθαρότης, καὶ ἡ ἑκάστων ἰδιότης πολλῷ τελεώτερον τῆς τῶν εἰδῶν ἑτερότητος, ἀσύγχυτα τηροῦσα τὰ θεῖα καὶ διακεκριμένας τὰς οἰκείας δυνάμεις (Procl. *In Prm.* Steel).

29. Chlup, *Proclus*, 116.

fusion," namely because each henad is said to internally contain all the other henads, with respect to each individual henad (Procl. *In Parm.* 1048.14–15 Steel). The henads are also described as gods, with each god being a specific manifestation of any given henad.[30] Every order of henad anticipates a divine stratum of gods on lower levels (*ET* 125). These lower levels participate in the henad that appears to them as a plurality at the lower ranks. When taken together, the gods are said to have an "undivided union (*henosis*) and all-perfect communion with one another," and yet their own essences are separated to preserve their "peculiar hypostasis unconfused (*asynchytos*)" (Procl. *Theol. Plat.* 1.97.25 Saffrey Westerink and *ET* 125 Dodds). Proclus calls this order of causes "unconfused" (*asynchytos*) (Procl. *Theol. Plat.* 1.89.1 Saffrey Westerink), which is to say that each monadic cause (the henad in its pure form) has a separate essence or *idiotēs* (Procl. *Theol. Plat.* 1.89.5 Saffrey Westerink) Thus the unity of each henad maintains a rank of gods that are hierarchically arranged below it. The gods differ from one another with respect to their potency (*dynamis*)—the closer a god is to its monadic cause, the more power it has (*ET* 145 and 126).

Thus, to summarize, Syrianus shows how the forms interrelate without confusion in the unified essence of Intellect. Still, these forms maintain their identity—an important aspect as that individuality gives rise to distinction in the universe. Proclus likewise describes the forms as Syrianus does. Moreover, he uses the same language to describe henads interpenetrating one another without confusion as they exist unified in the One (and yet still distinct). The henads (also considered "gods") are monadic entities at the heads of series that provide unity throughout the world. Still, they also provide diversity, giving rise to particular series, each noted for a different characteristic. The henads—contained within the One as aspects of the One—have distinction in their modes of differentiation. This concept plays a key role in the way the Father and Son retain distinction in the unified Godhead in Cyril's Trinitarian theology.

Cyril on Union without Confusion within the Trinity

Cyril demonstrates that the Holy Spirit, Father, and Son maintain their individual properties, and yet they interpenetrate without confusion:

---

30. "Every god is self-complete henad or unit and every self-complete henad is a god." Procl. *ET* 114 Dodds.

Ἅγιον δὲ Πνεῦμα προσερεῖς τὸ ἐκ Θεοῦ Πατρὸς δι᾽ Υἱοῦ προχεόμενον φυσικῶς καὶ καθάπερ ἐν τύπῳ τῆς ἐκ στομάτων διεκπνοῆς τὴν ἰδίαν ἡμῖν κατασημαῖνον ὕπαρξιν, οὕτω τε σαφῆ καὶ ἀσύγχυτον τὴν τῶν τριῶν ὑποστάσεων ἐν ὑπάρξεσιν ἰδικαῖς ἰδιότητα τηρῶν, μίαν τε καὶ ὁμοούσιον τὴν ἁπάντων βασιλίδα προσκυνήσεις φύσιν. (Cyr. *Dial. Trin.* 423.4–11 Durand)

Finally, you will qualify the Holy Spirit as the one who, through its nature, is brought forth from the nature of the Father through the Son, who, just as breath moves from the mouth, he reveals his own existence. In so doing, you will preserve clearly and without confusion (*asynchyton*) the property (*idiotēta*) of the three hypostases in their own existences, while adoring the unique and consubstantial nature (*homousion*), queen of all beings.

The three have one consubstantial nature or essence and yet they have three hypostases—the mark of the three hypostases is that each hypostasis has its own characteristic that is preserved without confusion. Cyril says that the Father and Son unite without confusion and maintain equal power:

Ὅπου μὲν γὰρ οὐκ ἐν σαρκὶ γεγονὼς Θεὸς ἦν ὁ Λόγος, γεγεννημένος ἐκ Πατρός, ἐκεῖ κατασκέπτου τὸ ἀμίκτως ἔτι θεοπρεπὲς ἀξίωμα, τὴν εἰλικρινῆ καὶ ἀσύγχυτον δόξαν, τὸ ἐξηρημένως ἐλεύθερον, τὸ ἰσοσθενὲς τῷ Πατρί. (Cyr. *Dial. Trin.* 516.25–30 Durand)

On the one hand, or, while having engendered from the father, the Word is not yet a God come into the flesh—one must then contemplate the honor without mixture, a glory pure and without confusion, a supreme freedom, equal in power with the father.

Here Cyril describes the relationship between Father and Son as without mixture, without confusion, and equal in power. Likewise, in his *Commentary on the Gospel of John*, Cyril says that while the three share substance (*homoousios*), they retain individual properties; if otherwise, the Father would have the same substance (*to eikos*) as the Son. Identity of nature would overturn the distinction of person, something he calls absurd (*atopon*) (I.54).

This description of members of the Trinity differs from Proclus's description of henads or Syrianus's descriptions of the difference among orders of forms. Forms can be differentiated from each other depending on their distance from their monad—the distance from their monad determines how much power each one has. Because the Father, Son, and Holy Spirit share one *ousia* and exist within the Godhead together, they share the same rank and have the same degree of power. The hypostases for Cyril share one *ousia*—in this way, his terminology differs from Proclus's understanding of the henads that exist beyond the realm of being. The unity among henads in no way depends on a shared *ousia* as they exist beyond substance.

Unmixed Unity in the Trinity

When Cyril describes the *henosis* of the three divine principles, his concept of unity rests on a shared *ousia*—a concept fundamentally different from Proclus's understanding of unity among henads. Cyril uses the concept of consubstantiality throughout his writings in *Dialogues on the Holy Trinity* and his *Commentary on the Gospel of John*. By declaring that the Father, Son, and Holy Spirit are consubstantial, he understands the likeness of their substance as a fact of their nature.[31] Thus he claims that the Son is like the Father according to substance, making him neither a creature nor a production.[32] When he explains the principle of shared substance, Cyril emphasizes that the two principles share substance as one proceeds from the other (cf. this to Plotinus's description of Intellect proceeding from the One in Plot. 5.1.Henry Schwyzer)[33] In his *Commentary on the Gospel of John* (Cyr. *Io.* 1.45 Meunier), Cyril says that even as the Son proceeds from the Father, one item clearly exists in the other, and they are the same in substance. In Cyril's *Commentary on the Gospel of John*, the Son is of the same substance as the Father, although they are not one in the same number (Cyr. *Io.* 1.25). However, Cyril—as with Proclus—also calls the members of the Trinity "beyond substance." Despite his frequent use of *homoousios*, Cyril says that we discuss the substance of God only according to our own limitations in human speech. As with Proclus, Cyril says that God is supersubstantial[34] or hypersubstantial.[35] The term *hyperousios*, moreover, is not a Plotinian term but appears in the Porph. *In Prm.* 2.11 Hadot and *Sent.* 10 Lamberz; it likewise appears Syrian. *In Metaph.* 6.1. 18.25 Kroll, where it is used thirteen times, and Procl. *ET* 115 Dodds.[36] Cyril also uses the

---

31. Boulnois, *La Paradoxe Trinitaire chez Cyrille d'Alexandrie*, 238.

32. Cyr., *Thes.* 15.250D Durand and Cyr. *Festal Letter*, 12.5, 689B Burns.

33. Plot. 5.1 [10] 6, 39–49 Henry Schwyzer; Plot. 5.1.3.6–10 Henry Schwyzer; cf. these passages with Cyr. *Io.* 1. 5, 46e Meunier. See Boulnois, *La Paradoxe Trinitaire chez Cyrille d'Alexandrie*, 222, on a comparison between Plotinus and Cyril on procession of the Intellect from One with the procession of Son from the Father.

34. Supersubstantial: Cyr. *Thes.* 3.36B Durand.

35. *Hypoerousios*: Cyr. *Festal Letter* XII, 3, 681D Burns. The nature that exercises its authority over other things is incorporeal and supersubstantial. See also Cyr. *Io.* 1. 5.48c.

36. Boulnois, "Patristique et historie des dogmes," 231.

phrase "beyond substance" (*epkeina tēs ousias*) in both Cyr. *De Trinitate* (Durand) VI, 598a and 625a , where the divinity is beyond everything because it surpasses all beings by a superiority of its substance (Cyr. IV, 511ab Durand). This seeming contradiction—how God the Father can possess transcendence as an ontological characteristic while the three hypostases are consubstantial—is explained in Cyr. *Thes.* 3.36a. For Cyril, to say that God is substance signifies that God is. God is not part of substance or one of beings; *ousia* merely indicates that he is that which is, a reading of Exodus 3:14.[37] He declares that naming God as substance signifies that God is, here using the infinitive (Cyr. *Thes.* 3.36A); the use of the noun *ousia* reflects the original verbal sense here. This thought thus mirrors Fragment 5 of Porph. *In Parm.* 11–12 Hadot.[38] While Cyril makes a shared *ousia* the basis for unity in the Godhead, he also points out that the Godhead exists beyond substance and any discussion of *ousia* stems from a limitation in human discourse.

Mode and Property in Cyril and Proclus

Because Cyril makes substance the foundation for unity in his discussion of the relationship between Father, Son, and Holy Spirit, differentiation among hypostases thus arises not in the substance itself (as the three hypostases share one *ousia*), but rather in the mode of being. Because a unity of substance (*ousia*) necessitates a unity of operation (*energeia*), all three hypostases work together in a unity of operation (Cyr. *Dial. Trin.* 3. 468C Durand). Cyril argues that a single substance can only make a single cooperation (Cyr. *Io.* 10.2, 859D; 4.3.367a Meunier). They differ, however, in the mode of operation; the Father is the initiator, the Son the executor, and the operation is achieved through the Holy Spirit (Cyr. *Io.* 10. 259CD Meunier); thus "those which have a unique operation carry also a unique concept of the mode of being" (Cyr. *Thes.* 24. 605D).[39]

Mode of being is linked with *idiōmata* and participation in late Platonist thought. In Porphyry's *Sentence* 10, "all things are in all, but in a mode proper to the essence of each; in the intellect, intellectually; in the soul, discursively; in plants, seminally; in bodies, imagistically; and in the Beyond, non-intellectually and supra-essentially."[40] Porphyry says any given es-

---

37. Boulnois, "Patristique et historie des dogmes," 233.

38. Porph. *In Prm.*, 99–107; Boulnois, "Patristique et historie des dogmes," 234.

39. Boulnois, *La Paradoxe Trinitaire chez Cyrille d'Alexandrie*, 284.

40. Porphyrye, *Sentences* (ed. Brisson).

sence manifests one mode. Cyril's thought differs from Porphyry's here as he presents each hypostasis as sharing an essence but manifesting itself in a different mode. Still, the basic concept of mode exists in Proclus's thought on henads, as seen in Procl. *In Parm.* 756.12–18, 23 Steel, where all henads are in all, but each expresses the One in a different mode. Mode and property are connected as the manner of participation manifests itself as a unique property of the entity experiencing participation. In Hermias's *Commentary on the Phaedrus*, Hermias says that each rational soul administers a cosmic series depending on its properties (*idiōmata* Herm. *In Phdr.* 136.3 Lucarini Moreschini). Properties used here indicate characteristics of essence—property is shared in a series but in different degrees. Proclus links property with capacity; the same property of a thing in a species is shared but shared unequally. Property is common to all in a series but in different degrees. Souls are linked to a god in a chain and imitate the property of that god; still, some imitate that god more than others (Procl. *ET* 79 Dodds and *In Prm.* 707.5–31 Steel). The henads, for instance, exhibit union (*henosis*) as well as distinction from one another according to their individual distinction (*idiotēs*) (Procl. *ET* 118.1–3; 119.7, 135.5 Dodds).

Cyril uses his argument that differences exist in mode of being, rather than in operation or substance, to describe how the three hypostases differ with respect to property (*idiotes*). Property resides in a substance but does not exist by itself (Cyr. *Dial. Trin.* 2. 421d Durand). Cyril distinguishes two kinds of properties: natural and hypostatic.[41] Properties that are natural are traits that all three members will have in common (Cyr. *Thes.* 5. 57D–60A)—for instance, unity[42]— and that speak to the substance itself. Because the Son is created without generation, he possesses the divine properties of the Father; everything is common to the Father and Son (Cyr. *Dial. Trin.* 5.554a Durand; Cyr. *Thes.* 9.117A). In fact, it is the commonality of natural properties that shows how the one is in the other and that Father and Son are consubstantial (Cyr. *Io.* 11. 7.962d Meunier). The procession of the one from the other implies a communication of natural properties because the Son is issued from the Father by nature (Cyr. *Io.* 1.4.36c Meunier). But the Son still differs from the Father in the way he manifests the properties; the Son manifests what characterizes the Father because his being reveals the property of the Father's nature.[43] The property of the Father passes to the Son; he is himself in the Father and he is one with him by the

<hr>

41. Boulnois, *La Paradoxe Trinitaire chez Cyrille d'Alexandrie*, 314.
42. Boulnois, *La Paradoxe Trinitaire chez Cyrille d'Alexandrie*, 314.
43. Boulnois, *La Paradoxe Trinitaire chez Cyrille d'Alexandrie*, 321.

identity of nature, differing only in the fact of being a Son (Cyr. Juln. 8.908A Brüggemann). The properties shared between Father, Son, and Holy Spirit are not shared by creation. Yet Cyril notes that the immutability that exists in God's nature is not shared by us precisely, but we do share in a kind of stability, the creature's version of immutability (I.448). Thus the Son manifests the property of the Father in a way knowable to us. One may reasonably compare Cyril's notion of property with Proclus's, whereby henads convey oneness to the lower strata according to those that participate in it.

Still, despite sharing substance and natural properties, the three hypostases remain distinct—this distinction is also conveyed through the use of the term *idiotēs* or *idiōma*.[44] There is a paradoxical use of the term property—it at once indicates what unites persons in substance when it points to property of nature, and it differentiates particular hypostases when it points to individual property in what is termed "hypostatic property." According to hypostatic property, what distinguishes the Father from the Son is the original relationship between the two—the Son is that which is engendered from the Father. In his *Commentary on the Gospel of John*, Cyril explains this difference in hypostatic property as a difference in mode of being: "The Son may be heir to all the properties which are by nature in the Father, yet he will never possess the fact of being a father" (Cyr. *Io.* I, 4, 37e–38a Meunier). Thus the Son inherits all the traits of the Father, with the exception of being a father and being a son (Cyr. *Thes.* 7.100D). Cyril further explains that when one calls him God, one indicates by this appellation the master of the universe; this divinity is common to all three members of the Trinity. But when one calls him Father, the expression speaks to his own property, since it manifests that he is the one who engenders (Cyr. *Io.* 11. 7.961b Meunier). Cyril prioritizes the name of Father precisely because it is proper to the mode of being of his hypostasis (Cyr. *Io.* XI, 7, 961C Meunier).[45]

Conclusion

To summarize, Cyril describes the Father, Son, and Holy Spirit existing in an unmixed unity. The Son contains all the traits of the Father so

---

44. Boulnois states that "properties" in the plural (*idiōmata*) tends to indicate shared natural property, while "property" in the singular (*idiōma* or *idiotēs*) tends to indicate hypostatic property particular to one member of the Trinity. See *La Paradoxe Trinitaire chez Cyrille d'Alexandrie*, 325.

45. Boulnois, *La Paradoxe Trinitaire chez Cyrille d'Alexandrie*, 386.

that Christ can say to his disciples, "the one who has seen me has seen the Father." Everything that the Father possesses Christ also possesses (Cyr *Io.* 11.1. 931C). Likewise, for Proclus, there is a mutual unity of the heands so that all are in all—everything that can be said of one henad can be said of all (Procl. *In Prm.* 1048.14 Steel). Distinction occurs between the members of the Trinity and between the henads in their mode, particularly in their mode with respect to participation. The Father differs from the Son insofar as he engenders the Son. Still, the Son is substantially identical to the Father. Christ's being fully reveals the properties of the Father to us—that is, the Son's mode of being manifests the characteristics of the Father to us (Cyr. *Juln.* 8.908A).[46] Proclus's henads, likewise, are unified aspects of God. Internally, they exist in an unmixed unity. Every god exists wholly in every other god. Differentiation exists in the form of peculiarity (*idiotēs*) for supra-essential entities.[47] Proclus explains this in Procl. *In Prm.* 1048.16–20 Steel: "And yet, in spite of this degree of unity in that realm [of the One], how marvelous and unmixed is their purity, and the individuality of each of them is a much more perfect thing than the otherness of the Forms, preserving as it does unmixed all the divine entities and their proper powers distinct" (trans. Morrow and Dillon).

Because the henads appear in the realm of the One, they are unitary rather than unified—their source of unity is their own selves, rather than a participation in the One.[48] No difference exists between the henads and the One. It is only from an external perspective that henads appear multiple; when lower orders participate in them, they seem to participate in particular aspects of them. In this way, lower orders come to participate in aspects of the transcendent One. One may argue that the key element to hypostatic difference among members of the Trinity has to do with their mode of being.[49]

46. Boulnois, *La Paradoxe Trinitaire chez Cyrille d'Alexandrie*, 321.
47. Chlup, *Proclus*, 116.
48. Chlup, *Proclus*, 116.
49. On the relationship between the Father and Son and creation, see Boulnois (2007).

CHAPTER 5 ‖ Proclus and the Tripartite Soul in Plato's *Republic*

John F. Finamore

In Treatise 7 of his *Republic* commentary, Proclus takes up the topic of the three elements of the soul and their relation to the four virtues. The discussion of the tripartite soul has a long history among the Neoplatonists. Both Porphyry in his "On the Powers of the Soul" and Iamblichus in his *De Anima* discuss the topic. Proclus, although his treatment is much wider-ranging, continues their discussion. In this essay, I wish to explore Proclus's discussion in light of those of his predecessors and argue that Proclus's treatise helps fill in the gaps in his predecessors' doctrine, especially as regards the relationship between the three elements and the grades of virtue.

Platonic Background

The problem arises in the Platonic dialogues.[1] In the *Phaedo*, Socrates presents the soul as a single entity without parts that is opposed to the workings of the body. In Book IV of the *Republic*, after laying out the four cardinal virtues (wisdom, courage, self-control, and justice) in the three segments of his state (rulers, guardians, and workers) (Pl. R. 427d–434d

---

1. For a more detailed account of the Platonic background, including views of modern philosophers, see Finamore, "Tripartite Soul in Plato's Republic and Phaedrus," 36–44.

Slings), Socrates argues that the equivalent of these three elements of society will be found in the soul as well (Pl. R. 435b Slings). From the interrelations of these three elements will come the definitions of the virtues and especially of justice.[2] Plato argues that there are three elements
in the soul (the rational, spirited, and appetitive). He does so on the basis
of the proposition that "the same thing does not wish to perform or suffer
opposites at the same time in the same respect with regard to the same
thing" (ταὐτὸν τἀναντία ποιεῖν ἢ πάσχειν κατὰ ταὐτόν γε καὶ πρὸς ταὐτὸν
οὐκ ἐθελήσει ἅμα, Pl. R. Slings 436b8–9). When something acts or is affected in opposite ways, Plato assures us, we have not one thing but many.
Thus, since the same person at the same time is thirsty and does not want
to drink, the person must have two separate elements, one of which thirsts
and the other of which fights against this desire; namely, the appetitive (τὸ
ἐπιθυμητικόν) and the rational (τὸ λογιστικόν) elements (Pl. R. 437b–439e
Slings). So too, since the same person (Leontion in Plato's example) both
wants to look at a corpse and is angry that he wants to do so, there are
again distinct elements at play, the appetitive and the spirited (τὸ θυμοειδές,
Pl. R. 439e–441c Slings). Thus there are three elements of the soul, and
the virtues are defined in accordance with these three elements. Justice is
defined as each psychic element doing its own work with the rational aspect in charge (Pl. R. 441d12–e7 Slings); courage as the spirited element
agreeing with reason about what is to be feared (Pl. R. 442b12–c4 Slings);
wisdom as the rational element controlling what is best for all the psychic
aspects (Pl. R. 442c5–9 Slings); self-control as the harmony among all three
elements (Pl. R. 442c10–d1 Slings). Whereas in the *Phaedo* the soul was a
purely rational entity at war not with itself but with the body that housed
it, in the *Republic* the soul was more dynamic internally, in opposition with
different aspects of itself, until reason could bring it into harmony. All three
elements make up the soul and all are immortal, a point that becomes even
more clear in the *Phaedrus* where the charioteer myth demonstrates that
the soul is tripartite before it ever enters a body and some aspects cause the
soul's descent.[3]

2. These three elements become known as the "parts" of the soul, but Plato is not metic-
ulous about the vocabulary he uses for these so-called parts. He calls them "classes" (γένη) in
Pl. R. 435b5 and 7, 441c6, 442b2, 443d3, 444b5; "kinds" (εἴδη) in 435b9, c5, e2, 439e2, 440e8–9
Slings; and most often he resorts simply to the neuter of the adjective coupled with the definite
article (Pl. R. 436a8–c1, 439b3–6, 439c5–d8, 440e2–6, 441a5–6, 441d12–e2, 442c10–d1, 443b1–2
Slings). In fact, Plato uses the word "part" (μέρος) only twice at Pl. R. 442b11 and c5 Slings, and
he never uses the word "power" (δύναμις) to describe the elements of the soul.

3. See Finamore, "Tripartite Soul in Plato's Republic and Phaedrus," 45–50. The soul is

The *Timaeus* also presents a tripartite soul, but with a difference.[4] The three elements are placed in different parts of the body, a placement that keeps them separate from each other. The rational element is in the head (Pl. Tim. 69d6–e4 Burnet), the spirited in the midriff (Pl. Tim. 69e5–70a3 Burnet), and the irrational between the midriff and the navel (Pl. Tim. 70d7–71a3 Burnet). An even more important difference is that in this dialogue Plato specifically says that the two lower elements are mortal (Pl. Tim. 41d1–3 Burnet). Only the rational aspect is immortal.

Porphyry and Iamblichus

This discrepancy in the Platonic texts concerning the tripartite soul was discussed in similar terms by both Porphyry and Iamblichus.[5] Both philosophers draw a distinction between parts and powers. "Parts" are defined as aspects of soul that exist in specific areas of the body.[6] "Powers," however, do not require specific body parts in which to function. Both Porphyry and Iamblichus give the example of an apple.[7] An apple has many powers (its taste, its texture, etc.), and these are present throughout the apple, not confined to specific parts of the apple. Applying this distinction to the soul, one may say that the soul as a whole (when it is disembodied) has multiple powers but no parts. Once the soul is embodied, however, it may be considered as having its three parts each located in different areas of the body. Thus in one sense the soul is without parts, and in another it is partitioned in different bodily substrates. Thus what Porphyry and Iamblichus have done is combine the *Timaeus* (which presents the tripartite human soul as divided into three parts in the body) with the *Republic* (where the soul itself consists of three parts), but both philosophers also insist that the soul in its separated state has no parts. The soul's partedness, as it were, is a function of its corporeal existence.

There remains, however, the problem of whether we should call the soul "tripartite" or not. Both Porphyry and Iamblichus address this ques-

---

conceived as a charioteer (= τὸ λογιστικόν) driving a pair of horses, one good and controllable (= τὸ θυμοειδές) and the other recalcitrant and hard to control (= τὸ ἐπιθυμητικόν).

4. For the problem presented by the *Timaeus*, see Finamore, "Plato's Timaean Psychology," 11–25.

5. I have discussed the similarities between the two Neoplatonists on this matter in Finamore and Dillon, *Iamblichus' De Anima*, 103–17. All translations herein are from this edition.

6. Porphyry, *Concerning the Powers of the Soul* 253F.272.29–273.42 and 276.110–22 Smith. Iamblichus, *De Anima* sections 11–12 Finamore-Dillon.

7. Porphyry, *Concerning the Powers of the Soul* 253F.274.68–70 Smith; Iamblichus, *De An.* section 11, 36.4–7.

tion and state that the tripartition in the *Republic* has a pedagogical purpose. Porphyry writes that many think that Plato[8] said that the soul was tripartite, but they fail to notice that the division was for the sake of the virtues; Porphyry adds that the division into three parts is incomplete since it does not include the imaginative, perceptive, intellectual, and nutritive aspects.[9] Iamblichus writes that Plato divided the soul into three parts "for these are useful for establishing the system of virtues."[10] Thus the division of the soul into three parts in the *Timaeus* is accurate because the embodied soul does have separate parts in three different areas of the body, but the tripartism of the *Republic* (and, presumably, the *Phaedrus*) would not be literally true of the *disembodied* soul but would help to explain the doctrine of virtues that Porphyry and Iamblichus espoused.

Neither Porphyry nor Iamblichus in their surviving works or fragments explains the significance of the four virtues to understanding the tripartite division of the embodied soul. We know that each espoused his own ranking of the four virtues at various levels of their metaphysical system, and we will examine their doctrine below in the next section. It will be in Proclus's *Republic* commentary that we find an explanation of the pedagogical value of the virtues to tripartism.

Neoplatonism and the Four Virtues

Neoplatonists embraced a doctrine that the four virtues exist in different ways at different psychic levels. Plotinus differentiated the Civic Virtues

8. And, he adds, "Aristotle in the *Ethics*" (253F.272.1–2 Smith). Smith (*ad loc.*) cites Arist. *EN* 1102b28*ff.*

9. *Concerning the Powers of the Soul* 253F.272.11–18 Smith: "For Plato and Aristotle in the *Ethics*, the soul is said to be tripartite, and this prevails among the many who fail to understand that the division was taken up for the sake of the system of virtues. For this simply is not inclusive of all the parts. The imaginative, perceptive, intellective, and nutritive are surely not included in this division." (Παρὰ δὲ Πλάτωνι καὶ Ἀριστοτέλει ἐν τοῖς Ἠθικοῖς τριμερὴς ἡ ψυχὴ λέγεται εἶναι, καὶ κεκράτηκε τοῦτο παρὰ τοῖς πολλοῖς ἀγνοοῦσιν ὡς ἡ διαίρεσις τῆς συστάσεως ἕνεκα τῶν ἀρετῶν παρείληπται· οὐ γὰρ ἁπλῶς εἰς σύλληψιν πάντων τῶν μερῶν. Τὸ γὰρ φανταστικὸν καὶ αἰσθητικὸν καὶ τὸ νοερὸν καὶ <τὸ> φυτικὸν οὐ δήπου ἐν τῇ διαιρέσει ταύτῃ περιληφθήσεται.)

10. "Plato and his school, Archytas, and the rest of the Pythagoreans assert that the soul is tripartite, dividing it into reason, spirit, and desire, for these are useful for establishing the system of virtues. As to the powers of the soul, these philosophers include the powers of growth, imagination, perception, opinion, thought that moves the body, desire for good and evil, and intellection." (Οἱ δὲ περὶ Πλάτωνα καὶ Ἀρχύτας καὶ οἱ λοιποὶ Πυθαγόρειοι τὴν ψυχὴν τριμερῆ ἀποφαίνονται, διαιροῦντες εἰς λογισμὸν καὶ θυμὸν καὶ ἐπιθυμίαν· ταῦτα γὰρ εἶναι χρήσιμα πρὸς τὴν τῶν ἀρετῶν σύστασιν. Δυνάμεις δὲ τῆς ψυχῆς ἀναλογίζονται φύσιν καὶ φαντασίαν καὶ αἴσθησιν καὶ δόξαν καὶ κινητικὴν σωμάτων διάνοιαν καὶ ὄρεξιν καλῶν κἀγαθῶν καὶ νοήσεις (Porph. *De An.* section 12, 36.21–26 Finamore-Dillon).

(found in the *Republic*) from the Purificatory Virtues (found in the *Phaedo*).[11] The Civic Virtues are those of the virtuous citizen, while the Purificatory are associated with the soul as it is being purified and made ready to escape the body and ascend to the Intellect.[12] Porphyry added to the Plotinian list of virtues. To the Civic and Purificatory Virtues, he added above them one without a name (occurring when the soul entered into union with the Intellect) and the Paradigmatic (which were not virtues per se but were the lower virtues' preexistence in the Intellect) (Porph. *Sent.* 32).[13] Iamblichus added three more classifications (two below the Civic Virtues and one above the Paradigmatic), bringing the total to seven:[14]

> Hieratic/Theurgic (ἱερατικαί/θεουργικαί)
> Paradigmatic (παραδειγματικαί)
> Contemplative (θεωρητικαί)
> Purificatory (καθαρτικαί)
> Civic (πολιτικαί)
> Ethical (ἠθικαί)
> Natural (φυσικαί)

All animals and human beings are born with the Natural Virtues. They are akin to innate drives toward or away from just, brave, wise, self-controlled behaviors. The Ethical Virtues are the result of training on the Natural Virtues, such as parental discipline put to bear on improper conduct of children. True virtues begin at the Civic level. As we ascend through the grades of virtue, the person makes use of higher forms of thought and cognition. The Civic Virtues involve rational thinking, the Purificatory a move toward a higher form of thought, the Contemplative and Paradigmatic make use of intellection, and the Hieratic/Theurgic occur when the soul unites with the One.[15] Thus the human being moves away from the irratio-

11. For the virtues in Plotinus, see Baltzly, "Virtues and 'Becoming Like God,'" 301–3, and Ahbel-Rappe, "Contemplative and Practical Virtue."

12. For these virtues, see Marin. *Procl.* 14–18 and 21 Saffrey, Segonds, Luna; Dam. *In Phd.* I.140–41 Westerink; and Olymp. *In Phd.* I.8.119.9–11 Westerink.

13. For Porphyry and the virtues, see Brisson, "Doctrine of the Degrees of Virtues in the Neoplatonists," 93–99, and Baltzly, "Virtues and 'Becoming Like God,'", 303–5.

14. For the evidence that we possess of Iamblichus's grades of virtue, the evidence of what each level of virtue signifies, and an account of the role that the hierarchy of virtues plays in Iamblichean philosophy, see my "Iamblichus on the Grades of Virtue," 113–24, and "Ethics, Virtue, and Theurgy."

15. On these higher virtues, see Marin. *Procl.* 22–28; Dam. *In Phd.* I.142–44 Westerink; and Olymp. *In Phd.* I.8.119.11–12 and 123.6–17 Westerink. See also my "Iamblichus on the Grades of Virtue," 120–24.

nal and discursive toward the higher modes of thinking and to pure unity. These grades involve ever higher and more purified forms of theurgy and contact with ever higher divinities. When souls have attained their highest level, they must return again to their bodies and live in the human society, as the parable of the Cave in the *Republic* teaches (Pl. *R.* 7.514a1–518b5). When they do so, they can bring that higher order of understanding with them to the practical problems of the polis.

As we have seen, both Porphyry and Iamblichus held that the tripartite division of the soul in the *Republic* was somehow connected to the Civic Virtues, the virtues affiliated with statecraft.[16] Unfortunately, we do not possess the treatises in which either philosopher discussed how the Civic Virtues corresponded with the three parts of the soul. For that topic, we must turn to Proclus.

Proclus's Commentary on the *Republic*

Proclus tackles the question of the relationship between the tripartite soul and the grades of virtue in Essay 7 of his commentary on the *Republic* (1.206.1–235.21). After a brief introduction to the three parts of the soul and the four virtues and their interrelationship (206.6–13), Proclus draws a distinction between looking at anything in itself (καθ> αὐτὸ, 207.17) and looking at it in relation to something else (κατὰ τὴν πρὸς ἄλλο σχέσιν, 207.18). Proclus explains this distinction by using the case of the soul *qua* soul and the soul *qua* ruler of the body:[17]

οὐδὲ ταὐτὸν ψυχὴν ἁπλῶς ὁρᾶν καὶ ψυχὴν σώματος ἄρχουσαν. δῆλον δὲ τοῦτο καὶ ἐξ ὧν αὐτὸς ἐν Τιμαίῳ λέγει τὴν γὰρ ἀσκήσεσιν χρωμένην ψυχὴν συντονωτέραις τοῦ σώματος μὴ εἶναι ὡς σώματος ἄρχουσαν ἐπαινετήν, φθείρουσαν τὸ ἀρχόμενον. (207.22–26)

To observe the soul unqualifiedly is not the same thing as [to observe] the soul ruling the body. This is evident from what [Plato] himself says in the *Timaeus*,[18] that the soul that makes use of exercise that is too intense for the body ought not be praised as a ruler of the body since it destroys what is ruled.

---

16. Olympiodorus also connects the Civic Virtues with the tripartite soul: "The Civic Virtues make use of the tripartition of the soul, but the Purificatory and Contemplative do not do so" αἱ μὲν πολιτικαὶ τῇ τριμερείᾳ τῆς ψυχῆς χρῶνται, αἱ δὲ καθαρτικαὶ καὶ θεωρητικαὶ οὐχ οὕτως (Olymp. *In Phd.* I.8.123.6–7 Westerink).

17. All translations from the *Republic* commentary are my own.

18. Pl., *Tim.* 88b5–c6, where he argues that there must be a balance between the needs of the soul and the needs of the body. One should prioritize neither the life of the mind nor that of the body, but practice both physical and mental exercise.

The soul that looks to its own good exclusively will neglect the body and so will ruin the body instead of ruling it. What is good for the soul itself *qua* soul is not necessarily what is best for the body, and so one must be wary of seeking the καθ' αὑτὸ good lest it interfere with the good that is κατὰ τὴν πρὸς τὸ σῶμα σχέσιν.

Proclus next brings this doctrine into play with the three elements of the soul and the four virtues (208.5–10 and 11–13):

For example, when the rational [element] in us lives in a purificatory or[19] contemplative manner it is performing its own proper function and is naturally disposed to live in accordance with its own essence, but it is not [performing] the function of ruling the irrational elements since it is contributing nothing to them when its activity is for itself... Thus, whenever the rational [element] furnishes the good only for itself by purifying itself and seeking itself, it does not lead the life of the ruler.

οἷον τὸ λογικὸν τὸ ἐν ἡμῖν καθαρτικῶς ζῶν [ἢ] θεωρητικῶς ἑαυτοῦ τὸ μὲν οἰκεῖον ἔργον πράττει, πεφυκὸς οὕτω ζῆν κατὰ τὴν αὐτοῦ οὐσίαν, οὐ μέντοι τὸ τοῦ ἄρχοντος τῶν ἀλόγων μορίων, οὐδὲν ἐκείνοις συμβαλλόμενον ἐν τῷ πρὸς ἑαυτὸ ἐνεργεῖν.... ὥσθ> ὅταν τὸ λογικὸν ἑαυτῷ μόνον τὸ ἀγαθὸν ἐκπορίζῃ καθαῖρον ἑαυτὸ καὶ ζητοῦν ἑαυτό, τὴν τοῦ ἄρχοντος οὐκ ἔχει ζωήν.

Proclus is laying out guidelines for the rulers of the ideal polis. As in the parable of the Cave, the soul must ascend in order to intellegize the Forms, but it must also descend again to apply its knowledge to governing the polis. In Neoplatonic terms, ascension means that we must first purify our vehicle and soul (exchanging the Civic Virtues for the Purificatory ones) and then ascend to contemplation of the Intellect (exchanging the Purificatory Virtues for the Contemplative ones). Each rung on the ladder of ascent represents a purer sort of virtue and a concomitant higher kind of cognition of reality. But this ascent to the less material, more unified divinities is also a movement away from the life of civic activity, and the soul must return to its body to bring its new knowledge to bear on civic issues.[20]

19. The Greek text has no conjunction between the words καθαρτικῶς ζῶν and θεωρητικῶς. Kroll inserts καὶ ("and"), which both Festugière, *Proclus: Commentaire sur la République*, 15, and Abbate, *Proclo: Commento alla "Repubblica" di Platone*, 119, adopt without comment. Dirk Baltzly, one of the translators of the *Republic* commentary (along with Graeme Miles and me), has suggested inserting ἢ ("or") instead. He offered this explanation to me: "given that the kathartic and theoretic virtues are the gradations above the civic ones, it is tempting to read this remark in light of the scale of virtues. If that were warranted, it would be perhaps better to insert ἢ rather than καὶ. One might then translate more freely: 'lives at the level of purificatory or theoretic [virtue].'" I am adopting Baltzly's reading here.

20. Proclus will reference the parable of the Cave just below at 209.6–13. In this passage he

When it does so, the soul reenters the corporeal body, reconnects with the two lower elements of the soul, and reactivates the Civic Virtues associated with them, but it also has a memory of its higher form of life, which will help it administer the state better because it understands the four virtues in a higher, purer form. Thus, although the knowledge gained above is useful for the civic life, it must be converted (as it were) into the kind of virtue that is useful for the polis, so that the higher virtue and intellection reinforces and invigorates Civic Virtue.[21] It should be noted as well that the ascent of the soul is, strictly speaking, the ascent of the rational element of the soul alone. Thus in the Intelligible the rational element does not have the lower elements to harmonize with itself. Indeed, the harmony of the three elements is the foundation for the purification of the rational element, which allows the rational element to separate from the lower elements in the ascent. The kind of thought associated with the ascent to the Intellect is no longer discursive but is pure intellection, a kind of thought that is alien to the embodied tripartite soul. Just as intellection differs from discursive reasoning, so too the four Contemplative Virtues differ from the Civic Virtues, as we shall see.

A passage from the end of Essay 7 (Procl. In R. 7.233.29–234.30 Kroll) helps illustrate what Proclus has in mind here. Proclus is there addressing the question of how anything composite can be a unity. For Platonists (as opposed to materialists like the Stoics), the answer is assisted by the fact that the soul is incorporeal (Procl. In R. 7.233.29–234.17 Kroll). "Incorporeal [substances] are united without confusion," he says (τῶν ἀσωμάτων ἀσυγχύτως ἡνωμένων, Procl. In R. 234.15 Kroll).[22] Thus the three soul elements can be said to interpenetrate each other (existing all together as

---

writes that the guardian who ascends as high even as the One "actualizes an activity that belongs to him/herself but jettisons the life of a ruler" (ἐνεργεῖ τὴν ἑαυτῷ προσήκουσαν ἐνέργειαν, τὴν δὲ ἀρχικὴν ἀφῆκε ζωήν, Procl. In R. 209.8–9 Kroll). Proclus then writes (Procl. In R. 209.13–210.6 Kroll) that any auxiliaries who do not obey the rulers or any members of the worker class who live a private life conducting business however they might wish "destroy the virtue relative to [the other classes]" (διέφθειρεν τὴν σχετικὴν ἀρετήν, Procl. In R. 209.21 Kroll). If any of the three classes act independently for their own good exclusively, the harmony among the classes is broken. Thus, again, in the society as in the soul, all three elements must work in harmony for Civic Virtue to exist. See also Abbate, *Proclo: Commento alla "Repubblica" di Platone*, 358n6.

21. On the benefits in Iamblichean philosophy of using the higher virtues in this lower realm, see Finamore, "Ethics, Virtue, and Theurgy."

22. For the term ἀσύγχυτος (without confusion), see Proclus *ET* Prop. 176, p. 154.8 and 10 Dodds, where Intelligible Forms are said to interpenetrate but keep their distinctness from one another in their union and Prop. 197, p. 172.14, where the soul's vital and cognitive (ζωτικὴ καὶ γνωστική, 172.1) essences are unconfusedly distinct (διήρηται … ἀσυγχύτως, 172.13–14). Incorporeal entities interpenetrate each other but also keep their distinct natures.

a unity) while retaining their own unique features. The soul complex is a multiplicity that has become unified. Proclus then continues, adding a second argument that makes use of the *Timaeus*'s tripartite doctrine (Procl. In R. 234.17–25 Kroll):

Nevertheless there is also another way that Plato's account is able to gain leeway, when he says that reason arises from a more divine essence but the irrational from another that is much inferior, and that the former preserves and orders while the latter is preserved and ordered. Just as Form when it is associated with matter introduces unity to it (and we have no need for any other thing to unite these with one another), in the same way also reason, which holds the rank of Form, itself unifies the irrational life and does not require any third thing to bind both.

οὐ μὴν ἀλλὰ καὶ ἕτερον τρόπον εὐοδεῖν τῷ Πλάτωνι τὸν λόγον δυνατόν, λέγοντι τὸν μὲν λόγον ἄλλης οὐσίας εἶναι θειοτέρας, τὸ δὲ ἄλογον ἄλλης καὶ πολλῷ λειπομένης, καὶ τὸν μὲν συνέχειν καὶ κοσμεῖν, τὸ δὲ συνέχεσθαι καὶ κοσμεῖσθαι. καθάπερ οὖν τὸ εἶδος τῇ ὕλῃ συγγενόμενον ἐπάγει τὸ ἕν, καὶ οὐδὲν ἄλλου δεόμεθα ταῦτα ἀλλήλοις ἐνοῦντος, κατὰ τὰ αὐτὰ δὴ καὶ ὁ λόγος εἴδους ἔχων τάξιν αὐτὸς ἐνίζει τὴν ἄλογον ζωὴν καὶ οὐ δεῖ τρίτου τινὸς ἄμφω συνδέοντος.

Since the reasoning element is in essence Intelligible (since it was fashioned by the Demiurge), it acts as a unifier of the two lower elements with itself. Proclus says that it "preserves and orders" (συνέχειν καὶ κοσμεῖν, 234.20) the other two, thereby binding them together with itself and also arranging them so that they work in cooperation with it. The comparison Proclus draws with Intelligible Form and material objects clarifies his doctrine. Just as individual Forms provide qualities for the object, thereby making the object one specific object but nonetheless a unity of multiple Forms-in-matter, so too the reasoning element organizes the lower elements to produce a unified soul. No third thing is needed. This allows the reasoning element to play its essential double role as both a separate Intelligible agent above and the lead element in the embodied soul below.[23]

Returning to Proclus's distinction between what belongs to anything in

---

23. Finally, building on the doctrine that the soul has an Intelligible origin, Proclus concludes (Procl. In R. 234.26–30 Kroll), since the Demiurge is the primary cause of the rational soul and—because he created the younger gods who in their turn created the lower two elements—is also the secondary cause of the lower elements themselves, it is the Demiurge that is the cause of the three elements' coherence with each other and unity (τὴν πρὸς ἄλληλα συνέχειαν καὶ ἕνωσιν, Procl. In R. 234.30 Kroll) Thus the soul is unified by its incorporeality, by the reasoning element's superiority over the lower elements, and by the oversight of the Demiurge. The soul is a unity of interpenetrated elements, ruled by reason and held in union by the Demiurgic will.

itself (καθ᾽ αὑτὸ) and what belongs to it in relation to something else (κατὰ τὴν πρὸς ἄλλο σχέσιν), we can see now that the soul in itself is the separated rational element engaging in pure intellection of the Forms, while the soul in relation to the body engages in discursive thought, but that its ability to think discursively depends on the cooperation of the other two elements.[24] What is true of the reasoning element is also true in an appropriate manner of the lower elements. When the spirited element lives according to itself, it does not obey reason, and when the irrational element lives according to itself, it selfishly desires everything without regard for the other elements of the soul. None of the three elements can live the life most suited to itself if the citizen of the polis is to be virtuous. Rather, the three elements must form a unity in relation to each other (Procl. *In R.* 208.14–25 Kroll). What brings about this harmonious unity in the tripartite soul is Civic Virtue (Procl. *In R.* 208.26–209.2 Kroll):

Since all [the elements of the soul] are yoked together with one another and make up a single form of life, one must examine also the activity of all of them in relation to one another. In this way we shall see the virtue and vice of each and define this [activity of the elements in relation to one another] as Civic Virtue,[25] when it is a state that is perfective of the life of the elements of the soul in relation to one another, but [define] as vice the opposite of this [activity] inasmuch as it destroys the [harmonious] state [of the soul], which is the vital natural relation of [the elements] to one another.

24. Proclus makes a similar distinction between the disembodied and embodied soul in Procl. *in R.* 6, 171.24–172.6 Kroll. Drawing on a discussion in the *Alcibiades* (Pl. *Alc.* 129b1–130c7 Burnet) about what "our very self" (αὐτὸ τὸ αὑτό, Pl. *Alc.* 130d5 Burnet) may be, Proclus distinguishes it from the body (which is the self's instrument) and the combination of body and soul, and he associates "our very self" with the disembodied rational soul. ("The true self is the intellectual form of the soul," τὸ δὲ ὄντως αὐτὸ τοῦτο ἄρα ἦν ἐκεῖνο τὸ νοερὸν εἶδος τῆς ψυχῆς Procl. *in R.* 172.5–6. Kroll) Proclus says that this separated soul rules the embodied soul. On this passage, see also Opsomer, "Proclus," 129–30. In Essay 7, it is this separated soul that returns to the body to rule the other two elements of the soul.

25. A problematic phrase: ταύτην ὁρίζεσθαι πολιτικὴν ἀρετὴν (Procl. *in R.* 208.29 Kroll). To what does ταύτην refer? Festugière, *Proclus: Commentaire sur la République*, 15n3, thinks that the feminine demonstrative takes the place of the neuter (τοῦτο) and refers to the following participial clause (ἕξιν οὖσαν τελειωτικὴν τῆς σχετικῆς τῶν τῆς ψυχῆς μορίων ζωῆς, 208.29–30). He translates: "definir comme ceci la vertu politique, 'un habitus qui perfectionne la vie des parties de l'ame dans leur relation l'une à l'autre.'" Abbate, *Proclo: Commento alla "Repubblica" di Platone*, 358n5, thinks that ταύτην refers to τὴν σχετικὴν ἐνέργειαν (208.27) and that πολιτικὴν ἀρετὴν (208.29) complements it. He translates: "definire virtù politica l'attività di relazione, in quanto è condizione che perfeziona la vita di relazione propria delle parti dell'anima." I agree with Abbate about the referent of ταύτην, about ταύτην being the direct object of ὁρίζεσθαι, and about πολιτικὴν ἀρετὴν being in apposition with ταύτην. This interpretation makes πολιτικὴν ἀρετὴν the referent of οὖσαν (208.29).

ἐπειδὴ δὲ συνέζευκται πάντα ἀλλήλοις καὶ μίαν συμπληροῖ ζωήν, δεῖ σκοπεῖν αὐτῶν πάντων καὶ τὴν σχετικὴν ἐνέργειαν, καὶ οὕτως ὁρᾶν τήν τε ἀρετὴν ἑκάστου καὶ τὴν κακίαν, καὶ ταύτην ὁρίζεσθαι πολιτικὴν ἀρετὴν ἕξιν οὖσαν τελειωτικὴν τῆς σχετικῆς τῶν τῆς ψυχῆς μορίων ζωῆς, τὴν δὲ ἐναντίαν ταύτης κακίαν ἕξιν διαφθείρουσαν τὴν κατὰ φύσιν αὐτῶν πρὸς ἄλληλα ζωτικὴν σχέσιν.

Thus, in order for an embodied soul to be virtuous (to have Civic Virtue), it must have ordered its three elements so that the rational element is in charge and the other two elements follow its lead. When any of the elements, including the rational element, goes its own way without regard for the others, the individual citizen ceases to be virtuous. Civic Virtue is possible only when the rational element agrees to rule the whole for the good of the whole and when the spirited and irrational elements agree to be so ruled.

How do the three grades of virtue (Civic, Purificatory, and Contemplative) differ in accordance with this dual life of the rational element? The Civic Virtues, as we have seen, are those involved in harmonizing the three soul elements with one another in such a way that the reasoning element is in charge. Purificatory Virtues do not merely control the lower elements but begin the separation of the rational element from the rest.[26] As we have seen, the Purificatory and Contemplative Virtues belong to the disembodied soul, the former freeing the reasoning element from the soul/body complex and the latter belonging to it as it intellegizes apart from the complex. Thus, according to Marinus, Proclus exercised the Civic Virtues by taking an active role in Athenian politics and urging right action in the city (Marin. *Procl.* 15 Masullo); his activities were aimed at those in this lower realm and ipso facto helped others order their tripartite souls properly as well. In Marin. *Procl.* 21.1–9 Masullo, Marinus describes the Purificatory Virtues as they appeared in Proclus. The reasoning element "engages in pure intellection itself by itself and, having turned toward itself, it no longer engaged in doxastic sympathy[27] with the body" (αὐτὸ δὲ καθ᾽ αὐτὸ εἰλικρινὲς τὸ νοεῖν καὶ τὸ πρὸς ἑαυτὴν ἐστράφθαι, μηδαμοῦ συνδοξάζειν τῷ σώματι, 21.8–9). Unlike the Civic Virtues, which involve engagement with the body, the Purificatory Virtues leave the body and its reliance on discursive thinking and opining behind. Finally, Marinus relates that once Proclus had freed himself

---

26. For the differences between these two sorts of virtues, see Marin., *Procl.* 18. Edwards, *Neoplatonic Saints*, 84n184, cites John Dillon's explanation that the Civic Virtues "merely restrain the appetites" while the Purificatory "expel them from the soul altogether."

27. For the meaning of the verb συνδοξάζειν, see Edwards, *Neoplatonic Saints*, 90n230: "The term sundoxazein … implies participation in *doxa* or opinion, which for Plato, *Republic* 510ab is a lower cognitive state than genuine knowledge."

from the body and the lower elements completely and contemplated the Forms directly, he ascended from practical knowledge (φρόνησις) to wisdom (σοφία) (Marin. *Procl.* 22.5–15 Masullo) and thereby from Purificatory to Contemplative Virtue. Thus Marinus verifies what we found in Proclus's *Republic* commentary. The grades of virtue are directly related to the life of the soul, whether it is embodied or separated from the body.

Conclusion

We have examined the issue of the tripartite soul in the later Neoplatonists. We encountered a tension in the Platonic dialogues between the presence of the lower elements of the soul in the soul's disembodied life in the *Republic* and *Phaedrus* and their absence in the disembodied life in the *Timaeus*. We next examined the treatments of the problem in Porphyry and Iamblichus, where we discovered that they argued that the embodied soul was tripartite but the disembodied soul was not, and that they believed that the reason for the tripartism of the embodied soul was Plato's discussion in the *Republic* of the four virtues being defined in accordance with the three elements. Since neither Porphyry nor Iamblichus explained the relation between the virtues and embodied soul in the *Republic*, we turned to Proclus's commentary on the *Republic*, where we discovered a discussion on this topic. For Proclus, the four virtues belonged to all three elements of the soul when the soul was embodied but belonged to the rational element alone when it was freed from the body. Virtue in the embodied soul required that all three parts worked together harmoniously, thereby creating a unified soul. In the disembodied soul, however, no such harmony was required since the rational element was in itself unitary. Nonetheless, in order for the separated rational element to use the knowledge it gained in the Intelligible after it again becomes embodied, it is necessary for it to retain the Civic Virtue that it had possessed previously and therefore to retain the former harmony of all three elements. In this way the embodied soul continues to be ruled by the rational element, which is now endowed with its acquired Intelligible knowledge. Thus, for Proclus, the higher soul possesses a higher form of knowledge, which it retains and uses when it is again embodied. The rational element in the soul, after it has acquired the Purificatory and Contemplative Virtues and then has reunited with the body and with the spirited and irrational elements, is once again engaged with the Civic Virtues.

CHAPTER 6 ‖ Damascius

New Insights in the Platonic Tradition

Marilena Vlad

In this essay, I discuss Damascius's reading of the negative hypotheses in Plato's *Parmenides* (160b–166c), trying to show that this interpretation sustains his overall perspective about the structure of reality; namely, the presence of an ineffable principle, beyond the One.

The five positive hypotheses, based on the assumption that "the one is," are interpreted by Damascius (and by Proclus) as describing the absolute One, the intellect, the soul, the forms, and the intelligible matter. In what concerns the negative hypotheses, starting from the assumption that "the one is *not*," there are two major types of interpretation before Damascius. Porphyry and Iamblichus considered that they simply follow the line of the previous deductions, revealing new levels of reality. Proclus strongly opposes this perspective. For him, as for Syrianus, nothing can exist in the absence of the one. Therefore the last four deductions are not describing any reality but conclude to impossibilities. Their function is to demonstrate the absolute One and its productive power, through the absurd consequences that follow when suppressing the one.[1] Why? Because for Proclus the pri-

This essay was developed in the project PN-III-P4-ID-PCE-2016-0712, funded by CNCS–UEFISCDI.

1. Procl. *In Prm.* 1055.25–1057.5 Cousin; *Theol. Plat.* 1.12, p. 58.12–22 Saffrey-Westerink.

mordial generative cause is the One, which produces everything through the power of negation, instantiating everything that it is not itself.[2] This is a negation by excellence, which shows that the One transcends everything, and not that it lacks anything. On the contrary, the negations in the last hypotheses, which indicate the total lack of power resulting from the suppression of the one, cannot produce anything else. In these hypotheses, the one is suppressed, and the negation no longer has the generating power it had in the first hypothesis.

Proclus's interpretation relies on Plato's remark—close to the end of the dialogue—that "if the one is not, nothing is." For Proclus, this seems to be the general conclusion of the four negative hypotheses. Damascius does not agree. For him, this conclusion only concerns hypothesis nine—which leads to nothingness—but not all the four negative hypotheses.[3]

Rejecting the two lines of interpretation of his predecessors, Damascius argues that not *all* the negative hypotheses reveal new levels of reality. In fact, numbers seven and nine culminate into pure nothingness, since in both cases nothing can be said about the one (or about the others). He also rejects the idea that *all* the negative deductions turn to impossibilities. He notices that, in some of them—despite the fact that the one *is not*—Plato still refers to it in positive terms, listing its attributes and suggesting that it is knowable.[4] Moreover, Damascius argues, if all the negative hypotheses would be impossible, then Plato's division in the *Parmenides* would be incomplete because it would oppose the one that *is* (both absolutely and relatively) to the one that *is not* (but only in an absolute sense). If the division is to be complete, we have to admit not only that the one is (absolutely and relatively), but also that the one is not (both absolutely and *relatively*). We should thus assume that at least some of the negative hypotheses do not lead to absurdities, but to relative manners in which the one is not. Damascius therefore proposes a mixed perspective. He argues that only two hypotheses (seven and nine) turn to impossibilities, while the other two (six and eight) describe the last level of reality; namely, the sensible world.[5]

For Proclus, the one cannot be denied but only affirmed, which leads us either to the existence of the One as first principle (in the first hypothesis), or to the productive power of the One as cause of the reality (in the rest of

2. See on this Casas, "L'indicible comme principe paradigme néoplatonicien de l'apophatisme."

3. Dam. *In Prm.* 4.135.10–15 Westerink.

4. Pl. *Prm.* 160 c7 Burnet.

5. See also Doull, "Neoplatonism and the Origin of the Older Modern Philosophy," 507.

the affirmative hypotheses). For Damascius, the one can be affirmed, but also denied. When affirmed, it indicates the One (which eventually is not even one), or the reality down to the level of the forms and the intelligible matter (in hypotheses two to five). When denied, it indicates the apparent reality, that is, the world of becoming (in hypotheses six and eight), while its radical negation ultimately leads to pure nothingness (in hypotheses seven and nine).

Departing from all his predecessors, Damascius both admits that the procession of the reality continues below the intelligible matter and introduces explicit paradigms of the pure, inferior nothingness, which bring the development of the reality to a halt. In order to support this interpretation, he explains that the *nonbeing* (from the expression "the one *is not*") should be taken in two different senses. He follows Plato's distinction in the *Sophist*, between absolute nonbeing, which does not exist in any way, and relative nonbeing, which still is, inasmuch as we say that it *is* nonbeing,[6] so that the last degree of being is a relative nonbeing. In an analogous manner, the last degree of one is this "one-that-is-not," which he also calls "non-one," taken in a relative manner.[7] Accordingly, the last one is actually a relative non-one.[8] For Damascius, the fact that the nonbeing is still thought in the terms of the being means that the being has gone down to the level of nonbeing, integrating relative nonbeing.[9] The procession of the one (which is the general subject of the *Parmenides*) does not stop at the level of the intelligible world (described in the positive hypotheses) but goes down to the level of this "one-that-is-not" (ἐν μὴ εἶναι) or simply "non-one." In a paradoxical expression, Damascius says that the one-that-is-not participates to the one-that-is, simply because it is still called "one."

Damascius's interpretative choice should be understood in relationship with his general outlay of the reality and with his main goal: that of establishing the ineffable as absolute principle above the One.[10] If he departs from Proclus, it is because Proclus's perspective does not match his own structure of reality, which culminates with the ineffable.[11] If all the negative hypotheses indicated levels of reality, it would no longer be possible to con-

<hr>

6. Pl. *Sph.* 256 d11–12 Burnet.

7. ἐν τῷ μὴ εἶναι ἓν ἔχει τὸ εἶναι ἕν (Dam. *In Prm.* 4.81.15 Westerink).

8. μὴ ἓν οἷον εἶναι ἔσχατον ἑνός. (Dam. *In Prm.* 4.81.32 Westerink).

9. Dam. *In Prm.* 4.84.18–23 Westerink.

10. On Damascius's manner of introducing the ineffable principle, see Caluori, "*Aporia* and the Limits of Reason and of Language in Damascius."

11. Concerning this principle and its function in Damascius's thinking, see Napoli, Ἐπέκεινα τοῦ ἑνός; Béguin, "Ineffable et indicible chez Damascius"; Vlad, *Damascius et l'ineffable*.

ceive an absolute nothingness. But Damascius proposes the ineffable using a distinction between two manners of nothingness: superior to the One and inferior to any reality. Conversely, if all the negative deductions would lead to absurdity, the power of the One would be unsurpassable and insuppressible. This is what Proclus is trying to say. But for Damascius, the suppression of the one is necessary both in the negative sense and primarily in the superior sense, as a step toward the ineffable. He needs this suppression of the one in a totally different manner than Proclus: not as absurd but rather positively, as productive of some level of reality, and also negatively, as ultimately leading to nothingness. Accordingly, he suggests that below the intelligible matter we still have a non-one that produces some reality and a corresponding plurality, before engulfing into pure nothingness. Let's see what he means by this.

The Apparent One: Hypothesis Six

The one in hypothesis six—which is not *really* one but only apparently one (τὸ φαινόμενον ἕν) and rather non-one—should not be confounded with the inferior nothingness (which is not even one) or with the proper One (τὸ κυρίως ἕν, from the first hypothesis), which, in the conclusion, is not even one, but in a superior sense.[12] Rather, it is one only in a relative and apparent sense, and also "it is not," and it is not one, but still in a relative sense. This one is not suppressed completely, but only inasmuch as it is not the others. It is an ambiguous reality, which both is one and is not one.

The one-that-is-not is still considered one, and it is analyzed in the terms of the one and in the terms of being, even if we affirm nonbeing about it. Moreover, just as the nonbeing still has a share in the being,[13] this one-that-is-not still *is* in a way and Plato refers to it as *being*. Therefore the one-that-is-not is a last manifestation and a remote presence of the absolute One itself.

Nevertheless, the one in hypothesis six is not the One itself, and therefore it is assumed as nonbeing and is called non-one. In order to find a place for this contradictory one in the structure of reality, Damascius continues the analogy with the nonbeing in the *Sophist* and notices that nonbeing exists in the intelligible realm (as difference between the intelligible kinds), but nonbeing also appears—in a more proper manner—in the world of

---

12. Dam. *In Prm.* 4.92.4–5 Westerink.
13. Dam. *In Prm.* 4.86 Westerink.

becoming.[14] The same thing can be said about the non-one. It exits in the intelligible realm, for instance, when we speak about the others and declare them different from the one, so that, in a certain sense, they are non-one. Yet, in a more proper manner, this non-one appears in the world of becoming, and this is precisely what hypothesis six shows. This "non-one" is a simulacrum of the One (εἴδωλον τοῦ ἑνός), just as the relative nonbeing is an image of the real being.[15] The "non-one" is introduced by Damascius[16] in analogy with the nonbeing. Just as the nonbeing is not simply *nothing* but can also exist as relative nonbeing, so the-one-that-is-not (which would correspond to the nonbeing and thus will also be called non-one) is not pure and absurd nothingness (as Proclus suggested) but is a relative non-one, a one that is not properly one.

What is the role of this non-one? What exactly does it do in the frame of reality? After the first three positive deductions, concerning the one that *is*, numbers four and five show what happens with the "others," in the assumption that "the one *is*." For Damascius as well as for Proclus, these two hypotheses describe the forms and the matter. Both of them are types of intelligible "others." These two types of "others" are also intelligible types of "non-one," since the others are different from the one, as Plato constantly reminds us in the second part of the dialogue. Therefore Damascius implies that these two intelligible types of non-one actually join into the non-one of hypothesis six, which would thus be a compound of all the senses in which Parmenides discussed the "others" so far:[17] as forms and as matter. Since the forms and the matter (despite their specificity and difference) share this property of being "others," the one in hypothesis six would be an entity that combines them and accomplishes their unity, their community into being others. It is a compound of the two general types of others that exist, which are themselves compound, through their plural nature.

The-One-That-Is-Not as Principle of the Sensible World

This apparent one, which is a simulacrum of the real One, is the principle of the sensible world.[18] But how is it possible that two *intelligible* types

---

14. Dam. *In Prm.* 4.82.4–10. Cf. Pl. *Sph.* 240 a5–c5 Burnet.

15. εἴδωλον τοῦ ὄντος (Dam. *In Prm.* 4.82.8–9 Westerink); Pl. *Sph.* 240 a–c Burnet.

16. Dam. *In Prm.* 4.81.23 Westerink.

17. πᾶν τὸ σύνθετον (Dam. *In Prm.* IV.83.12 Westerink) and τὸ ἐκ τῶν ἄλλων συγκείμενον (Dam. *In Prm.* 4.83.13 Westerink).

18. εἴδωλον τοῦ ἑνὸς ἐν τῇ γενέσει τυγχάνει ὄν (Dam. *In Prm.* 4.82.8–9 Westerink).

of "others" (viz., the forms and the matter) combine into a *sensible* non-one? This is because in hypotheses four and five, the forms are discussed in themselves, unmixed with matter, just as matter is discussed in itself, as an intelligible entity, not determined by forms. Once Damascius proposes the mixture of these two "others," we obtain forms that are *in* the matter or matter that is determined by forms, which is precisely what we call the sensible. Thus hypothesis six would give us the law of constitution of the compound of these two, which is the sensible world.[19] He also relies on the idea that the world of becoming is produced by the celestial gods.[20] This production is envisaged by Damascius as a type of composition of the last two intelligible genera: the forms and the matter. This one is a compound of its elements (matter and forms), but the compound destroys its own elements by combining them,[21] joining the "in power" of the matter (in the fifth hypothesis) with the "in the act" of the forms (from the fourth hypothesis), which thus perfects the matter.[22] Similar to the one-that-is, the matter plays the role of the one, while the forms play the role of being,[23] which here, in hypothesis six, strengthens the one (of the matter) and makes it be what it is.[24] Damascius considers that, just as the third one (i.e., the soul) combines the two previous hypotheses, so the sixth one combines the fourth and fifth hypotheses.

Even though it is located at the furthest end of the reality, right before the pure nothingness, this non-one is still considered to be "a kind of principle" (τοιάδε τις ἀρχή).[25] It works like a principle, combining the matter and the forms and producing a particular nature: that of the world that undergoes change, and even a particular manner of self-constitution, because the sensible is constituted out of matter and forms, but not as a pure superposition of these two previous levels. Here Damascius opposes

---

19. Dam. *In Prm.* 4.84.15–18 Westerink. Cf. Combès, Études néoplatoniciennes, 134, who notices that the forms (hypothesis four) and the matter (hypothesis five) are the conditions of possibility for the sensible to appear. Nevertheless, they are not "ses principes efficaces. Espèces et matière ne sont pas encore mêlées. C'est pourquoi Damascius, dans son commentaire du *Parménide*, se tourne vers les hypothèses négatives (si l'un n'est pas) pour leur demander des principes constitutifs de la manifestation du sensible. Jamais, dans la philosophie antique, le vœux d'une procession intégrale n'a été poussé aussi loin que dans cette ultime expression."

20. Dam. *In Prm.* 4.101.26–27 Westerink.

21. Dam. *In Prm.* 4.86.19–20 and 4.94.19–21 Westerink.

22. Dam. *In Prm.* 4.96.3–4; 4.94.19–21.

23. Ἀναλογεῖ δὲ τῷ μὲν ὄντι τὸ εἶδος, τῷ δὲ ἑνὶ ἡ δυνάμει ὕλη (Dam. *In Prm.* 4.97.1–2; 4.94.19–21).

24. Dam. *In Prm.* 4.95.25–27 Westerink.

25. Dam. *In Prm.* 4.84.3–18 Westerink.

Proclus, for whom the composite cannot be a principle but can only result from a principle.[26] For Damascius, the very status of a principle changes. He relies on Iamblichus, for whom the composite can still be a principle.[27] In fact, Damascius notices that, for the sensible world to appear for real, we have to put the two hypotheses (the fourth and the fifth) together, to combine their subjects and make them interact; otherwise, there would be no sensible sublunary world.

This principle of the sensible world has an unstable nature. Parmenides himself presents it as changing and constantly becoming something else, *different* from the others and different from itself, even though it is also un-moved.[28] This one—which is not properly one—is conceived as combining the others (i.e., the forms and the matter). It is the compound of what is different from the proper one. This implies that, even though this sixth one combines the others, it is not determined as a unity of these others. The result of the combination does not have a permanent identity and is never stable and unitary. On the contrary, it is in constant change. This principle is *one*, not as a constantly subsisting nature, but only as becoming. It is the one of the others, which are different from the proper one and thus are constantly becoming different, so that the nature of the sixth one is undermining its own identity. What is stable and unitary in this principle is precisely its *changing* character. Iamblichus and Plutarch had already suggested that this hypothesis refers to the sensible.[29] Damascius continues this perspective. Yet, for him, the hypotheses do not simply follow the way down the series of realities, but they spring from distinct manners of nonbeing. Thus the sensible is not just the subsequent level of reality (after the matter and the specific forms), but it is the first sense in which the nonbeing can be applied to the one, the first manner in which the one functions in its reverse manner, not as properly one, but as being different from the other ones and from the others in general (i.e., different from the others of the matter and of the specific forms). Thus Damascius relies on Iamblichus when he describes the object of this hypothesis as being the sensible, but in fact he understands the sensible differently. What matters for Damascius is not the sensible in itself but the completeness of the reality that can thus spring

---

26. Procl. *Theol. Plat.* 1.9.38.4–7, 40.13–18 Saffrey-Westerink; *In Prm.*, 6.1048.4–6 Cousin. See Dam. *In Prm.* 4.74.6–8 Westerink.

27. Dam. *In Prm.* 4.74.8–12 Westerink.

28. Pl. *Prm.* 163 a2–b6 Burnet. Dam. *In Prm.* 4.86.17–22 Westerink. As Combès, *Études néoplatoniciennes*, 136, notices, "Dans la 6ème hypothèse, la déperdition de l'être n'est plus compensée par l'indivision de l'un. Celui-ci est affecté en lui-même, il se divise et s'écoule avec l'être."

29. Dam. *In Prm.* 4.84.5–9 Westerink. Cf. Procl. *In Prm.* 6.1055.15–17 Cousin.

from the One. The one is not just affirmed but also denied and even denied the quality of being one, so that, in the end, the one is not really one but only imitates the one and functions in a unifying manner, without having the nature of a one.

The very status of this so-called principle is contradictory: it is one, but it is not properly one. It imitates the one because it acts like a unifying principle, since it is a mixture of the others,[30] accomplishing their compound unity. Yet for the same reason it is not genuinely one,[31] because the one refuses any duality and composition.[32] So, it is one through its unifying function, through its effect, but not through its nature.

While unifying the others, it becomes itself non-one, because it unifies the pluralities of the "others." Its very unifying act makes it plural, composite, and thus non-one. Damascius describes it as being "one in a certain manner" and says that it is "like a one" (οἷον ἓν)[33] and that it is accompanied by the property of not being what it seems to be.[34] It *seems* to be one, because it is called one in the hypothesis, but in fact it is not one, because the hypothesis denies its being and, implicitly, its being one.[35] Moreover, it is not composed of ones but of the others (of the other of the matter and of the others of the forms). It is not a unitary nature because it is not made up of ones (like a unified of henads, for instance). It is not the One itself (οὐκ αὐτοὲν), but it "introduces the others" (τὰ ἄλλα εἰσάγειν), it consists of the others (ἐξ ἄλλων σύγκειται), and it is the one of the others. It has the character of the others (ἀλλοῖον ἕν).[36] Though it seems to be one, it is not a true one but a deceitful one (ψευδόμενον ἕν).[37] It is an ambiguous nature (ἀμφίβολον φύσιν), which *is* considered *not to be*.[38]

This one is differentiated from "the others". We can understand the "others" in three manners. First, it is different from the proper others, that is, from the specified forms (in the fourth hypothesis) and the matter (of the fifth hypothesis). Through their own nature, the others are different from the one (since this is how Plato defines the others). Therefore the one—

---

30. Dam. *In Prm.* 4.83.18–19 Westerink.

31. ἅμα δὲ οὐκ ἔστιν ἕν (Dam. *In Prm.* 4.83.19 Westerink).

32. ἀναίνεται γὰρ τὸ ἓν πᾶσαν διπλόην καὶ μάλιστα σύνθεσιν (Dam. *In Prm.* 4.83.20–21 Westerink).

33. Dam. *In Prm.* 4.85.18–19 Westerink.

34. Dam. *In Prm.* 4.90.1–2 Westerink.

35. Dam. *In Prm.* 4.83.18–21 and καὶ τὸ ἓν ἔσται τε καὶ οὐκ ἔσται ἕν (Dam. In Prm. 4.86.16 Westerink).

36. Dam. *In Prm.* 4.83.26 Westerink.

37. Dam. *In Prm.* 4.83.26 Westerink.

38. Dam. *In Prm.* 4.87.3–4 Westerink.

that-is-not is composed of the others, which are (by their nature) different from the one. This is precisely why this one is untruthful (ψευδόμενον).[39] Nevertheless, in a second interpretation, these others are the ones—that is, the henads—so that the one in hypothesis six is different from the ones examined in the previous hypotheses.[40] The subject of this sixth hypothesis is still the one, yet it is a one assumed as *not being*. This does not mean that it is not at all, that it simply does not exist, in an absolute sense, but rather that it is not "the others." *It is not* in the sense in which it is different from the other ones, and as such it is not the one in its affirmative sense (from the first five hypotheses). For Damascius, it is important to show that this one in hypothesis six is not just another level of unity, in the series of ones previously discussed. This one is different from the previous ones because it is not properly one. In a third sense, this one is different from the others, that is, from its own others,[41] which appear in hypothesis eight. This one-that-is-not is a compound of the others that precede it (i.e., a compound of the form and matter that are the subjects of the two previous hypotheses, four and five), and it is a one that unifies the others that follow it (i.e., the others in hypothesis eight).[42]

Its ambiguous nature shows forth even when we try to express it in some way. Parmenides mentions that this one is knowable.[43] There is science about it, because otherwise we would not even know what it means that "the one is not."[44] This is one of the arguments Damascius turns against Proclus: since this one is known, it cannot be completely absurd and contradictory, as Proclus had it. Nevertheless, for Damascius, this one is not known in a direct and complete manner, but rather through an obscure knowledge,[45] because, as sensible, it is the subject of sensation and opinion.[46]

On a closer look, Damascius notices that, in an essential manner, this one is founded in the ineffable of the matter, which enters into its composition[47] and was discussed in hypothesis five. The trace of the ineffable goes down to this very last principle. All the forms that enter into this com-

---

39. Dam. *In Prm.* 4.83.21–84.1 Westerink.
40. Dam. *In Prm.* 4.90–92 Westerink.
41. Dam. *In Prm.* 4.104.20 Westerink.
42. ἓν δὲ τῶν ἄλλων καὶ ἐκ τῶν ἄλλων ὑφεστὼς (Dam. *In Prm.* 4.89.3–8 Westerink).
43. Dam. *In Prm.* 4.105 Westerink.
44. Pl. *Prm.* 160 d4–6 Burnet.
45. ἀμυδρὰν ἐνδείκνυται γνῶσιν (Dam. *In Prm.* 4.105.17 Westerink).
46. Dam. *In Prm.* 4.105.13–14 Westerink.
47. Dam. *In Prm.* 4.96.7 Westerink.

pound are trying to approximate the ineffable of the matter, but in fact it is impossible to express it. There is, even at this level of reality, an unfulfilled knowledge, precisely as it happens in the first hypothesis, where the One tends to express the ineffable, but all that it can do is to suggest it through its own suppression. Here, at the other end of the reality, the one-that-is-not tends to grasp this ineffable of the matter (in which its hypostasis is rooted); it pursuits it, but it cannot grasp it because the ineffable evades.[48] Thus the one in this one-that-is-not corresponds to the matter, and more-over it suggests or anticipates the "ineffable of the matter."[49] Thus the non-one ultimately remains ineffable.

Consequently, this non-one cannot be described in a proper manner; it only *seems* to be everything that we say about it in the hypothesis, for instance, one, changing and unchanging, and all the others characteristics that we attribute to it, but it remains essentially impossible to determine.

The Plurality of the Apparent One: Hypothesis Eight

Hypothesis eight discusses the plurality associated with the apparent one; namely, the sensible individuals that are generated into this world and are also apparent. Parmenides discusses the others than the one, when we assume that the one does not exist. Whereas the non-one represents the phenomenal all, the total world of becoming, the others are the individuals generated into this world,[50] the sensible things, like animals, vegetables, or inanimate things. These sensible individuals are the images of the forms. The one-that-is-not has a slight trace of being one, when compared to its own others. These others (which are others in relationship to each other, and not to the one, because here the one is not) are simulacra and pseud-onyms (εἰδωλικῶν καὶ ψευδωνύμων), and they undergo constant change.[51] Moreover, because all of these others seem one (even though they are not one), each of them is "one-that-is-not."[52] These are the elements of the phe-nomenal one,[53] its constitutive parts. And they present the same charac-teristics as the non-one in hypothesis six: they are also phenomenal and apparent.[54]

48. Dam. *In Prm.* 4.96.7–10 Westerink.

49. Dam. *In Prm.* 4.98.5–6 Westerink.

50. τὰ δὲ καθέκαστα καὶ ἄτομα (Dam. *In Prm.* 4.123.3–5 Westerink).

51. Dam. *In Prm.* 4.125.14–17 Westerink.

52. Dam. *In Prm.* 4.128.3–5 Westerink.

53. τὰ σύνθετα μέρη τοῦ συνθέτου ἑνός (Dam. *In Prm.* 4.122.15–16 Westerink).

54. Dam. *In Prm.* 4.122.8–10 Westerink. As Combès, *Études néoplatoniciennes*, 126, notices,

The Absolute Nothingness: Hypotheses Seven and Nine

It is only after this sensible level that Damascius introduces the complete nothingness, which implies a total impossibility of the discourse. Described in hypotheses seven and nine, the nothingness results from the suppression of any determination, including that of the apparent one, just as in the *Sophist*, the real nothing is not the nonbeing (as negation of the being, which still is considered to be) but consists in the complete privation of being (τὸ μηδαμῶς ὄν).[55] Hypothesis seven shows that if the one—taken in itself[56]—is not, then we cannot apply any discourse and any determination to it. Hypothesis nine also analyzes the absolute nothingness, not in relationship with the non-one, but in relationship with its others (discussed in hypothesis eight).

For Damascius, it is risky to admit a pure inferior nothingness, because in his perspective, the real nothing is the ineffable. Therefore he explicitly rejects any similarity of nature between these two. The nothingness is not nothing in the sense in which the ineffable is said to be nothing in *De principiis*, nor is it a last reflection of this superior nothingness. He intimates that Proclus would have suggested such an analogy: whereas the first principle is productive of everything, the inferior nothing would be receptive of everything that perishes.[57] Damascius rejects this perspective.[58] The nothingness in hypothesis seven is neither the ineffable cause of all things nor the ineffable of the matter, which is the last reflection of the ineffable, into the reality.[59] In fact, the ineffable is "nothing *of* all" (μηδὲν ᾗ τῶν πάντων),[60] and it cannot even be called "nothing" because it is a reality that surpasses any description. On the contrary, the inferior nothing is neither one nor the ineffable, but an absolute suppression of any property, subsistence, or reality. This nothing purely does not exist and does not have any nature of

---

the objects of hypotheses six and eight are "des échos plus affaiblis de *l'hyparxis* de l'un, qui tendra ici sur le mode du non-être vers sa limite de séparation avec l'être."

55. Dam. *In Prm.* 4.82.8–12 Westerink.

56. On the distinction, πρὸς ἑαυτό - πρὸς τὰ ἄλλα; see Karfík, "Par rapport à soi-même et par rapport aux autres."

57. Dam. *In Prm.* 4.116.10–16 Westerink.

58. Dam. *In Prm.* 4.118.6–14 Westerink.

59. Dam. *In Prm.* 4.115.6–8 Westerink. See also Gersh, "*More Neoplatonism after Derrida*" 126: "In the *Commentarius in Parmenidem*, he establishes the premise that 'the Ineffable is in all things' (*to aporrhēton en pasin*) in order to prove that, since it is impossible to maintain that the absolutely non-existent is similarly omnipresent because that would undermine the foundation of all beings, the Ineffable must be distinguished from the absolutely non-existent."

60. Dam. *In Prm.* 4.115.13 Westerink.

its own. If the nothingness would have some community of nature with the ineffable, we would either give some function to the inferior nothingness (and thus we would objectify it, so that it would not really be nothing), or the very meaning of the ineffable would be affected, if the last trace of the principle of all things (productive of all things) would be found in the nothingness. The very "nature" or particularity of the ineffable would be annihilated, since it would also be present in the nothingness. Damascius argues that if this last nothingness would be an effect of the ineffable, then just as the ineffable traverses all things, the absolute nothingness would also be present in the reality, which would overturn the hearth of the being.[61]

Moreover, if the nothingness itself would be produced from the ineffable, it would also be produced in a certain manner from the other principles after the ineffable, and thus it would be a last trace and effect of the ineffable; it would be a last offshoot (γέννημα) of the reality.[62] This offshoot would contain all the impossible things that we can imagine, and moreover it would not be completely unsayable, but still expressible, as inferior to the absolute ineffable. Being expressible, it would still have a certain being; it would still be something, which would be absurd, since it should be the absolute nothingness.[63] In this manner, we would infinitely advance into this offshoot because we would never reach a final, pure nothingness. In order to avoid the risk of confounding the two types of nothing, Damascius proposes a formal analogy between them, but without any similarity of nature. The two "nothings" do not have anything essential in common. They only have in common the effect that they have on our discourse, that is, the type of blockage that they produce in the discourse.

It is of paramount importance for Damascius that this inferior nothingness be isolated and not extended to all the negative hypotheses. He speaks about this nothing as such, as the absolute suppression of the being of the one, which corresponds to the pure nonbeing in the *Sophist*. If, however, all the negative hypotheses would lead to absurdity and contradiction, this would mean that denying the being of the one is simply impossible, and as such, it would not even be possible to speak about an absolute nothingness. Thus, when Damascius does accept that some hypotheses (seven and nine) lead to impossibilities, he means this in a different manner than Proclus: he does not mean that it is simply contradictory to say that the one is not, but he means to say that *it is possible* to suppress the being of the one in an

---

61. Dam. *In Prm.* 4.117.9–13 Westerink.
62. Dam. *In Prm.* 4.117.15–16 Westerink.
63. Dam. *In Prm.* 4.117.16–27 Westerink.

absolute manner, even though the result of this suppression leaves us in the incapacity to hold any discourse.

Damascius needs the absolute nothingness. First, because it is in contrast with this inferior nothing that he describes the existence of a superior nothing: the ineffable.[64] Second, he needs to put a limit to the reality. Otherwise, we would have another level even lower than the material world, and we would infinitely advance into a kind of offshoot of the reality.

Why is Damascius's perspective relevant? We can answer this question in two manners: first inside Damascius's own perspective about the reality as a whole, and second looking from the effects that his perspective produces at a philosophical level.

Damascius ends the history of Neoplatonic interpretations to the *Parmenides* with a new perspective, trying to integrate all the hypotheses and all the possible senses of the one: he sees the one both as being and as not being, both relatively and absolutely. His interpretation restores the completeness of Parmenides's project. The one functions as productive principle, both when it is and when it is not. Moreover, even when it is suppressed in an absolute manner, when we say that the one is not at all, we reach the border of reality, the pure nothingness. Nevertheless, this nothingness is not a pure contradiction, but it is a constitutive limit, which guarantees that the reality no longer proliferates below the material individuals.

Indirect Proof of the Ineffable

But even more important is the conclusion that Damascius is trying to draw from the completeness of this project. For Proclus, the One is the absolute principle, which cannot be suppressed, because the suppression of the one would lead to absurdities. For Damascius, even the suppression of the one reveals new types of reality. Thus the power of the One is not exclusive, and reality is not solely dependent on the One. While interpreting the negative hypotheses, Damascius is actually presenting the positive hypotheses in a different light. If only the positive hypotheses would be possible and productive of some sort of reality, then the whole reality would enter into the exclusive dominion of the One. But Damascius is challenging the One in two manners. First, he invokes the fact that the One is still thought (in fact, Plato speaks about the One in the *Sophist*, while in the *Parmenides* the One appears as the principle of the discourse, this being the reason why

64. Dam. *Pr.* 1.7.24–8.5 Westerink.

Plato cannot deny the One in the first hypothesis). Second, he challenges the One starting from the negative hypotheses, inasmuch as he shows that it is still possible (already for Plato himself) to think outside of the hypothesis of the one, that is, under a hypothesis that the one be suppressed. The one is not just a positive principle that continues to produce realities down to the very end of the scale of reality (as other Neoplatonists have suggested). On the contrary, the one itself can be suppressed and considered as nonexistent (either in a relative or in an absolute manner). In both cases, we can still think and deduce a certain nature: either that of the material individuals or that of the pure nothingness. Thus the One is not unsurpassable. For Damascius, the One is only the dynamic vehicle that suggests a higher principle: the ineffable. This other principle traverses all things and all levels of reality,[65] but it can no longer enter into this dialectic, into this game of hypotheses. We can only grasp it indirectly, through the unsayable character of every level of reality: from the unspeakable nature of the One in the first hypothesis, to the unsayable character of the matter, which no form can express. For Damascius, the suppression of the one is not impossible and absurd, but on the contrary, it is the sign that Plato tacitly admits of a previous principle: the ineffable. Damascius sees the suppression of the one in two matters. In the first hypothesis, if the One is, we get to the conclusion that the One is not; that is, we get to the suppression of the One itself, which is the sign that we should look above the One itself. On the contrary, in the negative hypotheses (viz., six and eight), we admit the-one-that-is-not, and this relative suppression is still a manner in which the one can manifest and can still be productive. In fact, this is precisely what happens in the first hypothesis, in a superior manner, whereas here it happens in an inferior manner.

For Damascius, the other levels of reality that he distinguishes, like the One, the unified and even the soul, already have a deeply aporetical character. They are not easy to comprehend and are not so "positive" as we might think, or as his predecessor might want us to think. Damascius pumps a lot of energy in proving this. But if they remain impossible to determine and to comprise positively, it is because some sort of ineffable presence (inaccessible and incomprehensible) is already infiltrated in them at all levels. This means that the levels of reality cannot be explained only by appealing to the productive power of the One (as Proclus would have suggested). In other words, the power of the "one that is" is not the only one active in the

---

65. ἀπόρρητον ἐν πᾶσιν (Dam. *In Prm.* 4.117.11 Westerink).

reality. On the contrary, some productive power subsists even when suppressing the one in both senses: in the first aporia, but also in the negative hypotheses.

Thus Damascius does not stop at the One as first principle but goes beyond, toward a totally ineffable principle. This ineffable produces everything, in an ineffable manner. This is why, after the positive levels, Damascius identifies "negative" levels (phenomena, simulacra, the nothing with respect to the one, and the nothing with respect to the others). First, it is important for him to show that reality expands out of the limits imposed by the One. Second, the last four hypotheses include phenomena that are ineffable in a negative manner and emerge in the absence of the one. This shows that the influence of the ineffable is larger than that of the One and that we can still think, even if we suppress the one. Thus the negative hypotheses are the counterpart of Damascius's interpretation of the first hypothesis, which also surpasses Proclus's perspective, suggesting the ineffable as absolute principle. If the reality can develop even after the "positive" levels, this means that the principle of the whole reality does not appear in opposition to the reality (as the One is opposed to the plurality), but it can include in its productive power both sides of the reality: that in which the one functions positively and that which appears through the suppression of the one. For Damascius, the negative deductions in the *Parmenides* become an indirect proof that the absolute principle must be above the One, since suppressing the one does not suppress all reality.

The Ontological Dignity of the Sensible

Damascius's analysis has an important impact even outside of his own overall perspective. What is remarkable is that he discusses the *sensible* world as an *intelligible* possibility, as a particular case in which the one in the *Parmenides* can manifest. He treats the sensible as a philosophical problem, giving it a logical structure. He thus reduces the gap between intelligible and sensible worlds and restores the ontological dignity of the sensible. The sensible world appears as a consequence of the intelligible levels.[66]

What is more interesting is that, even though this sixth one is negative and appears as *not being*, still, this one is considered to be superior to matter and forms (the subjects of hypotheses four and five), at least inasmuch as

---

66. Proclus considered that the sensible world is produced by the gods, as an expression of the ideal paradigm. Cf. Procl. *In Ti.* 1.217.18–27 Diehl.

the compound is superior to its elements.[67] This superiority has nothing contradictory. In fact, since all the reality is a system of symbols, in a way, the absolute One is definitely superior to anything that follows, because it is closer to the ineffable. Nevertheless, since every other symbol intervenes in order to amend some incongruence of the previous symbols, in this much, every inferior symbol is superior to the previous symbols.

Moreover, Damascius introduces a change of paradigm in the Neoplatonic thinking. For Proclus, the major distinction was that between a unitary principle and a plural reality. Damascius proposes the ineffable as first principle and traces its presence down to the level of the sensible world. The opposition between the principle and the reality is no longer that between unity and multiplicity. The ineffable does not produce everything in the manner in which the One produces the plurals, but it produces everything in an ineffable manner.[68] The problem is no longer how to get from the One to less unified pluralities, but rather how to get from the ineffable to different symbols of this ungraspable principle. The One itself is already a symbol of the ineffable.[69] Everything after the ineffable suggests this principle and constantly amends the inadequacy of any possible symbol of the principle. Damascius notices that not only the one in hypothesis six is apparent, but also in a different sense, the one itself (the general subject of the dialogue) appears in different manners, throughout the nine hypotheses.[70] The reality looks like the conclusion that Plato draws at the end of the *Parmenides*; namely, that if the one is or is not, it will appear in all the possible ways: both as being everything and as not being anything. For Damascius, this game of appearing of the reality is nothing but a reminder of the ineffable principle of the all. From the transcendent One down to the physical world, everything is a manner of appearance—a mode of projecting (προβολή) different images of the principle. The reality is an appearance of something unapparent—because everything is less than the principle and a mere approximation of it. The ineffable is only the unseen part of a world of appearances. Therefore it is important for Damascius to explain how the sensible (which essentially *is* a world of appearance) is possible. The negative hypotheses become a logical counterpart of the ineffable, a final demonstration of the ineffable principle, not through *reductio ad absurdum*, but rather through showing how phenomena are possible and how even

---

67. Dam. *In Prm.* 4.85.10 Westerink: ἀεὶ γὰρ τὸ σύνθετον κρεῖττον τῶν οἰκείων στοιχείων.
68. Dam. *Pr.* 1.8.6–11 Westerink.
69. Dam. *Pr.* 2.11.22–25 Westerink.
70. Dam. *In Prm.* 4.94.1–3 Westerink.

this realm of appearance is still ineffable. As Damascius mentions, the one-that-is-not is already present in the positive hypotheses, though in a relative manner. Therefore what happens in hypothesis six (this one-that-is-not) is ultimately infiltrated in all the reality. Eventually, anything that can be identified in the reality already has an aspect of unreality, of appearance, since it is not totally ineffable, but only a symbol of it.

The Double-Reference Scheme and Its Meaning

Ilaria Ramelli

The powerful but elusive figure of Dionysius the Areopagite is indebted to both "pagan" Platonists, such as Plotinus and especially Proclus, and
Christians, primarily Origen. He often offers what I call a double-reference
scheme, which points to both the "pagan" Platonic and the Christian traditions at the same time. Like Origen, Dionysius alludes to both Plato and
Scripture together or uses "pagan" Platonic concepts and terminology in
reference to Christian ideas or vice versa. For instance, he applies ἀνάμνησις
to both Jesus's Eucharistic command and Plato's reminiscence doctrine;
he cites 1 Timothy 6:20 (Merk-Barbaglio) but with the addition of καλέ to
"Timothy" (Dion. Ar. *DN* 1.8 Suchla), from Plato's *Phaedrus*, where Socrates addresses a "fair youth"; in Dion. Ar. *Ep.* 8.6 Ritter Heil, Jesus appears
"on the ridge of heaven" (from Pl. *Phdr.* 247BC Burnet). His throne is "beyond heaven," ὑπερουράνιος, like Plato's ὑπερουράνιος.[1] The most important examples of the double-reference scheme, as I shall point out, include
(1) the works attributed to Dionysius's master (which can refer to both

1. Petroff, "*Corpus Areopagiticum* as a Project in Intertextuality," 253–75.

92

Origen and Proclus), (2) the notion of *apokatastasis* and reversion, and (3) that of love, *agape* and *eros*.

I do not tackle the issue of the relation between the Greek and the Syriac *Corpus*. Dionysius, in Greek, presents the Origenian thought as the true Christian philosophy, not in an Origenistic, radical form (as in Sudhaili or post-Evagrian thought), but in an *Origenian* form, closer to Origen's genuine philosophical theology, who inspired the Corpus along with his followers Nyssen and Evagrius.[2]

Dionysius in the footsteps of Nyssen, called God "beautiful and good" as the motivation of all things' desire and love of God.[3] Now, Dionysius found the connection between the desire for God–Good and the Platonist third metaphysical movement of reversion (ἐπιστροφή), both in Proclus (Procl. *ET* 31 Dodds: all things desire the Good and revert to it) and in Origen and Nyssen, and applied this connection to *apokatastasis*. Dionysius takes over both traditions, "pagan" and Christian: "Every being is from the Beautiful and Good, and in the Beautiful and the Good, and is reverted to the Beautiful and Good,"[4] and takes on the connection between love-desire and reversion. For the Good is what all beings desire, and to which all beings revert.[5] The link between love, God as Beautiful and Good, and reversion is even stronger in Dion Ar. *DN* 4.12.709D Suchla: "Love is a power that unifies, connects, and distributively combines; it preexists in the Beautiful and Good, through the Beautiful and Good, and is given out from the Beautiful and Good through the Beautiful and Good … it moves the first beings to providence and establishes the reversion of the needier towards their superiors." Dionysius, I shall point out, repeatedly and expressly assimilates reversion (ἐπιστροφή) and restoration (ἀποκατάστασις), using both lexica in the same text or replacing one with the other, and employs both ἀγάπη and ἔρως in reference to God. These are some examples of the double-reference scheme.

Dionysius joins the Christian tradition of *agape* with the "pagan" Platonic tradition of *eros*. This assimilation comes from Origen and Nyssen. For Origen, love is the principle that guarantees the stability of *apokatastasis*, based on the Pauline tenet that "Love (ἀγάπη) never falls."[6] Ἀγάπη guar-

---

2. Argument in Ramelli, "Origen, Evagrios, and Dionysios."

3. Dion. Ar. *DN* 4.10.708A, 4.7.701C, 704AB Suchla. Other occurrences of "beautiful and good": Dion. Ar. *DN* 4.7.704B, 4.8.704D, 4.10.705C–708A, 4.18.713D Suchla.

4. Dion. Ar. *DN* 4.10.705C Suchla.

5. Dion. Ar. *DN* 4.4.700B Suchla.

6. *C. Rom.* 5.10.195–226 Bammel. Discussion in Ramelli, *Christian Doctrine of Apokatastasis*, chapter on Origen.

antees the eternity of *apokatastasis*, which can happen only *after* God's love was manifested in Christ's inhumanation and crucifixion.[7] This is also why Origen identified the cause of the Fall in the weakening of love. Origen based his tenet on Paul, who, we shall see, was both Origen's and Dionysius's hero—and Dionysius pretended to be his disciple.

Origen's *Commentary on Canticles* interpreted the Song of Songs (SS) spiritually as expressing the soul's (or the Church's) mystical union with Christ. Origen's interpretation inspired Dionysius, who, as I shall point out, alluded to Origen's commentary. Origen describes *mystica* as the highest part of Christian philosophy: the ascent to the contemplation of the divinity through love: "through pure, spiritual love [*amor* = ἔρως], one ascends to the mystical level, to the contemplation of the divinity."[8] The soul's love for Christ is salvific: the soul is "on fire with salvific love for him"; "will receive from him a salvific wound and burn with his love's blessed fire."[9] The "grace of love is preeminent" since, with Paul, "love is greater than all, the only one that never falls."[10] This is because love has rational creatures "adhere to God entirely."[11] This is why Origen deemed the end better than the beginning: in the end, rational creatures will adhere to God voluntarily, after rejecting evil, in endless love striving.[12]

Origen stresses the role of the bonds of love in the ascent to God: if rational creatures reach Christ's true being, incomprehensible and ineffable, they will be "tied by the bonds of Christ's love, will adhere to it and have no longer the force to move again, because they will be one and the same spirit with Christ."[13] This will fulfill Jesus's prayer in John 17 (Merk-Barbaglio; translation mine, as ever): "As you, Father, are in me and I am in you, and we are One, so may also they be one in Us." Origen identified ἀγάπη with perfection in his *Commentary on Canticles*, followed by Gregory in his Homilies.[14] Out

---

7. To the objection that love could not impede Satan's fall, or Adam's, Origen replies exactly that this fall took place *before* the manifestation of Christ's love (Or. *Comm in Rom.* 5.10.227–230 Bammel).

8. Or. *Cant.* prol. 3.16 (Brésard–Crouzel): *Ad mystica atque ad divinitatis contemplationem sincero et spiritali amore conscenditur.*

9. *Salutari in eum amore succendi,* Or. *Cant.* prol. 3.23 Brésard–Crouzel; *salutare ab ipso vulnus accipiet et beato igne amoris eius ardebit,* prol. 2.17. Cf. Or. *Cant.* prol. 2.17 Brésard–Crouzel: *amore caelesti agitur anima … vulnus amoris acceperit.*

10. Or. *Cant.* 3.7.27; the same in Or. *Comm. in Rom.* 5.10 Bammel.

11. Or. *Hom. in Ier.* 5.2: ἡ ἀγάπη κολλᾷ ἡμᾶς τῷ Θεῷ Husson–Nautin.

12. Origen here influenced Gregory's doctrine of *epektasis*, as argued by Ramelli, "Apokatastasis and Epektasis in *In Cant.*," 312–39.

13. Or. *Cant.* 1.4.9, GCS 8.103.

14. *Summa perfectionis in caritate consistit: caritas nihil iniquitatis admittit* (1.6.8); *in caritatis perfectione et omne mandatum restaurari dicitur et legis virtus prophetarumque pendere* (prol. 2.43).

of love, some *logika* descend onto earth to assist the process of salvation and restoration.[15] Restoration and liberation from evil begin the infinite process of tension toward God and beatitude.[16] The ardent love of God is light to the just and purifying fire to sinners.[17]

Nyssen was deeply influenced by Origen in his mystical exegesis of Canticles and in the role of love (both *agape* and *eros*) in the mystical ascent to God. Gregory interpreted SS as describing the soul's mystical union with God, an allegorical expression of the soul's infinite tension (ἐπέκτασις) toward God. Gregory explicitly refers to Origen's allegorical exegesis and calls Origen "laborious,"[18] like Athanasius, who called Origen φιλοπονώτατος.[19] Gregory also knew Plotinus, who also attributed Eros to the Good in *Enneads*. 6.8.15. Gregory sometimes even echoes Origen's *Commentary on Canticles* word for word but orients his own interpretation toward the main themes dear to him.[20] The most important is the soul's tension out of itself (*epektasis*) toward the knowledge of God, in an apophatic theological context.[21] This is a progression without end, as God's nature is infinite and beyond creatural reach: ascent to God takes place through love.

Gregory shared Origen's position that *Canticles* is about love, which he, like Origen, calls both ἀγάπη and ἔρως. In *Homilies on Canticles* 1 GNO VI 15, Gregory declares that in *Canticles* God, "who wants all humans to be saved and reach the knowledge of truth,"[22] reveals "the most perfect way of salvation: through ἀγάπη." The programmatic declaration of God's universally saving will is, for Gregory and Origen, a buttress of apokatastasis.

Canticles has love as its main topic, and love is God, according to John, repeatedly quoted in Nyssen's *Homilies on Canticles*.[23] But for Origen and Gregory, God's essence is ungraspable; it can be known by a mystical union with Christ-Logos, symbolized by a love union.[24] Origen referred to Plato's *Symposium* when stating that Greek philosophers already explored love's nature in "banquets of discourses," rightly concluding that "love's power

15. Or. *Io.* 2.31.187–88 Preuschen; Or. *Princ.* 2.9.7 Behr.

16. Or. *H.Ez.* 1.12 Borret.

17. *Lux … iustis et ignis efficitur peccatoribus, ut consumat in iis omne quod in anima eorum corruptibilitatis et fragilitatis invenerit* (Or. *Comm. in Cant.* 2.2.21 Brésard–Crouzel).

18. φιλόπονος, Greg. Nyss. *H.Cant.* 13.3 Langerbeck.

19. See Ramelli, "Dialogue of Adamantius," 71–98.

20. Placida, "La presenza di Origene nelle omelie sul Cantico di Gregorio di Nissa," 33–49.

21. See Ramelli, "Divine as Inaccessible Object of Knowledge in Ancient Platonism," 167–88.

22. 1 Tim 2:4 (Merk-Barbaglio).

23. Greg. Nyss. GNO VI 214.10; cf. 120.17, 370.12 Langerbeck.

24. See Ramelli, "Harmony between *Arkhē* and *Telos* in Patristic Platonism," 1–49.

is none other than that which leads the soul from earth to heaven's lofty heights and the highest beatitude can be attained solely under the stimulus of love's desire." Although using both terms—as Dionysius was aware—Origen distinguished passionate love (ἔρως) from charity-love (ἀγάπη) and insists that love must be oriented toward God. Scripture generally uses ἀγάπη, and sometimes ἔρως, only when there is no possibility of mistaking it for a passion; with this proviso, ἀγάπη and ἔρως in Scripture are interchangeable.[25]

Similarly, Nyssen expressed the God-soul relation in terms of ἀγάπη, and even ἔρως, already used by Origen in reference to divine love in a Christianization of Plato's ἔρως. With regard to divine love, Gregory defines ἔρως as "intense ἀγάπη,"[26] expressing the soul's love for God: "Wisdom speaks clearly in Proverbs, describing ἔρως of the divine Beauty: This love is irreproachable, a passion without passion oriented toward incorporeal objects"; "ἔρως for God derives from sentiments opposite to those which produce corporeal desire."[27] This is the same distinction as Origen's in the prologue to his *Commentary on Canticles*. Gregory applied the ἔρως terminology to God and the ascent to God, for instance, stating: "the soul, tending towards the inaccessible beauty of the divine nature, necessarily is caught by desiring love (ἐρᾶν) for It … It will transform its desire into impassibility (μετενεγκοῦσαν εἰς ἀπάθειαν τὸ πάθος) and eliminate every material affection, and therefore the soul will burn with passion (ζέειν ἐρωτικῶς), heated only by that fire which the Lord came to bring upon earth."[28]

The connection between love and *apokatastasis* was prominent in Origen and Nyssen and resurfaces in Dionysius. For Origen, love will guarantee the eternity of *apokatastasis* by preventing new falls, since, as seen above, "love never falls [(ἐκ)πίπτει]." Gregory echoes Origen, declaring that "no creature of God will fall out" of God's Kingdom.[29] Sin, as lack of love, caused the initial fall, and love produces the opposite, apokatastasis: "Sin separated rational creatures from one another, but once *the love of God has joined them again*, they will utter again that hymn of praise" (*Inscr.* 1.9). Nyssen emphasizes the link between *eros*-desire and ascent to God also in

<hr>

25. Or. *Cant.* prol. 2.22–23,25,33 Brésard–Crouzel. Rufinus renders ἀγάπη by *caritas vel dilectio* and ἔρως by *cupido seu amor* (Or. *Cant.* prol. 2.20).

26. Ἐπιτεταμένη, Greg. Nyss. *Cant* 13 GNO VI 383.9 Langerbeck.

27. Greg. Nyss. *Cant* 1, GNO VI 23.12, 192.1 Langerbeck.

28. Greg. Nyss. *Cant* 1, GNO 6.27.8–15 Langerbeck.

29. Μηδενὸς ἀποπίπτοντος, Greg. Nyss. *Tunc et ipse* GNO III/2.13–14 Downing.

Inst. 50.1–4: this ascent, provoked by desire, must take place through virtue, which produces one's restoration/*apokatastasis* to God: "the one who desires to become the bride of Christ must be assimilated to the beauty of Christ through virtue according to his ability."

Again within his double-reference scheme, Dionysius built on Origen's and Nyssen's reflections on love and its role in *apokatastasis*, as well as on those by Proclus (and by Plotinus's noble ἔρως in *Enn.* 6.9.9.35). Indeed, Dionysius was heavily influenced by Proclus. István Perczel even suggested that Dionysius's literary and philosophical strategy was to offer a "broken paraphrase" of Proclus's *Platonic Theology*.[30] This was likely a late work by Proclus, not read outside the inner circle of the Athenian Platonic school for a while.[31] Thus Dionysius might have been closely connected to Proclus's school. But it is unnecessary to hypothesize that he was a "pagan."[32]

Dionysius was aware of the use of ἔρως in Proclus. Proclus attributed love to the gods and anticipated Dionysius's link between love and reversion (ἐπιστροφή, the third Neoplatonic movement after μονή and πρόοδος): the superior gods love the inferior providentially, and the inferior the superior revertively (ἐπιστρεπτικῶς, *In Alc.* 55–56). This nexus might come from Origen, who theorized the role of love in apokatastasis and assimilated the latter to reversion.[33] Unlike Proclus, and like Origen, Dionysius, qua *Christian* Platonist, attributes love not only to the inferior gods (gods for Proclus, not for Dionysius) but also to the supreme deity, the One. Proclus contemplated both a providential ἔρως of the superior toward the inferior and an anagogic ἔρως of the inferior toward the superior. He constructed anagogic ἔρως in master-disciple relationships.[34] The master had to reorient desire (ἔρως) from sensible to intelligible beauty and help the disciple to become like god and attain union with the divine (the same last two

30. Perczel, "Pseudo-Dionysius and the Platonic Theology, 498–99; "Dionysius the Areopagite," 214–15.

31. Lankila, "Corpus Areopagiticum as a Crypto-Pagan Project."

32. Mainoldi, *Dietro Dionigi l'Areopagita*, 486–503, identifies the main author of the *Corpus* with an Athenian "pagan" Neoplatonist who converted to Christianity; hence his excellent knowledge of the doctrines of Proclus and Damascius and his use of "theurgy" for Christian liturgy. He might be Hegias, the son of Theagenes, who was covertly accused by Damascius of conversion to Christianity (510). I agree (499) that the critiques of Theagenes of having preferred νέα ἀξιώματα, having fallen into "the life of the multitude," and having "detached himself from the Hellenes" allude to a conversion to Christianity (Suda, s.v. *Theagenes*). The same accusation of detaching himself from philosophy was levelled against Hegias (Suda, s.v. *Hegias*).

33. I cannot investigate here Origen's impact on Proclus. Hints in Ramelli, "Proclus and Christian Neoplatonism," 37–70; idem, "Origen to Evagrius," 271–91.

34. On which see Markus, "Anagogic Love between Neoplatonic Philosophers," 1–39.

stages posited by Origen: likeness to God and unity). Anagogic ἔρως was therefore a form of pedagogy. For Origen it was a divine pedagogy, as is clear from his *Commentary on Canticles*. The *First Alcibiades*, according to Proclus, is concerned with the proper orientation of ἔρως, which leads the perfectly loving souls (ἐρωτικαὶ ψυχαί) to union with the real beauty and the avoidance of misguided ἔρως. Socrates's love is providential, related to the Form of the Good, and it is elevating/anagogic (ἀναγωγός, *In Alc.* 45.5). In Proclus's *Commentary on the First Alcibiades*, anagogic ἔρως is, as mentioned, "the cause of reversion (ἐπιστροφή) to the divine beauty, which … elevates (ἀνάγουσα) all things that come second." Reversion is connected with apokatastasis in Proclus and Dionysius, as shall be indicated, and both relate it to anagogic love.

The notion of love of both Proclus, on the one side, and Origen and Nyssen in their exegesis of *Canticles* on the other influenced Dionysius's concept of love. As Paul was the model of ecstasy and *epektasis* for Gregory, so too is he for Dionysius. And he is so precisely through love. Dionysius calls Paul "the great lover" who suffers ecstasy for God (2 Cor 5:13) and withdraws to make room for Christ (Gal 2:20; *DN* 4.13). Origen also inspired Dionysius with the notion of the perfect who can state, "I no longer live, but Christ lives in me" (Gal 2:20), in *C.Io.* 4.23, in his ideal of the perfect who "becomes Christ" and be Mary's child.[35]

Saying "theologians," Dionysius may mean Origen's tradition[36] and at the same time Proclus, with his typical double system of "pagan" and Christian references. Dionysius's revered teacher Hierotheus, whose teaching Dionysius declares to explicate in his own corpus,[37] might point to Origen.[38] In *DN* 2.11, Paul is described as a "common guide" of Dionysius and his "instructor" Hierotheus; Hierotheus is Dionysius's inspirer after "the divine Paul" (*DN* 3.2). As Paul inspired Origen's doctrine of *apokatastasis*, that of love, Christology, and much else, this backs the suspicion that "Hierotheus" may point to Origen. His name features in the title of Stephen Bar Sudhaili's pantheistic *Book of the Holy Hierotheus*, and Dionysius represents him as his own teacher, a contemporary of the Apostles—like "Dionysius"—superior to all other Christian sages after the Apostles (*DN* 3.2,

---

35. Jn 19:26 Merk-Barbaglio.

36. Argument in Ramelli, "Origen, Evagrios, and Dionysios."

37. Dion. Ar. *DN* 3.2–3 Suchla. So did Clement with Pantaenus, and Plotinus with Ammonius.

38. Suggested in Ramelli, *Christian Doctrine of Apokatastasis*, 694–700; further hints here and below.

like Origen in Didymus's and Jerome's definition), a sublime mystical theologian (παθὼν τὰ θεῖα) whose writings are a "second Scripture." This would fit Origen's mystical exegesis, especially the *Commentary on Canticles* and *On First Principles*, which was commented on by Didymus like a "second Scripture" (all previous Christian commentaries were on Scripture).

Dionysius quotes two passages from Hierotheus's *Elements of Theology* (Θεολογικαὶ στοιχειώσεις, a pendant to Dionysius's *Outlines of Theology*, Θεολογικαὶ ὑποτυπώσεις) and *Hymns on Love* (*DN* 2.9–10, 4.15–17). These Ἐρωτικοὶ ὕμνοι may refer to Origen's *Commentary on Canticles*, known to Dionysius (who, as will be pointed out, seems to allude to it), and the Θεολογικαὶ στοιχειώσεις to Origen's *First Principles*, or the whole of his theological work. At the same time, within Dionysius's double-reference scheme, the Θεολογικαὶ στοιχειώσεις and *Hymns on Love* may point to Proclus's Στοιχείωσις θεολογική and *Hymns*, seven of which are preserved (which celebrate inferior, encosmic, and hypercosmic deities, not the One, who befits silence).[39]

The first extract treats Christ-Logos, who keeps the harmony of parts and whole, transcending the parts and the whole (*DN* 2.9–10): this concept resembles Origen's Logos theology.[40] The second extract presents the gradation of love, whose forms and powers are reduced to unity (*DN* 4.15–17): love is a unifying power that moves all,[41] from the Good (God) to the last being and from this to the Good. This, as will be pointed out, may refer to Origen's *Commentary on Canticles*.

Besides love, another doctrine that shows Dionysius's double-reference scheme is that of apokatastasis,[42] related to reversion (ἐπιστροφή). This connects him to (1) Origen and Gregory (like the concept of *anastasis* as *apokatastasis*,[43] typical of Nyssen and rooted in Origen,[44] and (2) to Proclus and Damascius.[45] Dionysius explicitly assimilates ἐπιστροφή, the Neoplatonic movement after μονή and πρόοδος, with ἀποκατάστασις, in at least four passages,[46] even to the point of using, for ἐπιστροφή, the terminolo-

<hr>

39. Van der Berg, *Proclus' Hymns.*

40. Examined in Ramelli, "Logos/Nous One-Many between 'Pagan' and Christian Platonism."

41. Sassi, "Mystical Union as Acknowledgment," 771–84.

42. See Ramelli, *Christian Doctrine of Apokatastasis*, 694–721.

43. In *TM* 7.9 p. 130 H.-R.

44. See Ramelli, "Christian Soteriology and Christian Platonism," 313–56.

45. See my "Question of Origen's Conversion." Further work will be conducted on the notions of *apokatastasis* and reversion in ancient philosophy, down to late Neoplatonism, and their relation to Christian philosophy.

46. Dion. Ar. *EH* 82.17, 83.7 Ritter Heil; Dion. Ar. *DN* 4.14, 160.15, 202.14 Suchla

gy of *apokatastasis. Apokatastasis* is the return to the proper and familiar Monad (οἰκείαν μονάδα) and unification (Dion. Ar. *EH* 82.17, 83.7 Ritter Heil): Dionysius's application of the lexicon of *oikeiōsis* to the notion of apokatastasis is inherited from Origen and Nyssen.[47] Dionysius observes:

In an inspired way one can see the priest, who holds the holy power, go from the divine altar to the most extreme parts of the temple (μέχρι τῶν ἐσχάτων τοῦ ἱεροῦ) with the perfume (of incense), and then return back [literally, "be restored"] to the same altar, having fulfilled all to perfection (πάλιν ἐπ᾽ αὐτῷ τελειωτικῶς ἀποκαθιστάμενον). Indeed, also God's sovereign beatitude (θεαρχικὴ μακαριότης), which transcends all, even if, out of its divine goodness, it proceeds (πρόεισιν) to the communion of those holy creatures who participate in it (τῶν μετεχόντων αὐτῆς), nevertheless does not exit the immobile rest and stability that characterize its own nature (τῆς κατ᾽ οὐσίαν ἀκινήτου στάσεως καὶ ἱδρύσεως), and yet it shines forth in the very same way to all ... In the same way, the divine mystery of the office, although it has a single, simple, and unified principle (ἐνιαίαν καὶ ἁπλῆν ἔχουσα καὶ συνεπτυγμένην ἀρχήν), multiplies itself into a sacred variety of symbols out of love for the human beings, and extends down to all the holy iconography, but from all this in turn *it gathers itself back into its own monad* in a unified way, and *unifies those who are led back up to itself* in a holy manner (αὖθις εἰς τὴν οἰκείαν μονάδα συνάγεται καὶ ἑνοποιεῖ τοὺς ἐπ᾽ αὐτὴν ἱερῶς ἀναγομένους) ... The priest is restored to his original principle (εἰς τὴν οἰκείαν ἀρχὴν ἀμειώτως ἀποκαθίσταται) without suffering any diminution, qua free and independent of his inferiors. And, having made his intellectual entrance into the One, he sees in a pure way the unitary *logoi* of the ceremonies celebrated, making *the goal and perfecting of the procession* (νοερὰν εἴσοδον) toward the second realities, dictated by love for human beings, *the divine return to the first realities* (τὴν εἰς τὰ πρῶτα θειοτέραν ἐπιστροφὴν ποιούμενος).

Here we can clearly see the Neoplatonic terminology of reversion (ἐπιστροφήν), as opposed to procession (εἴσοδον), assimilated to that of apokatastasis (εἰς τὴν οἰκείαν ἀρχὴν ... ἀποκαθίσταται), for the same movement, which is applied to that of the Christian priest.

　　Dionysius's third and fourth passages on apokatastasis (Dion. Ar. *DN* 4.14, 160.15, and 202.14 Suchla) also identify the Neoplatonic metaphysical movement of ἐπιστροφή (εἰς τἀγαθὸν ἐπιστρεφομένην), after that of πρόοδος (ἀγαθὴν πρόοδον), with *apokatastasis*. In 202.14, there is a lexical substitution: God's power is said to proceed down to all beings, preserve them by leading them to their own good, preserve angels uncontaminated, order the *apokatastasis* of heavenly bodies, and offer deification as a gift, providing

---

47. See Ramelli, "Stoic Doctrine of Oikeiosis," 116–40.

the relevant capacity to those who will be deified (ἐκθεούμενοι).[48] Here Dionysius uses "procession" (πρόοδος) and then *apokatastasis* instead of "reversion" (ἐπιστροφή). The fusion of the two terminologies was already operated by Origen,[49] and the union between *apokatastasis* and deification, evident in Dionysius's passage, is Origenian.

Apokatastasis terminology replaces that of ἐπιστροφή also in Dion. Ar. *DN* 4.14 (160.15) Suchla: God's love (Platonically ἔρως) forms a circle that proceeds from the Good—God is "Beauty and Good itself" (as in Nyssen, as mentioned)—and returns to the Good; it "always proceeds, remains, and returns (ἀποκαθιστάμενος) to the same Good." First, Dionysius mentions *epistrophē* (ἐπιστρεφομένην) after *proodos*; then, instead of mentioning *monē*, *proodos*, and *epistrophē*, Dionysius speaks of *proodos*, *monē*, and *apokatastasis*, manifestly replacing reversion with *apokatastasis*. Dionysius ascribes this doctrine to Hierotheus, likely meaning, in his double-reference scheme, Origen and Proclus (who both used both terminologies and spoke of divine love).

The only one who is Beauty and Good itself (καλὸν καὶ ἀγαθόν) is the manifestation, so to say, of itself through itself, the good procession (πρόοδον) of the transcendent unity, and simple movement of love, self-moving, self-operating, proceeding in the Good and gushing out from the Good to the beings and returning again to the Good (ἐπιστρεφομένην). In this the divine love (ὁ θεῖος ἔρως) shows exceptionally clearly its own lack of an end and a beginning, like a kind of infinite[50] and absolutely eternal circle (ἀίδιος κύκλος) for the Good, from the Good, in the Good, and toward the Good, proceeding around in an introversive, non-wandering spiral, *always proceeding, remaining, and returning* (προϊὼν ἀεὶ καὶ μένων καὶ ἀποκαθιστάμενος) in the same movement and way. These truths were also explained, in his divinely inspired exegesis (ἐνθέως ὑφηγήσατο), by my illustrious and holy initiator throughout the / according to the *Hymns on Love* (κατὰ τοὺς ἐρωτικοὺς ὕμνους). It will be particularly appropriate to quote from these *Hymns* and thus provide my own discourse on love with a sacred introduction, as it were: "Love (τὸν ἔρωτα), be it divine, angelic, intellectual, psychic, or physical, should be understood as a unitive and commingling force that gathers together (ἑνωτικήν τινα καὶ συγκρατικὴν δύναμιν) and induces the superior to provide for the inferior, the peer to be in communion with the peer, and the inferior *to revert* to the superior."[51]

---

48. Πρόεισι δὲ τὰ τῆς ἀνεκλείπτου δυνάμεως καὶ εἰς ἀνθρώπους … συνάγει δὲ ταῖς ἀποκαταστάσεσι … καὶ τὴν τοῦ παντὸς ἀδιάλυτον μονὴν ἀσφαλίζεται καὶ τὴν θέωσιν αὐτὴν δωρεῖται δύναμιν εἰς τοῦτο τοῖς ἐκθεουμένοις παρέχουσα (Dion. Ar. *DN* 202.14 Suchla).

49. See Ramelli, "Question of Origen's Conversion."

50. Note again the influence of Nyssen about God as infinite.

51. Dion. Ar. *DN* 4.14.712C–713AB (p. 160.15) Suchla.

The lexicon of *apokatastasis* is employed for ἐπιστροφή and is related to love: God's *eros* forms a circle that proceeds from the Good and returns to the Good. The use of *apokatastasis* terminology in place of reversion terminology can be read against the backdrop of Dionysius's double-reference scheme. In his day, both terminologies were used on the "pagan" and the Christian side.[52]

The inspired exegete who expounded this doctrine is both Proclus, the author of *Hymns*, who used the similar expression "circle without beginning or end,"[53] and Origen in his *Commentary on Canticles*. Dionysius is paraphrasing the initial sections of Origen's commentary (he paraphrases Origen also elsewhere),[54] and "divinely inspired exegesis" suits well Origen's *Commentary on Canticles*. The reference to Origen is supported by the connection between love, unity, and reversion/restoration. So, the ἐρωτικοὶ ὕμνοι may refer to Origen's *Commentary on Canticles*, where Origen used ἔρως, besides ἀγάπη, to refer to God's love, and, like Hierotheus, conceived it as a unifying force.[55] In prol. 2.16, he remarks that besides *carnalis amor/cupido* one should admit of *spiritalis amor* (ἔρως), relevant to the inner human. Dionysius likely meant Origen and Nyssen when observing that "the theologians regarded ἔρως and ἀγάπη as having the same meaning" and thus treated ἀγάπη and ἔρως as synonyms, as Origen and Nyssen did. But this ἔρως, appropriate to God, must be distinguished from the divided, physical, and partial ἔρως, which is not true ἔρως but its empty image (Dion. Ar. *DN* 4.12.709BC Suchla). Origen put forward the same distinction.

That Dionysius points to Origen and Nyssen is evident when in 4.12.709B he remarks that some Christian theological authors deemed the title Eros more divine than Agape. Now, Gregory exactly argued that ἔρως is a more intense form of ἀγάπη.[56] The mystical application of ἔρως to God and apokatastasis can be ascribed to Origen as "Hierotheus" (with his followers Nyssen and Methodius[57]).

Moreover, Dionysius cites Ignatius's words, "my love has been crucified,"[58] to explain his application of ἔρως to divine love, thus doing what

---

52. A specific work, *Caelo volente*, will be devoted to this.

53. Procl. ET 146 Dodds = Dion. Ar. *DN* 4.14.712D Suchla: the divine love has neither beginning nor end (ἀτελεύτητον καὶ ἄναρχον), like "an eternal (ἀίδιον) circle."

54. Collected in Ramelli, "Origen, Evagrios, and Dionysios."

55. Ramelli, "Love," 611–26.

56. Greg. Nyss. *H.Cant.* 13, GNO VI 383.9 Langerbeck.

57. See Ramelli, "Love."

58. ὁ ἔρως μου ἐσταύρωται, Dion. Ar. *DN* 4.12 Suchla.

Origen did in his *Commentary on Canticles*: "It is no fault if one calls God Eros, as John called God Agape. For I remember that a saint, named Ignatius, said about Christ: My Eros was crucified."[59] Origen used Platonic ἔρως, besides ἀγάπη, to refer to God's love and in the *Commentary* did conceive it as a unifying force, as Hierotheus did according to Dionysius.

Therefore Dionysius ascribes ἔρως to God in *DN* 4.10: "the cause of all beings, by excess of goodness, *loves* (ἐρᾷ) all beings, creates, perfects, sustains, and *reverts* all beings" (*DN* 4.10.708AB). Dionysius relates again love-desire to reversion. His notion of the "ecstatic" excess of God's love as the cause of all beings[60] and their "ecstatic" return comes—once more with double reference—from Proclus's idea of "excess" (περιουσία) as the cause of all beings (*ET* 27), and probably Nyssen's idea of *epektasis*: going out of oneself toward God.

Origen's mystical exegesis of Canticles influenced also Dionysius's *Theologia mystica*. In 3.103BC, Dionysius links the darkness with "the absence of words and thought" (ἀλογία, ἀνοησία) and silence, on which Nyssen already insisted for his apophatic theology.[61] For "the one who is above all being also transcends all knowledge" (*DN* 1.4.593A), so the union with God can only be "above intellect" (*DN* 7.3.872B) and implies the "cessation of intellectual activities" (*DN* 2.4.592D), but God even transcends ineffability and unknowing, being ὑπεράρρητος, ὑπεράγνωστος (*DN* 1.4.592B). Now, with his double-reference strategy, in at least four passages, Dionysius inserted a quotation from Plotinus (ἄφελε πάντα for the union with the One), who inspired Nyssen too in this respect.[62] Dionysius, like Origen and Nyssen, thought that God's essence is inaccessible, but God's operations, names—explored in a specific work[63]—and powers, reflected in God's names, are accessible.

Dionysius, as seen, quotes two excerpts from Hierotheus, *Elements of Theology* and *Hymns on Love*, which perhaps allude to Origen and Proclus, in the usual double-reference scheme. This scheme is evident in Diony-

---

59. *Nec puto quod culpari possit si quis Deum, sicut Iohannes caritatem* (ἀγάπη), *ita ipse amorem* (ἔρως) *nominet. Denique memini aliquem sanctorum dixisse, Ignatium nomine, de Christo: Meus autem amor* (ἔρως) *crucifixus est* (Or. *Cant.* prol. 2.36 Brésard–Crouzel).

60. Dion. Ar. *DN* 4.13.712AB Suchla: "going out of himself," "excess of erotic goodness," etc.

61. Ramelli, "Silenzio apofatico in Gregorio di Nissa," 367–88.

62. Plot. 5.3.[49.]17.39; cf. 6.7.36, 6.8.21 Henry–Schwyzer; Ramelli, "Mysticism and Mystic Apophaticism." The verbal form appears in Dion. Ar. *Myst.* 1.1.1001A, Ritter Heil (πάντα ἀφελών; 2.1.1025B, τὰ πάντα ἀφαιροῦμεν; the nominal form appears in Dion. Ar. *DN* 2.4.641A Suchla, ἡ πάντων ἀφαίρεσις; 1.5.593C, τῆς πάντων τῶν ὄντων ἀφαιρέσεως.

63. *De divinis nominibus*; see the edition with commentary, *Les Noms divins* De Andia.

sius's reflections on love and on *apokatastasis*. Many hints, in his preserved and lost works, suggest that Dionysius supported *apokatastasis*,[64] following authors he knew, such as Origen, Nyssen, Evagrius, and Proclus, from whom he also inherited the μονή-πρόοδος-ἐπιστροφή movement.[65] As I pointed out, Dionysius directly used the terminology of apokatastasis for ἐπιστροφή: he followed here, too, the double-reference scheme. Moreover, he supported apokatastasis both continually (as in Proclus) and in the *telos* (as in Origen, who, however, also had the notion of the present apokatastasis of the soul).[66] Apokatastasis for Dionysius—just as for Eriugena, who read Dionysius with the scholia of John of Scythopolis and Maximus the Confessor,[67] but also for Proclus[68]—is related to the culmination of ἐπιστροφή.

Dionysius explains: "The Cause of All is 'all in all,' according to the saying (κατὰ τὸ λόγιον), and certainly it must be praised in that it is the Giver of existence to all, the Originator of all beings, *who brings all to perfection* (τελειωτική), holding them together and protecting them; their seat, which has *them all revert to itself* (πρὸς ἑαυτὴν ἐπιστρεπτική), and this in a unified, *irresistible* and *absolute* (ἀσχέτως), and transcendent way" (*DN* 1.7.596c–597a). Τὸ λόγιον, "sacred utterance," also meant "oracular response/utterance"; by the fifth century, τὰ λόγια referred to the *Chaldaean Oracles*.[69] Dionysius, here and elsewhere, by using τὰ λόγια, was therefore opposing Christian Scripture and Christian Platonism (primarily Origen) to the *Chaldaean Oracles* and their use in "pagan" Platonism. Here, in Dionysius's usual double-reference scheme, the "saying" at stake is both biblical-Origenian and Procline: "all in all"—cited in both *DN* 1.7.596C and 9.4.912D—is (1) the tenet of 1 Corinthians 15:28, God as eschatologically "all in all" (πάντα ἐν πᾶσι), one of the main pillars of Origen's and Nyssen's doctrine of *apokatastasis* (so it is biblical and is a tenet of Christian Platonism), and (2) the principle supported by Proclus, "all in all but appropriately" (πάντα ἐν πᾶσι ἀλλ᾽ οἰκείως), an expression of later "pagan" Neoplatonism.[70]

64. These may be lost, invented, or preserved under a different name/author. The first two possibilities are held as equally probable by Perl, "Ps. Dionysius the Areopagite," 767.

65. On the centrality of this scheme especially in *De divinis nominibus*, see Schäfer, *Philosophy of Dionysius the Areopagite*.

66. See Ramelli, "Proclus of Constantinople and Apokatastasis."

67. See Ramelli, *Christian Doctrine of Apokatastasis*, the section on Eriugena.

68. As I have argued in "Proclus of Constantinople and Apokatastasis," 95–122; "Proclus and Christian Neoplatonism," 37–70.

69. Addey, *Divination and Theurgy in Neoplatonism*, 7.

70. See Ramelli, "Proclus of Constantinople and Apokatastasis." On "all in all" in "pagan"

That all beings are brought to perfection by God, will all return to God, and God's goodness and providence are the cause of all, is consistent with the theory of *apokatastasis*. Dionysius also mentions an eschatological παλιγγενεσία (*EH* 7.1.1.3; 7.3.1), originally a Stoic term, which Christian sources also connected with apokatastasis.[71]

Both the application of ἔρως to God and *apokatastasis*, as seen, obey the double-reference scheme. The *joining* of love and *apokatastasis* (in Dion. Ar. *DN* 4.14.712C–713AB Suchla) comes from Origen, who posited *apokatastasis* as guaranteed by love, as I pointed out.[72] In *DN* 4.10.708AB, Dionysius links again love and *apokatastasis*. He describes God, Beauty–Good, as ἐραστόν and ἀγαπητόν—according to the double-reference scheme—and declares that "the Cause of all beings loves all beings in the superabundance of its goodness," because of which God creates all, perfects all, keeps all together, and restores all. "Divine love (θεῖος ἔρως) is Good seeking Good for the sake of Good." Therefore the "endless circle" of ἔρως (*DN* 4.14–15.712D–713AB, examined above) moves "through the Good, from the Good, in the Good, and to the Good" in a movement of *monē–proodos–epistrophē* that becomes *monē–proodos–apokatastasis*, through the substitution of *epistrophē* with *apokatastasis* that I have pointed out: "always proceeding, remaining, and *being restored* [instead of *reverting*] to itself." Dionysius introduces here Hierotheus's definition of love-Eros, as seen: that Hierotheus conceals Origen is suggested, among else, by the reference to Ignatius, the paraphrases of Origen's *Commentary*, and the connection between love, unity, and *apokatastasis/epistrophē*.

The return to God is manifest in Dionysius's postulate that the aim of all hierarchy is ἀγάπη toward God (*EH* 1.3.376A). Dionysius uses many terms related to hierarchy.[73] I suspect that his neologism "Thearchy" (θεαρχία), the divine unity of the three Hypostases of the Trinity who are the three ἀρχαί or Principles of all, derives from Origen's *First Principles* (Περὶ ἀρχῶν), where the ἀρχαί are the three Hypostases of the Trinity. Origen likely influenced Porphyry's choice of entitling a treatise of Plotinus

---

and Christian Platonism, see my "Father in the Son." The potential reciprocal influences will be the object of a specific study; it is not possible to investigate them here.

71. See Ramelli, *Christian Doctrine of Apokatastasis*, introduction. Work on the ancient philosophical concepts of apokatastasis is needed and underway.

72. As I argued in Ramelli, "Apokatastasis and Epektasis in *In Cant.*"; further arguments in my "Mystical Theology in Evagrius."

73. Κυριαρχία, ἱεραρχία (Dion. Ar. *CH* 8.1.240B Ritter Heil), ἐναρχία (Dion. Ar. *DN* 2.4.641A, etc. Suchla), οὐσιαρχία (Dion. Ar. *DN* 5.1.816B, etc. Suchla), ἐξουσιαρχία, ἀγαθαρχία (Dion. Ar. *DN* 1.5.593C, 3.1.680B, etc. Suchla), and θεαρχία.

The Three Principal Hypostases (περὶ τῶν τριῶν ἀρχικῶν ὑποστάσεων):[74] "the three Hypostases that are the ἀρχαί." From God are "the ἀρχαί of beings," "every being owes its ἀρχή to God" (*DN* 5.6, 4.28): these ἀρχαί are such by virtue of their participation in God (*DN* 5.5; cf. 4.4). God is repeatedly called θεαρχικὴ ἀγαθότης in *MT* 7.4.125H–R[75]: this combines ἀγαθαρχία, "the principle that is Good," and θεαρχία, "the Principle that is God." In Dionysius the Trinity is θεαρχία and θεαρχικὴ ἀγαθότης, expressions probably inspired by Origen's God as three ἀρχαί or "Trinity of ἀρχαί" (ἀρχικὴ τριάς), and God as supreme ἀγαθότης.[76] Περὶ ἀρχῶν, which referred primarily to God in Origen and had a long philosophical history,[77] was also the title of Damascius's treatise. Dionysius's "Principle above the Principle" (ὑπεράρχιος ἀρχή, *DN* 1.3.589C, *CH* 1.2.121B, etc.) may further refer to Damascius's idea of a principle before the principle. If so, we would see again a double reference.

Dionysius's definition of God, "Monad and Henad" (μονὰς καὶ ἑνάς, *DN* 1.4), derives from both Origen (*Princ.* 1.1.6) and Proclus, with the double-allusion strategy once more. Though the reference is more to Origen: only rarely does Proclus place Monad and Henad on the same plane, and never in reference to the First Principle, while Origen in *Princ.* 1.1.6 defines God as μονάς and ἑνάς—preserved in Greek by Rufinus—and called Henad the union of Father and Son (*Dial. Her.* 4.4). Dionysius's Origenian passage on God–Monad–Henad (*DN* 1.4)[78] develops the doctrine of apokatastasis as restoration to unity and to God's image and likeness, as Origen and Nyssen understood it: "The whole *hymnology of the theologians* prepares the divine names in a revelatory and hymnic way according to the beneficent procession of the principle of the divinity. For this reason, practically in the whole *theological doctrine* we see the principle of the divinity celebrated as *Monad and Henad* (μονὰς καὶ ἑνάς), because of the simplicity and unity of its supernatural indivisibility, by which *we are unified as by a unifying power*, and by a super-cosmic act of *reunion of our divisible alterities, we are assembled in a monad that is an image of God* (θεοειδής) *and in a*

74. Argument in Ramelli "Origen, Greek Philosophy, and the Birth of the Trinitarian Meaning of Hypostasis," 302–50.

75. Ritter and Heil, *Corpus Dionysiacum II*. Commentary: *Les Noms divins* De Andia.

76. Ramelli, "Origen, Greek Philosophy, and the Birth of the Trinitarian Meaning of Hypostasis."

77. Analyzed in Ramelli, "Origen, Patristic Philosophy, and Christian Platonism."

78. In the *Outlines of Theodicy*, Dionysius maintained that the names of God must be ascribed to the three Persons of the Trinity indivisibly, since the Trinity is a "Superunited Henad" (ἡ ὑπερηνωμένη ἑνάς, *DN* p. 122.11 Suchla).

union that is in the likeness of God (θεομίμητος)." Dionysius here telescopes Origen's stages of image—likeness—unity.[79] The biblical concepts of εἰκών ("image") and ὁμοίωσις ("likeness") are expressed by "pagan" synonyms (θεοειδής, θεομίμητος), with Dionysius's usual move of double reference.

Dionysius here, as often, speaks in the *present* tense, not in the *future*, of God's activities of reunion, unification, and making creatures a monad as image and likeness of God. This is because God is beyond time: God is "the eternity of things that are, the time of things that come to be," and even God "transcends both time and eternity and all things in time and eternity" (*DN* 5.4.817C, 5.10.825B). God, being eternal, needs the use of the present or imperfect tense, as in the Johannine Prologue. This does not mean that Dionysius rejected apokatastasis. Dionysius stresses that God is the Eternal, from which all times and aeons derive—as Origen taught.[80]

Dionysius calls "the theological doctrine" Origen's tradition; his reference to the "hymnology of the theologians" seems to point again to the *Hymns on Love*, meaning Proclus with his hymns, as mentioned, but also Origen's *Commentary on Canticles* (*DN* 1.4). Origen indeed introduced the equivalence between "hymns" and "theology."[81]

Again with the double-reference scheme, "divine names" here in 1.4 may refer both to Porphyry's work *On divine names* (Περὶ θείων ὀνομάτων)[82] and to Origen's systematic study of Christ's *epinoiai* in his *Commentary on John*. What in Origen were mainly the *epinoiai* of Christ are in Nyssen the *epinoiai* of the Trinity, although in *De perfectione*, Nyssen analyzes the *epinoiai* of Christ. Dionysius declares to have drawn his divine names from Scripture (*DN* 1.8.597B): this is what Origen and Nyssen did. Dionysius seems to follow the latter in identifying not only the Father, but also all the three Persons of the Trinity, with the Platonic One or Good. Therefore not only the Father but also the Son is beyond Being (ὑπερούσιος, *MT* 1.1).

In *Princ.* 2.1.1 Origen calls *unitas–ἑνάς* the original unity of creation, a conception furthered by Evagrius. Likewise, in our Dionysian passage, the unity of the Henad is applied to the original unity that is restored in *apokatastasis*, according to the assimilation of ἀρχή and τέλος—supported not only by Origen but also by Plotinus—which is reflected in the circle of

79. See Ramelli, "Harmony between *Arkhē* and *Telos* in Patristic Platonism," 1–49 (emphasis added).

80. Ramelli and Konstan, *Terms for Eternity*, sections on Origen and Dionysius. See further my "Time and Eternity."

81. θεολογεῖν ἐν ὕμνοις πνευματικοῖς. (Or. *Fr. Eph.* 3.69 Gregg).

82. This reference is rightly caught by Mainoldi, *Dietro Dionigi l'Areopagita* , 424.

μονή-πρόοδος-ἐπιστροφή. In 1.4, God's unifying power will restore humans to unity and to the image and likeness of God, as they were initially created (Gn 1:26).

Dionysius avers that, based on many biblical quotations, he had written about the universal peace and restoration foreseen from eternity: these will occur when, through Christ, God will be "all in all." Dionysius had treated this in his lost *Outlines of Theology* (Θεολογικαὶ ὑποτυπώσεις): "What could be said of Christ's love for humanity, which gives peace in profusion (εἰρηνοχύτου φιλανθρωπίας)? Jesus, who operates *all in all* (τὰ πάντα ἐν πᾶσι ἐνεργοῦντος) and realizes an *unspeakable peace* (ποιοῦντος εἰρήνην ἄρρητον) established *from eternity* (ἐξ αἰῶνος προωρισμένην), and *reconciles us to him* (ἀποκαταλλάσσοντος ἡμᾶς ἑαυτῷ) in spirit, and, *through himself and in himself, to the Father* (δι' ἑαυτοῦ καὶ ἐν ἑαυτῷ τῷ πατρί). Of these wonderful gifts I have abundantly and sufficiently spoken (ἱκανῶς εἴρηται) in the *Theological Outlines*, where to our testimony is joined that of the holy inspiration of Scriptures / the sages / the oracles (λογίων)." "All in all," as seen, is a double-tradition concept, biblical-Origenian and Procline. The link with peace and reconciliation, which Origen attached to apokatastasis, and the reference to both Proclus and 1 Corinthians 15:28 (Origen's, Gregory of Nyssa's, and Evagrius's favorite passage in support of apokatastasis) suggest that Dionysius in his lost work treated the theory of apokatastasis in terms close to those of Origen and of Nyssen's *In Illud: Tunc et Ipse Filius*.[83] Like Origen and Nyssen, Dionysius buttressed *apokatastasis* through Scripture. Λογίων may derive from λόγια, meaning "Scriptures," but also "oracles," or from λόγιοι, sages, that is, earlier theologians (Origen, Nyssen, Evagrius). This ambiguous term, too, points to a double-reference scheme.

The state foreseen in 1 Corinthians 15:28, God's being "all in all," in *DN* 9.5 is related both to "the providence of God" and to "the salvation of all beings": "in his providence, God is close to every being," assisting each of them, "and [thus] becomes 'all in all.'" This takes place διὰ τὴν πάντων σωτηρίαν, which is both the *preservation* of all beings now (a Platonic, Procline notion) and their eventual *salvation* (a Christian, Origenian notion). Again a double reference. Dionysius echoes 1 Corinthians 15:28 in two more passages, *DN* 7.3 and 1.7. This is a *Pauline* verse but can also have, as seen, Proclean overtones, in Dionysius's double-tradition scheme. Paul

---

83. Argument in Ramelli, "*In Illud: Tunc et Ipse Filius*," 259–74; idem, "Gregory of Nyssa's Trinitarian Theology in *In Illud*," 445–78.

was Origen's great inspirer in major respects. We have seen that Dionysius presents Paul as the common teacher of both himself and Hierotheus, his master, who is likely to conceal a reference to Origen.

In the excursus on evil in *DN* 4.18.35, in a section that, unlike most of the rest, is not a paraphrase of Proclus's *De malorum subsistentia*, Dionysius in §21 insists on two elements that probably derive from Origen, thus displaying again a double reference to both Origen and Proclus:

1. Protological monism in the statement "the principle cannot be any duality" and must be simple (ἁπλῆ).

2. Evil is a consequence of free choice—the very tenet of Origen's theology of freedom, grounded in theodicy and followed by Nyssen.[84] The principle that evil is without cause (ἀναίτιον, *DN* 4.30.732A, 4.32.732D), so as to remove God from any responsibility for evil, seems to me to take over Plato's famous definition of God as ἀναίτιος (meaning "not responsible for evil") in the myth of Er. Origen and Nyssen often repeated this tenet as the foundation of theodicy.

Dionysius reports that in his *Outlines of Theology* he had discussed the main points of cataphatic theology, such as God's unity and trinity, the three Persons of the Trinity, the generation of the Son, and his assumption of human nature, always basing himself on Scripture.[85] This is what Origen did in *First Principles* (Περὶ ἀρχῶν). Soon after, Dionysius claims that in *Symbolic Theology* he allegorized biblical anthropomorphisms attributed to God. Now, Origen explained biblical references to God's anger, threats, and the like, in the selfsame way, thereby reconciling anthropomorphisms with his doctrine of *apokatastasis*.

Dionysius then explains the reasons why the *Outlines of Theology* were more concise (βραχυλογώτερα) than the *Symbolic Theology*: because they

84. On Gregory's indebtedness to Origen's theology of freedom, see Ramelli, *Social Justice and the Legitimacy of Slavery*, chaps. 5–6. Origen's freedom theology is also stressed by Lekkas, *Liberté et progrès chez Origène*; Hengstermann, *Origenes und der Ursprung der Freiheitsmetaphysik*; Fürst, *Origenes*.

85. *TM* 3.1 (p. 146.1–9): "In the *Theological Outlines* I sang the main points of cataphatic theology, how the divine and good nature is called one, forming a unity (ἑνική), and how it is called triune (τριαδική); what is paternity in it and what sonship; what theological discourse concerning the Spirit means; how from the immaterial Good, deprived of parts, lights sprang off, from the heart of Goodness, and how these have remained inseparable from the eternal *manentia*, coeternal with the bud, *manentia* of the Father in himself, *manentia* of the Father in himself *and* the Son in himself, and of the Father and the Son reciprocally; how superessential Jesus has substantiated himself with the truth of the human nature, and all the rest that is sung in the *Theological Outlines*, revealed by Scriptures/the sages (λογίων)."

proceeded from on high, from the beginning (ἄνω), from God qua first Principle, down to creatures and their existence in time, until "the last things," τὰ ἔσχατα (which has the usual double meaning, in reference to eschatology but also in reference to the last beings, the farthest removed from God: but the former is more probable given the previous reference to beings' existence in time).[86] Therefore the *Outlines of Theology* began with God as first ἀρχή, as in Origen's Περὶ Ἀρχῶν, and likely arrived, as there, to the eventual *apokatastasis*. Even in case this work never existed, it would be significant that Dionysius indicates its structure as similar to that of Origen's masterpiece (and perhaps to Proclus's *Elements of Theology*, while the *Symbolic Theology* might allude to Proclus's *Platonic Theology*).

What Is the Meaning of the Double-Reference Scheme?

István Perczel thinks that the Dionysian corpus stems from an Origenistic milieu, which prudentially adopted pseudonymity.[87] But it soon became prominent among "orthodox" Christian writings. Its author, in my view not a radical Origenist but an Origenian, chose to ascribe his ideas to Dionysius the Areopagite, so as to present the Origenian thought as the true Christian philosophy. The corpus was soon translated into Syriac by Sergius of Resh'aina, who also wrote a substantial introduction to his translation. Sergius's translation, according to Perczel, is closer to the original Greek than the Greek *textus receptus* (ultimately based on the edition of John of Scythopolis, who also commented on the Corpus in scholia).[88] The sixth-century manuscript containing Sergius's translation is the most ancient manuscript of the corpus, anterior to all Greek ones available. Mainoldi agrees that the corpus is "not polemical against the doctrinal contents of Origenism"[89] but much more against "pagan" philosophy (*qua* responding to Damascius's anti-Christian polemics) and Manichaeism, in the excursus on evil in *DN* 4.

Dionysius brought together Plato and Scripture, like Origen earlier,[90] and referred to "pagan" and Christian Platonism in a double-reference scheme throughout the corpus, as pointed out. One clue may indicate the aim of this operation: he was accused of "using the ideas of the Greeks

---

86. Κἀκεῖ μὲν ἀπὸ τοῦ ἄνω πρὸς τὰ ἔσχατα κατιὼν ὁ λόγος.

87. Perczel, "God as Monad and Henad," 1209.

88. PG 4; Rorem and Lamoreaux, *John of Scythopolis and the Dionysian Corpus*.

89. Mainoldi, *Dietro Dionigi l'Areopagita*, 485.

90. I provide many examples in a monograph that is in preparation.

against the Greeks" (τοῖς Ἑλλήνων ἐπὶ τοὺς Ἕλληνας, *Ep.* 7). This charge likely came from the Athenian Platonic school against Christian Platonists, including Dionysius after he became a Christian—if he was a convert[91]— and probably also against Origen. For Origen had already used the ideas of the Greeks (as Porphyry remarked in *C.Chr.* F39[92]) "against the Greeks," in rational support of Christianity, and applied them and allegoresis, a philosophical tool, to the interpretation of Scripture (Porphyry deemed this move illegitimate in *C.Chr.* F39).[93]

Dionysius followed Origen not only in the concepts of love and apokatastasis, as argued, but also regarding the allegorico-symbolical method. Not by chance, Dionysius retorted, I suspect, Porphyry's attack on Origen's application of Greek allegoresis to Scripture, labeled "an absurdity" (ἀτοπία, F39). Dionysius, rejoining, remarks that "uninitiated" (ἀτελέσι) deemed scriptural allegoresis, which explains "what the λόγια say about the divine mysteries" in "riddles," an "outstanding absurdity" (ἀτοπίαν δεινήν, *Letter* 9). Dionysius was replying to Porphyry *qua* Origen's accuser here in *Letter* 9. And *Letter* 7 and likely his whole double-reference system in the corpus responded to the whole "pagan" Platonic charge of using Hellenic ideas against the Hellenes that was leveled against Dionysius and the whole line of Christian Platonism.[94] This had Origen as initiator. Proclus speaks of Origen as a Platonist and admires him although he criticizes his protology, but if he is speaking of the Christian Origen, he never mentions that he was a Christian.

Both Origen and Dionysius could have been charged with being "parricides" of "pagan'" Platonism: "the sophist Apollophanes is attacking me,

91. As Panayiotis Tzamalikos, Ernesto Mainoldi, and others have hypothesized. Others deem him a "pagan," such as Carlo Maria Mazzucchi, Vanneste, Hathaway, Brons, and Tuomo Lankila, suggesting Agapius. Like Perczel, Paul Rorem, Ysabel de Andia, Alexander Golitzin, Ernesto Mainoldi, and others, among whom Gavrilyuk, "Did Ps.-Dionysius Live in Constantinople?," 505–14, Louth sees in Dionysius a Christian, a hypothesis already envisaged by Hausherr and Balthasar. Mainoldi, *Dietro Dionigi l'Areopagita*, plausibly deems Dionysius a Christian who drew on Proclus and Damascius but transformed their ideas with puns against "paganism" (*DN* 11.6): God has nothing to do with "gods"; those who confound the two have no proper knowledge. Mainoldi deems the corpus a work of several authors, reflecting Justinian's positions and possibly commissioned by him (*Dietro Dionigi l'Areopagita*, 491). I only note that Justinian was averse to Origen (without knowing his real ideas) and Origenism, whereas the corpus is profoundly Origenian, although not Origenistic.

92. Analyzed in Ramelli, "Origen, Patristic Philosophy, and Christian Platonism," as well as in my monograph in preparation.

93. Argument in Ramelli, "Philosophical Stance of Allegory in Stoicism," 335–71; "Role of Allegory, Allegoresis, and Metaphor," 130–57.

94. This descriptive category, which I defend in many works, is also defended in Hampton and Kenney, *Christian Platonism.* My invited review is forthcoming in *The Thomist.*

calling me 'parricide,' charging me of making unholy use of Greek things … *but it is the Greeks who make unholy use of godly things to attack God!"* (*Ep.* 7.2). This is Origen's position, and Dionysius's. Therefore the double-reference scheme used by Dionysius throughout his work should likely be seen within the framework of this polemic.

CHAPTER 8 ‖ Body and Soul in
Dionysius the Areopagite

Filip Ivanović

When discussing one of the theonyms—namely, Power—in his *Divine Names*, Dionysius the Areopagite says, among other things, that it "reinforces the bonds of soul and body,"[1] but also that it grants the power of deification to those made godlike and provides the possibility of nourishment and growth to plants. The Power of God, as a matter of fact, is beneficial for the whole creation—humans, animals, and plants.[2] Like many other passages that discuss divine names, this one is not just a mere philosophy of language or an exhibition of cataphatic theology, but it is rather a concise recapitulation of the Areopagite's understanding of God, the world, and created beings. What one learns here is yet another example of that genuinely Dionysian view of the cosmos as unitary, harmonious, and purposeful, with God as its creator and human being as his eminent creation. This is evident if we take a look at the passage as a whole:

[The benefits of Power] enable the assembly of all things to achieve mutual harmony and communion and they enable the distinguished to be so in accordance with the natural laws and qualities of each and without any confusion or intermingling of their characteristics. This Power ensures that the orders and directions of the universe achieve their proper good and it preserves in immortality

1. Dion. Ar. *DN* VIII.5.893A Suchla.
2. Dion. Ar. *DN* VIII.5, 892B Suchla.

113

the unharmed lives of the angelic henads. It keeps the stars of heaven in their shining and unchanging orders. It gives them the power to be eternal. It distinguishes the circlings of time from its procession and duly brings them back to base. It fashions the unquenchability of fire and the ceaseless moisture of water. It keeps the atmosphere fluid, founds the earth upon the void, making its labors endlessly fruitful. It preserves the shared harmony and mixture of the linked elements in their distinctiveness and their separateness. It reinforces the bonds of soul and body. It stirs the powers which give nourishment and growth to plants. It guides the powers which keep each creature in being. It establishes the unshakable remaining of the world. To those made godlike it grants the power for deification itself. In short, nothing in the world lacks the almighty power of God to support and to surround it.[3]

The Deity, as Power, thus holds the whole world together, provides harmony, keeps the natural laws, preserves life, maintains the order and position of celestial bodies, and, most importantly in the Dionysian context, deifies. While at first sight this enumeration of various "benefits" of divine power might seem rather self-evident, given that it is a list of things that Creator *qua* Creator does, I decided to use this passage as an opening to my chapter precisely because it clearly references body and soul from the chapter's title, but also because I find the place of body and soul here important. Having in mind the usual perception of Christianity as emphasizing asceticism and spiritual departing from the body, I believe that the contemporary reader might expect the phrasing to be put as "loosening," rather than "reinforcing the bonds of soul and body."[4] Contrary to the expectations, though, Dionysius lists the soul-body link among the natural laws and includes it within the God-created universe, and he does it not as an example of some aberration or error to be disdained or corrected, but as a relation that is established and supported by God's power.

A contemporary reader's possible surprise by the affirmation of the body-soul link is not, however, a consequence of the postmodern understanding of Christian spirituality. It rather has roots in both pagan and early Christian reflections on the body. For example, Origen reports that Celsus regarded God as happy, good, and beautiful, and that for him to become a man would mean to change from good to evil, from beautiful

---

3. Dion. Ar. *DN* IV.5, 892C–893A. All Dionysius's quotations are given in Colm Luibheld's translation.

4. If one reads, e.g., Onfray's *Atheist Manifesto* and trusts his judgment that "[St.] Paul's pen drips *ad nauseam* a hatred, a contempt, a permanent mistrust for the things of the body," then Dionysius's phrase should come as a surprise.

to shameful,[5] while Tertullian condemns Marcion, a prominent figure of early Christianity, for considering the flesh as "full of dung";[6] Plato's view of the body as the prison of the soul is yet another commonplace.[7] The Neoplatonists, who greatly influenced Dionysius, had different views on body/matter issues, which come to light when their theories of evil are taken into account.

Namely, Plotinus defines evil as privation, that is, as an absolute lack, because if something shows a particular type of lack, it cannot be considered evil, since it would still have the possibility of being perfected. That which absolutely lacks is precisely matter: "But when something is absolutely lacking—which is what matter is—this is really evil, having no share of good."[8] In line with his idea that to be means to participate in the good, Plotinus must deny the very existence of matter. Thus one cannot talk about an evil being, but rather about a nonbeing that constitutes sensible things instead of pure forms, so "we say that 'existence' is said of it [matter] equivocally, so that the true way to speak of it is as non-existent."[9] If matter is evil, then it seems that it is a necessary evil, because without it, without the "material substrate," the sensible world would not exist. However, the matter corrupts and destroys, it is its characteristic, because it juxtaposes its own nature over the forms: "The forms in matter are not identical with what they would be if they existed by themselves, but rather are enmattered expressed principles corrupted and infected by that nature."[10] Similarly, "if the body is the [proximate] cause of evils, matter would be the [ultimate] cause of evils."[11] The evils that a human being does therefore come from the soul's surrender to body and matter as causes of evil, as it fails to be fully intellectual—it is not the soul but the body in which the soul is encased, that is evil.[12]

If Plotinus considers matter to be evil, though not absolute evil, Proclus breaks away from such conception.[13] In the famous treatise *On the Subsistence of Evil*, which is precisely where the Areopagite found the source of

5. Or. *Cels.*, III.28 Chadwick.
6. Tertullian *Marc.*, III.10 Evans.
7. Pl. *Phdr.*, 250C Burnet.
8. Plot. I.8.5. Quotations form the *Enneads* are given according to the translation by George Boys-Stones and others.
9. Plot. I.8.5 Henry Schwyzer.
10. Plot. I.8.8 Henry Schwyzer.
11. Plot. I.8.8 Henry Schwyzer.
12. See Plot. I.8.4 Henry Schwyzer.
13. For a detailed discussion, see Opsomer, "Proclus vs Plotinus on Matter," 154–88.

his doctrine on evil, Proclus states that evil is privation of being, and since matter is used in the fabrication of the world, then it cannot really be evil:

If, however, matter is necessary to the universe, and the world, this absolutely great and "blessed god," would not exist in the absence of matter, how can one still refer the nature of evil to matter? For evil is one thing, but the necessary is something else; the necessary is that without which it is impossible to be, whereas evil is the privation of being itself. If, then, matter offers itself to be used in the fabrication of the whole world, and has been produced primarily for the sake of being "the receptacle of generation, and as it were as a wet-nurse" and "mother," how can it still be said to be evil, and even the primary evil?[14]

Proclus arrives at this conclusion by positing that matter must stem from a principle, that is, from the Good and thus receive its being from the Good, or that matter must be a principle itself; this would imply the existence of two principles, one primary good and the other primary evil, which, he concludes, is impossible.[15] Clearly, Proclus rejects Plotinus's idea that matter is both evil and coming from the Good: "The good as the cause of evil would be evil, and evil, as being produced from the good, would be good."[16] Finally, he concludes that it can no longer be held that "weakness and evil in general occur in souls because of matter."[17]

That Dionysius based his discussion on evil precisely upon Proclus's views has been known for more than a century.[18] Just like Proclus, who writes that "all evil comes about through impotence and lack,"[19] so the Areopagite states that "evil is a deficiency and a lack of perfection of the inherent virtues."[20] He continues by affirming that evil is not inherent to irrational animals, demons, or humans, and that it actually does not belong to nature as a whole.[21] In doing so, Dionysius extends Proclus's theory to all levels of reality, since, as Eric. D. Perl writes, whereas Proclus's doctrine of evil as deficiency works only at the level of human souls and of natural bodies, "Dionysius uses this procedure to explain, on the one hand, that evil is no positive reality in anything, and, on the other, that it can occur as a deficiency of proper perfection at any level of being whatsoever."[22]

---

14. Procl. *De mal.*, 32.1–10 Boese. Translation by Jan Opsomer and Carlos Steel.

15. Procl. *De mal.*, 31.5–12 Boese.

16. Procl. *De mal.*, 31.16–18 Boese.

17. Procl. *De mal.*, 33.15 Boese.

18. Stiglmayr, "Der Neuplatoniker Proklos als Vorlage des sog," 253–73, 721–48.

19. Procl. *De mal.*, 42.10 Boese.

20. Dion. Ar. *DN* IV.24, 728A Suchla.

21. Dion. Ar. *DN* IV.24–26, 725D–728C Suchla.

22. Perl, *Theophany*, 58.

There is no evil, then, in the body, nor can the body be seen as the cause of evil:

And there is no evil in our bodies, for ugliness and disease are a defect in form and a lack of due order. What is here is not pure evil but a lesser beauty. If beauty, form, and order could be destroyed completely the body itself would disappear. It is also obvious that the body is not the cause of evil in the soul. Evil does not require a body to be nearby, as is clear in the case of demons. Evil in minds, in souls, and in bodies is a weakness and a defect in the condition of their natural virtues.[23]

What I would like to note here is the strong both ethical and aesthetic dimension of Dionysius's claims. The Areopagite is famous for his highly aestheticized language and for putting a strong emphasis on beauty as one of the divine names and, consequently, one of the most important attributes of the whole cosmos. As a matter of fact, God as Beauty gives beauty to every creature:

We call "beautiful" that which has a share in beauty, and we give the name of "beauty" to that ingredient which is the cause of beauty in everything. But the "beautiful" (καλόν) which is beyond individual being is called "beauty" (κάλλος) because of that beauty (καλλονὴν) bestowed by it on all things each in accordance with what it is. It is given this name because it is the cause of the harmony and splendor in everything, because like a light it flashes onto everything the beauty causing impartations of its own well-sprang ray. Beauty "calls" (καλοῦν), whence it is called beauty, all things to itself and gathers everything into itself.[24]

Furthermore, Beauty is not just the cause of beauty in all creatures, but it is the cause of very being: "From this beauty comes the existence of everything, each being exhibiting its own way of beauty."[25] God is thus present in each being as its cause, and each being manifests its creator. If this is true for each being, then it is even more valid for humans, created in the image and likeness of God, who "has made us in his image and . . . has given us a share of the divine condition and uplifting."[26] This made it possible for humans to ascend to God and to participate in the divine ἕξις. The ultimate proof of God's care for humankind was his taking on our own nature—the Incarnation. He became a man, a fact that "allowed us, as those equal in birth, to enter into communion with it and to acquire a share of its

23. Dion. Ar. *DN* IV.27, 728CD Suchla.
24. Dion. Ar. *DN* IV.7, 701CD Suchla.
25. Dion. Ar. *DN* IV.7, 704A Suchla.
26. Dion. Ar. *EH* III.3.7, 436C Ritter Heil.

own true beauty."[27] The event of the Incarnation represents the watershed of all human life; it is a calling to communion with the divine, a complete change of nature, and a reception of mysterious divine light, which makes all shadows vanish, saves souls, and adorns minds with a formless beauty (ἀνείδεον κάλλεσι).[28] Here the formless beauty does not mean ugliness or lesser beauty, as in the realm of perceptible, but means transcendent beauty, which is on the other side, beyond the perceptible world; and it is precisely in that realm beyond that a deified mind is found, and it is that transcendent beauty that adorns it in that state.[29] The importance of the Incarnation thus lies not only in the possibility of spiritual communion with the divine, but also in the affirmation of the full human being, composed of both body and soul—by his complete humanization, God opened the way to human deification, but also provided a validation for the goodness of the body. It was therefore not difficult for the Areopagite to exclaim that God's power reinforces the bonds between body and soul, and that the destruction of beauty and form annihilates the body itself. The body is actually an integral part of human nature, and a possible evil of the body comes not from the body per se, but in the distortion of the true nature and in deficiency of natural powers.

Evil, as a matter of fact, is a condition in which a being stands out of its place, as an opposition to the proper arrangement, since "it is not principles (λόγοι) and powers which produce evil."[30] Dionysius defines λόγοι as exemplars, "predefining, divine and good acts of will (προορισμοὺς καλεῖ καὶ θεῖα καὶ ἀγαθὰ θελήματα),"[31] that is, paradigmatic causes by which essence of beings is established or, to put it more simply, principles according to which a being is what it is and ought to be. Thus to move toward evil means to move away from nature, to abandon one's own place in the whole cosmic structure—a state that is remedied by setting a thing "where it ought to be, adding on lost virtue, bringing back order and arrangement where there was disorder and derangement, making it perfect and liberating it from defects."[32] This redemption is, in fact, worked out by Righteousness, which is yet another divine name. When a thing does not act according to its own nature, which is its best actualization,[33] then evil comes into play—in

---

27. Dion. Ar. *EH* III.3.11, 441B Ritter Heil.
28. Dion. Ar. *EH* III.3.11, 441B Ritter Heil.
29. Ivanović, *Desiring the Beautiful*, 72.
30. Dion. Ar. *DN* IV.31 732B Suchla.
31. Dion. Ar. *DN* V.8, 824C Suchla.
32. Dion. Ar. *DN* VIII.9, 897B Suchla.
33. Schäfer, *Philosophy of Dionysius the Areopagite*, 145.

souls as an "activity contrary to nature" and in bodies as "the renunciation of what is natural."[34] If evil is something not proper to nature, then it must be an accident, just like when one does something with good intentions but with bad outcome, as Dionysius states it in very simple words:

We have to assume that evil exists as an accident. It is there by means of something else. Its source does not lie within itself. Hence something we do for the sake of the Good looks right and yet is not really so when we consider to be good what is actually not so. Desire and event are clearly different.[35]

Now, if evil is an "accident" and if it is there "by means of something else," how are humans then susceptible to it? The answer is in reason, with which humans are endowed, and freedom, which is always associated with reason—the freedom to choose then may lead to the proper use of one's natural faculties or to their abuse. As the peak of creation, humans are gifted with nature that includes freedom, and not even God would interfere with it:

Therefore we should ignore the popular notion that Providence will lead us to virtue even against our will. Providence does not destroy nature. Indeed its character as Providence is shown by the fact that it saves the nature of each individual, so that the free may freely act as individual or as groups.[36]

Freedom, inherent in human nature, which is a composite nature, thus refers to both soul and body—it depends on us whether we will use them or misuse them. Since God bestowed on human beings the capacities needed to do good, then "there can be no excuse for any sin in the realm of one's own good, for any turning aside, any desertion, any lapse."[37] The punishment for the misuse of capacities provided to do good is reminiscent of Plato's account of the creation of humans in *Timaeus*. There Plato talks about the constitution of the human body, how the souls are encapsulated in them, and what purpose various organs have. But what is important here is that such teleology for Plato is not physiological, but rather moral. As the bodies associated with the souls are mortal, the use they make of them would determine their future life:

And he explained that whether they lived moral or immoral lives would depend on whether they were in control of these things or were controlled by them. Any soul which made good use of its allotted time would return to dwell once more

34. Dion. Ar. *DN* IV.32, 733A Suchla.
35. Dion. Ar. *DN* IV.32, 732C Suchla.
36. Dion. Ar. *DN* IV.33, 733B Suchla.
37. Dion. Ar. *DN* IV.35, 736A Suchla.

on the star with which it had been paired, to live a blessed life in keeping with its character; but any soul that fell short would, for its second incarnation, become a woman instead of a man.[38]

If, however, they do not free themselves from wickedness, in subsequent incarnations they would be turned into animals, until they are restored to their best state. Again, freedom plays the most important role—the Demiurge bestows the soul with all the capacities to do good, and the only evil they could suffer would only be self-inflicted:

Once he had gone through all these decrees for them, which freed him of responsibility for any wickedness any of them might subsequently perform, he set about planting some of them in the earth, some in the moon, and others in the other instruments of time. After this, he handed over to the younger gods the task of forming their mortal bodies. When they had also created any further attributes a human soul might require, and whatever went along with such attributes, he left it up to them to govern and steer every mortal creature as best they could, so that each one would be as noble and good as it might be, apart from any self-caused evils.[39]

The moral of the narrative is clear—gods are not to be blamed for any harm or unhappiness humans might suffer, as the cause of the suffering is neither in the world nor in the body. The physical world and the constitution of the body are not valid excuses for the vices or misdoings committed by exercising our own free will. Quite the contrary, the younger gods were ordered to create mortal bodies in the best possible way, precisely to ensure that reason would be in charge and that they would serve the purpose of the good life.[40] This purpose is explained by Plato's discussion of all the vital organs in human body, but he does it not with the intention of describing their physiological functions, but instead to prove how the proper use of them should make human life good. In a quite similar way, Dionysius writes a passage in which he describes various body parts explicitly and implicitly mentioned in the Bible (and some that do not appear in the Scripture) in order to show how their function is not purely biological but can be used to grasp "the powers of heaven":

One could say that the powers of sight suggest their ability to gaze up directly toward the lights of God and, at the same time, to receive softly, clearly, without resistance but flexibly, purely and openly the enlightenments coming from the

---

38. Pl. *Tim.*, 42BC Burnet. Translation by Robin Waterfield.
39. Pl. *Tim.*, 42DE Burnet.
40. See Steel, "Moral Purpose of the Human Body," 125*ff.*

Deity, yet without emotion. The powers to discern smells indicate their capacity to welcome fully those fragrances which elude the understanding and to discern with understanding those opposites which must be utterly avoided. The powers of hearing signify the ability to have a knowing share of divine inspiration. Taste has to do with the fill of conceptual nourishment and their receptiveness to the divine and nourishing streams. Touch is understanding how to distinguish the profitable from the harmful. Eyelids and eyebrows signify the guarding of what the mind has observed of God. Adolescence and youth indicate the perennial vigor of living power. Teeth have to do with the skill which produces divisions in the intake of nourishing perfection, for it is a fact that every intelligent being, having received from one which is more divine the gift of a unified conception, proceeds to divide it and to make provision for its diffusion in order that an inferior may be lifted up as far as possible. Shoulders, arms, and also the hands signify acting, achieving. The heart symbolizes life lived in conformity to God, benevolently dispensing the life-giving power to those in its care.[41]

The senses—sight, hearing, taste, touch, smell—and various body parts all serve to physically perceive the intelligible world, to rise beyond pure perceptions, and to use their faculties in an appropriate manner in order to know God. Sense perceptions are actually described by Dionysius as "echoes of wisdom,"[42] by which the mind can "read" the Creator and the creation. The mind is inseparable from the body, and the Areopagite denies that this bond can ever be broken, at the same time rejecting the possibility of reincarnation and affirming deification of the whole human being:

Among the unholy there are some who ridiculously believe that our bodies experience a dissolution of being. Others think that the link of body and soul is broken forever since, as they imagine, it would be inappropriate for souls to be trammeled with a body in the midst of the godlike life and blessedness. Such people, because of their inadequate acquaintance with divine understanding (ἐπιστήμη), overlook the fact that Christ has already provided the example of a human life conforming perfectly to God. And there are others who would assign other bodies to the souls, thereby, in my opinion, holding an unfair view of the bodies which have shared in the struggles of divine souls … No sacred men will ever fall into such error, for they know that their whole being will be granted the peace which will make them Christlike.[43]

Thus Dionysius seems to break away from many of the ancient doctrines on the body-soul relationship, such as Epicureans, Pythagoreans, but also (Neo)Platonists that adhere to either of the views from *Phaedrus* or

41. Dion. Ar. *CH* XV.3, 332AC Ritter Heil.
42. Dion. Ar. *DN* VII.2, 868C Suchla.
43. Dion. Ar. *EH* VII.1.2, 553CD Ritter Heil.

Timaeus, discussed earlier. On the contrary, the Incarnation here represents for Dionysius a proof of the body-soul union, while Christ becomes an example of good life in the entirety of the composite human being. Dionysius is quite aware of the difficulties that stand before human persona—a variety of passions, pains, desires can seduce the soul and set it on a wrong way; the exaggerated satisfaction of everyday needs can surely lead to the misuse of natural faculties. Living the good life is not an easy task, but still the Areopagite can point out Christ, who proved it possible to harmonize the body and soul, so that the whole person can be made godlike. Guided by his example and aided by the sacraments, humankind gains access to the divine life.[44] If the body is important in the earthly life, so it remains in the afterlife. Dionysius clearly states it when discussing funeral rites, which he describes in detail. The attention given to the body during the burial affirms its inseparable connection to the soul, with which it shared the same way of life:

If the deceased lived, body and soul, a life pleasing to God, his body will deserve to have a share of the honors bestowed on the soul which was its companion in the sacred struggle. That is why divine justice links the body with the soul when final judgment is rendered to the soul, for the body also took part in the same journey along the road of holiness or impiety.[45]

The rite, which does not consist only of prayers but includes physical treatment of the body as well, denies the possibility of radical dualism or parallelism between soul and body in the Dionysian cosmos. Contemplation and understanding for the soul, and ointment for the body, are the constituent elements of giving "divine communion" to both elements of human being: "Thus the entire person is made holy, the work of his salvation is all-embracing, and the full rites make known the totality of the resurrection that is to come."[46]

The treatment of body and soul that Dionysius offers is unfortunately not as detailed and systematic as one would hope. We cannot gather his ideas on the issue as we can do in Plato, despite clear divergences between earlier and later dialogues and consequently obvious difficulty in defining Plato's unitary psychology, especially in relation to the body.[47] Unlike the master of the Academy, Dionysius does not give a thorough account of the

44. See Roques, *L'univers Dionysien,* 292–93.
45. Dion. Ar. *EH* VII.3.9, 565B Ritter Heil.
46. Dion. Ar. *EH* VII.3.9, 565B Ritter Heil.
47. See, e.g., Robinson, "Rasgos distintivos del dualismo mente-cuerpo en los escritos de Platón."

relationship between body and soul, but he does constantly affirm their unbreakable union. What exactly is the kind of that union it is impossible to infer, although the author mentions that he wrote a treatise *The Soul*,[48] where he allegedly described the soul's qualities. This book has never been found, however, and most probably was never written. We can neverthe-less summarize a few points deriving from our discussion. First, Dionysius is obviously indebted to Neoplatonists, especially Proclus, from whom he inherits the views on evil and denies the possibility of evil to be found in body or matter, but he does extend this theory of evil as deficiency to all levels of reality. Second, his understanding of the right or wrong use of mental and physical realities comes close to the one expounded by Plato in *Timaeus*, in the sense of the good life and punishment for the misuse of God-given qualities, but he completely rejects the possibility of metem-psychosis and any kind of separation of body and soul, in which he goes against not only Plato, but also most of the ancient philosophical schools. Third, by strongly affirming the union between body and soul, Dionysius conjoins his anthropology and eschatology, the foundation of which he finds in Christology in terms of the resurrection of the entire human being. Furthermore, Christology becomes the basis for his ethics, since Christ, as being not just God but true man as well, is proclaimed the true example of a good life, that a human being should lead "body and soul."

48. Dion. Ar. *DN* IV.2, 696C.

CHAPTER 9 ❙ "Chalcedonian Participation"

St. Maximus the Confessor's Christian Neoplatonism

Dionysios Skliris

Introduction

If transcendence and participation are the two ontological quests that are most characteristic of Platonism, then the version of Christian Neoplatonism that prevailed in the teaching of the Byzantine Fathers is arguably the most radical form of Platonism, since it combines the most absolute divine transcendence with the fullest possible human participation in it. Admitting the possibility of such a combination required a bold reformation of Platonism that could oppose some of its basic tenets and negate some of its intuitions. But what the Christian Fathers seemed to have affirmed is the deepest existential demand of Platonism; namely, communion with a divine reality that transcends the world of the sensibles. The Fathers thus responded to the most profound thirst of Platonists while altering or even reversing the right order, that is, the hierarchy that was perceived as necessary by the philosophers.

In this chapter we shall observe the philosophical outlook of St. Maximus the Confessor (ca. 580–662), who was arguably one of the last thinkers of late antiquity before the demise of the ancient polis, having recapitulated many demands of Greek thought in his contemplative system. We shall examine how the striving for participation in the transcendent God is a recurrent feature in the Confessor's thought, echoing the relevant preoccupation of the prominent Neoplatonist philosophers. This striving is evident in Maximian Trinitarian theology, cosmology, soteriology, spirituality, and theory of evil. The absolute character of divine transcendence entails a radical natural gap between God and the cosmos. This means that unlike the Neoplatonic Trinity, the Christian one shares in the same ontological alterity in relation to the world without a natural hierarchy that would be intrinsic to it. But absolute transcendence and full participation run in tandem: if there is no natural relation between God and the world, then there is no privileged part of created nature in the participation of the divine. The body is a candidate for *methexis* at least as much as the intellect. This is the meaning of "Chalcedonian participation"; namely, the fact that man does not need to leave something aside when he participates in God but can include his full hypostasis in his ecstasis. In this view, evil is nonbeing but is not detected in one particular ontological domain that is the most remote from God; it is rather something that emerges in history from voluntarily severing the beings from their source. In all such cases, one witnesses a common theme with Neoplatonism that has undergone some original twist: Trinity without hierarchy, participation including the body, the notion of evil as nonbeing yet in a de-reified way.

The differences—namely, egalitarian Trinitarianism with a natural gap in relation to the world, the emphasis on the body, and the non-identification of evil with matter—could be seen as a betrayal of Platonism's most valuable insights. Conversely, they could also be seen as a surprising and unexpected way to fulfill the underlying goals and demands of the Platonist project in a more radical way. In other words, if participation in transcendence is considered as the Platonist project par excellence, then its Christian twist entails participation in an absolutely transcendent God that does not present any natural continuity with the cosmos whatsoever. The latter means an extreme apophaticism where the "hypostases" of the Trinity are not put in a "vertical" hierarchy but share the same supra-substantial apophatic "reality" in a "homoousion" that is rather "horizontal" than "vertical." Participation in this divine reality is performed not by focusing on man's higher constituents of selfhood, such as the intellect, but thanks to a divine initiative, by including what is most remote from the immaterial God; namely, the body. The latter arguably leads to the most complete and integral participation that is possible, thus enhancing Platonism rather that betraying it. Evil is consequently detached from matter: it is a "parhypostasis" as in Proclus, but one that emerges inside the historical dialogue between God and man through a deviation of natural capacities and a turning of them toward created goals, not one that constitutes a simple "fading away" from Goodness. Evil thus becomes a genuine historical tragedy that requires an equally historical redemption, while at the same time retaining the fundamental thrust of Neoplatonist ontological optimism that only the Good really exists. I have termed this Maximian twist of the Neoplatonist program "Chalcedonian participation" in order to imply that it responds to the most profound Neoplatonist goal—namely, participation in transcendence—while at the same time it is inspired by the Chalcedonian Christology in which the union with the divine happens without confusion nor separation.

Of course this "Chalcedonian participation" means a "crucifixion" of Platonism and a "resurrection" of it in an alternative form. The Christian Platonist philosopher does not have the self-pride that indulging in his intellectual selfhood could automatically bring him to the deeper divine selfhood of the entire cosmos. The intellect of the wise man is rather invited to contemplate the *logoi* of beings as God's volitional acts and utterances for the future of a cosmos that is ontologically other than God. The Neoplatonic Energeia thus becomes a personal act,[1] and philosophy is centered in Christ as the One Logos of God who encompasses the many *logoi*. The corollary of this is that the wise man is called not to abandon his body but to transform it. But what the wise man gains by modifying the Platonic insights is participation to the most radically apophatic divine "reality" in the most inclusive way that comprehends also the body. For the sake of this endeavor, I will rather focus on the similarities between the Maximian project and the Neoplatonist one, examining cases where St. Maximus was deeply influenced by Neoplatonism and tried a peculiar Byzantine synthesis with the biblical vision.

Possible Philosophical Sources of St. Maximus's Thought

It is not possible to ascertain from the writings of Maximus the Confessor (ca. 580–662) whether he had any direct acquaintance with partic-

---

1. Tollefsen, *Activity and Participation in Late Antique and Early Christian Thought*, 214.

ular philosophical texts by specific Neoplatonist authors. In general, most scholars seem to agree that what Maximus the Confessor had received from the Greek philosophical tradition is neither an unmediated Aristotelianism nor pure Neoplatonism, but rather a Neoplatonist interpretation of Aristotle due to commentators of late antiquity. In the age of Maximus, the philosophical instruction was based on the writings of Plato and Aristotle, as they were interpreted by Proclus, Iamblichus, Alexander from Aphrodisias, Amonius, and Porphyry.[2] Maximus had of course integrated this Neoplatonic synthesis of Plato and Aristotle in a Christian contemplative vision.[3] This is famously the case with the triad essence-potentiality/power-actualization/activity (οὐσία-δύναμις-ἐνέργεια), which is not used by Maximus in an unmediated Aristotelian fashion but is received through Proclus[4] and, most of all, the Christian interpretation of the latter by Ps.-Dionysius.[5]

Maximus is familiar with the kind of logic that stems from Aristotle's *Categories*, but it is not certain whether he had actually read Porphyry's *Isagoge*. Having read Porphyry is a possibility, but he could also have known the logic of the *Isagoge* through the Fathers. In his major work, the *Ambigua ad Ioannem*, Maximus lists the Aristotelian categories[6] and seems to understand them in a Neoplatonic fashion.[7] The hypothesis could be constructed that Maximus knew the logic of the *Isagoge* from logical compendia and textbooks of the sixth and early seventh centuries. Antoine Lévy has tried to show that Maximus's knowledge of the Aristotelian *Categories* as well as his use of notions such as ἐνέργεια (activity), σχέσις (relation), and ἐπιτηδειότης (fitness) are indebted particularly to Simplicius.[8]

It is characteristic that at least two logical compendia are attributed to Maximus, the likeliest explanation being, as Mossman Roueché notes, that they were found among his papers after his death and mistakenly transmitted in his name.[9] An alternative hypothesis is formulated by Torstein Tollefsen, who thinks that the editors of Maximus's works could have con-

---

2. Sherwood, "Notes on Maximus the Confessor," 348.

3. Tollefsen, *Christocentric Cosmology of St Maximus the Confessor*, 15.

4. Procl. *ET* 169 Dodds.

5. Dion. Ar. *C.H.* 11.2 Heil and Ritter.

6. Max. *Ambig.* 1.294–96 Constas (PG 91,1181B).

7. For the use of Aristotelian categories by Maximus, see Mueller-Jourdan, *Typologie spatio-temporelle de l'Ecclesia byzantine*, 44–98.

8. See Lévy, *Le Créé et l'incréé*, 143–95, and the general assessment in Portaru, "Classical Philosophical Influences," 130–34.

9. Roueché, "Byzantine Philosophical Texts of the Seventh Century."

sidered these logical texts as a useful tool in understanding his thought.[10] These logical compendia contain and explain some of the technical vocabulary of Aristotelian-Neoplatonic (Porphyrian) logic and treat the Aristotelian categories that also expose the Porphyrian tree.[11] According to Mossman Roueché, the compendia are ultimately based on Porphyry's *Isagoge* and Aristotle's *Categories* and are directly dependent on sixth-century Aristotelian lectures in Alexandria. They show familiarity particularly with the *Prolegomena* of the commentators Elias and David. They were, however, destined for a Christian audience, as they have a Christian mold.

One specific philosophical acquaintance might have been the Christian Neoplatonist Stephanus, a disciple of John Philoponus in Alexandria. Stephanus was the author of commentaries on Aristotle—for example, on *De Anima* III and on *De Interpretatione*—and he was lecturing on both Plato and Aristotle.[12] His definition of philosophy seems to have been integrated in the *Mystagogy*.[13] It is possibly through Stephanus that St. Maximus came into contact with the thought of John Philoponus and the latter's effort to correct Proclus from a Christian point of view.[14] It is equally through Stephanus that Maximus might have known the works of the Christian Neoplatonists of Alexandria such as Elias and David, as well as Ps.-Elias. David has offered us a commentary on the *Isagoge*,[15] while Elias has written commentaries on both the *Isagoge* and the *Categories*.[16] W. Lackner had proposed a lengthy textual parallelism between the first *Opusculum Theologicum et Polemicum*, by Maximus (*PG* 91, 20A–B), and the *Prolegomena* 47.1–2, by David.[17] Pascal Mueller-Jourdan finds textual parallels between the same *Opusculum* and Ps.-Elias.[18] It is to be noted that Elias and David were also the sources for John of Damascus's *Dialectic*, which has in a certain sense replaced the manuals of philosophy and the florilegia.[19]

---

10. Tollefsen, *Christocentric Cosmology of St Maximus the Confessor*, 15.

11. Tollefsen, *Christocentric Cosmology of St Maximus the Confessor*, 15.

12. Tollefsen, *Christocentric Cosmology of St Maximus the Confessor*, 16.

13. Ouzounian, "David l'Invincible," 614–15; Mueller-Jourdan, *Typologie spatio-temporelle de l'Ecclesia byzantine*, 31.

14. Tollefsen, *Activity and Participation in Late Antique and Early Christian Thought*, 119. For example, cf. Max. *Ambig.* 1.294–96 Constas (PG 91,1181B), Max. *Carit.* 4.4 PG 90,1048D with Phlp. *Procl.* 36, 74, 76, 78, 79 Rabe. Cf. Max. *Cap. Theol.* 1,10 PG 90,1085D–1088A with Phlp. *Procl.* 88 Rabe.

15. David. *In Porph.* 18,2. Busse.

16. Elias. *In Porph.* 18,1. Busse.

17. Lackner, *Studien zur philosophischen Schultradition*.

18. Ps.-Elias, *in Porph.* 17.16–20 Westerink; see Mueller-Jourdan, *Une initiation à la philosophie de l'antiquité tardive*, xxi–xxvi.

19. Portaru, "Classical Philosophical Influences," 134.

But in many cases, Maximus seems to draw notions of Greek philosophers in a mediated way through the Fathers and the Christian authors of late antiquity, such as the Cappadocians,[20] Nemesius of Emesa, St. Cyril, Leontius of Byzantium, and Leontius of Jerusalem. For example, his dependence on Nemesius of Emesa (fourth century) concerning Aristotelian psychology was shown convincingly already by R.-A. Gauthier.[21] His Proclean use of the triad essence-power-energy (οὐσία-δύναμις-ἐνέργεια)[22] is probably inherited by Ps.-Dionysius,[23] as was already noted. In general, there seems to be a certain familiarity of Maximus with the vocabulary and the ideas of the tradition of Iamblichus, as it was reformulated by the eminent members of the Neoplatonic School of Athens, such as Proclus, Damascius, and Simplicius.[24] As there seems to be no reason to postulate an immediate relation between Maximus and the Athenian Neoplatonic School, the dependence of Maximus on the latter is probably due to the influence of Ps.-Dionysius. Pascal Mueller-Jourdan has shown convincingly the influence of this particular school on the *Mystagogy*. The latter does not cite the Neoplatonic philosophers directly, but it does contain a citation of the *Celestial Hierarchy* in the introduction[25] and a reference to the *Nomina Sacra* in chapter 23.[26] St. Maximus contemplates the *ecclesia* in a way that reminds of the contemplation of the intelligible world by philosophers like Proclus.[27] The Maximian imagery about the Church as supreme participatory unification[28] of the human community is one of supporting angle or of the sun, its center and its rays thus echoing the Proclean tradition.[29] What is decidedly Platonic is the close relation between the intellectual *theoria* of the first principles and the political organization of the human community.[30] But before examining this theory of participation, it would be more fruitful to start from a comparison between Maximian and Neoplatonist Trinitarian theology.

20. For example, Tollefsen thinks that Maximus draws a part of his knowledge of logic from Gregory of Nyssa's *De hominis opificio* (*Christocentric Cosmology of St Maximus the Confessor*, 84).

21. Gauthier, "Saint Maxime le Confesseur et la psychologie de l'acte humain."

22. See Procl. *ET* 169 Dodds.

23. See Dion. Ar. *C.H.* 11.2 Heil and Ritter.

24. Mueller-Jourdan, *Typologie spatio-temporelle de l'Ecclesia byzantine*, 34, 193.

25. Max. *Myst.* CCSG 69,6,54–7,74 Boudignon (PG 91,660D–661A).

26. Max. *Myst.* CCSG 69,54,875–55,882 Boudignon (PG 91,701C).

27. See Procl. *In Euc.* 19.20 Friedlein and the comparison with Maximus in Mueller-Jourdan, *Typologie spatio-temporelle de l'Ecclesia byzantine*, 25.

28. See Max. *Myst.* CCSG 69,43,693–44,713 Boudignon (PG 91,692D–693B); 67,1110–69,1165 (PG 91,713A–716A).

29. Max. *Myst.* CCSG 69,13,184–14,198 Boudignon (PG 91,668A–B).

30. Mueller-Jourdan, *Typologie spatio-temporelle de l'Ecclesia byzantine*, 30.

Trinitarian Theology

Maximus's theology is characterized by an effort to bring Neoplatonic apophaticism to the extreme. In the *Mystagogy* he writes that if the being is referred to the world, then God is nonbeing.[31] In *De Charitate* 3,28 (PG 90,1025B–C) we find a strange twist of Aristotelianism. God is "defined" in an eminent way as the One who does not have any contrary whatsoever. Unlike Aristotle, Maximus thinks that the substance does have a contrary; namely, nonbeing. Maximus does not believe in the eternity of the world, which means that he relativizes the being of the created substance: it is a being that is constantly threatened by nonbeing and cannot acquire stability. Conversely, God in himself is beyond substance, as he is beyond every affirmation and negation, according to the Dionysian doctrine. God in himself is beyond everything that has a contrary, including Goodness, Truth, Simplicity, and Being. It seems that Being proper is to be found neither in God, who is above it, nor in the world, which is under the menace of nonbeing but in the intermediary ontological sphere of the activity "around God" (περὶ Θεόν) that is communicated to the creation through Christ in an eschatological perspective. It is through the activity of God and man's participation in it through Christ that being actually arises or rather is awaited for its full manifestation in the eschatological life after the end of history. But before turning to the subject of the ontological "emergence" of being, we should note the Trinitarian structure of Maximian theology, which also reflects his view on participation.

St. Maximus does give a philosophical grounding for Christian Trinitarianism. He thinks that the Monad entails ontological sterility, while the Dyad means imperfection pointing to the division between form and matter. Only the Trinity is a perfect reality combining wealth and perfection that is impossibility of division. In the *Ambiguum* 1, St. Maximus follows St. Gregory of Nazianzus in contemplating a movement that is interior to the Trinity.[32] He speaks about this movement of intra-Trinitarian relations in terms of causality, but also of relation and mutual implication (σχέσις, συνένδειξις).[33] Apart from the biblical Trinity of Father, Son, and Spirit, Maximus employs a psychological one of Nous (Intellect), Logos

---

31. Max. *Myst.* CCSG 69,9,103–10,126 Boudignon (PG 91,664A–C).

32. Max. *Ambig.* 1.6–8 Constas (PG 91,1033D–1036C).

33. Tollefsen thinks that St. Maximus avoids the terminology of causality (*Activity and Participation in Late Antique and Early Christian Thought*, 78). But there is a notion of causality in the begetting of the Logos from the Son in the *Mystagogy*.

(Reason), and Pneuma (Spirit). The latter is common in the Fathers, but Maximus gives it a systematic development in relation to its created image; namely, the human soul. It would be interesting to compare this Christian Trinity to the Neoplatonic one of the One, the Intellect, and the Psyche.[34]

In Patristic theology, following the Gospel of John, the Christ is named both Son and Word (Logos). The term "Son" obviously implies a net of existential relations. As noted by Gregory of Nazianzus, cited by Maximus, the Father cannot be conceived without his Son.[35] Maximus is persistently trying to establish a correlation between the divine Trinity and the Trinitarian character of the human soul. That is the fact that the human soul comprises intellect (νοῦς), reason (λόγος), and spirit (πνεῦμα) is considered by Maximus to be an "icon," a reflection of the Divine Trinity in human personhood. In the divine Trinity, the Father is the Intellect (Νοῦς) who is generating the Word (Λόγος) and processing the Spirit (Πνεῦμα).

Maximus is synthesizing the "social"[36] and the "psychological" Trinity, too, when he considers the "generation" of the Son by the Father as tantamount to a "generation" of the Logos-Word by the Intellect-Nous.[37] Likewise, the fact that the Son is personally caused by the Father is connected to the fact that, generally speaking, the logos is caused by the nous.[38] Besides, at the anthropological level, the detailed description of the correlations between nous and logos in the *Mystagogy* is concluded as follows: "The logos-reason is the energy/act and the manifestation of the intellect, like an effect is the act and manifestation of its cause."[39] In general, for Maximus, the nous is the part of the soul in which rationality exists in a transcendent and absolutely simple way. It is only at the level of the logos that rationality is articulated as a structure with a logical content and where there are distinctions and alterities. The intellect is addressing primordial simplicity, whereas the logos is progressing logically through distinctions[40] (without, however,

---

34. For a more detailed account of the consequences of the Trinity for spirituality, see Skliris, "Saint Maximus the Confessor's Trinitarian Theology."

35. See Max. *Ambig.* 2.20 Constas (PG 91,1265D), where Maximus is analyzing a passage from the *Oratio* 29 of Gregory of Nazianzus. See Gr. Naz. *Or.* 29, 210 Gallay.

36. The "Social Trinity" is a modern theological term that denotes those Trinitarian theologies in which the three hypostases are considered as three distinct persons in relations of loving communion, in contradistinction to the "psychological" Trinitarian theologies, in which the three hypostases are compared to capacities of the soul.

37. Max. *Qu. Thal.* CCSG 7,161,46–50 Laga and Steel (PG 90,332B); Max. *Qu. Thal.* CCSG 7,163,72–74 Laga and Steel (PG 90,332D).

38. Max. *Qu. Thal.* CCSG 7,167,158–159 Laga and Steel (PG 90,336C).

39. Max. *Myst.* CCSG 69,28,437–438 Boudignon (PG 91,680B).

40. Max. *Qu. Thal.* CCSG 22,65,307–328 Laga and Steel (PG 90,616C–D).

being equated to discursive *dianoia*). Such a conception of the difference between the nous and the logos runs in tandem with the Trinitarian reality of these terms that is characterized by the following traits: as the Father is the divine Intellect, he constitutes the primordial cause of Divinity (just like *mutatis mutandis* the human intellect is the primordial cause of the soul[41]), and by extension he is the origin of every divine movement toward the creation. By being the Nous, the Father is equally formless. He is therefore accessible to creatures only through his Logos.[42] The Word is the Logos of the Father because he is articulating in a structured content with distinction between alterities that subsists in the Father in a sort of transcendental simplicity.[43] This causality of a psychological type is also valid for the Holy Spirit: "Just as the Nous is the cause of the Logos, He is equally the cause of the Spirit but through the Logos; and just as we cannot say that speech (logos) comes from the voice, in the same way we cannot say that the Logos comes from the Pneuma-breath."[44] In other words, there is a hypostatic order of the Trinity, where the Father is the cause of the two other persons; namely, of the Son and of the Spirit (through the Son). This hypostatic order is founded in a psychological Trinitarianism, where the intellect-nous is the cause of its Logos-speech and through it of the spirit-breath (the latter being compared to human voice in relation to speech). It is interesting that in a teleological context the speech is considered to be the cause of the voice. In a mechanistic context it could have been the opposite; namely, the voice being a cause of speech.

What is more, the fact that Christ is the eternal Logos of the Trinity seems to be connected to the fact that he is the only one to be incarnated. On the one hand, the Son is eternally the Logos of the Father because he is articulating in a structured content with distinctions between alterities what subsists at the level of the Father only as an eminent transcendent simplicity. On the other hand, it is in this sense that the Son is par excellence the creator of the world. It is true of course that all three persons participate in the creative act.[45] But the Son is the one who is par excellence the author of creation, in almost (but of course not completely) the same way in which he is the only one of the three to be incarnated. Maximus is

41. See *Myst.* Boudignon (PG 91,680B).

42. Max. *Qu. Thal.* CCSG 7,161,54–163,80 Laga and Steel (PG 90,332C–333A).

43. For the relation between Logos and Nous in the Trinity as well as in human psychology, see *Qu. Thal.* CCSG 7,159–67 Laga and Steel (PG 90,329C–336C).

44. Max. *Qu. Dub.* CCSG 10,151,4–7 Declerck (PG 90,813B).

45. Max. *Qu. Thal.* CCSG 7,207,70–90 Laga and Steel (PG 90,364B).

distinguishing between three distinct modes by which the three persons participate in the economy of God's incarnation: These are the εὐδοκία ("goodwill") of the Father, the αὐτουργία of the Son, and the συνέργεια ("cooperation") of the Spirit.[46] Maximus is then connecting the αὐτουργία to the act of creation: "this mystery [the Incarnation] was preconceived before all ages solely by the Father and the Son and the Holy Spirit, that is it was willed by the Father and was accomplished by the Son with the participation of the Holy Spirit."[47] Maximus then adds: "Because He who was truly the creator of the essence of beings according to nature had to also become the One who would accomplish Himself the divinization according to grace of the things that came to be, so that the One who granted them the [well-]being might prove to be the same with the One who granted them the eternal well-being."[48] The term αὐτουργία designates the specific role of the Son in the Incarnation, the fact that he became himself part of creation and history, which is applicable to neither the Father nor the Spirit. But this distinct role of the αὐτουργία is connected here to the act of creation in the sense that the realization of our divinization by the Logos according to grace is a fulfillment of our creation by the same Logos according to nature. What can be concluded from these and many other passages[49] is that the Father as Nous is the hypostatic cause of the divine hypostases, but he also is the primordial cause of creation toward which he manifests his goodwill (εὐδοκία).

The Son has the following characteristics. (1) He is the Logos of the Father-Nous, in the sense that he is articulating divine rationality in a structured content. (2) By extension, he is the "author" (αὐτουργία) par excellence of the act of creation, which is founded on the rational principles (logoi) that he is bearing in his hypostasis. (3) He is the sole divine hypostasis to be incarnated. He is also therefore the "author" (αὐτουργός) par excellence of divinization in the sense of a hypostatic union between God and human nature. The latter also has important eschatological implications. In a similar drawing of consequences from theology to economy, the Spirit is inside the Trinity a hypostasized principle of vitality and spirituality, and as such he is also the hypostasis that vivifies creation and brings it to its perfect eschatological fulfillment.

46. Max. *Qu. Thal.* CCSG 22,79,94–81,130 Laga and Steel (PG 90,624B–625A).

47. Max. *Qu. Thal.* CCSG 22,79,94–97 Laga and Steel (PG 90,624B–C).

48. Max. *Qu. Thal.* CCSG 22,79,117–20 Laga and Steel (PG 90, 624D).

49. See, e.g., Max. *Qu. Thal.* CCSG 7,225–27 Laga and Steel (PG 90,372B–D); Max. *Ambig.* 2.266 Constas (PG 91,1385D–1388A).

From the above it is evident that St. Maximus is following a peculiar kind of Patristic Neoplatonism. Nevertheless, it is perhaps more interesting to detect the differences of Maximian Trinitarianism from the Neoplatonic one as, for example, the Plotinian or the Proclean one. In Plotinus, the "first" "hypostasis"—namely, the One—is absolutely transcendent to intellection and conscious volition.[50] (Of course, both the term "first" and the term "hypostasis" are used abusively; it could be claimed that by comparing Plotinus with Christianity we cannot but betray some particularities of Plotinus, such as the fact that the One is not a "hypostasis" among many, nor exactly the "first" one in a series of three hypostases.) The Nous is the "second" hypostasis and not the "first" one. What is more, for Plotinus, the logos is situated in the third hypostasis—namely, the Soul—which also assumes the formation of the inferior material world. On the contrary, in the Maximian system the Nous is elevated from the "second" place to the "first" one, and the Logos from the third one to the second. These changes have important consequences for their conception. The Maximian nous is transcendent, simple, and not formed. Nevertheless, it is not as simple as the Neoplatonic One: the Maximian nous is neither above intellection nor above conscious volition. But it is not "full" of an intelligible articulated structure like the Plotinian nous, either. If we might draw an analogy, the Maximian nous is like the "first moment"[51] of the Plotinian nous, "when" the One is acquiring self-consciousness and with it the simplest possible intellection, which is not "yet" articulated as a structure that would comprise the totality of the intelligible universe. What is more, the Maximian nous does have volition, the latter being arguably the most fundamental aspect of its being[52] along with intellection. In Plotinus, on the contrary, the One does not have conscious volition, even though it might be regarded as having a simple "thelema" that is identified with its own existence. Then, in Plotinus at least, the procession of the world is the work of the "third" hypostasis, the Soul, and it is there that we find the creative logos.

But in Maximus, the Logos is placed in the "second" place, and Logos is personally "undertaking" the creation of the world directly and not through the intermediary of the "third" hypostasis. In Maximus, the second hypostasis comprises elements of the third Plotinian hypostasis, as it is the Logos who is par excellence the creation. The principles that are

---

50. Plot. 5.3.10.31–51 Henry and Schwyzer. The One might be considered as having a sort of eminent nonconscious "volition" that is completely identical with its absolute simplicity.

51. This is obviously an eternal and nontemporal process.

52. Max. *Ambig.* 2.8–10 Constas (PG 91,1261B–1264B).

termed in Plotinus as "species" (εἴδη), "ideas" (ἰδέαι), "intellects" (νόες), or "intellections" (νοήσεις) are termed in Maximus as "logoi" since they are not only intellectual principles but also creative ones. In other words, there is a fusion in Maximus between the second and the third ontological level that is between the principle of intellection and the efficient cause of the world. Finally, in Maximus, the third hypostasis, the Spirit, even if the Spirit not the creator par excellence, is participating in the common divine act of creation, and what is more peculiar to him, he vivifies it and brings it to its perfect eschatological fulfillment. In other words, the third hypostasis is indeed a principle of life as in the Neoplatonists, but also of perfection in a rather Judeo-Christian eschatological sense. One could add that Maximus's metaphysics are closer to Proclus than to Plotinus. There is no smooth degradation from the higher hypostasis to the lower reality. Sometimes the higher and the lower interact directly.

One could also add that the Patristic version of Neoplatonism, including the Maximian one, is arguably closer to Middle Platonism, as Torstein Tollefsen remarks.[53] According to Antiochus of Ascalo (ca. 125 to ca. 68 BC), the divine ideas are conceived as dynamic logoi in God, while in Plutarch (46–120 AD) the ideas are contained by the Logos. In Philo of Alexandria (ca. 20 BC to ca. 50 AD) God is the Intellect, transcending every predicate, but the paradigm is created by God, existing in the divine thought, that is, in the divine Logos.[54] In Origen (184–253) the divine wisdom and providence are thoughts that constitute an intelligible world inside the Logos.[55] Thus one could see the Maximian version of Neoplatonism either as a Christian novelty that was destined to respond to the needs of Judeo-Christian soteriology or as an archaism, because the Confessor was inspired by the Alexandrinian Patristic tradition that preserved some currents of thought that were antecedent to Plotinus. What is peculiar to Maximus is his sharp distinction between on the one hand the logoi as dynamic uncreated principles and the universals as created ones.[56] For Maximus, universals are created, unlike what Dexippus and Ammonius have to say about them existing in the Intellect.[57] On the other hand, the logoi are not necessarily connected with the universals, since

53. Tollefsen, *Christocentric Cosmology of St Maximus the Confessor*, 33.

54. See the analysis of *De Opificio Mundi* in Tollefsen, *Christocentric Cosmology of St Maximus the Confessor*, 34.

55. See the analysis in Tollefsen, *Christocentric Cosmology of St Maximus the Confessor*, 36.

56. Max. *Ambig.* 1.290 Constas Amb.7 (PG 91,1080A).

57. See Max. *Ambig.* 1.290 Constas Amb.7 (PG 91,1080A) and its analysis in Tollefsen, *Christocentric Cosmology of St Maximus the Confessor*, 87.

there are logoi not only for genera and species, but also for individuals.[58] It is true, however, that the logoi open the created beings to the catholicity of meaning and to wide universal interconnections owing to their assumption by Christ. For the needs of the current endeavor, I see the thought of the Confessor more as a genuine Christian synthesis that follows in the steps of Ps.-Dionysius, who in turn follows the Proclean tradition. At the same time, it could be argued that this synthesis repeats in a more elaborate way some efforts of early Alexandrinian Christian philosophy, which was prior to Plotinus's theology of the eminent One that evades thought and intellection.

These particularities of the Maximian conception, which arguably bring him closer to Proclus than to Plotinus, have consequences for the subject that I would like to develop; namely, participation in the transcendent God. The logoi are both logoi of God and logoi of beings. They are logoi of God in the sense that God is the subject of logoi: God speaks through the logoi and thus expresses his will. And they are logoi of beings in the sense that the beings are the objects(-to-be) of logoi. There is thus continuity between the logoi of God that is the manifestation of God, his wills and his energies, and the logoi of beings that is the logical principles that explain beings and maintain them in consistence. These logoi as divine wills (a notion inherited by Ps.-Dionysius and Clement of Alexandria) concern God in his totality but are situated par excellence in the second hypostasis of Son the Logos.

We can now assess the Maximian Trinitarian theology in comparison to the Neoplatonic one in a more complete way: St. Maximus is following the Judeo-Christian tradition in stressing the absolute natural otherness of the uncreated God in relation to the created world. There is no natural continuity between the two whatsoever. The other side of this belief is a lack of ontological or natural hierarchy between the hypostases of the Trinity. The three persons share in the same nature and activity. In St. Maximus, however, there is a sort of hypostatic or personal order between them, which is also contemplated in a psychological way, thus echoing Neoplatonism. The Father is the cause of the Son as the Intellect is the cause of Reason. The Spirit is also caused by the Intellect and accompanies the Reason in the latter's "generation." What Maximus receives from Neoplatonism is a certain generation of structured formative content from absolute eminent

---

58. Max. *Ambig.* 1.290 Constas Amb.7 (PG 91,1080A); Max. *Ambig.* 2.114–16 Constas (PG 91,1312B–D).

simplicity and the relation between the two. In doing so, he is arguably performing a genuine synthesis between Christianity and Platonism and not just a superficial Christianization of Platonism. But it is equally important to note the differences and their existential consequences for the type of methexis that is possible for man. (1) In Maximus, there is no divine simplicity that transcends divine intellection and volition. (2) St. Maximus is less interested in the intellectual forms (ἰδέαι, εἴδη) as contents of the divine intellect and more interested in the logoi as active utterances of the God of the Bible, who creates through what one might be tempted to call "speech-acts," if one is allowed to use a term of contemporary performance studies. Thus man is called to participate not in eternal forms, but in dynamic wills of God that accompany his activity.

These logoi can be contemplated by the human intellect, but not as forms. They are rather uncreated wills[59] that precede the forms, the latter being considered rather as created results of the logoi. This means that the participation of man in the divine Logos is more mystical in character since it does not involve the intellection of a divine formative principle; it is rather an intellectual coordination with a personal will. And even if one agrees with Torstein Tollefsen that the doctrine of the logoi is a form of exemplarism[60] that follows in the steps of Platonic exemplarism, one should qualify this assertion by the remark that the examples are more like biblical utterances or speech-acts than Hellenic Forms, though one cannot totally exclude the latter. What is more, the logoi are centered in Christ the Logos precisely in the sense that he is the person that assumes what is most remote from divine immateriality; namely, matter. The hypostatic union of the material world with the immaterial Logos is for Maximus the absolute final goal of the creation of the cosmos in a surprising version of Aristotelian teleology. Ironically enough, Christ as Logos saves the notion of exemplarism but only through the anti-Platonic act of the Incarnation and of the assumption of informed matter. Through the Maximian Christology, the Judaistic mentality of the logoi as formless utterances is synthesized with the Hellenic emphasis on the forms, but only if the latter includes the salvation of matter. This is indeed the most counterintuitive Christian twist of Maximian Neoplatonism, even though it was in some sense foreshadowed by Proclus's insistence that there is a direct interaction of what is most remote in the ontological scale. (3) The Spirit is not a mediator or

---

59. Max. *Qu. Thal.* CCSG 7,95 Laga and Steel (PG 90,293D–296B).
60. Tollefsen, *Christocentric Cosmology of St Maximus the Confessor*, 21.

an efficient cause of creation, but rather the One who opens creation to its post-historical future, accompanying the Word and constituting his eschatological character. The Trinitarian structure of human participation in the divine transcendence could thus be regarded as a methexis of the divine Logos in the Spirit so that man can be referred to the absolute simplicity of the divine Intellect, that is, the Father. Or, in Maximian psychological terms, the human intellect contemplates the logoi in the Spirit in order to arrive through them to the hypostatic principle of the Logos and through him to the Father as the most eminent simplicity of intellectual selfhood. In this participation, man does not abandon the body, the latter being completely valorized by Chalcedonian Christology, as we shall now observe.

Analogical Participation, Motion, and Eschatology

The Trinitarian theology of the logos corresponds to a relevant anthropology, since the human soul is considered as being an image of the divine one. According to its Trinitarian structure, the human soul comprises the nous (intellect), the logos (reason but also speech, discourse, verb, language), and the pneuma (spirit but also breath, voice). Thus the human logos corresponds to the divine Logos. Man can undertake a dialogue, a dia-logos, with God because he is given the gift of logos. And just as God possesses the Logos who manifests divine being, in the same sense man can be expressed and manifested through his own logos. This dialogue between God and man necessarily takes place at the level of the contingent historical modes (tropoi) by which the created nature is activated.[61] But the human logos as a natural power or faculty is an indispensable presupposition.

This dia-logical notion of participation is based on a more rudimentary ontology, according to which participation is a communication of being.[62] As I have already noted, there is a threefold schema in Maximus: (1) God in himself is above being; (2) his activities or energies constitute an ontological "realm" "around God"[63] where being proper as well as eternity, simplicity, goodness, infinity, immutability, life, virtue, holiness, and the like are to be found; and (3) created beings lack being because they are constantly threatened by nonbeing.[64] Maximus's particularly Christian

---

61. Skliris, "Le concept de 'tropos' chez Maxime le Confesseur."
62. Portaru, "Classical Philosophical Influences," 130.
63. Max. *Ambig.* 1.372 Constas PG 91,1220C.
64. In the *Chapters on Theology*, Maximus distinguishes between the "works" that God has

outlook is that the participation of created beings in being proper as an activity of the transcendent God happens through Christ and the hypostatic union. The Confessor thus inherits the Neoplatonic schema of remaining- procession and return (μονή-πρόοδος-ἐπιστροφή) with the following twists. (1) The procession is primarily a procession of divine energies since beings in themselves are only results of these energies, being created ex nihilo.[65] (2) The return acquires in Maximus a historical, Christological, and eschatological character. The logoi of beings point to the manifestation of God's will in the eschaton. They are situated inside the Logos also in the sense that Christ realizes the raison d'être of created nature through his incarnation, the full ontological consequences of which will only be manifested in the eschaton. The logoi as divine wills also mean the way in which particular natural capacities are assumed by the incarnated Christ. Thus, inside history, the wise man is invited to discern the logoi—that is, the divine wills—behind creatures and to conform his life to them, thus participating in the divine energy that acts through the logoi. Participation thus leads to deification, which is but the supreme form of participation.[66] As in Neoplatonism, the ontological notion of participation is intermingled with an ethical one, but the latter acquires a historical and eschatological perspective in a way that is foreign to the Platonic emphasis on protology.

Maximus wishes to formulate this itinerary from protology to eschatology in a philosophical idiom. He uses a theory of motion according to which movement is a passage from potentiality to actualization in view of a final goal in an Aristotelian fashion,[67] but in an eclectic way he combines it with a Neoplatonic conception of the divine efficient cause of motion.[68] The final goal of motion is participation in God, but in order to understand the Maximian notion of participation, one has to study first the polysemy of the notion of energeia,[69] since the participation of beings in God is considered as tantamount to God being active and operating in them.[70] The energeia can mean the actualization of a being's capacities as in Aristotle.

---

started (τὰ ἔργα ὧν ἤρξατο) and those that he has not started (ὧν οὐκ ἤρξατο). The latter are the eternal activities that are participated in (τὰ ὄντα μεθεκτὰ), whereas the former are the created beings that participate in them (τὰ ὄντα μετέχοντα). See Max. *Cap. Theol.* I,47–48 PG 90, 1100B–1101A. In Max. *Carit.* 3,25 PG 90,1024B–C they are also called God's "properties" (ἰδιώματα).

65. Portaru, "Classical Philosophical Influences," 137.

66. Portaru, "Classical Philosophical Influences," 137.

67. Compare Max. *Ambig.* I 82 Constas (PG 91,1072C) and Arist. *Met.* A, 2,994B16 Ross.

68. Portaru, "Classical Philosophical Influences," 139–40.

69. Ayroulet, *De l'image à l'image*, 244–48.

70. Tollefsen, *Activity and Participation in Late Antique and Early Christian Thought*, 210.

As such, it can mean the natural constitutive power (συστατική δύναμις) of a nature, its first and most particular characteristic or the one that gives it its specific form.[71] In the *Dispute with Pyrrhus*, the natural energeia is considered as an innate distinctive mark (ἔμφυτος χαρακτήρ) of nature.[72] In this sense, essence is constituted by the proper energeia of a being: "essence is basically energeia," as Torstein Tollefsen puts it.[73] Sometimes, the Maximian notion of energeia is closer to the Plotinian one, as it means a productive natural power or capacity.[74]

According to Torstein Tollefsen, we could better understand Maximus if we consider the Plotinian theory of double activity.[75] The internal activity of each being is its actuality. The external activity is dependent on the internal one but also distinct from it. The external energeia is the power that manifests the essence; it is the natural movement by which the essence is participated. In God the internal activity is unknown, while the external one is participated by created beings. But unlike Plotinus, the bringing forth of the cosmos is not an incidental result.[76] God, who is unmovable by nature, can even be said to move out of love for the beings he creates in an unexpected Maximian (but also Dionysian) twist of Hellenic philosophy.[77] Thus, in the Maximian schema of remaining, procession, and return, God's activity is exercised to creation through the logoi that are volitional utterances for the creation, the providence, and the eschatological future of created beings. The divine energeia is considered as a whole in which beings participate according to logical principles limiting their receptive capacity.[78] God is both active everywhere as a whole in a common way (κοινῶς) and in a particular manner in each different being (ἰδιαζόντως).[79] The sheer act of being is already a participation in the divine energeia. But beings with the capacity of self-movement (αὐτεξούσιον) can participate more fully according to their deliberate fitness (ἐπιτηδειότης).[80] The no-

---

71. See Max. *Ambig.* 1.30–58 Constas (PG 91,1045D–1060D) and its assessment in Portaru, "Classical Philosophical Influences," 141.

72. Max. *Pyrr.* 603 Doucet (PG 91,348A).

73. Tollefsen, *Activity and Participation in Late Antique and Early Christian Thought*, 75.

74. Plot. 5.4.2 Henry and Schwyzer.

75. Tollefsen, *Activity and Participation in Late Antique and Early Christian Thought*, 76–77.

76. Tollefsen, *Activity and Participation in Late Antique and Early Christian Thought*, 122.

77. Max. *Ambig.* 1.340 Constas (PG 91,1204D–1205A).

78. Tollefsen, *Activity and Participation in Late Antique and Early Christian Thought*, 211.

79. Max. *Ambig.* 1.448–50 Constas (PG 91,1257A–C).

80. See Max. *Carit.* 3,25 PG 90, 1024B–C; *Cap. Theol.* 1,47–48 PG 90,1100B–1101A; *Ambig.* 1.278–80 Constas (PG 91,1172B–C); *Ambig.* 1.290–92 Constas (PG 91,1080B). Being and eternal being are given to the essence of creatures, while goodness and wisdom are given to the gnomic fitness. The human will is in a condition of being prepared for the divine grace.

tion of fitness was introduced by the commentators of Aristotle in late antiquity exactly as an amelioration of the Stagirite's doctrine of potency and actualization, since the commentators have realized that potentiality is a necessary condition for actualization, but not a sufficient one.[81] But the schema of πρόοδος and ἐπιστροφή is developed in later Neoplatonists, such as Proclus, stemming from Plotinus's theory about the double activity. In the Proclean version of the Plotinian double activity, "every effect remains in its cause, proceeds from it, and converts to it."[82] The effect is brought forward by an activity of the cause that is initially internal.[83]

In the *Ambiguum 7*, Maximus employs a terminology of Proclean inspiration (συνεκτικὴ πρόοδος-ἐπιστρεπτικὴ ἀναφορά)[84] but gives a different signification. Maximus does inherit the notion that the effect undergoes a procession, then a conversion, and remains in its cause, but for him this happens through the contingent adventure of history and its eschatological fulfillment. The conversion means a free coordination of the motion of intellectual beings with their logos.[85] The triad of remaining-procession-returning is joined to those of beginning-middle-end (ἀρχή-μεσότης-τέλος) and essence-power/potentiality-activity/actualization (οὐσία-δύναμις-ἐνέργεια).[86] The energeia is an actualization, as to act in a virtuous way means to initiate the state of virtue.[87] But the final goal transcends this actualization, since it is beyond nature. The actualization of human nature in Christ entails a radical novelty: it is a novel mode of existence (τρόπος) of created nature. The human nature of Christ is modified in a divine way, and even the divine nature receives a new mode of permanent coexistence with the human one. Since, for Maximus, this does not bring about a change of either nature in its logos, the new mode of each nature takes place at the level of its activity. But this new conception of activity takes us far from both Neoplatonism and Aristotelianism. In the eschatological end, the final deification is a rest (stasis), which is also a cessation (telos) of becoming. In a paradoxical way, the peak of the natural energeia is identical to the passive reception of divinization.[88] At the same time, this is not a restriction of

<hr>

81. Tollefsen, *Christocentric Cosmology of St Maximus the Confessor*, 185; Sambursky, *Physical World of Late Antiquity*, 106.

82. Procl. *ET* 35 Dodds.

83. Procl. *ET* 25–39 Dodds.

84. Max. *Ambig.* I 100–102 Constas (PG 91,1081C).

85. Max. *Ambig.* I 96–98 Constas (PG 91,1080C).

86. Tollefsen, *Activity and Participation in Late Antique and Early Christian Thought*, 145.

87. Tollefsen, *Activity and Participation in Late Antique and Early Christian Thought*, 146.

88. Max. *Ambig.* 1.96 Constas (PG 91,1080B); I 372–74 (Constas PG 91,1220D). I develop this in Skliris, "Ontological Implications of Maximus the Confessor's Eschatology."

human capacities, but an infinite expansion. This eminent coincidence of activity and passivity in the act of divinization is more reminiscent of the Iamblichan theurgy.[89]

Conclusions

The notions of participation and activity are linked in the sense that the participation in the uncreated is the presence of the uncreated in the created through its activity. But the created participates in this presence with its own activity. For Maximus, even being entails participation, but participation in virtue and goodness is a higher form of participation that is enjoyed only by intellectual beings when they turn their intellect toward God.[90] This participation takes place in the *ecclesia*, which is considered as the mystical body of Christ that can coincide with the whole of the human political community or even with the intelligible world.[91] It seems that this intimate connection of the psyche and the polis was the everlasting legacy of Platonism to Patristic thought, with the important qualification that the Christian Fathers like St. Maximus saw the soul as an image of the Trinity and replaced the polis by the new polis of the *ecclesia*. There is thus a deep interconnection between the Trinity, the soul, and the new polis of the *ecclesia* that constitutes a profound echo of Neoplatonism in Maximian thought.

89. Portaru, "Classical Philosophical Influences," 141–42.
90. Tollefsen, *Activity and Participation in Late Antique and Early Christian Thought*, 183.
91. Mueller-Jourdan, *Typologie spatio-temporelle de l'Ecclesia byzantine*, 129–32.

CHAPTER 10 ❙ Plato's *Parmenides* in
Seventh-Century Constantinople

George of Pisidia's *Hexameron*,
1639–93

Frederick Lauritzen

Plato's *Parmenides* is one of the most influential texts in Byzantine philosophy. Its influence is so pervasive that many of the notions and conclusions written by Plato are familiar from philosophical texts between 284 and 1453. The first hypothesis concerning the One (137c4–142b1) contains a number of negative definitions that become the backbone of Byzantine negative theology, both pagan and Christian.[1] The ancients, like contemporary scholars, have questioned what Plato intended by the contrast one and many. The Neoplatonists, followed by the Byzantines, understood the hypotheses as levels of reality. Proclus is explicit that the dialogue is not a logical exercise,[2] as the Middle Platonists had claimed.[3] Dillon and Morrow

1. The list in Appendix A will be familiar to scholars of Plato, but also to Byzantinists.

2. ἀλλ᾽ οὐχ, ὥς τινες ᾠήθησαν, ἄψυχόν τινα καὶ κενὴν τῶν πραγμάτων μετιὼν τὴν λογικὴν γυμνασίαν (Procl. *In Prm* 1051.30–1052.2 Steel). Procl. *Theol. Plat.* 1.9 Saffrey Westerink.

3. Alb. *Intr.* 3 Hermann; Alb. *Didasc.* 6.6 Louis. While Middle Platonists seem to limit the Parmenides to a logical exercise, Dodds has discussed the origin of the metaphysical reading at this time ("Parmenides of Plato and the Origin of the Neoplatonic One").

point out that orthodox Platonism adopted the ontological reading starting from Plotinus onward (*Enn.* 5.1.8).[4] Plotinus's *Enneads* were published in 301,[5] and therefore during the period 284–1453 the most familiar reading was the ontological one. Such a reading was widely accepted: Plotinus, Porphyry, Iamblichus, Proclus, and Damascius accept the idea that Plato's *Parmenides* is an ontological treatise defining the One and the structure of reality. That means that between 301 and 529,[6] such a reading was part of orthodox Platonism. This was accepted also by Dionysius the Areopagite,[7] who uses such an interpretation of the *Parmenides* without referring to either the dialogue or the author.

The seventh century is the main concern here, specifically the period between 610 and 681, the period of debate on the relation between an unknowable or generally unparticipated divine and the structure of reality or nature. Much of the surviving philosophy in the decades after 529 seems focused on Aristotelian commentaries,[8] even if through a Platonic lens.[9] For this reason, the poem the *Hexameron* of George of Pisidia, is important. It is dedicated to Sergius patriarch of Constantinople and therefore may be dated between 610 and 638. Moreover, it was written in Constantinople. It is therefore essential proof that the Platonic texts were in Constantinople before the rise of Islamic scholarship, in Damascus or Baghdad. This is obvious given that the oldest Greek manuscripts of Plato originate from Constantinople.[10]

The question of George of Pisidia is philosophical. This essay will prove that he read Plato's *Parmenides* either directly or through a Platonic commentary. One will focus only on the section of his poem dealing with the

---

4. While Dodds, "Parmenides of Plato and the Origin of the Neoplatonic One," explored previous cases, he explains that Plot. 5.1.8 Henry Schwyzer (dated ca. 253–63) is the first major metaphysical reading of the second half of the Parmenides. See Proclus's *Commentary on Plato's Parmenides*, xxvii.

5. Porphyry was sixty-eight years old when he published the *Enneads* (Porph. *Plot.* 23 Henry Schwyzer). Porphyry was thirty when he met Plotinus first during the tenth year of emperor Gallienus's reign (253–68) (Porph. *Plot.* 4 Henry Schwyzer). This would mean that Porphyry published the *Enneads* during the reign of Diocletian (284–305) and specifically when Diocletian became Augustus in residence at Antioch (299–302).

6. Cameron, "Last Days of the Academy at Athens."

7. Corsini, *Il trattato 'De divinis nominibus.'* Dillon and Wear, *Dionysius the Areopagite and the Neoplatonist Tradition*, chap. 8, is about Plato's *Parmenides*, hypothesis 1.

8. Some names are Philoponus, Olympiodorus, Priscian, Simplicius.

9. Some examples of the exegetical techniques are discussed in Sorabji, *Philoponus and the Rejection of Aristotelian Science*; Perkams, "Priscian of Lydia"; Baltussen, *Philosophy and Exegesis in Simplicius*.

10. Wilson, "List of Plato Manuscripts."

divine, specifically lines 1639–93.[11] Sometimes George of Pisidia follows closely the notions present in the *Parmenides*, mainly the question of parts and wholes, place and movement. He summarizes the question of comparison with the term ἀόριστος, older/younger and becoming with the term ἄχρονος and knowability with ἄγνωστος. Fundamentally, George of Pisidia seems to subdivide the first hypothesis into six categories: (1) wholes/parts, (2) place, (3) movement, (4) definition, (5) time, and (6) knowability. The first three seem important to him; the latter three are defined more briefly.

This is extraordinary. The poem is about nature and yet there is an overlap with the themes present in the first hypothesis of Plato's *Parmenides*. This could be because of the overarching influence of the ontological reading of the hypotheses since Plotinus.[12] Such an interpretation avoids the point of the poem, however. George of Pisidia says Porphyry is wrong,[13] Proclus is wrong.[14] He says Aristotle missed the point and needs to be corrected by Plato.[15] Therefore Pisides thinks Aristotle wrong and that a Platonic interpretation is necessary. Yet he indicates that Proclus's interpretation is also wrong within the Platonic tradition, and it may be argued that Pisides believes Proclus is wrong about the One, that is, wrong about first hypothesis of Plato's *Parmenides*. Therefore the passage of 1639–93 indicates that there is a plurality within the highest principle. Neoplatonists believe this is a question of interpretation of hypothesis one of Plato's *Parmenides*.[16] Proclus claims that the first hypothesis concerns the One.[17] Iamblichus claims that there is a plurality within this hypothesis.[18] Damascius claims

11. The text and translation may be found in appendix A.

12. Plot. 5.1.8 Henry Schwyzer (treatise 10 Porph. Plot. and therefore dated 253–63 but published 301).

13. τῷ Πορφυρίῳ γλῶσσα μὲν τεθηγμένη, | γνώμης δὲ φύρσις ἀστατεῖν εἰθισμένη (Geo. Pis. *Hex.* 1058–59 Gonnelli).

14. Geo. Pis. *Hex.* 61–80 Gonnelli.

15. Ἀλλ᾽ εἰπὲ λοιπὸν τῷ Σταγειρίτῃ, Πλάτων, // καὶ τὸν μαθητὴν πεῖσον, εἰ πείσεις λέγων, // ἐκ τῶν ἄνω κάτελθε, καὶ λάλει κάτω, // μήπως ἐπαρθεὶς τῷ μεταρσίῳ θράσει, // ὥσπερ νεοττὸς αἰετοῦ, καὶ μὴ θέλων // αὖθις κατέλθῃς, μὴ φέρων τὸν ἥλιον (Geo. Pis. *Hex.* 581–86).

16. Proclus gives an overview of previous interpretations in Procl. *In Prm.* 1052–54 Steel.

17. Procl. *In Prm.* 1065.1 Steel. Procl. *Theol. Plat.* 1.7 Saffrey Westerink.

18. Iamblichus claims there are two principles: Μετὰ δὲ ταῦτα ἐκεῖνο προβαλλώμεθα εἰς ἐπίσκεψιν, πότερον δύο εἰσὶν αἱ πρῶται ἀρχαὶ πρὸ τῆς νοητῆς πρώτης τριάδος, ἥτε πάντη ἄρρητος καὶ ἡ ἀσύντακτος πρὸς τὴν τριάδα, καθάπερ ἠξίωσεν ὁ μέγας Ἰάμβλιχος ἐν τῷ ΚΗῳ βιβλίῳ τῆς χαλδαϊκῆς τελειοτάτης θεολογίας, ἢ ὡς οἱ πλεῖστοι τῶν μετ᾽ αὐτὸν ἐδοκίμασαν, μετὰ τὴν ἄρρητον αἰτίαν καὶ μίαν εἶναι τὴν πρώτην τριάδα τῶν νοητῶν (Dam. *Pr.* 1.86.2–7 Ruelle). Proclus says the two interpretations of hypothesis one are: it concerns God or it concerns the Gods (Procl. *In Prm.* 1065.1 Steel).

that for this reason it is necessary to postulate a higher principle[19] not discussed in Plato's Parmenides. This implies there is a plurality within the first hypothesis: the One is not really one. Damascius claims the first hypothesis discusses the "unified one" ἡνωμένον.[20] Proclus is aware of this opinion and criticizes it in *Elements of Theology*, proposition 20.

καὶ οὐκέτι τοῦ ἑνὸς ἄλλο ἐπέκεινα. ταὐτὸν γὰρ ἓν καὶ τἀγαθόν· ἀρχὴ ἄρα πάντων, ὡς δέδεικται. (Procl., ET 20.31–32 Dodds)

Beyond the one there is no further principle: for unity is identical with the Good (prop. 13) and therefore the principium of all things, as has been shown (prop. 12). (Trans. Dodds)

Thus Proclus confirms that the first hypothesis is the revelation of the ultimate principle. George of Pisidia, like Iamblichus and Damascius, claims there is a plurality within the divine. He says that God is both One and Many (1678), Everywhere and Nowhere (1677). The notion of a unified one also explains the expression τὸ ἓν μονωθέν (Pisid. *Hexaemeron* 1680), which Damascius refers to as τὸ ἡνωμένον.[21] This further explains George of Pisidia's attack on Proclus. The disagreement is not just about the nature of the Divine, but also on how to interpret hypothesis one of Plato's *Parmenides*. Therefore George of Pisidia was aware of the debates surrounding the hypotheses of Plato's *Parmenides*. He opted for opinions that were expressed by Iamblichus and Damascius. The first hypothesis represented a plurality that contained also contradictory opinions. The One could break the law of non-contradiction. But it also meant there was something superior to the One, something that Proclus denied. Therefore Plotinus and Proclus claimed that the first hypothesis referred to the One (the first principle/the divine). The One above being and above knowledge. Christians agreed since Paul had said it in the Acts of the Apostles.[22] But it also implied that the hypotheses other than the first defined what was within being. In other words, the definition of the divine was present in hypothesis one, but other hypotheses dealt with nature. They also dealt with the relation with the One. Since the One cannot be known,

---

19. καὶ πρὸ τοῦ ἑνὸς ἄρα τὸ ἁπλῶς καὶ πάντη ἄρρητον, ἄθετον, ἀσύντακτον καὶ ἀνεπινόητον κατὰ πάντα τρόπον· (Dam. *Pr.* 1.38.22–23 Ruelle).

20. Dam. *Pr.* 1.2–3 Ruelle.

21. Διὸ καὶ πάντα ἀπ' αὐτοῦ, ὅ τι πάντα, καὶ αὐτὸ πρὸ τῶν πάντων· ὥσπερ τὸ ἡνωμένον πρὸ τῶν διακεκριμένων, οὕτω τὸ ἓν πρὸ τῶν πολλῶν τὰ πάντα ἐστίν (Dam. *Pr.* 1.3.3–5 Ruelle).

22. "For as I passed by, and beheld your devotions, I found an altar with this inscription, To The Unknown God. Whom therefore ye ignorantly worship, him declare I unto you" (Acts 17:23 KJV).

when something is knowable, it is something that is below the level of the One.

Thus Proclus believes the first hypothesis is about the first principle. Iamblichus, Damascius, and George of Pisidia believe the first hypothesis somehow contains a plurality of principles. In 681, the Sixth Ecumenical Council condemned John Philoponus[23] because he argued for a plurality of principles (tritheism).[24] It also condemned the patriarch Sergius,[25] the dedicatee of George of Pisidia's poem. The point of their condemnation was the relation between the One and the Many, between the Divine and Nature. George of Pisidia's poem is not about the One or the divine, but the relation between creation and the One. Indeed, it is seventeen hundred verses concerning creation, and the theme is based on a verse of the psalm,[26] which he paraphrases thus: "how the creative and wise creation // of all creatures of God is magnified."[27] The poem is about the relation between the One and the Many. In Christian terms it is the relation between the hypostases of the Trinity and nature.

George of Pisidia's understanding of hypothesis one of the *Parmenides* hinges on the nature of Christ. In the fifth century, the Council of Chalcedon had already solved these questions (two natures of Christ, human and divine) in 451, almost two centuries before George of Pisidia's *Hexameron*. In the seventh century the debate was about the energies/activities of Christ. Both George of Pisidia and Maximus the Confessor (580–662) worry, from opposite points of view, that the Trinity would become a tetrad if

23. Condemnation of Philoponos: Ἰωάννης ὁ γραμματικός, ὁ τὴν ἐπωνυμίαν Φιλόπονος, μᾶλλον δὲ ματαιόπονος, Κόνων τε καὶ Εὐγένιος, οἱ τρεῖς τῆς τριθεΐας τρισκατάρατοι πρόμαχοι (CCP [681] act. 11, March 20, 681 480.14–16 Riedinger).

24. ἀριθμεῖται γοῦν ἡ μακαρία τριὰς οὐκ οὐσίαις καὶ φύσεσι καὶ διαφόροις θεότησιν ἢ τρισσαῖς κυριότησιν, ἄπαγε, ὡς Ἄρειοι μαίνονται καὶ οἱ τῆς νέας τριθεΐας λυττῶσιν ἡγούμενοι, οὐσίας τρεῖς καὶ φύσεις τρεῖς καὶ τρεῖς κυριότητας καὶ τρεῖς ὁμοίως κενολογοῦντες θεότητας, ἀλλ'ὑποστάσεσι καὶ ἰδιότησι νοεραῖς τελείαις καθ' ἑαυτὰς ὑφεστώσαις, ἀριθμῷ διαιρεταῖς καὶ οὐ διαιρεταῖς τῇ θεότητι (CCP [681] act. 11, March 20, 681, 424.4–9 Riedinger).

25. Θεοδώρῳ αἱρετικῷ τῷ Φαρανίτῃ ἀνάθεμα· Σεργίῳ αἱρετικῷ ἀνάθεμα· Κύρῳ αἱρετικῷ ἀνάθεμα· Ὀνωρίῳ αἱρετικῷ ἀνάθεμα· Πύρρῳ αἱρετικῷ ἀνάθεμα· Παύλῳ αἱρετικῷ ἀνάθεμα· Πέτρῳ αἱρετικῷ ἀνάθεμα· Μακαρίῳ καὶ Στεφάνῳ καὶ Πολυχρονίῳ αἱρετικοῖς ἀνάθεμα· Ἀπεργίῳ τῷ Πέργης ἐπισκοπήσαντι ἀνάθεμα· ὅλοις τοῖς αἱρετικοῖς ἀνάθεμα· πᾶσι τοῖς ἀντιποιουμένοις τῶν αἱρετικῶν ἀνάθεμα (CCP [681] act. 16, August 9, 681, 702.18–22 Riedinger).

26. Psalm 103:24 Septuaginta, which he paraphrases thus: ὡς ἐμεγαλύνθη τὰ ἔργα σου, κύριε· // πάντα ἐν σοφίᾳ ἐποίησας, // ἐπληρώθη ἡ γῆ τῆς κτήσεώς σου. "O Lord, how manifold are thy works! // in wisdom hast thou made them all: // the earth is full of thy riches" (Ps 104:24, KJV).

27. ὡς ἐμεγαλύνθη τοῦ Θεοῦ τῶν κτισμάτων // ἡ δημιουργὸς καὶ σοφὴ παντουργία (Geo. Pis. *Hex.* 9.55*ff.*=1863*ff.* Gonnelli).

one adopted the wrong theory. George of Pisidia thought that each person of the Trinity has a different activity/energy. If Christ has two energies, that would make four energies/activities.[28] Thus each activity defines a hypostasis. He understands that four activities would imply the existence of four hypostases within the Trinity. It would thus become a tetrad.[29] Conversely, Maximus the Confessor thinks that if Christ has a single activity/energy, that means that the body has an activity, which is the same as each person of the Trinity. Thus the human Jesus would become a separate substance of the same type as each person of the trinity.[30] Both George of Pisidia and Maximus the Confessor, from opposite points of view, see the question as concerning the connection between energy and hypostasis (Pisidia) or nature (Maximus). Maximus indicates that choice is between a ὑποστατικὴ ἐνέργεια and a φυσικὴ ἐνέργεια. Maximus thinks that each physical activity implies a different being.

If God is to be One, his activity is divine, according to Maximus the Confessor. His nature is divine, and therefore his activity is divine. This fits with Proclus's view that hypothesis one of the *Parmenides* contains no plurality. The ultimate principle is the source of unity and has one activity. If each person of the Trinity has an activity, there is a plurality within the first principle, according to John Philoponus. He was condemned for tritheism at the same time Sergius was condemned for monoergism. The synod

28. Energy of God the Father, energy of Holy Ghost, divine energy of Christ, human energy of Christ.

29. ἐκφαντικῇ τρανοῦντες ὀρθοδοξίᾳ // τὴν υἱότητα τοῦ λόγου σαρκουμένην // εἰς ἀλλόφυλον μὴ ῥυῆναι τετράδα, // ἀλλ᾽ ἓν πρόσωπον καὶ θεαρχίαν μίαν (190) // πρὸ σαρκὸς ὑμνεῖν καὶ μετὰ σαρκὸς λόγον, // τὸν αὐτὸν ἄνθρωπόν τε καὶ θεὸν φύσει, // μὴ προσθέσει χυθέντα, μὴ διαιρέσει // τομὴν παθόντα, μὴ τραπέντα συγχύσει, // διπλοῦν τὸν ἁπλοῦν, μηδαμοῦ πεφυρμένον (Geo. Pis. *Hex.* 187–95 Gonnelli).

30. γὰρ ὑποστατικὴν λέγομεν τοῦ Χριστοῦ τὴν μίαν ἐνέργειαν, οὐ συμβαίνει δὲ κατὰ τὴν ὑπόστασιν τῷ Πατρὶ καὶ Πνεύματι ὁ Υἱός, δῆλον ὅτι οὔτε κατὰ τὴν ὑποστατικὴν ἐνέργειαν· ἀναγκαζόμεθα δὲ ὥσπερ τῷ Υἱῷ, οὕτω καὶ τῷ Πατρί καὶ τῷ Πνεύματι ὑποστατικὰς ἐνεργείας ἀπονεῖμαι· καὶ καθ᾽ ὑμᾶς, τέσσαρας ἐνεργείας ἕξει μακαρία Θεότης· τρεῖς ἀφοριστικὰς τῶν ἐν οἷς ἐστι προσώπων, καὶ μίαν κοινὴν σημαντικὴν τῆς κατὰ φύσιν τῶν τριῶν ὑποστάσεων κοινότητος· καὶ κατὰ τοὺς Πατέρας, εἴπερ αὐτῶν δεχόμεθα τὴν διδασκαλίαν, τετραθεῖαν νοσήσομεν. Φυσικὴν γὰρ, ἀλλ᾽ οὐχ ὑποστατικὴν πᾶσαν εἶναι διαγορεύουσιν ἐνέργειαν. Καί εἰ τοῦτό ἐστιν ἀληθῶς, ὡς οὖν καὶ ἔστι, τέσσαρας φύσεις, τέσσαρας θεούς, διαφέροντας ἀλλήλων ὑποστάσει τε καὶ φύσει δειχθησόμεθα λέγοντες (Max. *Bizya* 2.14 PG 90.150D–152A Migne). ΘΕΟΔ. Τί γὰρ κακὸν ὁμολογοῦμεν, ἵνα χωρισθῇς τῆς κοινωνίας ἡμῶν; ΜΑΞ. Ὅτι μίαν ἐνέργειαν λέγοντες θεότητος καὶ ἀνθρωπότητος τοῦ Θεοῦ καὶ Σωτῆρος ἡμῶν Ἰησοῦ Χριστοῦ, συγχέετε τὸν τε τῆς θεολογίας, καὶ τῆς οἰκονομίας λόγον. Εἰ γὰρ πεισθῆναι δεῖ τοῖς ἁγίοις Πατράσι, λέγουσιν, Ὧν ἡ ἐνέργεια μία, τούτων καὶ ἡ οὐσία μία· τετράδα ποιεῖτε τὴν ἁγίαν Τριάδα, ὡς ὁμοφυοῦς τῷ Λόγῳ γενομένης τῆς αὐτοῦ σαρκός, καὶ ἐκστάσης τῆς πρὸς ἡμᾶς καὶ τῆς αὐτὸν τεκούσης συγγενοῦς κατὰ φύσιν ταυτότητος (Max. *Bizya* 1.5 PG 90.141A).

of 681 saw the two ideas as closely connected. A single energy of Jesus would imply tritheism. Thus George of Pisidia is correct to identify Proclus as his problem. One has here argued that the problem was Proclus's identification of the first hypothesis of the *Parmenides* as the actual (negative) definition of the divine, in contrast with a sort of immanent plurality present in the divine according to Iamblichus, Damascius, John Philoponus, and George of Pisidia.

One may add a curious detail. Damascius points out the problem of identifying the ultimate principle with the first hypothesis of Plato's *Parmenides* is the fact that there is always some sort of plurality. One way of thinking differently about this is by opposition through antonymia.[31] John Philoponus also often employed this same term with an interest in its grammatical sense, and finally George of Pisidia employs the term to refer to the creator declining creation according to grammatical categories in the poem. This interest in grammatical forms is present in these three writers. The term never appears in Plato, Aristotle, Plotinus, Iamblichus, or Proclus. This may indicate a specific linguistic and philological interest in the linguistic analysis and influence of Aristotle's commentators in the sixth century.

George of Pisidia had a direct interest in the *Parmenides*, and specifically hypothesis one. He employs concepts that reveal a close study of a commentator to this text. This would imply that he had read the actual dialogue of Plato. His endorsement of Plato versus Aristotle also implies that he simply preferred a commentary by such a thinker as Damascius rather than Proclus. He did not simply read the commentary; he engaged with the notions and consequences of the argument and applied them to Trinitarian thought. His choice of monoergism/monothelitism as well as the physics of John Philoponus means his ideas were condemned together with his patriarch Sergius at the council of Constantinople of 680–81.[32] Therefore one sees a direct concern for the meaning of hypothesis one of Plato's *Parmenides* in seventh-century Constantinople. A non-Proclean reading of this part of the dialogue requires ideas that were condemned in the Sixth Ecumenical Council of 681 as not orthodox.

31. Εἰ τοίνυν μηδὲ ἓν εἴη, μήτε πρὸς τὸ ἓν ἀντιδιαστελλόμενον διὰ τῆς ἀντωνυμίας, οὐκ ἔσται αὐτοῦ τὸ μὴ εἶναι καθ᾽ ἑτερότητα τὴν πρὸς τὸ κυρίως ἕν (Dam. *In Prm.* 306.17–19 Ruelle).

32. See Lauritzen, "Late Antique Philosophy and the Poetry of George of Pisidia."

Appendix A

The terms employed in Plato's Parmenides are familiar in Byzantine theology, and one may find them in Dionysius the Areopagite, in the Ambigua of Maximus Confessor (A), and in the Triads of Gregory Palamas (T).

	Plato	Dion.Areop.	Maximus Conf.	Palamas
ἀμέριστον	137c	136.16	A22.3.6	T3.1.34
ἄναρχον	[137d]	153.16	A16.1.5	T1.1.14
ἀτελεύτητον	[137d]	153.16	A10.46.11	T1.3.27
ἄπειρον	137d	220.20	A10.46.12	T2.3.31
ἀσχημάχιστος	[137d]	114.5	A17.11.5	T2.3.23
ἀμερές	138a	213.22	A22.3.6	T1.3.45
ἄτοπον	[138b]	194.5	—	—
ἄστατον	[138b]	220.20	A10.13.10	T2.1.9.7
ἀστασίαστος	—	220.8	A1.22	—
ἀκίνητον	138b	213.15	A10.88.17	T2.2.19.26
ἀναλλοιωτόν	[138c]	130.11	A16.1.5	T1.3.30.15
ἀόριστον	—	220.20	A10.58.1	—
οὐκ ὅμοιον	139e	207.7	A20.7.12	T2.3.31.4
οὐκ ἀνόμοιον	139e	207.7	A16.2.1	—
οὐκ ἴσον	140b	213.22	A17.12.9	—
οὐκ ἄνισον	140b		A67.10.5	—
οὐ μεῖζον	140bc	164.15	A17.12.8	T3.1.13.4
οὐκ ἔλαττον	140bc	164.15		T3.1.13.5
οὐ πρεσβύτερον	141a	215.19	A10.97.10	
οὐ νεώτερον	141a	215.19		
ἀγένητον	141e	210.1	A10.90.15	T3.17.15
ἀνώνυμος	142a	118.2	—	—
ἄλογος	142a	196.10	A10.91.14	—
ἀνεπίστατος	142a	—	—	—
ἄνους		196.9		
ἀναίσθητος	142a	196.9	—	T2.2.8
ἀδόξαστος	142a			

Appendix B: George of Pisidia's Definition of God (*Hexaemeron*, 1639–93 Gonnelli)

[ἄπειρον, ἄστατος, ἀκίνητος, ἄμορφος, ἄδηλος]
τὸ σὸν γὰρ εἰς ἄπειρον ἐκτείνας κράτος
φαίνῃ καλύπτῃ καὶ προέρχῃ καὶ μένεις (1640)
στάσει τρεχούσῃ καὶ φορᾷ πεπηγμένῃ
καὶ τὰς ἀμόρφους εἰδοποιῶν οὐσίας.
[ἀμέριστον, ἄναρχον, ἀσχήματον, ἄγνωστος, ἀόριστος]
αὐτὸς δὲ τοῦ σύμπαντος ἐξῃρημένος
ὑπερτελὴς εἶ· καὶ γὰρ ἀρχὴν οὐκ ἔχεις,
τέλους ἀπέστης καὶ διέστης τοῦ μέσου, (1645)
ἐκτὸς βεβηκὼς τῶν τριῶν καὶ τῶν ὅλων
ἐντὸς πεφυκὼς τῶν ὅλων ἐκτὸς μένεις·
πρόδηλος ὢν ἄδηλος, οὐκ ἔχων ὅρους,
ἀλλ' ὢν ὁρισμὸς τῶν ὁριζόντων ὅρων·
[ἄναρχος, ἄχρονος]
ἄρχων ἀνάρχως, οὐ μετρούμενος χρόνῳ, (1650)
ῥοπῇ δὲ ποιῶν ἀχρόνῳ τὰ τοῦ χρόνου.
[grammatical concepts]
Ὡς ἔντεχνος δὲ τῶν φρενῶν ἐπιστάτης
πᾶσάν τε πρᾶξιν τεχνολογεῖν ἠσκημένος
καὶ πᾶν μὲν εἰδὼς ὄνομα καὶ ῥῆμα ξένον
καὶ λεπτὸν ἄρθρον καὶ μετοχὴν κεκρυμμένην, (1655)
ἀντωνυμίαν δὲ πᾶσαν ἠκριβωμένος,
προθέσει δὲ πάσῃ μέτρα δοὺς ἡρμοσμένα
τὸν πάντα κόσμον εἰς ἐπίρρημα τρέπεις,
εἰ μὴ τὸ σὸν συνεῖδεν ἀρρήτως κράτος,
συζευκτικὸν σύνδεσμον ἐμβαλεῖς ὅλοις. (1660)
ἀεὶ δὲ δεικνὺς τεχνικὰς ἐπεκτάσεις
ἄπαντα γίνῃ πρὸς τό σοι δεδογμένον,
μέλλων ἐνεστὼς παρατατικὸς παρακείμενος,
σὺν τοῖς δε … ἄμα
ἀόριστος ὑπερσυντελικός· ἐγκλίσεις νέμων, (1665)
ὁριστικὴν ἀπαρέμφατον εὐκτικὴν πλέον.
[ἄρρητος, ἄμορφος, ἄστατον, ἀκίνητον, ἄγνωστος]
ἐνθεὶς δὲ ταῦτα τῇ τέχνῃ τῇ ἀρρήτῳ
προστακτικῷ δὲ πάντα μορφώσας λόγῳ,
ὑποτακτικήν σοι δημιουργεῖς τὴν κτίσιν
πάμμορφος ὢν ἄμορφος, οὐκ ἔχων στάσιν, (1670)
οὐκ ἴχνος οὐ κίνησιν οὐ γνωστὴν βάσιν·
πάντων γὰρ εἰ κίνησις ἢ πάντων βάσις,

ἁπλοῦς μεθεκτὸς πρῶτος ἔσχατος μέσος,
ὑψηλὸς εὐρὺς ἀπλατὴς βαθὺς μέγας,
οὐδὲν δὲ τούτων, ἀλλ᾽ ἐν ἀβάτοις ὅροις (1675)
τῆς σῆς ἐπήξω μυστικῆς ἐξουσίας.
[πανταχοῦ, οὐδαμοῦ, πάντα καὶ ἕν, ἀναίσθητος, ἀπερίληπτος]
Ὁ πανταχοῦ μὲν οὐδαμοῦ δὲ καὶ πάλιν
καὶ πάντα καὶ ἕν (ταῦτα γὰρ συναπτέον),
μήπως ὑπαχθῇ τοῖς κατ᾽ αἴσθησιν τύποις
τὸ ἓν μονωθέν, τῇ δὲ πάντα συνθέσει (1680)
δηλοῦντες αὐτοῦ τὴν ἀπερίληπτον φύσιν,
αὖθις τό γ᾽ ἐγκρίνωμεν ἠκριβωμένως,
μήπως τὰ πάντα σχῇ κακὴν ὑποψίαν,
καὶ δῶμεν εἱρμὸν τῇ ῥεούσῃ συνθέσει.
[πανταχοῦ, ἄτοπος, ἀμέριστος, ἀνούσιος]
τὸ πανταχοῦ δὲ τὸν θεὸν πεφυκέναι (1685)
τῇ μηδαμοῦ πρόσεστιν ἀντισυνθέσει,
μήπως μερισθὲν τῇ διχῇ διαστάσει
τὸ μηδαμοῦ μὲν εἰς ἀνούσιον ῥέπῃ,
τὸ πανταχοῦ δὲ τοῖς μεριστοῖς ἁρμόσῃ,
ἀλλ᾽ ἀντιγόμφοις ὡς ἂν εἴποι τις λόγοις (1690)
τὸ πάντα καὶ ἓν καὶ τὸ μηδαμοῦ πάλιν
τῇ πανταχοῦ σφίγγοντες ἀντιφθεγγίᾳ
στερρὸν τὸ βάθρον πήξομεν τῶν δογμάτων.

You have extended your power to infinity,
You appear, hide, advance and remain (1640)
with running rest and fixed movement.
You also give form to shapeless beings.
You yourself, transcend everything,
you are superior: and you do not have a beginning
you were away from the end and distant from the middle. (1645)
you have gone outside the Trinity and outside of everything.
Though born within everything, you remain outside everything.
Visible though invisible: you do not have a limit,
though you are the definition of the defining limits.
Ruling through anarchy, not measured by time, (1650)
You create time by a timeless influence.
You are the artful master of minds,
taking care to elaborate each action.
You know every noun, unusual verb,
fine article and hidden conjunction. (1655)
You are precise about each opposition.
You gave proportioned balance with every adjective,

You turn the entire world into an adverb,
Even if it did not recognise your ineffable power.
You will apply a connecting conjunction to everything. (1660)
You always show artistic evolutions.
Everything occurs according to your decision
Future, present, past, perfect
With the … together
Aorist, plusperfect: you distribute moods (1665)
Indicative, infinitive, optative, more.
You set it with ineffable art,
you shaped everything with your command,
you create the subordinate creation.
All-shaped though shapeless: you do not have rest (1670)
nor trace, nor movement nor known foundation.
You are the movement of all, the foundation of all.
Simple, participated, the first, the last, the middle,
High, wide, without breadth, deep, great,
None of these, but on untrodden mountains (1675)
You established your secret power.
The one who is nowhere and again,
Both everything and one (this must be understood).
May it not be led by sensible types,
The unified one, always by combination (1680)
We reveal its unreachable nature.
And once more we may judge him precisely
So that everything does not have a bad suspicion
And we may start with a flowing combination
God is everywhere. (1685)
He is present by his being nowhere by opposition.
Yet he is not divided by separate division.
His being nowhere does not incline towards non-being.
His being everywhere fits with the divided beings
But with opposing words one would say (1690)
That he is everything and one and nowhere again.
We bind them by contradictions which are everywhere
And we will establish them as the solid foundation of beliefs.

Appendix C

	Plato	Pisides *Hexameron*	
ἀμέριστον	137c	1645	
ἄναρχον	137d	1644; 1650	
ἀτέλευτον	137d	ὑπερτελής 1644	
ἄπειρον	137d	1700?	
ἀσχήματον	137d	1645, 1670?	
ἀμερές	138a	1645	
οὐ τόπος	138b	1686	
ἄστατον	138b	1670	
ἀκίνητον	138b	1671	
ἀναλλοιωτόν	138c	—	[687]
ἀόριστον	—	1648; 1665	
ἀδιάστατος		1687	
οὐκ ὅμοιον	139e	—	
οὐκ ἀνόμοιον	139e	—	
οὐκ ἴσον	140b	—	
οὐκ ἄνισον	140b	—	
οὐ μεῖζον	140bc	—	
οὐκ ἔλαττον	140bc	—	
ἄχρονος	1651		
οὐ πρεσβύτερον	141a	—	
οὐ νεώτερον	141a	—	
ἀγένητον	141e	—	
ἄγνωστος		622/873	
ἀνόμαντος	142a		
ἄλογος	142a		
ἀνεπίστατος	142a		
ἀναίσθητος	142a		
ἀδόξαστος	142a		

George Diamantopoulos

Introduction

There is no systematic study about the reception in Byzantium of the cardinal virtues' theory[1]—namely, prudence, temperance, courage, justice—which was first taught in the fourth book of Plato's *Res Publica*.[2] This doctrine is attested in several works of Nicetas Stethatos.[3] I consider his analysis on the treatise *De anima* to be the culmination of an evolution, since it is one of his last works and derives material from the *Centuriae*, which he modifies on the basis of the purpose of the treatise and the prob-

1. For the cardinal virtues in the Middle Ages, see Bejczy, *Cardinal Virtues in the Middle Ages*, based on Western Patristic and medieval sources; for further literature on Western sources, see also Shlenov, "Учение прп I," 193n4. For a short reference to Stethatos's doctrine, see also in Pentzopoulou-Valala, "Reading Nikitas Stethatos' 'On the Soul,'" 29–30. I could not access the monograph of Sotiropoulos on the four cardinal virtues (Ἡ ἀξία τῶν τεσσάρων γενικῶν ἀρετῶν εἰς τὸν ἄνθρωπον).

2. Pl. *R.* 427d–445e Slings. On Plato's teaching on the cardinal virtues in *Res Publica*, see among others Slings, *Critical Notes on Plato's "Politeia,"* 60–70; Sheppard, *Plato's Republic*, 60–68; Becker, *Platons "Politeia,"* 106–33. For the cardinal virtues in general, see also Hilpert, "Kardinaltugenden." For the cardinal virtues in the ancient world, see also Shlenov, "Учение прп II," 180–83.

3. For Nicetas Stethatos's life and works, see the literature mentioned in Diamantopoulos, *Die Hermeneutik des Niketas Stethatos*, 13–15nn2–3 (also passim and mainly 600–654). He was hieromonk and later abbot of the Stoudios monastery in the eleventh century, disciple of Symeon the New Theologian, and significant author of theological works with various content.

lems of his times. In the preamble of *De anima*, the question of the cardinal virtues is raised as one of the main issues for examination.[4] In this chapter, I present the concepts connected to the cardinal virtues in Stethatos's thought. The sources and context of the teaching will also be examined.

In a recent study in two parts, D. Shlenov[5] discussed the cardinal virtues' theory in Stethatos's thought, where the ancient and Byzantine contexts of this concept were also presented. It is a useful contribution that highlighted the originality of Stethatos and expounded the history of the concept in the Patristic and Byzantine literature. I will also discuss this paper in my study.

Terminology

Stethatos mainly uses the term γενικαὶ ἀρεταί.[6] Shlenov sees in this term the meaning "main" virtues.[7] According to him, this is explained by the fact that the four virtues govern the others.[8] Stethatos also uses the *termini* τετρακτύς[9] and ἀρχαί.[10] The latter is most likely drawn from the biblical narrative of the four rivers in Eden, which appears in Genesis 2:10. The four rivers concept is part of the *imago mundi* concept. There the cardinal virtues are regarded as constituent principles of the soul's being. I will thematize

4. Nic. Steth. *Anim.* 1.19–20 Darrouzès.

5. Shlenov, "Учение прп I" and "Учение прп II."

6. Nic. Steth. *Cap.* 1.12, PG 120, 856D; 1.72, PG 120, 884C; 1.96, PG 120, 897A; 2.12, PG 120, 905B; 3.95, PG 120, 1005B Migne; Nic. Steth. *Intr. Hymn.* 11, 168–69 Kambylis; Nic. Steth. *Ep. Prox.* 3.10 Darrouzès; Nic. Steth. *Anim.* 1.20 (paraphrase); 26.4, 27.5, 28.9, 29.2; 50.14; 54.2, 68.3 Darrouzès.

7. Shlenov, "Учение прп I," 194–95. For a short presentation of the term and its meaning in Patristic literature (also in Russian and Slavonic) and in Stethatos's works, see Shlenov, "Учение прп I," 193–95 (also ancient sources); "Учение прп II," 186–89; he did not consider all the testimonies in Stethatos's works; see notes 13, 14, 39, 54, 111, 115, and 137 in this chapter.

8. Shlenov, "Учение прп I," 204. Indeed, Stethatos teaches in Nic. Steth. *Cap.* 2.12, PG 120, 905B Migne: αἱ γενικαὶ καὶ ἄρχουσαι τὸ λοιπὸν ἀρεταί. See also Nic. Steth. *Anim.* 28.8–11 Darrouzès. In Nic. Steth. *Anim.* 54.6–7 Darrouzès, however, he believes that the highest virtue is piety enriched by love. He does not highlight explicitly any cardinal virtue against another, a distinction that is attested in the Patristic literature. See for that Shlenov, "Учение прп II," 186–89, but I think it is clear that he assumes prudence as a more important one; see more in " Knowledge of Divine and Human Things and Cardinal Virtues" below.

9. Nic. Steth. *Cap.* 3.43, PG 120, 973B; 3.49, PG 120, 977A Migne; here the τετρακτύς of the cardinal virtues is distinguished from the general virtues (γενικαὶ ἀρεταί); the latter belong together with the natural virtues (φυσικαὶ ἀρεταί) to a group of eight virtues (ὀγδοάς); Nic. Steth. *Ep. Prox.* 3.10 Darrouzès. The term is thus not used in the treatise *De anima*. The mentioned letter was attached to it, however.

10. Nic. Steth. *Anim.* 27.4, 28.10 Darrouzès; Nic. Steth. *Cap.* 2.12, PG 120, 905B; 3.49, PG 120, 977B; 3.95, PG 120, 1005B–C Migne.

this concept in the third section. Stethatos also joins the term ἀρχαί with the mentioned meaning of the γενικαὶ ἀρεταί, that the cardinal virtues rule the others; he thus means by ἀρχαί also principles that rule other things.[11] I will discuss the term τετρακτύς further in the fourth part of this chapter.

Concepts

Four-Horse Chariot

Stethatos links the four virtues to the image of a fiery four-horse chariot, which he draws from the story of the ascension of the prophet Elias.[12] We find it in the *Canon in Sanctum Nicolaum*[13] and also in the *Centuriae*,[14] but not in *De anima*. The chariot is a means of warfare against the three principal passions (avarice, carnality, ambition).[15] It is a feature of the one who has reached the second stage of spiritual perfection,[16] where apathy predominates; it then raises man to an intelligible sky. It is linked to the other characteristics, works, and goals of this stage—for example, knowledge of beings, contemplation of the creation's rational principles, intellect's purification, sublime meanings, knowledge of divine and human things, and revelation of mysteries[17]—this state is related to the life on earth (ἔτι ζῶν). A similar exaltation occurs to the one who will subdue the senses to the four virtues; the body then moves stolidly, and the passive part of the soul submits to the rational part.[18] That is, it is a means against passions, and it also lifts the soul after the victory over them. In general, the four-horse chariot is associated with the state according to nature, or the return to it.[19]

11. In some cases, both terms (ἀρχαί and γενικαὶ ἀρεταί) appear together; see Nic. Steth. *Cap.* 3.95, PG 120, 1005B; Nic. Steth. *Anim.* 27.4–5, 28.9–10 Darrouzès.

12. 2 Kgs 2:11–12 Brooke, McLean and Thackeray.

13. Nic. Steth. *Can. Nic.* 7. Ode, 2. Troparion Schirò and Kominis. This troparion mentions only virtues, not cardinal, and also the chariot of fire, not a four-horsed one, but in the other Stethatos's testimonies the four-horse chariot of fire relates to the four virtues. Shlenov, "Учение прп I" and "Учение прп II," did not discuss this passage.

14. Nic. Steth. *Cap.* 1.12, PG 120, 905B; 3.43, PG 120, 973B–C; 3.95, PG 120, 1005B–C Migne. Shlenov, "Учение прп I" and "Учение прп II," did not mention Nic. Steth. *Cap.* 3.43, PG 120, Migne. This chapter is of importance for the concept of φυσικὴ θεωρία (see below); Shlenov also did not thematize the cardinal virtues' concept of the four-horsed chariot at all.

15. Nic. Steth. *Cap.* 1.12, PG 120, 905B Migne. See on this chapter also Shlenov, "Учение прп I," 202.

16. See on this "Contemplation of Nature."

17. Nic. Steth. *Cap.* 3.3, PG 120, 973B Migne.

18. Nic. Steth. *Cap.* 3.95, PG 120, 1005B–C Migne. On this chapter, see also Shlenov, "Учение прп I," 204.

19. See on that "Κατὰ φύσιν and Virtues."

Κατὰ φύσιν and Virtues

Stethatos emphasizes that the four virtues are not acquired but constitute a creation of God and they are inherent in man.[20] They relate to man's state according to nature (κατὰ φύσιν). God set in the intelligible world of virtues the Holy Spirit so that the former would move eternally κατὰ φύσιν and not be separated from God.[21] Also, a characteristic of courage is the cut of a παρὰ φύσιν movement from the κατὰ φύσιν one.[22]

The pursuit of virtue and justice relates to the state according to nature, when the forces of the soul's tripartite (λογιστικόν, ἐπιθυμητικόν, θυμοειδές) are moving properly. Then the soul will be joined with the angels.[23] This doctrine is taught in chapter 7, where Stethatos expounds the doctrine about the movement of the soul's tripartite κατὰ φύσιν.

Thus justice is linked to the proper functioning of the tripartite.[24] Stethatos more explicitly combines the four virtues with the harmonious movement of the three forces of the soul, such as Plato,[25] in the *Centuriae*.[26] The virtues' connection to the tripartite is also evident in the attribution of the four virtues at the reason (λογιστικόν),[27] the main part of the tripartite. This also explains their relationship with the angelic life.[28]

---

20. In addition to the passages mentioned in "Four Material Elements as Paradigm for the Four Virtues" from the treatise *De anima* that speak of the creation of an intelligible world, presupposing a state κατά φύσιν, see also the passages Nic. Steth. *Cap.* 1.72, PG 120, 884C: συμπεφύκασιν ἡμῖν (the four virtues) ἐκ δημιουργίας; 2.12 Migne: Φύσει τοῖς ἀνθρώποις αἱ γενικαὶ καὶ ἄρχουσαι τὸ λοιπὸν ἀρεταὶ συνεκτίσθησαν.

21. Nic. Steth. *Anim.* 28.1–8 Darrouzès. In the parallel passage Nic. Steth. *Cap.* 3.49, PG 120, 977B–C Migne, the reference to the movement according to nature (κατὰ φύσιν) is missing; this proves that Stethatos wants to emphasize this aspect in *De anima*.

22. Nic. Steth. *Anim.* 29.23–25 Darrouzès.

23. Nic. Steth. *Anim.* 33.6–13 Darrouzès. See also, 54.1–3 Darrouzès and below in this paragraph.

24. Shlenov, "Учение прп I," 197, also observed the connection between tripartite and cardinal virtues, but without exploring exactly how this connection is described. He saw Stethatos's reference to the tripartite structure as a simple occasion for a spiritual teaching and not an adoption of platonic teachings. But the tripartite's concept is an essential element of the cardinal virtues' *imago mundi* concept and man's spiritual progress; see "*Imago Mundi, Imago Dei* and Secret Union."

25. See Pl. *R.* 434d–44d Slings.

26. See Nic. Steth. *Cap.* 1.72, PG 120, 884C; 3.95, PG 120, 1005B Migne. In Nic. Steth. *Anim.* 33.10–13 Darrouzès, however, it is taught that virtuous life leads to the victory of the rational part of the soul against the irrational. It seems, however, that according to Stethatos it is this victory that leads to the union of virtues with the soul; that is to say, the union is preceded by the sovereignty of the rational and not the other way around. See also Nic. Steth. *Anim.* 54.1–3 Darrouzès.

27. Nic. Steth. *Anim.* 68.3 Darrouzès; see also "Eschatology" below.

28. Nic. Steth. *Anim.* 32, mainly 8–10 Darrouzès.

The same reference to κατὰ φύσιν is also found in the teaching about the basis (βάσις) of the soul: the cardinal virtues stand κατὰ φύσιν and are united with the intellect's forces.[29] The condition for this union is that the activity of the bodily senses is turned to the soul's senses.[30] The soul is then united with the cardinal virtues and with the angels.[31] The perspective of the four virtues is the union of the soul with the world of angels, but at the same time they are assumed as separated from them. They constitute a preliminary stage before the angelic life. The virtues mainly concern the earthly world. The soul's βάσις doctrine is included in chapter 8. The cardinal virtues must be thus regarded also in the context of the teachings of chapters 7 and 8.

One can of course conclude that the cardinal virtues as elements, without their use for the creation of the intelligible world, do not constitute the κατὰ φύσιν state. There is a need to create an intelligible world in order to be harmonized with the material, since also in the latter the four elements in themselves are useless. The intelligible world symbolically includes all other elements of the material[32] (stars, sun, moon, light, plants, Holy Spirit as its moving force, etc.[33]) as well as the properties of the elements.[34]

The creation of the intelligible world concerns not only the prelapsarian but also the postlapsarian human, as the latter can seek the four virtues within him. This is about the recovering of the κατὰ φύσιν. The four virtues are located in the second stage of spiritual perfection, where, however, first the ascetical practice has been overcome and man has returned to κατὰ φύσιν.[35] This is when the senses submit to the four virtues. Then the latter become a four-horse chariot that leads to heavenly kingdom.[36]

29. Nic. Steth. *Anim.* 50.14–20 Darrouzès and the whole paragraph 50 with Shlenov, "Учение прп I," 201, where he made no mention of the βάσις context of this chapter. See also Nic. Steth. *Cap.* 1.72, PG 120, 884C–D Migne for the concept of the cardinal virtues' activity according to nature.

30. Nic. Steth. *Anim.* 50.1–14 Darrouzès; see also Nic. Steth. *Cap.* 3.95, PG 120, 1005B–C Migne.

31. Nic. Steth. *Anim.* 54.1–5 Darrouzès.

32. See for these material elements the chapter 2 of the treatise *De anima.*

33. See Nic. Steth. *Anim.* paragraph 27 Darrouzès and Shlenov, "Учение прп I," 197–98; Tsames, Ἡ τελείωσις τοῦ ἀνθρώπου κατὰ Νικήταν τὸν Στηθᾶτον, 24n3.

34. See Nic. Steth. *Anim.* paragraph 29 Darrouzès and Shlenov, "Учение прп I," 199–201.

35. Nic. Steth. *Cap.* 3.43, PG 120, 973B–C Migne. See also "Contemplation of Nature."

36. Nic. Steth. *Cap.* 3.95, PG 120, 1005B–C Migne. See also the passages from the *Centuriae* mentioned in "Four-Horse Chariot."

Cardinal Virtues' παρὰ φύσιν State

The four virtues as four elements, insofar as they are related to κατὰ φύσιν and angelization, do not appear to resemble the irrational part of the soul (ἐπιθυμητικόν/θυμοειδές), which, because it has a counterpart element in the material world, brutalizes the soul when it dominates,[37] even though they also have their counterpart in the material world, that is, the four material elements. That is to say, one could see a spiritualization of the four material elements in their connection to the four virtues. Yet Stethatos teaches about the virtues' state against man's nature. What exactly does Stethatos mean under the cardinal virtues' παρὰ φύσιν state? How can we understand this concept with more precision?

Stethatos talks about the demise of the cardinal virtues and the need to stay unshakable or be rebuilt through repentance.[38] He also recommends their guarding,[39] which means there is a risk of destruction. In addition, God has set the Holy Spirit as the moving force of the intelligible world of virtues;[40] therefore one can infer from this *e contrario* the possibility of the dissolution of the world of virtues.

Since Stethatos attributes virtues to the reason (λογιστικόν), we can also conceive the παρὰ φύσιν of virtues as demonization, the illness of the λογιστικόν through arrogance.[41] It is also stated, as I mentioned, that at the base of the soul the cardinal virtues stand according to nature (κατὰ φύσιν ἑστώσας) and are united with the forces of the intellect,[42] which indicates that a παρὰ φύσιν state is also presupposed, which creates a problem for their union with the intellect. The dominance of the rational part on the irrational is also assumed, which indicates that virtues may otherwise be misled. Stethatos thus considers the separation of the cardinal virtues from the forces of the intellect, the main soul's instrument for the mystical experience, as an unnatural state, which allows him to assume his positions in the context of the eleventh century's ethical debate, which I discuss in "Contextualization" below.

The four virtues can further be subdued to the senses, with the result

---

37. Nic. Steth. *Anim.* paragraphs 32–34, 36, 40, 45–47, 55–56 Darrouzès.

38. Nic. Steth. *Cap.* 2.12, PG 120, 905B Migne.

39. Nic. Steth. *Intr. Hymn.* 11.168–69 Kambylis. Shlenov, "Учение прп I" and "Учение прп II," did not mention this passage.

40. Nic. Steth. *Anim.* 28.1–8 Darrouzès.

41. See on that Nic. Steth. *Anim.* 56.1–2 Darrouzès.

42. Nic. Steth. *Anim.* 50.14–20 Darrouzès; see also Nic. Steth. *Cap.* 1.72, PG 120, 884C–D Migne.

that the body, being made up also of four elements, diverts the soul, as is inferred *e contrario* by *Centuria* 3.95. Also, in the letter *Amico proximo* the reader is urged to nourish the four virtues with spiritual teachings as the four elements of the body. In this way the reader would pay homage to them.[43] That is to say, their non-spiritual nourishment entails their death and their dishonor, in the sense that man believes that he consists only of four material and not spiritual elements. Finally, Stethatos teaches that we must seek the cardinal virtues within ourselves by restoring the activity of the soul's tripartite and converging them, aiming at their activity according to nature.[44] Consequently, their unnatural state is not their absence but their scattering.

Cardinal Virtues and *Imago Mundi*

According to this concept the soul is an image of the world, where the essential element is that they are the constituent elements of this spiritual world, as the material consists of four fundamental material elements.[45] The virtues are only a part of this image, as the soul portrays through their symbolism not only the world of matter, but also the world of angels through its rational nature and thus the whole universe and its beings.[46]

Simultaneous Creation   The existence of four virtues as four elements seems to be explained by the doctrine that the soul was built simultaneously with the body. The fact that Stethatos mentions the simultaneous doctrine in his thought that the soul was built in a similar way to the sensible world permits this hypothesis:[47] since the soul was created from the

43. Nic. Steth. *Ep. Prox.* 3.8–11 Darrouzès. See Shlenov "Учение прп I," 196, where the analogy between body's and soul's elements in this passage was not discussed.

44. Nic. Steth. *Cap.* 1.72, PG 120, 884C–D Migne. See on this chapter Shlenov, "Учение прп I," 203.

45. On these four elements, see Böhme and Böhme, *Feuer, Wasser, Erde, Luft,* and Crowley, "On the Use of Stoicheion in the Sense of 'Element.'"

46. Nic. Steth. *Anim.* chapter 6 (paragraphs 26–30) Darrouzès makes no explicit reference to the depiction of the angelic world. However, see Nic. Steth. *Anim.* chapter 4 (paragraphs 18–20) Darrouzès and in "*Imago Mundi, Imago Dei,* and Secret Union," mainly concerning the concept of the image of God. The fact that man communicates with both worlds is also emphasized in Nic. Steth. *Anim.* paragraph 32 of chapter 7 Darrouzès.

47. Nic. Steth. *Anim.* 26 Darrouzès. The causal ὡς that accompanies the *termini* συνύπαρκτον and ὁμόχρονον explains the whole preceding period, where Stethatos teaches that the soul was formed of four elements similar to the four elements of the material creation: Οἶμαι δέ … κτισθῆναι ταύτην παραπλησίως τῇ ὁρωμένῃ κτίσει καὶ αἰσθητῇ πρὸς Θεοῦ ἐκ τεσσάρων ὥσπερ στοιχείων, τῶν γενικῶν ἀρετῶν … καὶ ἐν τῇ συνδρομῇ τούτων … συντεθῆναι καὶ ἀπαρτισθῆναι αὐτὴν ἐν τῇ πλάσει ἅμα τοῦ σώματος ὡς συνύπαρκτον τούτῳ οὖσαν αὐτὴν καὶ ὁμόχρονον κατὰ τὸν καιρὸν καὶ τὴν ῥοπὴν τῆς ἐκείνου πλάσεως.

beginning and simultaneously with the body, it must have been built in a same way, that is, with constituent main elements. One could claim that Stethatos uses this image to *defend* an orthodox anthropological doctrine against Origenism, that is, against the preexistence of the soul. On the other side, the four virtues' analogy with the four material elements could cause an accusation of heresy: the concept of the four virtues as elements and subject matter, from which God takes the material to create a spiritual world of virtues,[48] could lead to Origenes's doctrine. Stethatos thus emphasizes the simultaneous creation of body and soul because he wants to *avoid* this accusation. I argue, however, that the main reason of the virtues' connection to the four material elements is the promotion of the concept of *imago mundi*.

Four Material Elements as Paradigm for the Four Virtues   In the *imago mundi* concept, the connection of the four virtues with the four material elements is essential.[49] The creation of the visible world[50]—namely, of four material elements of the material world and of the animals' and humans' body—functions as a pattern. The body was created not directly from the elements but through the four humors,[51] which emerged from the four qualities[52] of the elements.[53] The soul was created with four virtues as four constituent elements in comparison with and parallel to the body[54] and to the visible creation.[55]

This means that prudence corresponds to fire,[56] temperance to air, for-

---

48. λαμβάνων ἐκ τῶν ὑποκειμένων ἀρχῶν τὴν ἐξ ἑκατέρας ὕλην (Nic. Steth. *Cap.* 3.49, PG 120, 977B Migne); ἐκ τῶν ὑποκειμένων τοίνυν τεσσάρων ἀρχῶν) (Nic. Steth. *Anim.* 27.4 Darrouzès); these passages concern not the material elements but the virtues.

49. Empedocles first taught about the four elements; see, e.g., Emp. *Vorsokr.* 31 B 6; 17 Diels and Kranz.

50. See on this chapter 2 (paragraphs 8–12) of *De anima* Darrouzès.

51. Blood, yellow bile, phlegm, and black bile. Hippocrates (460–370 BC) and his school and Galen (129–201 AD) systemized this doctrine and connected it with the four elements see Böhme and Böhme, *Feuer, Wasser, Erde, Luft*, 164–69.

52. Hot, dry, wet, cold. Aristoteles taught a connection of them with the four elements in his treatise *De generatione et corruptione*: fire is hot and dry, air hot and wet, water cold and wet, earth cold and dry. See Böhme and Böhme, *Feuer, Wasser, Erde, Luft*, 114–15, 164–65.

53. Nic. Steth. *Anim.*11.5–19, 13.1–8, 19.2–7 Darrouzès. See also Nic. Steth. *Ep. Prox.* 3.9–11 Darrouzès; Nic. Steth. *Cap.* 3.95, PG 120, 1005B Migne.

54. Nic. Steth. *Anim.* 13.18–20 Darrouzès. Shlenov, "Учение прп I" and "Учение прп II" did not mention this passage.

55. Nic. Steth. *Anim.* 26.1–5 Darrouzès.

56. More precisely, prudence relates to sky, wherein αἰθήρ is the fire (πῦρ) of the spiritual desire; see Nic. Steth. *Anim.* 27.9–11 Darrouzès. Stethatos connects indirectly fire to prudence because he sees fire as the illuminating element of this sky—namely, of prudence—also, he

titude to water, and justice to earth. Taken together they constitute a whole intelligible world with αἰθήρ, stars, sun, moon, plants. Each virtue of the intelligible world functions in correspondence with one of the four visible elements.[57]

Stethatos makes some references to how each virtue is related to each element, but there is no absolute correspondence.[58] Prudence is connected to fire because prudence is the intelligible sky, where also αἰθήρ is the fire of the spiritual desire; therefore prudence is a source of the illumination of the sky's stars.[59] This illumination, however, does not concern the intelligible sun and moon because the latter are illuminated by the Holy Spirit. But the fact that the Holy Spirit illuminates the whole world (καταφωτίζειν τὸν ὅλον τοῦτον κόσμον ποιεῖ) leads to the conclusion that the sky, the stars, and αἰθήρ are illuminated by the Holy Spirit. Prudence is then illuminated from the latter and illuminates the stars through its intelligible αἰθήρ.[60]

Justice is connected to earth, where plants of ascesis are mentioned,[61] perhaps because of Eden's allegory of ascesis (πρακτικὴ φιλοσοφία). Stethatos allegorizes Eden, the sensible paradise—that is, the place on *earth* where Adam and Eve were destined to live—with ascesis in his treatise *De Paradiso*.[62] In this paradise the virtues are considered as plants that adorn the ascetics,[63] where we must assume that justice is essential. As I will show, however, Stethatos considers the cardinal virtues rather separated from the ascesis in his treatise *De anima*. He further assumes the mentioned concept of the soul's base (βάσις), where the cardinal virtues stand κατὰ φύσιν, as an intelligible paradise, and characterizes the latter as the meeks' *earth* (Mt 5:5).[64]

---

makes no distinction between fire and αἰθήρ; see also his third letter to Nicetas Chartophylax, Nic. Steth. *Ep. Nic. Chart.* paragraph 3 Darrouzès. In the philosophical cosmology, αἰθήρ is a fifth element (πεμπτουσία); see Böhme and Böhme, *Feuer, Wasser, Erde, Luft*, 143–45.

57. Nic. Steth. *Anim.* 27 Darrouzès. See on this paragraph also Shlenov, "Учение прп I," 197–98.

58. I thank M. Edwards for his useful query concerning this issue to my speech at the conference in Venice on October 3, 2019, "Platonismo bizantino, pensiero occidentale, influenze veneziane," concerning this volume.

59. Nic. Steth. *Anim.* 27.9–17 Darrouzès.

60. See, e.g., the parallel passage Νοῦς ἰλύος πάσης ἐκκαθαρθεὶς, οὐρανὸς κατάστερος ἐν λαμπροῖς καὶ φωτεινοτάτοις νοήμασι γίνεται τῇ ψυχῇ, τὸν Ἥλιον τῆς δικαιοσύνης ἔχων λάμποντα ἐν ἑαυτῷ, καὶ φαιδρὰς τὰς ἀκτῖνας τῆς θεολογίας εἰς τὸν κόσμον ἐκπέμποντα (Nic. Steth. *Cap.* 2.67, PG 120, 933A).

61. Nic. Steth. *Anim.* 27.17–20 Darrouzès.

62. See Nic. Steth. *Parad.* 30 Darrouzès and the whole chapter 6 (paragraphs 30–33).

63. Nic. Steth. *Parad.* 30.3, 8–9 Darrouzès.

64. Nic. Steth. *Anim.*51.1–3 Darrouzès.

Temperance is connected with air by the fact that the former "cools" the soul by its fight against the warmth of the passions, but it is not clear which exactly is the connection between temperance as an intelligible air, with the fact that it supplies the soul with clear spirit.[65]

Courage is joined with water because Stethatos allegorizes the human's weakness with the sand, which refers to man's creation with earth, a symbol of man's weakness.[66] On this sand demonic castles are built, which the spiritual water of courage destroys helping man to overcome the weakness.[67]

The need for a perfect match between the four material elements and the soul implies that each virtue has two properties, such as the material elements.[68] As mentioned, the humors and the animals' bodies derive from these material qualities. The intelligible qualities are, for prudence: (a) the regal, the sovereign[69] and (b) the investigation of the depth of the meanings with thoughtfulness and the attention on the senses; for justice, (a) equality by all judgments, division of the unlike and incompatible and their right handling, and (b) just weighing of the thoughts; for temperance, (a) chastity and purity as well as (b) joy of the spirits' freedom and honesty's perfume and immortality's scent; for courage, (a) stubbornness, unbendingness in pains, and (b) the cutting through of the παρὰ φύσιν movements with reason, the pierce of fear with patience.[70]

Stethatos probably drew the concept of each virtue's two qualities from *Centuria* 3.49,[71] where two more virtues are attached to each cardinal virtue. In some cases, there is a perfect connection between the two texts.[72] In any case, Stethatos drew from that chapter the idea that each cardinal virtue has two others for the sake of the essential concept, that there is an absolute analogy between the visible and invisible world, concerning also the qualities of each element (material and intelligible).[73]

---

65. Nic. Steth. *Anim.* 27.20–24 Darrouzès.

66. See on that Nic. Steth. *Anim.* paragraph 14; 16.10–17 Darrouzès.

67. Nic. Steth. *Anim.* 27.24–28 Darrouzès.

68. Stethatos expounded the qualities of the material elements in Nic. Steth. *Anim.* 11.5–11 Darrouzès.

69. Stethatos seems to divide the enumeration of properties into two major categories for each virtue; there is no clear criterium for each of this division. I propose the use of the phrases καὶ πρὸς τούτοις for prudence, καὶ προσέτι for justice, καὶ πρὸς τούτοις for temperance, and οὐ μόνον δὲ ἀλλὰ for courage, which divides the qualities' groups by each virtue.

70. Nic. Steth. *Anim.* 29 Darrouzès. See on this paragraph also Shlenov, "Учение прп I," 199–201.

71. Nic. Steth. *Cap.* 3.49, PG 120, 977A–C Migne.

72. See, e.g., chastity for temperance, discretion for justice, and patience for courage, which appear in both texts.

73. See also "*Centuriae.*"

The qualities of virtues are therefore essential to the formation and functioning of the intelligible world. Without them there is no such conceivable world, and the virtues are useless. But one cannot find a semantic analogy between them and the properties of the material elements, dryness, coldness, moisture, and warmness: they correspond only to the *virtues'* semantic context.

Stethatos cites teachings by John Damascene, in which virtues belong to both the body and the soul but are ultimately attributed to the soul,[74] but he disagrees.[75] In any case, however, we have seen that he links the virtues also with the body, but with the meaning that matter is a model of the spirit. Stethatos also parallelizes the cease of the virtues after death with the rest of the body:[76] he assumes them thus as quasi functions of the body. This is connected to the abovementioned idea that they are part of the earthly life.[77]

This dependence of the structure of the soul on the body and on the material world at large is fundamental to the concept of *imago mundi*. At the same time, however, Stethatos points out that the analogy is relative and not absolute.[78]

Contemplation of Nature   The image of the intelligible world of virtues is not a mere metaphor: the four virtues are looked into as an image that must be examined through contemplation of nature,[79] like the material creation.[80] They are considered as something external that needs to be internalized through contemplation.

Stethatos stresses the need to see through contemplation (θεωρῆσαι δεῖ[81]) how a human being was created as a big world into a small via the vir-

---

74. Nic. Steth. *Anim.* 64.7–9 Darrouzès and the critical apparatus. Stethatos cites Jo. D. *f.o.* 26.91–93 Kotter. Stethatos seems to integrate the passage and his reference to virtues in the special issue of the cardinal virtues; see Nic. Steth. *Anim.* 65.3–9, 68.1–3 Darrouzès.

75. In the two passages cited in note 74 above, he states that the cardinal virtues belong solely to the logical part of the soul (λογιστικόν).

76. Nic. Steth. *Anim.* 70.6–7 Darrouzès. See more in "Eschatology."

77. See also "Eschatology."

78. Nic. Steth. *Anim.* 13.18–19 (οἱονεὶ), 26.3 (ὥσπερ); 29.1 (τρόπον τινά), 2–3 (οἷα δὴ στοιχεῖα) Darrouzès.

79. For natural contemplation by Stethatos, see Tsames, Ἡ τελείωσις τοῦ ἀνθρώπου κατὰ Νικήταν τὸν Στηθᾶτον, 95–108; Diamantopoulos, *Die Hermeneutik des Niketas Stethatos*, 101–9, 767–79 and passim; Krausmüller, "An Embattled Charismatic," 107–10; for the contemplation of nature in general, see Lollar, *To See in the Life of Things*, 134–65.

80. One can find out this also through the pseudo-areopagitic teaching about the material world, the Bible, and the liturgy as symbols taught and modified by Stethatos; see Diamantopoulos, *Die Hermeneutik des Niketas Stethatos*, 174–82.

81. Θεωρῆσαι means not only examine, as Darrouzès, *Nicétas Stéthatos*, 89 translates it (considérer), but also mainly a spiritual contemplation.

tues; this is described explicitly as something that can be seen (ὁρᾶται).[82] The purpose of the intelligible world's creation from the four virtues is not only to exist but also to be seen (εἰς τὸ … ὁρᾶσθαι) in the soul close to the visible, that is, to be an object of spiritual contemplation: its purpose is the φυσικὴ θεωρία.[83]

As I have shown, the virtues have qualities, like the four elements. Stethatos stresses that we also need to know (εἰδέναι χρή) the qualities of the intelligible elements as the material ones.[84] The need to find an absolute analogy between the material and the intelligible world, which goes into detail, is emphasized. This presupposes that in principle this analogy is possible. The possibility exists through the creation of the intelligible world, which man is then called upon to examine through contemplation.

However, natural contemplation is not only a method of seeing and research but also a necessary stage of spiritual development. The four virtues accompany the mystic in the second stage of natural contemplation, called also φωτιστική.[85] It is one of the three stages that man must go through to attain spiritual perfection. Elsewhere, Stethatos teaches that guarding the four virtues is a prerequisite for the preparation of hymns and melodies and in general for theology.[86] The four virtues are distinguished from ascesis in this reference, which shows that they do not purely belong to practical philosophy. Additionally, they precede the third stage of mystical theology. So, connecting the material to the intelligible world through the virtues, the contemplation described by Stethatos is an essential feature of the spiritual path of the mystic, part of the second stage. That is also why the image of the intelligible world is not just an artificial comparison to the visible one.

It is no coincidence that in the chapters about the four virtues taken from the *Centuriae,* all the passages regarding the virtues as instruments of battle against the devil and the passions have been eliminated in *De anima.* These concepts relate mainly to the first stage of spiritual perfection (πρακτικὴ φιλοσοφία). In *De anima* dominates the integration of the chapters from the *Centuriae* rather in the *imago mundi* concept, the state according to nature, the intelligible paradise, which is related to the stage

---

82. Nic. Steth. *Anim.* 27.1–3 Darrouzès.

83. Nic. Steth. *Anim.* 27.4–8 Darrouzès.

84. Nic. Steth. *Anim.* 29 Darrouzès, esp. 1–4.

85. Nic. Steth. *Cap.* 3.43, PG 120, 973B–C Migne. On the alternation of the euagrian term φυσικὴ θεωρία with the pseudo-areopagitic φωτιστική by Stethatos, see Diamantopoulos, *Die Hermeneutik des Niketas Stethatos,* 180n33.

86. Nic. Steth. *Intr. Hymn.* 11.168–69 Kambylis.

of contemplation of nature.[87] What exactly is contemplated in the four virtues through natural contemplation?

***Imago Mundi, Imago Dei,* and Secret Union**   The *imago mundi* is not just a parallel and analogous picture of the material world: it leads to self-knowledge. According to Stethatos, self-knowledge[88] is attained by knowing the rational principles (λόγοι) and nature of beings through natural contemplation, after one has passed the stage of purification.[89] Through this argument man can understand the importance of the parallelization of the structure of the world with that of the soul in Stethatos's thought. This self-knowledge refers primarily to the knowledge of the image of God[90] within us. Achieving self-awareness based on the awareness of *imago mundi* and *imago Dei* is one of Stethatos's basic goals in *De anima*.[91]

But what exactly does the knowledge of the image of the world and through this of the image of God mean as self-knowledge? The image of the world is fundamental for the image of God. In the exposition of the teaching that God created in the soul an intelligible world, it is emphasized that man was created in the image of God: Stethatos thinks that the intelligible world is explained by the fact that man is an image of God.[92] In the same context the infinitive ὁρᾶσθαι is used,[93] which, as I mentioned, shows that the intelligible world is something to be seen, an *imago*. The latter symbolically depicts the visible world. So, the intelligible world of virtues, the *imago mundi*, is a form and part of the *imago Dei* that must be contemplated.

How exactly does the image of the world relate to the image of God? Is it enough just that both as *imagines* are objects of a contemplation? The concept that founds the image of God in the image of the world is raised as

87. See more on this in "*Centuriae.*"

88. On self-knowledge by Stethatos, see Shlenov, "Принцип 'Познай себя' у прп"; however, I suggest here a different analysis.

89. Nic. Steth. *Cap.* 2.36, PG 120, 916C Migne.

90. On *imago Dei* by Stethatos, see Tsames, Ἡ τελείωσις τοῦ ἀνθρώπου κατὰ Νικήταν τὸν Στηθᾶτον, 28–33; Chouliaras, "Imago Trinitatis in St Symeon the New Theologian and Niketas Stethatos," 498–99; the latter discusses "briefly" only the triadological *imago Dei* of Stethatos and its relation to the respective of Symeon the New Theologian and Gregorios Palamas.

91. Nic. Steth. *Anim.* 1.8–11 Darrouzès. See also Shlenov, "Принцип 'Познай себя' у прп," 103–4.

92. Nic. Steth. *Anim.* 27.6–8 Darrouzès: συνδημιουργεῖ τῇ ψυχῇ ἐν ὅλῳ **τῷ κατ᾽ εἰκόνα κτισθέντι αὐτοῦ ἀνθρώπῳ** τὸν νοητὸν καὶ ἀόρατον κόσμον (my emphasis in boldface).

93. Nic. Steth. *Anim.* 27.8 Darrouzès. See also 40.25, where the verb ὁρᾶται is used; namely, the soul is seen as a picture between the intelligible and the sensible having the logical and the passive part, depicting with them the material and the spiritual world.

a central theme in the preamble of *De anima*.[94] Stethatos asks there how man is the image of God, and at the same time he is associated with the earth and what is the reason for the connection in man of two opposing worlds (material and intelligible) as basic sub-questions of the question of self-knowledge. This connection of cosmology to the *imago Dei* is expounded in chapter 4.[95] Stethatos teaches there that man, as a whole, soul and body, contains all the nature of beings, logical and irrational/material, and depicts the whole world. Thus, as that kind of *imago mundi*, he is an image of God because he depicts God, who also has in him all beings. Consequently, chapter's 4 iconology, which deals with the psychosomatic person, is transferred to the subject of the chapter's 6 intelligible world of the soul. It thus proved that also the soul *itself*, without the body, is an image of God, for it contains all the nature of beings, not only intangibles but also materials. The four virtues belong to the material beings symbolically. *Imago mundi* is therefore part of *imago Dei* in a cosmological/ontological sense.

In the treatise *De Paradiso*[96] a parallel idea is attested: that in the Bible many names are ascribed to the human being (e.g., light, plant, tree), which can be allegorized through many contemplations, is explained by the fact that he is an image of God, who also has many names. Thus God's *plurality* and *variety* constitute in both concepts the *imago Dei* in man. Here the plurality of names, and in the parallel concept in *De anima*, the plurality of beings and soul's forces.[97]

This is a basic self-knowledge giving a first answer to the preamble's question about the image of God.[98] This self-knowledge aims again at a deeper meaning. We do not simply know through *imago mundi* that we are

94. Nic. Steth. *Anim.* 1.8–19 Darrouzès.

95. Nic. Steth. *Anim.* paragraphs 18–19 Darrouzès; see esp. 18.8–15. The question about the union of two contrary elements (spiritual and material) in the creation of man is also raised in the treatise Nic. Steth. *Limit. Vit.*, 14.6–15 Darrouzès. Stethatos connects the question of the union of the two worlds also with self-knowledge in the same treatise, paragraph 15; see also 32.7. The idea is discussed in the context of the problem of the limits of life.

96. Nic. Steth. *Parad.* 9.17–21 Darrouzès.

97. See also Nic. Steth. *Anim.* 15.6–8 Darrouzès (connection of *imago Dei* to the richness of the soul's forces). See on the πολυώνυμον concept also Diamantopoulos, *Die Hermeneutik des Niketas Stethatos*, 249–51, 256, 260.

98. Also, Tsames, Ἡ τελείωσις τοῦ ἀνθρώπου κατὰ Νικήταν τὸν Στηθᾶτον, 23–25, explained Stethatos's mentioned doctrine, that man communicates with all beings and thus resembles God, where the four elements' and the four virtues' theory play a dominating role, as aiming at God's knowledge, but he did not connect it to self-knowledge. He did this by the triadological *imago mundi*, however (Ἡ τελείωσις τοῦ ἀνθρώπου κατὰ Νικήταν τὸν Στηθᾶτον, 29–31); see on that below, note 114, with my critical remarks. Tsames did not discuss Stethatos's concept that man *depicts* the world (*imago mundi*) at all; this is yet fundamental for the aspect of the φυσικὴ θεωρία and thus for self-knowledge.

an image of God: Stethatos, after showing that the soul was also built close to the visible creation from four elements, then emphasizes that the soul is a *higher* world: he is a macrocosm in a microcosm.[99] The image of God therefore contains also this axiological element. This supremacy has as a fundamental condition the cosmological concept of *imago mundi* because it gives an essential element so that man can understand his value and superiority: the human soul contains a second world, similar to the material, which he depicts; it is, however, essential for man's superiority that this world is intelligible and not material. Additionally, with this second world the human soul is shown as the only intelligible being that contains similarities also with the material world, which are not to be found in the angels. Only humans depict the whole universe.

The idea that through the awareness that man is a great world in a small world leads us to self-knowledge—that is, to the knowledge of the highest value of man—is developed also in chapter 3, which speaks of man, as a whole, as a soul and body, as macrocosm.[100] Stethatos connects there the greater world's concept (οἷόν τινα κόσμου κόσμον ἕτερον, κρείττονά τε καὶ ὑψηλότερον) with the whole human (body and soul) because it is mentioned in a context where the elements of the two worlds appear and explain this concept. Man is a greater world—namely, visible and invisible, mortal and immortal—between magnitude and humility, earthly and heavenly, spirit and flesh.[101] But it is certain that the macrocosm idea also applies to the soul itself, and especially to the intelligible world of the four virtues of chapter 6: Stethatos transfers thus this idea to chapter 6.[102] From chapter 4, as I mentioned, he conveys the ontological idea that the image of God contains all beings. Consequently, the notions of the macrocosm and the image of God as a universe are combined in a new composition in chapter 6, dealing with the four virtues.

99. Nic. Steth. *Anim.* 27.1–3, 30.1–2 Darrouzès. See also the title of chapter 6; Nic. Steth. *Parad.* 3.15–18, 19.1–9 Darrouzès. In the last passage, Stethatos connects this concept also with *imago Dei.* See for that also in Nic. Steth. *Limit. Vit.* 25.6–15 Darrouzès. See also Golitzin, "Hierarchy versus Anarchy?," 143–45; Delli, "La phantasia selon Michel Psellos," 112–13, where she finds similarities with Psellos. This doctrine appears first by Greg. Naz. *Or. 38* 11, PG 36, 324A Migne and then by Jo. D. *f.o.* 26.25–26 Kotter, where man is considered as a small world in a great one. Stethatos follows Gregorius's concept; see also Darrouzès, *Nicétas Stéthatos,* 88–89n1; Tsames, Ἡ τελείωσις τοῦ ἀνθρώπου κατὰ Νικήταν τὸν Στηθᾶτον, 26.

100. Nic. Steth. *Anim.* paragraph 16 Darrouzès, esp. 3–5.

101. Nic. Steth. *Anim.* 16.4–5, 11–12 Darrouzès. The same concept is taught also by Gregorius Nazianzenus in his mentioned passage.

102. For the connection with Nic. Steth. *Anim.* chapter 6 Darrouzès, see also Darrouzès, *Nicétas Stéthatos,* 88na, in the critical apparatus.

Stethatos joins this *imago mundi* thought also to the tripartite of the soul (λογιστικόν, ἐπιθυμητικόν, θυμοειδές),[103] as also the latter is connected to the rational and irrational world and depicts them.[104] The use of the term μεθόριος[105] in the teaching about the tripartite refers to the *imago mundi*.[106] He calls the ἐπιθυμητικόν and θυμικόν a material dyad (ὑλικὴ δυάδα),[107] which shows that he sees these two parts as *quasi* part of the material world, which they thus depict, because we find them also in the animals.[108] Stethatos considers the soul's irrational part (ἐπιθυμητικόν, θυμοειδές) as the invisible creation in man, which corresponds to the visible one, that is, as a picture of the material world.[109] In the teaching of the dual movement of the irrational/rational of the tripartite according to or against nature is further emphasized the grandeur of the divine image (τῷ μεγαλείῳ τῆς θείας εἰκόνος),[110] which refers to the concept of the great world in a small and therefore of the *imago Dei*. The *imago mundi* concept of the four virtues is thus part of the *imago mundi* concept of the tripartite and both of the *imago Dei* concept. That is why it is taught that the tripartite together with the four virtues constitute the soul.[111]

However, Stethatos teaches not only in chapter 4, but mainly in chapter 5, about the image of God.[112] He relies now on triadology: the image of God in man is that it consists of mind (νοῦς), word (λόγος), and soul (ψυχή), consubstantially, like the Holy Trinity of Νοῦς, Λόγος, and

103. This is again a Platonic notion, which appears in the mentioned fourth book of the *Res Publica*.

104. Nic. Steth. *Anim.* paragraphs 31–32; see also 36.1–10, 40.6–26 Darrouzès. Stethatos teaches in the last passage that the soul is seen between sensible and invisible beings. He doesn't refer explicitly to the irrational part of the soul; however, he means that the soul's irrational part is connected to the sensible world. See especially Nic. Steth. *Anim.* paragraphs 45–47 Darrouzès.

105. Nic. Steth. *Anim.* 36, 10 Darrouzès.

106. See also the preamble of Nic. Steth. *Anim.* (specifically 1.13 Darrouzès), chapter 3 (specifically 14.2), on the use of the term in the sense that man or his soul lie between two worlds that they contain. See also chapter 10 (especially 57.5) for the use of the term in relation to anger, where the same logic is used, of something between two worlds.

107. Nic. Steth. *Parad.* 27.9–10, 32.6–12 Darrouzès; Nic. Steth. *Limit. Vit.* 15.8 Darrouzès (see on this passage Darrouzès, *Nicétas Stéthatos*, 380n1). This term appears in Greg. Naz. *Or.* 21.2.114.8 Mossay and Lafontaine. Stethatos probably drew this concept from Max. *Ambig.* 10 Constas, where Maximus interprets Gregorius's abovementioned passage.

108. See on this Nic. Steth. *Anim.* 13.9–11, 19.9–10, 36.1–10 Darrouzès.

109. Nic. Steth. *Anim.* 46.6–8 Darrouzès.

110. Nic. Steth. *Anim.* 40.23–24 Darrouzès.

111. Nic. Steth. *Anim.* 1.19–20, the title of chapter 6 and 26.1–9 Darrouzès. Shlenov, "Учение прп I" and "Учение прп II," did not mention the first passage; however, he also noted the virtues' connection to the tripartite on the ground of paragraph 26 ("Учение прп I," 197).

112. Nic. Steth. *Anim.* paragraphs 21–22, Darrouzès.

Πνεῦμα.[113] Consequently, knowing this, we are led to the self-knowledge that we are images of God because we depict the Trinity (*imago Trinitatis*). This is an additional answer to the original question of the preamble of *De anima*.[114]

The triadological *imago Dei*, however, is related to the four virtues directly in chapter 49 of Stethatos's third *Centuria*.[115] There the creation by God's Word of the four virtues as an intelligible world in the soul is taught. God the Father is enthroned over the four virtues and their eight auxiliaries in the throne of the soul's νοῦς and sends his Word for the creation of an intelligible world from the four virtues as subject elements. The Word places then the Holy Spirit in him as a moving and cohesive force. The creation of the intelligible world presupposes the indwelling of the Trinity. This happened by the creation, but we can assume that it can occur also after the Fall, if man repents.

Therefore the fact that we have a νοῦς is not only linked to knowing the image of God within us through its reference to the Holy Trinity, which also has Νοῦς, Λόγος and Πνεῦμα, but also primarily we know and must seek the possibility of secret union with the Trinity's Νοῦς through our νοῦς.[116] Stethatos teaches elsewhere that man's νοῦς seeks its union with God's Νοῦς and tends to imitate the latter; therefore the former begets its word and creates with him also in other's people soul an intelligible world, a macrocosm, imitating by that the Creator (ὁρᾶται δημιουργὸς καὶ αὐτὸς τῆς νοητῆς κτίσεως καὶ τοῦ μεγάλου κόσμου), where the virtues strengthen the soul.[117]

Stethatos is interested in restoring the physical function of the intellect (νοῦς),[118] which is the fundamental instrument of the mystical contemplation. For this reason, elsewhere is emphasized the union of the four

113. Stethatos differs here from the Patristic tradition of the triadological *imago Dei*, which assumes the elements νοῦς, λόγος, and πνεῦμα instead of ψυχή, in man's soul as the corresponding ones to the Trinity; see also Tsames, Ἡ τελείωσις τοῦ ἀνθρώπου κατὰ Νικήταν τὸν Στηθᾶτον, 29–30; Chouliaras, "Imago Trinitatis in St Symeon the New Theologian and Niketas Stethatos," 494–95, 498–500.

114. Tsames, Ἡ τελείωσις τοῦ ἀνθρώπου κατὰ Νικήταν τὸν Στηθᾶτον, 29–31, also considers the triadological *imago Dei* connected to self-knowledge by Stethatos, but he makes no mention to the cardinal virtues on that issue. On Stethatos's triadological *imago Dei*, see also Krausmüller, "Hiding in Plain Sight."

115. Nic. Steth. *Cap.* 3.49, PG 120, 977A–C Migne is a key source for chapter 6 of the treatise *De anima*. Shlenov, "Учение прп I" and "Учение прп II," neither mentioned nor discussed Nic. Steth. *Cap.* 3.49, PG 120, Migne.

116. See on that also Tsames, Ἡ τελείωσις τοῦ ἀνθρώπου κατὰ Νικήταν τὸν Στηθᾶτον, 29–32.

117. Nic. Steth. *Cap.* 3.12, PG 120, 960C–D Migne.

118. See also Tsames, Ἡ τελείωσις τοῦ ἀνθρώπου κατὰ Νικήταν τὸν Στηθᾶτον, 33–34, 43. On the physical operation of the intellect, see Nic. Steth. *Anim.* 34.8 Darrouzès.

virtues with the four general powers of the intellect in the natural state of the soul.[119] He understands the cardinal virtues not only cosmologically but also mystically. But this secret union is mainly associated with the state according to nature and the second stage (φυσικὴ θεωρία), not the super-natural one (ὑπὲρ φύσιν), as it is traced to the prelapsarian man upon his creation or to the return to this state as a re-creation.

The self-knowledge of the secret union is achieved only through the consideration of the four virtues as the intelligible world, which depicts the visible. Only when there are four virtues as raw materials can the Trinity indwell within us, which then creates the intelligible world. Man is called to spiritually regard the creation of the world as a secret union with the Holy Trinity, which then creates an intelligible world of virtues. The virtues are therefore linked not only to the cosmological *imago Dei* but also to the triadological one, which leads to their deeper understanding and self-knowledge, as the virtues lead to the latter and to the secret indwelling of the Trinity in the soul.

Stethatos did not include the teaching about the indwelling of the Trin-ity in the soul of the *Centuria* 3.49 in *De anima*, probably because he wanted to emphasize that the four virtues mainly concern the second stage of the contemplation, although the secret union in the *Centuria* 3.49 is related, as I have shown, rather to the second stage. But there is a triadological refer-ence also in *De anima* to the creation of the intelligible world by the Father through the Word, also to the Holy Spirit in him.[120]

Consequently, Stethatos intimately and creatively connects the con-cepts of the four virtues as elements, the intelligible world of these virtues, the self-knowledge, the image of God, the triadology, and the secret union with him in a creative composition aimed at bringing out the secret theol-ogy and experience.

Intelligible Paradise   The four virtues as constituents are regarded also as the four rivers of Eden.[121] The virtues are not only the fundamental ele-ments of an intelligible world in general, but especially of its intelligible paradise. From the world of cardinal virtues spring the rivers of the other virtues and water the intelligible paradise.[122]

---

119. For the linking of the human's intellect with four virtues, see Nic. Steth. *Cap.* 1.12, PG 120, 856D Migne; Nic. Steth. *Anim.* 50.14–20 Darrouzès. See also Shlenov, "Учение прп I," 201–2.

120. Nic. Steth. *Anim.* 27.16–17, 28.1–6, 29. 2 Darrouzès. See also Darrouzès, *Nicétas Stétha-tos,* 91n1.

121. Gn 2:10–14 Brooke, McLean and Thackeray.

122. Nic. Steth. *Anim.* 28.8–13 Darrouzès; see also Nic. Steth. *Cap.* 2.12, PG 120, 905B Migne.

This connection between the cardinal virtues and the four rivers of Eden is not random. Stethatos mentions in his work *De Paradiso* that the purpose of *De anima* was the philosophy—that is, the interpretation—about paradise; namely, *De Paradiso*.[123] *De anima* prepares the reader for the basic doctrine of *De Paradiso*, that the human soul is an intelligible paradise. Stethatos teaches there that there is an intelligible paradise in the world outside Eden, which is the invisible creation in man's soul.[124] He further bases the concept of the intelligible paradise on the fact that man is a big world in a small one.[125] The macrocosm's idea is emphasized in chapter 6 of *De anima*. There, as I showed, he tends to find an absolute analogy between the invisible and the invisible worlds in man's soul, where the cardinal virtues' assumption as the four elements of the soul serves essential. This is expounded on the base of the *imago mundi* and macrocosm concepts. This founds thus the fundamental idea of *De Paradiso*, that the soul can also include a noetic paradise because exactly the soul as an invisible world, depicting the material one, contains and depicts all the elements of the latter, and is thus also an Eden. This explains the virtues' assumption not only as four basic elements of the intelligible creation but also as four basic rivers of its intelligible Eden. The intelligible world in man is thus the conceptual fundament of the main argument of *De Paradiso*, which highlights the existence and the necessity of the intelligible paradise. As I will show in "Contextualization" below, however, Stethatos's connection of the cardinal virtues to the *imago mundi* concept is related also with the intellectual conflicts of his time.

Remarks on Shlenov's Study   Shlenov commented only briefly that chapter 6 of *De anima* is about the soul being an intelligible and a greater world in a small one.[126] I think instead that chapter's 6 *imago mundi* concept is one of the main doctrines about the four virtues. Shlenov considered the connection of the noetic world to the material of secondary importance.[127] The material world, its elements, and numbers are according to Shlenov

123. Nic. Steth. *Parad.* 1.2–3 Darrouzès.

124. Nic. Steth. *Parad.* 6.1–3 Darrouzès.

125. Nic. Steth. *Parad.* 3.15–18, 19.1–7 Darrouzès. See also Shlenov, "Учение прп I," 198–99, where he didn't see a direct connection between *De anima* and Nic. Steth. *Parad.* on the ground of these passages; he referred only to the fact that Stethatos in Nic. Steth. *Parad.* highlighted the comparison between Eden and the soul.

126. Shlenov, "Учение прп I," 198. He pointed out that Stethatos in comparison with Gregorius Nazianzenus and John Damascene parallelized with details the analogy of the virtues to the material world. But see "Sources" below.

127. Shlenov, "Учение прп I," 203.

a simple occasion (повод) for an artificial *comparison* with the four virtues and the soul, which aims at spiritual elevation.[128] He thought that the four virtues basically help as a tool (инструментом) in focusing on the right function of the intellect (νοῦς) and its four forces:[129] as the material elements and the creation of the material world are an occasion for comparison with the four virtues (where Shlenov did not explain sufficiently why this comparison dominates in Stethatos's thought), and the five senses of the body are similarly compared with the five senses of the soul, so are the four virtues an occasion for comparison with the intellect and its four forces.[130] He assumed that Stethatos instrumentalizes the four virtues for the battle against passions helping the intellect's right function. Their higher importance is that they're working as weapons against passions and must coordinate with the intellect, which guides the battle against them.[131] The cardinal virtues lead to self-knowledge and must not be overestimated because they are part of a broader morale doctrine, where also the main Christian virtues dominate, focusing on the virtue of love.[132] One can conclude that Shlenov considers that Stethatos places them rather in the first stage of spiritual progress.

Shlenov did not assume the soul's base (βάσις), the soul's state according to nature (κατὰ φύσιν), the contemplation of nature, as frame of reference for the four virtues.[133] Additionally, he did not look into their mystic aspect, where the intellect is united with the Trinity, which leads to the creation of the intelligible world of virtues using them as raw elements. Finally, he misinterpreted some of Stethatos's essential passages.[134]

128. Shlenov, "Учение прп I," 197–201, 204.

129. Shlenov, "Учение прп I,", 202.

130. Shlenov, "Учение прп I," 204.

131. Shlenov, "Учение прп I," 202–3.

132. Shlenov, "Учение прп I," 203–4. Shlenov did not quote in this argument a Stethatos passage on the connection between self-knowledge and the cardinal virtues. For this connection, see rather above, "*Imago Mundi, Imago Dei* and Secret Union."

133. He made only a brief reference (Shlenov, "Учение прп II," 193–94) to contemplation as a method of interpretation, as the Stethatos method, when the latter presents the image of the soul correlating with other cosmological elements, where Shlenov assumed that Stethatos follows Church Fathers like Maximus the Confessor. But this was not Shlenov's main argument, and also in this reference he insists to assume Stethatos's concept as a product of a spiritual interpretation, perhaps as simple metaphor and not as a fundamental stage of a spiritual progress.

134. Shlenov, "Учение прп I," 200–201, describing the connection of the material elements' qualities to the cardinal virtues' qualities (see Nic. Steth. *Anim.* paragraph 29 Darrouzès), assumed a connection between the enumeration of the material elements' qualities mentioned in Nic. Steth. *Anim.* 29.4–8 Darrouzès and the enumeration of the virtues' qualities mentioned in Nic. Steth. *Anim.* 29.8–26 Darrouzès; so he understood that justice's qualities, mentioned in the second place, are "compared" with the qualities of earth—that is, moisture and warmth—which

In my opinion, the noetic world's concept of the cardinal virtues is not a simple matter of comparison of the two worlds, a simple excuse for a higher teaching, only an instrument for focusing on νοῦς or a weapon against passions, but an essential spiritual contemplation, part of the doctrine about the φυσικὴ θεωρία and as *imago mundi* vital for the spiritual perfection. The importance of the cardinal virtues has further not only to do with the fact that they together with the soul's tripartite constitute the soul: they function mainly as raw materials for the creation of an intelligible world. This world is further essential for the existence of the intellect. Especially in the concept of the secret union of God's Νοῦς with man's νοῦς, as I have shown, one can find the necessity of the cardinal virtues' concept of *imago mundi*, not only as fundament but also as aim: without them the Trinity would not create their intelligible world. The virtues are thus not only tools (as four raw elements) but also mainly the *aim* of the right function of the intellect by its union with God, which must lead to the creation of their intelligible world. This can be seen not only in *Centuria* 3.49 Migne but also in the modified chapter 6 of *De anima*.

I argue thus that the cardinal virtues' concepts as *imago mundi* are of the same and of greater importance than their correlation with the intellect and its four forces: they are in all cases an indispensable part of the latter. The creation of this intelligible world is a θεωρία that the soul *must* contemplate to achieve perfection and is therefore not just a metaphor. This contemplation includes also a web of other fundamental concepts: the image of God, triadology, and self-knowledge.[135]

---

according to him appear also in the second place. But first, the qualities of earth are dryness and coldness (see Nic. Steth. *Anim.* 11.8–9 Darrouzès); second and most important, Stethatos apparently does not connect in paragraph 29 the enumeration of the material elements' qualities with the enumeration of the virtues' qualities. Dryness and coldness, earth's qualities, equivalent to justice, take the third place in the enumeration, while justice's qualities, as mentioned, appear in the second place. See Nic. Steth. *Anim.* 29.11–18 Darrouzès; this shows exactly that Stethatos is not interested in a perfect symmetry and thus an exact correspondence between the two enumerations. The same problem occurs in the discussion of the qualities of air, which are not cold and dry, as Shlenov assumed, but wet and warm (see Nic. Steth. *Anim.* 11.10–11 Darrouzès). Shlenov accepted that connection because temperance, air's equivalent, comes in the third place (see Nic. Steth. *Anim.* 29.18–21 Darrouzès), and cold and dry come also in the third place (Nic. Steth. *Anim.* 29.6–7 Darrouzès). The air's qualities come in the second place (Nic. Steth. *Anim.* 29.6 Darrouzès). Lastly, even though Stethatos divides the qualities by each virtue in two categories, he does not state explicitly which virtue's quality corresponds to which material element's quality.

135. In his study on Stethatos's concept of self-knowledge, Shlenov, "Принцип 'Познай себя' у прп," 103–4, argued that Stethatos set in his treatise *De anima* as his primary purpose to achieve self-knowledge. Although he cited the relevant mentioned passage in the preamble of *De anima* that links self-knowledge and iconology, also the mentioned parallel passage 18.8–15

This presupposes an *essential* connection to the material world: the analogy and relation between matter and spirit are not simply metaphoric but ontological—they really exist and are based on the assumption of hidden reasons of beings (λόγοι τῶν ὄντων), ideas about God in the material entities, accessed through φυσικὴ θεωρία.[136] The virtues' contemplation is conceivable only *through* the material world, and *this* contemplation is then a prerequisite to achieve the third stage of perfection, the μυστικὴ θεολογία.

I also emphasize the preparatory role of the cardinal virtues' *imago mundi* concept in *De anima* for *De Paradiso*, which was not assumed by Shlenov: it shows that the virtues are not only connected to the intellect's problem but also refer mainly to the fundamental teaching of the mystics about the intelligible paradise. This helps essentially in understanding the context and the aim of the elaboration of this doctrine in *De anima*.

Eschatology

The four virtues are also part of the eschatological question of *De anima* about the middle state of the soul; namely, the state after death, before the Second Coming of Christ.[137] According to Stethatos, the cardinal virtues belong to the soul's reason (λογιστικόν).[138] In the posthumous state the soul takes together only reason, and from that a few elements, to which the cardinal virtues do not belong.[139] The soul does not take from the properties of the λογιστικόν after death either the sciences, the principles of

---

Darrouzès, where Nicetas makes this connection again; he did not explore deeper this relationship, and the same appears in his study on the virtues ("Учение прп I" and "Учение прп II"), which did not mention the preamble at all. Additionally, Shlenov did not cite any passage that connects directly self-knowledge and the cardinal virtues in all his mentioned studies.

136. On this concept in the Patristic thought and Stethatos, see Diamantopoulos, *Die Hermeneutik des Niketas Stethatos*, 286n503.

137. Nic. Steth. *Anim.* chapters 12–15 Darrouzès. For a discussion of these chapters, see Constas, "'To Sleep, Perchance to Dream,'" and Marinis, "'He Who Is at the Point of Death'" and *Death and the Afterlife in Byzantium*, where yet the cardinal virtues' problem in the middle state is not discussed. Shlenov, "Учение прп I" and "Учение прп II," did not make a reference to the related paragraphs 65 and 70 *De anima* Darrouzès. He referred only to the passage Nic. Steth. *Anim.* 68.1–7 Darrouzès, where Stethatos teaches that the cardinal virtues are qualities of the λογιστικόν, but also that the soul does not take with her all the qualities of the λογιστικόν after death. Shlenov mentioned only the first teaching and made no reference to the middle state doctrine of this passage; see Shlenov, "Учение прп I," 201–2. The eschatological discussion is essential, however, because it helps understanding the context of the treatise, the conflict between mystics and intellectuals (see "Contextualization").

138. Nic. Steth. *Anim.* 65.9, 68.3 Darrouzès. This can also be linked to the above teaching that the virtues are innate, not acquired.

139. Nic. Steth. *Anim.* paragraph 70 Darrouzès.

the arts, the deliberation (βουλευτικόν), and the volition (προαιρετικόν).[140] It takes together only the knowledge of the beings, the noetic perception (νοερὰ αἴσθησις), the intellections of the intelligible beings (νοήσεις νοητῶν), and the memory.[141] The characteristic properties (ἴδια) of the λογιστικόν, from which the soul ceases, are paralleled with the works of the body, from which the soul ceases after death.[142]

In the Stethatos research, a broader conflict is assumed between mystics and Italos about θνητοψυχιτισμός as context of *De anima*: Stethatos fights against the doctrine that the soul sleeps and is unconscious after death. I assumed a broader background connected rather to Psellos:[143] by fighting the θνητοψυχιτισμός, Stethatos defends the νοερὰ αἴσθησις. The latter is the soul's faculty to sense the mystical experience of direct communion with God in the third stage of spiritual perfection as real, and thus the main condition and confirmation of this experience not only after death but also in the earthly life. Stethatos thus defends the conditions of mystical theology. This also explains the absence of the cardinal virtues in the middle state: there the νοερὰ αἴσθησις is the most essential element. Therefore it is highlighted that in the mystical experience the virtues are not needed.

But this state is in Stethatos's thought a mirror of the soul's abilities, which are prerequisites for the mystic experience in the life in earth. It is, however, a preliminary stage, not a perfect model of mystical theology, as the middle state is ending in the union with angels, according to a concept based on the treatise *De hierarchia*,[144] while the third stage speaks of a direct communion with God, where no creatures, even the angels, mediate.[145] But the posthumous state of the soul is a state depicting closer the

140. Nic. Steth. *Anim.* 65.3–11, 68.1–5 Darrouzès.

141. Nic. Steth. *Anim.* 70.1–6 Darrouzès.

142. Nic. Steth. *Anim.* 70.6–8 Darrouzès. For the mentioned translations of the *termini* βουλευτικόν, προαιρετικόν, νοήσεις νοητῶν, νοερὰ αἴσθησις, see Palmer, Sherrard, and Ware, *Philokalia*, 81; Krausmüller, "What Is Mortal in the Soul?," 6.

143. See Diamantopoulos, *Die Hermeneutik des Niketas Stethatos*, 607–13, 671–73, where I also discuss mainly Psell. *Theol.* 1.27 Gautier, which is relevant to the hypothesis that follows; there also Italos's and Psellos's sources (mainly Italos's *Op.* 37 and 50 Joannou and Psellos's Psell. *Phil. Min.* 2.20 O' Meara) on θνητοψυχιτισμός and critical discussion of the literature on that issue.

144. See Nic. Steth. *Anim.* 72.4–7, 83.11–13 Darrouzès, which teach that the souls in the middle state expect something higher after the Second Coming of Christ. For the parallelism between middle state and the third stage of spiritual progress, see also, e.g., Nic. Steth. *Parad.* 52.10–14 Darrouzès, where Stethatos by describing the entry into that stage uses the same terminology concerning the soul's cease from works mentioned in the middle state (καταπαῦσαι).

145. See Diamantopoulos, *Die Hermeneutik des Niketas Stethatos*, 355–56, 665–66, 672–73, 679, 681, 681n707.

mystical experience, while the life on the body, thus also with the virtues, symbolizes rather the second stage of perfection.

The intelligible world of four virtues, their image of the four-horse chariot, relate to this life, to κατὰ φύσιν and to the second stage of spiritual progress. But in the third stage of mystical theology and ὑπὲρ φύσιν they are not required.[146] However, Stethatos defends the doctrine that the third stage is fully achievable in the earthly life and thus that also in this life the virtues are not needed by the mystical experience, despite the fact that they are part of the higher part of the soul.

Sources

Maximus the Confessor

It is known in general that Stethatos draws from Maximus the Confessor.[147] The latter often refers to the four virtues,[148] but Stethatos's source is *Ambiguum ad Ioannem* 21, where the consideration of the four virtues as four elements is systematically taught.[149] Shlenov[150] also assumed an indirect relation to Maximus's *Quaestio* 87, where also a connection of the four elements to the cardinal virtues is attested,[151] but he did not discuss this *Ambiguum* at all.[152]

Maximus associates the four elements with the four virtues in a different context: he discusses why Gregorius Nazianzenus named the evangelist John "the Forerunner."[153] This is explained with the idea that John's Gospel

146. On Nic. Steth. *Cap.* 3.49, PG 120, 977A–C Migne, which concerns rather the κατὰ φύσιν state and not the third stage, see my thoughts above.

147. See Krausmüller, "An Embattled Charismatic," 107–10, 112, 123, and Diamantopoulos, *Die Hermeneutik des Niketas Stethatos*, 86n189, for further bibliography.

148. Max. *Ambig.* 66.3.3, 67.5.3–4 Constas; Max. *Qu. Dub.* 41.15, 46.13–14; 48.10–14, 116.17–18, I. 68, 49–50 Declerck.

149. Max. *Ambig.* 21.3–10 Constas. See on this *Ambiguum* Steel, "'Elementatio Evangelica'"; Grigoras, "Commentaires par le Père Dumitru Staniloae," 467–73; Cristiani, "Κόσμος αἰσθητός," 459–62; Moreschini, *Massimo il Confessore*, 184–87, 679–83; Max. *Ambig.* Constas, vol. 1, 500. Tsames, Ἡ τελείωσις τοῦ ἀνθρώπου κατὰ Νικήταν τὸν Στηθᾶτον, 24, argues that the cardinal virtues' and the four material elements' ancient theory was adopted from the mystic writers mainly through Maximus the Confessor, despite the fact that it was used also from the Alexandrinian and Cappadocian Church Fathers.

150. Shlenov, "Учение прп I," 196.

151. Max. *Qu. Dub.* 87 Declerck: such as the four elements are principle (ἀρχή) and basic material (στοιχείωσις) of the human body, so the basic material and principle of the soul from the four cardinal virtues achieve the righteousness (κατόρθωσις ἠθῶν).

152. Shlenov, "Учение прп I," 196, also assumed that Stethatos draws the term γενικαὶ ἀρεταί from an unspecified source from the previous ascetic tradition.

153. καὶ ἃ μηδ' ἂν «αὐτὸν δυνηθῆναι χωρῆσαι τὸν κάτω κόσμον» Ἰωάννης ὁ τοῦ Λόγου πρόδρομος, ἡ μεγάλη τῆς ἀληθείας φωνή, διωρίζετο (Greg. Naz. *Or.* 28.20.16–18 Gallay).

and all Gospels as a written word are a preparation; they forerun the mystical, eschatological, and unwritten God the Word and correspond to the four elements of the material world. The written word of the Gospels is considered as elementary because it is based on the letters, which are the elementary parts of the speech. This enables the connection of the Gospel's word to the four basic elements of the material world.[154] This concerns the readers of the Gospels, subject to the four elements with their senses. The four elements refer also to noetic elements; namely, the four virtues. The Gospels synthesize these two worlds because in both an analogy is found between element and higher form.[155] There is constantly an element of preparation for something higher and a synthesis of these elements for the purpose of higher knowledge.[156]

A similar synthesis is taught for the human being: the four virtues are elements for preparation and part of this synthesis. They unite the soul's tripartite and prepare it for the union with the spirit. The soul by uniting its powers with the senses creates a noetic world of virtues.[157] The latter are subjected to a process of compositions that lead to the virtue of love,[158] and another process where virtues are linked to the powers of the soul, the latter with the λόγοι hidden in the cardinal virtues, and the virtues' λόγοι with the intellect (νοῦς) hidden in the former. This process leads to union with God.[159] All the elements of the visible and invisible world (four elements, Gospels, virtues, senses, powers of the soul) are basically different manifestations of the one incarnated God-Word; through their syntheses, man is united to God.[160]

Stethatos received from Maximus's *Ambiguum ad Ioannem* 21 the concept of the cardinal virtues' correspondence to the four material elements; the idea of the creation of an intelligible world of virtues. Maximus, as Stethatos, attributes the cardinal virtues rather to this world, as a preparation for mystical experience.[161] Maximus, however, associates virtues and elements with the four Gospels and with the concept of elementary

154. Cristiani, "Κόσμος αἰσθητός," 460.

155. Max. *Ambig.* 21.3–6 Constas.

156. See also Grigoras, "Commentaires par le Père Dumitru Staniloae," 469nn282–83 on this, mainly on the ground of paragraphs 7–8 of Max. *Ambig.* 21 Constas.

157. Max. *Ambig.* 21.7–8 Constas.

158. Max. *Ambig.* 21.9 Constas. From the synthesis of the four virtues occur two (wisdom and mildness), and from the latter's synthesis occurs love. See also Grigoras, "Commentaires par le Père Dumitru Staniloae," 469–70n284.

159. Max. *Ambig.* 21.10 Constas.

160. Cristiani, "Κόσμος αἰσθητός," 460–62.

161. See Max. *Ambig.* 21, paragraphs 10, 11 Constas.

teaching (στοιχείωσις).[162] Stethatos and Maximus teach that the virtues are joined with something else (Gospels, senses, soul's powers, etc.). In the synthesis process, however, it seems that the cardinal virtues are eliminated, which is not attested by Stethatos (e.g., by the union of the virtues with the intellect's forces). Additionally, virtues according to Maximus prepare for something higher, while for Stethatos they do not have a "forerunning" function. Furthermore, no references to the properties of the elements and the virtues are made by Maximus. Stethatos is unique with the last idea because no author until him had ever made such a connection. No triadic God is assumed as creator of the noetic world; the latter is a creation of the human's free choice (κατὰ προαίρεσιν).[163] Therefore no mention is found to the indwelling of the Trinity in the soul, nor to that the virtues are innate. Additionally, Maximus does not refer to the concepts of four-horse chariot and the important theme of the soul's middle state, even though he teaches about the eschatological Word. Differences in correspondence of virtues and material elements are also found: for Maximus, fire corresponds to prudence, air to courage, water to temperance, and earth to justice.[164] Stethatos agrees with Maximus about prudence (partly because he adds the concept of a sky) and justice. I couldn't find a deeper reason why Stethatos modified Maximus's concept of temperance and courage.

Most of all, Maximus makes no explicit mention of the *imago mundi*, the soul's macrocosm concept, nor to the *imago Dei*. The noetic world does not reflect the material:[165] he talks only about two categories of beings, material and intelligible, in each of which preparatory elements exist, synthesized in a higher form. Stethatos uses further these concepts for the foundation of the intelligible paradise concept, which is not mentioned by Maximus and introduces the virtues' theory in the dispute with his contemporary intellectuals against the autonomization of philosophy, as I will show. This shows their essential contextual difference.

---

162. The term στοιχείωσις was used for the scientific manuals of the late antiquity philosophy. Maximus makes thus a pun with στοιχεῖον and στοιχείωσις. See Moreschini, *Massimo il Confessore*, 680n11, there also sources and literature.

163. *Max. Ambig.* 21.8 Constas. This happens when the soul's forces activate their energy through their connection with their corresponding bodily sense and organ; this presupposes the submission of the latter to the former.

164. *Max. Ambig.* 21.5 Constas.

165. See, however, Grigoras, "Commentaires par le Père Dumitru Staniloae," 469n282, where he assumes a mirror function of the material world by Maximus, but this is not explicitly mentioned in *Ambiguum* 21.

Philo Judaeus

Stethatos uses also Philo Judaeus's allegoresis of the four rivers of Eden (Gn 2:10–14), probably from *Legum Allegoriarum*[166] for the concept of the virtues as the four rivers of an intelligible paradise.[167] Unlike Philo, he does not attribute the virtues to every one of the four rivers. Stethatos probably draws directly from Philo, not only because this allegoresis appears only in Philo, but also because it is likely that Stethatos draws from him directly other concepts and passages as well.[168]

Centuriae

Stethatos also uses material from his own *Centuriae*,[169] mainly for the concept that the cardinal virtues where created from God like the four material elements and like the material world from these elements.[170] He omits from that material the concepts that associate the four virtues with ascetic practice[171] or with eremitic life,[172] the image of the four-horse char-

166. Ph. *leg.* 1.63–87 Cohn. See also Philo *posterit.* 128–29 Wendland. For the cardinal virtues in Philo, see Shlenov, "Учение прп II," 185, where no mention to Stethatos appeared, however; he assumed that through Philo the term γενικαὶ ἀρεταί became common in Christian doctrine; see also Shlenov, "Учение прп II," 184–85, also on the Old Testament. Stethatos draws also from Philo *congr.* 98–99 Wendland the concept of the four forces of the νοῦς (σύνεσις, ἀγχίνοια, κατάληψις, ἐντρέχεια; see Nic. Steth. *Cap.* 1.12, 856D Migne; Nic. Steth. *Anim.* 50.15–20 Darrouzès), except for ἐντρέχεια, which is not attested by Philo. These forces are to be connected to the virtues.

167. The four rivers of Eden are dealt with allegorically also by Leont. B. *Hom.* 11 46–70 Allen and Datema and by Anast. S. *Hex.* 8.2–7 Baggarly and Kuehn, but these authors make no mention of the four virtues.

168. See on that Diamantopoulos, *Die Hermeneutik des Niketas Stethatos*, 233n271, 291–92.

169. Nic. Steth. *Cap.* 1.12, 13, 72; 2.12; 3.49, PG 120, Migne.

170. See Nic. Steth. *Anim.* paragraphs 13, 26, 27, 29 Darrouzès, which draw from Nic. Steth. *Cap.* 1.72; 2.12; 3.49, PG 120, Migne that the virtues where created from God, like the four elements of the material world; *De anima* paragraph 27 Darrouzès draws from Nic. Steth. *Cap.* 3.49, PG 120, Migne the correspondence between the creation of the whole material world (not only its elements) to the intelligible; Nic. Steth. *Anim.* 28 Darrouzès draws from Nic. Steth. *Cap.* 2.12, PG 120, Migne the virtues' concept as four rivers; Nic. Steth. *Anim.* 29 Darrouzès draws from Nic. Steth. *Cap.* 3.49, PG 120, Migne the virtues' qualities' idea; Nic. Steth. *Anim.* 50 Darrouzès draws from Nic. Steth. *Cap.* 1.12, 72; 2.12; 3.95, PG 120, Migne the connection of the virtues to the intellect's forces and the κατὰ φύσιν idea. See also Nic. Steth. *Cap.* 3.95, PG 120, Migne for the concept in Nic. Steth. *Anim.* paragraph 13 Darrouzès that the soul consists of four elements *like the body*. See also the notes from Darrouzès, *Nicétas Stéthatos*, 88, 90, in the critical apparatus. Shlenov, "Учение прп I" and "Учение прп II," did not compare the material from the *Centuriae* with that in *De anima*, except for a short reference to Nic. Steth. *Cap.* 2.12, PG 120, Migne for the mentioned passage Nic. Steth. *Anim.* paragraph 28 Darrouzès; see Shlenov, "Учение прп I," 198–99.

171. Attested in Nic. Steth. *Cap.* 1.12, 13; 2.12; 3.95, PG 120, Migne. The relevant Nic. Steth. *Cap.* 1.96, PG 120, Migne was omitted at all. Stethatos teaches there that the general virtues are used against ghosts and embodiments of demons in sleep. See on this chapter also Shlenov, "Учение прп I," 203–4.

172. Nic. Steth. *Cap.* 1.72, PG 120, 856D Migne. Stethatos criticizes in this chapter the

iot,[173] God's enthronement,[174] the concept of the virtues' collapse or rebuilding,[175] and some definitions of the four virtues: according to *Centuria* 1.13, justice is ἡ πρὸς τὸ ὁμογενὲς ἐλεήμεων συμπάθεια ("consists in merciful compassion for one's fellow beings"); temperance is ἡ περιεκτικὴ ἐγκράτεια ("all-inclusive self-control"), and prudence is ἡ εὐδιάκριτος διάκρισις τῶν θείων καὶ ἀνθρωπίνων πραγμάτων ("exact discrimination in things human and divine").[176] These definitions concern mainly the ascetical stage.

He also modifies the content of the *Centuria* 1.13. In *De anima* the knowledge of the human and divine things is not identified with prudence, which is the intelligible sky, but is part of it: it corresponds to the intelligible sun and moon of this intelligible sky;[177] in *Centuria* 1.13, prudence is the distinction of the human and divine things.[178] Modifications are also attested by *Centuria* 3.49. For example, concerning the intelligible sky, in *Centuria* 3.49, the αἰθήρ and the νοήματα as stars of the intelligible sky (prudence) are missing (the stars appear, but not as νοήματα); the sun and moon are the γνῶσις and φυσικὴ θεωρία,[179] where in *De anima* they are the γνῶσις τῶν θείων and γνῶσις τῶν ἀνθρωπίνων πραγμάτων;[180] in *Centuria* 3.49, the Holy Spirit is not mentioned as the element that gives light to sun and moon.

The fact that Stethatos in other passages of *De anima* refers to the *Centuriae*[181] and to other of his works,[182] but he makes no mention to the *Cen-*

---

extreme emphasis on eremitism as a way of achieving virtues and highlights that the cardinal virtues are innate in man; thus no special place, such as a desert, is needed, but an internal spiritual life that would revive the virtues, which already exist in man. Additionally, the chapter's explicit formulation that the virtues are innate is omitted in *De anima*; however, this can be logically concluded with the idea that God creates them by the creation of the soul.

173. See the passages in "Four-Horse Chariot."

174. Attested in Nic. Steth. *Cap.* 3.49, PG 120, 977A–B Migne.

175. Nic. Steth. *Cap.* 2.12, PG 120, 905B Migne.

176. Nic. Steth. *Cap.* 1.13, PG 120, 856D–857A Migne; for the translations, see Palmer, Sherrard and Ware, *Philokalia*, 82. Courage is not mentioned at all. Although Shlenov, "Учение прп I," 195, mentioned chapter 13 by his presentation of the passages, where the cardinal virtues' theory appears, he did not discuss it further. For the connection of prudence to discretion in Patristic literature, see Shlenov, "Учение прп II," 187.

177. Nic. Steth. *Anim.* 27.9–15 Darrouzès.

178. Nic. Steth. *Cap.* 1.13, PG 120, 857A Migne.

179. Nic. Steth. *Cap.* 3.49, PG 120, 977B Migne.

180. Nic. Steth. *Anim.* 27, 12–14 Darrouzès. More on this in "Knowledge of Divine and Human Things and Cardinal Virtues."

181. Nic. Steth. *Anim.* 19.4, 21.1–3, 52.2–4, 57.4–5, 58.4–5 (see on this passage Darrouzès, *Nicétas Stéthatos*, 121n1), 71.25–26 Darrouzès.

182. Nic. Steth. *Anim.* 44.6–7 (reference to lost letter *Ad Cosmam*); 71.26–27 (*Hier.*) Darrouzès.

turiae in the passages where he teaches about the four virtues, strengthens my hypothesis, that he aims with this elaboration to emphasize on their connection to the second stage of spiritual progress (φυσικὴ θεωρία) and with the *imago mundi* concept. Except for *Centuria* 3.49 in all the *Centuriae's* chapters, where the cardinal virtues are discussed, the aspect of the first stage (πρακτικὴ φιλοσοφία) is well attested, and the second stage (φυσικὴ θεωρία) is rare.[183] The *imago mundi* concept is not attested in them at all.[184] With his silence, Stethatos aims to leave the doctrine concerning ascesis and the first stage unnoticed.

This also indicates that Stethatos elaborated his material for the mentioned function of *De anima* as an anthropological fundament of the main concept of *De Paradiso*, that the human soul as an *imago mundi* is and depicts also an intelligible paradise. This can be proved additionally with reference to the modification of *Centuria* 2.12 in *De anima*: in the former the four rivers water the city of God—that is, the heart of man that is purified—and in the latter they water the intelligible paradise.[185] Stethatos emphasizes the concept of an intelligible paradise and modifies his material for this purpose.

The Term τετρακτύς

Neither Maximus nor Philo uses the *terminus* τετρακτύς for the cardinal virtues,[186] which indicates that Stethatos draws also from another source. The term appears in the cardinal virtues' context before Stethatos in six texts[187] from Christian writers.[188] It is quite possible that Stethatos drew this term from one of them, probably from the *Canon in Sanctos Menam, Victorem, Vicentium, Stephanidem et in Sanctum Theodorum Studitam.*[189] The

183. The only direct connection of the virtues with φυσικὴ θεωρία in the *Centuriae* is attested in Nic. Steth. *Cap.* 3.43, PG 120, 973B–C Migne. This chapter highlights the aspect that φυσικὴ θεωρία is a stage; however, its investigation aspect is certainly implied; see Contemplation of Nature. This chapter is otherwise not used in the treatise *De anima*.

184. Nic. Steth. *Cap.* 3.49, PG 120, 977A–C Migne teaches about the creation of the intelligible world of virtues, but there is no mention either that it must be contemplated or that it is an *imago*, which is taught and emphasized in the treatise *De anima*.

185. See Nic. Steth. *Cap.* 2.12, PG 120, 905B Migne and Nic. Steth. *Anim.* 28.8–13 Darrouzès.

186. According to a search of the *Thesaurus Linguae Graecae* accessed on May 6, 2021.

187. According to a search of the *Thesaurus Linguae Graecae* accessed on May 6, 2021.

188. An., *Epig.* 93, 1 Beckby; Evagr. Pont. *Or.*, PG 79, 1166C Migne; Synes. *Ep.* 140.36 Garzya; Phot. *Luc.* 160 Antonopoulou; Theoph. Cont. *Chron.* 72.28–29 Ševcenko. Roques, commenting on Synesius's mentioned passage, thinks that the meaning is rather Neoplatonic but that of the *Epig.* Platonic (Synes. *Ep.* Garzya, 404–5); see also there for older literature on Synesius's *Ep.* 140. For the *Epig.*, see also Wehrhahn, "Spätkarolingische Wandmalerei in Reichenau-Oberzell?," 342–44.

189. Jo. D. et Cos. mel. *can.* 9. Ode, 8. Troparion Kominis and Schirò.

fact that this troparion refers to Theodorus Studita[190] enables us to assume that Stethatos could have been influenced from this canon. In his *Vita Symeonis*, Stethatos says that he composed canons on Theodorus Studita as an exercise for the composition of canons on Symeon the New Theologian.[191] We therefore cannot exclude the hypothesis that during this preparatory period he had read this canon as a pattern. Perhaps he is the author of its troparia on Theodorus, which were added later to this canon; the remaining troparia (on Menas, Victor, and Stephanis) are attributed to a period before Stethatos; namely, to John Damascene and Cosmas of Jerusalem.[192] The term τετρακτύς is otherwise not attested in another canon apart from Stethatos's *Canon in Sanctum Nicolaum*.[193] This would make this hypothesis more reasonable. But if Stethatos is not the author of the troparia on Theodorus, then, if he drew the term from a canon,[194] he most likely drew the term from this canon because it would be the only one possible.[195]

Contextualization

We must now answer several questions. Why does Stethatos draw from Philo or Maximus? What are the problems that caused Stethatos's doctrine? Does Stethatos try only to found his doctrine about the intelligible paradise?

Philo Judaeus

I will discuss first Philo's mentioned image of the four rivers by Stethatos. In my study about the hermeneutics of Stethatos, I assumed that the latter proposes a hermeneutic mysticism, where Philo's concepts are fundamental,[196] mainly because he discusses with intellectuals, which I assume also here, in his aretology.

Additionally, I would not rule out the hypothesis of a competition

190. See also the commentary to Jo. D. et Cos. mel. *can.* Kominis and Schirò, 600–602.

191. Nic. Steth. *Symeon.* 136.1–3 Hausherr. Kaklamanos edited a canon on Theodorus Studita (*Can. Th.*), which he attributed to Stethatos (see introduction, 106–7).

192. Jo. D. et Cos. mel. *can.* Kominis and Schirò, 601.

193. According to a search of the *Thesaurus Linguae Graecae* on May 6, 2021. The mentioned canon, edited by Kaklamanos, does not include the *terminus*.

194. This is possible because Stethatos does not otherwise draw from the other five texts in his works.

195. Shlenov, "Учение прп II," did not discuss the problem of this term by Stethatos. He made a short reference to the term in general and *in abstracto* (179n3); namely, in the fact that it was used for the four virtues together.

196. Diamantopoulos, *Die Hermeneutik des Niketas Stethatos*, 232–38, 594–95.

between Stethatos and Michael Psellos[197] on who understands and better uses Philo, because Psellos also uses Philo's allegoresis by his exegesis of Genesis 2:6.[198] As I have already assumed,[199] Stethatos's hermeneutic arguments against Psellos, included also in his treatise *De Paradiso*, not only concern a theoretical field but also obviously presuppose a competition between the hermeneutic praxis of the schools of the Stoudios's monastery and of Psellos.

Maximus the Confessor

The main question is rather Maximus, because Stethatos draws mainly from him for the cardinal virtues' theory. In the eleventh century, a conflict about Maximus is attested between mystics and philosophers, mainly Psellos, summarized in the question, Who is the better user and interpreter of Maximus?[200] Psellos, who is involved in this debate, discusses the cardinal virtues in some of his works.[201] But he does not quote Maximus's mentioned doctrine, although he often comments and criticizes his other works.[202]

I think we must see Stethatos's insistence on Maximus's doctrine, especially its elaboration from Stethatos, in the context of that debate: he wants to prove that he understands Maximus better than Psellos by modifying and adjusting Maximus's teaching about the virtues, which Psellos does not discuss at all, to the needs of his treatise. This dispute must be seen further in the wider debate between mysticism and philosophy of the eleventh century,[203] where Stethatos inserts the Platonic doctrine in a mystic context on the fundaments of Maximus's doctrine. Psellos thematizes the four virtues only in a philosophical context.[204] Important is thus not only

197. On Psellos as intellectual, see Jenkins, "Michael Psellos."

198. Psell. *Theol.* 2.24.9–16 Westerink and Duffy. On Psellos and Philo, see also Diamantopoulos, *Die Hermeneutik des Niketas Stethatos*, 594–96.

199. Diamantopoulos, *Die Hermeneutik des Niketas Stethatos*, 706–27.

200. Diamantopoulos, *Die Hermeneutik des Niketas Stethatos*, 775–77, see also the relevant bibliography, where one may find the literature about this matter; see esp. Simonopetrites, "St Maximos the Confessor," 39–42. I thank F. Lauritzen for his useful critical remarks and questions concerning this idea at the conference in Venice, mentioned in note 58.

201. Psell. *Theol.* 2.24 Westerink and Duffy; Psell. *Omn.* 68, 69, 70, 76, 79 Westerink; Psell. *Phil. Min.* 2.32 O'Meara.

202. Diamantopoulos, *Die Hermeneutik des Niketas Stethatos*, 565–66.

203. See on that the literature mentioned in Diamantopoulos, *Die Hermeneutik des Niketas Stethatos*, 15–16n6, and the second part of the study. See esp. also Lauritzen, "Debate on Faith and Reason."

204. Psellos discusses only in one case the cardinal virtues in a pure Patristic context in the mentioned Psell. *Phil. Min.* 2.32 O'Meara, where he interprets passages from Synesius Cyrenensis's

Maximus's reception and elaboration from Stethatos, but also the inclusion of the former in this dispute.

This is further thinkable when the mentioned deeper aim of *De anima* is considered; namely, the foundation of a basis of arguments to prove the existence of the intelligible paradise, the main argument of *De Paradiso*. Stethatos would try to show then that he understands and uses Maximus better in the sense that he can prove that the latter "belongs" to the mystics, because the intelligible paradise concept was their symbol of the mystical experience.[205] The adaption and elaboration of Maximus's cardinal virtues' concept as corresponding with the four material elements would then serve as a fundament of the mystical theology against the intellectuals' appeal on Maximus as "their" philosopher.[206]

Knowledge of Divine and Human Things and Cardinal Virtues

The debate between mystics and philosophers as a background can be considered in a broader perspective: Stethatos teaches that in the world of virtues in the noetic sky of prudence, the sun and moon are the knowledge of divine things and the knowledge of human things; they illuminate the whole noetic world.[207] This reference is the second definition of philosophy of stoic origin, which was taught together with five others[208] in the Neoplatonic school of Alexandria; Stethatos draws him from John Damascene.[209] For Stethatos, philosophy is the mystical doctrine that illuminates all over the world.

This emphasis on the definition of philosophy is explained with the conflicts of the eleventh century, caused by the attempt to autonomize philosophy from intellectuals such as Psellos or Italos. Stethatos stands in this

---

Ep. 140; however, there he also refers to Neoplatonic sources. See also "Aretological Debate" about the moral discussion.

205. See Rigo, "Teodoro diacono della Madre di Dio delle Blacherne," 309–10, and the literature mentioned in Diamantopoulos, *Die Hermeneutik des Niketas Stethatos*, 657n657.

206. Psellos many times calls Maximus his philosopher (ὁ ἐμὸς φιλόσοφος). See, apart from Simonopetrites, "St Maximos the Confessor," 40, sources and literature on that also in Diamantopoulos, *Die Hermeneutik des Niketas Stethatos*, 566 and esp. 566n333.

207. Nic. Steth. *Anim.* 27.12–15 Darrouzès.

208. Philosophy is: (a) knowledge of beings as beings, (b) knowledge of human and divine things, (c) study of death, (d) assimilation to God as far as possible for humans, (e) art of arts and science of sciences, and (f) love of wisdom. See my note 209 below for literature on this.

209. See on this definition in general Chroust, "Late Hellenistic 'Textbook Definitions' of Philosophy"; Roueché, "Middle Byzantine Handbook of Logical Terminology"; and Diamantopoulos, *Die Hermeneutik des Niketas Stethatos*, 230–32, 316–17.

dispute for the mysticism as the real philosophy against its secularization. He modifies for this purpose in *De anima* the chapter 49 of his third *Centuria*, where he also speaks about the creation of the intelligible world, here especially about the intelligible fire, which one finds in the intelligible sky, that is, prudence. There the two luminaries are the divine knowledge and φυσικὴ θεωρία; in *De anima* he uses the mentioned definition for the two luminaries, which proves his aim to emphasize the definition of philosophy and his mystical understanding of it against the intellectuals' one.[210] The mystic philosophy is thus the light of prudence and of the whole world of the virtues. It is important to know that divine knowledge and φυσικὴ θεωρία, mentioned in chapter 49, are the two last stages of mystics, inaccessible to the impure or via rationality. The fact that Stethatos chooses to replace the cardinal virtues' connection to φυσικὴ θεωρία of chapter 49, where φυσικὴ θεωρία, as I showed, is essential for his cardinal virtues' concept, with a connection to the definition of philosophy, proves his involvement in the intellectual debate of his times and his aim to emphasize on the "right" understanding of philosophy.

Stethatos also connects the four virtues with the second definition of philosophy in chapter 43 of his third *Centuria*: virtues and knowledge of divine and human things are also there clearly part of the second stage (φυσικὴ θεωρία), where ascetical practice is presupposed.[211] Prudence and philosophy thus belong, according to Stethatos, not to the intellectuals-philosophers but to the mystics-philosophers, who after purification contemplate the beings. There cannot exist any wisdom without the mystic's spirituality.

Aretological Debate

In this context I also assume an aretological conflict. Contemplation of nature as research of beings and as a spiritual stage is related closely to aretology in Stethatos's thought. The virtues are accepted only in a broader system of a noetic world, which depicts the material one (*imago mundi*) and God (*imago Dei*), where the Trinity is also united with the soul. The

---

210. Psellos also taught about the second definition of philosophy together with the five others, if the treatise Psell. *Phil. Min.* 1.49 Duffy can be attributed to him. There are, however, other Psellos passages concerning the θεῖα καὶ ἀνθρώπινα πράγματα, a phrase from this definition. See, e.g., Psell. *Or. Paneg.* 15.89 Dennis. Italos also refers to this definition in a pure philosophical context in Ital. *Quaest.* 16.31 Joannou.

211. Nic. Steth. *Cap.* 3.43, PG 120, 973B Migne. In the also relevant Nic. Steth. *Cap.* 1.13, PG 120, 857A Migne, prudence is the distinction between divine and human things.

virtues themselves, without the creation of the intelligible world and not as part of the spiritual progress, are rather meaningless.[212] Stethatos also unites the virtues with the intellect's forces, the heart of mysticism, as also Shlenov showed. I argue that he criticizes with that the autonomization of ethics against mysticism or their conceptualization with Neoplatonism's mystic.

This tendency can be seen, for example, in the irony of Psellos against the Ναζιραίους, with which he means probably ascetics with extreme ascetical ideals, which lead to mystical experience, probably also Stethatos himself.[213] Psellos defends the middle way in the ethics against the "extremism" of mystics.[214]

Also, E. Delli,[215] briefly referring to the moral teaching of Stethatos on the cardinal virtues, indicated that it is based on the Patristic tradition. She found parallel references to Psellos's teaching on the four virtues, but based on Platonism, Neoplatonism, or Synesius Cyrenensis.[216] Delli assumed not only an ethic of μεσότης but also a concept of union with God in Psellos's ethics, which man finds also in Stethatos. However, comparing Stethatos's with Psellos's anthropology and psychology on the ground of aretology, where she explored also knowledge of God and deification according to Psellos,[217] she saw them as quite different concepts. Although Psellos accepted an unmediated union with God, he based it on Neoplatonic foundations (mainly aretological); further and most important, the union is achieved only through education and philosophical knowledge. Delli emphasized in this context Psellos's concept of the σπουδαῖος, a man of civic

212. See also Tsames, Ἡ τελείωσις τοῦ ἀνθρώπου κατὰ Νικήταν τὸν Στηθᾶτον, 33.

213. Psell. *Chron.* 6a18 Reinsch; see also Psell. *Ep. Cer.* 2.32–41 Criscuolo; see also the literature and discussion on these passages and on *Chron.* 6a8 Reinsch (Psellos rejects the extreme ascetism as an element of a politician's character and stands for the middle way in ethics) in Diamantopoulos, *Die Hermeneutik des Niketas Stethatos,* 139–41, esp. 140–41n406. See there also for this group of ascetics and for Stethatos's positive attitude toward them. See esp. for *Chron.* 6a8 Reinsch Lauritzen, "Mixed Life of Plato's Philebus in Psellos' Chronographia."

214. See note 213 above. For Psellos's ethics, see also Walter, *Michael Psellos,* 102–79. For the middle ethical way by Psellos, where the abovementioned passages from Psellos, also Psell. *Chron.* 6a7 Reinsch and the literature about them are discussed, see Walter, *Michael Psellos,* 103–7, 160. For a short reference on his teaching about the cardinal virtues, see Walter, *Michael Psellos,* 176–77.

215. Delli, "La phantasia selon Michel Psellos," 116–17.

216. For these sources, see Delli, "La phantasia selon Michel Psellos," 116n320. A main Neoplatonic source comes Porph. *Sent.* 32 Lamberz. For Synesius, see in "The Term τετρακτύς" about *Ep.* 140, which also draws from Porphyrius; see the commentary on Synes. *Ep.* 140 Garzya, 405; there also more literature on the Neoplatonic virtues' hierarchy, which include the cardinal virtues.

217. Delli, "La phantasia selon Michel Psellos," 117–21.

virtues within human society based on the principle of metropathy.[218] This is in other words the mentioned idea of the middle way in ethics. Psellos's account of faith is according to Delli not naive and spontaneous. Divination is achieved with the wisdom in this earthly world through civic virtues. Erudition is the basic virtue for the knowledge of God. Psellos differs significantly from Stethatos's concept of isolation (μονότροπος)—that is, far from the world and alone with God, where no need for education exists[219]— which is essentially the mentioned criticism against the Ναζιραίους.[220] Delli assumed thus also in Psellos's thought an ascension through virtues, but with a philosophical method (Neoplatonic), which also requires friendship, the arts, and sciences and not the ascetic one of Stethatos.[221]

Even though *De omnifaria doctrina* could be dated later than *De anima*,[222] because it is addressed to the young emperor and pupil of Psellos, Michael VII (1071–78), we must assume that Psellos had held similar positions in the previous decades, mainly in the 40s and 50s, and thus it is safe at least chronologically to accept that Stethatos answers them in *De anima*. Shlenov[223] assumed that the material from *Phil. Min.* 2.32 O'Meara, which shows parallel teachings with the one in *De omnifaria doctrina*, attests the teaching method of aretology, where the cardinal virtues are included, in the profane schools of Constantinople in the eleventh century.[224] Shlenov compared this teaching with Stethatos's one and inferred that the latter is a simpler concept about the harmonious connection of the cardinal virtues with the soul's forces.[225] Thus, even though Shlenov did not systematical-

218. See on σπουδαῖος Delli, "La phantasia selon Michel Psellos," 117n329; Diamantopoulos, *Die Hermeneutik des Niketas Stethatos*, 212n184.

219. See on this concept of Stethatos Delli, "La phantasia selon Michel Psellos," 115–17.

220. Delli was based for her mentioned analysis mainly on Psell. *Theol.* 1.63.2–9 Gautier, on the mentioned passages from *De omnifaria doctrina*, and on Psell. *Phil. Min.* 2.32 O'Meara, but also on other Psellian sources. She made no references to the mentioned passages from *Chronographia*, however.

221. Stethatos is against an extreme eremitic life, however; see note 172 above. Walter, *Michael Psellos*, 105, argued that the Neoplatonic ideas about the hierarchy of virtues in the mentioned passages in *De omnifaria doctrina* contradict the concept of accumulation of scientific knowledge. See also his criticism on Delli ("La phantasia selon Michel Psellos," 106–7).

222. If my dating of *De anima* to 1050 is correct. It is in general accepted that *De anima* was written around 1080; see for that and my chronology Diamantopoulos, *Die Hermeneutik des Niketas Stethatos*, 600–654.

223. Shlenov, "Учение прп II," 184.

224. See also an eleventh-century *Miscellaneum*, which drew from Psellos: An. *Misc.*, chapter 13 Pontikos. See also Shlenov, "Учение прп II," 183–84.

225. For the parallelism with Psellos, see also a brief reference in Shlenov, "Учение прп I," 197, where he did not assume a conflict.

ly compare the concepts, he importantly also accepted the possibility of a chronological and conceptual parallelism between the two authors. I also showed that Delli compared Stethatos's and Psellos's teachings on the basis of *De omnifaria doctrina*, where also the cardinal virtues are discussed. Additionally, Walter compared briefly the ethics of Stethatos and Psellos, even though he assumed Stethatos to be an earlier author.[226]

The ability to compare Stethatos's and Psellos's concepts can further be proved not only on the basis of Psellos's other mentioned passages (mainly *Chronographia*, *Theol.* 1.63, *Phil. Min.* 2.32), which are or can be dated much earlier, but also on the fact of an attested tendency in the works of other intellectuals of the early eleventh century to introduce the cardinal virtues in a philosophical and not Christian context. A few years before Psellos, an important teacher of rhetoric, Ioannes Siceliotes,[227] inserted some of the cardinal virtues' theory in his lectures on Hermogenes's rhetoric,[228] where also Neoplatonic elements appear, so that one can speak about a philosophization of rhetoric.[229] The cardinal virtues' discussion is attested in two more eleventh-century texts, dated a few decades later than Stethatos and Psellos; namely, in the already mentioned *Miscellaneum*[230] and in the *Dioptra* of Philippos Monotropos,[231] who draws directly from Stethatos's *De anima*. In them, as in *Phil. Min.* 2.32 O'Meara, the term τετρακτύς, which I discussed in "The Term τετρακτύς," is additionally attested. The fact that this term appears in four texts in the eleventh century and one from the twelfth century that draws directly from them, a frequency that is not attested in its use in the earlier centuries, is a further evidence that the cardinal virtues' theory became a *locus communis* in the eleventh century's aretology.

It is thus well attested that in the eleventh century the cardinal virtues' theory became an essential part of the intellectuals' teaching activity and was joined with Neoplatonic doctrines. This, together with concepts about the middle way in ethics, caused the reaction of the mystics. We must see

226. Walter, *Michael Psellos*, 101–2, 141, 150, 170. He made no comparison on the ground of the cardinal virtues, however.

227. See on him Papaioannou, "Sicily, Constantinople, Miletos," 274–77. He taught in Constantinople and flourished in the eleventh century, probably in the 20s.

228. Sicel. *Proleg.* 398.27–401.22 Rabe; he discusses temperance and prudence. See Roilos, *Amphoteroglossia*, 144, and Diamantopoulos, *Die Hermeneutik des Niketas Stethatos*, 516.

229. See Magdalino, "From 'Encyclopaedism' to 'Humanism,'" 11–14, and Diamantopoulos, *Die Hermeneutik des Niketas Stethatos*, 495–505, with discussion of further literature on this matter.

230. An. *Misc.*, 13.33–35 Pontikos. The passages repeat Psell. *Phil. Min.* 2.32 O'Meara.

231. Phil. Monotr. *Dioptr.* 4.7.1488–95, 1825–37 Lauriotes. In the last passage, Philippos draws directly from *De anima*, paragraph 29, Darrouzès.

Stethatos's doctrine in this context as a "mystic" answer to such challenges. Nicetas points out the necessity to connect the virtues with the second stage of contemplation of nature, after purification, as condition of mystical theology. The κατὰ φύσιν human is called not only to be virtuous, but also to represent in himself an intelligible world secretly united with the Triadic God. This world includes also an intelligible paradise, which the virtues nourish.

CHAPTER 12 ⫼ John Italos on *Authypostaton* and *Authyparkton* in *Quaestio* 7 and His Processing of Psellos's *Phil. min.* I, Op. 7

Denis Walter

Introduction

John Italos (1025–82), student of the famous Michael Psellos (1018–76) and his successor as *hypathos tôn philosophôn*, was not born in Constantinople and learned the Greek language only to a certain extent, as Anna Komnena tells us in her *Alexiad*,[1] not positively and without sensitivity for problems that come with migration. Italos is furthermore known for having been condemned because of several philosophical positions he was said to hold that might have been against Christian doctrine. The anathema was pronounced on his teachings, about which much has been written in literature.[2] Anna Komnene's negative judgment of Italos, which mainly refers to his character and behavior, does not make her ignore that Italos was an expert of Aristotle. In fact, we find in his writings many arguments with Aristotelian themes, as can be seen not least in his commentary on Books 2,

1. Anna Komnene, *Alexiad* V 8 Kambylis, Reinsch.
2. Clucas, *Trial of John Italos*; Gulliard, "Le Process official de Jean l'Italien"; Kraft and Perczel, "John Italos on the Eternity of the World." See Melloni, "Great Councils of the Orthodox Churches," 2013.

3, and 4 of *Topica, De dialectica, De syllogismis, De rhetorica*, and *Quaestiones quodlibetales*.[3] This is one of the reasons why older research has contrasted the "Platonist" Psellos with the "Aristotelian" Italos.

We will here investigate whether Italos explains two terms that do not originate from Aristotle but became extremely important in the later Platonic tradition and were taken up by Christian Neoplatonists: *authypostaton* and *authyparkon*.

Can We Identify Constant Philosophical Positions of John Italos?

Finding out the philosophical positions of John Italos is probably even more difficult than with other Byzantine philosophers, since we have only few of his writings. Especially in the *Quaestiones*, he takes up and elaborates a multitude of arguments from the ancient commentary tradition, partly by interpreting Aristotle with the help of Proclus.[4] The literature discussed his strange attempt to refute the "Hellenic" concept of matter in *Quaestio* 92, in which he tries to play off the Plotinian position against the Proclean.[5] This kind of "sophistic" mixing of positions is not a constant feature of his writings, as he mostly refers precisely to the similarities and differences of the views of the classical philosophers he investigates. In *Quaestio* 42, for example, he argues that the Platonic *dodekahedron* from Timaeus[6] corresponds to the Aristotelian *aether*[7] from *De caelo*.[8] The Aristotelian *nous pathêtikos*[9] also finds its counterpart in Plato's *phantasia* concept, which corresponds to an inferior way of thinking.[10] But he also refers to the differences between the traditions that go back to Plato and Aristotle.[11] In fact, he writes

3. Kraft and Perczel, "John Italos on the Eternity of the World," 666n25. There might have been other works that did not survive. The date of the *Questiones* is not clear. Some of the texts of the *Questiones* could have been composed as answers to the anathemas after a possible rehabilitation of Italos.

4. Ital. *Quaest.* 26 (p. 27), 28 (p. 29) and 74 (p. 125) Joannou.

5. E.g., Trizio, "Late Antique Debate on Matter-Evil." A new interpretation was presented by Kraft and Perczel, "John Italos on the Eternity of the World," 701n91: "Italos' purpose in *Ital. Quaest.* 92 is to refute that matter is an eternal substrate." See Lauritzen, "Psello discepolo di Stethato," and "Psellos and Plotinus."

6. Pl. *Tim.* 55b Burnet.

7. Arist. *Cael.* I 2–4 Moraux.

8. Ital. *Quaest.* 42, 33–37. Joannou

9. Cf. Ital. *Quaest.* 37; *Arist. De. An.* 3.4.429a10 Ross.

10. Pl. *Phd.* 66d Burnet; *Pl. Sph.* 232a Burnet.

11. Ital. *Quaest.* 3 (p. 4, 12) Joannou.

in one passage, Plato is the greatest philosopher, while Aristotle was only praised for his *Physics* and his teachings about the soul.[12] This kind of particular praise of one philosopher over the other must not lead us—as it is also the case in Psellos's writings—to assume that this is always an indication of a general preference for them.

But there is also another line of argument in his writings, which is not only evident in the abovementioned *Quaestio* 92: the presentation of Christian positions.[13] He argues for the immortality of the soul,[14] the resurrection of the body,[15] about the Trinity,[16] and presents his conviction that the world is finite.[17] Among all these approaches, statements, concepts, and argumentative strategies, one of the few constant elements that has been worked out in research from the writings of Italos is the ontological position called by Linos Benakis "conceptual realism" or "moderate realism."[18] The "moderate realism" goes back to Ammonios Hermeious's *Commentary on the Isagoge* of Porphyrios, in which it is said that universals existed in three ways: as ideas in God (*pro tôn pollôn*), then in matter (*en tois pollois*), and as abstractions by the human soul from the many things (*epi tois pollois*).[19] A further element of his teaching, which not only belongs to the basic concepts of philosophy in Byzantium but also recurs in several of his *Quaestiones*, is the *authypostaton* and the *authyparkton*, which will now be examined in more detail.

Authypostaton and *Authyparkton*

As Christophe Erismann writes, *authypostaton* is the traditional Byzantine name of substance.[20] In fact, the term has a long tradition that has its roots in Stoicism[21] but became particularly prominent in the Neoplatonic tradition. Thus the "self-constitutive," as it is often translated, is in a relevant manner first found in Plotinus, who uses it to describe the ori-

12. Ital. *Quaest.* 50 (p. 64, 32–34) Joannou.
13. Ierodiakonou, "John Italos on Universals," 26.
14. Ital. *Quaest.* 36 (p. 44), 37 (p. 45), 50 (p. 63), 56 (p. 79) Joannou.
15. Ital. *Quaest.* 71 (p. 44). 120), 86 (p. 134), 89 (p. 135) Joannou.
16. Ital. *Quaest.* 68 (p. 109), 69 (p. 114), 71 (p. 120), 88 (p. 134) Joannou.
17. Kraft and Perczel, "John Italos on the Eternity of the World."
18. Benakis, "To problêma tôn genikôn ennoiôn," 311–40; Ierodiakonou, "John Italos on Universals," 232–40.
19. Ital. *Quaest.* 3 (s. 4.36–5.8), 4 (s. 6.4–8) and 23 (s. 25.7–12) Joannou.
20. Erismann, "Logic in Byzantium," 372.
21. Beierwaltes, *Das wahre Selbst*, 161; Whittaker, "Historical Background of Proclus' Doctrine of the Authypostaton," 193–230.

gin of all beings, the One.[22] His view evoked the criticism of Proclus, who considered the plurality of the self-constitutive from its two elements, the "constituting" and the "constituted" "part" to be inappropriate for the One, which could not consist of such a plurality.[23] Proclus therefore finds the *authypostaton* no longer in the first principle but in the subsequent intellect and soul. It is important to note that the criterion for the self-constitution is according to him the immanence of reversion. This can be found as the reversion of the *nous* toward itself. The reversion to itself can be also found in a similar manner in the soul.[24]

Apart from these two uses, there is another strand of interpretation that stems from the Alexandrian tradition. In contrast to Proclus, Ammonius Hermeiou[25] and David use *authypostaton* in their commentaries to the *Isagoge* of Porphyry as the basis for accidents. David even refers directly to Aristotle (who does not use the term).[26] *Authypostaton* thus in a sense takes on the role of the Aristotelian *ousia*, as that which exists in the first sense, and on which the accidentals depend. In contrast to the aforementioned interpretation of the *authypostaton* of Plotinus and Proclus, we find here a strong turn "downward," which appears in a similar way in John of Damascus,[27] whom Italos consults for his own investigation. According to G. Richter, John of Damascus does indeed process elements of an Aristotelian tradition[28] but can in principle be described neither as an Aristotelian nor as a Neoplatonist.[29] However, he seems not only to follow the Alexandrian understanding of *authypostaton* but also to focus on the individual thing and even uses the body as an example for it.[30] *Authypostaton* and *au-*

22. Beierwaltes, *Das wahre Selbst*, 179–81; Plot. 6.8.13,57*ff.*; Plot. 6.8.16,17.

23. Beierwaltes, *Das wahre Selbst*, 178:"Proklos ist allerdings nicht der Erste, der Plotin in diesem Punkte kritisiert, dies hat bereits *Iamblich* getan." Procl. *In Prm.* 1145,34*ff.*, 1146,8*ff.*, 1149,32*ff.*, 1150,16*ff.* Steel; Procl. *Theol. Plat.* II 2.18,15–17 Saffrey Westerink.

24. Beierwaltes, *Das wahre Selbst*, 174; Gersh, *From Iamblichus to Eriugena*, 126n5.

25. λέγω δὴ τὴν οὐσίαν, ἥτις αὐθυπόστατον ὑπάρχει (*Ammon. In Porph.* 70.8 Busse) πρᾶγμα καὶ γενικώτατον γένος· αἱ γὰρ ἄλλαι κατηγορίαι συμβεβηκότα ὑπάρχουσιν αὐτῆς·

26. Τὸ ἀχώριστον διαιρεῖ εἰς συμβεβηκὸς καὶ οὐσίαν, καὶ ἐν μὲν τῷ λέγειν καθ' ἑαυτάς δηλοῖ τὰς οὐσιώδεις (οὕτω γὰρ καὶ ὁ Ἀριστοτέλης· τοῦτο γὰρ δηλοῖ τὸ αὐθυπόστατον), ἐν δὲ τῷ λέγειν κατὰ συμβεβηκός ῥᾷστα τὰ συμβεβηκότα δηλοῖ, ἅτινα καθ' ἑαυτὰ μὲν οὔκ εἰσιν, ἐν ἑτέρῳ δέ (David. Porph. 184, 9–12 Busse). Richter, *Die Dialektik des Johannes von Damaskos*, 247n593.

27. Who uses Ammonios Hermeiou's position.

28. Richter, *Die Dialektik des Johannes von Damaskos*, 8–22; we can find, e.g., *ousia* as described by John Damascene in Ammon. *Porph.* 70, 11–13.

29. Richter, *Die Dialektik des Johannes von Damaskos*, 247.

30. He uses a position that is contrary to the one found in οὐδὲν γὰρ σῶμα αὐθυπόστατον (*Procl. In R.* 2.14.12 Kroll); Οὐ γάρ ἐστιν αὐθυπόστατον οὐδὲ αὐτογενὲς τῶν σωμάτων οὐδέν, ἀλλὰ πᾶν τὸ τοιοῦτον, ἐν ἑνὶ τὴν αἰτίαν καὶ τὸ ἀπ' αἰτίας συνηρηκός, ἀσώματόν ἐστι καὶ ἀμερές (*Procl. Theol. Plat.* 3.20.13–16 Saffrey Westerink); Ἡ οὐσία δὲ τέμνεται εἰς σῶμα καὶ ἀσώματον. Ἰδοὺ τὸ

thyparkton are also used by John of Damascus basically in the same meaning, even if they have completely different histories; for *authyparkton* is not used regularly in the Neoplatonic tradition but is found almost exclusively in Christian writings. The origin seems to lie in a definition of the *ousia* that we can find in Ps.-Archytas, however. It is almost identical in word to that of John of Damascus.[31]

Psellos's Theory of *Authypostaton* and *Authyparkton* in *Phil. Min.* 1.7

Before we can come back to John Italos, we must examine a further station of reception of these concepts that, as we will see, is extremely important for Italos; namely, that of his teacher Michael Psellos, who wrote a treatise specifically dedicated to the *authyparkton*.[32] This extremely carefully composed and content-wise demanding work requires a more intensive examination in order that we can compare it to Italos's position. As is often the case in the texts of Psellos, he seems to take a stance closely to skepticism by employing statements on different levels without (on a first glance) clearly taking sides. He interweaves his own position in several passages into the text that are difficult to carve out, but, as we are going to see, Psellos offers rigid criteria for what he considers to be *authypostaton* and *authyparkton*. Both these statements appear without different significations in his *Op.* 7. Besides the subtle inclusion of his own positions into the writing,

σῶμα καὶ τὸ ἀσώματον εἴδη εἰσὶ τῆς οὐσίας· ἕκαστον γὰρ αὐτῶν καὶ τὸ ὄνομα καὶ τέλειον τὸν ὅρον τῆς οὐσίας ἐπιδέχεται. Ὥστε ἡ οὐσία οὐκ ἔστιν εἶδος μὴ ἔχουσα ἐπάνω αὐτῆς γένος, ἀλλ' αὐτή ἐστι πρῶτον καὶ γενικώτατον γένος. Πάλιν τὸ σῶμα τέμνεται εἰς ἔμψυχον καὶ ἄψυχον· (Jo. D. *dialect. fus.* 10 Kotter). Οὐσία ἐστὶ πρᾶγμα αὐθύπαρκτον μὴ δεόμενον ἑτέρου πρὸς σύστασιν· καὶ πάλιν οὐσία ἐστὶ πᾶν, ὅτιπερ αὐθυπόστατόν ἐστι καὶ μὴ ἐν ἑτέρῳ ἔχει τὸ εἶναι ἤγουν τὸ μὴ δι' ἄλλο ὂν μηδὲ ἐν ἑτέρῳ ἔχον τὴν ὕπαρξιν μηδὲ δεόμενον ἑτέρου πρὸς σύστασιν, ἀλλ' ἐν αὐτῷ ὄν, ἐν ᾧ καὶ τὸ συμβεβηκὸς ἔχει τὴν ὕπαρξιν· τὸ γὰρ χρῶμα διὰ τὸ σῶμα γέγονεν, ἵνα χρῴζῃ αὐτό, καὶ οὐ τὸ σῶμα διὰ τὸ χρῶμα. Καὶ τὸ χρῶμα ἐν τῷ σώματι ὑπάρχει καὶ οὐ τὸ σῶμα ἐν τῷ χρώματι· ὅθεν καὶ τὸ χρῶμα τοῦ σώματος λέγεται καὶ οὐ τὸ σῶμα τοῦ χρώματος. Πολλάκις τοιγαροῦν ἀλλασσομένου τοῦ χρώματος καὶ μεταβαλλομένου ἡ οὐσία οὐ μεταβάλλεται ἤγουν τὸ σῶμα, ἀλλὰ μένει τὸ αὐτό. Λέγεται δὲ οὐσία παρὰ τὸ εἶναι (Jo. D. *dialect. fus.* 40 Kotter). Ἔστι δὲ οὐσία πρᾶγμα ὑφεστὸς αὐθυπόστατον. Οὐσία ἐστὶ πᾶν τὸ κατ' ἰδίαν ὕπαρξιν ὑφεστὸς καὶ μὴ ἐν ἄλλῳ τὸ εἶναι ἔχον (Jo. D. *fr. Phil.* 11.5–7 Kotter).

31. καὶ ὁ μὲν πρᾶτος λόγος, ἡ οὐσία, πρᾶγμα αὐθύπαρκτον καὶ ὑφεστός, μὴ δεόμενον ἑτέρου πρὸς σύστασιν, κἂν γενέσει ὑπόκειται καθὸ γέγονε (Ps. Archyt. Fr. 3,13 Thesleff). Only John Philoponos uses this definition of *ousia*, with the difference that instead of *authyparkton* in his *Commentary on Aristotelian Physics* he writes *authypostaton*, thus mixing the two traditions terminologically. ἐνταῦθα οὖν τὴν οὐσίαν τὸ αὐθυπόστατόν φησι καὶ μὴ δεόμενον ὑποκειμένου πρὸς τὸ εἶναι, ὥσπερ καὶ ἐν ταῖς Κατηγορίαις (Phlp. *In Ph.* 16.137.27 Vitelli). Cf. also οὐσία (Suda 961).

32. Psell. *Phil. Min.* 1.7. He is also using the two notions without significant difference.

we can distinguish two main historical components: the first regarding the more "theological" positions of authors like Plotinus and Proclus (56–126) and the second regarding more Aristotelian inspired positions (127–73). These are framed by an introduction (2–55) and the conclusion (173–81). In terms of content, we find on the one side the rejection of many possible significations of these terms, and on the other side the presentation of the positive criteria he elaborates. It is extremely interesting to read this complex text with its historical and systematic sides under the heading of lines 53–55: "For not every Hellenic *dogma* conflicts with ours, but it is true that some of them are helpers of our *dogmata*."[33] By working out his criteria, we will see how he understands the two notions.

What Does Not Fall under *Authypostaton* or *Authyparkton* in Its Classical Signification

In *Op.* 7 of the *Philosophica minora* I, Psellos first lists all the possibilities where the notion of *authyparkton* could come into play. The candidates are: (a) God (8–9) and the One (56–57); (b) the (i) first or (ii) second *ousia* of the Aristotelian tradition (9–10), whereby the first *ousia* as an individual thing (*atomon*) has to be divided again into (i) *eidos* and (ii) *hylê* (10–11); (c) (i) the "Platonic" *eidê* (13) and (ii) the *enhylon on* (18); (d) the *nous* (20); (e) the *on*; (f) the *noes* (161); the (g) *psychai* (161); and (h) the body (162–64). Psellos now disproves the majority of the candidates by rejecting the independence of these "entities" with various reasons.

(a) In describing God as *authyparkton*, because analytically no higher cause is necessary for his existence, one disregards the fact that he transcends all human designations (76). For God "is" even above being (84–85), and also one, but neither as *atomon*, nor as *eidos*, nor as genos (81). If, however, someone wants to call God an *authyparkton* because he is eternal, the answer would be that he even transcends eternity (70). This hyperbolic description of God, reminiscent of Ps.-Dionysius Areopagites, not only works as a counterargument against a Plotinian use[34] of the *authypostaton* concept, but also shows that Psellos sees *authyparkton* in close connection with being. *Authypostaton* or *authyparkton* could not be superordinate to existence in any way. God is also not self-sufficient (*autarkês*), since something that is "only" self-sufficient would not communicate itself beyond itself, he argues (92).

---

33. οὐ γὰρ πᾶσα Ἑλληνὶς δόξα διαβέβληται πρὸς ἡμῶν, τινὲς δὲ καὶ συνεργοὶ τοῦ ἡμετέρου τυγχάνουσι δόγματος (Psell. *Phil. Min.* 1.7.53–55 Duffy).

34. Cf. *Plot.* 6.8, [39] 14, 41 Henry Schwytzer.

(b) The reason why (i) the first or (ii) the second *ousia* cannot be considered an *authyparkton* is as follows: the first *ousia*, understood as an individual being, fails because it requires form and matter, which are its "parts" (13–15), and on which it would thus obviously be in a certain sense dependent.

(c) If, however, one wanted to understand (i) the forms that constitute the individual things as Platonic ideas, one would have to assume that they themselves depend in turn on the higher genera (11–13), whereby independence is also not given. But if one wanted to see them (ii) as *enhylon on* (18), they would need "the seat" at which they occur, that is, matter.

(d) The *nous* as a subject of discussion emerges from the continuation of argument (c), (i), since the Platonic ideas also require a "creator" (*hupostatês*), who is here identified in a peculiar way by the *nous* in question (20). Thus the *nous* as God cannot be *authypostaton* according to (a).

Finally, (e) the *on*, (f) the *noes*, (g) the *psychai* (161), and (h) the body appear as independent objects of investigation in a complicated argumentation, the meaning of which must first be put aside in order to be able to trace the course of the argumentation and its content a bit better. Psellos, in fact, shortly before this, sets out the Aristotelian-looking position, which states that the *ousia* is *authyparkton* because the further categories depend on it, while it itself does not depend on other things (156).[35] According to what has been said for (b) and (c), however, it should be excluded as *authyparkton* precisely because it is dependent and in need of its elements, so that we must ask why it now appears again in an argument from the Aristotelian *authypartkon* tradition. Without leaving it at that, Psellos adds a further criterion immediately afterward when he includes the paradigm image motif: the *ousia* is an image (*indalma*) of the first being (158) and images (*apeikasmena*) of the first being also somehow (*tropon tina*) exhibit the characteristic of independence (160). The first being, however, was also rejected in the first part as not being an *authyparkton*, since it surpasses self-sufficiency. This ambiguity is because of the transcendence of God (which is mentioned) and his immanence (which is not explicitly mentioned) but seems to be presupposed.[36]

The Positive Criteria for *Authypostaton* or *Authyparkton*

Psellôs's own definitions occur in several passages that are interwoven into the argumentation. In *Op.* 7 he states:

35. Ammon. *Porph.* 70.11–13 Busse; David. *In Porph.* 184.9–12 Busse.
36. Gersh, *From Iamblichus to Eriugena*, 233, and more on Ps.-Dionysios Areopagites and Maximus Confessor.

ἡμεῖς δὲ οὐ φαμεν εἶναι ταύτην τὴν σημασίαν τοῦ ὀνόματος, ἀλλ᾽ ὃ παρὰ κρείττονος μὲν γένους τὴν ὑπόστασιν εἴληχεν, ἀμέσως δὲ τῆς πρώτης ἀπολαῦσαν αἰτίας ὅλην ἅπαξ τὴν ἐκεῖθεν ἐκλάμπουσαν δύναμιν ἐν ἑαυτῷ συνείληφεν, ὥστε αὐτὸ ἑαυτῷ πρὸς σύστασιν ἐξαρκεῖν. (*Psell. Phil. Min.* 1.42–46 Duffy)

We do not say, however, that this is the meaning of the denomination [i.e., *authyparkton*, DW], but that which has attained existence from higher kinds, has received furthermore the whole radiant power originating from there at once, enjoying immediately the first cause, so that it is sufficient for itself to exist.

οὐδὲν οὖν τῶν ὄντων αὐθυπόστατον ὡς ἀφ᾽ ἑαυτοῦ τὴν γέννησιν ἔχον. αὐθυποστάτους δέ φαμεν τὰς οὐσίας οὐχ ὅτι μὴ παρ᾽ ἑτέρου παρήχθησαν, ἀλλ᾽ ὅτι ἀπὸ κρειττόνων αἰτίων παραχθεῖσαι ἀρκοῦσιν ἑαυταῖς πρὸς τὴν ὕπαρξιν. (*Psell. Phil. Min.* 1.172–175 Duffy)

So, none of the beings is a self-constitutive, as if it had the generation out of itself. But, we do not call the beings self-constitutive, because they were not produced from another, but originating from stronger causes they are sufficient for existence by themselves.

It is therefore not the absence of an independent cause of being that is decisive for something to be *authypostaton* or *authyparkton*. This *ad litteram* understanding of the word was the reason for denying to nearly everything this status in the first part of the text, since the majority of the entities (a)–(d) (except God) have an origin (167–72). It is also not about being one's own cause, since nothing is one's own cause, not even God, who is without cause. Rather, what is able to exist by itself having its origin in the first cause is a decisive criterion for the adequate designation as *authypostaton* and *authyparkton*. In fact, the "new" definition makes it possible to find various things in creation that match these first criteria, which we will discuss in more detail but shall first be enumerated: according to these criteria, Psellos designates mainly four types of entities that come into closer consideration; these include (b), (i) the first *ousia*, (e) the *on*, (f) *noes*, and (g) *psychai*. Psellos furthermore introduces toward the end of the text another type; namely, (h) the bodies (*sômata*, 162–63) into the discussion who incorporate it in a lesser degree because, he says, they are more distant from their origin.[37] The accidents, however, exist only indirectly in the *ousiai*, so that Psellos does not refer to them ever as *authypostata* and *authyparkta*,[38] a

---

37. See below, Psell. *Phil. Min* 1.7.162–163; Psell. *Theol.* 1.10.33–35.

38. οὐ μὴν οὕτως ἔχει ἐπὶ τοῦ πράγματος, ἀλλὰ τὰ ἐννέα γένη καθ᾽ ἑαυτὰ εἶναι μὴ δυνάμενα τῇ οὐσίᾳ ὑποβεβήκασι, μόνη δὲ αὕτη ἑτέρων οὐκ ἐπιδεῖται εἰς ὕπαρξιν (Psell. *Phil. Min.* 1.7.155–56 Duffy).

strategy he maintains throughout his work.[39] *Authyparkta* and *authypostata* now seem to him to be the things of creation that have independent principles of existence within them. Looking more closely, we can identify as a common characteristic for all these entities that the only cause they can depend on in order to be *authyparkta* and *authypostata* is God, who transfers the principle of existence to the entity without remaining in connection with it. The detachment from the producing cause is explicitly mentioned for the *on* (84–86)[40] and hinted at regarding the Aristotelian *ousia* (131),[41] while it is not clearly mentioned for the other objects. The core of the argument for dealing with the problem within creation can be found in lines 98–103, where Psellos uses an analogy for clarification of his position. He refers to and presents somewhat cryptically an ontology that at first is not directly identifiable:

ὥσπερ γὰρ τὸ ὂν ὑποβεβηκὸς τὸ ἓν ἄλλο τι παρ' ἐκεῖνο γέγονεν, οὕτω δὴ τὸ αὐτοκίνητον μετὰ τὸ ὂν γεγονὸς οὐκέτι μεμένηκεν ὥσπερ ἐκεῖνο ἀκίνητον, ἀλλ' ὑπέμεινε κίνησιν, ἐπειδὴ ἐν ἑαυτῷ ὡσανεὶ τὴν πηγὴν τοῦ κινεῖσθαι εἴληχε, καὶ ἅπαξ κινηθὲν οὐ δεῖται ἐς ἀεὶ τοῦ κινοῦντος. διὰ ταῦτα αὐτοκίνητον τοῦτο λέγεται οἷον τὸ ἐν ἑαυτῷ ἔχον τὴν ἀρχὴν τῆς ὑποστάσεως. (Psell. *Phil. Min.* 1.98–103 Duffy)

For just as being standing under the One has become something else next to that, so then what is self-moved has become after being, and has no longer remained unmoved like that, but took up movement, since it has somehow taken the source of being moved within itself, and what is simply moved does not forever need the moving. This is why it is also called self-motion like that which has in itself the principle of existence.

This first part of the passage could go back to *Phaedrus* 245c9–e6, which has been widely received, such as by Proclus,[42] John Philoponus,[43] or Simplicius.[44] But it is curious that Psellos addresses Plato's position directly in the following lines 103–16, identifying it with what is said in the *Timaeus*, and in clear contrast to 98–103 (ὁ δὲ Πλάτων ἑτέρως ἐφερμηνεύει τὸ αὐτοκίνητον τῇ ψυχῇ·), by attributing this kind of identification of the soul with the self-moving only to him—whereas in lines 98–103 no such

39. Psell. *Phil. Min.* 1.51.290.

40. ἀφ' οὗ δὴ πρόεισι πρώτως τὸ ὄν, ὃ δὴ ἀμέσως ἐντυγχάνον τῷ ἑνὶ ὂν μέν ἐστι κατὰ οὐσίαν, ἓν δὲ κατὰ μετοχήν. τοῦτο δὲ καὶ αὐθυπόστατόν ἐστιν, ὅτι μὴ δεῖται διηνεκῶς τῆς ὑφιστώσης αὐτὸ χειρός· (Psell. *Phil. Min.* 1.7.84–86 Duffy).

41. Even if *ousia*, *noes*, *psychai* should also be included into the discussion, as we have seen.

42. Procl. *In R.* 5, p. 115, 24; p.116, 13–14 Kroll.

43. Phlp. *De An.* 15.81.28–29 Hayduck.

44. Simp. *In Ph.* 9.234.22; 10.1247.33 Diels.

identification takes place.[45] One could therefore be inclined to assume that Psellos misappropriates the source of 98–103, which would identify his own conviction with the Platonic interpretation, speaking of the One (*hen*), the intellect (which would then be designated here by *on*), and the soul (which would thus hide behind *autokinêton*). But it seems impossible that potential recipients of this writing, who have just been confronted in the first part of the text with the Neoplatonic ontology, would not recognize the source of this position.

Psellos provides a brief explanation of how the *ousiai* are exactly described as things that are *authyparkton* and *authypostaton*. His argument is remarkable because the ontological explanation is presented in analogy to the physical explanation of how beings move and are moved: the principle of movement, he says, is taken over by the following entity (ἐν ἑαυτῷ ὡσανεὶ τὴν πηγὴν τοῦ κινεῖσθαι εἴληχε) as the principle of existence (οἷον τὸ ἐν ἑαυτῷ ἔχον τὴν ἀρχὴν τῆς ὑποστάσεως). The moved does not need the external moving cause forever, speaking of a separation (ἅπαξ κινηθὲν οὐ ἐς ἀεὶ τοῦ κινοῦντος). These passages that remember Gregory's *Contra Eunomium* II, 243: ἅπαξ γὰρ τὴν ἀρχὴν λαβοῦσα παρὰ τοῦ πεποιηκότος ἡ φύσις ἑαυτὴν κινεῖ τε καὶ διεξάγει πρὸς τὸ ἑκάστοτε δοκοῦν ἐνεργοῦσα τὴν κίνησιν would explain why in the following Psellos distances himself from the Platonic position. Psellos uses this "Greagorian" line of thought already in lines 85–86, where the same position is stated in a somewhat different manner (τοῦτο δὲ καὶ αὐθυπόστατόν ἐστιν, ὅτι μὴ δεῖται διηνεκῶς τῆς ὑφιστώσης αὐτὸ χειρός·).

The bottom line of the argument is that in the same way as the movement continues independently of its first cause, an *authyparkton* or *authypostaton* continues to exist by itself independently of the cause that created it.[46] This unusual mixture of physical and ontological argument reappears in 164–75:

εἰ μὲν οὖν τὸ αὐθυπόστατον ἐπὶ ταύτης λήψῃ τῆς σημασίας, ὥσπερ ἐγὼ ἐθεώρησα, ἀνεπίληπτος ὁ ὅρος ἐστίν, εἰ δ' ὥσπερ ἐπὶ τῆς παραγωγῆς καὶ τῆς ἀπογεννήσεως, πολὺ τούτῳ τὸ ἐπιλήψιμον· οὐδὲν γὰρ τῶν ὄντων <ἀν>αίτιον, ἀλλ' ἀτμοὶ μὲν ἀπὸ

---

45. ὁ δὲ Πλάτων ἑτέρως ἐφερμηνεύει τὸ αὐτοκίνητον τῇ ψυχῇ (Psell. *Phil. Min.* 1.7.103–4 Duffy).

46. One could assume that Psellos takes a position similar to that of Philoponos with regard to the external movement of projectiles. Philoponos was the first to apply the so-called impetus theory to bodies (Sorabji, "Infinite Power Impressed," 195–96). With Michael Wolff, Sorabji summarizes his position as follows: "Philoponus transforms Proclus' ideas by insisting that the transmitted power finds its monê, or, as he guardedly says, its monê, so to speak, not in the original source of motion, but in the thing moved instead."

γῆς ὑγρανθείσης εἶτα θαλφθείσης ὑπὸ ἡλίου, νέφη δὲ ἐξ ἀτμῶν, ὑετοὶ δὲ ἀπὸ νεφῶν, καὶ τὸ εἶδος ἀπὸ τοῦ σπέρματος, τὸ δὲ σπέρμα ἀπὸ τοῦ γεννήσαντος, ὁ δὲ γεννήσας ἐκ τοῦ πατρός, καὶ οὕτως ἀφ' ἑτέρου χωρῶν πρὸς ἕτερον οὐκ ἂν σταίης πρὶν ἂν εἰς τὴν προτέραν ἀρχὴν ἀναβῇς. οὐδὲν οὖν τῶν ὄντων αὐθυπόστατον ὡς ἀφ' ἑαυτοῦ τὴν γέννησιν ἔχον. αὐθυποστάτους δέ φαμεν τὰς οὐσίας οὐχ ὅτι μὴ παρ' ἑτέρου παρήχθησαν, ἀλλ' ὅτι ἀπὸ κρειττόνων αἰτίων παραχθεῖσαι ἀρκοῦσιν ἑαυταῖς πρὸς τὴν ὕπαρξιν. (*Psell. Phil. Min.* 1. 7. 164–175 Duffy)

So if you will grasp the self-constitutive in this meaning, as I have considered it, the definition is unassailable, but if in the sense of a derivation and of generation, it is liable to seizure: For none of the beings is without cause, but vapours come out of the earth after it has become damp and then warmed by the sun, but clouds come out of vapours, rain from clouds and form from seed, but seed from the begetter, and the begetter from the Father, and in this way you may not stop going from one place to another before going up to the first origin. For, none of the existing is a self-constitutive, as having the generation from itself. So, none of the beings is a self-constitutive, as if it had the generation out of itself. But, we do not call the beings self-constitutive, because they were not produced from another, but originating from stronger causes they are sufficient for existence by themselves.

The many objects named in this passage are, however, not only examples for the process of becoming and passing away. They also take up the position from 162–64 that also (g) bodies are self-constitutive in a diminished sense:[47]

ὅσα δὲ πλέον ἀφέστηκεν, ὥσπερ τὰ σώματα ταῦτα, ἔστ' ἂν μένῃ, ἑαυτοῖς ἐξαρκοῦσι πρὸς ὕπαρξιν, ἐπεὶ δὲ πόρρω τυγχάνει τοῦ ὄντος, ἀμενηνά πώς εἰσι καὶ ταχὺ διαπίπτει καὶ ἀπόλλυται. (Psell. *Phil. Min.* 1. 7. 162–164 Duffy)

But all those who are further away, like these bodies—as long as they last they are for themselves sufficient for existence—but since it happens that they are further away from being, they are also somehow unstable and soon fall apart and perish.

So, another subordinated criterion is added—namely, the distance from the creator—according to which something can be called more or less *authyparkton* and *authypostaton*. Thus Psellos characterizes *noes* and

---

47. Cf. also Psell. *Theol.* 1.46.58–60; Psellos thus takes up a point from the explication of John of Damascus. That bodies are also called *ousiai* in a certain sense seems to be a concession to his position. Οὐσία ἐστὶ πρᾶγμα αὐθύπαρκτον μὴ δεόμενον ἑτέρου πρὸς σύστασιν· καὶ πάλιν οὐσία ἐστὶ πᾶν, ὅτιπερ αὐθυπόστατόν ἐστι καὶ μὴ ἐν ἑτέρῳ ἔχει τὸ εἶναι ἤγουν τὸ μὴ δι' ἄλλο ὂν μηδὲ ἐν ἑτέρῳ ἔχον τὴν ὕπαρξιν μηδὲ δεόμενον ἑτέρου πρὸς σύστασιν, ἀλλ' ἐν αὑτῷ ὄν, ἐν ᾧ καὶ τὸ συμβεβηκὸς ἔχει τὴν ὕπαρξιν· τὸ γὰρ χρῶμα διὰ τὸ σῶμα γέγονεν, ἵνα χρώζῃ αὐτό, καὶ οὐ τὸ σῶμα διὰ τὸ χρῶμα. Καὶ τὸ χρῶμα ἐν τῷ σώματι ὑπάρχει καὶ οὐ τὸ σῶμα ἐν τῷ χρώματι (Jo. D. *dialect. Fus.* 40).

psychai, in turn, as particularly *authyparkta* (160–62) because of their proximity to the first origin.[48] All in all, (b), (i) the first *ousia,* (e) *on,* (f) *noes,* (g) *psychai,* and (h) bodies fall under the criteria that Psellos enumerates for *authypostaton* and *authyparkton,*[49] which are as follows: (i) being created directly by God, (ii) having a principle of existence in themselves, and (iii) being separated, as well as the subordinated criterion (iv) that the intensity to what degree something is *authypostaton* and *authyparkton* depends on the distance to the creator. As a distinguishing feature from the pagan Neoplatonic tradition, however, two points emerge in the Psellian text: on the one hand, the treatment of reversion (*epistrophê*) in connection with *authypostaton* or *authyparktos* is completely missing.[50] The only possible reference is *anaphora* (24), but this term is more likely to refer to Maximus Confessor *Ambiguum* 7,20.[51] On the other hand, the text shows that corporeality also has a status of self-subsistence—even if it is a reduced one.[52] This subtle difference to the "classical" Neoplatonic position allows Psellos to get closer to the Damascene reasoning.

John Italos's Position

Psellos's text is extremely difficult and presuppositional. We will see, however, that some elements can also be found in John Italos's writings.

48. Being, from which bodies are further away than other entities, is not the category of *ousia,* but it is the origin of creation, God, whose "images" we are talking about (*indalmata tou protou ontos,* 158). Psellos in many places leaves out the graduality of the concept and often, without further differentiation, assigns the status of *ousia* primarily to incorporeal things; cf. also Walter, *Michael Psellos,* 64–67. *Noes* as well as *psychai* can be found in the pagan Neoplatonic tradition—e.g., in Proclus—as well as in the Christian Neoplatonic tradition—e.g., in Ps.-Dionysios Areopagites (Gersh, *From Iamblichus to Eriugena,* 154, 169–71). "The respective cognitive roles of angel and men" (169n196) zitiert: Διὰ τὴν θείαν σοφίαν καὶ ψυχαὶ τὸ λογικὸν ἔχουσι διεξοδικῶς μὲν καὶ κύκλῳ περὶ τὴν τῶν ὄντων ἀλήθειαν περιπορευόμεναι καὶ τῷ μεριστῷ καὶ παντοδαπῷ τῆς ποικιλίας ἀπολειπόμεναι τῶν ἑνιαίων νοῶν, τῇ δὲ τῶν πολλῶν εἰς τὸ ἓν συνελίξει καὶ τῶν ἰσαγγέλων νοήσεων, ἐφ' ψυχαῖς οἰκεῖον καὶ ἐφικτόν, ἀξιούμεναι (Dion. Ar. *DN* 195.12–16 Suchla); FN 206 cites Εἰ δὲ καὶ εἰσὶν οἱ θεῖοι νόες ὑπὲρ τὰ λοιπὰ ὄντα καὶ ζῶσιν ὑπὲρ τὰ ἄλλα ζῶντα καὶ νοοῦσι καὶ γινώσκουσιν ὑπὲρ αἴσθησιν καὶ λόγον καὶ παρὰ πάντα τὰ ὄντα τοῦ καλοῦ καὶ ἀγαθοῦ ἐφίενται καὶ μετέχουσιν (Dion. Ar. *DN* 182 Suchla).

49. For an overview of Psellos's understanding of *authypostaton, ousia,* and "Aristotelian" *eidos,* and furthermore for his ontology of *synamphoteron,* see Walter, *Michael Psellos,* 54–67.

50. The only hint could be the anaphora in 24, but see Constas, "Maximus the Confessor."

51. Constas, "Maximus the Confessor," 9.

52. It is true that Psellos, at least in one place, uses the *epistrophê* conception as a determinant of being: only God turns to himself, while the *nous* and the *psychê* turn to themselves and to another. He excludes the extended body from the possibility of turning back. An attempt to explain this exclusionary position appears in Walter, *Michael Psellos,* 44–45.

After these preliminary investigations, we can now attempt to interpret the position of John Italos, who also treats *authypostaton* and *authypartkon* in *Quaestiones* 7 (p. 9), 14 (p. 16), 32 (p. 41), and 33 (p. 42) without major differences in its signification. Although his elaboration is not as detailed as that of Psellos, he nevertheless treats the problem at various points in his work. In *Quaestio* 7 (p. 9), it becomes clear that his course of argumentation has certain similarities to that of his teacher Psellos. Italos also starts from the definition of John of Damascus when he describes the *authypark-ton* in such a way that no other is needed for its *systasin*.[53] He also continues by saying that opinions differ as to exactly what it means, since the term is ultimately homonymous (Ital. *Quaest.* 7 p 9, 24 Joannou; Psellos processed in Op. 7 Plato, Aristotle,[54] the Neoplatonists, briefly names the Stoics, as well as his "own" definition). Therefore the opinions of the Hellenes in this regard are given next, even if they often contradict the "pious" *dogmata*.[55] Furthermore, the same division into "theological" interpretations and others is found.[56] Some of the more theological Hellenes claimed that the *au-thyparkton* means self-constitution.[57] This, however, was to be understood as containing two distinct moments, since one was the generating and the other the generated "element."[58] Above the latter, however, is the first thing they call both One and Good.[59] Unlike Psellos, Italos attributes this super-abundance of God (*hyperplêres*) and the transcending of the self-sufficient (*hyperautarkes*) to the Hellenes, while Psellos sees this as Christian opin-ion.[60] In the following, Italos alludes to the Proclean position that regards as *authyparkton* that which is inclined to itself, which could refer to the in-tellect and the soul.[61,62] Like Psellos, he then attributes the *authyparkton* to the fact that, although it is sufficient in itself, it has its origin in that which exceeds the self-sufficiency.[63] The other Hellenes, who are not theological, called the *ousia authypostaton*[64] since they said it did not need anything

<hr>

53. Ital. *Quaest.* 7 p 9, 20 Joannou; vs. Psellos Phil. min. 1, Op. 7, 2. Duffy

54. Whose theory of categories, as was often the case in antiquity, was considered to have been adopted from Archytas the Pythagorean.

55. Ital. *Quaest.* 7 p 9, 27 Joannou; cf. Psell. *Phil. Min.* 1.7.118–19 Duffy.

56. Ital. *Quaest.* 7 p 9, 28 ; p 10, 5; cf. Psell. *Phil. Min.* 1.7.56–116, 127–56 Duffy.

57. Ital. *Quaest.* 7 p. 9, 30 Joannou; cf. Psell. *Phil. Min.* 1.7.5 Duffy.

58. *Paragon, paragomenon*, p. 9, 31; an argument of Proclus against Plotinus's understanding of the One as *authypostaton*, which Psellos does not take over in *Op. 7*.

59. Ital. *Quaest.* 7 p. 9, 33 Joannou; cf. Psell. *Phil. Min.* 1.7.56–57 Duffy.

60. Ital. *Quaest.* 7 p. 9, 33–34 Joannou; cf. Psell. *Phil. Min.* 1.7.93; cf. also 70 Duffy.

61. Ital. *Quaest.* 7 p. 9, 34–35 Joannou.

62. Cf. for Proclus Beierwaltes, *Das wahre Selbst*, 174.

63. *Ital. Quaest.* 7 p. 10, 3–4 Joannou; cf. *Psell. Phil. Min.* 1.7.42–46, 173–75 Duffy.

64. *Ital. Quaest.* 7 p. 10, 5 Joannou; cf. *Psell. Phil. Min.* 1.7.127–56 Duffy.

else for its existence.[65] Italos's own opinion seems to be exactly this one, since he states clearly that the *ousia* is to be described as *authyparkton*.[66] Apart from this longer discussion of the term, he also uses it in *Quaestio* 14 (p. 16) with an identical definition, in *Quaestio* 32 (pp. 41–42), and again shortened in *Quaestio* 33 (p. 42).

One element that is not found in Italos's account from *Quaestio* 7 (pp. 9–10) concerns the bodies to which Psellos, following in part John of Damascus's *Dialectica*, attributed a diminished status as independent being. In *Quaestio* 8 (pp. 10–11), however, we find an analysis of the incorporeal, which can provide clues as to how he treats the body. First of all, he presents different ways of meaning of "incorporeal," which could be understood either in the actual sense (*kyrios*) or as an accidental that one encounters through abstraction. An example of the first are *psychai* and *daimones*,[67] which do not need the body to exist but are only connected to the bodies by their effects. To the other category belong, for example, the point, the appearance, the time, the place, in a similar way the body,[68] the light of the sun, and the so-called *sterêsis*. In the last part of the text he summarizes his view as follows:

Οὐκοῦν περὶ τῆς ὕλης καὶ τοῦ εἴδους ἡμῖν τανῦν λεκτέον· λεγέσθω τοίνυν περὶ τούτων ὡς ἑκάτερον ἑκατέρου χωρὶς ἀνυπόστατόν ἐστιν καὶ ὅλως ἀνύπαρκτον καὶ καθάπερ ἐν θατέρῳ νοούμενον τὸ εἶναι θατέρῳ παρέχεται καὶ οὐ τοῦτο μόνον, ἀλλὰ καὶ ὃ δέδωκε λαβὸν καὶ δεδωκὸς ὃ ἔλαβε· καὶ τούτων μὲν ἅμα ὄντων τὸ φυσικὸν ἔσται σῶμα, μὴ ὄντων δὲ οὐκ ἔσται· διὰ τοῦτο καὶ ἀσώματον λέγεται ὅτι ἐξ ἀμφοτέρων τὸ σῶμα. (Joannou)

About matter and form, then, we must now say the following: it must be said about them, then, that separate from one another, none is an *authypostaton* and is entirely inexistent, just as what is thought in another supplies being to another; and not only that, but it also gives what it is taking and takes what it is giving. And out of these beings will indeed be the physical body, but if they are not, it will not be. Therefore, it is called incorporeal, too, because the body consists of both.

Since Italos here not only presents an investigation of the body, which is similar to Psellos's, but also uses the terms *authypostaton* and *authyparktos* once again, the two writings have a common structure. Italos's position is interesting because, just like Psellos, he ascribes a status as *authypostaton*

---

65. Ital. *Quaest.* 7 p. 10, 8–11 Joannou; cf. Psell. *Phil. Min.* 1.7.154–56 Duffy.

66. Ital. *Quaest.* 7 p. 10, 19 Joannou.

67. Ital. *Quaest.* 7 p. 10, 35 Joannou.

68. The body is sometimes called incorporeal because of its components, form, and matter. See Ital. *Quaest.* 8 p. 11, 17–18 Joannou.

to the body, although it consists of the two "elements" form and matter, which are not called *authypostata* by themselves. Only composed they can be called *authypostaton*. One difference between the two philosophers concerns the fact that Italos does not name the *noes* in this text. Nevertheless, Italos seems to follow also the line of thought prefigured by John of Damascus, discussing the positions of Neoplatonic philosophers.

Summary

John Italos follows his teacher Psellos in describing *ousia* as *authypostaton* or *authyparkton*: while in Psellos *on, ousia, noes,* and *psychai* are paradigmatic examples, bodies also fall into this category to a lesser degree. Italos is not so detailed in the manner of fine subtlety but adopts the same scheme. Both authors are in the tradition of John of Damascus, who is their first authority for dealing with this problem. Psellos offers different criteria, while Italos follows more clearly the traditional explanations and choses between them the one he considers most plausible.

Christian Förstel

Nikephoros Choumnos is not among the authors whom we quote first when we speak about philosophy in Byzantium.[1] Less well known and less important than Psellos or Pachymeres, Choumnos suffers also from comparison with Theodoros Metochites, his younger contemporary, friend, and then enemy,[2] who replaced him in his function as *mesazon*, the highest (even if not clearly defined) office the Byzantine administration had to offer.[3] Metochites owes his notoriety above all to the restoration of the Chora monastery—whose founder (κτήτωρ) he was—which is still today one of the most beautiful Byzantine churches preserved. Choumnos, too, restored monasteries, among them that of the Mother of God of quick suc-

The author is grateful to the organisers, Frederick Lauritzen and Sarah Wear, as well as to the director of the Polo Culturale e Museale della Scuola Grande di San Marco, Mario Po, for the invitation to take part at the Venice conference on Byzantine Platonism. The author also thanks Eugenio Amato, Konstantinos P. Christou, Michael Featherstone, and Frederick Lauritzen for their most valuable help and suggestions in preparing the written version.

1. The most complete biography is still Verpeaux, *Nicéphore Choumnos*. About Choumnos as philosopher, see Kapriev, "Nikephoros Chumnos."

2. Cf. Ševčenko, Études sur la polémique entre Théodore Métochite et Nicéphore Choumnos.

3. See Ševčenko, Études sur la polémique entre Théodore Métochite et Nicéphore Choumnos, 147–50; idem, "Theodore Metochites, the Chora, and the Intellectual Trends of His Time," 27–28.

cour (Gorgoepekoos) in Constantinople.[4] Even more important was the foundation completed by his daughter Irene, who had joined the imperial family by marrying the Despot John, son of Andronicos II. After the death of her husband, in 1307, Irene, only sixteen years old, refounded with her father the monastery of Christ Philanthropos,[5] in which Choumnos would retire a few years later under the monastic name of Nathanael. This monastery was located in a central area on the Propontis shore, in the immediate neighborhood of the Mangana monastery and therefore also close to St. Sophia; but unlike Metochites's foundation, it has not been preserved except for a few fragments still visible today.[6]

Less famous than Metochites, since fewer traces of his patronage have survived, Choumnos nevertheless resembles his successor on account of his similar political career and his abundant literary output, in which philosophical writings occupy a prominent place. Jean Verpeaux, the French scholar to whom we owe the most thorough study of the life and of the works of Choumnos, estimated that his philosophical writings constituted about a quarter of his entire literary production,[7] an estimate that perhaps needs to be corrected because it does not take into account the letters, some of which are clearly philosophical in content.[8] But at any rate, among the twenty-four treatises by Choumnos that are preserved in the manuscripts—leaving aside his chancellery texts and correspondence—nine are exclusively philosophical in nature.[9] These philosophical treatises are significantly placed at the beginning of both of the oldest manuscripts of the writings of Choumnos, which were probably commissioned by the author himself.[10]

A brief look at the titles of these treatises allows us to distinguish two main categories. First, there are six on physical and cosmological subjects:[11]

1. *On the universe and its nature.*[12]
2. *On the first and simple bodies.*[13]

4. Laurent, "Une fondation monastique de Nicéphore Choumnos."

5. See Talbot, "*Philanthropos.*"

6. Müller-Wiener, *Bildlexikon zur Topographie Istanbuls*, 109.

7. Verpeaux, *Nicéphore Choumnos*, 124.

8. See Riehle, "Epistolography as Autobiography," 9–11. Alexander Riehle is preparing a new edition and translation of the letters of Nikephoros Choumnos.

9. Edition of all treatises by Konstantinos P. Christou. For other editions, see bibliography.

10. See below my remarks on the manuscripts of Choumnos and Plotinus.

11. Verpeaux, *Nicéphore Choumnos*, 126.

12. Niceph. Chumn. *Mund.* See Verpeaux, *Nicéphore Choumnos*, 126–28.

13. Niceph. Chumn. *Prim.* See Verpeaux, *Nicéphore Choumnos*, 128–30. For a new edition,

3. *That the earth is at the center of the universe and that nothing is underneath it.*[14]

7. *It is neither impossible nor difficult to admit that water was placed above the firmament when the world was created.*[15]

8. *On the air, why and for which reason, in spite of its being naturally warm, it becomes cold when it is blown; on the generation of hail; on the nature of the winds and their oblique blowing and movement.*[16]

9. *Refutation of the wise men of antiquity who did not say the same things on the same object and the same problem.*[17]

Then there are three treatises concerning the soul:

4. *Neither is matter anterior to bodies nor are their forms separate, but both exist together.*[18]

5. *Refutation of Plotinus on the soul.*[19]

6. *On the vegetative and sensitive soul, the rational soul having already been sufficiently examined and discussed by us previously.*[20]

In simple terms, we can say that in his physical writings Choumnos presents himself as an Aristotelian, but his Aristotelianism is not dogmatic in nature because he refers from time to time—usually implicitly—to Plato and does not refrain from criticizing and even rejecting both Plato and Aristotle. This occurs, for example, in the first treatise when he raises the question of the eternity of the world that is accepted by the Platonic and the Peripatetic tradition.[21] Choumnos's rejection of the eternity of the world is obviously a result of the Christian dogma of creation ex nihilo,

---

translation, and an important commentary see Amato and Ramelli, "Filosofia *rhetoricans* in Niceforo Cumno."

14. Niceph. Chumn. *Terra.* See Verpeaux, *Nicéphore Choumnos,* 132.

15. Niceph. Chumn. *Imposs.* See Verpeaux, *Nicéphore Choumnos,* 138–40.

16. Niceph. Chumn. *Aer.* See Verpeaux, *Nicéphore Choumnos,* 131–32. Previous edition: Boissonade (1831, 392–97).

17. Niceph. Chumn. *Antithet.* See Verpeaux, *Nicéphore Choumnos,* 132. Previous edition: Boissonade (1831, 398–406).

18. Niceph. Chumn. *Mater.* See Verpeaux, *Nicéphore Choumnos,* 133–40. Previous edition: Boissonade (1844, 191–201).

19. Niceph. Chumn. *Plot.* See Verpeaux, *Nicéphore Choumnos,* 141–43. A summary of the main arguments of the treatise is offered by Benakis, "Nikephoros Choumnos." Previous edition: Niceph. Chumn. *Plot.* Creuzer (1416–30), reprinted in *Patrologia Graeca* Migne (1404–38).

20. Niceph. Chumn. *Anim.* See Verpeaux, *Nicéphore Choumnos,* 143–45. This long title appears, however, only at the real beginning of the treatise after the preface (Christou, Τὸ φιλοσοφικὸ ἔργο τοῦ Νικηφόρου Χούμνου, 92). The whole text has a shortened title (Περὶ – κινήσεων; Christou, 87).

21. Niceph. Chum. *Mund.* 3.1–9 Christou.

which is in direct contradiction to pagan theories of antiquity. But it must be said immediately that Choumnos does not limit himself to opposing Christian dogma and the doctrines of ancient philosophers. At the beginning of his first treatise, *On the Universe and Its Nature*, Choumnos explains the method he intends to pursue: rather than polemicizing against his predecessors, "we must rely on firmly established principles and definitions, in order to produce demonstrations that prevent those who want to express their disagreement from speaking." Choumnos continues: "No one can accept principles and premises and then escape the necessary consequences which derive from them if he is a philosopher."[22]

Thus Choumnos poses as an authentic philosopher who wants to demonstrate the truth as a philosopher. A similar attitude is expressed in the very title of Treatise 7:[23] the text of Genesis, according to which God created the firmament in the middle of the waters, does not contradict physical laws. This, at least, is what Choumnos aims to demonstrate in the treatise.

In his six physical treatises, Choumnos refers sometimes to Plato, as we have seen. These references concern in most cases the *Timaeus*.[24] But Platonism is much more present in his three psychological treatises, which might be called, with good reason, "anti-Platonic": Treatise 5[25] is explicitly directed against Plotinus; Treatise 6[26] presents itself as the continuation of the preceding one. Choumnos devotes his text to the sensitive and vegetative soul "as the rational soul has already been sufficiently examined and discussed by us previously." Concerning Treatise 4, its title does not leave room for doubt about the identity of the philosophers whom Choumnos wants to refute: the preexistence of matter is, roughly speaking, admitted by both Aristotle and Plato,[27] but the autonomous and separate existence of forms or ideas outside any hylemorphic compound is obviously a point of doctrine that is central to the Platonic philosophical system while it is rejected by Aristotle and the Peripatetics.

22. δεῖ δὲ μᾶλλον τῶν ἀρχῶν καὶ τῶν ὅρων ἀσφαλῶς κειμένων τῶν καὶ πᾶσιν ἀνωμολογημένων ἐκ τούτων τὰς ἀποδείξεις πειρᾶσθαι ποιεῖσθαι, καὶ οὕτω γε τοὺς βουλομένους ἀντιλέγειν ἀφαιρεῖσθαι τὸ λέγειν. οὐδεὶς γὰρ τὰς ἀρχὰς καὶ προτάσεις διδούς, τὸ ἐκ τούτων ἐξανάγκης συμβαῖνον, φιλοσοφῶν ἂν φύγοι (Niceph. Chum. *Mund.* 1.14–20 Christou).

23. Niceph. Chum. *Imposs.* 143.1–6 Christou.

24. Niceph. Chum. *Mund.* 15.1–8, 17.7–8, 18.24–19.3, 20.2–3, 22.6–7, 23, 20–21 Christou; Niceph. Chum. *Prim.*, 28.24–25 Christou; Niceph. Chum. *Aer.*, 166.25–167.2 Christou; Niceph. Chum. *Antithet.*, 174.2–4 Christou.

25. Niceph. Chum. *Plot.*

26. Niceph. Chum. *Anim.*

27. See, e.g., Mesch, "Materie/Material (*hylè*)," 195–96; Brisson, "À quelles conditions peut-on parler," 7–9; and the conclusions of Happ, *Hyle*, 804–7.

But let us turn to the treatise against Plotinus: its content is summarized in its long title, which lists the principal themes addressed by Choumnos as follows:

Refutation of Plotinus: (i) souls are not anterior to bodies, (ii) nor do they migrate from one body to another; (iii) there is no intellect in irrational beings nor could there ever be one; (iv) [the author] uses numerous arguments to refute the theory that science is reminiscence; (v) by relying on this doctrine Plotinus and before him Plato deduced that souls are anterior with respect to bodies; (vi) he discusses the awakening of dead bodies and proves it with other irrefutable arguments; (vii) from the very theories of Plato concerning the rebirth of souls [the author] demonstrates the enjoyment of eternal goods and at the same time the eternal punishment of souls and bodies.[28]

This summary is of the greatest interest, as it contains *in nuce* a presentation of Platonism that aims to explain the very genesis of the Platonic system. In Choumnos's eyes, the concept of science precedes other Platonic key doctrines. By claiming that science or (real) knowledge is based on recollection or anamnesis, Plato, Plotinus, and hence all the Platonists had to admit that souls had a life before entering the body. It is from this supposed anteriority that arises, in turn, the necessity for the Platonists to conceive the doctrine of metempsychosis or transmigration of souls. Choumnos does not state explicitly the relation between both positions, but the logical link can be easily reconstructed.

In the treatise itself, after having rejected the theory of anamnesis and anteriority of the soul in relation to the body, Choumnos tries to prove that science, which he considers as an energy of the soul, acts through the body and its organs. It is therefore impossible to completely separate the soul from the body: the soul is born at the same time as the body, she does not reject the body, nor flee from it, and she cannot but preserve the body for which she is born. The Platonists themselves never stop establishing links between body and soul: that is the very reason why they conceived the doctrine of metempsychosis. Thus, according to Choumnos, the doctrine of metempsychosis, however erroneous it may be, shows that even the

28. Ἀντιθετικὸς πρὸς Πλωτῖνον ὅτι μήτε τῶν σωμάτων προϋπάρχουσιν αἱ ψυχαί, μήτε ἐξ ἑτέρων μεταχωροῦσιν εἰς ἕτερα, ἀλλ'οὐδ'ἐν τοῖς ἀλόγοις ἔστι νοῦς, οὐδ'οὐ μήποτε γένοιτο. πολλαῖς δὲ καὶ ταῖς ἀποδείξεσι κέχρηται πρὸς ἐκεῖνο ἀπαντῶν, τὸ τὰς ἐπιστήμας ἀναμνήσεις εἶναι· ἐξ οὗ δὴ δόγματος αὐτῷ τῷ Πλωτίνῳ καὶ πρὸ αὐτοῦ Πλάτωνι κατεσκεύασται πρὸ τῶν σωμάτων τὰς ψυχὰς εἶναι· καὶ περὶ ἐγέρσεως σωμάτων τεθνεώτων ἀγωνίζεται, καὶ δείκνυσι ταύτην ἄλλαις δὴ ἀνάγκαις· καί γ'ἐξ αὐτῶν τῶν τοῦ Πλάτωνος περὶ τοῦ τὰς ψυχὰς ἀναβιώσκεσθαι θέσεων καὶ ἀπόλαυσιν δείκνυσιν ἀεὶ μενόντων ἀγαθῶν καὶ κόλασιν ψυχῶν ὁμοῦ καὶ σωμάτων μηδέποτε λήγουσαν (Niceph. Chumn. *Plot.* 58.1–14 Christou = Creuzer, 1416).

Platonists are aware of the strong bond that connects the soul to the body.

Without going into detail, it seems to me that Choumnos's purpose is to refute the Platonic doctrines that are incompatible with Christian dogma, starting from the Platonic conceptions themselves. Until now I have treated Platonism as a homogeneous philosophical system, but Choumnos himself informs us that his refutation is specifically directed against Plotinus. Why does Plotinus appear here? How can we explain this reference to him?

In the text of the treatise, Choumnos seems to use above all themes that are Platonic in the strict sense, as numerous expressions reflect a thorough reading of Plato's *Phaedo*. Such a direct knowledge of the Platonic dialogues appears also in the other writings of Choumnos: I have already mentioned the *Timaeus*,[29] and we can add at least the *Republic*.[30] Such knowledge of Plato is not surprising in Byzantine writers of the Palaeologan period.

But where is Plotinus in the treatise that pretends to be a refutation of Plotinus? At the very beginning of the treatise, Choumnos gives us an important precision: the text is directed, he tells us, "against Plotinus and his writings on the incorruptible soul,"[31] but the question arises: Does this precision have any value?

The name of Plotinus is mentioned only seven times in the text (I do not take into account mention in the title and that which is directly related to the title at the beginning and the end of the treatise). It is worthwhile to have a closer look at these explicit mentions.

At the beginning of the treatise, Choumnos insists on a point of doctrine that is common to both the Platonists and himself: our intellect (ὁ ἐν ἡμῖν νοῦς) is simple (ἁπλοῦς), non-composite (ἀσύνθετος), self-subsistent (καθ' ἑαυτὸν ὑφεστώς), and having life in itself (ζωὴν ἐν ἑαυτῷ ἔχων). This, explains Choumnos, "has also been well demonstrated by Plotinus' writings,"[32] and a couple of lines later, he repeats his appreciation: "Plotinus and all those who, before and after him, shared his opinion have well recognised the nature of the intellective soul."[33] But this positive evaluation only prepares for the criticism to come soon after:

29. See note 25 above.

30. See the apparatus fontium in Christou's edition.

31. Ἐμοὶ τὸ παρὸν σπούδασμα πρὸς Πλωτῖνον καὶ τοὺς ἐκείνου περὶ ἀφθάρτου ψυχῆς λόγους (Niceph. Chumn. *Plot.* 58.15–16 Christou = Creuzer, 1416).

32. τόγε πρὸς τοῦτο φέρον καὶ τοῖς Πλωτίνου λόγοις καλῶς ἀποδεδειγμένον (Niceph. Chumn. *Plot.* 59.2–3 Christou = Creuzer, 1416).

33. καὶ μὴν καὶ Πλωτῖνος καὶ εἴτις μετ' ἐκείνου πρὸ αὐτοῦ ἢ μετ' αὐτὸν ὀρθῶς καὶ καλῶς ἐπέγνωσαν τὴν αὐτῆς [i.e., τῆς ψυχῆς νοερᾶς] φύσιν ἁπλῆν ταύτην εἰδότες καὶ μηδὲν μήτε κατὰ σῶμα μήτε κατὰ σύνθεσιν οὖσαν, ἄλλο δέ τι παρὰ ταῦτα, λύσιν μηδεμίαν μήτε φθορὰν καταδεδεγμένον (Niceph. Chumn. *Plot.* 60.3–8 Christou = Creuzer, 1417).

But that he creates and causes the subsistence of these souls which we spoke about [i.e., the intellective souls] previously to the bodies, that he puts them in the world above and fastens them to the first [principle] which is alone, unique and immobile, and then tears them from there and throws them down and pushes them into bodies, moving them from one body to another and from those bodies, which are better and more convenient, to those, which are worse and not convenient at all, that he imposes such a great wandering on them and that the ever-thinking intellect out of folly suffers such terrible things which do not even happen to the irrational soul, all this, I am ashamed to say, has been badly imagined by our dear Plotinus.[34]

Thus Choumnos blames Plotinus not so much for having installed the soul in the intelligible realm as for having supposedly perverted the soul's dignity by letting her change bodies and go down to the lowest levels of being, that is, even to plants.[35] But in all this there is no specifically Plotinian material: Choumnos only repeats here the classical orthodox position, which condemns the preexistence of souls as well as what is presented as its consequence: the transmigration of souls. These points were already at the heart of the anti-Origenist polemics of the Church Fathers in the fourth century as well as central points in the condemnation of Origen by the Council of Constantinople in 553.[36] As far as Plotinus is concerned, metempsychosis is indeed accepted in the *Enneads* in its whole extent as Plotinus accepts also the migration of souls in animals and plants,[37] whereas these latter forms of migration are rejected by Porphyrius and Proclus. But Choumnos is not at all precise here, and his rebuke concerns only metempsychosis as a whole without going into detail.

The next mention of the name of Plotinus is still related to the problem of the descent of the soul:

34. ὅτι δ' αὐτὰς ταύτας ἃς ἔφημεν ψυχὰς προδημιουργεῖ καὶ προυφιστᾷ τῶν σωμάτων καὶ ἄνω τίθησι καὶ τοῦ πρώτου ἐξάπτει καὶ μόνου ὄντος καὶ ἑνὸς μόνου καὶ ἀκινήτου ὄντος, εἶτ' ἐκεῖθεν ἀποσπᾷ καὶ βάλλει κάτω καὶ ὠθεῖ ἐπὶ σώματα καὶ ἐξ ἑτέρων εἰς ἕτερα ἐμβιβάζει καὶ ἐξ ἀμεινόνων καὶ γνησίων αὐταῖς μᾶλλον ἐπὶ χείρω καὶ μηθὲν ταύταις προσήκοντα καὶ πολλήν τινα τίθησι τὴν πλάνην αὐτῶν, καὶ τὰ δεινὰ ταῦτα ἐξ ἀνοίας ὁ τὰ πολλὰ φρονῶν πάσχει νοῦς, ἃ μηδὲ τῇ παντάπασιν ἀλόγῳ ψυχῇ συμβαίνει, τοῦτο δὴ καὶ αἰσχύνομαι τῷ καλῷ Πλωτίνῳ μὴ καλῶς δεδογμένον (Niceph. Chumn. *Plot.* 60.9–19 Christou = Creuzer, 1417).

35. See, e.g., Plot. 4.7.14.1–8 Henry Schwyzer.

36. See Diekamp, *Die origenistischen Streitigkeiten*, and Perczel, "Philosophical Myth in the Service of Christian Apologetics?," 207–11. The doctrine of metempsychosis is also condemned in the Synod of Constantinople of 1082, directed against John Italos; cf. Clucas, *Trial of John Italos*, 142, and Anna Comnena, *Al.* V 9, 2 and 7 Reinsch Kambylis.

37. See Rich, "Reincarnation in Plotinus," 236–38; Dörrie, "Kontroversen um die Seelenwanderung im kaiserzeitlichen Platonismus," 419–20.

Concerning the soul which is immortal and suffers neither from irrational life nor from sensible perception, what else could be the object of her desire (ὀρέξει) and longing, if not the eternal beings? Plotinus tells us that the souls were first among these eternal beings, but under the influence of other desires (ὀρέξεσιν ἄλλαις) they turned themselves in another direction and fell away from where they were; however some of them failed, although they wanted to embellish these (inferior) realities—that is why they came down—and they missed their aim and became themselves disordered. We do not agree with him, but that which we have recognised concerning the rational soul has already been presented.[38]

What is at stake here is the typical Plotinian doctrine of the undescended soul. If one accepts this doctrine and agrees with the idea, that a part of the soul remains among the eternal, intelligible beings, how can we explain the soul's descent? As many authors before him and as nearly all the Neoplatonists,[39] Choumnos rejects the doctrine of the undescended soul, but he does not limit himself to refusing this peculiar aspect of Plotinian psychology; he wants to show how this theory is contradictory to the role Plotinus assigns to the soul in the sensible world. In so doing—and this is an important point—he uses Plotinus's very words, or more precisely, he turns against Plotinus the words Plotinus is using when he describes the descent of the soul in treatise 4.7.13. Plotinus's text reads as follows:

How then, since the intelligible is separate, does soul come into body? It is in this way: as much of it as is only intellect has a purely intellectual life in the intelligible and stays there forever, without impulse or desire (ὄρεξις); but that which acquires desire (ὄρεξιν), which follows immediately on that intellect, goes out further in a way by its acquisition of desire (ὀρέξεως), and desiring to impart order and beauty according to the pattern which it sees in Intellect, is as if pregnant by the intelligible and laboring to give birth, and so is eager to make, and constructs the world.[40]

---

38. ψυχὴ δ' ἀθάνατος καὶ μὴ λωβηθεῖσα μηδὲν ἐξ ἀλόγου ζωῆς καὶ αἰσθήσεως, τίνος ἂν ἄλλου ἢ τῶν ἀεὶ ὄντων ἐν ὀρέξει καὶ πόθῳ γένοιτο ; ἐν οἷς καὶ τὰς ψυχὰς Πλωτῖνος φησι πρῶτον οὔσας, ὀρέξεσιν ἄλλαις ἐφ' ἕτερα τραπείσας, ἐκείνων τε ἐκπεσεῖν, καὶ ἐν οἷς ἐγένοντο, ἔστιν ἃς τούτων σφαλῆναι, κοσμῆσαι μὲν ταῦτα βουληθείσας καὶ πρὸς τοῦθ' ἱκέσθαι κάτω, ὁμοῦ δ' ἀποτυχεῖν τούτου, καὶ ἀκόσμους ταύτας γεγενῆσθαι. ἀλλ' οὐχ ἡμεῖς οὕτως, ἀλλ' ὅσον ἐσμὲν ἐπεγνωκότες καὶ ψυχῆς νοερᾶς ἕνεκεν ἤδη λέλεκται (Niceph. Chumn. *Plot.* 71.18–72.2 Christou = Creuzer, 1423).

39. See, e.g., Dillon, "Iamblichus' Criticisms of Plotinus' Doctrine of the Undescended Soul."

40. Πῶς οὖν τοῦ νοητοῦ χωριστοῦ ὄντος ἥδε εἰς σῶμα ἔρχεται; ὅτι, ὅσος μὲν νοῦς μόνος, ἀπαθὴς ἐν τοῖς νοητοῖς ζωὴν μόνον νοερὰν ἔχων ἐκεῖ ἀεὶ μένει—οὐ γὰρ ἔνι ὁρμὴ οὐδ' ὄρεξις—ὃ δ' ἂν ὄρεξιν προσλάβῃ ἐφεξῆς ἐκείνῳ τῷ νῷ ὄν, τῇ προσθήκῃ τῆς ὀρέξεως οἷον πρόεισιν ἤδη ἐπιπλέον καὶ κοσμεῖν ὀρεγόμενον καθὰ ἐν νῷ εἶδεν, ὥσπερ κινοῦν ἀπ' αὐτῶν καὶ ὠδῖνον γεννῆσαι, ποιεῖν σπεύδει καὶ δημιουργεῖ (Plot. 4.7.13.1–8 Henry, Schwyzer, trans. Armstrong; Wiitala, "Desire and the Good in Plotinus," 651, based on Armstrong).

For Choumnos, the only desire (ὄρεξις) that could affect the soul that is in the intelligible is the desire for the first, eternal principles. In Choumnos's eyes, it is absurd to imagine an intelligible reality feeling desire for lower realities, as it is not touched at all by passions or affections coming from the sensible world. Thus Plotinus is in contradiction with himself when he postulates on the one hand (1) the presence of the human soul or part of it in the intelligible—the so-called doctrine of the undescended soul—and simultaneously (2) advocates the idea that soul's descent from "above" is due to desire. The consequence of all this is clear: the soul or part of the soul cannot remain always in the intelligible world, nor can she migrate into various bodies of humans, to say nothing of animals or plants. The ultimate target of Choumnos's arguments here and in the whole treatise is the Plotinian and more generally Platonic conception of preexistence of the soul and of metempsychosis.

The two other mentions of Plotinus's name appear in the same polemical context, and in both cases Plotinus is named at the same time as Plato: if we accept the unity of the soul and the doctrine of metempsychosis, as Plato and Plotinus do, this implies that "neither the great Plato nor Plotinus would be different from dogs, cranes and ants."[41] Mentioning these animals rather than others, Choumnos has possibly in mind the guard-dog analogy in Plato's *Republic*[42] as well as Plato's evocations of cranes and of ants in the *Statesman*[43] and in the *Phaedo*, respectively.[44] Plato and Plotinus are again associated at the very end of the treatise: here Choumnos makes the point that in the case of transmigration of souls, the individual coming later in the succession of incarnations is paying for the sins committed by another, earlier, individual. It is "as if, because Plato was at fault, Plotinus or anyone else not subject to punishment was brandmarked."[45] In other words, metempsychosis is not compatible with the concept of individual responsibility and justice.

41. καὶ γοῦν τόνδε δὴ τὸν λόγον Πλάτων ὁ μέγας καὶ Πλωτῖνος οὐδὲν ἂν εἶεν κυνῶν καὶ γεράνων καὶ μυρμήκων διενηνοχότες (Niceph. Chumn. *Plot.* 72.22–24 Christou = Creuzer, 1423–24).

42. Pl., *R.* II 375a–376c Slings; cf. Neuhausen, "Platons 'philosophischer' Hund bei Sextus Empiricus," 244–48, and Hotes, "Du chien au philosophe," 21–29.

43. Pl. *Plt.* 263d3–e1 Burnet; cf. White, *Myth, Metaphysics and Dialectic,* 27–28, and Schäfer, "Herrschen und Selbstbeherrschung," 204, 217–24.

44. Pl. *Phd.* 82b5–8 Burnet, where ants are mentioned with bees and wasps as example of "a civic and tame species" in the context of metempsychosis.

45. ὥσπερ ἂν εἰ τοῦ Πλάτωνος ἡμαρτηκότος ἐστίζετο Πλωτῖνος ἢ ἄλλος τις τῶν μὴ ταῖς δίκαις ἐνεχομένων (Niceph. Chumn. *Plot.* 86.20–21 Christou = Creuzer, 1430).

Most of the mentions of Plotinus in Choumnos's treatise appear then to be only general references to mainstream Platonic doctrines. An important exception, however, is the reference to the "desire of the soul" quoted above. If my identification is correct and if Choumnos is really reacting in this case to the passage 4.7.13 of Plotinus, this would mean that Choumnos had direct knowledge of part of the *Enneads* and would connect with the reference to the Plotinian writings about "the incorruptible soul" made by Choumnos at the beginning of his treatise.

From a philological point of view, this hypothesis could have interesting consequences also for our knowledge of the direct tradition of Plotinus. In fact, the oldest manuscripts of the *Enneads* are not earlier than the beginning of the fourteenth century and, for one of the most important of them, the Laurentianus 87,3, a relation has been established with Nikephoros Choumnos, as it is sometimes attributed to the scribe who is responsible for the copying of the two manuscript editions of Choumnos's works in Parisinus gr. 2105 and the Patmiacus 127. This identification is not correct, however, as the handwriting of both scribes intervening in the Laurentianus is clearly different from the one displayed in the collections of Choumnos's works.[46] Nevertheless, a relation exists between the so-called Choumnos Schreiber and the text of Plotinus, as is evident in Marcianus gr. 209, a manuscript containing several writings of, or attributed to, Aristotle—*De anima, De motu animalium, De sensu, De memoria, De somno, De insomniis, De divinatione*—and three treatises of Plotinus; namely, IV 7, I 1, and IV 2. The Marcianus was dated by Paul Henry to the twelfth century. Later publications on, or editions of, the *Enneads* repeated Henry's dating or changed it only slightly moving the date to the thirteenth century. But such an early date is not consistent with the archaizing and rather artificial character of the handwriting that can be assigned to the beginning of the fourteenth century. Thus the codex Marcianus is in all probability roughly contemporary with the earliest witnesses of the complete *Enneads*; namely, Laurentianus 87,3 and Parisinus gr. 1976. But even more important for us is the fact that the script of the Marcianus is similar to that in both of Choumnos's manuscripts, and in my opinion we can even identify the scribe of Marcianus gr. 209 with the "Chumnos-Schreiber." If this hypothesis is correct, the Marcianus would become a good candidate for being the very ex-

---

46. Förstel, "Untersuchungen zur Rezeption Plotins in der Palaiologenzeit," 421. In this paper, written several years ago, I expressed a pessimistic view of Choumnos's knowledge of Plotinus, which I have to correct here.

emplar in which Choumnos might have read some Aristotelian texts as well as the treatises "on the incorruptible soul," or at least some of Plotinus's psychological writings that he aims to refute in his text.

In conclusion, summarizing the points we have made, we can say that Nikephoros Choumnos presents himself in the whole of his philosophical production as an eclectic philosopher who faces Platonism from a position similar to that of the Church Fathers—this relation with the Church Fathers has also been highlighted by Eugenio Amato and Ilaria Ramelli.[47] Choumnos accepts some of the Platonic doctrines insofar as they are compatible with Christianity but rejects all that is in contradiction to Christian dogma, often adopting himself an Aristotelian point of view. By using "his Aristotle," to paraphrase the expression employed by Metochites speaking of Choumnos,[48] he is able to challenge and to contest the radical separation between intelligible and sensible world, between soul and body, which is propagated by the Platonists, especially by Plato and Plotinus. But Choumnos does not limit himself to such a rather common position; he tries also to act as authentic philosopher and to defend from a philosophical point of view and sometimes with personal arguments the main doctrines of the Christian faith. Such originality, as basic as it may be, does not facilitate the identification of his philosophical and literary sources. It seems nevertheless possible to state, at least provisionally, that, in addition to authors and texts already identified in previous studies, the difficult writings of Plotinus—or, more precisely, a part of these writings—were among the Platonic texts studied by Choumnos.

47. Amato and Ramelli, "Filosofia *rhetoricans* in Niceforo Cumno," 29–30, 40).

48. ὁ σὸς Ἀριστοτέλης, letter of Metochites to Choumnos transmitted among the letters of Choumnos (Niceph. Chumn. *Epist.* 134 Boissonade, 1844, 157).

 ❘❘❘ "It Will Overcome
Its Own Nature"

The Topic of Self-Reversion of the Intellect in *Logos on Saint Peter of Athos* by St. Gregory Palamas and in *Ennead* V.3

Timur Shchukin

Ioannis Polemis has recently drawn attention[1] to the fact that the earliest work of Gregory Palamas, *Logos on Saint Peter of Athos*, dated 1332–33,[2]

The author expresses his gratitude to S. Akishin for his help in preparing the English version of this paper. The Russian version was published as "'On prevzojdyot sobstvennuyu prirodu': Tema samoobrashchyonnosti uma v 'Slove na zhitie prepodobnogo Petra Afonskogo' svyatitelya Grigoriya Palamy i v Enneades V.3," *Bibliya i hristianskaya drevnost* 1, no. 2 (2019): 212–30. The work was supported by RFBR grant 21-011-44263, "Formation of the concept of 'theology' as a science and its conceptual apparatus in the Byzantine Christian theological thought of the late 5th–early 8th centuries in the context of scientific and philosophical knowledge of late antiquity."

1. Polemis, "Neoplatonic and Hesychastic Elements in the Early Teaching of Gregorios Palamas."

2. Palamas's work was published as a critical edition by P. Chrestou in 1992. A reprint of the text prepared by Chrestou, taking into account various readings of Moscow manuscript copy from the State Historical Museum (Mosq. GIM gr. 212 = Syn. gr. 98), with Russian translation was published as Pospelov, *Grigorij Palama*, 36-134. In this edition also a translation of Antonio Rigo's research ("La Vita di Pietro l'Athonita") can be found, containing general information

contains several allusions to the *Enneads*. Polemis admits both direct and indirect influence of Plotinus's texts to Palamas as a classifier of hesychast practice. He is nearly assured that the early theology of Gregory Palamas was of Neoplatonic disposition, but the influence of this philosophic school could be traced in his later texts as well. Polemis underlines that in the *Logos* there is neither doctrine on descension of intellect into the heart nor description of respective psychosomatic practices or words on importance of contemplation of the divine light.[3] In this period, Palamas emphasizes the contemplation of God by self-revertible intellect. While relying upon the testimonies of Anti-Palamites, Polemis attributes the teaching on uncreated light as divine energy to the later period of Palamas's creative work.[4] Nevertheless, according to the author, the hesychast denied the sensual nature of the uncreated light precisely over the dependence on Plotinus (or Neoplatonism in general). Thus Neoplatonism has remained the constant of his philosophical approach despite all the transformations of his theological agenda. In the present article, without rejecting the key proposition of Polemis, we intend, first, to contour the early version of his "Neoplatonic" anthropology and, second, to highlight more sharply the motives driving Palamas, particularly with respect to Plotinus.

In the *Logos on Saint Peter of Athos*, Gregory Palamas not only represents for us an image of the ideal hermit, a proto-hesychast, but also suggests a theoretical pattern of how a hermit can gain the state of theosis and God-seeing. For this purpose, the saint engages a Neoplatonic framework while remaining within the tradition of Eastern Christianity:[5] the human intellect, while reverting to itself and abstracting from any sensual and all the more passionate content, calms itself; however, in this state of calm it gains the real activity and gets an ability not only to contemplate God, but also to become God itself. Nevertheless, it is not only the intellect that reaches theosis, but also the whole compound of a human, including

---

on the cult of Peter of the Athos, the "Logos" of Gregory Palamas, together with several notes on the ascetic doctrine and terminology of this treatise, as well as an article by A. Vinogradov on the literary sources of this writing ("Istochniki, ispolzuemye svyatitelem Grigoriem Palamoj"), or rather biography compiled by Nicholas the Monk in the tenth century, whereupon Gregory Palamas has leaned. It was also D. Mitrea who wrote extensively on hagiographical strategy of the saint in his recent article "'Old Wine in New Bottles'?"

3. Polemis, "Neoplatonic and Hesychastic Elements in the Early Teaching of Gregorios Palamas," 215-16.

4. Polemis, "Neoplatonic and Hesychastic Elements in the Early Teaching of Gregorios Palamas," 216-20.

5. See Meyendorff, "Le thème du 'retour en soi' dans la doctrine palamite."

the body.[6] This thought, quite popular in the Orthodox tradition, was interlaced by Gregory Palamas into a purely ascetic discourse. Therefore it is naturally indeed that neither J. Meyendorff[7] nor A. Rigo[8] and other authors[9] paid attention to the specific terminology of the respective fragments of the *Logos*. The observations made by I. Polemis are important in this context: for if Gregory Palamas at the early stage of his creative work turns to Neoplatonism not as a commonplace hardly distinct from the Christian tradition and mediated by the ecclesial Platonist writers like Evagrius of Pontus and Dionysius Areopagita, this focusing appears a marker of a specific intellectual interest.

Polemis puts forward three excerpts from the *Enneads*[10] that, in his opinion, serve as a parallel to certain places in *Logos*. Here are these excerpts in a broadened form:

If it is [the intellect], it is empty of everything, for it thinks nothing. Yet if it is in itself such that it is everything, then when it thinks [only] itself, it thinks everything altogether. For this reason, on the one hand, such [intellect] by reverting to itself and actually contemplating itself contains everything [in itself], while, on the other hand, [in reverting to and actually contemplating] everything, it contains itself [within itself].[11]

6. Greg. Pal. *Laud. Pet. Ath.* 171, I.17–173, I.9 Chrestou.

7. J. Meyendorff, who has undoubtedly descried the Neoplatonic background of various of Palamas's expressions, underlined the general critical attitude the saint has had for ancient philosophy (see, e.g., "Le thème du 'retour en soi' dans la doctrine palamite," 200; *Introduction a l'étude de Grégoire Palamas*, 189-90, 193-94). He besides suggested that Plotinus's terminology has been borrowed by Gregory Palamas from Gregory of Nyssa and Dionysius Areopagita (194).

8. Oddly enough, Rigo holds the term ἐπιστροφή and its derivative verbs as the terminological novelties of Gregory Palamas (Rigo, "La Vita di Pietro l'Athonita," 19), though their Neoplatonic origin is an evident fact.

9. On the acknowledgment of Gregory Palamas with the writings of Plotinus in its entirety, see Dimitrakopoulos, "Γρηγορίου Παλαμά, Κεφάλαια εκατόν πεντήκοντα," 319-21; Dimitrakopoulos, "Υστεροβυζαντινή κοσμολογία," 175-91; Dimitrakopoulos, "Υστεροβυζαντινή κοσμολογία Β," 111-32. Other references include Polemis, "Neoplatonic and Hesychastic Elements in the Early Teaching of Gregorios Palamas," 214n49.

10. A necessary bibliography on the doctrine of self-contemplation of intellect is also given in Polemis, "Neoplatonic and Hesychastic Elements in the Early Teaching of Gregorios Palamas," 210-11. On the topic in general, see Courcelle, *Connais-toi toi-meme*, 83-111. Especially on Plotinus, see O'Daly, *Plotinus's Philosophy of the Self*; Hadot, "La conception plotinienne"; Reuter, "Plotinus on the Role of Nous in Self-Knowledge"; Remes, *Plotinus on Self*. Of the latest works, see Hutchinson, *Plotinus on Consciousness*.

11. Ἤ, εἰ μὲν αὐτὸς κενός ἐστι παντός, ὅταν μηδὲν νοῇ. Εἰ δέ ἐστιν αὐτὸς τοιοῦτος οἷος πάντα εἶναι ὅταν αὐτὸν νοῇ, πάντα ὁμοῦ νοεῖ· ὥστε τῇ μὲν εἰς ἑαυτὸν ὁ τοιοῦτος ἐπιβολῇ καὶ ἐνεργείᾳ ἑαυτὸν ὁρῶν τὰ πάντα ἐμπεριεχόμενα ἔχει, τῇ δὲ πρὸς τὰ πάντα ἐμπεριεχόμενον ἑαυτόν (Plot. 4.4.2.10-14 Henry Schwyzer). Hereinafter all the translations are by T. Shchukin and S. Akishin.

We would say, it [the intellect] contemplates God. Yet should someone admit that it knows God, he would necessarily come to an idea that it knows itself the same way. For the intellect will know what it has got from God, both what he has given and what he may. And having learned and recognized that, it will the same way know itself.[12]

Polemis asserts that in both excerpts there is one and the same thought; however, he suggests that in the second one it is closer to what Gregory Palamas thinks, especially with respect to the identity of the intellect and God. It should be appreciated that Polemis further quotes the later "Triads for the defense of those who practice sacred quietude" together with the places from the *Enneads*, which seem to him parallel to them. The majority of these references (three of five, while the other two are obviously facultative) are to the same treatise "On cognizant hypostasis and on what is higher than it" (*Enn.* V.3). The assembly of these facts, as well as, namely, the mentioned treatise of Plotinus, was intentionally dedicated to the problem field of self-consciousness,[13] precisely to the sense in which it is adherent to the intellect or the soul, convinces us that Gregory Palamas in the *Logos* has relied upon this work and that it has been especially significant for the founder of hesychasm in the later period as well. Finally, it is worthwhile to cite a parallel between the *Logos* with *Enneads* V.3, which was not paid attention to by Polemis, although it has serious importance:

Plotinus

What else can we attribute to the intellect? Swear by Zeus, quietude (ἡσυχίαν). Yet for the intellect, the quietude is not an exit of intellect.[14] Rather, the quietude of the intellect is an action delivering to the intellect rest of other things.[15]

12. Ἀλλὰ τὸν θεὸν θεωρεῖ, εἴποιμεν ἄν. Ἀλλ> εἰ τὸν θεὸν γινώσκειν αὐτόν τις ὁμολογήσει, καὶ ταύτῃ συγχωρεῖν ἀναγκασθήσεται καὶ ἑαυτὸν γινώσκειν. Καὶ γὰρ ὅσα ἔχει παρ> ἐκείνου γνώσεται, καὶ ἃ ἔδωκε, καὶ ἃ δύναται ἐκεῖνος. Ταῦτα δὲ μαθὼν καὶ γνοὺς καὶ ταύτῃ ἑαυτὸν γνώσεται (Plot. 5.3.7.1-5 Henry Schwyzer).

13. The treatise "On the doubts of the soul" (Plot. 4.2) is dedicated to the topic more specialized and proper to Neoplatonism of interrelations between the intellect and the soul with their identity and difference. It seems that this treatise could not be applied to the hesychasm theory, whereas Plot. *En.* 5.3 suits it quite well.

14. The latest English translation suggests here "self-transcending experience" (Gerson, *Enneads*, 561), which conceptually overloads the phrase with the interpretation of the movement of the intellect as a vertical one heading for the One. We incline to assume that in this context only the "exit" of the intellect beyond the limits of its nature, or its natural state, is discussed. For it is proper to the intellect to be in motion (Plotinus further writes about this: Plot. 5.3.18), and its quietude is not a negation of this natural motion. J. Bussanich shares this opinion (*The One and Its Relation to Intellect in Plotinus*, 171) in translating ἔκστασις as "departure from its true nature"

15. Τί γὰρ ἂν καὶ δοίημεν αὐτῷ ἄλλο; Ἡσυχίαν, νὴ Δία. Ἀλλὰ νῷ ἡσυχία οὐ νοῦ ἐστιν

Gregory Palamas

For when the intellect settles out of all the sensual things and resurface from the whirl of turmoil over them and look into the inner human, then, having perceived the disgusting mask which is drawn close [to him] due to prowlings through the low, it hurries up to wash it away through grievance. And as soon as this ugly coverage is torn off, right at the moment the soul is no longer lacerated by variegated low affections, the intellect acquires peace with hardship and reaches the true quietude and remains in itself while intellecting itself, or rather God, by whom it is, via itself in a degree it can comprise him.[16]

In spite of different rhetoric shaping of these excerpts, there are three key points coinciding in them: (1) the idea that self-reversion of the intellect suggests purity of the intellect, its freedom from any sensual, secondary, casual, singular content; (2) the idea that quietude of the intellect does not mean interruption of its activity but rather signifies a qualitatively new stage of activity not depending on other things beyond the intellect; and (3) the idea that contemplating itself means rather contemplating God as a source of being for the intellect. There is also a fourth coincidence in Plotinus densely using the term ἡσυχία, which is discovered five times in total within the given treatise, out of twenty-seven cases in the whole corpus of the *Enneads*. Finally, in the previous fragment,[17] the contemplation of God is discussed, that is, that the self-reversion of the intellect is the primary aim, compliant with Gregory Palamas. In our opinion, all the aforesaid, with adding the materials presented by I. Polemis, suggests that the source of inspiration for Gregory Palamas was the given treatise of the *Enneads*. It is significant that later, while quoting himself, like in the "Word promised in the letter to John and Theodor Philosophers," Gregory Palamas omits the Neoplatonic part of his expression, precisely what was said on self-reversion of the intellect and especially on the hesychia as an uninterruptible activity.[18] The Neoplatonic

ἔκστασις, ἀλλ› ἔστιν ἡσυχία τοῦ νοῦ σχολὴν ἄγουσα ἀπὸ τῶν ἄλλων ἐνέργεια (Plot. 55.3.7.12-15 Henry Schwyzer).

16. Ὅταν γὰρ ὁ νοῦς αἰσθητοῦ παντὸς ἀπαναστῇ καὶ τοῦ κατακλυσμοῦ τῆς περὶ ταῦτα τύρβης ἀνακύψῃ καὶ κατόπτευσῃ τὸν ἐντὸς ἄνθρωπον, τέως μὲν ἐνιδὼν τὸ προσγενόμενον εἰδεχθὲς προσωπεῖον ἐκ τῆς κάτω περιπλανήσεως, τοῦτο διὰ πένθους ἀπονίψασθαι σπεύδει· κἀπειδὰν περιέλη τὸ δυσειδὲς τοῦτο κάλυμμα, τότε δή, τότε μὴ ποικίλαις σχέσεσι τῆς ψυχῆς ἀγεννῶς διασπωμένης, μόγις εἰρήνην ἄγει καὶ τῆς ὄντως ἡσυχίας ἅπτεται καὶ καθ᾽ ἑαυτὸν μένει νοῶν αὐτὸς ἑαυτὸν μᾶλλον δὲ δι᾽ ἑαυτοῦ, καθ᾽ ὅσον ἐγχωρεῖ, τὸν θεόν, δι᾽ ὅν ἐστιν (Greg. Pal. *Laud. Pet. Ath.* 171.24–172.4 Chrestou).

17. Plot. 55.3.7.1-11 Henry Schwyzer.

18. See Greg. Pal. *Epist. Jo. et Th.* 237.18–238.15 Chrestou. In 237.18-24, factually the same text is found as in the excerpt cited above, from "For when the intellect settles out" till "the soul is

loaning was probably situational and sufficient only in the course of writing the "Biography."

In *Ennead* V.3,[19] Plotinus inquires how self-contemplation and self-cognition are possible. His answer is that it is possible by the self-reversion of the cognizing subject on the account of "simplification," overcoming the sensual content, any external objectness and further the discursive (rational) thought ever suggesting a sensual object.[20] The indicated type of cognition is accessible not only to the intellect but also to the soul or, more strictly, its higher part,[21] not only to the intellect as the second hypostasis, but also by participating to particular human intellects.[22] In resuming the reflections of exclusiveness of the intellect in comparison with the other elements of hierarchy, Plotinus writes:

For it [the intellect] is not practical. Since to the one gazing upon the external things and not remaining in himself, any knowledge would appear external, on the one hand, and on the other hand, there would be no necessity to know himself, if actually he is fully involved in practical matters. Indeed, to what does not relate to practical activity—for the pure intellect aims not for the absent—the reversion to itself reveals the knowledge of one's self not only to be fair (εὔλογον), but also necessary. For what would be its life to it, since it is not involved in activity and exists within the intellect?[23]

Plotinus faces the problem of the object of self-contemplation.[24] While denying the possibility of discursive self-thought suggesting a split

---

no longer lacerated," while further instead of a brief Neoplatonic passage a long narration on ascetic virtues follows finishing by the same Gospel quote as the relevant excerpt in the *Logos*.

19. In this case we do not seek to explain the main ideas of the given treatise, all the more in their interconnection with the other treatises. It is necessary only to specify the points of tangency between Plotinus and Gregory Palamas and mark the crossroads they could have come together. For more profound studying of this text, one should address the following commented editions: Oosthout, *Modes of Knowledge and the Transcendental*; Beierwaltes, *Selbsterkenntnis und Erfahrung der Einheit*; Ham, *Plotin: Traite 49*; and also a collective monograph, Dixaut, *La connaissance de Soi*.

20. Plot. 5.3.1 Henry Schwyzer.

21. Plot. 5.3.2-3 Henry Schwyzer.

22. Plot. 5.3.4 Henry Schwyzer.

23. Οὐ γὰρ δὴ πρακτικός γε οὗτος· ὡς πρὸς τὸ ἔξω βλέποντι τῷ πρακτικῷ καὶ μὴ ἐν αὐτῷ μένοντι εἴη ἂν τῶν μὲν ἔξω τις γνῶσις, ἀνάγκη δὲ οὐκ ἔνεστιν, εἴπερ τὸ πᾶν πρακτικὸς εἴη, γινώσκειν ἑαυτόν. Ὧι δὲ μὴ πρᾶξις—οὐδὲ γὰρ ὄρεξις τῷ καθαρῷ νῷ ἀπόντος—τούτῳ ἡ ἐπιστροφὴ πρὸς αὐτὸν οὖσα οὐ μόνον εὔλογον ὑποδείκνυσιν [τὴν ἑαυτοῦ], ἀλλὰ καὶ ἀναγκαίαν [αὐτοῦ] τὴν <ἑαυτοῦ> γνῶσιν· τίς γὰρ ἂν καὶ ἡ ζωὴ αὐτοῦ εἴη πράξεως ἀπηλλαγμένῳ καὶ ἐν νῷ ὄντι (Plot. 5.3.6.35-43 Henry, Schwyzer).

24. Plot. 5.3.5 Henry Schwyzer. I. V. Berestov, taking namely Plot. 5.3 as a base, writes that for Plotinus two patterns of constructing an object of pure intellect were actual. On the one hand, the intellect could intellect not itself, but some set of its own properties. On the other

of the contemplating substance to intellectual and intelligible, subject and object with any degree of abstraction and purity,[25] he nevertheless speaks on "cognizing one's self" in which God reveals himself to him.

> We would say, it [the intellect] contemplates God. Yet should someone admit that it knows God, he would necessarily come to an idea that it knows itself the same way. For the intellect will know what it has got from God, both what he has given and what he may. And having learned and recognized that, it will the same way know itself, for it is by itself one of what has been bestowed, or rather it is all that has been bestowed. And if it knows God, having cognized his powers, it will also know itself, for it has emerged therefrom and has been nourished with what it is empowered. If, however, it is unable to clearly see God, while contemplation is probably the same with what is contemplated, then thus it is by excellence left to him to see and know itself, if this vision is the same with what is contemplated.[26]

In this context, the subject discussed is the One, as Plotinus apparently antithesizes the vague knowledge of what surpasses the intellect and is its source and the knowledge of itself by the intellect, which is quite clear.[27] Finally, for Plotinus in this text, the contemplation of the One appears a source of self-cognition, an initial point, an imperceptible moment, where the sought "clear knowing itself" takes its place. Still after that the "fall" of the discursive thought necessarily follows, because while contemplating

---

hand, again, it thought not itself but the One. According to Berestov, "both cases do not exclude but supplement each other" (*Svoboda v filosofii Plotina*, 301-2). It should be understood that the second and the first patterns refer to different stages of relation of the intellect to itself. They could be legally called self-contemplation (the intellect contemplates the One) and self-thinking, where the intellect contemplates the multiplicity of intelligible within itself.

25. Plot. 5I.7.39.11–13; 5.3.5.9–15 Henry Schwyzer. See the interpretation by Berestov (*Svoboda v filosofii Plotina*, 178-79), which suggests that "in Plotinus' understanding of 'action,' a very important feature is impossibility for an action of a subject to be directed to that subject. 'Active' in Plotinus' view cannot be 'suffering' in the relation it acts, according to the law of prohibition of contradiction." In these fragments, however, the narration goes rather on necessary "split" of the active into active and suffering, than on prohibition of the active to be simultaneously one and another.

26. Ἀλλὰ τὸν θεὸν θεωρεῖ, εἴποιμεν ἄν. Ἀλλ> εἰ τὸν θεὸν γινώσκειν αὐτόν τις ὁμολογήσει, καὶ ταύτῃ συγχωρεῖν ἀναγκασθήσεται καὶ ἑαυτὸν γινώσκειν. Καὶ γὰρ ὅσα ἔχει παρ> ἐκείνου γνώσεται, καὶ ἃ ἔδωκε, καὶ ἃ δύναται ἐκεῖνος. Ταῦτα δὲ μαθὼν καὶ γνοὺς καὶ ταύτῃ ἑαυτὸν γνώσεται· καὶ γὰρ ἕν τι τῶν δοθέντων αὐτός, μᾶλλον δὲ πάντα τὰ δοθέντα αὐτός. Εἰ μὲν οὖν κἀκεῖνο γνώσεται κατὰ τὰς δυνάμεις αὐτοῦ μαθών, καὶ ἑαυτὸν γνώσεται ἐκεῖθεν γενόμενος καὶ ἃ δύναται κομισάμενος· εἰ δὲ ἀδυνατήσει ἰδεῖν σαφῶς ἐκεῖνον, ἐπειδὴ τὸ ἰδεῖν ἴσως αὐτό ἐστι τὸ ὁρώμενον, ταύτῃ μάλιστα λείποιτ> ἂν αὐτῷ ἰδεῖν ἑαυτὸν καὶ εἰδέναι, εἰ τὸ ἰδεῖν τοῦτό ἐστι τὸ αὐτὸ εἶναι τὸ ὁρώμενον (Plot. 5.3.7.1-13 Henry Schwyzer).

27. See a collection of parallel places and an analysis in Bussanich, *The One and Its Relation to Intellect in Plotinus*, 229.

the One, the intellect defines itself in regard to it, creates its own multiplicity and all the multiplicity of the intelligible.[28] The intellect pursues the One, but in this pursuit it discovers only what it has accepted from the One, that is, itself. It tries to catch sight of the One but sees just its own vision. It wishes to cognize the supreme beginning, but only receives the "knowledge of knowledge." It is namely for this reason that Plotinus insists that the contemplation of the One is a sign that activity is uninterrupted. On the contrary, such contemplation is a starting point for its activity as intellect.

Let us single out two important issues. First, for Plotinus, the One and the intellect (at least in this text, while it is important solely here) cannot be unified; they are divided, and the entire description of their interaction is aimed at underlining this division. If some unified and divided presence within the intellect is possible for the soul,[29] a complete unification with the One is unattainable for the intellect. Second, the highest point of being for intellect is not an exit beyond its limits in contemplating the One but, on the contrary, attainment of its own limits in this contemplation. The vision of God does not liberate in the sense that it resolves the limits of nature, but in that it establishes these limits.

In the above cited text of Gregory Palamas, there is another dispute. The presence of the intellect is not an end in itself, but rather a degree or an instrument to gain what surpasses the intellect. Being in agreement with Plotinus that "the intellect acquires peace with hardship and reaches the true quietude and remains in itself while contemplating itself, or rather God, by whom it is,"[30] Gregory Palamas writes further something in contradiction to Plotinus: "[The intellect] will overcome its own nature and will be deified through junction ever advancing to the better."[31] That means that in a single phrase the founder of hesychasm refutes both theses we have marked of the respective Plotinus's treatise. Yes, it is real that self-contemplation of the intellect is in a strict sense contemplation of God, who—there is no possible contradiction between the pagan and Christian thinkers in this point—is a source both of the being of intellect and its ability to think. But precisely for that reason, it is not the contemplation of God that reveals the intellect to itself, but the self-contemplation of the

28. Plot. 5.3.11 Henry Schwyzer.
29. See Plot. 4.4.2 Henry Schwyzer.
30. Greg. Pal. *Laud. Pet. Ath.* 172.1-4 Chrestou.
31. Greg. Pal. *Laud. Pet. Ath.* 172.4-5 Chrestou. Here we find an evident reference to the doctrine of eternal increment of soul (or intellect), which is also traditional for the Eastern patristics. See Blowers, "Maximus the Confessor, Gregory of Nyssa and the Concept of 'Perpetual Progress,'" 151–71; Emerson, "The Work of Christ According to Gregory of Nyssa," 149–94.

intellect that reveals God to it; the latter does not take a stand at this self-contemplation but advances beyond its own nature. *Eo ipso*, for Plotinus, the correlation of the intellect and its source is self-definition of the intellect, establishment of limits of its being, affixment of its possibilities, whereas for Gregory Palamas, it is resolution of limits and extension of "possibilities." In the end, as we find in the second point of discrepancies between the thinkers, the intellect and God convene to the highest degree of unity, whereby the full identification is impossible, while also the distinction is constantly overcome on the account of "advancement to the better." For while Plotinus holds important the definition of God as an object of contemplation, owing to what its inner nature and capability to creative evolving ad extra is highlighted in maximum degree, for Gregory Palamas, God is a desired goal of junction, with recognition of unattainability of this goal in a full measure.

To summarize: Gregory Palamas comes round with Plotinus in that (1) reversion of the intellect to itself suggests its liberation from any external content; (2) it means acquisition of proper nature[32] simultaneously with attaining the contemplation of God; and (3) the intellect in this state reaches quietude, but such quietude does not signify termination of activity. Yet the Byzantine thinker, as different from the Hellenic, supposes that (1) in contemplation of God the nature of the intellect is not only acquired but also overcome up to deification, as well as that (2) the supreme activity of the intellect provides not so much its natural and creative functions as moving gradually (with complete unattainability) closer to God. Thus Gregory Palamas not only situationally loans the terminology and logical steps of Plotinus, but also polemicizes with the text of the *Enneads*. To speak more exactly, he does it addressing those who regarded the *Enneads* for themselves; namely, those for whom the text of *Logos on Saint Peter of Athos* was written.

The *Logos*, according to the biography of Gregory Palamas, compiled by Philotheus Coccinus, was written after the hesychast received clear notifications from God not to keep his mystical experience and intellectual

---

32. As a probable parallel to the teaching of Plotinus on contemplating of God as an initial point of creativity of the intellect, the words of Gregory Palamas could be counted that when the intellect stands before God, "the law of the matter is restricted by the intellect and the intellect is sculptured in full safety as a supreme creation, for there is no more passion that is knocking to the intellect, because the grace received from beyond attune it whole to the best concord. Therefore, the participated to so much good intellect transfers also to the body conjoined to it many features of divine beauty, being a mediator between the divine grace and rudeness of the flesh and making the impossible possible" (Greg. Pal. *Laud. Pet. Ath.* 172.22–27 Chrestou).

talent under wraps but to convert them first into an oral and then into a written sermon.[33] Certainly, the addressees of these texts were not solely the Athone monks, but also the intellectuals of Thessaloniki and Constantinople, who formed connected groups with the monkhood. Moreover, the *Logos* seems to appear a manifest of the hesychast movement, addressed to the whole world, proposing a program of salvation for everybody, not only for the elected ones.[34] It also seems to be evident with this that the "Neoplatonic passages" were directed namely to the intellectual elite.

The most significant and influential person in the intellectual circles of that period was Nicephorus Gregoras, who by that time had been neither conceptual enemy nor adversary or competitor of Gregory Palamas. At that time, polemics might carry a peaceful and friendly air. It is probable, for example, that in the second text, *On Entrance of Theotokos into the Temple*, written immediately after the *Logos*, Gregory Palamas disputes with Nicephorus Gregoras; nevertheless, it does not follow immediately from the text.[35] It could be suggested that also the *Logos*, a work that is not in itself polemical but rather popularizing, proposes an intellectual alternative to the writings of the humanist. We know from the letter of another friend of Palamas, Gregory Akindynos, that the latter has been intellectually influenced by him, and circa 1330, Gregory Palamas gave Akindynos one of his treatises.[36] It was possibly the treatise on calculation of the Easter date.[37] But from this very source it comes that Akindynos has been acquainted also with other Nicephorus Gregoras's texts,[38] while the letter sent to him by the latter contained a "multitude of arguments from the treasuries of

33. Philoth. *Laud. Greg. Pal.* 466–467 Tsames.

34. There are some substantial observations made by Michael Mitreu. First, the episode appropriated from Nicholas the Monk with the hunter asking Peter of Athone admission to stay in reclusion with him, but receiving an order to stay in the world with prayer, contemplation, and spiritual grievance represents here the hesychast doctrine as something accessible for laypeople, for any human (Mitrea, "'Old Wine in New Bottles'?," 256–57). Second, the rhetoric framework of the "Homily," the introduction, and especially the conclusion describes Peter of Athone as a universal saint both in the light of universal usefulness of his asceticism as important for all people and in the sense of dispersion of his worship (259).

35. Philotheus Coccinus notifies of the matters for writing the treatise: Philoth. *Laud. Greg. Pal.* 467 Tsames. J. Meyendorff convincingly writes on the fact that the addressee of the text was Nicephorus Gregoras ("Spiritual Trends in Byzantium," 102–3; *Introduction a l'étude de Grégoire Palamas*, 60).

36. See Greg. Acind. *Ep.* 1.30-38 Hero; Meyendorff, *Introduction a l'étude de Grégoire Palamas*, 48.

37. See the hypothesis in Hero, "Commentary," 311, based on that both in the letter of Akindynos and in the heading of one of the manuscripts the initial addressee of the treatise is philosopher Joseph Rhakendytes.

38. Greg. Acind. *Ep.* 1.1-6, 28-30 Hero.

Plato."[39] Upon that, it is admissible to affirm with some credibility that the polemics with the *Enneads* is an attempt to create by the material familiar to the addressees an intellectual pattern opposite to the one habitual to the communicants like Nicephorus Gregoras or Gregory Akindynos.

A year before the compilation of *Logos on Saint Peter of Athos*, in 1331 or a little earlier, a dispute between the "rising star" of the Byzantine theology Barlaam of Calabria and Nicephorus Gregoras became a prominent event in the intellectual life of Constantinople. The latter is recognized a winner in this dispute and, a fact sufficient for us, has left a literary description of the discussion, a dialogue "Florentius or on Wisdom."[40] Sergey Mariev has drawn noticeable attention in this work to the influence of the treatise "On Dialectics" (*Enn.* I.3),[41] but the description of dynamics of cognition process produced by Gregoras in this text is more valuable:

Who, therefore, cannot initiate the study of what is from above and according to the nature but, still lacking such wings, stays in the need of leadership from below; if he, having started, goes up all the way as like being led through a stairway, and returns to the plain of the true knowledge, he would be justly praised, though not wondered at, for he probably seems to expose himself from the weak side of nature in regard of the duty, while acting on his own. Yet the one who would contact with the wisdom decisively and in a natural way, and then with the excessive ambitiousness pursues the secondary matters, coming down from what is united by nature and divagating among what comes before the senses and watching as if from the root the disintegration of the one into the multitude—for the reason that, having gathered together once more a single variegated entwinement out of everything and make it as one thing, sees everything, it is he who much deserves, to my mind, being excited at for his loftiness, for he clearly displays that what belongs to the art, is secondary after what is by nature.[42]

39. Greg. Acind. *Ep.* 1.12-13 Hero.

40. On the treatise and conditions of its creation, see Leone, "Alcune osservazioni sul Florentios di Niceforo Gregora"; idem, "Appunti e note su alcuni opuscoli di Niceforo Gregora"; idem, "Introduzione"; Krasikov, "Vizantijskoe myshlenie"; Bydén, "Criticism of Aristotle in Nikephoros Gregoras' Florentius"; Manolova, "Nikephoros Gregoras's Philomathes and Phlorentios."

41. Mariev, "Plotinus in the Phlorentios of Nikephoros Gregoras." See on the significance of Plotinus for Nicephorus Gregoras in general: Beyer, "Nikephoros Gregoras als Theologe," 182-83; Ierodiakonou, "Anti-Logical Movement in the Fourteenth Century," 223–24. While polemicizing in the "Roman History" with the doctrine of Gregory Palamas on substance and energies, Nicephorus Gregoras starts namely with Plotinus in enumerating the pagan philosophers who "disagreed" with the hesychast: Nic. Greg. *H. R.* 23.6 Migne.

42. ὅστις οὖν μὴ δυνάμενος ἐκ τῆς ἄνωθεν ἀρχῆς καὶ κατὰ φύσιν τὰ τῆς ἐπιστήμης ποιεῖσθαι προοίμια, ἀλλ' ἀχορήγητος ὢν ἔτι τοιούτων πτερῶν, δεῖται τῆς κάτωθεν ἀγωγῆς, ἐὰν μὲν ἀρξάμενος ὅλην ἀνέλθῃ τὴν οἱονεὶ διὰ κλίμακος ἄγουσαν καὶ πρὸς τὸ τῆς ἀληθευούσης γνώσεως ἀναλύσῃ πεδίον, ἔπαινον μὲν προσάγεσθαι δίκαιος, θαῦμα δ' οὔ, τοῦ γε ὀφειλομένου καὶ ὅσον εἰκὸς

Here we deal with an evident contraposition of two types of thought. The first is *ab ovo* focused on interaction of cognizing intellect and sensual object (the type of thought ascribed by the author of the dialog to his adversary, Barlaam of Calabria), where the apt mastering of the logical tool kit appears to be the maximum the human is able to attain, while the diversity of sensitivity is a mere given that has no obvious origin. The cognizing intellect and diversified sensuality stand forth as initial abstract oppositions that convene only in a cognitive act and have no common unique source (at least the one this or other way cognizable). For this type of thought, the logical tool kit serves as a "support from below" due to which it is possible to reach some degree of generalization and succeed in the "true knowledge," that is, in this case, in cognition of sensual things within their non-sensual unity. Nevertheless, such thought is, without addressing the initial unity, eventually helpless and imperfect. The second type of thought, whereof Nicephorus Gregoras himself was a supporter, supposes as a "starting point" of its process what surpasses the dyad of cognizing intellect and sensual object, something unique that is a source of this dyad. The intellect starts with that it defines itself not in regard of the sensual but in regard of the one, and in this self-definition it discloses both the limits of its nature and the one as a source of this self-definition. As the "second stage" of thought, the division of the one in sensual things stands, which is certainly an intellectual procedure and such an action of the intellect that is performed over the impulse proposed by contemplation of the unity and by the true nature of the intellect shaped by this contemplation. At this stage, the relation of the intellect to the sensual objects acquires quite different features: the intellect comprehends both itself and its object as a result of the same process of "division" of the one. It is because of this that a natural result of this is junction is performed by the very intellect.

Based on the passages above, Plotinus states that the intellect (in its self-reversion) reveals itself as a pure object behind which the One "hides itself" as a true object. It is a source of any content; any powers of the intellect are probably reflected in this passage and in its logic. In the end, the intellect exposes its nature as different and separated from the One,

---

ἀρρωστούσῃ φύσει φανεὶς αὐτουργός. ὅστις δ' ἐρρωμένως καὶ κατὰ φύσιν ἄπτοιτο τῆς σοφίας, ἔπειτα φιλοτιμίας περιουσίᾳ καὶ τῶν δευτέρων ἐφίεται, κατιὼν ἐκ τοῦ φύσει ἑνὸς καὶ σκιδνάμενος καθ' ὁπόσα αἰσθήσει ὑπόκειται καὶ βλέπων ὡς ἀπὸ ῥίζης τὴν τοῦ ἑνὸς πρὸς τὰ πλείω διαίρεσιν, ἵν' αὖθις συνηθροικὼς καὶ μίαν πλοκὴν διὰ πάντων ποικίλην, πεποιηκὼς ὡς ἓν ὁρᾷ τὸ πᾶν, οὗτος ἐμοὶ τῆς εὐφυΐας μάλα θαυμάζεσθαι δίκαιος, δεικνὺς ἐναργῶς ὁπόσα τῆς τέχνης τῆς φύσεως δεύτερα (Niceph. Greg. *Phlor.* 949-64 Leone).

and "at the same moment" falls apart from being present in the unity and simplicity in order to get down to the level of discursive thinking up to comprehension of one or another partial and sensual content. Considering all the nuances, we find that here are identical patterns of correlation of God, intellect and sensual world, where the key aspect is the presence of the intellect within its own nature, and the ascension is interpreted as acquisition of this nature on the account of self-definition in regard of God and discerning the principal unconnectibility of God and the intellect.

As we see, for Gregory Palamas this interpretation of communication with God is strange and unacceptable, because the *Logos on Saint Peter of Athos* is manifest of the hesychast movement addressed not only to the monks but also to the Byzantine educated class. It contains references to the philosophical topics familiar to it with a simultaneous controversion with them over their incompatibility with the views of hesychasm. Although for Nicephorus Gregoras, the most popular thinker of that period, Plotinus was an influence[43] not only at the level of speech but also in key concepts, Palamas could not fail to take regard of this. While Gregoras's main idea of incommunicability of the human intellect with God was based on the *Enneads* of Plotinus, Gregory Palamas could not avoid addressing this text. Finally, we should suggest that here we have the first attempt to lay down a theory that, in the course of cognizing God and participating with the deity, a human being becomes someone greater than he is in his natural givenness and that his self-definition is simply a step to the unspeakable identity with God.

43. Yet one can judge of distinctive actuality of Plotinus for the discussed period, for example, by the fact that ca. 1315 Nikephoros Choumnos, the classical author of the Byzantine humanism, compiled a special writing against Plotinus, "On the Soul against Plotinus" (Benakis, "To problêma tôn genikôn ennoiôn kai o ennoiologikos realismos tôn Byzantinôn"; Mariev, "Neoplatonic Philosophy in Byzantium," 14-15), where he, while rejecting the overtly pagan ideas like metempsychosis, solidifies with the Hellenic philosopher namely in interpretation of the intellect (Niceph. Chumn. *Plot.* 1405 Migne). It should be noted that right in those years, Gregory Palamas studied the ancient philosophy, and he certainly was able to get acquainted with Choumnos's treatise as well as with the *Enneads* immediately (Meyendorff, *Introduction a l'étude de Grégoire Palamas*, 46–49).

CHAPTER 15 ‖ Cardinal Bessarion and the *Corpus Dionysiacum*

Platonic Love between East and West

Denis J.-J. Robichaud

It has become canonical history that Joseph Stiglmayr and Hugo Koch first established the dependence of the *Corpus Dionysiacum* on Proclus's concepts and terminology in 1895.[1] For many, the demonstration of Dionysius's reliance on Proclus was the final coup de grâce to the old legends that the author of the *Corpus Dionysiacum* was the same person as Paul of Tarsus's convert on the Areopagite (Acts 17:34) and as the martyred Bishop of Athens or Paris. As is also often acknowledged, Lorenzo Valla (1407–57)

The author presented different parts of his evidence and arguments at the conference "Dimensione Teologica & Percezione del Contributo Bessarioneo / Θεολογική διάσταση και πρόσληψη του έργου του βησσαρίωνα" at the Istituto Ellenico di Studi Bizantini e Postbizantini di Venezia / Ελληνικό Ινστιτούτο Βυζαντινών και Μεταβυζαντινών Σπουδών Βενετίας; at a collaborative workshop between the University of Notre Dame and the De Wulf-Mansion Centre for Ancient, Medieval and Renaissance Philosophy of KU Leuven; during an invited lecture at the Instituto de Investigaciones Filosóficas of the Universidad Nacional Autónoma de México; and at the III Convegno di Studi Bizantini of the Scuola Grande di San Marco on Platonismo Byzantino. The author thanks the organizers and the audiences for their questions. He also wishes to thank John Monfasani for reading the final draft of this article. All translations are the author's unless otherwise indicated.

1. Stiglmayr, "Der Neuplatoniker Proklos als Vorlage des sog"; Koch, "Proklus als Quelle des Pseudo-Dionysius Areopagita."

and Desiderius Erasmus (1466–1536) had long before demonstrated the pseudepigraphic nature of the *Corpus Dionysiacum* through a number of philological and historical arguments, none of which, however, investigated Ps.-Dionysius's dependence on Proclus.[2] Besides, that Proclus and Ps.-Dionysius employed similar concepts and terminology was not a new revelation in 1895, nor even in Valla's time. In fact, the earliest known evidence of someone detecting similarities between the *Corpus Dionysiacum* and Athenian Neoplatonism comes from introductory *scholia* to the *Corpus* that sought to disabuse readers of any suggestions that its theological writings might have been influenced by Proclus, which would of course expose the name Dionysius the Areopagite as a fictitious. If the late ancient *scholia* is evidence of early discussions of Ps.-Dionysius's relationship to Proclus, there is further evidence that the question of the *Corpus Dionysiacum*'s Platonism developed into a full investigation among Byzantine émigrés in the community of Cardinal Bessarion in fifteenth-century Italy.

Valla traveled in similar circles as Cardinal Bessarion. Not only did Valla eventually receive the title of Apostolic secretary under Pope Nicholas V, but he also counted Bessarion as a patron. But it is important to emphasize that he had begun to make up his mind about the pseudepigraphic nature of the *Corpus Dionysiacum* before he arrived in Rome. This probably accounts for why his arguments are by and large independent from his colleague's inquiries into Dionysius's Platonism. His arguments appear in his annotation to Acts 17:34 from around 1442–44, which he revised and dedicated to Pope Nicholas V in 1448 when he came to Rome. I will not dwell too long on his arguments since I have discussed them (along with Erasmus's expansion of them) elsewhere at length.[3] Valla's reasons why the *Corpus Dionysiacum* is pseudepigraphic can be broken down into seven arguments: (1) that the Areopagite is a legal site for judges, not a philosophical school; (2) that the author's claims that an eclipse's shadow covered the whole world during the crucifixion of Jesus of Nazareth are problematic for a number of reasons, including that there is no other evidence and that it contradicts the Bible; (3) Dionysius's letters about the eclipse contradict his own statements about the event; (4) there is no evidence of Dionysius's writings before Gregory the Great; (5) Gregory does not specify which Dionysius he is consulting; (6) some contemporary Greeks in Italy (*quid-*

---

2. Monfasani, "Pseudo-Dionysius the Areopagite in Mid-Quattrocento Rome"; Moreschini, "Aspetti della difesa del cristianesimo"; idem, "L'Autenticità del *Corpus Dionysianum*"; Robichaud, "Valla and Erasmus on the Dionysian Question."

3. Robichaud, "Valla and Erasmus on the Dionysian Question."

am nostrae aetatis eruditissimi Graeci) attribute the *Corpus Dionysiacum* not to St. Paul's disciple but to the fourth-century heretic Apollinaris; and (7) whoever wrote the *De coelesti hierarchia* does not write in a style that seems ancient (*nec antiquitatem sapit*).[4]

Valla keeps *in pectore* the name of the erudite Greeks who might have harbored doubts that the author of the *Corpus Dionysiacum* was Apollinaris and not Dionysius the Areopagite, but John Monfasani has established that Valla had in mind the Byzantine émigré Theodore Gaza (ca. 1398 to ca. 1475). Although Gaza wrote to Pope Nicholas V in his preface to his translation of Ps.-Alexander of Aphrodiasias's *Problemata* that he thought that the *Corpus Dionysiacum* was a forgery, Monfasani argues that he did not publish his reasoning out of fear of offending his patrons, who were none other than Pope Nicholas V and Cardinal Bessarion.[5] Monfasani's argument is also confirmed by a letter, published by Claudio Moreschini, from Gianfrancesco Pico della Mirandola (1470–1533) to Giampietro Carafa, later Pope Paul IV, defending the Apostolic authorship of Dionysius the Areopagite against Valla and Gaza.[6] Like the question of Proclus's influence on Dionysius, the possible attribution of the *Corpus Dionysiacum* to Apollinaris circulated in a portion of the *scholia* to the *Corpus* that is attributed to John of Scythopolis (ca. 536–50), as it did also in Photius (ca. 810/20–93), who referred to an attribution by Ephraim the sixth-century Patriarch of Antioch. In fact, in one of the earliest mentions of the *Corpus Dionysiacum*, during a controversy in 532 in Constantinople between Catholic devotees of the Council of Chalcedon of 451 and Severian Monophysites, Hypatius of Ephesus voiced his suspicion that the pseudonym Dionysius was invented by followers of the heretic Apollinaris.[7] Valla's recognition that some erudite Byzantines attributed the *Corpus Dionysiacum* to Apollinaris

4. For a detailed analysis of Valla's arguments, see the literature cited in note 2 above, as well as Valla, *In latinam novi testamenti interpretationem*; idem, *Collatio Novi Testamenti*; Camporeale, *Lorenzo Valla*.

5. Monfasani, "Pseudo-Dionysius the Areopagite in Mid-Quattrocento Rome."

6. Moreschini, "Aspetti della difesa del cristianesimo"; idem, "L'Autenticità del *Corpus Dionysianum*."

7. *Sancti Maximi Scholia* in *PG* 4: 21D–23A; Innocentius of Maronea, *Epistola de collatione cum severianis* in Schwartz and Straub, *Acta Concilium Oecumenicorum*, 172:5, 173:12–18; Suchla, "Die sogenannten Maximus-Scholien des *Corpus Dionysiacum Areopagiticum*"; idem, "Die Überlieferung des Prologs des Johannes von Skythopolis"; idem, "Eine Redaktion des griechischen *Corpus Dionysiacum Areopagiticum*"; idem, "Die Überlieferung von Prolog und Scholien des Johannes von Skythopolis"; idem, "Verteidigung eines platonischen Denkmodells einer christlichen Welt"; Rorem and Lamoreaux, *John of Scythopolis and the Dionysian Corpus*; Lilla, *Dionigi l'Areopagita e il platonismo cristiano*, 159; Mainoldi, *Dietro Dionigi l'Areopagita*, 62, 76; and Robichaud, "Valla and Erasmus on the Dionysian Question."

is the clearest evidence of his knowledge of earlier "Greek" doubts about the authorship of the *Corpus*, but despite the circulation of all of these earlier suspicions in mid-fifteenth-century Rome, neither Valla nor even Gaza addresses Ps.-Dionysius's connection to Proclus and the Athenian school of Platonism.

If Cardinal Bessarion tried to sweep Gaza's arguments under the rug, as Monfasani maintains, he nonetheless had to grapple with Dionysius's relationship to Platonism because his intellectual adversary, another Byzantine émigré, George of Trebizond (1395–84), forced him to do so.[8] In his voluminous critique of Plato and the Platonists, the *Comparatio philosophorum Platonis et Aristotelis*, George presented an interesting theory regarding the author of the *Corpus Dionysiacum*'s relationship to late ancient Platonism:

But among the Platonists, Numenius and especially Proclus tried to show that Plato set up three trinities and an order of nine in the heavens. Proclus made it absolutely clear that he appropriated for himself by theft the books of the most holy of men Dionysius the Areopagite, especially when he uses the same abstract and uncommon words as Dionysius. Numenius took expressions from both the Old and the New Testament, and imitating them to accommodate Plato's language, he created a forgery, for he plucks a word from somewhere in Plato, never three at a time, very rarely two, but frequently only a single word, and never indicating the place from which he took them, and he cuts and pastes them together, and claims that Plato wrote these pastiches so that he can easily make it seem as though these Platonists drew from the Gospels rather than Plato himself.[9]

It needs to be said at the outset that George did not just target dead Platonists but the revival of Platonism taking place in Bessarion's court. George's logic seems to be that by attacking ancient sources he should be able to prevent his contemporaries from reviving them, and we shall see how Bessarion defends his position by engaging in competing source criticism. To critique Numenius of Apamea (second century), George works largely with Eusebius's *Praeparatio Evangelica*, which he had translated into Latin for the first time, and an important *scholion* to the *Corpus Dionysiacum*. Eusebius, everyone knows, quotes Numenius's saying that "Plato

8. For George of Trebizond, see esp. Monfasani, *George of Trebizond*; *Collectanea Trapezuntiania*; and "Pseudo-Dionysius the Areopagite in Mid-Quattrocento Rome."

9. "Sed inter alios Proculus maxime atque Numenius, quorum alter tres trinitates, et novem ordines in divinis Platonem posuisse conatus ostendere, ipsa re manifestum fecit areopagite Dionisii viri omnino celestis libros furto sibi arrogasse, praesertim cum sepius eisdem vocabulis abstractis atque inusitatis quibus etiam Dyonisius utitur." George of Trebizond, *Comparatio platonis et aristotelis*, G8r.

is none other than Moses speaking in Attic Greek."[10] But this statement, according to George, reveals that Numenius was simply a plagiarist who cut Plato's writings into pieces and pasted his words back together in order to make his doctrines resemble and compete with Christianity. While these comments might reveal an interesting dimension to George's attempts to drive a wedge between Platonism and Christianity, they do not present any compelling arguments or evidence for his polemical claims.

Regarding George's critique of Proclus, even though his statements about Proclus's relationship to Dionysius the Areopagite do not provide evidence that he undertook a careful philological examination of the similarities between Proclus's and Dionysius's "abstract and uncommon terminology," it is clear that George is familiar enough with Proclus's language and his systematic multiplication of triadic hypostases into three groups of three to find similarities with Dionysius's hierarchy, which is also composed of nine grades or three levels that are, again like Proclus, multiplied into three further orders. Rather than a philological comparison of the two late ancient sources, George is drawing on some of his general knowledge of Proclus in order to elaborate on scant information in a *scholion* that introduces a number of Greek manuscripts of the *Corpus Dionysiacum*. Some of this material, which seems to have originated with Philoponus, addresses the Platonic dimension of the *Corpus Dionysiacum* but turns Platonism's influence on Dionysius upside down by writing a history of Platonic thievery. It points the finger at Proclus's theft from Dionysius as a late occurrence of Platonists robbing Christians but also quotes the opinion of Basil of Caesarea (330–79) that like the Devil, Platonists steal from Christian theology. To cap off the history, the scholiast quotes the aforementioned opinion from the Pythagorean Numenius (also found in Eusebius) that Plato is an Atticizing Moses to show that Platonists were stealing from the Bible even before the advent of Christ. The message is clear; Proclus stole from Ps.-Dionysius and even Plato stole from the Hebrews. It should also be noted that since a similar version of the accusations also circulated in the *Souda*'s entry on Dionysius the Areopagite from the tenth century and later in George Pachymeres's (1242 to ca. 1310) introduction to the *Corpus Dionysiacum*, which refers to a passage from Basil the Great that includes the accusations against Proclus but does not quote Numenius, I can establish that George

10. See the fragments of Numenius from Eus. *p.e.* 11.10.14 and Clem. *Str.* 1.22.150 as edited by Des Places (Numénius, *Fragments*).

of Trebizond was in all likelihood working with the manuscript *scholion* to the *Corpus Dionysiacum* and not the *Souda*, nor Pachymeres.

George was not the sole reader of this *scholion* in the fifteenth century, however. It was also discussed by others near and dear to Cardinal Bessarion. Bessarion's close friend Pietro Balbi (1399–79) translated it for Cardinal Nicholas of Cusa (1401–64) between January and September 1462 as part of a longer note accompanying Robert Grosseteste's (ca. 1168–1253) translation and commentary on Ps.-Dionysius.[11] As is clear from the fact that Balbi also translated Proclus's *Platonic Theology* for Cusanus in the 1460s, Balbi's translations were part of a larger research agenda. Therefore, unlike George, Balbi would have recognized from his close studies of the *Platonic Theology* the terminological similarities between Proclus and Dionysius. As a matter of fact, in Cusanus's own work of Platonic theology, the dialogue titled *De non aliud*, Balbi speaks as one of the interlocutors questioning Dionysius relationship to Proclus: "In the past few days, in fact, I translated from Greek into Latin the famous Platonist Proclus's work about the divine Plato's theology, and I discovered in them the same things as in Dionysius and nearly in the same style and mode of speaking. On account of which, I would also like to hear you speak about Proclus's *Platonic Theology*." To which Cusanus responds, "It is certainly the case, Pietro, that your Proclus is chronologically later than Dionysius the Areopagite. However, it is not certain whether he read the writings of Dionysius."[12] Quoting Dionysius's interpretation of Romans 1:19, Cusanus explains that all wise men, if they are truly wise, wish to say the same thing about the divine first principle of reality, even if they express themselves differently. Cusanus continues to explain that Proclus followed Plato as though he were his God, and that he could have arrived at true conclusions about the nature of the divine by intellect alone and without revelation.

But the notes that Balbi translated for Cardinal Cusanus must have ended up nagging him because they not only contained the claim found in

11. Denis the Carthusian (1402–71) also translated the *scholion*, which Jacques Lefèvre d'Etaples (ca. 1455–1536) printed with the mistaken attribution to Ambrogio Traversari (1386–1439). See Monfasani, "Pseudo-Dionysius the Areopagite in Mid-Quattrocento Rome," 218–19; and Robichaud, "Valla and Erasmus on the Dionysian Question." Balbi's translation is in MS. Kues-Bernkastel, St.-Nikolaus-Hospital, Cus. 44. On Balbi, see Saffrey, "Pietro Balbi et la première traduction latine de la *Théologie Platonicienne* de Proclus"; Pratesi, "Balbi, Pietro"; Monfasani, "Quality Control in Renaissance Translations."

12. "Petrus Balbus Pisanus: Cum enim Proculum illum Platonicum in libro de Platonis divini theologia de Graeco verterem hiis diebus in Latinum, ea ipsa quasi eodem quoque expressionis tenore ac modo repperi, quam ob rem de Platonica etiam te audire theologia aliquid cupio. Nicolaus: Proculum tuum, Petre, Dionysio Areopagita tempore posteriorem fuisse certum est. An autem Dionysii scripta viderit, est incertum" (Cusanus, *De non aliud*, 1546–48).

the *scholion* that the Athenian Platonists stole Dionysius's writings and hid them for centuries, using them, as Proclus supposedly did, to compete with Christianity, but they also included the troubling assertion taken from John of Scythopolis's comments (later attributed to Maximus the Confessor) in the preface to his commentary on the *Corpus Dionysiacum*: "However, since some say that this treatise is not Dionysius' but of some later author, it is necessary also [for them] to admit that he [Dionysius] asserted some absurd and useless things, having counterfeited his works in this way as if he had been together with the Apostles and had sent letters to them who were not his contemporaries and to whom he could not send letters."[13] Therefore, for any reader who happened to be convinced that the terminological and conceptual similarities between Proclean and Dionysian theologies were too close to be accidental, Balbi's notes on the *Corpus Dionysiacum* would have in effect offered two options to solve the dilemma: (1) either Proclus and the Platonists stole and plagiarized from the Apostolic Dionysius the Areopagite, or (2) Dionysius the Areopagite is a pseudonym for a later author influenced by Proclean philosophy.

Balbi's translation of the *scholia* to the *Corpus Dionysiacum* and Proclus's *Platonic Theology* surely had an impact on Cusanus, since the following year he revised the position he expressed in the *De non aliud* on the Dionysian Question in his *De venatione sapientiae*. Because he now understood that Proclus and Dionysius were just too close for comfort on certain points that differ from Plato to claim that they both learned them from Plato—for example, Dionysius's negative theology was similar to Proclus's aphaeretic method—he argues that Proclus must have followed Dionysius: "Dionysius, who imitates Plato, made a similar hunt in the field of unity, and claims that negations, which are not privations but excellent affirmations filled with meaning, are truer than affirmations. But Proclus, who mentions Origen, came after Dionysius. Following Dionysius, he negates about the First, which is completely ineffable, the names One and Good, although Plato called the First with these names."[14] In short, rather than

13. "At cum quidam hunc tractatum sancti esse Dionisii negent sed cuiusdam posteriorum, necesse est [et] fateri hunc absurda quedam et supervacanea posuisse: sua eiusmodi mentitus ac si una cum apostolis fuisset misissetque epistolas illis qui neque contemporanei sibi fuerint neque mittere epistolas quiret." Translated and edited by Monfasani, "Pseudo-Dionysius the Areopagite in Mid-Quattrocento Rome," 218–19, MS. Kues-Bernkastel, St.-Nikolaus-Hospita, Cus. 44., f. 1v. For the scholarship on the *scholia* to the *Corpus Dionysiacum*, see note 7 above.

14. "Proclus vero, qui Origen allegat, post Dionysium venit. Dionysium sequendo, unum et bonum—licet ita Plato primum nominaverit—de primo negat, quod penitus est ineffabile" (Cusanus, *De non aliud*, 1674).

questioning the identity of the author of the *Corpus Dionysiacum*, Cusanus chooses the first solution to the dilemma. But there is still further evidence buried in the marginal notes of Cusanus's manuscript of Athanasius that Cusanus began to consider the second option, perhaps under the influence of Valla, who pursues a similar line of reasoning, that Dionysius might have been a pseudonym for a later author since there is a prompt in these notes to check whether Athanasius refers to Dionysius because there seems to be no mention of him in Ambrose, Augustine, and Jerome. Only Gregory and John of Damascus speak of him.[15]

In addition to Valla, Gaza, and Balbi, we now have a clear picture of how two of Bessarion's other contemporaries, George of Trebizond and Cardinal Cusanus, wrestled with the Dionysius Question. In George's historical reconstruction of Ps.-Dionysius's relationship to Proclus, the author of the *Corpus Dionysiacum* is still Paul of Tarsus's first convert and the font of Christian theology, while Proclus is nothing more than a plagiarist, stealing concepts and terminology from Christian theology to erect a nefarious Platonic pagan theology to rival Christianity. George's story of a Platonic heist of the bank vaults of Apostolic Christian theology inverts the common trope in medieval Latin Christendom from Augustine's *De doctrina christiana* that Christian theologians can take from pagan philosophers and convert their thinking to Christianity in the manner of the Israelites stealing from the Egyptians. In comparison, Cusanus finally agrees with George's chronology and belief that Proclus depended on Dionysius, but disagrees with his conclusion. Where George sees a case of Proclus's theft, Cusanus finds grounds for agreement and a reason to continue cautiously employing Proclean arguments and concepts in his theology.

Turning to Cardinal Bessarion, he invokes the authority of Dionysius's *De coelesti hierarchia* and *De ecclesiastica hierarchia* to compose his *De sacramento eucharistiae*, but in his *In Calumniatorem platonis* (published in 1469 but completed probably by 1459) he deploys specific philological strategies to show that the *De divinis nominibus* is strongly influenced by Plato's *Parmenides* and especially by Plato's *Symposium* and philosophy of love.[16]

---

15. Baur, *Cusanus Texte*, 19; Rice, *Prefatory Epistles of Jacques Lefèvre d'Etaples*, 68n10; Vansteenbergh, *Le cardinal Nicolas de Cues*, 26n5; Massaut, *Critique et Tradition à la Veille de la Réforme en France*, 180; Robichaud, "Valla and Erasmus on the Dionysian Question."

16. There is much scholarship on Bessarion. The classic is still Mohler, *Kardinal Bessarion als Theologe, Humanist und Staatsmann*, but see also Monfasani, *Byzantine Scholars in Renaissance Italy*; idem, *Bessarion Scholasticus*; Bianca, *Da Bisanzio a Roma*; Coluccia, *Basilio Bessarione*; Märtl et al., *"Inter graecos latinissimus, inter latinos graecissimus"*; and Soldato, *Basilio Bessarione, Contro il calunniatore di Platone*.

Nowhere does Bessarion explicitly challenge the traditional chronology and authorship of the *Corpus Dionysiacum*, but evidence from his *In Calumniatorem Platonis* survives that shows that he engaged in these debates.

George of Trebizond, as I mentioned, elaborated on the accusation that he had read in the manuscript *scholia* to the *Corpus Dionysiacum* that the Platonists stole Dionysius's terminology and concepts to try to convince Christians to leave their faith. Bessarion uses Dionysius's *De divinis nominibus* in the *In Calumniatorem platonis* specifically to argue against this claim. If there are any similarities between Ps.-Dionysius and Neoplatonists, he reasons, it is not because they stole from the *Corpus Dionysiacum*, perhaps even hiding his writings for centuries, but because Dionysius like the Neoplatonists draw on the same source: the Platonic *Corpus*. Bessarion's position therefore rests on a kind of source criticism. To make his case, Bessarion quotes large passages from the *Corpus Dionysiacum* and Plato. This not only has the net effect of making the Neoplatonists useful for Christian theology, but also directly refutes George's goal of making Plato a heretic and anti-Christ by raising Plato to the status of being the divine teacher of Dionysius.

To understand George and Bessarion's disagreement over the *Corpus Dionysiacum*, it is important to keep in mind that their arguments emerged from broader Plato-Aristotle controversies and that they wrote their respective books for Latin audiences. They knew that they had a privileged knowledge of Plato's writings, and they vied with each other to control his message. A particular point of contention between the two Byzantine transplants was the correct interpretation of Platonic *eros*. George drew from his extensive knowledge of Plato's *Laws*, the *Parmenides*, both of which he had translated into Latin, and especially the *Phaedrus* and the *Symposium* (in addition to Aristotle and the Church Fathers) to argue that Plato was at best a confusing writer and a poor philosopher, but at worst—and according to George the worst interpretation of Plato is the correct interpretation of Plato—Plato's philosophy taught nothing but sexual hedonism and heresy. He presents Latin readers with a truly strange revisionist history of philosophy in which Platonic philosophy is a virus of Platonic love that originates in Plato and passes, like a sexually transmitted disease, first to the Epicureans, who infect the Roman Empire with decadent hedonism, then to the late ancient Neoplatonists, who in turn contaminate Christians with hedonistic and pagan Platonic *eros*. It is in this Platonic intoxication, he believes, that late Christian heresies propagate and Mohammad, a new hedonistic Plato, emerges. Finally, in his own day, Bessarion's own teacher, the philosopher Gemistus Pletho, another Mohammad and another Plato, as George characterizes him, drew from Plato's philosophy of love to spread his pagan "creed of *voluptas*."[17] In short, like a fifteenth-century Anders Nygren, George concludes that Platonic *eros* has nothing to do with Christian *agape*.

Bessarion points out absurdities in George's understanding of Plato's philosophy of love. Instead of being a breeding ground for heresies and hedonism, Bessarion contends that Platonic *eros* agrees with Christian love. It is to make this very point that Bessarion quotes most extensively from the *Corpus Dionysiacum*. In particular, Book 4 of the *De divinis nominibus* provides him with ammunition because it contains Dionysius's extensive examination of the first principle as good, beauty, and *eros* (along with related considerations on light and ecstasy). George had argued in his *Comparatio* that Diotima's speech in the *Symposium* is nothing more than the ravings of an old woman, but Bessarion counters that none other than Dionysius the Areopagite quotes a long section of the *Symposium* in the fourth book of the *De divinis nominibus* precisely to introduce his examination of love (*eros*) as one of God's names: "But my adversary attributes the knowledge of *eros* that in this dialogue [the *Symposium*] Socrates pretends to have learned from the wise woman Diotima, neither to Socrates, nor to Plato, but to Diotima, and proceeds to call an old wives' tale what the holy Dionysius the Areopagite explained (theologized, θεολογεῖ) about divine love by employing Plato's very own words (τοῖς αὐτοῖς τῷ Πλάτωνι χρησάμενος ῥήμασιν; *verbis iisdem Platonis scribens*)."[18] Bessarion is correct; in *De divinis nominibus* (*DN*, 4.7), Ps.-Dionysius does not just simply express the same opinion as Plato on *eros*; he actually quotes a fairly long passage from Diotima's speech in the *Symposium* (*Symp.* 211). This is a fine example of Bessarion's philology at work. Even though Ps.-Dionysius never explicitly states that he is quoting from Plato's *Symposium* in this passage, Bessa-

---

17. Quoted in Monfasani, *George of Trebizond*, 158–59.

18. Ὁ κατήγορος μέντοι, ἃ Σωκράτης ἐν διαλόγῳ πλάττει παρὰ γυναικὸς Διοτίμης σοφῆς τὰ ἐρωτικὰ παρειληφέναι, οὐ Σωκράτει οὐδὲ Πλάτωνι, ἀλλὰ γυναικὶ τῇ Διοτίμῃ ἀπονέμει καὶ γραϊδίων καλεῖ μύθους, ἅπερ ὁ ἱερὸς Διονύσιος ὁ Ἀρεοπαγίτης τοῖς αὐτοῖς τῷ Πλάτωνι χρησάμενος ῥήμασιν περὶ τοῦ θείου θεολογεῖ ἔρωτος. "At hic adversarius, quae Socrates in dialogo fingit se accepisse ex muliere Diotima, non Socrati, non Platoni, sed Diotimae attribuit atque aniles fabulas vocat, quae divus Dionusius Areopagita verbis iisdem Platonis scribens de divino amore exposuit" (Bessar. *Calumn. Plat.* 2.246 Mohler). I quote both the Greek and Latin versions of the *In calumniatorem platonis* because the texts sometimes contain differences, but I have translated from the Latin version unless otherwise indicated. I have also translated Bessarion's quotations of Greek authors (e.g., Plato and Ps.-Dionysius) directly from the Greek.

rion rightly demonstrates that he is citing the *Symposium* verbatim. And when nineteenth-century German scholars began to examine the Platonic sources behind the *Corpus Dionysiacum*, they acknowledged their fifteenth-century predecessor's originality in identifying this passage as a quotation from the *Symposium*.[19]

Bessarion's source criticism helps him in two ways. First, it proves that Plato's philosophy of *eros* agrees with Christian theology because it serves as a foundation for the *Corpus Dionysiacum*'s teachings on love, which according to Bessarion is an Apostolic document and the oldest surviving body of Christian theological texts. Instead of understanding Platonic *eros* a form of hedonistic lust, Bessarion argues that if Plato's words are interpreted correctly, his philosophy of *eros* agrees with the biblical notions of *agape* and *philanthropia*. To corroborate his argument, Bessarion, like Ps.-Dionysius and Origen before him, quotes the Ignatian phrase "my eros is crucified" as well as the scriptural passages of Proverbs 4:6–8 and Wisdom 8:2. Second, it replies to George that the reason why Proclus's and Dionysius's terminology resemble one another is not because the Neoplatonists stole from Dionysius but because they both drew on Plato's Corpus.

Bessarion therefore offers Ps.-Dionysius to his Latin readers as a model for how to read Plato correctly. Taking Plato's account of love as a literal form of madness, George describes this sickness as the worst kind of venereal disease; Bessarion counters by quoting long passages from both Ps.-Dionysius and Plato to explain that the correct interpretation of Plato's *furor amoris* is as desire to connect and unite with God, that is, as *henosis*. Platonic love, according to Ps.-Dionysius and Bessarion, is equivalent to the Neoplatonic principle of conversion (ἐπιστροφή) toward unification—that is, the principle of return in the triad μονή-πρόοδος-ἐπιστροφή—which is especially prevalent in the *Corpus Dionysiacum* in its hierarchal formulation of love as purgative, illuminating, and perfecting ἐπιστροφή, and is found earlier in Proclus's *Commentary on the First Alcibiades*. Proclus explains in this text that all things fall under the providence of a savior, *eros*, connecting all things in the series beneath it to this higher divine principle. To explain this, Bessarion quotes from Ps.-Dionysius's famous fourfold schema of *eros*: "Dionysius, following his master [Hierotheus who explains that love is a capacity to connect and unite] says: 'All things want, desire, and love the beautiful and the good, and either through it or on account of it, the lower loves the higher by turning towards it, equals love equals commonly, the

19. Jahn, *Dionysiaca*, 61; Dräseke, "Zu Dionysius"; Koch, *Pseudo-Dionysius Areopagita*, 63.

higher love the lower providentially, and each conserves themselves.'"[20] Bessarion continues to compare quotations from Dionysius and Plato's *Phaedrus* to show once more that not only does Dionysius agree with Plato, but he also actually cites Plato's very words without acknowledgment:

In fact, Plato holds that madness isn't simple, he divides it into two parts so that one comes from human sickness and the other gives a divine madness to the intellect. He then differentiates this positive madness into four parts … Therefore, he expresses the goods, the uses, and the merits of each madness that he just explained, and so that no one can reject the word "love / or *eros*" as ambiguous he writes: "Therefore let us not be afraid on that point, and let no one disturb and frighten us by saying that the reasonable friend should be preferred to him who is in a frenzy. Let him show in addition that love is not sent from heaven for the advantage of lover and beloved alike, and we will grant him the prize of victory." [Pl. *Phdr.*, 245b–c Burnet]

From this quotation we should note how Dionysius, in that passage that I cited earlier, employs not only Plato's meaning but also his very words when he speaks about love.

Bessarion thereafter quotes more Dionysius to drive the point home:
"therefore we should not fear this word *eros* at all. No nothing in fact that could disturb or frighten us is caused by it." [Dion. Ar. *DN*, 4.12 Suchla][21]

---

20. Bessarion, quoting Dion. Ar. *DN*, 4.10: Διονύσιος δὲ καὶ αὐτὸς τῷ καθηγητῇ ἑπόμενος· 'πᾶσίν ἐστι, φησί, τὸ καλὸν καὶ ἀγαθόν, ἐφετὸν καὶ ἐραστὸν καὶ ἀγαπητὸν καὶ δι' αὐτὸ καὶ αὐτοῦ ἕνεκα. καὶ τὰ ἥττω τῶν κρειττόνων ἐπιστρεπτικῶς ἐρῶσι, καὶ κοινωνικῶς τὰ ὁμόστοιχα τῶν ὁμοταγῶν, καὶ τὰ κρείττονα τῶν ἡττόνων προνοητικῶς, καὶ αὐτὰ ἑαυτῶν ἕκαστα συνεκτικῶς. "Hunc praeceptorem suum Dionysius secutus: 'Omnia, inquit, summum bonum, honestum et pulchrum petunt, affectant, diligunt tum propter ipsum, tum ipsius gratia. Et superiora a suis inferioribus amantur per conversionis respectu, inferiora a suis superioribus per providentiam, paria a suis paribus per communicationem, quaeque se ipsa amant per conservationem.'" Bessar. *Calumn. Plat.* 2.446 Mohler.

21. μανίαν' μὲν οὖν αὐτὸν καλεῖ, μανίαν δὲ ἔνθεον καὶ ἐνθουσιασμὸν ὅλως. εἶναι γὰρ δὴ μὴ ἁπλοῦν τι τὴν μανίαν μηδὲ κακὸν ἁπλῶς, ἀλλὰ τετραπλοῦν τε καὶ πολλῶν ἀγαθῶν καὶ μεγίστων ἡμῖν αἴτιον, θείᾳ μέντοι δόσει διδόμενον, καὶ τὴν μὲν 'μαντικήν,' τὴν δὲ 'τελεστικήν.' τὴν δὲ τὴν ποιητῶν εἶναι 'μανίαν τε καὶ κατακωχὴν' ἀπὸ θεῶν. τετάρτην δὲ τὴν τοῦ θείου καὶ σεμνοῦ ἔρωτος εἶναί φησι. καὶ καταριθμεῖ τὰ ἐξ αὐτῶν ἀνθρώποις γιγνόμενα ἀγαθά. μεθ' ἅ φησι· 'τοσαῦτα μέντοι καὶ ἔτι πλείω ἔχω μανίας γινομένης ἀπὸ θεῶν λέγειν καλὰ ἔργα,' μανίαν τε ὁμοίως καὶ τὸν ἔρωτα ὀνομάζει. φησί τε· 'ὥστε τοῦτό γε αὐτὸ μὴ φοβώμεθα, μηδέ τις ἡμᾶς λόγος θορυβείτω δεδιττόμενος, ὡς πρὸ τοῦ κεκινημένου τὸν σώφρονα δεῖ προαιρεῖσθαι φίλον.' [Plato, Phdr., 245b–c] ὅπου καὶ ἐπίστησον ὡς ὁ θεῖος Διονύσιος ἐν οἷς προείπομεν οὐ τῇ διανοίᾳ μόνον, ἀλλὰ αὐταῖς ταῖς Πλάτωνος λέξεσι περὶ τοῦ ἔρωτος χρῆται λέγων· ὥστε δὴ τὸ τοῦ ἔρωτος ὄνομα μὴ φοβηθῶμεν, μήδε τις ἡμᾶς θορυβείτω λόγος περὶ τούτου δεδιττόμενος [Dion. Ar. *DN* 4.12 Suchla]. Furorem enim haud simplicem esse Plato existimat, sed primo bifariam dividit, ut unus ab humanis morbis fiat, alter divina quadam mentis alienatione. Mox partem hanc laudabilem quadripartito distribuit. Unum divinatione contineri statuit, alterum initiationibus, tertium poësi, postremum sancto felicique amore. Tum bona et utilitatem et commoda singulorum furorum, quae modo enumeravi, commemorat et, ne quis amoris nomen velut anceps repudiet: "**Ne id, inquit, vereamur**

Bessarion is correct in one respect: the author of the *Corpus Dionysiacum* not only employs Plato's arguments but also quotes him literally, first at *De Divinis Nominibus* 4, 7 and then at 4, 12 without acknowledging his source—and indeed some modern editions still do not recognize these quotations in their notes. But in another respect, Bessarion misses the mark. The Platonic scheme that he quotes from *De divinis nominibus* 4, 10 is taken not from Plato but from Proclus's *Commentary on the First Alcibiades*:

i. A lower lover can turn toward a higher beloved, which is the perfecting union of love (ἔρως ἐπιστρεπτικός).

ii. A lover can turn toward an equal lover, which is common bond of unity in the world (ἔρως κοινωνικός).

iii. A higher lover can turn toward a lower beloved, which is providential love (ἔρως προνοητικός).

iv. Someone can love oneself, which is a unifying love of self-preservation and self-knowledge (ἔρως συνεκτικός).[22]

Πᾶσιν οὖν ἐστι τὸ καλὸν καὶ ἀγαθὸν ἐφετὸν καὶ ἐραστὸν καὶ ἀγαπητόν, καὶ δι᾽ αὐτὸ καὶ αὐτοῦ ἕνεκα καὶ τὰ ἥττω τῶν κρειττόνων **ἐπιστρεπτικῶς** ἐρῶσι καὶ **κοινωνικῶς** τὰ ὁμόστοιχα τῶν ὁμοταγῶν καὶ τὰ κρείττω τῶν ἡττόνων **προνοητικῶς** καὶ αὐτὰ ἑαυτῶν ἕκαστα **συνεκτικῶς**, καὶ πάντα τοῦ καλοῦ καὶ ἀγαθοῦ ἐφιέμενα ποιεῖ καὶ βούλεται πάντα ὅσα ποιεῖ καὶ βούλεται. [Dion. Ar. *DN*, 4.10 Suchla][23]

---

nec ratio nos ulla deterreat, quasi homo mente constans potius quam alienatus in amicum deligendus sit. Sed illud si demonstret, vincat genus hoc amoris, quod ego probo non utile a diis immortalibus datum amanti atque amato" [Plato, *Phdr.*, 245b–c]. Quo in loco animadvertendum est, quomodo Dionysius in iis, quae superius retuli, non modo sensu, sed verbis ipsis Platonis usus sit, cum de amore loqueretur. "Ergo hoc nomen amoris, inquit, minime formidare debemus. Nihil est enim, quod nos hac de causa turbare possit aut deterrere" [Dion. Ar. *DN*, 4.12 Suchla] Bessar. *Calumn. Plat.* 2.462 Mohler. N.B. To facilitate the source criticism—both Bessarion's and my own—I provide the passages of the *Corpus Dionysiacum* that are compared to Plato and the Platonists in bold.

22. The *Corpus Dionysiacum*'s dependence on Platonic and Proclean philosophies of love is now recognized, though not without some controversy, in part owing to Anders Nygren's famous and provocative thesis that Christian *agape* owes nothing to Platonic *eros*: Jahn, *Dionysiaca*; Dräseke, "Zu Dionysius"; Koch, *Pseudo-Dionysius Areopagita*, esp. 63–72; Horn, "Amour et Extase d'après Denys l'Aréopagite"; Armstrong, "Platonic Eros and Christian Agape"; Rist, "Note on Eros and Agape in Pseudo-Dionysius"; de Vogel, "Amor quo caelum regitur"; idem, "Greek Cosmic Love and the Christian Love of God"; Esposito Buckley, "Ecstatic and Emanating, Providential and Unifying"; de Andia, *Henosis*; Podolak, "L'Amore divino nella tradizione platonica"; Vasilakis, "Platonic Eros, Moral Egoism, and Proclus."

23. Cf. with Proclus: Οὐχ ὅτι **προνοητικός** ἐστιν ὁ τοιοῦτος ἔρως καὶ **σωστικὸς** τῶν ἐρωμένων καὶ **τελειωτικὸς** αὐτῶν καὶ **συνεκτικός**; . . . Πᾶν γὰρ ὅτιπερ ἂν ἀγαθὸν καὶ **σωτήριον** ἐν ταῖς ψυχαῖς ᾖ τὴν αἰτίαν ἀπὸ τῶν θεῶν ὡρισμένην ἔχει· διὸ καὶ τῶν ἀρετῶν πασῶν καὶ τῶν σωματικῶν ἀγαθῶν ἐκεῖ προϋπάρχειν τὰ παραδείγματά φησιν ὁ Πλάτων, οἷον ὑγείας ἰσχύος δικαιοσύνης σωφροσύνης. Πόσῳ δὴ μᾶλλον τῆς ἐρωτικῆς ἐν θεοῖς εἶναι τὴν προτουργὸν αἰτίαν ὑποθησόμεθα /

Dionysius employs this schema elsewhere at times in a binary or tripartite form, which suggests a certain connection in his mind between ἔρως κοινωνικός and ἔρως συνεκτικός, insofar as these manifestations of love move neither vertically upward or downward but turn on a horizontal plane, as it were, either outward or inward.

Ἱεροθέου τοῦ ἁγιωτάτου ἐκ τῶν ἐρωτικῶν ὕμνων. Τὸ ἔρωτα, εἴτα θεῖον εἴτε ἀγγελικὸν εἴτε νοερὸν εἴτε ψυχικὸν εἴτε φυσίκον εἴποιμεν, ἑνωτικήν τινα καὶ συγκρατικὴν ἐννοήσωμεν δύναμιν τὰ μὲν ὑπέρτερα κινοῦσαν ἐπὶ **πρόνοιαν** τῶν καταδεεστέρων, τὰ δὲ ὁμόστοιχα πάλιν εἰς **κοινωνικὴν** ἀλληλουχίαν καὶ ἐπ᾽ ἐσχάτων τὰ ὑφειμένα πρὸς τὴν τῶν κρειττόνων καὶ ὑπερκειμένων **ἐπιστροφήν**.[24]

In fact, the difference between the binary schema consisting of movements (i) and (iii), the tripartite schema consisting of (i), (ii), and (iii), or the fourfold sequence should not be thought of as different systems of love but as the unfolding of a singular and unified form of love (ἑνοειδὲς) into four movements or moments of a singular and unified erotic series, as Proclus and Dionysius both emphasize.[25]

Bessarion continues with his strategy of philological source criticism, showing how Ps.-Dionysius appropriates Plato not only from the *Symposium* and the *Phaedrus*, as I have shown, but also from the *Statesman*, the *Phaedo*, the *Philebus*, the *Timaeus*, the *Republic*, the *Laws*, and the *Parmenides*. To take what is perhaps the most important example from the

---

θείᾳ δόσει διδομένης, ὡς αὐτὸς φησιν ὁ ἐν τῷ Φαιδρῳ Σωκράτης; **Καὶ θεοὶ τοίνυν θεῶν ἐρῶσιν, οἱ πρεσβύτεροι τῶν καταδεεστέρων, ἀλλὰ προνοητικῶς, καὶ οἱ καταδεέστεροι τῶν ὑπερτέρων, ἀλλ᾽ ἐπιστρεπτικῶς** (Proclus, *In Alc.* 55.13–56.5 Segonds). Καὶ δεῖ τὸν ἐρωτικὸν ἑνί τινι καλῷ τοῦ ἐρωμένου προσέχειν, ἵνα καὶ τελειότερος ᾖ καὶ προσεχῶς ὑπεριδρυμένος. Οὕτω γὰρ ἂν καὶ ὁ μὲν ἀνάγοι, ὁ δὲ ἀνάγοιτο, καὶ μετά τινος συμπαθείας ποιοῖτο τὴν **πρόνοιαν**· τὸ γὰρ παντελῶς ἀσύντακτον οὐδεμίαν ἔχει πρὸς τὸ καταδεέστερον **κοινωνίαν**· ὁ δὲ ἔρως ἐν τοῖς δυναμένοις **κοινωνεῖν** ἀλλήλοις ἔχει τὴν ὑπόστασιν, ἐπειδὴ καὶ αὐτὸς δι᾽ ὁμοιότητος ἐπιτελεῖται τῶν ὑφειμένων πρὸς τὰ κρείττονα καὶ διὰ συνδέσεως τῶν ἀτελεστέρων πρὸς τὰ τελειότερα καὶ **δι᾽ ἐπιστροφῆς** τῶν πληρουμένων πρὸς τὰ τῆς πληρώσεως αἴτια (Procl., *In Alc.*, 140.19–141.14 Segonds). Cf. Proclus *In Alc.*, 20.1–21.9 Segonds; 328.14 sq; 336,5 sq; *In Alc.*, 53.1–17; 56.2 sq; *In Cra.* 82.8 sq; *In Prm.* 4.213; 5.110; 5.118; *ET.*, 21; 97 Dodds

24. Cf. with Proclus: Ἔστι μὲν οὖν **τὰ εἴδη τῆς ἐπιστροφῆς τριττά**· πᾶν γὰρ τὸ **ἐπιστρεφόμενον ἢ πρὸς τὸ χεῖρον ἐπιστρέφει** ἑαυτοῦ διὰ τὴν ἀπόπτωσιν τῆς εἰκείας τελειότητος ἢ πρὸς τὸ κρεῖττον ἀνάγεται διὰ τῆς ἑαυτοῦ ζωῆς καὶ τῆς κατὰ φύσιν ἐνεργείας **ἢ πρὸς ἑαυτὸ ἐπιστρέφει** κατὰ τὴν σύστοιχον ἑαυτῷ γνῶσιν καὶ τὸ μέσον εἶδος τῆς κινήσεως. Ἀλλ᾽ **ἡ μὲν πρὸς τὸ χεῖρον ἐπιστροφὴ** ψυχῆς ἐστι πάθος πτερορρυησάσης καὶ γενομένης ἐν λήθῃ καὶ ἑαυτῆς ἅμα καὶ τῶν πρὸ αὐτῆς· **ἡ δὲ καὶ πρὸς ἑαυτὸ καὶ πρὸς τὸ κρεῖττον** οὐκ ἐν ψυχαῖς ἐστι μόναις ἀλλὰ καὶ ἐν αὐτοῖς τοῖς θείοις, ὥσπερ ἡμᾶς ὁ Παρμενίδης ἀναδιδάσκει **διττὰ τὰ τῆς ἐπιστροφῆς εἴδη** τιθέμενος καὶ δεικνύς, ὅπως **μὲν εἰς ἑαυτὸ τὸ θεῖον ἐπέστραπται** καὶ ἐν ἑαυτῷ ἐστίν, ὅπως δὲ **εἰς τὸ πρὸ αὐτοῦ**, καθ᾽ ὃ δὴ καὶ ἐν ἄλλῳ περιέχεται καὶ συνήνωται πρὸς τὴν κρείττονα φύσιν (Procl., *In Alc.* 20.1–16 Segonds). Cf. Procl., *In Alc.* 30.7–8 sq Segonds; 63.12 sq.; 64.11 sq.; *In Prm.*, 4.213; 5.110.

25. See my discussion of Dion. Ar. *DN*, 4.12 Suchla and Procl., *In Alc.*, 31.9–14 Segonds below.

list, scholars today know that the theological arguments in the *De divinis nominibus* depend largely on the Neoplatonic interpretation of the first two hypotheses of Plato's *Parmenides*, the One and the One-Being.[26] In the fifteenth century, philosophers, theologians, and humanist scholars — Bessarion, Cusanus, Balbi, George of Trebizond, Giovanni Pico della Mirandola, and Marsilio Ficino, among others—were rediscovering the Neoplatonic understanding of the *Parmenides* as a work of theology. It is remarkable to see how Bessarion addresses the relationship between the *Corpus Dionysiacum* and the *Parmenides*. In an early chapter devoted to explaining Plato's theology from the *Parmenides*, Bessarion demonstrates to his readers how it is probably this dialogue, above all others, that is at the heart of Dionysius's theology. After Bessarion quotes a long passage from the *Parmenides* (*Prm.* 137c–142a) on the nature of the One and Being, he quotes again from the *De divinis nominibus* in order to write an extensive defense of Dionysius the Areopagite's dependence on Plato:

But Plato's theology pleases the holiest doctors of our faith so much that every time they write something about God they wish to use not only his opinions but also his words. For the most holy Dionysius the Areopagite, who was the first and greatest author of Christian theology, which had no one to write about its divine matters before him, except for the Apostle Paul and the Athenian Pontiff Hierotheus who were his teachers, wrote in his book entitled *De divinis nominibus* as follows:

> "Indeed the supersubstantial infinity lies beyond substances and the superintelligible unity lies beyond intelligences; and the One that is beyond thought is unthinkable to all thoughts; and the Good beyond words is ineffable to all words." [Dion. Ar. *DN*, 1.1 Suchla]

Again:

> "The unifying unity of all unities, the supersubstantial substance, the unintelligible intellect, the ineffable logos, the irrational and unintelligible and anonymous, is not like beings and is the cause of all being, but it itself is not being, as it is completely beyond being." [Dion. Ar. *DN*, 1.1 Suchla]

Again:

> "there is no sensation of it, nor imagination, nor opinion, nor name, nor word, nor contact, nor knowledge." [Dion. Ar. *DN*, 1.5 Suchla]

---

26. To keep the list short, see Corsini, *Il trattato 'De divinis nominibus' dello Pseudo-Dionigi*; Lilla, *Dionigi l'Areopagita e il platonismo cristiano*; Gersh, *From Iamblichus to Eriugena*; Beierwaltes, "Dionigi Areopagita—Un Proclo cristiano?," which is an expanded version of idem, "Dionysios Areopagites—Ein christlicher Proklos"; de Andia, *Henosis*; as well as Dillon and Wear, *Dionysius the Areopagite and the Neoplatonist Tradition*.

And shortly thereafter:

"So the supersubstantiality of the divine principle, seeing that it is ever super-existence of what is beyond good, cannot be recalled either as logos, or power, or intellect, or life, or being by anyone who might love truth that is beyond all truth, but as most distant from all habit, movement, life, imagination, opinion, name, word, reasoning, intelligence, being, state, foundation, union, limit, unlimittedness, and all that exists." [Dion. Ar. *DN*, 1.5 Suchla]

Where, by God, did Dionysius take these expressions unless he took them literally from Plato's words?

Once more, one notices that Bessarion is pursing the same twofold method to argue against George. First, he contends that George is wrong in arguing that Plato's *Parmenides* does not support Christian theology since it turns out that Dionysius's theology is actually grounded in Plato's *Parmenides*. Second, this in turn demonstrates that the similar vocabulary employed by Neoplatonists is not stolen from Dionysius but shared through a common older source: Plato himself. But even a cursory glance of the Greek reveals that only one sentence from all of this material from *De divinis nominibus* 1, 1 and 1, 5 quoted by Bessarion comes almost verbatim from Plato's *Parmenides*, but on closer examination it is also apparent that most of the sources for Dionysius terminology—for instance, in his piling up superlatives on superlatives—is not from Plato per se, but from the lexical and conceptual fields of the Athenian school of Neoplatonism:

οὕτω δὲ ἡ τοιαύτη αὐτοῦ θεολογία τοῖς ἡμετέροις πατράσι καὶ διδασκάλοις ἤρεσεν, ὡς μὴ αἰσχυνθῆναι ἐν τοῖς ἑαυτῶν συγγράμμασι περὶ θεοῦ ποιουμένους τὸν λόγον καὶ αὐτοῖς ῥήμασι τοῖς Πλατωνικοῖς, οὐ μόνον τῇ διανοίᾳ χρήσασθαι. Αὐτίκα ὁ μακάριος Διονύσιος ὁ Ἀρεοπαγίτης, ὁ πρώτιστός τε καὶ ἄριστος τῶν μετ' αὐτὸν ἁπάντων τῆς Χριστιανικῆς θεολογίας διδασκάλων γενομένων—πρὸ αὐτοῦ γὰρ οὐδεὶς πλὴν Παύλου τοῦ μεγάλου καὶ Ἱεροθέου Ἀθηνῶν, οἷς καὶ ἐμαθήτευσεν, ἄλλος ὑπῆρξεν—ἐν τῷ περὶ θείων ὀνομάτων·

ὑπέρκειται, φησί, τῶν οὐσιῶν ἡ ὑπερούσιος ἀπειρία καὶ τῶν νοῶν ἡ ὑπὲρ νοῦν ἑνότης, καὶ πάσαις διανοίαις ἀδιανόητόν ἐστι τὸ ὑπὲρ διάνοιαν ἓν ἄρρητόν τε λόγῳ παντὶ[27] **τὸ ὑπὲρ λόγον ἀγαθόν.** [Dion. Ar. *DN*, 1.1 Suchla]
καὶ πάλιν·
ἑνὰς ἑνοποιὸς ἁπάσης ἑνάδος καὶ ὑπερούσιος οὐσία καὶ νοῦς ἀνόητος καὶ λόγος ἄρρητος, ἀλογία καὶ ἀνοησία καὶ ἀνωνυμία, κατὰ μηδὲν τῶν ὄντων οὖσα. καὶ αἴτιον μὲν τοῦ εἶναι πᾶσιν· αὐτὸ δὲ μὴ ὄν, ὡς πάσης **οὐσίας ἐπέκεινα.**[28] [Dion. Ar. *DN*, 1.1 Suchla]

---

27. **ἄρρητος μὲν παντὶ λόγῳ** καὶ ἄφραστος, ἄγνωστος δὲ πάσῃ γνώσει καὶ ἄληπτος (Procl. *Theol. Plat.* 3.7. Saffrey Westerink).

28. καὶ τοῖς γιγνωσκομένοις τοίνυν μὴ μόνον τὸ γιγνώσκεσθαι φάναιὑπὸ τοῦ ἀγαθοῦ παρεῖναι,

καὶ αὖ·

οὔτε αἴσθησις αὐτῆς ἐστιν οὔτε φαντασία οὔτε δόξα οὔτε ὄνομα οὔτε λόγος οὔτε ἐπαφὴ οὔτε ἐπιστήμη.[29] [Dion. Ar. *DN*, 1.5 Suchla]

καὶ μετά τινα·

τὴν μὲν οὖν ὑπερουσιότητα τὴν θεαρχικήν, ὅτι ποτέ ἐστιν ἡ τῆς **ὑπεραγαθότητος ὑπερύπαρξις,**[30] οὔτε ὡς λόγον ἢ δύναμιν οὔτε ὡς νοῦν ἢ ζωὴν ἢ οὐσίαν ὑπομνῆσαι θεμιτὸν οὐδενὶ τῶν ὅσοι τῆς ὑπὲρ πᾶσαν **ἀλήθειαν ἀληθείας εἰσὶν ἐρασταί·** ἀλλ᾽ ὡς πάσης ἕξεως, κινήσεως, ζωῆς, φαντασίας, δόξης, ὀνόματος, λόγου, διανοίας, νοήσεως, οὐσίας, στάσεως, ἱδρύσεως, ἑνώσεως, πέρατος, ἀπειρίας, ἁπάντων ὅσα ἐστίν, ὑπεροχικῶς ἀφῃρημένην. [Dion. Ar. *DN*, 1.5 Suchla]

Ταῦτα, πρὸς θεοῦ, οὐκ αὐτοῖς ῥήμασιν ἐκ τῶν Πλάτωνος εἴληπται.[31]

This brings me to a final but essential point: that Bessarion conflates Plato's terminology with the Neoplatonists'. Even though the *In Calumniatorem platonis* exists in both Greek and Latin versions, since Bessarion primarily wrote it for a Latin audience, it is not altogether surprising to find him citing the authority of Thomas Aquinas on three occasions as a precedent for his philological examination of Dionysius's terminology, specifically from his commentary *Super De divinis nominibus*: "Dionysius

---

ἀλλὰ καὶ τὸ εἶναί τε **καὶ τὴν οὐσίαν ὑπ᾽ ἐκείνου** αὐτοῖς προσεῖναι, οὐκ οὐσίας ὄντος τοῦ ἀγαθοῦ, ἀλλ᾽ἔτιἐπέκεινα τῆς οὐσίας πρεσβείᾳ καὶ δυνάμει ὑπερέχοντος (Pl. *R*.., 509b Burnet). Cf. Procl. *Theol. Plat.*, 2.4. Saffrey Westerink.

29. οὐδ᾽ ἄρα ὄνομα ἔστιν αὐτῷ οὐδὲ λόγος οὐδέ τις ἐπιστήμη οὐδὲ αἴσθησις οὐδὲ δόξα (Plato *Prm*. 142a. Burnet).

30. Πᾶν τὸ θεῖον **ὕπαρξιν** μὲν ἔχει τὴν **ἀγαθότητα,** δύναμιν δὲ ἑνιαίαν καὶ γνῶσιν κρύφιον καὶ ἄληπτον πᾶσιν ὁμοῦ τοῖς δευτέροις (Proclus, *ET*., Prop. 121 Dodds); πᾶν γὰρ τὸ θεῖον κατ᾽ αὐτὴν τὴν θείαν **ὕπαρξιν** ἀγαθόν ἐστιν· (Procl., *In Alc*., 318.6–7 Segonds).

31. "Adeo autem haec Platonis theologia sanctissimis fidei nostrae doctoribus grata fuit, ut quotiescumque de deo aliquid scripserunt, non modo sententiis eius, sed etiam verbis uti voluerint. Nam vir sanctissimus Dionysius Areopagita, qui primus et summus Christianae theologiae auctor fuit neminemque ante se habuit divinarum rerum scriptorem praeter apostolum Paulum et Hierotheum Athenarum pontificem, quibus ipse praeceptoribus usus est, in libro, quem de divinis nominibus edidit, ita scripsit: 'Manet quidem supra omnes substantias supersubstantialis infinitudo et supra mentes supermentalis unitas, et omnibus intellegentiis inintelligibilie est, quod omnem intellegentiam superat unum et ineffabile, quod omnem dicendi rationem excedit, bonum.' Et rursus: 'Unitas unifica omnis unitatis supersubstantialis substantia, mens inintelligibilis, ratio ineffabilis, irrationabilitas, inintelligibilitas, innominabilitas est, nullius entis similitudinem gerit et causa est entium omnium, ipsum autem est non ens, utpote **quod ultra omnem substantiam est.**' [Dion. Ar. *DN*, 1.1] Item: '**Non sensus eius est, non imaginatio, non opinio, non ratio, non scientia, non nomen.**' Et paulo post: 'Supersubstantiale divinum principium, quod sit **superessentia superbonitatis**, minime intellegi potest. Nec enim ut rationem aut virtutem, nec ut mentem aut vitam aut substantiam memorare fas est cuiquam eorum, **qui veritatis omnem veritatem superantis amore** tenentur; sed ut ab omni habitu, vita, magnitudine, opinione, nomine, ratione, mente, intellegentia, substantia, motu, statu, loco, unione, fine, infinitudine, omnibus denique rebus superlative abstractum perinde intellegendum est' [Dion. Ar. *DN*, 1.5]. Haec, per immortalem deum, nonne a Platone per eadem fere verba Dionysius sumpsit?" (Bessar. *Calumn. Plat.* 2.88 Mohler).

often writes in the style and in the way of speaking of the Platonists, which is out of fashion among moderns."[32] But despite the fact that Bessarion had a better knowledge of the texts of Plato and of Dionysius than Thomas Aquinas, who was ignorant of Greek and who did not actually undertake a philological examination of the *De divinis nominibus*, Aquinas rightly says that Dionysius writes not like Plato but like the Platonists. This brings us to the crux of Bessarion's answer to the Dionysian Question; namely, that for Bessarion's philological strategy to succeed, he needs to find Plato's own words in the *Corpus Dionysiacum*, where they certainly are, but at the same time in a number of sections of the *In Calumniatorem Platonis*, Bessarion argues that the author of the *Corpus Dionysiacum* is employing Plato's own words when he is clearly using later Neoplatonic terminology.

One last example from *In Calumniatorem Platonis* 4, 2 suffices to prove the point. The whole chapter is devoted to examining the nature of *eros*. Bessarion is once more in the process of explaining how Platonic *eros* is not simply hedonism but a force that converts and unifies all things with God. His strategy is the same as before: to compare Plato and Dionysius. He quotes portions of Plato from the *Symposium* and the *Phaedrus* to prove that Ps.-Dionysius had quoted from these dialogues without acknowledgment in his *De Divinis nominibus*, including the fact that his plea not to fear using the word *eros* to speak about the divine (*DN*, 4, 12) is based on Plato's *Phaedrus* (245b). Bessarion deploys a number of passages from Plato and the *De divinis nominibus* to marshal evidence that the Apostolic fathers agreed with Plato: true love converts the lover to the unifying contemplation of true and divine beauty:

And all understand Plato's *eros* in this manner, starting first of all with the holy Dionysius, disciple of the holy Hierotheos and the holy Apostle Paul, the first doctor of our religion:

"The true love [*eros*] I not only praise in a manner appropriate to God, but by these Holy Scriptures, the many cannot grasp the henadic form (ἐνοειδὲς) of the erotic divine name since each according to their capacity get lost in a partial love, appropriate to the body, and divided, which is not the true *eros*, but an image or rather a loss of the true *eros*." [Dion. Ar. *DN*, 4.12 Suchla]

That most holy man uses the same words as Plato when he speaks about *eros* in the fourth book *De divinis nominibus*, as I already stated and demonstrated. This whole chapter on love is a praise and recommendation of *eros*, and was taken not only from the sense, but also from the very words of Plato's dialogue. And if

---

32. "Plurumque utitur stilo et modo loquendi quo utebantur Platonici, qui apud modernos est inconsuetus" (Aquinas, *In libr. Dion. De div. nom.*, prooemium Pera).

that calumniator vituperates against Plato's teachings, what will he say about the most holy doctors of our religion who not only think but speak like Plato?

To be more compliant with his evidence, Bessarion might have said that the Apostolic Dionysius the Areopagite and the most holy Christian doctors think and speak like Proclus. While it is true that Dionysius's terminology for the image of love (εἴδωλον) in these passages comes from Plato's *Phaedrus* and the *Symposium*, nearly everything else seems to come directly from Proclus, and as we already saw with the fourth book of the *De divinis nominibus*, especially from Proclus's *Commentary on the First Alcibiades*:

θεοπρεπῶς γάρ,' φησὶ Διονύσιος ὁ μέγας, 'τοῦ ὄντος ἔρωτος οὐχ ὑφ' ἡμῶν μόνον, ἀλλὰ καὶ πρὸς τῶν λογίων αὐτῶν ὑμνουμένου τὰ πλήθη μὴ χωρήσαντα τὸ ἑνοειδὲς τῆς ἐρωτικῆς θεωνυμίας οἰκείως ἑαυτοῖς³³ ἐπὶ τὸν μεριστὸν καὶ σωματοπρεπῆ καὶ διῃρημένον ἐξωλίσθησαν, ὃς οὐκ ἔστιν ἀληθὴς ἔρως, ἀλλ' εἴδωλον, ἢ μᾶλλον ἔκπτωσις τοῦ ὄντως ἔρωτος.³⁴ [Dion. Ar. *DN*, 4.12 Suchla]

33. Κατὰ δὴ τὴν ἰδιότητα ταύτην ἁπάσης **τῆς ἐρωτικῆς σειρᾶς** ἐν τοῖς θεοῖς ὑφισταμένης, τὴν μὲν **ἑνοειδῆ** καὶ κρύφιον αὐτῆς ἀκρότητα νοήσωμεν ἐν αὐτοῖς τοῖς πρωτίστοις διακόσμοις τῶν θεῶν ἀρρήτως ἱδρυμένην καὶ τῷ πρωτίστῳ καὶ νοητῷ κάλλει συνηνωμένην χωριστῶς ἀφ' ὅλων τῶν ὄντων· (Procl., *In Alc.*, 31.9–14 Segonds); Πέμπτον **ἀπ' αὐτῶν τῶν ῥημάτων** λάβοις ἂν τὸ τὸν μὲν **θεῖον ἐραστὴν ἕνα λέγεσθαι καὶ πρῶτον καὶ μόνον** ἅτε οἰκεῖον ὄντα **τῷ ἑνὶ καὶ τῷ ἀγαθῷ** καὶ πρὸς τὸ ἁπλοῦν καὶ **ἑνοειδὲς παράδειγμα** τῶν καλῶν ἀνατεινόμενον, τὸν δὲ φορτικὸν πολὺ καὶ εἰκῆ συμπεφορημένον· τὸ γὰρ ἄλλους μὲν προσειπεῖν τοὺς τῶν **εἰδώλων ἐραστάς, πρῶτον δὲ καὶ μόνον** τὸν ἔνθεον φίλον, ἐκείνων μὲν τὴν ἀόριστον καὶ μεριστὴν καὶ πάντῃ διεσκεδασμένην ἀπελέγχει ζωήν, τούτου δὲ **τὴν θεοπρεπῆ** καὶ πόρρω τοῦ ἐνύλου πλήθους οὖσαν καὶ πάντων τῶν γενεσιουργῶν παθῶν ἐξῃρημένην ἀρετὴν ἀποσεμνύνει (Procl., *In Alc.*, 36.12–16 Segonds); Ἔτι τοίνυν ἑξῆς ἀναζητήσωμεν τὴν αἰτίαν δι' ἣν ὁ μὲν ἀκόλαστος οὐκ ἂν ἀξιώσειεν ἑαυτόν **ποτε τῆς τοῦ σώφρονος ἐπωνυμίας**, οὐδέ γε ὁ ἄδικος οὐδὲ ὁ δειλὸς ὁ μὲν τῆς τοῦ ἀνδρείου προσηγορίας, ὁ δὲ τῆς τοῦ δικαίου· οἱ δὲ **φορτικοὶ περὶ τοὺς ἔρωτας καὶ διαπεπτωκότες τῆς τοῦ ἐπιτηδεύματος ὀρθότητος ἐρασταὶ καλεῖσθαι βούλονται καὶ κοινωνεῖν τῆς αὐτῆς τοῖς ἐν θέποις προσρήσεως οἱ μὴ τῆς αὐτῆς προαιρέσεως κεκοινωνηκότες**, ἀλλὰ καὶ ἐναντίως διακείμενοι πρὸς αὐτούς. **Οἱ μέν γε πρὸς τὸ θεῖον καὶ τὸ φανὸν καὶ τὸ ἑνοειδὲς ἀνατείνουσι τοὺς ἐρωμένους,** οἱ δὲ πρὸς τὸ ἄθεον καὶ σκοτεινὸν καὶ τὸ σκεδαστὸν κατασπῶσιν αὐτῶν τὰς ψυχάς ... κατὰ τοῦτο τοίνων καὶ τῆς αὐτῆς ἐπωνυμίας μεταλαγχάνει· πανταχοῦ γὰρ **τὰ εἴδωλα κοινωνεῖν τῆς προσηγορίας τοῖς ἑαυτῶν ἐφίεται παραδείγμασι** (Procl., *In. Alc.*, 47.16–48.6 Segonds); Ἔτι δὴ οὖν τὸ τρίτον λέγομεν ὅτι τὰ θειότερα τῶν πραγμάτων διὰ περιουσίαν δυνάμεως καὶ τὰς ἀποπτώσεις ἑαυτῶν κατακοσμεῖ καὶ δίδωσι καὶ ταύταις **εἰδωλικήν** τινα τῆς ἑαυτῶν ἰδιότητος ἔμφασιν. Ἡ μὲν οὖν σωφροσύνη τοῦτο δρᾶν εἰς τὴν ἀκολασίαν οὐ δύναται, **ἡ δὲ ἔνοθεος ἐρωτικὴ θειοτέρα** τῆς σωφροσύνης οὖσα δίδωσί τι καὶ τῷ ἑαυτῆς **εἰδώλῳ** καὶ ἀμυδρὸν ἴχνος εἰς αὐτὸ καταπέμπει, διὸ καὶ **εἴδωλον** λέγεται. Κατὰ τοῦτο τοίνυν καὶ τῆς αὐτῆς ἐπωνυμίας μεταλαγχάνει· πανταχοῦ γὰρ **τὰ εἴδωλα** κοινωνεῖν τῆς προσηγορίας τοῖς ἑαυτῶν ἐφίεται παραδείγμασι (Procl. *In Alc.*, 49.12–13 Segonds); ἐνεργήσας οὖν εὐεργετικῶς καὶ **θεοπρεπῶς** ἐν τῇ ἐνεργείᾳ τὸ τέλος ἔχει, καὶ εἰ μὴ τὸ ἐνδεχόμενον αὐτῷ κατὰ τὴν ἐκτὸς ἐνέργειαν τετελείωται. / Ταῦτά μοι δοκεῖ καὶ τῷ Πλάτωνι σύμφωνα καὶ τοῖς πράγμασιν ὑπὸ τῶν ἐξηγητῶν εἰρῆσθαι πρὸς τὴν τῆς ἀπορίας διάλυσιν (Procl., *In Alc.*, 91.20–25 Segonds).

34. καὶ ὅταν μὲν ἐκεῖνος παρῇ, λήγει κατὰ ταὐτὰ ἐκείνῳ τῆς ὀδύνης, ὅταν δὲ ἀπῇ, κατὰ ταὐτὰ αὖ ποθεῖ καὶ ποθεῖται, **εἴδωλον ἔρωτος** ἀντέρωτα ἔχων· καλεῖ δὲ αὐτὸν καὶ οἴεται οὐκ ἔρωτα ἀλλὰ φιλίαν εἶναι (Plato, *Phdr.*, 255c–d Burnet); ἢ οὐκ ἐνθυμῇ, ἔφη, ὅτι ἐνταῦθα αὐτῷ μοναχοῦ

ὃν δηλονότι ὁ κατήγορος ὡς καὶ αὐτὸς εἷς τῶν τοῦ πλήθους ὢν καὶ οὐδαμοῦ τοῦ ἑνιαίου, τοῦ θείου καὶ ἑνὸς ἔρωτος ἐκείνου χωρητικὸς τοῖς ἀνδράσι προφέρει ὡς δὴ κατ᾽ αὐτὸν καὶ ὁμοίοις αὐτῷ οὖσιν. τοῦτο δὲ πάμπολυ διαφέρει. οὕτω γὰρ θεῖοι καὶ σεβάσμιοί εἰσι δὴ καὶ δοκοῦσι πᾶσι σοφοῖς οἱ περὶ ἔρωτος Σωκράτους καὶ Πλάτωνος λόγοι, ὡς καὶ τὸν θεῖον καὶ ἱερὸν Διονύσιον, τὸν Ἱεροθέου τοῦ μεγάλου μαθητήν, τοῦ Παύλου τοῦ μετὰ Πέτρου κορυφαίου τῶν ἀποστόλων φοιτητήν, τὸν τῆς θεολογίας ἡμῖν πρῶτον γενόμενον καθηγητήν, μὴ ἐπαισχυνθῆναι αὐταῖς λέξεσιν, αὐτοῖς ῥήμασιν, ὡς ἐνταῦθα ἡμεῖς ἐξεθήκαμεν, ἐν τῷ τετάρτῳ περὶ Θείων Ὀνομάτων, ἢ καὶ πρότερον εἴρηται, κεφαλαίῳ περὶ τούτου μεγαληγορῆσαι. ἀναγνώτω πᾶν ἐκεῖνο μακρότατον ὂν τὸ κεφάλειον ὁ βουλόμενος, καὶ εὑρήσει πολλὰ μὲν ἔνθεα καὶ θεῖα νοήματα περὶ ἔρωτος ἐκεῖ ἐγκείμενα, πολλὰ δὲ εἰς ὕμνον αὐτοῦ εἰρημένα. πάντα δὲ ἐκ τῶν τοῦ Πλάτωνος οὐ διανοίᾳ μόνον, ἀλλὰ καὶ λέξεσι ταῖς αὐταῖς εἰλημμένα. εἰ δ᾽ ὁ κατήγορος οὗτος καὶ τὰ ῥήματα καὶ τὴν διάνοιαν Πλάτωνος διασύρει, τί περὶ τῶν ἱερῶν τῆς ἐκκλησίας διδασκάλων ἐρεῖ ταῦτα τῷ Πλάτωνι καὶ διανοησαμένων καὶ φθεγξαμένων;

Ita cum ceteri omnes, tum imprimis divus Dionysius discipulus divi Hierothei divique Pauli apostoli, doctor nostrae religionis primus, accipiunt Platonis amorem.

"Et veri, inquit Dionysius, **amoris, qui non solum a nobis, sed etiam a sacris litteris laudatur, uniformem rationem multitudo capere sibique accommodare non potuit, sed ad dividuum, corporeum, multiplicem et dispartitum amorem dilapsa est, qui non verus est amor, sed simulacrum, vel potius lapsus veri amoris."** [Dion. Ar. *DN*, 4.12 Suchla]

Iisdem etiam verbis sanctissimus vir, quibus Plato usus est, cum de amore quarto de Divinis Nominibus libro loqueretur, ut dicutum iam atque ostensum est. Totum illud de amore caput laus et commendatio amoris est ex Platonis sermone deducta non modo sensu, sed etiam vocabulis iisdem. Quodsi obiurgator iste sententiam Platonis vituperat, quid de sanctissimis nostrae religionis doctoribus dicet, qui eadem cum Platone et sentiunt et loquuntur?[35]

The precise terminology to explain the problem that both Bessarion and Dionysius confront in these pages—namely, why different types of love share the same name—comes from Proclus's *Commentary on the First Alcibiades*, as does the solution to the problem, that true *eros* is only one—namely, the one love that unifies all grades of love that participate in its chain or series (τάξεις, σειραί) headed by a daemon that is also a God, exemplified, for Proclus, by Socrates's daemonic God, which in Dionysius's account finds an equivalent in Christ *qua* leader of the angelic hierarchy.

γενήσεται, ὁρῶντι ᾧ ὁρατὸν τὸ καλόν, τίκτειν οὐκ **εἴδωλα** ἀρετῆς, ἄτε οὐκ εἰδώλου ἐφαπτομένῳ, ἀλλ᾽ ἀληθῆ, ἄτε τοῦ ἀληθοῦς ἐφπτομένῳ· (Pl. *Symp.* 212a Burnet).

35. Bessar. *Calumn. Plat.* 488 Mohler. I quote the Latin and Greek texts since they do not exactly match.

Like Dionysius and Bessarion, Proclus's love, moreover, is a unified love expressed appropriately for the One God (θεοπρεπής) in a unified divine erotic name, *eros* (τὸ ἑνοειδὲς τῆς ἐρωτικῆς θεωνυμίας). Again, like Proclus, Dionysius and Bessarion claim that this cannot be grasped by the many who have not yet attained the capacity to do so, because they are ensnared by loves that are of a lower rank, that is, partial loves that are divided and divide, loves that are appropriately called bodily instead of divine (σωματοπρεπής instead of θεοπρεπής). These arguments and terms are as Proclean as the day is long.

Bessarion would have recognized this in Proclus since we know that he read Proclus's extended explanation of love in his manuscript copy of Proclus's *Commentary on the First Alcibiades*. The manuscript contains *scholia* but is not heavily annotated. There are, however, two additional marginal markings next to passages about Proclus's philosophy of love. The first note flags a passage in Proclus's commentary where Proclus quotes from Plato to discuss how the Gods love humans providentially and inspire them to convert toward the divine:

But as it is said, all are awakened, rekindled, and warmed up again around the emanation of beauty [cf. Plato *Phdr.*, 251b]. And indeed, human souls partake of this inspiration, and because of their intimacy with God they are set in motion around the beautiful and descend into the place of generation to do good works for more imperfect souls, and to exercise their providence over souls in need of salvation. For the Gods and the attendants of the Gods, holding strong in their habit [cf. Plato *Ti.*, 42e], do good works for and convert all inferiors towards themselves. And human souls descend and lay hold of generation to make an image of the boniform providence of the Gods.[36]

All of this is relevant because it reveals how Proclus conceives of love's power as conversion (ἔρως ἐπιστρεπτικός) and providential love (ἔρως προνοητικός), as Ps.-Dionysius will also argue afterward. The second marginal marking signals a key passage where Proclus assigns the place of the God *Eros* in the divine hierarchy:

36. πάντα δὲ ὡς εἰπεῖν ἐγείρεται καὶ ἀναζωπυρεῖται καὶ ἀναθάλπεται περὶ τὴν ἀπορροὴν τοῦ κάλλους· καὶ δὴ καὶ ἀνθρώπων ψυχαὶ μεταλαγχάνουσι τῆς τοιαύτης ἐπιπνοίας καὶ διὰ τὴν πρὸς τὸν θεὸν οἰκειότητα κινοῦνται περὶ τὸ καλὸν καὶ κατίασιν εἰς τὸν τῆς γενέσεως τόπον ἐπ᾽ εὐεργεσίᾳ μὲν τῶν ἀτελεστέρων ψυχῶν, προνοίᾳ δὲ τῶν σωτηρίας δεομένων. Θεοὶ μὲν γὰρ καὶ οἱ τῶν θεῶν ὀπαδοὶ μένοντες ἐν τοῖς ἑαυτῶν ἔθεσιν εὐεργετοῦσι τὰ δεύτερα πάντα καὶ πρὸς ἑαυτοὺς ἐπιστρέφουσι, ψυχαὶ δὲ ἀνθρώπων κατιοῦσαι καὶ γενέσεως ἐφαπτόμεναι τὴν ἀγαθοειδῆ πρόνοιαν ἀποτυποῦνται τῶν θεῶν (Procl., *In Alc.* 32.9–19 Segonds). For the first marginal bracket drawing attention to this passage in Bessarion's manuscript of Proclus's *In Alc.*, see MS. Venice, Biblioteca Marciana, Gr. Z. 190 (779), f. 275r.

Since there are three hypostases among the intelligible and hidden Gods and the first is characterized as Good (apprehending the Good itself, which is where one finds the paternal monad, as the Oracle says [cf. *Or. Chald.* 11]), then as Wisdom, which is where one finds the intelligence, and then the Beautiful, which is where one finds the most beautiful thoughts [cf. Plato, *Ti.*, 30d], as Timaeus reports. There came to be, moreover, three monads according to these three intelligible causes that exist in a causal mode and in henadic form among the intelligibles, and they first come to light in the order of the silent Gods: faith, truth, and *eros*. Faith settles all things and fixes them in the Good; truth brings to light the knowledge that exists in all things; and *eros* converts all things and collects them into the nature of the Good.[37]

The annotated passage is in fact much longer and continues into Proclus's discussion of *eros* as an intermediary power capable of converting, connecting, and unifying all separate beings, which is again of utmost relevance to the *De divinis nominibus*.

In sum, Bessarion quotes the *Corpus Dionysiacum* and claims that its author employs Plato's words. There are certainly instances where this might be the case, but there are other times too when Ps.-Dionysius the Areopagite clearly uses Neoplatonic terminology. Bessarion also seems to have been reading Neoplatonic sources to identify Dionysius's Neoplatonic terminology as Plato's. The implications of this evidence are actually quite significant. For, to go back to the dilemma outlined above, if Bessarion accepts the orthodox chronology that Dionysius is the disciple of Paul of Tarsus, it would mean that he ought to accept the thesis that the Neoplatonists appropriated (Cusanus's thesis) or stole (George's thesis) Dionysius's terminology. If he does not accept the orthodox chronology that Dionysius is the convert from the Areopagite, he can accommodate the similarities without accepting George's thesis that the Neoplatonists stole from Dionysius, but at the expense of the *Corpus Dionysiacum*'s Apostolicity. He does neither. Instead, he tries to find a middle ground, contending that Dionysius employs Plato's words when he clearly means later Neoplatonic terminology. I do not wish to make an argument *ex silentio* on Cardinal

---

37. τριττῶν τοίνυν ἐν τοῖς νοητοῖς καὶ κρυφίοις θεοῖς ὑποστάσεων οὐσῶν καὶ τῆς μὲν πρώτης τῷ ἀγαθῷ χαρακτηριζομένης (τἀγαθὸν αὐτὸ νοοῦσα, ὅπου πατρικὴ μονάς ἐστι, τὸ λόγιόν φησι), τῆς δὲ κατὰ τὸ σοφόν, ὅπου καὶ ἡ πρώτη νόησις, τῆς δὲ κατὰ τὸ καλόν, ὅπου καὶ τὸ τῶν νοητῶν ἐστὶ κάλλιστον, ὡς ὁ τοῦ Τιμαίου λόγος, καὶ τρεῖς κατὰ ταύτας τὰς νοητὰς αἰτίας ὑφίστανται μονάδες, κατ᾽ αἰτίαν μὲν ἐν τοῖς νοητοῖς οὖσαι καὶ ἑνοειδῶς, ἐκφαινόμεναι δὲ πρώτως ἐν τῇ ἀφθέγκτῳ τάξει τῶν θεῶν, πίστις καὶ ἀλήθεια καὶ ἔρως· ἡ μὲν ἐδράζουσα τὰ πάντα καὶ ἐνιδρύουσα τῷ ἀγαθῷ, ἡ δὲ ἐκφαίνουσα τὴν ἐν τοῖς οὖσιν ἅπασι γνῶσιν, ὁ δὲ ἐπιστρέφων πάντα καὶ συνάγων εἰς τὴν τοῦ καλοῦ φύσιν (Procl., *In Alc.* 51.10–52.1 Segonds). See MS. Venice, Biblioteca Marciana, Gr. Z. 190 (779), f. 278r.

Bessarion's motives for not mentioning the similarities between Proclus's language and the *Corpus Dionysiacum*; I wish merely to emphasize that it is important to take note of it.

There is evidence that Bessarion and Balbi might not have been working in a vacuum in studying the Platonism of the *Corpus Dionysiacum* and its possible connections to Proclus. Based on paleographic evidence brought to light by Dieter Harlfinger and studies by Alain Philippe Segonds, it is now clear that none other than Georges Pachymeres (1242–1310) not only studied Proclus's *In Alcibiadem*—formerly no one took notice of this work's influence among Byzantine philosophers—but, according to Harlfinger, he is also the copyist of the most important manuscript of this text (MS. Naples, Neapolit. Gr. 339). What is more, Pachymeres evidently drew some connections between Proclus and the *Corpus Dionysiacum* since, according to Segonds, he included a reference to his own commentary on the *Corpus Dionysiacum* in a marginal note in this Proclus manuscript and also filled his paraphrases of the *Corpus Dionysiacum* with allusions to and implicit citations from Proclus and other Neoplatonists.[38] Although Bessarion's manuscript (MS. Venice, Biblioteca Marciana, Gr. Z. 190 (779)) comes from a textual tradition independent from Pachymeres's manuscript, further studies are needed to understand the exact nature of Pachymeres's work on the *Corpus*'s Platonism and to determine whether Bessarion might have been influenced by this approach.

Bessarion was part of the first phase of critical studies of the *Corpus Dionysiacum* in the Latin West, and already he began to reorient the Dionysian Question, reframing its hermeneutics toward an attention to Platonism, as Marsilio Ficino (1433–99) a generation later demonstrated at length in his translations and commentaries on the *Theologia mystica* and the *De divinis nominibus*. But Bessarion's strategy to walk a narrow path between the two options to the dilemma by identifying the *Corpus Dionysiacum*'s Platonic sources while upholding its Apostolicity came at a risk of raising new questions about its dependence on late ancient Platonism. Perhaps because of this, when Bessarion says to his readers, quoting Plato and Dionysius, "don't be afraid to use the word *Eros*," one often thinks to have heard, if only *sotto voce*, "don't be afraid to love the writings of Plato and Platonists."

---

38. Procl., *In Alc.* I: cxv–cxix Segonds. Harlfinger's identification of Pachymeres as the scribe of MS. Naples, Neapolit. Gr. 339 is in a private letter to L. G. Westerink, dated February 18, 1976.

CHAPTER 16 ‖ Marsilio Ficino's Debt to George Gemistos Pletho

Recollection and Appropriation

Stephen Gersh

Introduction

It has been a commonplace among historians of Renaissance philosophy to draw attention to the relation between the philosophical doctrines of George Gemistos Pletho and Marsilio Ficino and to suggest that this was the key factor in stimulating the introduction in Italy and subsequently beyond Italy of a new genre of Platonism and a type of *Neo-Platonism* based on the careful study in the original language of ancient Greek philosophical texts. However, since there has been to date little agreement about the precise nature and extent of the doctrinal relation between Pletho and Ficino, and since the first modern edition of arguably the most relevant text—Ficino's *Commentary on Plotinus*—has now begun to appear,[1] it may be worth attempting one more time to cast some light on this tantalizingly elusive question. In the proem to the aforementioned work, Ficino writes:

Great Cosimo, the Father of his Country by senatorial degree, at the time when the Council between the Greeks and the Latins under the guidance of pope Eu-

---

1. For the edition, see Marsilio Ficino, *Commentary on Plotinus*, ed. Gersh.

254

genius was being held in Florence, frequently attended the lectures of the Greek philosopher named Gemistos and surnamed Pletho as he held forth regarding the Platonic mysteries, being as though another Plato. Having been immediately so inspired and aroused by this man's fervent utterance, Cosimo thereupon conceived a kind of "Academy" in the profundity of his mind with a view to bringing it to birth at the first opportune moment. Then, while that great Medici was somehow bringing to birth a conception of such magnitude, he assigned me, the son of his favourite physician Ficino, while I was still a boy, to the great undertaking, raising me day after day with that very end in mind.[2]

This statement assigns a decisive role to the famous Byzantine philosopher in inspiring the official foundation of the Florentine "Academy," of which Ficino was apparently the leading member.[3] But it is a curious fact that citations of Pletho's works appear only in Ficino's writings published in the 1490s, that there is only a kind of indirect reference in those produced between the 1470s and 1482, and that there are no citations or references at all in Ficino's works written immediately after the time of the "great undertaking" mentioned in the proem (1463). Even though a date of publication represents only a *terminus ad quem* for the germination of ideas, the reaction on the Florentine's part to this "other Plato" seems peculiarly muted or delayed.

Let us briefly review the most relevant facts. First, there is manuscript evidence of Ficino's relation to Pletho in the form of an extant codex—the Riccardianus graecus 76—which contains a number of Pletho's works together with a note in Ficino's hand recording his ownership.[4] The works are *On the Differences between Plato and Aristotle, Against the Objections of Scholarios in Favour of Aristotle, On Virtues, On Fate, Funeral Oration for Helen,* and *Funeral Oration for Cleopa.* In addition to these, the MS contains fragments of the ancient Platonist Atticus drawn from Eusebius, *Praeparatio Evangelica* XV; Julian, *Oration on the Sun*; Synesius, *On Dreams* together with Ficino's Latin translation; Demetrius Cydones, *On the Immortality of the Soul,* and some minor items. The index on fo. 187v compiled by Matthew Devaris provides us with the important additional information that

2. Ficino, *In Plotinum*, prooemium 1.

3. Ficino was a "member" in a metaphorical sense. Whatever Cosimo's original intention may have been, there is no real evidence that an "Academy" as a formal institution ever came about. When Ficino uses the word *Academia* in his letters and treatises, he invariably means either (a) the loose community of his Platonically inclined friends and correspondents or (b) Platonic philosophy as a discipline considered in the abstract. If anything, the latter usage is the predominant one.

4. On fo. 187v the note reads: *Marcilius. Hic liber Marcilii Ficini.* Further evidence in the MS shows that it later became the property of Ficino's nephew and then entered into the library of Cardinal Niccolo Rodolfi.

this manuscript had once contained also the *Oracles* with the *Exegesis* of Psellos and the *Commentary* of Pletho.[5] Second, there is literary evidence of Ficino's relation to Pletho that is partially direct and partially indirect. The direct evidence consists of six citations of Pletho by name in Ficinian writings in the following chronological order: *Platonic Theology* XV.1.1–2 (published 1482) on the Aristotelian interpretation of Averroes and Alexander [Text 1]; *Commentary on Plotinus*, pr. 1 (published 1492) [Text 2], the passage quoted above, and pr. 3 on the Aristotelian interpretation of Averroes and Alexander [Text 3]; *Commentary on Plotinus' Ennead II. 1. c.1*[6] on the fifth element according to "Aristotle" [Text 4]; *Commentary Plotinus' Ennead II. 1, c. 3*[7] on the psychic vehicle according to "Aristotle" [Text 5]; and *Commentary on Dionysius' On Divine Names c. 63*[8] (published 1496 or 1497) on divine transcendence [Text 6].[9] The indirect evidence consists of numerous citations of oracular verses that modern scholars normally call "Chaldaean" but whose labeling by Ficino as "Zoroastrian" links them securely with a compilation that Pletho had made and to which he had attached a commentary.[10] There are verbatim citations of these oracles throughout the *Platonic Theology*,[11] and a smaller number of allusions in the *Commentary on Plotinus' Enneads I* and *II*[12] and in the *Commentary on Dionysius' On Divine Names*.[13]

These facts have led to contrasting interpretations of the relation between Ficino and Pletho, which one might style the "maximal" and the

---

5. For a full description, see Gentile et al., *Marsilio Ficino e il Ritorno di Platone*, 55–7) [item #43].

6. Ficino, *Opera Omnia* [= Basel 1576] 1594.

7. Ficino, *Opera Omnia* 1596.

8. For the edition, see Marsilio Ficino, *On Dionysius the Areopagite*, ed. Allen (2015).

9. See Gall et al., *Marsilio Ficino*, 86, s.v. "Pletho."

10. Ficino cites these oracles either under the name of "Zoroaster" or under that of the "Magi," the latter being understood as the disciples of the former.

11. For a discussion of some of these, see Klutstein, *Marsilio Ficino et la Théologie Ancienne*, 1–20.

12. The passages are: Ficino, *In Enn.* I.9.3 Gersh—Plotinus inserts a poem of Zoroaster against suicide (= Pletho, *Orac. Chald.* 16 Tambrun-Krasker); *In Enn.* II.3, c. 8, *Opera Omnia* 1629—focusing the fiery mind on the work of piety and also saving the body (= Pletho, *Orac. Chald.* 17); *In Enn.* II.3, c. 9, *Opera Omnia* 1629—augmenting fate means ceding or not ceding to it (Pletho, *Orac. Chald.* 4); *In Enn.* II.9, c. 12, *Opera Omnia* 1670—the Gnostic heretics and their false books of Zoroaster.

13. The passages are: Ficino, *In Dion. Div. Nom.* c. 17, p. 136 Allen—resurrection of the human body by divine power (= Pletho, *Orac. Chald.* 17 Tambrun-Krasker); *In Dion. Div. Nom.* c. 67, p. 262—focusing all our love on the Good (= Pletho, *Orac. Chald.* 17). There is also a reference to a "Zoroastrian" oracle that is neither in Pletho's collection nor in Psellos's *Exegesis*: *In Dion. Div. Nom.* c. 11, p. 112—the power of divine names (= fr. 87 des Places).

"minimal," respectively. A maximal interpretation is that of B. Tambrun-Krasker,[14] who argues that the contexts in which the *Oracles* are inserted in the *Platonic Theology* often reveal the Plethonian background to Ficino's thought. Examples are: in the fifth book[15] the discussion of the relation between soul and its inherent principle of life; in the eleventh book[16] that of the soul's reception of Ideas from the divine mind; in the thirteenth book[17] the discussion of the soul's relation to fate where mind, idolum, and nature are said to be above, within, and under fate, respectively; and where the reference to augmenting fate is said to indicate either ceding or not ceding to it; in the same book[18] the discussion of the soul's relation to unity where the ecstasy achieved through the flower of intellect is compared to those experienced by Plato and St. Paul; and in the eighteenth book[19] that of the union of soul and body through the vehicle where the reference to not extending the vehicle to the planar dimension is said to indicate its near-incorporeality. However, there are problems with this interpretation. First, there is a difference between, on the one hand, simply deriving an oracle from Pletho's collection and, on the other, utilizing the oracle together with its accompanying commentary, and Ficino in most cases seems to adopt the former approach.[20] Second, the doctrines that might at first glance ap-

14. Tambrun-Krasker, *Pléthon, Le retour de Platon*, 241–64. For the examples to be cited, see especially her discussion on p. 247*ff*. This author attempts to bolster her case by arguing that Ficino had some knowledge of Pletho's *Laws* in addition to the excerpt "Concerning Fate," which is included in the MS. Riccardianus graecus 76. See her comment on p. 243 concerning Ficino's citation in his *Commentary on the Divine Names* of Pletho's doctrine concerning gods of the second and third order. But it seems more likely that Ficino is referring in the relevant passage simply to Pletho, *Scholar*. 412.20*ff*. and 486.22*ff*. Lagarde

15. Ficino, *Theol. Plat.* V.14.4, p. 94 Allen and Hankins. Cf. Pletho, *Orac. Chald.* 12 Tambrun-Krasker.

16. Ficino, *Theol. Plat.* XI.3.9, p. 224 Allen and Hankins. Cf. Pletho, *Orac. Chald.* 27 Tambrun-Krasker.

17. Ficino, *Theol. Plat.* XIII.2.17, p. 138 Allen and Hankins. Cf. Pletho, *Orac. Chald.* 4 Tambrun-Krasker.

18. Ficino, *Theol. Plat.* XIII.5.3, p. 212 Allen and Hankins. Cf. Pletho, *Orac. Chald.* 28b Tambrun-Krasker.

19. Ficino, *Theol. Plat.* XVIII.4.3, p. 106 Allen and Hankins. Cf. Pletho, *Orac. Chald.* 14 Tambrun-Krasker.

20. There is one notable exception, for at Ficino, *Theol. Plat.* IV.1.25, pp. 288–90 Allen and Hankins the use of Pletho's *Commentary*, p. 19 (on Pletho, *Orac. Chald.* 34 Tambrun-Krasker) is indicated by the presence of identical doxographies in Pletho and in Ficino. The Ficinian passage states that according to the Magi, the world has three chief rulers who leave three "traces" (*vestigia*) in the world: (1) *Oromasis* = God / his property is unity + from him alone comes unity of the world's whole and parts; (2) *Mitris* = Mind / his property is order + from him "through the power of God" (*virtute dei*) [i.e., of 1] comes the order of the unified parts; (3) *Arimanis* = Soul / his property is movement + from him "through the power of the higher" (*superiorum*

pear to be derived by Ficino from the Plethonian reading of an oracle are in almost all the cited instances actually elaborated in more detail in other sources frequently used by the Florentine such as Plotinus, Iamblichus, and Proclus.

A minimal interpretation of the relation between Ficino and Pletho is that of J. Monfasani,[21] who argues that Ficino was caught on the horns of an interpretative dilemma between, on the one hand, his personal dislike of Pletho's metaphysical doctrines in general and, on the other, his crucial dependence on his particular teaching regarding the tradition of ancient theology leading up to Plato.[22] His solution was, initially, when Pletho's dubious reputation for pagan polytheism was in the ascendant, to ignore him, but later, when the controversies surrounding the Byzantine intellectual had waned sufficiently, to cite him only briefly as it suited his own purposes. Thus in the proem to the *Commentary on Plotinus*, Ficino will remind Lorenzo de' Medici of his grandfather's enthusiastic patronage of Platonic studies, and in the same commentary and the *Platonic Theology* he will use him as an authority in order to separate Aristotle's doctrine from that of Averroes. This interpretation leads Monfasani to reduce to insignificance the three other explicit Ficinian citations of Pletho that he has conveniently presented to his reader.[23] He argues that in the *Commentary on Plotinus*, one citation "might reflect" certain passages in *On the Differences between Plato and Aristotle* and the *Against the Objections of Scholarios*, while another "conforms to nothing we have from Pletho —Ficino simply misremembered Pletho." Finally, he concludes that the reference in the *Commentary on Dionysius* "amounts to nothing more than a citation of Pletho as a Neoplatonic metaphysician."

The remainder of this essay aims to demonstrate that Ficino has a profound and genuine philosophical debt to Pletho and not simply an allegiance on a superficial or cosmetic level, even though the Florentine's undeniable dependence on the Plethonian collection of oracles is not per se sufficient evidence of a shared philosophical purpose on the two writers'

---

virtute) [i.e., of 1 + 2] comes the movement of the ordered work. Ficino adds that Plato seems to have been referring to this in his *Letter to King Dionysus* and refers to his more detailed discussion in *De Amore* II.4, pp. 31–5 Laurens. It is significant that there is no citation of a *verse* at this point: something in keeping with the use of Pletho's commentary on an oracle rather than the relevant oracle itself.

21. Monfasani, "Marsilio Ficino and the Plato-Aristotle Controversy," 184–86.

22. According to Monfasani, the antipathy toward Pletho on Ficino's part was primarily aroused by the Byzantine author's "anti-Aristotelianism." We will consider this question in detail below.

23. Monfasani, "Marsilio Ficino and the Plato-Aristotle Controversy," Appendix 1, 197–99.

part. Without anticipating the results of the more detailed discussion to follow, we may perhaps summarize the main points—and they are substantial ones—on which Ficino found himself to be in harmony with Pletho as follows: (1) Plato's thought invariably leads to theology—not least with respect to the central doctrine of the soul's immortality. It is interesting here to compare the passage in Ficino's *Platonic Theology* setting out this idea with an argument in Pletho's *Against the Objections of Scholarios*, for the Latin author emphasizes the fact that Plato's thought takes a theological turn irrespective of whether it is dealing with ethics, dialectic, mathematics, or physics,[24] while the Byzantine writer defends Plato against Scholarios's charge that he confuses physical, mathematical, and theological discussions by arguing that, since natural things depend on the divine, it is impossible to have an adequate science of the former without pursuing a knowledge of the latter.[25] (2) The Platonists' teaching agrees more closely with Christian doctrine than does that of Aristotle. This conclusion follows logically from Ficino's statement in the proem to the *Platonic Theology* regarding the greatest proximity of Platonism to Christianity,[26] although his rhetorical strategy is not to say this explicitly out of regard for the views of contemporary scholastics. As we will see, Ficino himself favors a kind of philosophical concord between Plato and Aristotle in which the former is the dominant factor. Pletho *does* explicitly argue for the greater concordance with Christian thought exhibited by Platonism in comparison with Aristotelianism in the course of *Against the Objections of Scholarios*,[27] the rhetorical strategy in this case being to enhance his polemic against a Christian and scholastic critic by engaging his opponent on familiar terrain. In reality, Pletho's philosophical agenda comprises a revival of Hellenic paganism in which Christianity plays only an accidental role.

24. Ficino, *Theol. Plat.*, pr. 2, p. 8 Allen and Hankins.

25. Pletho, *Scholar.* 446.17–448.19 Lagarde. Pletho continues by arguing that an ethics that does not touch upon theology might be compared to a kind of corpse, this being especially the case with Aristotle's attempt to define the virtue of "courage." In fact, the Aristotelian ethical project fails in two primary ways: in not considering the immortality of the human soul and in not making a distinction between the man "here" and the man "there."

26. Ficino, *Plat. Theol.*, pr. 2, pp. 8–10 Allen and Hankins. As we will see, Ficino himself favors a kind of concordance between Plato and Aristotle in which the former is the dominant tendency.

27. Pletho, *Scholar.* 374.24–376.13 Lagarde. Pletho stigmatizes the fallacy in Scholarios's attempt to reconcile Aristotle more than Plato with the Church—the lack of strong arguments driving him to the Church in the way that people in difficulties take refuge in monasteries—adding that it would be best to say that both thinkers are alien to the Church. Pletho then concludes that Scholarios's maladroit argumentation actually shows Plato's greater closeness to Christianity: something stated clearly by such Patristic authorities as Cyril of Alexandria.

Almost all the main questions meriting discussion with regard to the Ficino-Pletho relation are closely connected with the two fundamental positions mentioned above, which are also closely connected with one another. These questions, which should now be examined in detail, concern the ancient theological tradition leading up to Plato (documented in texts 2 and 6) and the relation between Platonic and Aristotelian thought in general (documented in texts 1, 3, 4, and 5), Ficino in both these cases accepting outright or at least adapting the teaching of Pletho. By way of contrast with this, we should also consider the question of the relation between determinism and freedom documented in Ficino's MS annotations, in which case Ficino's attitude to Pletho is definitely one of rejection.

Acceptance or Adaptation of Pletho

Ancient Theology

The notion that there was some unified and continuous tradition of theology from remote antiquity onward was not a standard tenet of ancient philosophical doxographers or their Renaissance successors but rather a metaphysical projection of history peculiar to Platonists in both periods.[28] In both cases, it has its roots in the tradition of Christian apologetics, that is, the notion that pagan thinkers borrowed ideas from the Judaic tradition.[29] Ficino's major contribution to the dissemination of this peculiar notion of ancient theology, which evolved somewhat over time, can perhaps be summarized by distinguishing three cultural or national traditions: (1) the "Egyptian" and Christian, (2) the Greek, and (3) the "Persian-Egyptian" and Christian. The question of the relation between Ficino and Pletho is illuminated by the former's citation of these traditions either separately or in combination.

In his *argumentum* ("analytical study") prefixed to his translation of the *Pimander* completed in 1463,[30] Ficino first draws upon evidence provided by Cicero, Augustine, and Lactantius[31] in order to explain the gene-

---

28. For a survey of philosophical doxography and the place of the "ancient theology" tradition within it (together with notes on the earlier extensive bibliography), see Monfasani, "*Prisca Theologia* in the Plato-Aristotle Controversy before Ficino," 47–51.

29. Examples from the Greek and Latin traditions can be found in Clement of Alexandria and Augustine, respectively.

30. Ficino, *Argumentum in Pimandrum, Opera Omnia* 1836.

31. See Augustine, *De Civitate Dei* XVIII.39 for the genealogical information, and Lactantius, *Divinae Institutiones* I.6 for the notion of *five* Mercuries, the account of Trismegistus's achievements, and the reference to Cicero (*De Natura Deorum* III.22.56).

alogy of *Mercurius Trismegistus* ("Thrice-Greatest Hermes),[32] the putative author of the thirteen treatises of the Hermetic Corpus.[33] He then places this Mercury at the head of a tradition of ancient thought passed on successively through Orpheus, Aglaophemus, Pythagoras, and Philolaus and ending with Plato, which external evidence suggests to have been derived from Proclus.[34] According to Ficino, the first Mercury was the grandson of Prometheus the physicist whose brother was Atlas the astronomer and who was a contemporary of Moses. This Mercury's grandson was the one called "Thoth" in Egypt, where he fled after slaying the Argus, being therefore the fifth in the order of generations. This Mercury-Thoth was called "thrice-greatest" because he was the greatest philosopher, the greatest priest, and the greatest king—indeed, Plato reports that in Egypt, priests were selected from philosophers, and kings from priests. This same Mercury established the Egyptian letters based on animals, trees, and so forth, was the first philosopher to transfer his attention from physics and mathematics to divine things, the first to dispute about God's majesty, the order of daemons, and the vicissitudes of souls, and was called the first writer of theology, concerning which he wrote many books revealing arcane mysteries and amazing oracles. He was followed in theology by Orpheus; Aglaophemus was initiated into the rites of Orpheus; he was followed in theology by Pythagoras; he was followed by Philolaus; finally, the divine Plato was taught by Philolaus. "Therefore, there was established a unitary school of ancient theology that was in every way consonant with itself in a certain wonderful six-fold order of theologians, taking its beginnings from Mercury and achieving complete perfection in the divine Plato" (*Itaque una priscae theologiae undique sibi consona secta ex theologis sex miro quodam ordine constata est, exordia sumens a Mercurio, a divo Platone penitus absoluta*).

This earliest presentation of Ficino's theory of ancient theology contains important features that are often missed by casual readers: especially its being defined on the one hand as unitary, consonant with itself, and sixfold, and also as being characterized on the other as both a philosophical and a hieratic tradition and as a repository of both doctrines and mysteries. The first set of properties confers a metaphysical status within a "Pythagorean" worldview and the second group theurgic or sacramental status redolent of both ancient pagan and ancient Christian thought. But the most

---

32. Or in alternative Latin: *Mercurius Termaximus.*

33. Ficino actually knew only twelve Greek treatises (as well as the Latin *Asclepius*).

34. On this point, see below.

important aspect of all from the viewpoint of Ficino's exegetical program is the insertion of Moses into the chronology and the placing of the first Mercury two generations after the Hebrew lawgiver and of "Thrice-Greatest" Mercury four generations after him. This suggests in a tentative manner that there is, if not some pedagogical or literary relation, at least some providentially ordained concordance between the traditions of paganism and Judeo-Christianity. Ficino goes further in his *Platonic Theology* by arguing that Mercurius Trismegistus has explained the world's generation even more clearly than has Plato—not surprisingly if he was the same man as Moses, as the historian Artapanus has shown using a number of conjectures.[35] Similarly, in *De Christiana Religione*, he reports the same Artapanus's statement that whatever things are said of Mercurius Trismegistus are in Moses's books and done by Moses, and that Moses was also called "Mercurius" and "Musaeus."[36]

The MS Riccardianus Graecus 70 contains a remark in Ficino's hand (fo. 4v): *Proculus dicit quod quinque fuerunt principes theologie graecorum; primo Orpheus a quo Aglaophemus, a quo Pythagoras, a quo Philolaus, a quo Plato habuit* ("Proclus says that there were five leaders in the theology of the Greeks, the first to have this theology being Orpheus, from whom Aglaophemus, Pythagoras, Philolaus, and Plato obtained it in turn").[37] The Florentine is here referring to a passage in Proclus's *Platonic Theology*[38] that explains how the principal doctrines of Plato are in agreement with the "secret traditions" (μυστικαὶ παραδόσεις) of the theologians. Indeed, the whole of Greek theology is the offspring of Orpheus's mystagogy,

35. Ficino, *Theol. Plat.* XVIII.1.14, p. 82 Allen and Hankins. Ficino has extracted this information from Eus. *p.e.* 9.27.6.

36. Ficino, *De Christiana Religione*, c. 26.49–51 Bartolucci. See Eus. *p.e.* 9.27.3. In addition to the sources cited by Ficino with respect to the genealogy and tradition of Hermes Trismegistus, it is important to remember that the Florentine would have been familiar with various medieval traditions and especially those in Arabic astrological texts translated into Latin. For instance, Abu Ma'shar distinguished three Hermes: one identified with Idris and Enoch, who was the first to have discussed higher things, wrote many books, was instructed by his grandfather Adam, predicted the flood, built pyramids, and carved inscriptions; a second who was a Chaldaean living in Babylon, revived the sciences after the flood, and taught Pythagoras; and a third who was a philosopher and physician, lived after the flood, wrote many books, and taught Asclepius. See Thorndike, *History of Magic and Experimental Science*, 340–41, for the identification of Hermes and Enoch and the influence of this idea in medieval tradition (e.g., Roger Bacon). More recently, see Burnett, "Establishment of Medieval Hermeticism," 111–30).

37. For a full description of the manuscript, see Gentile et al. *Marsilio Ficino e il Ritorno di Platone*, 35–37 [item #26]. The Ficinian notes at the beginning of the MS have been edited and published by Saffrey, "Notes platoniciennes de Marsile Ficin," 161–84.

38. Procl. *Theol. Plat.* 1.5, 25.24–26.22 Saffrey-Westerink.

since Pythagoras learned from Aglaophemos "the initiations relating to the gods" (τὰ περὶ θεῶν ὄργια), and Plato received the "all-perfect knowledge" (παντελὴς ἐπιστήμη) concerning those things from the Orphic and Pythagorean writings. Among illustrations of this legacy, Proclus continues by noting that the teaching concerning the principles of limit and infinity in the *Philebus* was derived from the Pythagoreans,[39] that regarding the order of the sublunary gods in the *Timaeus* from the theologians,[40] and that concerning the hierarchy of the divine worlds in the *Cratylus* from Homer, Hesiod, and Orpheus. However, although Plato's teaching is in conformity with the principles of the theologians, he always rejects the "tragic element in their mythical writing" (τῆς μυθοποιίας τὸ τραγικόν).

The passage in Proclus to which Ficino draws our attention is significant not only for rooting central tenets of Plato's theology in a more ancient milieu but also for depicting the pre-Platonic theology in terms of an articulated sequence of its main exponents, for indicating that this traditional theology includes both a philosophical and a hieratic component, and for suggesting that the theological element proper must be sifted interpretatively from the mythical fictions that accompany it. Irrespective of the date at which Ficino made his annotation, it seems likely that these features were added to the genealogy of Hermes Trismegistus derived from Augustine and Lactantius in the *argumentum* of the *Pimander* under the influence of Proclus.

Starting from around 1469, Ficino develops his doctrine concerning the ancient theology in a variety of ways.[41] In his *Commentary on Plato's Philebus*, he refers to this idea in two passages emphasizing the numerological aspect of the tradition, specifying the manner in which the theological doctrines were transmitted, and giving examples of the doctrines themselves. In one passage, he provides a list of six theologians—placing Zoroaster at the head of the list and omitting Philolaus—and explains that the theologians are the recipients of a single "ray of God" (*Dei radius*) that both "burns"[42] in the sense of purging their minds and souls of lower things

39. He adds: especially from Philolaus.

40. In referring simply to "theologians," Proclus here and elsewhere generally means the Orphics (as Saffrey notes in "Notes platoniciennes de Marsile Ficin").

41. The writing of the *Commentary on the Philebus* occupied its author over a long period (ending finally in 1492). Marsilio Ficino, *The 'Philebus' Commentary*, ed. Allen (introduction, p. 56 distinguishes three versions and dates the first to 1469. The passages discussed in this paragraph were already in the first version.

42. Or "heats"—the simile is complicated here.

and "illuminates" in that of revealing truths to those minds and souls.[43] In another passage, Ficino explains how the formative principles of God's works contained in his mind that Plato characterized as "Ideas" (*ideae*) were, having been named in various ways—as seeds, powers, models, and so forth—by the five theologians whom he followed, vainly believed to represent many gods.[44]

The same list of six theologians is standard in Ficino's *Platonic Theology* composed between 1469 and 1472. In this work we find one passage[45] which emphasizes the combination of philosophical theory and religious practice in the work of these theologians, for Ficino here notes that the philosophy of Zoroaster was nothing other than "wise piety and divine worship" (*sapiens pietas cultusque divinus*),[46] that Mercury Trismegistus always began his disputations with prayers and ended them with sacrifices, that the philosophy of Orpheus and Aglaophemus was entirely concerned with "praises of the divine" (*divinae laudes*), that Pythagoras used to start his studies of philosophy with the morning singing of sacred hymns, and that Plato taught us in every case of speaking or thinking "to begin with God" (*exordiri a Deo*).[47] Another passage in the same work[48] once again emphasizes the numerological aspect of the tradition, adding the notions that the six theologians "were in accord" (*consenserunt*) and that Plato embraced and expanded their "universal wisdom" (*universa sapientia*) in his writings.[49] Here, Ficino mentions for the first time a problem in the transmission. Because the ancient theologians "wrapped the sacred mysteries of the divine in poetic veils" (*sacra divinorum mysteria … poeticis umbraculis obtegebant*), in order to prevent them from becoming mixed with profane matters, the result was that their successors interpreted that theology in differing ways.

The doctrine of ancient theology as formulated in the *Platonic Theology* is restated in the proem to the *Commentary on Plotinus* together with an explanation of the reasons for the doctrinal agreement between the various theologians, a geographical classification, and a specification of the theo-

43. Ficino, *In Philebum* c. 26, p. 247 Allen

44. Ficino, *In Philebum* c. 17, p. 181 Allen. Cf. Ficino, *In Philebum* c. 29, pp. 271–73 Allen on the priority of Zoroaster to Mercurius as teachers of language and c. 35, p. 356 Allen on Zoroaster as founder of natural magic.

45. Ficino, *Theol. Plat.* XII.1.14, p. 24 Allen and Hankins.

46. Ficino attributes this information to Plato with an allusion to Plato: *I Alcibiades* 122a.

47. Here Ficino is recalling Plato, *Timaeus* 48de, etc.

48. Ficino, *Theol. Plat.* XVII.1.2, p. 6 Allen and Hankins.

49. A virtually identical statement occurs at Ficino, *De Christiana Religione* c. 22, 73–75 Bartolucci, a work dated to 1474.

logians' method of covering the sacred mysteries.[50] Having identified the contemporary problem of a separation between philosophy and religion, he notes that divine providence brought it about that there should be born at the same time "a certain pious philosophy" (*pia quaedam philosophia*) both among the Persians under Zoroaster and among the Egyptians under Hermes, whose doctrines were "in harmony with one another" (*sibimet consona*). After summarizing the next four stages in the transmission after its cofounders, and then explaining the ancient custom of the theologians of veiling the divine mysteries with both mathematical numbers and figures and poetic fictions in case they might be rashly shared with all and sundry, a statement implying that Plato was also complicit in this approach, Ficino states his crucially important thesis that it was Plotinus who finally and uniquely stripped away these veils in order to reveal the secrets of the ancients.[51]

At this point the question arises as to why Ficino posited Zoroaster as the founder of ancient theology by the time he started working on the *Commentary on the Philebus* and the *Platonic Theology*, having previously assigned the foundational role to Mercurius Trismegistus. Pletho now comes into the picture, given that the celebrated Byzantine thinker had not only placed Zoroaster at the head of his own version of the ancient theological tradition but also had associated an extant body of literature: the *Chaldaean Oracles*, with this figure and his disciples.

In the course of a discussion in *Against the Objections of Scholarios* that Ficino could not have failed to notice,[52] Pletho counters the charge that Aristotle is superior to Plato because he was expert in all the different branches of knowledge, whereas Plato never covered any field in a systematic manner. He explains that Plato did not write on all the sciences: first, because he had as predecessors the Pythagoreans who had already explored this territory; second, Plato preferred the oral transmission of doctrine with writing being used merely to rectify interruptions to the tradition; third, Plato has indeed left a few *aides-mémoires* about the first principles of various sciences. Finally, Plato wrote as he did because "he imparts not his own philosophy but that which came down to him from Zoroaster via the Pythagoreans (οὐκ ἰδίαν ἑαυτοῦ φιλοσοφίαν τεμῶν ἀλλὰ τὴν ἀπὸ Ζωροάστρου

---

50. Ficino, *In Plotinum*, pr. 2 Gersh.

51. The material in this passage reappears with identical wording in Ficino's letter to John of Hungary: *Epistulae* VIII.19 (*Opera Omnia* 871–72).

52. Ficino's MS has a marginal scholium in the copyist's hand (fo. 27v): ἀρχὴ Πλατωνικῆς θεολογίας ἀπὸ Ζωροάστρου ("the beginning of Platonic theology is from Zoroaster").

διὰ τῶν Πυθαγορείων ἐς ἑαυτὸν κατεληλυθυίαν).[53] After adding some historical information about the reports of Pythagoras's encounter in Asia with the magi who were disciples of Zoroaster, Pletho cites as evidence for his historical interpretation "the oracles of the tradition of Zoroaster that have come right down to us and are everywhere and entirely in harmony with Plato's opinions" (τὰ ἀπὸ Ζωροάστρου ἔτι καὶ ἐς ἡμᾶς σῳζόμενα λόγια … συνῳδὰ ὄντα ταῖς Πλάτωνος πάντῃ τε καὶ πάντως δόξαις).[54]

Now, if Ficino was inspired by Pletho to place Zoroaster at the head of the ancient theological tradition, as the insertion of numerous Chaldaean oracles together with their uniquely Plethonian attribution to Zoroaster himself or the magi who were his disciples suggests, then the demotion of Mercurius to second place in the succession was probably also under the Byzantine's influence.[55] Indeed, Pletho explicitly states that the Persian Zoroaster was the most ancient sage and legislator, and that even the *Egyptian* priests followed him in philosophy while remaining true to their Egyptian authority in ritual.[56]

53. We cannot enter here into the question where Pletho obtained his theory regarding the Zoroastrian origins of ancient theology. According to two of Scholarios's letters (*Oeuvres complètes*, 4:152–53 and 162), Pletho was influenced by an early Jewish Averroist teacher called "Elissaios" (= Elisha). For further development of this idea, see Tardieu, "Pléthon lecteur des Oracles," 141–64 and Pletho, *Orac. Chald.* pp. 41–47 Tambrun-Krasker. For a more skeptical reading, see Monfasani, "*Prisca Theologia* in the Plato-Aristotle Controversy before Ficino," 51–52. Whatever the truth is regarding the Pletho-Elissaios relation, it seems certain that the Byzantine could easily have constructed the theory from material in Plato, Plutarch, and especially Proclus.

54. Pletho, *Scholar.* 376.14–380.1 Lagarde.

55. There is also a passage in D.L., 1, prol. 2 and 8 Hicks that refers to the magi as disciples of Zoroaster, dating Zoroaster, and associating him with astrology and magic. Diogenes also quotes an unidentified passage of Aristotle: *De Philosophia* stating that the magi were more ancient than the Egyptian sages. Both Pletho and Ficino would have known this text.

56. Pletho, *Scholar.* 378.18–23 Lagarde. That Zoroaster rather than Mercurius Trismegistus was for Ficino from 1469 onward the founder of the ancient theological tradition is argued at length by Allen (*Synoptic Art*, 27–41). In order to reinforce his point, Allen underlines the connections between Zoroaster and the Judeo-Christian tradition that were (or would have been) noted by the Florentine: cf. Ficino, *De Christiana Religione* c. 26, 39–42 Bartolucci on Didymus the Blind's identification of Zoroaster with Canaan, the son of Cham, the son of Noah; *Praedicatio de Stella Magorum* (*Opera Omnia* 489–91), where the three wise men journeying to the Christ-child are identified as Zoroastrians. Ficino also knew of the ancient identification of Zoroaster and Er (in Eus. *p.e.*13. 13.30 Mras; Clem. *Str.* 5.14.157 Stählin), although no such identification occurs in Ficino's *Epitome of Republic* X. Finally, Allen argues that Ficino would have been hesitant to make Mercurius Trismegistus the founder of the ancient theology because of the inferiority of the Egyptians' material worship to the purer cult of the Chaldaeans; see Ficino, *In Epist. Pauli* c. 4 (*Opera Omnia* 432–33). However, on the view of the present writer, Ficino's position was not so dogmatic, and he eventually came to see Mercurius and Zoroaster as cofounders of ancient theology. See further below.

Plato and Aristotle

Whereas the evidence for Pletho as source of Ficino is indirect in the case of the Florentine's relation to the ancient theology tradition, we are on safer ground in the case of his relation to the Plato-Aristotle controversy. However, the two passages that have been discussed in this connection by earlier scholarship—to which we will eventually add two more in this essay—generate a whole new series of interpretative problems.[57]

At the beginning of *Platonic Theology* XV, Ficino begins to consider objections to his theory of soul, starting with a possible one formulated in Averroes's terms. The latter would argue that the "mind" (*mens*) of all men is one and eternal, while their "souls" (*animae*) are many and mortal, such that the eternity of this *mind* is of no benefit to human *souls* that will perish.[58] Ficino's reply to this argument is that, although Averroes was clearly devoted to Aristotle's teachings, he read him not in the original Greek but in translations that deformed the meaning. This is why according to "the Platonist Pletho and all the most learned Greeks" (*platonicus Pletho ac peritissimi quique graecorum*) on certain obscure matters this most succinct author's intent remained hidden from Averroes. In fact, the words of Aristotle in Greek contradict the Arabic commentator for, as the Platonist Pletho declares, the Stagirite undoubtedly considered human "souls" (*animi*) to be many and everlasting.[59]

In the proem to the *Commentary on Plotinus*, Ficino argues that almost the whole world is occupied by Peripatetics who are divided into two sects: namely, the adherents of Alexander who maintain that "our intellect" (*intellectus noster*) is mortal, and those of Averroes who maintain that our intellect "is the single one" (*unicum esse*). He adds that both these groups totally undermine religion, deny God's providence toward mankind, and traduce the Aristotle whom they admire. According to Ficino, few contemporary philosophers other than the Platonist Pico interpret the thought of Aristotle with "that same piety" (*ea pietate*) with which Theophrastus of old, then Themistius, Porphyry, Simplicius, and Avicenna, and more recently Pletho have interpreted it.[60]

A further passage in the same commentary, although not mentioning

57. These are Texts 1 and 3 in our inventory in this chapter's introduction.

58. My italics.

59. Ficino, *Theol. Plat.* XV.1.1–2, pp. 8–10 Allen and Hankins. The passage continues with a doxography of Alexander (and Ps.-Alexander), Themistius, and Proclus concerning the soul which is largely repeated in the passage of the *Commentary on Plotinus* to be considered below.

60. Ficino, *In Plotinum*, pr. 3 Gersh.

Pletho by name,[61] clearly represents an explanation in more detail of the interpretation of "Aristotelian" doctrine with which the Byzantine thinker has been linked. Here Ficino describes Plotinus's doctrine that the divine intellect is both communal—to the extent that it itself is undivided and as a whole everywhere—and particular—to the extent that it is received by individual souls in individual and proper ways. He then compares this relation between the divine intellect and the intellect of the individual soul to the relation between the sun's light and human eyes, adding that Themistius associated this doctrine with Aristotle and Theophrastus and that Avicenna and al-Ghazali followed them. Next, he returns to the conflict between the two Peripatetic authorities mentioned in the proem by arguing that Alexander agrees with Plotinus in attributing to us many intellects in addition to the one intellect but opposes him in asserting that these many intellects are mortal, whereas Averroes agrees with Plotinus in asserting that total intellect is immortal but opposes him in assigning the single intellect to us. Ficino concludes that if you take from Alexander the multiplicity of the human intellect, and from Averroes the immortal gift of total intelligence, you will have "the complete doctrine of our Plotinus" (*integra Plotini nostri sententia*).[62]

Ficino's information about the views of later Greek and medieval Arabic commentators on Aristotle was probably absorbed through Thomas Aquinas's *Summa contra Gentiles*[63] with possible further references to Averroes's *Commentarium Magnum in De Anima*,[64] Avicenna's *De Anima*,[65] and al-Ghazali's *Metaphysics*.[66] The Florentine is providing a compressed account in order to situate Plotinus as a mediator between two positions that might be set out more fully as follows. On the one hand, there is Averroes's doctrine contrasting a universal agent and possible intellect with the cogitative and imaginative components of the individual soul, these two being linked by a bidirectional process of abstracting sensory data.

61. For that reason, it has not been included in our inventory.

62. Ficino, *In Enneadem* I.1.15–16 Gersh. At I.1.8, there is a similar but briefer statement to the effect that Plotinus occupies the middle ground between Alexander, who maintains that the intellectual nature is able to be the proper life of the body, and Averroes, who holds that the intellectual nature is neither the life of the body nor infuses any life into the body. Cf. also I.2.6, heading.

63. See Aquinas, *Summa contra Gentiles* 2.46ff. and esp. 2.59–79.

64. See Averroes, *Commentarium Magnum In De Anima* III.5, p. 387ff. Crawford. For a summary of Averroes's position, see pp. 501–27. Views of Theophrastus and Themistius are discussed at pp. 57–116, and that of Alexander and others at p. 196ff.

65. See Avicenna, *Liber de Anima* 5.5, pp. 126–33 van Riet.

66. See Algazel, *Metaphysics* 2, tr. 4, c. 5, pp. 172–82 Muckle.

On the other hand, there is Alexander's doctrine contrasting the universal agent intellect with the individual possible intellect linked by a similar bi-directional process of abstraction from sense. It is between these extremes that one may situate Plotinus's mediating position contrasting a universal intellect containing the Platonic forms and an individual intellectual soul containing the images of those forms linked by a unidirectional process of emanative descent. For Ficino, the most important aspect of this discussion is the fact that the three positions imply immortality or mortality on the part of the system's various components which may be defined alternatively as souls and intellects.

A question arises concerning the correctness of Ficino's depiction of Pletho as a critic of Averroes's doctrine of soul and also as a careful reader of Aristotle's discussion of the same topic. Ficino seems to be right concerning Pletho and Averroes, for a combination of passages from *On the Differences between Plato and Aristotle* and *Against the Objections of Scholarios* shows that Pletho and his Aristotelian opponent have indeed clashed over the opinion of Averroes in this connection. Near the beginning of *On the Differences between Plato and Aristotle*, Pletho had asked why we should follow Averroes in his allegiance to Aristotelianism, given that this writer had declared that the human soul was mortal.[67] From *Against the Objections of Scholarios* we learn that Scholarios had complained that this was a false accusation against Averroes, since all the Latins and Jews understand him as saying that the human soul is indestructible, to which Pletho now counters that the most intelligent among these groups agree with his interpretation of Averroes: a thinker whose position has a subtlety that escapes Scholarios.[68]

Ficino also seems to be right concerning Pletho and Aristotle, for a passage in *Against the Objections of Scholarios* has Pletho taking his opponent to task for on the one hand acknowledging that Aristotle considers the human intellect to be immortal, but on the other hand not realizing that it necessarily follows that the human intellect does not begin together with the body. Scholarios has apparently attempted to argue that for Aristotle the intellect does indeed begin with the body, either in that God himself makes it directly at the moment of conception or in that God produces it subsequently by perfecting some part of the sperm. Now, if Aristotle does

67. Pletho, *De Diff.* 321.10–11 Lagarde.

68. Pletho, *Scholar.* 374. 15–24 Lagarde. He merely adds later in the same work a comment to the effect that he is mainly attacking Averroes in order to prevent anyone from being led unconsciously toward atheism by his doctrine: as is the case with "most westerners."

not hold the inconsistent position attributed to him by Scholarios but rather the logically coherent one attributed to him by Pletho, then he must subscribe to the doctrine of the soul's eternal existence normally associated with the Platonists. When Pletho goes on to criticize his opponent for on the one hand conceding that Aristotle maintains the eternity of the world, but on the other hand not realizing that it necessarily follows that the human soul is not only non-generated in a temporal sense but also subject to numerous descents into mortal bodies, the Platonic tendency of Aristotle's view becomes even more apparent.[69]

A further question arises concerning the correctness of Ficino's depiction of Pletho as holding a mediating position between Averroes and Alexander and at the same time holding the doctrine of Plato and Plotinus. If Ficino's depiction of Pletho as a critic of Averroes's doctrine of soul and as a careful reader of Aristotle's discussion of the same topic is also correct, then Pletho is by clear implication advocating some kind of harmony between Aristotelian and Platonic thought on this point. But this is problematic because Pletho is generally assumed to be someone who rejects this philosophical concordance in favor of an explicit valuation of Platonic thought as superior to Aristotelianism.

That Pletho sets himself squarely against the harmony of Plato and Aristotle seems to emerge from a passage where he responds to Scholarios's introduction of the notion that according to certain thinkers the difference between the two philosophers "is merely an appearance in connection with their use of language" (περὶ τὰ τῆς λέξεως φαινόμενον συμβῆναι μόνον). Pletho replies that this was the opinion only of Simplicius, who stated the issue in this manner in order to counter the argument of the Christian church, which contrasted its own agreement with the disagreement of the pagan philosophers.[70] Indeed, Simplicius "says nothing convincing" (οὐδ' ὁτιοῦν λέγων πιθανόν) in attempting to harmonize the two philosophers, while many other ancient writers have criticized Aristotle including Plotinus—an author far superior to Simplicius —who especially attacks the *Categories*, and also Proclus, especially writing in his *Theology*.[71]

However, a careful reading of Pletho's writing shows that he is here taking a seemingly extreme position as a result of Scholarios's provocations and that his view of the doctrinal relation between Plato and Aris-

69. Pletho, *Scholar.* 442.4–444.27 Lagarde.

70. Pletho is recalling passages such as Simp., *In Ph.* 1.2, 184b, pp. 28.32–29.5 Diels; 8.5, 258 b, p. 1249. 12–13; Simpl. *In De Cael.* 3.7, 306a, pp. 640, 27–29 Heiberg.

71. Pletho, *Scholar.* 370.7–23 Lagarde.

totle is much more nuanced. There are three particularly relevant texts. In the first passage, Pletho argues that we should not simply reject Aristotle but on the contrary read his books for the useful things they contain, realizing also that there is much mediocrity there.[72] We should not revere his errors because he has written on everything but be prepared, "while having as our leader Plato: a man much more divine than him" (Πλάτωνα ἔχοντες πολὺ αὐτοῦ θειότερον ἄνδρα προστάτην), to correct what Aristotle said badly.[73] Elsewhere, Pletho replies to Scholarios's favorable comparison of the comprehensive range of Aristotle's interests with the more restricted approach of Plato by pointing out that the latter only inserted the minimum necessary principles of philosophy in his dialogues and left it to his disciples to deduce what follows from them. Aristotle, he continues, had been a student of Plato but went over to sophistry under the cover of philosophy and sought prestige through the founding of his own school. He overthrew and corrupted "the first principles of philosophy written down by Plato as having come down to him from time immemorial" (τὰς μὲν ὑπὸ Πλάτωνος συγγεγραμμένας φιλοσοφίας ἀρχὰς ἐκ παμπόλλων ἐτῶν ἐς ἐκεῖνον κατεληλυθυίας). Moreover, "he himself appropriated the teachings that he had derived orally from Plato by writing them down" (ἃ δ' ἀπὸ φωνῆς Πλάτωνος διηκούσεν αὐτὸς συγγεγραφὼς ἑαυτοῦ ἐποιήσατο) while at the same time introducing many errors into them.[74] Being excessively preoccupied with things far from the first principles and insignificant, Aristotle published masses of writings to fascinate less intelligent people, whereas wisdom really deals only with the first principles of things and therefore uses relatively few words.[75] In the third passage, Pletho argues that Plato is better at unifying and distinguishing things because he always uses division, whereas Aristotle prefers the inferior method of induction and therefore cannot distinguish or order things. Division orders things starting from what is common, and unification cannot be accomplished by someone who does not "derive things causally from a single god" (ἀφ' ἑνὸς θεοῦ τὰ ὄντα παράγειν).[76]

72. Pletho adds that we should read him as Plutarch says we should read the poets.

73. Pletho, *Scholar.* 376.14–380.1 Lagarde. Throughout the *Contra Obiectiones Scholarii*, Pletho argues that Plato's use of Greek technical terminology is more precise than Aristotle's. This is not surprising because the former was a native Athenian and the latter a provincial from Macedonia. See Pletho, *Scholar.* 394.19–22 and 412.2–41 Lagarde.

74. Cf. Pletho, *Scholar.* 380.4–10 Lagarde.

75. Pletho, *Scholar.* 380.11–15 Lagarde.

76. Pletho, *Scholar.* 498.5–18 Lagarde. Pletho adds that this shows that Aristotle inclines towards atheism—a fact that Scholarios either does not recognize or covers up. At 486.19–23

Since these passages clearly show that he considered Aristotle to be a thinker who surreptitiously appropriated many Platonic doctrines while making a display of some of his disagreements with his predecessor, Pletho's apparently uncompromising attack on Simplicius's notion of a harmony between the two philosophers turns out to be something of an exaggeration, probably introduced for polemical reasons. He would certainly have known that this Aristotelian commentator was not the only ancient thinker to have advocated this interpretation but was summarizing a doctrine that had been traditional in the Platonic school since at least the time of Porphyry. It would also have been apparent to him that in quoting against the harmony thesis the first treatise of Plotinus's *Ennead* VI ,where the Aristotelian categories are criticized in preparation for a statement regarding the Platonic kinds,[77] and also the second book of Proclus's *Platonic Theology*, where the radical transcendence of the Platonic One is contrasted with the Aristotelian convertibility of unity and being,[78] he was at the same time ignoring numerous passages of these same authors where a combination and not an opposition of Platonic and Aristotelian elements is the dominant feature.

Therefore we may perhaps conclude that if Ficino considers Pletho—at least in connection with the doctrine of soul—as being at the same time a critic of Averroes, a careful reader of Aristotle's discussion, a mediator between Averroes and Alexander, a follower of Plato and Plotinus, and a believer in the harmony of Plato and Aristotle, then this understanding on Ficino's part is not totally far-fetched. In this case, it is not necessary to depend on the developmental thesis of J. Monfasani in order to make sense of the Florentine writer's relation to his Byzantine predecessor.[79] According to this view, Ficino's thought underwent a significant shift from an earlier belief in the harmony of Plato's and Aristotle's thought to a curious later position developed in response to Pletho where he was undoubtedly aware of the differences between the two thinkers but chose to ignore them as part of a rhetorical rather than a philosophical strategy.[80] In actual fact, Ficino always retains his belief in the harmony of Platonic and Aristotelian thought but, in

---

Lagarde, Pletho says that he does not accuse Aristotle himself of being an atheist—as Scholarios charges that he does—but as "inclining towards atheism" (ἐς ἀθεότητα ἀποκλίνειν).

77. Plot. 6.1, cc. 1–24 Henry and Schwyzer.

78. Procl, *Theol. Plat.* 2.2, pp. 16.22–23.12 Saffrey and Westerink.

79. Monfasani, "Marsilio Ficino and the Plato-Aristotle Controversy," 190–95.

80. There is some evidence of Ficino being more overt in stressing the superiority of Plato over Aristotle in his *Commentary on the Philebus*, c. 6, p. 113 Allen (concerning the supreme Good) and c. 16, p. 177 ed. Allen (concerning the Ideas). This may indicate that Ficino has recently been reading Pletho, especially since this commentary also has the earliest traces of Pletho's Zoroastrian theology.

line with Pletho, sees the harmony as something conceived on *Plato's* terms.

It therefore seems likely that Ficino was perfectly capable of reading between the lines of Pletho's somewhat intemperate polemic. In addition, he cannot have failed to admire the Byzantine Platonist for the expertise that he displays in precisely analyzing numerous Aristotelian passages in the course of his *Against the Objections of Scholarios*.[81] Indeed, it seems that the other two somewhat obscure references to Pletho in the *Commentary on Plotinus* are also concerned with his role as an Aristotelian commentator.

Other Topics

The Fifth Element   In his commentary on the first treatise of *Ennead* II,[82] Ficino argues that the world is everlasting not through the proper power of its body but (a) through its soul as though an internal cause of immortality and (b) through the divine will as though an external beginning and end. So, (1) if the world is considered in the immutable activity of God, it seems to be without beginning and end, but (2) if it is considered in relation to the free will of God, it seems to come into being. After quoting various authorities for the innovative theory (2) who argue either on the basis of (i) the priority of God to soul and body or (ii) the priority of soul's discursive motion to the world's bodily motion, Ficino adds a footnote indicated by the words "I now omit discussion of" (*mitto nunc*). Here he notes Heraclitus's opinion that the entire corporeal world including the stars and spheres is in a state of constant flux and reflux and therefore both comes to an end and is perpetually renewed—obviously a different kind of innovation from the one mentioned above—and also recalls Plato's similar view that the world is always in becoming and never in being. He then explains that this notion of the world as being in flux corresponds to the opinion of Plotinus in the present treatise, that Proclus agrees with it in commenting on the *Timaeus*,[83] that Pletho says that it is probable, and that he himself has argued for it in his *Platonic Theology*.[84]

Now, it is clear that the reference to Pletho is with respect to the foot-

81. E.g., see Pletho's correction of Scholarios's interpretation of Arist. *EN* 1.5, 1097a 28–34 and X.2, 1174a 8–1176a 26 Joachim—followed by correction of Aristotle's own errors—at Pletho, *Scholar.* 460.5–462.25 Lagarde; his correction of Scholarios's interpretation of Arist. *Ph.* 2.8, 199b 26–28 Ross at Pletho, *Scholar.* 480.9–484.15 Lagarde, and of his interpretation of Arist. *Metaph* Z.7, 1032a 30–33 Ross—followed by correction of Aristotle's own errors—at Pletho, *Scholar.* 490.1–18 Lagarde.

82. Ficino, *In Enn.* II.1, c. 1 (*Opera Omnia* 1594) [= Text 3].

83. See Procl. *In Ti.* 1.293.4–295.12 Diehl

84. Ficino, *Theol. Plat.* XI.4.15, p. 266 Allen and Hankins (quoting Heraclitus); XI.6.4, pp. 298–302 (quoting Heraclitus and Proclus); XVIII.1.13, pp. 80–82 (quoting Proclus).

note dealing with the world's continuous flux rather than with respect to the main argument concerning the world's relation to its prior cause.[85] In this case, Ficino seems to be recalling a passage in *Against the Objections of Scholarios* where the Byzantine writer is rejecting the Aristotelian doctrine of the fifth element in favor of a more Platonic theory in which the stars' bodies are of a fiery nature. He argues that it is because of their communal divine form—as well as the form of fire—through which God maintains their status that the stars' bodies are immortal and not because of a matter peculiar to them, that is, the fifth element. Moreover, there is no need for such a peculiar matter if they can achieve incorruptibility not only through the divine form but also through the primordial matter. That primordial matter which is potentially all the forms naturally "enters into" (ἐπιρρεῖν) and "exits from" (ἀπορρεῖν) from all living bodies, with the former prevailing over the latter in increasing bodies and the latter prevailing over the former in decreasing ones, the continuity of this flux being maintained by the "superfluity of power" (περιουσία δυνάμεως) in their controlling forms.[86]

The Vehicle Once again, in his commentary on the first treatise of *Ennead* II,[87] Ficino explains how all things are governed proximately by the heaven. In any animate thing, the soul continually puts forth a spirit infused in all the limbs, in some cases on its own, in other cases as enveloped by the humors, and in others as enveloped also by the limbs. He adds that particular souls put forth a spirit (a) toward the limbs that is a vapor of the blood, while rational souls also receive a spirit (b) from the heavens that is a fiery substance. Finally, he notes that Plotinus elsewhere says that we receive the latter spirit also from the soul of the earth, and that Aristotle thought our souls to be enwrapped with this spirit according to the testimony of Plutarch, John the Grammarian,[88] Proclus, and Pletho. Now, the combination of the cited authorities and especially the peculiar teaching attributed to Aristotle lead us to a precise passage in *Against the Objections of Scholarios* that furnishes the basis of this discussion.[89] Here Pletho re-

---

85. Monfasani, "Marsilio Ficino and the Plato-Aristotle Controversy," 197–98, attempts to connect the Plethonian citation with the main argument. Not surprisingly, he is therefore forced to conclude, "I could not track down a passage that corresponds exactly to Ficino's reference." Cf. 184–85, where some loose parallels in Pletho are suggested.

86. Pletho, *Scholar.* 474.3–20.

87. Ficino, *In Enn.* II.1, c. 3 (*Opera Omnia* 1596) [= Text 4].

88. I.e., John Philoponus.

89. Monfasani, "Marsilio Ficino and the Plato-Aristotle Controversy," 198, is therefore mistaken when he says, "nowhere in these pages [of *De Diff. Plat. et Arist.* and the *Contra Obiect.*

ports the doctrine of the Platonists that our soul immortalizes the "vehicle which is a certain fiery spirit" (ὄχημα, πνεῦμα δή τι ὂν πυρῶδες) that it uses as a medium between the imperishable incorporeal soul and the perishable body. He adds that this doctrine comes from the tradition of Zoroaster to the disciples of Plato, and that John[90] and before him Plutarch[91] attribute this doctrine to Aristotle "whether this pertains to him or not" (εἴτε δὴ προσήκουσα εἴτε μή).[92]

Transcendent God   If the two previous passages citing Pletho are concerned with the latter's role as a commentator of Aristotle or Pseudo-Aristotle, our last text takes us back more explicitly to Pletho as a "Zoroastrian" Platonist. In his *Commentary on Dionysius' On Divine Names*,[93] Ficino states that God is called being in a superessential way because he produces beings, but he is also said to surpass being in a superessential way, since he is not located on a highest level of beings with other things situated on secondary and tertiary levels. If the latter were the case, God would partly agree with the subsequent beings and partly differ from them and would therefore be a composite—especially if there is one univocal reason-principle of being itself that is common to all beings—as several illustrious metaphysicians and the Platonist Pletho point out.

Ficino could here be recalling one or more of several passages in Pletho's writings. In his *Commentary on the Oracles*, Pletho explains the verse: "the Father has snatched himself away, not enclosing his own fire in his intellective power" (ὁ πατὴρ ἥρπασεν ἑαυτὸν /οὐδ' ἐν ἑῇ δυνάμει νοερᾷ κλείσας ἴδιον πῦρ).[94] According to his exegesis, the oracle states that the first God has "a self-subsistence through which its divinity is distinguished from all other gods" (αὐτὸ δι' αὐτὸ ὄν, ᾧ ἡ αὐτοῦ θεότης τῶν ἄλλων πάντων ἐξήρηται), and further that it has a non-communicable status "because it is totally unable to encircle the contradiction of a thing" (τῷ δ' ὅλως οὐ δυνατῷ τοῦ πραγμάτος τὸ ἐς ἀντίφρασιν περιίστασθαι).[95] Pletho

---

Schol.] does he [Pletho] remotely suggest the opinion that Ficino says he attributed to Aristotle." Cf. 184–85 with reference to the same passage: "[it] conforms to nothing we have from Pletho. Ficino simply misremembered Pletho."

90. Once again, John Philoponus—with apparent reference to his *In De Anima* 255.8–14 Hayduck.

91. The source has not been identified; see Lagarde, p. 477n251.

92. Pletho, *Scholar.* 474.25–476.2 Lagarde.

93. Ficino, *In Dionysii De Divinis Nomnibus,* c. 63, pp. 250–52 Allen [= Text 6].

94. Orac. Chald. fr. 3 des Places.

95. Pletho, *Orac. Chald.* 33 Tambrun-Krasker p. 18—reading *to* (with MS *N*) in place of the *tōi* adopted by this editor on l. 19.

alludes to this same interpretation of Zoroaster—combining it with a reading of Plato's *Second Letter*—in a passage of his *Against the Objections of Scholarios* where he criticizes Aristotle for treating his highest god as being on the same level as the other gods, adding that this is a totally inappropriate way of talking about the God who is "king of all" according to Plato[96] and whom Zoroaster[97] describes as "pre-eminent and not numbered with the other gods" (ἐξαίρετος … καὶ θεοῖς τοῖς ἄλλοις οὐκ ἐνάριθμιος).[98] Later in the same work, he explains to Scholarios that he is not saying that Aristotle is an atheist, since the latter does speak generally of gods in the heavens, although he is fully justified in maintaining that he inclines toward atheism. This is for the following reasons: (i) Aristotle does not consider the leading god to be "pre-eminent in divinity" (τῇ θεότητι ἐξαίρετος)—as do Plato and all Zoroaster's disciples[99]—but as being "of a similar substance to the others" (παραπλησίας τοῖς ἄλλοις οὐσίας; (ii) he considers the first God as having an equal prerogative with the others in the distribution of the spheres; (iii) Aristotle does not consider the first God or any of the others as "the demiurge of the substance of the heaven" (τῆς τοῦ οὐρανοῦ οὐσίας … δημιουργός);[100] and (iv) he does not make any "divine intelligence" (νοῦς θεῖος) preside over things that come to be naturally.[101]

That Ficino is indeed recalling these passages seems to be confirmed especially by the close parallel between Pletho's notion of the highest God as "not encircling the contradiction of a thing" and Ficino's idea that this God cannot be rendered composite by agreeing with and differing from coordinate divinities, since this compositeness would certainly involve encircling such a contradiction: for instance, as the term "god" encircles the contradiction of "invisible [god]" and "visible [god]." Now, if this is the case, Ficino is engaging in an interpretation that can only be described as doubly ironic. He is citing Pletho in support of Dionysius the Areopagite's negative theology, a topic that this Byzantine author tended to avoid because of the associations it had acquired with the Hesychasts and Palamites.[102] At the same time, Ficino is citing material in Pletho that involves

96. Pl. *Ep.* 2.312e Burnet

97. I.e., in the oracle mentioned above.

98. Pletho, *Scholar.* 412.20–414.3 Lagarde.

99. I.e., in the two passages mentioned earlier.

100. Pletho adds that all the wise and most laypeople do this.

101. Pletho, *Scholar.* 486.23–488.6 Lagarde. He adds that this view opposes that of the most pious men.

102. On this general question, see Tambrun-Krasker, "Allusions antipalamites dans le *Commentaire* de Pléthon," 168–79.

a sharp critique of Aristotelian theology with which he would undoubtedly sympathize while being disinclined to admit this *in propria persona*.[103]

Rejection of Pletho

Determinism

Thus far, we have been studying Ficino's positive relation to Pletho's thought, and this has turned out to be significant albeit understated by the Florentine writer. But this clearly does not give us the entire picture of the relation between the two thinkers. In this final section, we must therefore turn to their main area of disagreement, where the tension is less between Platonic and Aristotelian than between Platonic and Stoic principles. It is well known that the *codex unicus* of Pletho's masterwork the *Laws* was destroyed on the orders of his arch-rival George Scholarios, when the latter had become the first orthodox patriarch of Constantinople under the Turkish regime. However, copies of parts of the work had already been circulating in Italy for some years. One such extract was of Book II, chapter 6, "On Fate" (Περὶ εἱμαρμένης),[104] an example of which is fortunately preserved in the MS Riccardianus graecus 76, which had belonged to Ficino and contains some of his annotations.[105] We will conclude with a brief paraphrase of Pletho's argument contextualized with Ficino's responses.

In brief, Pletho establishes a broad equation between fate, necessity, determination, and providence in the relevant chapter, whereas Ficino in his MS notes and in his published writings admits the equation between fate and necessity, treats determination as a broader category, and distinguishes providence clearly from fate and necessity.[106] Pletho's argument in the *Laws* is based on assumptions about the primacy of causality and its absolute identity with determination that are stated both in *On the Differences between Plato and Aristotle*[107] and in *Against the Objections of Scholarios*.[108]

---

103. Even if we have not made a full interpretation of the passages considered in this section, enough has perhaps been said to refute the view of Monfasani, "Marsilio Ficino and the Plato-Aristotle Controversy," 185, that we have here in Ficino's Dionysian commentary "nothing more than a citation of Pletho as a Neoplatonic metaphysician."

104. Pletho, *Lg.* 2.6, Alexandre pp. 64–78.

105. These appear on fo. 96r–98v. Transcription of the notes has been provided by Keller, "Two Byzantine Scholars and Their Reception in Italy," 365; and with some minor corrections by Monfasani, "Marsilio Ficino and the Plato-Aristotle Controversy," 199.

106. His position with respect to determination is more ambivalent.

107. Pletho, *Diff.* 332.29–32 Lagarde.

108. Pletho, *Scholar.* 492.12–15 Lagarde.

In both places he argues that (A) everything that comes about must of necessity come about through a cause, and that (B) every cause necessarily and determinately effects everything that it effects, typically citing Plato's authority for the two axioms while noting Aristotle's failure to observe the second one.[109] In his notes and published works, Ficino treats fate/necessity and providence as lower and higher levels, respectively, of dynamically emanative and divinely willed causality, and in commenting on Plotinus, he confines fate/necessity to formal and material causality while assimilating providence—in addition—to final causality.

The first part of the chapter "On Fate"[110] is devoted to an explanation of the relation between the divine dispensation and necessity. Pletho begins by arguing that everything is determined and fatal for, if something were not determined, either (A) it would come about without a cause or (B) the cause that produced it would act indeterminately, both of which are impossible. In fact, everything is determined from eternity "in the best possible way" (ὡς δυνατὸν αὐτοῖς) under Jupiter, who is the king of all. Jupiter alone is not subject to necessity because necessity is equivalent to determination by a higher cause, although Jupiter transmits necessity[111] to subsequent terms in a descending hierarchy to varying degrees. Those who abolish necessity and fate either (1) deny all providence to the gods regarding things here or (2) accuse the gods of being the authors of things that are not the best possible. Moreover, those who deny the determination of future events remove the possibility of foreknowledge for either gods or human beings. To this last point Ficino raises an objection, arguing that Boethius and Thomas Aquinas have both proven that God knows with certainty things that come about through undetermined causes.[112]

In the course of this discussion, Pletho has assumed the possibility of foreknowing future events not only on the part of the gods but also on that of certain men to whom the gods have chosen to reveal them. This naturally raises the question of whether it is possible for these chosen individuals themselves to evade or allow others to evade adverse future events, and Pletho replies that this avoidance will also be foreknown by the gods and therefore not outside their necessary dispensation. Ficino summarizes this argument in his note, adding a criticism to the effect that the indications of the gods to their chosen men will in this case be totally useless.[113]

---

109. The relevant texts are Pl. *Tim.* 28a Burnet and (probably) Pl. *Epin.* 982c Burnet.

110. Pletho, *Lg.* 2.6, pp. 64–72 Alexandre.

111. I.e., necessitating and being necessitated.

112. Fo. 96v.

113. Fo. 97r.

The second part of the chapter "on Fate"[114] is devoted to consideration of the relation between human freedom and divine justice. Regarding human freedom, Pletho argues that human beings are free not (1) in having nothing prior that rules them but (2) in having something in them that rules; namely, τὸ φρονοῦν ("soul/intellect"). Ficino summarizes this in his note.[115] Pletho further argues that human freedom is really equivalent to living as one wishes and that, since one wishes for the best and the best is determined by the gods, then freedom is equivalent to living according to the divine dispensation. Ficino also summarizes this argument in a note.[116] Regarding divine justice, Pletho argues that human beings are composed of two natures: an immortal one assimilating to the gods and a mortal one turning toward evils, and that the gods' punishment of the evil tendency is analogous to the physician's healing of a disease and is therefore a good for humanity. At this point, Ficino makes his most pointed criticism so far. He notes that Pletho has argued earlier that all things have been established for the best under Jupiter, whereas he now argues that the gods have established the evil tendency of mankind. Therefore Pletho has contradicted his own teaching.[117]

Although these autograph annotations give us some indication of Ficino's general attitude toward Pletho's doctrine of fate, they do not provide a detailed statement of what the Florentine's own position on this issue is. In order to obtain the latter, it will be most useful to turn once again to the text in which the majority of Ficino's Plethonian citations occur: the *Commentary on Plotinus*.

In the commentary on *Ennead* III.1, Ficino identifies the four doctrines concerning fate that Plotinus singles out for his own critique,[118] the most relevant of these in the present context being the fourth, which Ficino explicitly associates with Chrysippus. The commentator notes that according to this teaching there is a necessary succession of causes and no contingencies, and that Plotinus rejects this because it deprives the rational soul of freedom of choice.[119] In order to rectify this problem, Plotinus is said to have introduced two new distinctions not in the original Stoic theory: one between providence and fate/necessity, and the other between intellect, soul, and body. Applying these distinctions, the commentator says with

---

114. Pletho, *Lg.* 2.6, pp. 72–78 Alexandre.
115. Fo. 97v.
116. Fo. 98r.
117. Fo. 98v.
118. Ficino, *In Enn.* III.1.3 Gersh.
119. Ficino, *In Enn.* III.1.12 Gersh.

Plotinus that all things are under providence, and that under providence there are three kinds of cause: (a) "within fate" (*in fato*), the soul as governing the body and the bodily; (b) "outside fate" (*extra fatum*), the soul as separating/elevating itself from body and to intellect; and (c) "under fate" (*sub fato*), the soul as submitting to the body.[120]

This commentary in which Ficino follows the Plotinian text closely is followed by a kind of appendix called the *Summa Marsiliana*, in which Ficino sets out his more personal views with respect to the question of fate. Here the two distinctions not in the original Stoic theory—between providence and fate/necessity, and between intellect, soul, and body—are repeated together with statements of further ideas. These are, first, that necessity/fate should be reduced to either or both of a lower phase of world-soul and the power of celestial causes, and second, that necessity can be counteracted by either or both of matter and place. Most importantly, Ficino observes that, if necessity can be counteracted by natural things—that is, the matter and place just mentioned—it can certainly be counteracted by voluntary agents such as rational souls.[121]

At this point, the objection is anonymously introduced that everything must be according to necessity/fate because of the preexistence of effects in higher causes, to which Ficino's reply is that we must understand the aspect of dissimilarity as well as similarity between causes and effects.[122] The anonymous objector seems to be a *Platonic* rather than a Stoic fatalist and is apparently to be identified with "that legitimate Platonist" (*legitimus ille Platonicus*) mentioned in the next paragraph.[123] Now, it cannot be proven that Ficino is here referring with a certain wordplay to the Byzantine author of the *Laws* rather than to an advocate of Platonism in general. However, the possibility that he is making a specific albeit oblique reference is certainly an intriguing one.

120. Ficino, *In Enn.* III.1.13 Gersh.

121. Ficino, *In Enn.* III.1S.22 ed. Gersh.

122. Ficino, *In Enn.* III.1S.26, ed. Gersh. This metaphysical notion of preexistence is stated clearly in the first part of Pletho, *Lg.* 2.6 Alexandre and is—at least in its Plethonian version—the target of Ficino's hostile annotation on MS. Ricc. gr., fo. 98v.

123. Ficino, *In Enn.* III.1S.27, ed. Gersh.

Bibliography

Primary Sources

Albinus. "Introduction to Plato." (Alcin. *Intr.*) In *Platonis dialogi secundum Thrasylli tetralogias dispositi*, vol. 6. Edited by K. F. Hermann. Leipzig: Teubner, 1853.

——————. *Didascalicus.* (Alb. *Didasc.*) In *Albinos: Épitomé.* Edited and translated by P. Louis. Paris: Les Belles Lettres, 1945.

Alcinous. *Didaskalikos.* In *Alcinous: The Handbook of Platonism.* Translated with introduction and commentary by J. Dillon. Oxford: Oxford University Press, 1993.

Alexander of Aphrodisias. *De fato.* (Alex. Aphr. *Fat.*)

——————. *In Aristotelis Metaphysica commentaria.* (Alex. Aphr., *In Metaph.*) Edited by Michael Hayduck. Berlin: Reimer, 1891.

Algazel, *Metaphysics.* Edited by J. T. Muckle. Toronto: St. Michael's College, 1933.

Ammonius. *In Porphyrii isagogen sive quinque voces.* (Ammon. *Porph.*) Edited by A. Busse. Berlin: Reimer, 1891.

Anastasius Sinaita. *Anastasii Sinaitae in Hexaemeron anagogicarum contemplationum libros duodecim.* (Anast. S. *Hex.*) In *Anastasius of Sinai Hexaemeron.* Orientalia Christiana Analecta 278. Edited by D. Baggarly and C. A. Kuehn. Rome: Pontificio Istituto Orientale, 2007.

Anna Comnena, *Alexias.* (Anna Comn. *Al.*) Edited by D. R. Reinsch and A. Kambylis. Berlin: De Gruyter, 2001.

Anonymous. *Epigramma.* (An. *Epig.*) In *Anthologia Graeca.* Vol. 1, *Buch I–VI,* 164. Edited by H. Beckby. Munich: Heimeran, 1965.

——————. *Miscellanea Philosophica.* (An. *Misc.*) In *Anonymu philosophika symmeikta: A miscellany in the Tradition of Michael Psellos (Codex Baroccianus Greacus 131) = Anonymi miscellanea philosophica.* Corpus philosophorum medii aevi 6. Edited by N. Pontikos. Philosophi byzantini. Paris: Vrin, 1992.

Aquinas, Thomas. *Summa contra Gentiles.* Edited by P. Marc et al. Turin: Marietti, 1961–67.

Aristotle. *Ethica Nicomachea* (Arist. EN) Edited by Ingram Bywater. Oxford: Clarendon Press, 1894. Repr., 1962.

—————. *Metaphysics*. (Arist. *Metaph.*) Edited by W. D. Ross. Oxford: Clarendon Press, 1924.

—————. *Physica*. (Arist. *Ph.*) Edited by W. D. Ross. Oxford: Clarendon Press, 1950. Repr., 1966.

—————. *De Generatione et Corruptione*. In *Aristotle: On Sophistical Refutations. On Coming-to-Be and Passing Away. On the Cosmos*. Loeb Classical Library 400. Translated by E. S. Forster and D. J. Furley. Cambridge, MA: Harvard University Press, 1955.

—————. *De Anima* (Arist. De An.) Edited by W. D. Ross. Oxford: Clarendon Press, 1961. Repr., 1967.

—————. *De Caelo*. (Arist. *Cael.*) Edited by P. Moraux. Paris: Les Belles Lettres, 1965.

Athanasius Alexandrinus. *Epistulae ad Serapionem* (Ath. Ep. Serap.) Edited by H.-G. Opitz. Berlin: De Gruyter, 1940.

Averroes. *Commentarium Magnum in De Anima*. Edited by F. S. Crawford. Cambridge, MA: Mediaeval Academy of America, 1953.

Avicenna. *Liber de Anima (Avicenna Latinus)*. 2 vols. Edited by S. van Riet. Louvain: Peeters/Leiden: Brill, 1968, 1972.

Basile de Césarée. *Lettres*. (Bas. *Epist.*) 3 vols. Edited and translated by Y. Courtonne. Paris: Les Belles Lettres, 1957–66.

—————. *Sur le Saint-Esprit*. (Bas. *Spir.*) Greek ed. Translated by B. Pruche. Paris: Éditions du Cerf, 1968.

—————. *Contre Eunome*. (Bas. *Eun.*) 2 vols. Greek ed. Translated by B. Sesboüé, G. M. de Durand, and L. Doutreleau. Paris: Éditions du Cerf, 1982.

—————. *Hexaemeron*. (Bas. Hex.) Edited by S. Giet. Paris: Éditions du Cerf, 1968.

Bessarion. *In Calumniatorem Platonis*. (Bessar. *Calumn. Plat.*) In *Kardinal Bessarion als Theologe, Humanist und Staatsmann*. 3 vols. Edited by L. Mohler. Paderborn: Schöningh, 1923–42. Repr., 1967.

Clement of Alexandria. *Stromata*. (Clem. *Str.*) Edited by L. Früchtel, O. Stählin, and U. Treu. Berlin: Akademie Verlag, 1960, 1970.

Council of Constantinople 681. *Acta*. (CCP (681)) In *Acta conciliorum oecumenicorum Series secunda, volumen secundum: Concilium universale Constantinopolitanum tertium*, Pars 1–2. Edited by R. Riedinger. Berlin: De Gruyter, 1990–92.

Council of Ephesus 431. *Acta*. (C. Eph. (431)) In *Acta Conciliorum Oecumenicorum*, "Concilium Universale Ephesenum," Bk. I, vols. 1–5. Edited by E. Schwartz and J. Straub. Berlin: De Gruyter, 1927–30.

Cyril of Alexandria. *Commentary on John*. (Cyr. *Io.*) 3 vols. Edited by P. E. Pusey. Oxford: Clarendon, 1872. Repr., *Sancti patris nostril Cyrilli archiepiscopi Alexandrini Opera: Post Pontanum et Aubertum edidit P.E.Pusey, Bde. I–II: In XII prophetas, Bde. III–V: In D. Joannis Evangelium, Accedunt fragmenta varia necnon Tractatus ad Tiberium ad Tiberium diaconum duo, Oxonii 1868–1872*. 3 vols. Brussels: Culture et Civilization, 1965.

—————. *Deux dialogues christologiques*. Sources Chrétiennes 97. Edited by G.-M. de Durand. Paris: Éditions du Cerf, 1964. Quod Unus Sit Christus.

———. *Dialogues sur la Trinité.* (Cyr. *Dial. Trin.*) Sources Chrétiennes 231, 237, and 246. 3 vols. Edited and translated by G. M. D. Durand. Paris: Cerf, 1976–78.

———. "Epistula ad Nestorium." (Cyr. *Ep.* 17) In *Cyril of Alexandria: Select Letters.* Edited and translated by L. R. Wickham, 180–213. Oxford: Clarendon Press, 1983.

———. *Corpus.* In *Patrologia Graeca.* 1st ed., vols. 68–77. Edited by J.-P. Migne. Paris: Migne, 1859–64. Repr., Turnhout, 1991.

———. *Lettres Festales, Tome 1: Lettres 1–6.* Sources Chrétiennes 372. Edited by W. H. Burns and P. Évieux. Paris: Éditions du Cerf, 1991.

———. *Lettres Festales, Tome 2: Lettres 7–11.* Sources Chrétiennes 392. Edited by W. H. Burns and P. Évieux. Paris: Éditions du Cerf, 1993.

———. *Lettres Festales, Tome 3: Lettres 12–17.* Sources Chrétiennes 434. Edited by W. H. Burns. Paris: Éditions du Cerf, 1998.

———. *Festal Letters.* (Cyr. *Ep. Fest.*) Translated by Philip R. Amidon. Edited with introduction and notes by John J. O'Keefe, 1–30. Washington, DC: Catholic University of America Press, 2009.

———. *Commentary on John.* (Cyr. *Io.*) 2 vols. Translated by David R. Maxwell. Downers Gove, IL: IVP Academic Press, 2013.

———. *Gegen Julian, Buch 1–10 und Fragmente, Teil 1–2.* Die Griechischen Christlichen Schriftsteller der ersten Jahrhunderte Neue Folge 20–21. Edited by T. Brüggemann, W. Kinzig, and C. Riedweg. Berlin: De Gruyter, 2016–17.

———. *Gegen Julian.* (Cyr. *C. Jul.*). 2 vols. Edited by W. Kinzig and T. Brüggemann. Berlin: De Gruyter, 2017.

———. *Commentaire sur Jean.* Tome I: *Livre I.* (Cyr. *Io.*) Edited by B. Meunier. Paris: Cerf, 2018.

———. *Thesaurus de sancta consubstantiali trinitate.* (Cyr. *Thes.*) Edited by G. M. de Durand. Paris: Éditions du Cerf, 1976–78.

Damascius. *In Principiis.* (Dam. *Pr.*) In *Damascii successoris dubitationes et solutiones.* Edited by C. E. Ruelle. Paris: Klinsieck, 1889–99.

———. *De principiis.* (Dam. *Pr.*) Edited by L. G. Westerink. Paris: Les Belles Lettres, 1986–91.

———. *The Philosophical History.* (Dam. *Hist. Phil.*) Translated by Polymnia Athanassiadi. Athens: Apamea, 1999.

———. *In Parmenidem.* (Dam. *In Parm*) Edited by L. G. Westerink. Paris: Les Belles Lettres, 2002–3.

David. *Prolegomena et in Porphyrii Isagogen Commentarium.* (David *Prol.; in Porph.*) Commentaria in Aristotelem Graeca 18.2. Edited by A. Busse. Berlin: Reimer, 1904.

Dionysius the Areopagite. *De divinis nominibus.* (Dion. Ar. *DN*) Edited by B. R. Suchla. Berlin: De Gruyter, 1990.

———. *Corpus Dionysiacum,* vol. 2. (Dion. Ar. *CH; EH; Myst.; Ep.*) Patristische Texte und Studien 36. Edited by A. M. Ritter and G. Heil. Berlin: de Gruyter, 1991.

———. *Les Noms divins; la Théologie mystique.* (Dion Ar. *DN; Myst.*) Sources Chrétiennes 578–79. Translated by Y. De Andia. Paris: Cerf, 2016.

Diels, H., and W. Kranz, eds. *Die Fragmente der Vorsokratiker* (*Vorsokr.*), vol. 1. Berlin: Weidmann, 1951.

Elias. *In Porphyrii Isagogen et Aristotelis Categorias.* (Elias *in Porph.*; *In Cat.*) Commentaria in Aristotelem Graeca 18.1. Edited by A. Busse. Berlin: Reimer, 1900.

————. *In Porphyrii Isagogen.* (Pseud-Elias *in Porph.*) In *Lectures on Porphyry's Isagoge.* Edited by L. G. Westerink. Amsterdam: North-Holland, 1967.

Eunomius. *Apologia.* (Eun. Apol.) Edited by J.-P. Migne. *Patrologiae cursus completus.* Series Graeca 29. Paris: Migne, 1857–66.

Eusebius. *Preparatio Evangelica.* (Eus. P.e) Edited by K. Mras. Berlin: Akademie Verlag, 1956.

Evagrius Ponticus. *De oratione.* (Evagr. Pont. *Or.*) In *Patrologia Graeca*, vol. 79, 1165–200. Edited by J.-P. Migne. Paris: Migne, 1865.

George of Pisidia. *Carmi di Giorgio di Pisidia.* (Geo. Pis.) Edited by L. Tartaglia. Torino: Unione tipografico-editrice torinese, 1998.

————. *Hexaemeron.* (Geo. Pis. *Hex.*) Giorgio di Pisidia, Esamerone edited by F. Gonnelli. Pisa: 1998.

George of Trebizond. *Comparatio platonis et aristotelis a georgio trapezuntio edita.* Venezia: Jacobus Pentius de Leuco, 1523.

Gregory Acindynus. *Epistula.* (Greg. Acind. *Ep.*) In *Letters of Gregory Akindynos.* Edited by A. C. Hero. Washington, DC: Dumbarton Oaks Research Library and Collection, 1983.

Gregory Palamas. *Epistola ad Joannem et Theodorem.* (Greg. Pal. *Epist. Jo. et Th.*) In Γρηγορίου τοῦ Παλαμᾶ συγγράμματα, Τόμος Ε΄. Σ, 231–46. Edited by Π. Κ. Χρηστου. Θεσσαλονίκη: ΕΚΔΟΤΙΚΟΣ ΟΙΚΟΣ ΚΥΡΟΜΑΝΟΣ, 1992.

————. *Laudatio Petri Athonita.* (Greg. Pal. *Laud. Pet. Ath.*) In Γρηγορίου τοῦ Παλαμᾶ συγγράμματα. Τόμος Ε΄. Σ, 161–91. Edited by Π. Κ. Χρηστου. Θεσσαλονίκη: ΕΚΔΟΤΙΚΟΣ ΟΙΚΟΣ ΚΥΡΟΜΑΝΟΣ, 1992.

Gregory of Nazianzus. *Expositio Rectae Confessionis* 11. (Greg. Naz.) In *Patrologia Gracea.* Vol. 6, 1225 BC. Edited by J.-P. Migne. Paris: Migne, 1858.

————. *In Theophania.* (Greg. Naz. *Or. 38*) In *Patrologia Graeca.* Vol. 36, 311–34. Edited by J.-P. Migne. Paris: Migne, 1858.

————. *De theologia.* (Greg. Naz. *Or. 28*) In *Grégoire de Nazianz: Discours 27–31,* 100–175. Sources Chrétiennes 250. Edited by P. Gallay. Paris: Cerf, 1978.

————. *Oratio 29.* (Greg. Naz. *Or. 29*) In *Grégoire de Nazianze: Discours 27–31.* Sources Chrétiennes 250. Edited by P. Gallay. Paris: Cerf, 1978. *In laudem magni Athanasii episcopi Alexandrini.* (Greg. Naz. Or. 21) In *Grégoire de Nazianze: Discours 20–23,* 110–193. Sources Chrétiennes 270. Edited by J. Mossay and G. Lafontaine. Paris: Cerf, 1980.

Gregory of Nyssa. *Antirrheticus,* 2. (Greg. Nyss. *Apoll.*). In *Patrologia Graeca.* Vol. 45, 1128B. Edited by J.-P. Migne. Paris: Migne, 1863.

————. *De hominis opificio.* (Greg. Nyss. *Hom. Opif.*) In *La Création de l'homme.* Sources Chrétiennes 6. Edited by J. Place. Paris: Cerf, 1943.

————. *Gregorii Nysseni Opera.* (Greg. Nyss.) Edited by E. Mülenberg and G. Maspero. Leiden: Brill, 1960–present.

————. *In Canticum Canticorum*. Edited by H. Langerbeck, Leiden: Brill, 1960.

————. *Sermones de creatione hominis*. (Greg. Nyss. *Hom. creat.*) Gregorri Nysseni Opera, Supplementum. Edited by H. Hörner. Leiden: Brill, 1972.

————. *In illud: Tunc et ipse filius*. Edited by K. Kenneth Downing et al. Leiden: Brill, 1987.

————. *Sull' anima e la resurrezione*. (Greg. Nyss. *anim. et res.*) Edited by I. L. E. Ramelli. Milan: Bompania, 2007.

————. *De Opificio Hominis*. (Greg. Nyss. *Hom. Opif.*) Edited by L. Sels. Cologne: Böhlau, 2009.

Hermias Alexandrinus. *In Platonis Phaedrum Scholia*. (Herm. *In Phdr.*) Edited by C. M. Lucarini and C. Moreschini. Berlin: Walter de Gruyter, 2012.

Ioannes Italos. *Opuscula*. (Ital. *Quaest.*) In *Ioannes Italos: Quaestiones quodlibetales* (Ἀπορίαι καὶ λύσεις). Studia patristica et Byzantina 4. Edited by P. Joannou. Ettal: Buch-
Kunstverlag, 1956.

Ioannes Siceliotes. *Prolegomenon*. (Sicel. *Proleg.*) In *Prolegomenon Sylloge: Accedit maximi libellus de obiectionibus insolubilibus*, 393–420. Rhetores Graeci 14. Edited by H. Rabe. Leipzig: Teubner, 1931.

John Damascene. *Die Schriften des Johannes von Damaskos*, vol. 1. Edited by P. B. Kotter. Berlin: De Gruyter, 1969.

————. *Expositio fidei*. (Jo. D. *f.o.*) In *Die Schriften des Johannes von Damaskos*, vol. 2. Patristische Texte und Studien. Edited by B. Kotter. Berlin: Walter De Gruyter, 1973.

John Damascene and Cosmas of Jerusalem. *Canon in Sanctos Menam, Victorem, Vicentium, Stephanidem et in Sanctum Theodorum Studitam*. (Jo. D. et Cos. mel. *can.*) In *Analecta hymnica graeca e codicibus eruta Italiae inferioris*, vol. 3, 319–30. Edited by A. Kominis and G. Schirò. Rome: Istituto di Studi Bizantini e Neoellenici, Università di Roma, 1972.

John Damascus. (Jo. D. *dialect. Fus.*) In *Die Schriften des Johannes von Damaskos*, vols. 1–5. Patristische Texte und Studien. Edited by B. Kotter. Berlin: Walter De Gruyter, 1969–88.

John Italos. *Quaestiones Quodlibetales*. (Ital. *Quaest.*) Edited by Perikles Joannou. Buch-Kunstberlag, 1956.

John Philoponus. *In Aristotelis physicorum libros octo commentaria*. (Phlp. *In Ph.*) 2 vols. Edited by H. Vitelli. Berlin: Reimer, 1887–88.

————. *In Aristotelis de anima libros commentaria*. (Phlp. *De An.*) Edited by M. Hayduck. Berlin: Reimer, 1897.

————. *De Aeternitate Mundi contra Proclum*. (Phlp. *Procl.*) Edited by H. Rabe. Leipzig: Teubner, 1899.

Justinus Martyr. *Dialogus cum Tryphone*. (Just. *Dial.*) Edited by M. Marcovich. Berlin: de Gruyter, 1997.

Koetschau, P., ed. *Origenes, Werke 5: De Principiis*. Leipzig: Hinrichs, 1913.

Leontius of Byzantium. *In pentecosten*. (Leont. B. *Hom. 11*). In *Leontii presbyteri Constantinopolitani homiliae*, 347–65. Corpus Christianorum, Series Graeca 17. Edited by P. Allen and C. Datema. Turnhout: Brepols, 1987.

Marinus. *Vita di Proclo*. (Marin. *Procl.*) Edited by R. Masullo. Naples: M. D'Auria 1985. [Also in *Neoplatonic Saints: The Lives of Plotinus and Proclus by Their Students*. Translated with an introduction by M. Edwards. Liverpool: Liverpool University Press, 2000.]

Marsilio Ficino. *Florentini … Opera et quae hactenus extitere et quae in lucem nunc primum prodiere omnia*. 2 vols. Basel: Heinrich Petri, 1576. [Photographic repr., Turin: Bottega d'Erasmo, 1959. Later repr., Lucca: Société Marsile Ficin, 2011.]

———. *The 'Philebus' Commentary*. Edited by M. J. B. Allen. Berkeley: University of California Press, 1975.

———. *Platonic Theology*. 6 vols. Edited by M. J. B. Allen and J. Hankins. Cambridge, MA: Harvard University Press, 2001–6.

———. *Commentaire sur le Banquet de Platon. De l'Amour*. Edited by P. Laurens. Paris: Les Belles Lettres, 2002.

———. *On Dionysius the Areopagite*. 2 vols. Edited by M. J. B. Allen. Cambridge, MA: Harvard University Press, 2015.

———. *Commentary on Plotinus*. Edited by S. Gersh. Cambridge, MA: Harvard University Press, 2017–. [Two volumes to date.]

———. *De Christiana Religione*. Edited by G. Bartolucci. Pisa: Edizioni della Normale, 2019.

Maximus the Confessor. *Disputatio Biyzae*. (Max. *Bizya*) PG 90.

———. *Capitum de Charitate Centuria*. (Max. *Carit.*) In *Patrologia Graeca*, vol. 90, 959–1082. Edited by J.-P. Migne. Paris: Migne, 1857.

———. *Capitum de Theologia et Oeconomia Centuria*. (Max. *Cap. Theol.*) In *Patrologia Graeca*, vol. 90, 1084–173. Edited by J.-P. Migne. Paris: Migne, 1857.

———. *Opuscula Theologica et Polemica*. (Max. *Opusc.*) In *Patrologia Graeca*, vol. 91, 9–280. Edited by J.-P. Migne. Paris: Migne, 1863.

———. *Disputatio cum Pyrrho*. (Max. *Pyrr.*) In *Dispute de Maxime le Confesseur avec Pyrrhus*, 542–610. Edited by M. Doucet. Montréal: Université de Montreal, Institut d'Etudes Médiévales, 1972.

———. *Quaestiones ad Thalassium de scriptura*. (Max. *Qu. Thal.*) In *Maximi Confessoris Quaestiones ad Thalassium I, Quaestiones I–LV una cum latina interpretatione Ioannis Scotti Eriugenae iuxta posita*. Corpus Christianorum Series Graeca 7. Edited by C. Laga and C. Steel. Turnhout and Leuven: Brepols and Leuven University Press, 1980. [Also in *Maximi Confessoris Quaestiones ad Thalassium II, Quaestiones LVI–LXV una cum latina interpretatione Ioannis Scotti Eriugenae iuxta posita*, Corpus Christianorum Series Graeca 22. Edited by C. Laga and C. Steel. Turnhout and Leuven: Brepols and Leuven University Press, 1990.]

———. *Quaestiones et Dubia*. (Max. *Qu. Dub.*) In *Maximi Confessoris Quaestiones et Dubia*. Corpus Christianorum Series Graeca 10. Edited by J. Declerck. Turnhout and Leuven: Brepols and Leuven University Press, 1982.

———. *Mystagogia*. (Max. *Myst.*) In *Maximi Confessoris Mystagogia una cum Latina Interpretatione Anastasii Bibliothecarii*. Corpus Christianorum Series Graeca 69. Edited by C. Boudignon. Turnhout: Brepols, 2011.

———. *Ambiguorum Liber*. (Max. *Ambig.*) In *On Difficulties in the Church Fathers*, vol. 1. Dumbarton Oaks Medieval Library 28. Edited by N. Constas. Cambridge, MA: Harvard University Press, 2014.

Melloni, Alberto. "The Great Councils of the Orthodox Churches." In *Conciliorum oecumenicorum generaliumque decreta*. Brepols: Turnhout 2013.

Michael Psellos. *De omnifaria doctrina*. (Psell. *Omn.*) In "Michael Psellus: *De Omnifaria Doctrina*. Critical Text and Introduction." Dissertation by L. G. Westerink. Nijmegen, 1948.

———. *Theologica*, vol. 1. (Psell. *Theol.* 1) Edited by P. Gautier. Leipzig: Teubner, 1989.

———. *Epistola a Michele Cerulario*. (Psell. *Ep. Cer.*) Hellenica et Byzantina Neapolitana 15. Edited by U. Criscuolo. Napoli: Bibliopolis, 1990.

———. *Philosophica minora*. (Psell. *Phil. Min.*) Vols. 1–2. Bibliotheca scriptorum Graecorum et Romanorum Teubneriana. Edited by J. M. Duffy and D. J. O'Meara. Stuttgart: Teubner, 1992.

———. *Orationes panegyricae*. (Psell. *Or. Paneg.*) Scriptorum Graecorum et Romanorum Teubneriana. Edited by G. Dennis. Bibliotheca Stuttgart: Teubner, 1994.

———. *Theologica*, vol. 2. (Psell. *Theol.* 2) Bibliotheca scriptorum Graecorum et Romanorum Teubneriana. Edited by L. G. Westerink and J. M. Duffy. Munich: K. G. Saur, 2002.

———. *Chronographia*. (Psell. *Chron.*) Vols. 1–2. Millenium-Studien zu Kultur und Geschichte des ersten Jahrtausends 51. Edited by D. R. Reinsch. Berlin: Walter de Gruyter, 2014.

Nemesius. *De natura hominis*. (Nemes. *De Nat. Hom.*) In *Patrologia Graeca*, vol. 40, 604Aff. Edited by J.-P. Migne. Paris: Migne, 1863.

———. *On the Nature of Man*. (Nemes. *De Nat. Hom.*) Translated with introduction and notes by R. W. Sharples and P. J. Van der Eijk. Liverpool: Liverpool University Press, 2008.

Nicephorus Chumnos. *Anekdota*. (Niceph. Chumn. *Mund.; Aer.; Antithet.; Epist.*) In *Anecdota Graeca e codicibus regiis*, vol. 3, 356–408. Edited by J. F. Boissonade. Paris: F. G. Levrault, 1831.

———. *Against Plotinus*. (Niceph. Chumn. *Plot.*) In *Plotini Opera Omnia*, vol. 2, 1416–30. Edited by Friedrich Creuzer. Oxford: 1835.

———. *Ἐπιστολαί*. (Niceph. Chum. *Epist.*) In *Anecdota Nova*, 1–190. Edited by J.-F. Boissonade. Paris: Dumont, 1844.

———. "Nicephorus Chumnos." In *Patrologia Graeca*, vol. 140, 1397–526. Edited by J.-P. Migne. Paris: Garnier, 1887.

———. Ὅτι μήτε ἡ ὕλη πρὸ τῶν σωμάτων, μήτε τὰ εἴδη χωρίς, ἀλλ᾽ ὁμοῦ ταῦτα. (Niceph. Chum. *Mater.*) Edited by K. P. Christou. Thessaloniki: Kyromanos, 2002.

———. Περὶ τοῦ ὅτι μηδὲν ἀδύνατον οὔτ᾽ ἄπορον οὐδέν, οὐδὲ κατὰ λόγους τοὺςφυσικούς, ὕδωρ ἐπάνω τοῦ στερεώματος κατὰ τὴν τοῦ κόσμου γένεσιν ἀποτετάχθαι. (Niceph. Chumn. *Imposs.*) Edited by K. P. Christou. Thessaloniki: Kyromanos, 2002.

———. Περὶ τῶν πρώτων καὶ ἁπλῶν σωμάτων. (Niceph. Chumn. *Prim.*) Edited by K. P. Christou. Thessaloniki: Kyromanos, 2002.

————. Τὸ φιλοσοφικὸ ἔργο τοῦ Νικηφόρου Χούμνου. Edited by K. P. Christou. Thessaloniki: Kyromanos, 2002.

Nicephorus Gregoras. *Historia Romana.* (Nic. Greg. *H. R.*) In *Patrologia Graeca,* vol. 148, 119–450; vol. 149, 9–502. Edited by J.-P. Migne. Paris: Migne, 1865.

————. *Phlorentius.* (Niceph. Greg. *Phlor.*) In *Nikephoros Gregoras, Phlorentios, Fiorenzo o intorno alla Sapienza: Testo critico, introduzione, traduzione e commentario.* Edited by P. L. Leone. Napoli: Universita di Napoli, 1975.

Nicetas Stethatos. *Centuriae.* (Nic. Steth. *Cap.*) In *Patrologia Graeca,* vol. 120, 851–1010. Edited by J.-P. Migne. Paris: Migne, 1864. [Also in *Philokalia: The Complete Text, Compiled by St Nikodimos of the Holy Mountain and St Makarios of Corinth,* vol. 4, 79–174. Translated by G. E. H. Palmer, P. Sherrard, and K. Ware. London: Faber and Faber, 1998.]

————. *Vita Symeonis.* (Nic. Steth. *Symeon.*) In *Un grand mystique byzantin: Vie de Symeon le Nouveau Theologien (949–1022) par Nicetas Stethatos.* Orientalia Christiana 45. Edited by I. Hausherr. Translated by G. Horn. Roma: Pontificium Institutum Orientalium Studiorum, 1928.

————. *Ad Nicetam Chartophylax.* (Nic. Steth. *Ep. Nic. Chart.*) In *Nicétas Stéthatos: Opuscules et Lettres,* 234–44. Sources Chrétiennes 81. Edited by J. Darrouzès. Paris: Éditions du Cerf, 1961.

————. *Amico proximo.* (Nic. Steth. *Ep. Prox.*) In *Nicétas Stéthatos: Opuscules et Lettres,* 58–62. Sources Chrétiennes 81. Edited by J. Darrouzès. Paris: Cerf, 1961.

————. *De anima.* (Nic. Steth. *Anim.*) In *Nicétas Stéthatos: Opuscules et Lettres,* 89–126. Sources Chrétiennes 81. Edited by J. Darrouzès. Paris: Cerf, 1961.

————. *De hierarchia.* (Nic. Steth. *Hier.*) In *Nicétas Stéthatos: Opuscules et Lettres,* 300–365. Sources Chrétiennes 81. Edited by J. Darrouzès. Paris: Cerf, 1961.

————. *De paradiso.* (Nic. Steth. *Parad.*) In *Nicétas Stéthatos: Opuscules et Lettres,* 154–227. Sources Chrétiennes 81. Edited by J. Darrouzès. Paris: Cerf, 1961.

————. *De vitae limite.* (Nic. Steth. *Limit. Vit.*) In *Nicétas Stéthatos: Opuscules et Lettres,* 366–411. Sources Chrétiennes 81. Edited by J. Darrouzès. Paris: Cerf, 1961.

————. *Introductio in hymnos.* (Nic. Steth. *Intr. Hymn.*) In *Symeon Neos Theologos: Hymnen,* 13–24. Supplementa Byzantina 3. Edited by A. Kambylis. Berlin: Walter de Gruyter, 1976.

————. *Canon in Sanctum Nicolaum.* (Nic. Steth. *Can. Nic.*) In *Analecta Hymnica Greaca,* vol. 4, 179–89. Edited by G. Schirò and A. Kominis. Rome: Istituto di Studi Bizantini e Neoellenici—Università di Roma, 1976.

————. *Canon in Theodorum Studitam.* (Nic. Steth. *Can. Th.*) In D. A. Kaklamanos, "Un canon inédit de Nicétas Stéthatos en l'honneur de saint Théodore Stoudite." *Analecta Bollandiana* 137, no. 1 (2019): 103–19.

Nicholas Cusanus. *De non aliud.* Edited by E. Peroli. Milan: Bompiani, 2017.

Numénius. *Fragments.* Edited and translated by É. Des Places. Paris: Les Belles Lettres, 1973.

Oracles Chaldaïques. Edited by É. des Places. Paris: Les Belles Lettres, 1971.

Origen. *Scholia in Canticum canticorum* (Or. *Cant.*). Edited by J.-P. Migne. *Patrologiae cursus completus.* Series Graeca 75. Paris: Migne, 1857–66.

————. *In Celsum* (Or. *Cels.*) Edited by P. Koetschau. Leipzig: Hinrichs, 1897–99.

————. *Johanneskommentar.* (Orig. *Io.*) Edited by E. Preuschen. Leipzig: Hinrichs, 1899.

————. Homélies sur Jérémie. 2 vols. Edited by Pierre Husson and Pierre Nautin. Paris: Cerf, 1976–77.

————. *Homélies sur Ezéchiel.* Edited by Marcel Borret. Paris: Cerf, 1989.

————. *Der Römerbriefkommentar.* (*Comm. In Rom.*) 3 vols. Edited by C. P. Bammel. Freiburg: Herder, 1990–98.

————. *Commentaire sur le Cantique des Cantiques.* Edited by Luc Brésard and Henri Crouzel. Paris: Cerf, 1991.

————. *On First Principles.* (Or. *Prin.*) 2 vols. Edited by John Behr. Oxford. 2017.

Philip Monotropos. *Dioptra.* (Phil. Monotr. *Dioptr.*) Ὁ Ἄθως 1. Edited by S. Lauriotes. 1920; Repr., 2008, 331–504.

Philo Judaeus. *Legum allegoriarum.* (Philo *leg.*) In *Philonis Alexandrini: Opera quae supersunt,* vol. 1, 61–169. Edited by L. Cohn. Berlin: Reimer, 1896.

————. *De posteritate Caini.* (Philo *posterit.*) In *Philonis Alexandrini: Opera quae supersunt,* vol. 2, 1–41. Edited by P. Wendland. Berlin: Reimer, 1897.

————. *De congressu eruditionis gratia.* (Philo *congr.*) In *Philonis Alexandrini: Opera quae supersunt,* vol. 3, 72–109. Edited by P. Wendland. Berlin: Reimer, 1898.

Philoponus, Ioannes. *In De Anima commentaria.* Edited by M. Hayduck, Berlin: Reimer 1897.

Philotheus. *Laudatio Gregorii Palamas.* (Philoth. *Laud. Greg. Pal.*) In Φιλοθέου τοῦ Κωνσταντινουπόλεως τοῦ Κοκκίνου ἁγιολογικὰ ἔργα Α΄. Θεσσαλονικεῖς Ἅγιοι, Σ. 427–591. Edited by Δ. Γ. Τσάμης. Θεσσαλονίκη: Κέντρον Βυζαντινῶν Ερευνῶν, 1985.

Photius Diaconus. *Encomium in Sanctum Lucam.* (Phot. *Luc.*) In T. Antonopoulou, "Photios Deacon and Skeuophylax of the Holy Apostles and His Encomium on St Luke the Evangelist." *Jahrbuch der Österreichischen Byzantinistik* 55 (2005): 28–42.

Plato. *Platonis Opera.* (Pl.) Edited by J. Burnet. Oxford: Clarendon Press, 1899–1906. Repr., 1967–68.

————. *Res publica.* (Pl. *R.*) In *Platonis Rempublicam.* Scriptorum classicorum bibliotheca Oxoniensis. Edited by S. R. Slings. Oxford: Clarendon Press, 2003.

Pletho. *Traité des Lois: Ou Recueil des fragments.* (Pletho lg.) Edited by C. Alexandre. Translated by A. Pellissier. Paris: Firmin-Didot, 1858.

————. *Peri hōn Aristotelēs pros Platōna diapheretai.* (Pletho Diff.) In B. Lagarde, "Le *De Differentiis* de Pléthon d'après l'autographe de la Marcienne," *Byzantion* 43 (1973): 312–43.

————. *Pros tas Scholariou huper Aristotelous antilēpseis.* (Pletho Scholar.) In B. Lagarde, "Georges Gémiste Pléthon: *Contre les objections de Scholarios en faveur d'Aristote (Réplique).*" *Byzantion* 59 (1989): 354–507.

————. *Magika logia tōn apo Zōroastrou magōn … Oracles Chaldaïques, Recension de*

Georges Gémiste Pléthon. (Pletho Oracul. Chald.) Edited by B. Tambrun-Krasker. Athens: Academy of Athens/Paris: Vrin/Brussels: Ousia, 1995.

Plotinus. *Plotini opera.* (Plot.) 3 vols. Edited by P. Henry and H.-R. Schwyzer. Leiden: Brill, 1951; Paris: Desclée de Brouwer, 1959; Brussels: L'Édition universelle, 1959; Paris: Museum Lessianum, 1973; and Oxford: Oxford University Press, 1964–82.

——————. *Enneads.* Loeb Classical Library. Translated by A. H. Armstrong. Cambridge, MA: Harvard University Press, 1966–88.

Porphyry. *Life of Plotinus.* (Porph. *Plot.*) In *Plotini opera.* Edited by P. Henry and H.-R. Schwyzer. Leiden: Brill, 1951.

——————. *In Platonis Parmenidem.* (Porph. *In Prm.*) In *Porphyre et Victorius.* Edited by P. Hadot. Paris: Études augustiniennes, 1968.

——————. *Sententiae ad intelligibilia ducentes.* (Porph. *Sent.*) Bibliotheca Scriptorum Graecorum et Romanorum Teubneriana. Edited by E. Lamberz. Leipzig: Teubner, 1975.

——————. *Fragmenta.* (Porph. *Fr.*) Edited by A. Smith. Lepizig: Teubner, 1993.

——————. *Isagoge.* (Porph. *Intr.*) Edited by A. de Libera and A.-P. Segonds. Paris: Vrin, 1998.

——————. *Porphyre: Sentences. Études d'Introduction Texte Grec et Traduction Française, Commentaire de Luc Brisson avec une traduction anglaise de John Dillon.* (Porph. *Sent.*) 2 vols. Edited by L. Brisson. Translated by L. Brisson and J. Dillon. Paris: Vrin, 2005.

——————. *Sur la manière dont l'embryon reçoit l'âme.* (Porph. *Ad Gaur.*) Edited by L. Brisson. Paris: Vrin, 2009.

Proclus. *The Six Books of Proclus on the Theology of Plato.* (Procl. *Theol. Plat.*) 2 vols. Translated by T. Taylor. London: A. J. Valpy, 1816.

——————. *In primum Euclidis elementorum librum commentarii.* (Procl. *In Euc.*) Edited by G. Friedlein. Leipzig: Teubner, 1873.

——————. *In Platonis rem publicam commentarii.* (Procl. *In R.*) 2 vols. Edited by W. Kroll. Leipzig: Teubner, 1899–1901.

——————. *In Platonis Timaeum commentarii.* (Procl. *In Ti.*) Edited by E. Diehl. Leipzig: Teubner, 1903–6.

——————. *Elements of Theology.* (Procl. *ET.*) 2nd ed. Edited and translated with commentary by E. R. Dodds. Oxford: Oxford University Press, 1963.

——————. *Théologie platonicienne.* (Procl. *Theol. Plat.*) 6 vols. Edited and translated by H. D. Saffrey and L. G. Westerink. Paris: Les Belles Lettres, 1968–97.

——————. *De malorum substinentia* (Procl. De Mal.) Edited by D. Isaac. Paris: Les Belles Lettres, 1982.

——————. *Commentary on Plato's Parmenides.* (Procl. *In Parm.*) Translated by G. R. Morrow and J. M. Dillon. Introduction and notes by J. M. Dillon. Princeton, NJ: Princeton University Press, 1987.

——————. *In Cratylum* (Procl. Cra.) Edited by G. Pasquali, 1908. Repr., Stuttgart: Teubner, 1994.

——————. *Proclus' Hymns: Essays, Translations, Commentary.* (Procl. *H.*) Translated with introduction and commentary by R. van den Berg. Leiden: Brill, 2000.

————. *Sur le premier Alcibiade de Platon*. (Procl. *In Alc.*) 2 vols. Edited and translated by A.-P. Segonds. Paris: Les Belles Lettres, 2003.

————. *In Platonis Parmenidem commentaria*. (Procl. *In Prm.*) Edited by C. Steel. Oxford: Oxford University Press, 2007.

Schwartz, E., and J. Straub, eds. *Acta Concilium Oecumenicorum, Series Prima*. Berlin: Walter de Gruyter, 1914. Septuaginta. *The Old Testament in Greek*. 4 Vols. Edited by A. F. Brooke, N. McLean, and H. J. Thackeray. Cambridge: Cambridge University Press, 1906–40.

Simplicius. *In Aristotelis physicorum libros octo commentaria*. (Simp. *In Ph.*) 2 vols. Edited by H. Diels. Berlin: Reimer, 1882–95.

Synesius Cyrenensis. *Epistulae*. (Synes. *Ep.*) In *Synésios de Cyrène: Tome III; Correspondance; Lettres LXIV–CLVI*. Edited by A. Garzya. Translated with commentary by D. Roques. Paris: Les Belles Lettres, 2000.

Syrianus. *Syriani in Metaphysica Commentaria*. (Syrian. *In Metaph.*) Commentaria in Aristotelem Graeca 6.1. Edited by G. Kroll. Berlin: Reimer Verlag, 1902.

————. *On Aristotle's Metaphysics 3–4*. (Syrian. *In Metaph.* 3–4) Translated by D. O'Meara and J. Dillon. London: Duckworth, 2008.

————. *On Aristotle's Metaphysics 13–14*. (Syrian. *In Metaph.* 13–14) Translated by D. O'Meara and J. Dillon. London: Duckworth, 2014.

Tertullian. *Opera*. (Tert.) 2 vols. Edited by A. Gerlo. Turnhout: Brepols, 1954.

————. *De Anima*. (Tert.) Edited by J. H. Waszink. Amsterdam: Moehlenhoff, 1947.

Theophanes Continuatus. *Chronographia*. (Theoph. Cont. *Chron.*) In *Theophanis Continuati nomine fertur Liber V quo Vita Basilii imperatoris amplectitur*. Corpus fontium historiae Byzantinae 42. Series Berolinensis. Edited by I. Ševcenko. Berlin: De Gruyter, 2011.

Thesleff, H., ed. *The Pythagorean Texts of the Hellenistic Period*. Abo: Abo Akademi, 1965.

Thomas Aquinas. *In librum beati Dionysii De divinis nominibus*. Edited by C. Pera. Taurini: Marietti, 1950.

Valla, L. *In latinam novi testamenti interpretationem ex collatione graecorum exemplarium adnotationes apprime utiles*. Edited by D. Erasmus. Paris: Jehan Petit, 1505.

————. *Collatio Novi Testamenti, redazione inedita*. Edited by A. Perosa. Florence: Sansoni, 1970.

Secondary Sources

Abbate, M., trans. *Proclo: Commento alla "Repubblica" di Platone*. (Procl. *In R.*) Milan: Bompiani, 2004.

Addey, Crystal. *Divination and Theurgy in Neoplatonism: Oracles of the Gods*. Farnham: Ashgate, 2014.

Ahbel-Rappe, S. "Contemplative and Practical Virtue." In *The Reception of Greek Ethics in Late Antiquity and Byzantium*. Edited by A. Marmodoro and S. Xenofontos. Cambridge: Cambridge University Press, forthcoming.

Aland, K., M. Black, C. M. Martini, B. M. Metzger, and A. Wikgren, eds. *The Greek New Testament*. 2nd ed. Stuttgart: Württemberg Bible Society, 1968.

Allen, M. J. B. *Synoptic Art: Marsilio Ficino on the History of Platonic Interpretation*. Florence: Olschki, 1998.

Amato, E., and I. Ramelli. "Filosofia *rhetoricans* in Niceforo Cumno: L'inedito trattato *Sui corpi primi e semplici*." *Medioevo greco* 6 (2006): 1–40.

Anastos, M. V. "Basil's Κατὰ Εὐνομίου: A Critical Analysis." In *Basil of Caesarea: Christian, Humanist, Ascetic. A Sixteenth-Hundredth Anniversary Symposium*, 67–136. Edited by P. J. Fedwick. Toronto: Pontifical Institute of Medieval Studies, 1981.

Armstrong, A. H. "Platonic Eros and Christian Agape." *Downside Review* 75 (1961): 105–21.

Ayroulet, E. *De l'image à l'image:* Réflexions sur un concept clef de la doctrine de la divinisation de Saint Maxime le Confesseur. Rome: Institutum Patristicum Augustinianum, 2013.

Baltussen, H. *Philosophy and Exegesis in Simplicius: The Methodology of a Commentator*. London: Duckworth, 2008.

Baltzly, D. "The Virtues and 'Becoming Like God': Alcinous to Proclus." *Oxford Studies in Ancient Philosophy* 26 (2004): 297–321.

Barnes, J. *Porphyry: Introduction*. Oxford: Oxford University Press, 2003.

Baur, L. *Cusanus Texte. III. Marginalien. I. Nicolaus Cusanus und Ps. Dionysius im Lichte der Ziate und Randbemerkungen des Cusanus. Sitzungsberichte d. Heidl. Akad. d. Wissenschaften, Phil.-hist. Kl. Jahrg. 1940–1941*. 4 Abh. Heidelberg: Carl Winter, 1941.

Becker, A. *Platons "Politeia": Ein systematischer Kommentar*. Reclams Universal-Bibliothek. Ditzingen: Reclam, 2017.

Béguin, V. "Ineffable et indicible chez Damascius." *Les Études Philosophiques* 4 (2013): 553–69.

Beierwaltes, W. *Proklos*. Frankfurt: Vittorio Klostermann, 1979.

————. *Selbsterkenntnis und Erfahrung der Einheit: Plotinus Enneade V.3. Text, Übersetzung, Interpretation, Erläuterungen*. Frankfurt: Klostermann, 1991.

————. "Dionysios Areopagites—Ein christlicher Proklos." In *Platon in der abendländischen Gestesgeschichte*, 71–100. Edited by T. Kobusch and B. Mojsisch. Darmstadt: Wissenschatliche Buchgesellschaft, 1997.

————. "Dionigi Areopagita—Un Proclo cristiano?" In *Platonismo nel Cristianesimo*, 49–97. Edited by W. Beierwaltes. Milan: Vita e Pensiero, 2000.

————. *Das wahre Selbst*. Frankfurt: Vittorio Klostermann, 2001.

————. "Nous: Unity in Difference." In *Platonism and Forms of Intelligence*, 231–46. Edited by J. Dillon and M.-E. Zovko. Berlin: Akademie Verlag, 2008.

Bejczy, I. P. *The Cardinal Virtues in the Middle Ages: A Study in Moral Thought from the Fourth to the Fourteenth Century*. Leiden: Brill, 2011.

Benakis, L. G. "To problêma tôn genikôn ennoiôn kai o ennoiologikos realismos tôn Byzantinôn." *Philosophia* 8/9 (1978–79): 311–40.

————. "Nikephoros Choumnos (1250–1327), *Über die Seele gegen Plotin*." In *Néoplatonisme et philosophie médiévale, Actes du Colloque international de Corfou, 6-8 octobre 1995*, 319–26. Edited by L. G. Benakis. Turnhout: Brepols, 1997.

Berestov, I. V. *Svoboda v filosofii Plotina* [Freedom in the philosophy of Plotinus].
St. Petersburg: St. Petersburg State University Publishers, 2007.

Beyer, H.-V. "Nikephoros Gregoras als Theologe und sein erstes Auftreten gegen die
Hesychasten." *Jahrbuch der Österreichischen Byzantinistik* 20 (1971): 171–88.

Bianca, C. *Da Bisanzio a Roma: Studi sul cardinal Bessarione.* Rome: Roma nel Rinascimento, 1999.

Blowers, P. M. "Maximus the Confessor, Gregory of Nyssa and the Concept of
'Perpetual Progress.'" *Vigiliae Christianae* 46, no. 2 (1992): 151–71.

Boersma, H. *Embodiment and Virtue in Gregory of Nyssa.* Oxford: Oxford University
Press, 2013.

Böhme, G., and H. Böhme. *Feuer, Wasser, Erde, Luft: Eine Kulturgeschichte der Elemente.*
Beck'sche Reihe. Munich: C. H. Beck, 1996.

Boulnois, M.-O. *La Paradoxe Trinitaire chez Cyrille d'Alexandrie.* Paris. Institut
d'Etudes Augstustiniennes, 1994.

———. "The Mystery of the Trinity According to Cyril of Alexandria: The De-
velopment of the Triad and Its Recapitulation into the Unity of Divinity." In *The
Theology of St. Cyril of Alexandria: A Critical Appreciation,* 75–111. Edited by
T. G. Weinandy and D. A. Keating. London: T&T Clark, 2003.

———. "Le Dieu supreme peut-il entrer en contact avec le monde? Un débat entre
païens et chrétiens sur la transcendence divine à partir du Contre Julien de Cyrille
d'Alexandrie." In *La transcendence dans la philosophie grecque tardive et dans le pensée
chrétienne: Actes du Vie congrès international de philosophie grecque, Athènes, 22–27
septembre 2004,* 177–96. Edited by E. Moutsopoulos and G. Lekkas. Paris: Vrin, 2007.

———. "Patristique et historie des dogmes." *Annuaire de l'école pratique des hautes
études (EPHE), Section des sciences religieuses* 119 (2012): 163–72.

Boys-Stones, G. *Platonist Philosophy 80 BC to AD 250: An Introduction and Collection of
Sources in Translation.* Cambridge: Cambridge University Press, 2018.

Brisson, L. "À quelles conditions peut-on parler de 'matière' dans le *Timée* de Platon."
Revue de métaphysique et de morale 37 (2003): 5–21.

———. "The Doctrine of the Degrees of Virtues in the Neoplatonists: An Analysis
of Poprhyry's 'Sentence' 32, Its Antecedents, and Its Heritage." In *Reading Plato in
Antiquity,* 89–105. Edited by H. Tarrant and D. Baltzly. London: Duckworth, 2006.

Burnett, C. "The Establishment of Medieval Hermeticism." In *The Medieval World.*
Edited by P. Linehan and J. L. Nelson. London: Routledge, 2001.

Bussanich, J. *The One and Its Relation to Intellect in Plotinus: A Commentary on Selected
Texts.* Leiden: Brill, 1988.

Bydén, B. "The Criticism of Aristotle in Nikephoros Gregoras' Florentius." In
ΔΩΡΟΝ ΡΟΔΟΠΟΙΚΙΛΟΝ: *Studies in Honour of Jan Olof Rosenqvist,* 107-22.
Edited by D. Searby et al. Uppsala: Uppsala Universitet, 2012.

Callahan, J. F. "Basil of Caesarea: A New Source for St. Augustine's Theory of Time."
Harvard Studies in Classical Philology 63 (1958): 437–54.

Caluori, D. "*Aporia* and the Limits of Reason and of Language in Damascius." In *The
Aporetic Tradition in Ancient Philosophy,* 269–84. Edited by G. Karamanolis and
V. Politis. Cambridge University Press, 2018.

Cameron A. "The Last Days of the Academy at Athens." *Proceedings of the Cambridge Philological Society* 195 (1969): 7–29.

Camporeale, S. *Lorenzo Valla: Umanesimo e teologia.* Florence: Istituto Nazionale di Studi sul Rinascimento, 1972.

Casas, G. "L'indicible comme principe paradigme néoplatonicien de l'apophatisme." *Cahiers philosophiques* 158 (March 2019): 19–32.

Chase, M. "La subsistence néoplanicienne de Porphyre à Théodore de Raithu." *Revue d'études anciennes et médiévales* 7–8 (2009–10): 37–52.

Chlup, R. *Proclus: An Introduction.* Cambridge: Cambridge University Press, 2012.

Chouliaras, A. "The Imago Trinitatis in St Symeon the New Theologian and Niketas Stethatos: Is This the Basic Source of St Gregory Palamas' Own Approach?" In *Papers Presented at the Seventeenth International Conference on Patristic Studies Held in Oxford 2015.* Vol. 22, *The Second Half of the Fourth Century: From the Fifth Century Onwards (Greek Writers), Gregory Palamas' Epistula III,* 493–503. Studia Patristica 96. Edited by M. Vinzent. Leuven: Peeters, 2017.

Chroust, A. H. "Late Hellenistic 'Textbook Definitions' of Philosophy." *Laval théologique et philosophique* 28, no. 1 (1972): 15–25.

Clark, E. A. *The Origenist Controversy.* Princeton, NJ: Princeton University Press, 1992.

Clucas, L. *The Trial of John Italos and the Crisis of Intellectual Values in Byzantium in the Eleventh Century.* Munich: Institut für Byzantinistik, Neugriechische Philologie und Byzantinische Kunstgeschichte, 1981.

Coluccia, G. L. *Basilio Bessarione: Lo spirito greco e l'Occidente.* Florence: Olschki, 2009.

Combès, J. Études néoplatoniciennes. Grenoble: Millon, 1989.

Constas, M. "Maximus the Confessor, Dionysius the Areopagite, and the Transformation of Christian Neoplatonism." *Pempousia Journal of Theological Studies* 2, no. 1 (2017): 1–13.

Constas, N. "'To Sleep, Perchance to Dream': The Middle State of Souls in Patristic and Byzantine Literature." *Dumbarton Oaks Papers* 55 (2001): 91–124.

Corsini, E., ed. *Il trattato 'De divinis nominibus' dello Pseudo-Dionigi e i commenti neoplatonici al Parmenide.* Torino: Università di Torino, 1962.

Courcelle, P. *Connais-toi toi-meme: De Socrate a saint Bernard.* Vol. 1, *Histoire du précepte delphique.* Paris: Brepols, 1974.

Cristiani, M. "Κόσμος αἰσθητός: Le système des cinq sens dans les *Ambigua* de Maxime le Confesseur." *Micrologus* 10 (2002): 449–62.

Crowley, T. H. "On the Use of Stoicheion in the Sense of 'Element.'" *Oxford Studies in Ancient Philosophy* 29 (2005): 367–94.

Daley, B. "Nature and 'Mode of Union,' Late Patristic Models for Personal Unity in Christ." In *The Incarnation,* 164–96. Edited by S. T. Davis, D. Kendall, and G. O'Collins. Oxford: Oxford University Press, 2004.

de Andia, Y. *Henosis: L'union à Dieu Chez Denys l'Aréopagite.* Leiden: Brill, 1996.

DelCogliano, M. "Basil of Caesarea on Proverbs 8:22 and the Sources of Pro-Nicene Theology." *Journal of Theological Studies* 59, no. 1 (2008): 183–90.

———. "Basil of Caesarea, Didymus the Blind and the Anti-Pneumatomachian

Exegesis of *Amos* 4:13 and *John* 1:3." *Journal of Theological Studies* 61 (2010): 644–58.

——————. "Basil of Caesarea versus Eunomius of Cyzicus on the Nature of Time: A Patristic Reception of the Critique of Plato." *Vigiliae Christianae* 68 (2014): 498–532.

Delli, E. "La phantasia selon Michel Psellos et ses origines néoplatoniciennes: Une anthropologie de la médiété." 2 vols. PhD diss. École pratique des huates études, 2011.

de Vogel, C. J. "Amor quo caelum regitur." *Vivarium* 1 (1963): 2–34.

——————. "Greek Cosmic Love and the Christian Love of God: Boethius, Dionysius the Areopagite and the Author of the Fourth Gospel." *Vigiliae Christianae* 35, no. 1 (1981): 57–81.

Diamantopoulos, G. *Die Hermeneutik des Niketas Stethatos*. Münchner Arbeiten zur Byzantinistik 3.1–2. Neuried: Ars-Una, 2019.

Diekamp, F. *Die origenistischen Streitigkeiten im sechsten Jahrhundert und das fünfte allgemeine Concil*. Münster: Aschendorff, 1899.

Dillon, J. M. *Alcinous: The Handbook of Platonism*. Oxford: Clarendon Press, 1993.

——————. "Iamblichus' Criticisms of Plotinus' Doctrine of the Undescended Soul." In *Studi sull'anima in Plotino*, 337–51. Edited by R. Chiaradonna. Naples: Bibliopolis, 2005.

——————. "The Ideas as Thoughts of God." *Études Platoniciennes* 8 (2011): 31–42.

Dillon, J. M., and G. R. Morrow, trans. *Proclus' Commentary on Plato's Parmenides*. Princeton, NJ: Princeton University Press, 1987.

Dillon, J. M., and S. K. Wear. *Dionysius the Areopagite and the Neoplatonist Tradition: Despoiling the Hellenes*. Aldershot: Ashgate, 2007.

Dimitrakopoulos, I. "Γρηγορίου Παλαμά, Κεφάλαια εκατόν πεντήκοντα, 1-14: Ἱερὶ κόσμου.' Κείμενο, μετάφραση και ερμηνευτικά σχόλια." Βυζαντιακά 20 (2000): 293-348.

——————. "Ὑστεροβυζαντινή κοσμολογία. Η κριτική του Γρηγορίου Παλαμά στη διδασκαλία των Πλωτίνου και Πρόκλου περί κοσμικής ψυχής." Φιλοσοφία 31 (2001): 175-91.

——————. "Ὑστεροβυζαντινή κοσμολογία. Η κριτική του Γρηγορίου Παλαμά στη διδασκαλία των Πλωτίνου και Πρόκλου περί κοσμικής ψυχής. Β΄ μέρος." Φιλοσοφία 32 (2002): 111-32.

Dixaut, M. *La connaissance de Soi: Etudes sur le traité 49 de Plotin*. Paris: Vrin, 2002.

Dodds, E. R. "The Parmenides of Plato and the Origin of the Neoplatonic One." *Classical Quarterly* 22 (1928): 129–42.

——————, trans. *Proclus: The Elements of Theology*. (Procl. *ET*) 2nd ed. Oxford: Oxford University Press, 1963.

Dörrie, H. "Kontroversen um die Seelenwanderung im kaiserzeitlichen Platonismus." *Hermes* 85 (1957): 414–35.

Doull, J. "Neoplatonism and the Origin of the Older Modern Philosophy." In *The Perennial Tradition of Neoplatonism*, 486–516. Edited by J. C. Cleary. Leuven: Leuven University Press, 1997.

Dräseke, J. "Zu Dionysius." *Zeitschrift für Wissenschaftliche Theologie* 40 (1897): 613–17.

Edwards, M. J. *Neoplatonic Saints: The Lives of Plotinus and Proclus by Their Students.*
　　Liverpool: Liverpool University Press, 2001.
　　———. *Origen against Plato.* Farnham, UK: Ashgate, 2002.
　　———. "Porphyry and Cappadocian Logic." *Greek Orthodox Review* 60 (2015):
　　61–74.
　　———. "Dunamis and the Christian Trinity in Fourth-Century Theology." In
　　*Papers Presented at the Seventeenth International Conference on Patristic Studies
　　Held in Oxford 2015,* 105–22. Studia Patristica 84. Edited by M. Vinzent. Leuven:
　　Peeters, 2017.
　　———. "Origen and Gregory of Nyssa on the Song of Songs." In *Exploring Gregory
　　of Nyssa,* 74–92. Edited by A. Marmodoro and N. McLynn. Oxford: Oxford Uni-
　　versity Press, 2018.
　　———. *Aristotle and Early Christian Thought.* London: Routledge, 2019.
Emerson, S. D. "The Work of Christ According to Gregory of Nyssa." PhD diss., Van-
　　derbilt University, 1998.
Erismann, C. "Logic in Byzantium." In *The Cambridge Intellectual History of Byzantium,*
　　362–81. Edited by A. Kaldellis and N. Sinissoglou. Cambridge: Cambridge Uni-
　　versity Press, 2017.
Esposito Buckley, L. M. "Ecstatic and Emanating, Providential and Unifying: A Study
　　of Pseudo-Dionysian and Plotinian Concepts of Eros." *Journal of Neoplatonic
　　Studies* 1 (1992): 31–61.
Festugière, A. J., trans. *Proclus: Commentaire sur la République.* (Procl. *In R.*) Vol. 2.
　　Paris: Vrin, 1970.
Finamore, J. F. "The Tripartite Soul in Plato's Republic and Phaedrus." In *History of
　　Platonism: Plato Redivivus,* 35–51. Edited by J. F. Finamore and R. Berchman.
　　New Orleans: University Press of the South, 2005.
　　———. "Iamblichus on the Grades of Virtue." In *Iamblichus and the Foundation of
　　Late Platonism,* 113–32. Edited by E. Afonasin, J. Dillon, and J. Finamore. Leiden:
　　Brill, 2012.
　　———. "Plato's Timaean Psychology." In *Platonic Pathways: Papers from the
　　14th Annual Meeting for the International Society for Neoplatonic Studies,* 11–25.
　　Edited by J. F. Finamore and D. Layne. Bream, UK: Prometheus Trust, 2018.
　　———. "Ethics, Virtue, and Theurgy: On Being a Good Person in Late-
　　Neoplatonic Philosophy." In *The Reception of Greek Ethics in Late Antiquity
　　and Byzantium.* Edited by A. Marmodoro and S. Xenofontos. Cambridge:
　　Cambridge University Press, forthcoming.
Finamore, J. F., and J. M. Dillon, trans. *Iamblichus' De Anima: Text, Translation, and
　　Commentary.* (Iamb. *Anim.*) Leiden: Brill, 2002.
Fitzgerald, A. "Ambrose at the Well." *Revue des Études Augustiniennes* 48 (2002):
　　79–99.
Förstel, C. "Untersuchungen zur Rezeption Plotins in der Palaiologenzeit: Die
　　Handschriften A und E (*Laurentianus plut.* 87,3 und *Parisinus gr.* 1976)." In
　　Griechisch-byzantinische Handschriftenforschung: Traditionen, Entwicklungen, neue

Wege, 419–26. Edited by C. Brockmann, D. Deckers, D. Harlfinger, and S. Valente. Berlin: De Gruyter, 2020.

Frazze, C. A. "Anatolian Asceticism in the Fourth Century: Eustathios of Sebaste and Basil of Caesarea." *Catholic Historical Review* 66 (1980): 16–33.

Frede, M. "Monotheism and Pagan Philosophy in Antiquity." In *Pagan Monotheism in Late Antiquity*, 41–68. Edited by P. Athanassiadi and M. Frede. Oxford: Oxford University Press, 1999.

Fürst, A. *Origenes: Grieche und Christ in römischer Zeit.* Stuttgart: Hiersemann, 2018.

Gall, D., P. Riemer, U. Rombach, R. Simons, and C. Zintzen, eds. *Marsilio Ficino: Index nominum et index geographicus.* Hildesheim: Olms, 2003.

Gauthier, R. A. "Saint Maxime le Confesseur et la psychologie de l'acte humain." *Recherches de Théologie ancienne et médievale* 21 (1954): 51–100.

Gavrilyuk, P. "Did Ps.-Dionysius Live in Constantinople?" *Vigiliae Christianae* 62 (2008): 505–14.

Gentile, S., S. Niccoli, and P. Viti, eds. *Marsilio Ficino e il Ritorno di Platone: Mostra di manoscritti, stampe e documenti, 17 maggio – 16 giugno 1984, Catalogo.* Florence: Le Lettere, 1984.

Gersh, S. *From Iamblichus to Eriugena: An Investigation of the Prehistory and Evolution of the Pseudo-Dionysian Tradition.* Leiden: Brill, 1978.

————. "From the One to the Blank: Damascius." In *Being Different: More Neoplatonism after Derrida*, 115–68. Leiden: Brill, 2014.

Gerson, L. P. *Plotinus: Arguments of the Philosophers.* London: Routledge, 1994.

————, trans. *The Enneads.* Cambridge: Cambridge University Press, 2018.

Golitzin, A. "Hierarchy versus Anarchy? Dionysius Areopagita, Symeon the New Theologian, Nicetas Stethatos, and Their Common Roots in Ascetical Tradition." *St. Vladimir's Theological Quarterly* 38, no. 2 (1994): 131–79.

Grant, R. M. "Greek Literature in the Treatise *De Trinitate* and Cyril *Contra Julianum*." *Journal of Theological Studies* 15, no. 2 (1964): 265–79.

Greggs, T. *Barth, Origen and Universal Salvation.* Oxford: Oxford University Press, 2009.

Grigoras, A., trans. "Commentaires par le Père Dumitru Staniloae." In *Saint Maxime le Confesseur: Ambigua*, 375–540. Collection l'Arbre de Jessé. Translated by J. C. Larchet and E. Ponsoye. Paris: Les Éditions de l'Ancre, 1994. [Originally published as D. Staniloae, *Sfintul Maxim Mărturisitorul, Ambigua*. Părinţi si scrittori bisericeşti. Bucureşti: Editura Institutului biblic şi de misiune al Bisericii Ortodoxe Române, 1983.]

Gulliard, J. "Le Process official de Jean l'Italien: Les Actes et leurs sous-entendus." *Traveaux et Mémoires* 9 (1985): 133–74.

Hadot, P. "La conception plotinienne de l'identite entre l'intellect et son objet: Plotin et le De anima d'Aristote." In *Plotin, Porphyre: Etudes neoplatoniciennes*, 267-78. Paris: Les Belles Lettres, 1999.

Ham, B. *Plotin: Traite 49.* Vol. 3. Paris: Cerf, 2007.

Hampton, Alexander J. B., and John Peter Kenney. *Christian Platonism: A History.* Cambridge: Cambridge University Press, 2020.

Hanson, R. P. C. "Basil's Doctrine of Tradition in Relation to the Holy Spirit." *Vigiliae Christianae* 22 (1968): 241–55.

Happ, H. *Hyle: Studien zum aristotelischen Materie-Begriff*. Berlin: De Gruyter, 1971.

Hardy, E. R. "The Further Education of Cyril of Alexandria, 412–444: Questions and Problems." *Studia Patristica* 17, no. 1 (1982): 116–22.

Heine, R. *Origen: Homilies on Genesis and Exodus*. Washington, DC: Catholic University of America, 2010.

Hengstermann, C. *Origenes und der Ursprung der Freiheitsmetaphysik*. Münster: Aschendorff, 2015.

Hero, A. C. "Commentary." In *Letters of Gregory Akindynos*. Edited by A. C. Hero. Washington, DC: Dumbarton Oaks Research Library and Collection, 1983.

Hewitt, S. "God Is Not a Person (An Argument via Pantheism)." *International Journal for the Philosophy of Religion* 85 (2019): 281–96.

Hildebrand, S. M. *The Trinitarian Theology of Basil of Caesarea: A Synthesis of Greek Thought and Biblical Truth*. Washington, DC: Catholic University of America Press, 2007.

Hilpert, K. "Kardinaltugenden." In *Lexikon für Theologie und Kirche*. 3rd ed., vol. 5, 1232–34. Edited by W. Kaspar et al. Freiburg: Herder-Verlag, 1993–2001.

Horn, G. "Amour et Extase d'après Denys l'Aréopagite." *Revue d'ascétique et de mystique* 6 (1925): 278–89.

Hotes, M. "Du chien au philosophe: L'analogie du chien chez Diogène et Platon," *Revue de philosophie ancienne* 32 (2014): 3–33.

Humphries, T. L. *Who Is Chosen? Four Theories about Christian Salvation*. Eugene, OR: Wipf and Stock, 2017.

Hutchinson, D. M. *Plotinus on Consciousness*. Cambridge: Cambridge University Press, 2018.

Ierodiakonou, K. "The Anti-Logical Movement in the Fourteenth Century." In *Byzantine Philosophy and Its Ancient Sources*, 219–38. Edited by K. Ierodiakonou. Oxford: Oxford University Press, 2002.

————. "John Italos on Universals." *Documenti e Studi Sulla Tradizione Filosofica Medievale* 18 (2007): 231–47.

Ivanović, F. *Desiring the Beautiful: The Erotic-Aesthetic Dimension of Deification in Dionysius the Areopagite and Maximus the Confessor*. Washington, DC: Catholic University of America Press, 2019.

Jahn, A. *Dionysiaca: Sprachliche und Sachliche Platonische Blüthenlese aus Dionysios dem sog. Areopagiten*. Altona: Verlag von A. C. Reher, 1889.

Jenkins, D. "Michael Psellos." In *The Cambridge Intellectual History of Byzantium*, 447–61. Edited by A. Kaldellis and N. Siniossoglou. Cambridge: Cambridge University Press, 2017.

Joachim, H. H. "Aristotle's Conception of Chemical Combination." *Journal of Philology* 29 (1903): 72–86.

————. *Aristotle on Coming-to-Be and Passing-Away*. Oxford: Oxford University Press, 1922.

Johnson, A. P. "Astrology and the Will in Porphyry of Tyre." In *Causation and Creation in Late Antiquity,* 186–201. Edited by A. Marmodoro and B. D. Prince. Cambridge: Cambridge University Press, 2015.

Kapriev, G. "Nikephoros Chumnos." In *Die Philosophie des Mittelalters.* Vol. 1, *Byzanz, Judentum,* 110–11. Edited by A. Brungs, G. Kapriev, and V. Mudroch. Basel: Schwabe Verlag, 2019.

Karfík, F. "Par rapport à soi-même et par rapport aux autres: Une distinction clef dans le *Parménide* de Platon." In *Plato's Parmenides: Proceedings of the Fourth Symposium Platonicum Pragense,* 141–64. Edited by F. Karfík and A. Havlícek. Prague: Oikumene, 2005.

Keller, A. "Two Byzantine Scholars and Their Reception in Italy: 1. Marsiglio Ficino and Gemistos Plethon on Fate and Free Will; 2. Demetrios Raoul Kavakes on the Nature of the Sun." *Journal of the Warburg and Courtauld Institutes* 20 (1957): 363–70.

Klutstein, I. *Marsilio Ficino et la Théologie Ancienne—Oracles chaldaïques, hymnes orphiques, hymnes de Proclus.* Florence: Olschki, 1987.

Koch, H. "Proklus als Quelle des Pseudo-Dionysius Areopagita in der Lehre vom Bösen." *Philologus* 54 (1895): 438–54.

—————. *Pseudo-Dionysius Areopagita in seinen Beziehungen zum Neuplatonismus und Mysterienwesen.* Mainz: Verlag von Franz Kirchheim, 1900.

Kraft, A., and I. Perczel. "John Italos on the Eternity of the World: A New Critical Edition of Quaestio 71 with Translation and Commentary." *Byzantnische Zeitschrift* 111, no. 3 (2018): 659–720.

Krämer, H. J. *Der Ursprung der Geistmetaphysik.* Amsterdam: Schippers, 1964.

Krasikov, S. V. "Vizantijskoe myshlenie: Erudiciya protiv kreativnosti? (Nikifor Grigora i Varlaam Kalabrijskij)" ["Byzantine thought: erudition vs. creativity? (Nicephorus Gregoras and Barlaam of Calabria)"]. *Antichnaya drevnost i srednie veka* [*Antiquity and Middle Ages*] 31 (2000): 266-83.

Krausmüller, D. "Hiding in Plain Sight: Heterodox Trinitarian Speculation in the Writings of Niketas Stethatos." *Scrinium* 9 (2013): 255–84.

—————. "What Is Mortal in the Soul?" *Mukaddime* 6, no. 1 (2015): 1–17.

—————. "An Embattled Charismatic: Assertiveness and Invective in Niketas Stethatos' 'Spiritual Centuries.'" *Byzantine and Modern Greek Studies* 44, no. 1 (2020): 106–23.

Kretzmann, N., and E. Stump. "Absolute Simplicity." *Faith and Philosophy* 2, no. 4 (1985): 353–82.

Lackner, W. *Studien zur philosophischen Schultradition und zu dem Nemesioszitaten bei Maximos dem Bekenner.* Graz: Karl Franzes Universität zu Graz, 1962.

Lampert, J. "Origen on Time." *Laval théologique et philosophique* 52 (1996): 657.

Lankila, T. "The Corpus Areopagiticum as a Crypto-Pagan Project." *Journal for Late Antiquity Religion and Culture* 5 (2011): 14–40.

Laurent, V. "Une fondation monastique de Nicéphore Choumnos." *Revue des études byzantines* 12 (1954): 32–44.

Lauritzen, F. "The Debate on Faith and Reason." *Jahrbuch der Österreichischen Byzantinistik* 57 (2007): 75–82.

————. "Psello discepolo di Stethato." *Byzantinische Zeitschrift* 102, no. 2 (2008): 715–25.

————. "The Mixed Life of Plato's Philebus in Psellos' Chronographia (6a.8)." *Zbornik radova Vizantinološkog Instituta* 50 (2013): 399–409.

————. "Psellos and Plotinus." *Byzantinische Zeitschrift* 107, no. 2 (2014): 711–24.

————. "Late Antique Philosophy and the Poetry of George of Pisidia." *Wiener Studien Beiheft* 41 (2020): 59–68

Lauro, E. D. "Fall." In *The Westminster Handbook to Origen*. Edited by J. McGuckin, 1001–10. Louisville, KY: Westminster John Knox Press 2004.

Lekkas, G. *Liberté et progrès chez Origène*. Turnhout: Brepols, 2002.

Leone, P. L. "Alcune osservazioni sul Florentios di Niceforo Gregora." In *Byzantino-Sicula II: Miscellanea di scritti in memoria di Giuseppe Rossi Taibbi*, 335–45. Palermo: Istituto siciliano di studi bizantini e neoellenici, 1975.

————. "Appunti e note su alcuni opuscoli di Niceforo Gregora." *Nicolaus* 3, no. 2 (1975): 319–42.

————. "Introduzione." *Nikephoros Gregoras, Phlorentios, Fiorenzo o intorno alla sapienza*, 15-35. Edited by P. L. Leone. Napoli: Universita di Napoli, 1975.

Lévy, A. *Le Créé et l'incréé. Maxime le Confesseur et Thomas d'Aquin: Aux sources de la querelle palamienne*. Paris: Vrin, 2006.

Lienhard, J. T. "Ps-Athanasius Contra Sabellianos and Basil of Caesarea, Contra Sabellianos et Arium et Anomoes: Analysis and Comparison." *Vigiliae Christianae* 40 (1986): 365–89.

Lilla, S. *Dionigi l'Areopagita e il platonismo cristiano*. Brescia: Mocelliana, 2005.

Lollar, J. *To See in the Life of Things: The Contemplation of Nature in Maximus the Confessor and His Predecessors*. Monothéismes et philosophie 18. Turnhout: Brepols, 2013.

Magdalino, P. "From 'Encyclopaedism' to 'Humanism': The Turning Point of Basil II and the Millennium." In *Byzantium in the Eleventh Century: Being in Between. Papers from the 45th Spring Symposium of Byzantine Studies, Exeter College, Oxford, 24–6 March 2012*, 3–18. Edited by M. D. Lauxtermann and M. Whittow. Society for the Promotion of Byzantine Studies Publications 19. London: Routledge, 2017.

Mainoldi, E. *Dietro Dionigi l'Areopagita: La genesi e gli scopi del Corpus Dionysiacum*. Rome: Città Nuova, 2018.

Manolova, D. "Nikephoros Gregoras's Philomathes and Phlorentios." In *Dialogues and Debates from Late Antiquity to Late Byzantium*, 203-19. Edited by A. Cameron and N. Gaul. London: Routledge, 2017.

Mariev, S. "Plotinus in the Phlorentios of Nikephoros Gregoras." *Koinotaton Doron: Das späte Byzanz zwischen Machtlosigkeit und kultureller Blüte (1204–1461)*, 101-7. Edited by A. Berger et al. Berlin: De Gruyter, 2016.

————. "Neoplatonic Philosophy in Byzantium." In *Byzantine Perspectives on Neoplatonism*, 1-29. Edited by S. Mariev. Berlin: De Gruyter, 2017.

Marinis, V. "'He Who Is at the Point of Death': The Fate of the Soul in Byzantine Art and Liturgy." *Gesta* 54, no. 1 (2015): 59–84.

————. *Death and the Afterlife in Byzantium: The Fate of the Soul in Theology, Liturgy, and Art*. New York: Cambridge University Press, 2017.

Markus, D. "Anagogic Love between Neoplatonic Philosophers and Their Disciples in Late Antiquity." *International Journal of the Platonic Tradition* 10 (2016): 1–39.

Marmodoro, A. "Gregory of Nyssa on the Creation of the World." In *Causation and Creation in Late Antiquity*, 94–110. Edited by A. Marmodoro and B. D. Prince. Cambridge: Cambridge University Press, 2015.

Martens, P. M. "Embodiment, Heresy and the Hellenization of Christianity." *Harvard Theological Review* 108 (2015): 594–620.

————. "Response to Edwards." *Zeitschrift für Antikes Christentum* 23 (2019): 186–200.

Märtl, C., C. Kaiser, and T. Ricklin, eds. *"Inter graecos latinissimus, inter latinos graecissimus": Bessarion zwischen den Kulturen*. Berlin: De Gruyter, 2013.

Massaut, J.-P. *Critique et Tradition à la Veille de la Réforme en France*. Paris: Vrin, 1974.

McGuckin, J. A. *St. Cyril of Alexandria: The Christological Controversy*. Leiden: Brill, 1994.

McKinion, S. A. *Words, Imagery, and the Mystery of Christ: A Reconstruction of Cyril of Alexandria's Christology*. Leiden: Brill, 2000.

Meijering, E. P. "Cyril of Alexandria on the Platonists and the Trinity." In *God Being History: Studies in Patristic Philosophy*, 114–27. Oxford: Oxford University Press, 1975.

Mesch, W. "Materie/Material (*hylè*)." In *Platon-Lexikon: Begriffswörterbuch zu Platon und der platonischen Tradition*, 2 Auflage, 194–97. Darmstadt: Wissenschaftliche Buchgesellschaft, 2013.

Mesyats, S. "Iamblichus's Exegesis of Parmenides' Hypotheses and His Doctrine of the Divine Henads." In *Iamblichus and the Foundations of Late Platonism*, 151–75. Edited by E. Afonasin, J. Dillon, and J. Finamore. Leiden: Brill, 2012.

————. "Does the First Have a Hypostasis? Some Remarks to the History of the Term *Hypostasis* in Platonic and Christian Tradition of the 4th–5th Centuries AD." In *Papers Presented at the Sixteenth International Conference on Patristic Studies Held in Oxford 2011*. Vol. 10, *The Genres of Late Antique Literature; Foucault and the Practice of Patristics; Patristic Studies in Latin America; Historica*. Studia Patristica LXII, 41–56. Edited by M. Vinzent. Leuven: Peeters, 2013.

Meyendorff, J. "Le thème du 'retour en soi' dans la doctrine palamite du XIVe siècle." *Revue de l'historie des religions* 145, no. 2 (1954): 188–206.

————. "Spiritual Trends in Byzantium in the Late Thirteenth and Early Fourteenth Centuries." In *The Kariye Djami*. Vol. 4, *Studies in the Art of the Karije Djami and Its Intellectual Background*, 95–106. Edited by P. Underwood. Princeton, NJ: Princeton University Press, 1975.

————. *Introduction a l'étude de Grégoire Palamas*. Paris: Editions du Seuil, 1959.

Mitrea, D. "'Old Wine in New Bottles'? Gregory Palamas' Logos on Saint Peter of Athos (BHG 1506)." *Byzantine and Modern Greek Studies* 40, no. 2 (2016): 243-63.

Monfasani, J. *George of Trebizond: A Biography and a Study of His Rhetoric and Logic.* Leiden: Brill, 1976.

———, ed. *Collectanea Trapezuntiania: Texts, Documents and Bibliographies of George of Trebizond.* Binghamton, NY: Medieval and Renaissance Texts and Studies, 1984.

———. "Pseudo-Dionysius the Areopagite in Mid-Quattrocento Rome." In *Supplementum Festiuum: Studies in Honor of Paul Oskar Kristeller,* 189–219. Edited by J. Hankins, J. Monfasani, and F. Purnell Jr. Binghamton, NY: Medieval and Renaissance Texts and Studies, 1987.

———. *Byzantine Scholars in Renaissance Italy: Cardinal Bessarion and Other Emigrés.* Aldershot: Ashgate, 1995.

———. "Marsilio Ficino and the Plato-Aristotle Controversy." In *Marsilio Ficino: His Theology, His Philosophy, His Legacy,* 179–202. Edited by M. J. B. Allen and V. Rees. Leiden: Brill, 2002.

———. *Bessarion Scholasticus: A Study of Cardinal Bessarion's Latin Library.* Turnout: Brepols, 2011.

———. "Quality Control in Renaissance Translations: A Note of Pietro Balbi to Cardinal Oliviero Carafa." In *Roma e il papato nel Medioevo: Studi in onore di Massimo Miglio,* vol. 2, 129–40. Edited by A. Modigliani. Rome: Storia e Letteratura, 2012.

———. "*Prisca Theologia* in the Plato-Aristotle Controversy before Ficino." In *The Rebirth of Platonic Philosophy,* 47–59. Edited by J. Hankins and F. Meroi, Florence: Olschki, 2013. [Reprinted in his *Renaissance Humanism: From the Middle Ages to Modern Times.* Aldershot: Ashgate, 2015, item XII.]

Morani, M. *Nemesii Emeseni de natura hominis. Bibliotheca scriptorum Graecorum et Romanorum Teubneriana (BT).* Leipzig: Teubner, 1987.

Moreschini, C. "Aspetti della difesa del cristianesimo nell'attività letteraria di Gianfrancesco Pico della Mirandola." In *Giovanni e Giovanfrancesco Pico: L'opera e la fortuna di due studenti ferraresi,* 261–90. Edited by P. Castelli. Florence: Olschki, 1998.

———. "L'Autenticità del *Corpus Dionysianum*: Contestazione e difese." In *I Padri sotto il torchio: Le edizioni dell'antichità cristiana nei secoli xv–xvi,* 189–216. Edited by M. Cortesi. Florence: Sismel Edizioni del Galluzzo, 2002.

———. *Massimo il Confessore: Ambigua. Problemi metafisici e teologici su testi di Gregorio di Nazianzo e Dionigi Areopagita; Introduzione, traduzione, note e apparati di Claudio Moreschini.* Milan: Bompiani, 2003.

Mueller-Jourdan, P. *Typologie spatio-temporelle de l'Ecclesia byzantine: La Mystagogie de Maxime le Confesseur dans la culture philosophique de l'Antiquité tardive.* Leiden: Brill, 2005.

———. *Une initiation à la philosophie de l'antiquité tardive: Les leçons du pseudo-Elias.* Paris and Fribourg: Cerf and Academic Press, 2007.

Muhlenberg, E. *Apollinaris von Laodicea.* Göttingen: Vandenhoeck und Ruprecht, 1969.

Müller-Wiener, W. *Bildlexikon zur Topographie Istanbuls. Byzantion - Konstantinupolis*

———— *Istanbul bis zum Beginn des 17. Jahrhunderts*. Tübingen: Verlag Ernst Wasmuth, 1977.

Napoli, V. Ἐπέκεινα τοῦ ἑνός: *Il principio totalmente ineffabile tra dialettica ed esegesi in Damascio*. Catania, Palermo: CUECM–Officina di Studi Medievali, 2008.

Neuhausen, K. A. "Platons 'philosophischer' Hund bei Sextus Empiricus." *Rheinisches Museum* 118 (1975): 240–64.

O'Brien, C. S. "The Origin in Origen: Platonic Demiurgy or Christian Creation?" *Freiburger Zeitschrift für Philosophie und Theologie* 54, no. 1/2 (2007): 169–77.

————. "St Basil's Explanation of Creation." In *The Actuality of St Basil the Great*, 194–224. Edited by G. af Hällström. Turku: Åbo Akademi University Press, 2011.

————. "Creation, Cosmogony and Cappadocian Cosmology." In *The Ecumenical Legacy of the Cappadocians*, 7–20. Edited by N. Dumitrascu. New York: Palgrave Macmillan, 2015.

————. *The Demiurge in Ancient Thought: Secondary Gods and Divine Mediators*. Cambridge: Cambridge University Press, 2015.

————. "Middle Platonists and Pythagoreans." In *The Routledge Handbook of Early Christian Philosophy*, 280–92. Edited by M. Edwards. London: Routledge, 2021.

O'Daly, G. *Plotinus's Philosophy of the Self*. Shannon: Irish University Press, 1973.

Onfray, M. *Athiest Manifesto: The Case against Christianity, Judaism and Islam*. Translated by J. Leggatt. Serpent's Tail, 2008.

Oosthout, H. *Modes of Knowledge and the Transcendental: An Introduction to Plotinus Ennead 5, 3*. Amsterdam: Grüner, 1991.

Opsomer, J. "Proclus vs Plotinus on Matter." *Phronesis: A Journal of Ancient Philosophy* 46, no. 2 (2001): 154–88.

————. "Proclus." In *A History of Mind and Body in Late Antiquity*, 129–50. Edited by A. Marmodoro and S. Cartwright. Cambridge: Cambridge University Press, 2018.

Ouzounian, A. "David l'Invincible." In *Dictionnaire des Philosophes Antiques*. Vol. 2, 614–15. Edited by R. Goulet. Paris: CNRS Éditions, 1994.

Page, B. "Wherein Lies the Debate? Concerning Whether God Is a Person." *International Journal for Philosophy of Religion* 85 (2019): 297–317.

Papaioannou, S. "Sicily, Constantinople, Miletos: The Life of a Eunuch and the History of Byzantine Humanism." In *Myriobiblos: Essays on Byzantine Literature and Culture*, 261–84. Byzantinisches Archiv 29. Edited by T. Antonopoulou, S. Kotzabassi, and M. Lukaki. Berlin: De Gruyter, 2015.

Pelikan, J. "The 'Spiritual Sense' of Scripture: The Exegetical Basis for St Basil's Doctrine of the Holy Spirit." In *Basil of Caesarea: Christian, Humanist, Ascetic. A Sixteenth-Hundredth Anniversary Symposium*, 337–60. Edited by P. J. Fedwick. Toronto: Pontifical Institute of Medieval Studies, 1981.

Pentzopoulou-Valala, T. "Reading Nikitas Stethatos' 'On the Soul': The Problem of Free Will and Free Choice." *Philosophical Inquiry* 43, no. 3/4 (2019): 20–37.

Perczel, I. "Pseudo-Dionysius and the Platonic Theology." In *Proclus et la théologie platonicienne*, 491–532. Edited by A. P. Segonds and C. Steel. Leuven: Peeters, 2000.

————. "God as Monad and Henad: Dionysius the Areopagite and the Περὶ ἀρχῶν." In *Origeniana VIII*, 1193–209. Edited by L. Perrone. Leuven: Peeters, 2003.

————. "A Philosophical Myth in the Service of Christian Apologetics? Manichees and Origenists in the Sixth Century." In *Religious Apologetics—Philosophical Argumentation*, 205–36. Edited by Y. Schwartz and V. Krech. Tübingen: Mohr Siebeck, 2004.

————. "Dionysius the Areopagite." In *The Wiley-Blackwell Companion to Patristics*, 211–25. Edited by K. Parry, Oxford: Wiley-Blackwell, 2015.

Perkams, M. "Priscian of Lydia, Commentator on the De Anima in the Tradition of Iamblichus." *Mnemosyne* 58 (2005): 510–30.

Perl, E. D. *Theophany: The Neoplatonic Philosophy of Dionysius the Areopagite*. Albany: State University of New York Press, 2007.

————. "Ps. Dionysius the Areopagite." In *The Cambridge History of Philosophy in Late Antiquity*. Vol. 2, 767–87. Edited by L. P. Gerson. Cambridge: Cambridge University Press, 2010.

Petroff, V. "*Corpus Areopagiticum* as a Project in Intertextuality." In *Dire Dieu*, 253–75. Edited by B. Pouderon. Paris: Beauchesne, 2017.

Pitra, J. B. *Analecta sacra et classica spicilegio Solesmensi parata*. Vol. 5.1. Paris: Roger & Chernowitz, 1888.

Placida, R. "La presenza di Origene nelle omelie sul Cantico di Gregorio di Nissa." *Vetera Christianorum* 34 (1997): 33–49.

Plotini Opera. 3 vols. Edited by P. Henry and H.-R. Schwyzer. Paris: Desclée de Brouwer/Brussels: Édition Universelle/Leiden: Brill, 1951–73.

Podolak, P. "L'Amore divino nella tradizione platonica e nello Pseudo Dionigi Areopagita." *Adamantius* 14 (2008): 311–28.

Polemis, I. D. "Neoplatonic and Hesychastic Elements in the Early Teaching of Gregorios Palamas on the Union of Man with God: The Life of St. Peter of Athos." In *Pour une poétique de Byzance: Hommage à Vassilis Katsaros*, 205–21. Edited by S. Efthymiadis et al. Paris: Le Centre d'Études byzantines, néo-helléniques et sud-est européennes, École des Hautes études en Sciences sociales, 2015.

Portaru, M. "Classical Philosophical Influences: Aristotle and Platonism." In *The Oxford Handbook of Maximus the Confessor*, 127–48. Edited by P. Allen and N. Bronwen. Oxford: Oxford University Press, 2015.

Pospelov, D. A. *Grigorij Palama, svt. Slovo na zhitie prepodobnogo Petra Afonskogo*. Athone: Pustyn Novaya Fivaida Afonskogo Russkogo Svyato-Panteleimonova monastyrya, 2007.

Pratesi, P. "Balbi, Pietro." In *Dizionario Biografico degli Italiani*. Vol. 5. Rome: Treccani, 1963.

Radde-Gallwitz, A. *Basil of Caesarea, Gregory of Nyssa and the Transformation of Divine Simplicity*. Oxford: Oxford University Press, 2010.

Ramelli, I. L. E. "Christian Soteriology and Christian Platonism: Origen, Gregory of Nyssa, and the Biblical and Philosophical Basis of the Doctrine of Apokatastasis." *Vigiliae Christianae* 61, no. 3 (2007): 313–56.

————. "Origen, Patristic Philosophy, and Christian Platonism: Re-Thinking the Christianisation of Hellenism." *Vigiliae Christianae* 63 (2009): 217–63.

—————. "*In Illud: Tunc et Ipse Filius* … (1Cor 15,27–28): Gregory of Nyssa's Exegesis, Its Derivations from Origen, and Early Patristic Interpretations Related to Origen's." *Studia Patristica* 44 (2010): 259–74.

—————. "Gregory of Nyssa's Trinitarian Theology in *In Illud: Tunc et ipse Filius*: His Polemic against 'Arian' Subordinationism and Apokatastasis." In *Gregory of Nyssa: The Minor Treatises on Trinitarian Theology and Apollinarism. Proceedings of the 11th International Colloquium on Gregory of Nyssa (Tübingen, 17–20 September 2008)*, 445–78. Vigiliae Christianae Supplements 106. Edited by V. H. Drecoll and M. Berghaus. Leiden: Brill, 2011.

—————. "The Philosophical Stance of Allegory in Stoicism and Its Reception in Platonism, 'Pagan' and Christian: Origen in Dialogue with the Stoics and Plato." *International Journal of the Classical Tradition* 18 (2011): 335–71.

—————. "The Dialogue of Adamantius: Part One." *Studia Patristica* 52 (2012): 71–98.

—————. "Origen, Greek Philosophy, and the Birth of the Trinitarian Meaning of Hypostasis." *Harvard Theological Review* 105 (2012): 302–50.

—————. "Silenzio apofatico in Gregorio di Nissa." In *Silenzio e Parola*, 367–88. Edited by Vittorino Grossi. Rome: Augustinianum, 2012.

—————. *The Christian Doctrine of Apokatastasis: A Critical Assessment from the New Testament to Eriugena*. Vigiliae Christianae Supplements 120. Leiden: Brill, 2013.

—————. "Harmony between *Arkhē* and *Telos* in Patristic Platonism." *International Journal of the Platonic Tradition* 7 (2013): 1–49.

—————. "The Divine as Inaccessible Object of Knowledge in Ancient Platonism: A Common Philosophical Pattern across Religious Traditions." *Journal of the History of Ideas* 75, no. 2 (2014): 167–88.

—————. "Love." In *Encyclopedia of Ancient Christianity*. Vol. 2, 611–26. Edited by A. DiBerardino. Downers Grove, IL: InterVarsity, 2014.

—————. "The Stoic Doctrine of Oikeiosis and Its Transformation in Christian Platonism." *Apeiron* 47 (2014): 116–40.

—————. "Proclus and Christian Neoplatonism: A Case Study." In *The Ways of Byzantine Philosophy*, 37–70. Edited by Mikonja Knežević. Alhambra, CA: Sebastian Press, 2015.

—————. *Social Justice and the Legitimacy of Slavery: The Role of Philosophical Asceticism from Ancient Judaism to Late Antiquity*. Oxford: Oxford University Press, 2016.

—————. "Proclus of Constantinople and Apokatastasis." In *Proclus and His Legacy*, 95–122. Edited by D. Butorac and D. Layne. Berlin: de Gruyter, 2017.

—————. "Apokatastasis and Epektasis in *In Cant.*: The Relation between Two Core Doctrines in Gregory and Roots in Origen." In *Gregory of Nyssa: In Canticum Canticorum*, 312–39. Vigiliae Christianae Supplements 150. Edited by G. Maspero, M. Brugarolas, and I. Vigorelli. Leiden: Brill, 2018.

—————. "Mysticism and Mystic Apophaticism in Middle and Neoplatonism across Judaism, 'Paganism' and Christianity." In *Constructions of Mysticism as a Universal. Roots and Interactions across the Borders*. Studies in Oriental Religions Series 71. Edited by Annette Wilke. Wiesbaden: Harrassowitz, 2018.

—————. "Origen to Evagrius." In *Brill's Companion to the Reception of Plato in Antiquity*, 271–91. Edited by H. Tarrant, D. Baltzly, D. Layne, and F. Renaud. Leiden: Brill, 2018.

—————. "The Role of Allegory, Allegoresis, and Metaphor." *Journal of Greco-Roman Christianity and Judaism* 14 (2018): 130–57.

—————. "The Father in the Son, the Son in the Father in the Gospel of John: Sources and Reception of Dynamic Unity in Middle and Neoplatonism, 'Pagan' and Christian." *Journal of the Bible and Its Reception* 7 (2020): 31–66.

—————. "Time and Eternity." In *The Routledge Companion to Early Christian Philosophy*. Edited by M. Edwards. Oxford: Routledge, 2021.

—————. "The Logos/Nous One-Many between 'Pagan' and Christian Platonism, I–II." Lecture delivered at British Patristics, Cardiff, 2018; forthcoming in *Studia Patristica*.

—————. "Mystical Theology in Evagrius against the Backdrop of Gregory of Nyssa." In *Reappraising Mystical Theology in Eastern Christianity*. Edited by M. Pereira. Washington, DC: Catholic University of America Press, forthcoming.

—————. "Origen, Evagrios, and Dionysios." In *The Oxford Handbook to Dionysius the Areopagite*. Edited by Mark Edwards, Dimitrios Pallis, and Georgios Steiris. Oxford: Oxford University Press, forthcoming.

—————. "The Question of Origen's Conversion and His Philosophico-Theological Lexicon of *Epistrophē*." In *Religious and Philosophical Conversion*. Edited by H. Loehr and A. Despotis, Leiden: Brill, forthcoming.

Ramelli, I. L. E., and D. Konstan. *Terms for Eternity: Αἰώνιος and ἀίδιος in Classical and Christian Authors*. Piscataway, NJ: Gorgias Press, 2013.

Raven, C. E. *Apollinarism*. Cambridge: Cambridge University Press, 1923.

Remes, P. *Plotinus on Self: The Philosophy of the "We."* Cambridge: Cambridge University Press, 2009.

Reuter, M. "Plotinus on the Role of Nous in Self-Knowledge." PhD diss., University of Toronto, 1994.

Rice, E. F., Jr. *The Prefatory Epistles of Jacques Lefèvre d'Etaples and Related Texts*. New York: Columbia University Press, 1972.

Rich, A. N. M. "Reincarnation in Plotinus." *Mnemosyne* 10 (1957): 232–38.

Richter, G. *Die Dialektik des Johannes von Damaskos: Eine Untersuchung des Textes nach seinen Quellen und seiner Bedeutung*. Ettal: Buch-Kunstverlag, 1964.

Riehle, A. "Epistolography as Autobiography: Remarks on the Letter-Collections of Nikephoros Choumnos." *Parekbolai* 2 (2012): 1–22.

Rigo, A. "La Vita di Pietro l'Athonita (BHG 1506) scritta da Gregorio Palama." *Rivista di Studi Bizantini e Neoellenici* 32 (1995): 179–90.

—————. "Teodoro diacono della Madre di Dio delle Blacherne: La condanna (1094/1095) e le dottrine." *Rivista di Studi Bizantini e Neoellenici* 47 (2010): 293–318.

Rist, J. M. "A Note on Eros and Agape in Pseudo-Dionysius." *Vigiliae Christianae* 20, no. 4 (1966): 235–43.

—————. "Basil's 'Neoplatonism': Its Background and Nature." In *Basil of Caesarea: Christian, Humanist, Ascetic. A Sixteenth-Hundredth Anniversary Symposium*, 137–220. Edited by P. J. Fedwick. Toronto: Pontifical Institute of Medieval Studies, 1981.

—————. "Pseudo-Ammonius and the Soul/Body Problem in Some Platonic Texts of Late Antiquity." *American Journal of Philology* 109, no. 3 (1988): 402–15.

Robichaud, D. J.-J. "Valla and Erasmus on the Dionysian Question." In *Oxford Handbook to Dionysius the Areopagite*. Edited by M. Edwards, D. Pallis, and G. Steiris. Oxford: Oxford University Press, forthcoming.

Robinson, T. M. "Rasgos distintivos del dualismo mente-cuerpo en los escritos de Platón." *Arete: Revista de Filosofia* 12, no. 1 (2000): 43–66.

Roilos, P. *Amphoteroglossia: A Poetics of the Twelfth-Century Medieval Greek Novel*. Hellenic Studies 10. Washington, DC: Center for Hellenic Studies, 2005.

Roques, R. *L'univers Dionysien: Structure hiérarchique du monde selon le Pseudo-Denys*. Paris: Aubier, 1954.

Rorem, P., and J. C. Lamoreaux. *John of Scythopolis and the Dionysian Corpus: Annotating the Areopagite*. Oxford: Clarendon Press, 1998.

Rouerché, M. "Byzantine Philosophical Texts of the Seventh Century." *Jahrbuch der österreichischen Byzantinistik* 23 (1974): 61–76.

—————. "A Middle Byzantine Handbook of Logical Terminology." *Jahrbuch der österreichischen Byzantinistik* 29 (1980): 71–98.

—————. "The Definitions of Philosophy and a New Fragment of Stephanus the Philosopher." *Jahrbuch der* österreichischen *Byzantinistik* 40 (1990): 107–28.

Rousseau, P. *Basil of Caesarea*. Berkeley: University of California Press, 1994.

Saffrey, H. D. "Notes platoniciennes de Marsile Ficin dans un manuscrit de Proclus (Cod. Riccardianus 70)." *Bibliothèque d'humanisme et de renaissance* 21 (1959): 161–84.

—————. "Pietro Balbi et la première traduction latine de la *Théologie Platonicienne* de Proclus." In *Miscellanea codicologica F. Masai dicata*. 2 vols., 425–37. Edited by P. Cockshaw, M.-C. Garand, and P. Jodogne. Ghent: E. Story-Scientia, 1979–80.

Saffrey, H. D., A. P. Segonds, and C. Luna, trans. *Marinus: Proclus ou sur le Bonheur* (Marin. *Procl.*). Paris: Belles Lettres, 2002.

Sambursky, S. *The Physical World of Late Antiquity*. London: Routledge, 1962.

Sassi, N. "Mystical Union as Acknowledgment: Pseudo-Dionysius' Account of Henosis." *Greek, Roman, and Byzantine Studies* 56 (2016): 771–84.

Savvidis, K. *Athanasius: Werke, Band I. Die dogmatischen Schriften, Erster Teil, 4. Lieferung*. Berlin: De Gruyter, 2010.

Schäfer, C. *The Philosophy of Dionysius the Areopagite*. Leiden: Brill, 2006.

—————. "Herrschen und Selbstbeherrschung: der Mythos des *Politikos*." In *Platon als Mythologe*, 203–24. Edited by C. Schäfer. Darmstadt: Wissenschaftliche Buchgesellschaft, 2014.

Scholarios, George Gennadios. *Oeuvres completes*. 8 vols. Edited by L. Petit, X. A. Siderites, and M. Jugie. Paris: Maison de la bonne presse, 1928–36.

Ševčenko, I. Études sur la polémique entre Théodore Métochite et Nicéphore Choumnos. Brussels: Éditions de Byzantion, 1962.

—————. "Theodore Metochites, the Chora, and the Intellectual Trends of His Time." In *The Kariye Djami*. Vol. 4, *Studies in the Art of the Kariye Djami and Its Intellectual Background*. Edited by P. Underwood. Princeton, NJ: Princeton University Press, 1975.

Shchukin, T. A. "'On prevzojdyot sobstvennuyu prirodu': Tema samoobrashchyonnosti uma v 'Slove na zhitie prepodobnogo Petra Afonskogo' svyatitelya Grigoriya Palamy i v Enneades V.3 ["'It will overcome its own nature'. The topic of self-reversion of the intellect in the 'Logos on saint Peter of Athos' by Saint Gregory Palamas and in 'En.' V.3"]. *Bibliya i hristianskaya drevnost* [The Bible and Christian Antiquity] 1, no. 2 (2019): 212–30.

Sheppard, D. J. *Plato's Republic*. Edinburgh Philosophical Guides. Edinburgh: Edinburgh University Press, 2009.

Sherwood, P. "Notes on Maximus the Confessor." *American Benedictine Review* 1, no. 3 (1950): 347–56.

Shlenov, D. "'Принцип Познай себя' у прп. Никиты Стифата в контексте византийской традиции". *Богословский вестник* 28, no. 1 (2018): 96–126.

—————. "Учение прп. Никиты Стифата о 'четырех главных добродетелях' в контексте античной и византийской литературы. Часть I." *Богословский вестник* 32, no. 1 (2019): 192–209.

—————. "Учение прп. Никиты Стифата о 'четырех главных добродетелях' в контексте античной и византийской литературы. Часть II." *Богословский вестник* Богословский вестник 33, no. 2 (2019): 110–28.

Simonopetrites, M. (Nicholas Constas). "St Maximos the Confessor: The Reception of His Thought in East and West." In *Knowing the Purpose of Creation through the Resurrection: Proceedings of the Symposium on St Maximus the Confessor, Belgrade, October 18–21, 2012, 25–53*. Contemporary Christian Thought Series 20. Edited by M. Vasiljević. Alhambra, CA: Sebastian Press and the Faculty of Orthodox Theology, University of Belgrade, 2013.

Simplicius. *In Physica commentaria*. Edited by H. Diels. Berlin: Reimer, 1882–95.

—————. *In De Caelo commentaria*. Edited by J. L. Heiberg. Berlin: Reimer, 1884.

Skliris, D. "Le concept de 'tropos' chez Maxime le Confesseur." Diss., Université Paris IV-Sorbonne, 2015.

—————. "The Ontological Implications of Maximus the Confessor's Eschatology." In *Papers presented at the 17th International Conference on Patristic Studies Held in Oxford 2015*. Edited by V. Markus. *The Fountain and the Flood: Maximus the Confessor and Philosophical Enquiry*. Studia Patristica 89, 3–30. Edited by S. Mitralexis. Leuven, Paris, and Bristol, CT: Peeters, 2017.

—————. "Saint Maximus the Confessor's Trinitarian Theology of Nous, Logos and Spirit as a Model of Spirituality." In *Understanding Orthodox Christian Spirituality Today: Insights from Patristic and Contemporary Theology*, 41–51. Edited by O. Sevastyanova and N. Asproulis, Volos: Volos Academy, 2019.

Slings, S. R. *Critical Notes on Plato's "Politeia."* Mnemosyne 267. Edited by G. Boter and J. van Ophuijsen. Leiden: Brill, 2005.

Soldato, E. *Basilio Bessarione, Contro il calunniatore di Platone.* Rome: Edizioni di Storia e Letteratura, 2014.

Sorabji, R. ed. *Philoponus and the Rejection of Aristotelian Science.* London: Duckbacks, 1988.

——————. "Infinite Power Impressed: The Transformation of Aristotle's Physics and Theology." In *Aristotle Transformed: The Ancient Commentators and Their Influence,* 181–98. Edited by R. Sorabji. Ithaca, NY: Cornell University Press, 1990.

Sotiropoulos, C. G. Ἡ ἀξία τῶν τεσσάρων γενικῶν ἀρετῶν εἰς τὸν ἄνθρωπον. Athens: 1994.

Steel, C. "'Elementatio Evangelica': À propos de Maxime le Confesseur, Ambigua ad Ioh. XVII." In *The Four Gospels 1992: Festschrift Frans Neyrinck.* Vol. 3, 2419–32. Bibliotheca ephemeridum theologicarum Lovaniensium 100.3. Edited by F. van Segbroeck, C. M. Tuckett, G. Van Bell, and J. Verheyden. Leuven: Leuven University Press, 1992.

——————. "The Moral Purpose of the Human Body: A Reading of Timaeus 69–72." *Phronesis: A Journal for Ancient Philosophy* 46, no. 2 (2001).

Stiglmayr, J. "Der Neuplatoniker Proklos als Vorlage des sog. Dionysius Areopagita in der Lehre von Übel." *Historisches Jahrbuch* 16 (1895): 253–73, 721–48.

Suchla, B. R. "Die sogenannten Maximus-Scholien des *Corpus Dionysiacum Areopagiticum.*" *Nachrichten der Akademie der Wissenschaften in Göttingen. Philologisch-Historische Klasse* 3 (1980): 31–66.

——————. "Die Überlieferung des Prologs des Johannes von Skythopolis zum griechischen *Corpus Dionysiacum Areopagiticum.*" *Nachrichten der Akademie der Wissenschaften in Göttingen. Philologisch-Historische Klasse* 4 (1984): 176–88.

——————. "Eine Redaktion des griechischen *Corpus Dionysiacum Areopagiticum* im Umkreis des Johannes von Skythopolis, des Verfassers von Prolog und Scholien: ein dritter Beitrag zur Überlieferungsgeschichte des *Corpus Dionysiacum.*" *Nachrichten der Akademie der Wissenschaften in Göttingen. Philologisch-Historische Klasse* 4 (1985): 177–93.

——————. "Die Überlieferung von Prolog und Scholien des Johannes von Skythopolis zum griechischen *Corpus Dionysiacum Areopagiticum.*" *Studia Patristica* 18, no. 2 (1989): 79–83.

——————. "Verteidigung eines platonischen Denkmodells einer christlichen Welt: Die philosophie und theologiegeschichtliche Bedeutung des Scholienwerks des Johannes von Skythopolis zu den areopagitischen Traktaten." *Nachrichten der Akademie der Wissenschaften in Göttingen. Philologisch-Historische Klasse* 1 (1995): 1–28.

Swinburne, R. *The Coherence of Theism.* 2nd ed. Oxford: Oxford University Press, 2016.

Talbot, A.-M. "*Philanthropos: Typikon* of Irene Choumnaina Palaiologina for the Convent of Christ *Philanthropos* in Constantinople." In *Byzantine Monastic Foundation Documents: A Complete Translation of the Surviving Founders' Typika and Testaments,* 1383–88. Washington, DC: Dumbarton Oaks Research Library and Collection, 2000.

Tambrun-Krasker, B. "Allusions antipalamites dans le *Commentaire* de Pléthon sur les *Oracles chaldaïques.*" *Revue des études augustiniennes* 38 (1992): 168–79.

——————. *Pléthon, Le retour de Platon.* Paris: Vrin, 2006. Edited by J. Thomas and

A. Constantinides Hero. Washington, DC: Dumbarton Oaks Research Library and Collection, 2000.

Tardieu, M. "Pléthon lecteur des Oracles." *Métis* 2 (1987): 141–64.

Thorndike, L. *A History of Magic and Experimental Science during the First Thirteen Centuries of Our Era* I. New York: Columbia University Press, 1923.

Tollefsen, T. T. *The Christocentric Cosmology of St Maximus the Confessor.* Oxford: Oxford University Press, 2008.

—————. *Activity and Participation in Late Antique and Early Christian Thought.* Oxford: Oxford University Press, 2012.

Torrance, I. R. *Christology after Chalcedon: Severus of Antioch and Sergius the Monophysite.* Norwich, UK: Canterbury Press, 1988.

Trizio, M. "A Late Antique Debate on Matter-Evil Revisited in 11th Century Byzantium: John Italos and His 'Quaestio' 92." In *Fate, Providence and Moral Responsibility in Ancient, Medieval and Modern Thought: Studies in Honour of Carlos Steel,* 383–94. Edited by P. d'Hoine and C. Steel. Leuven: Leuven University Press, 2014.

Trostyanskiy, S. *St. Cyril of Alexandria's Metaphysics of the Incarnation.* New York: Peter Lang, 2016.

Tsames, D. G. *Ἡ τελείωσις τοῦ ἀνθρώπου κατὰ Νικήταν τὸν Στηθᾶτον. Ἀνάλεκτα Βλατάδων* 11. Thessalonike: Πατριαρχικὸν Ἵδρυμα Πατερικῶν Μελετῶν, 1971.

Turescu, L. "Prosopon and Hypostasis in Basil's Against Eunomius and the Epistles." *Vigiliae Christianae* 51 (1997): 374–93.

Vaggione, R. P. *Eunomius: The Extant Works.* Oxford Early Christian Texts. Oxford: Oxford University Press, 1987.

Van der Berg, Robert. *Proclus' Hymns.* Leiden: Brill, 2001.

Van Loon, H. *The Dyophysite Christology of Cyril of Alexandria.* Leiden: Brill, 2009.

Van Riel, G. *Plato's Gods.* London: Routledge, 2013.

Vansteenberghe, E. *Le cardinal Nicolas de Cues (1401–1461), l'action–la pensée.* Paris: Honoré Champion, 1920.

Vasilakis, D. A. "Platonic Eros, Moral Egoism, and Proclus." In *Proclus and His Legacy,* 45–52. Edited by D. Butorac and D. Layne. Berlin: de Gruyter, 2017.

Verpeaux, J. *Nicéphore Choumnos, homme d'État et humaniste byzantin (ca. 1250/1255–1327).* Paris: Éditions A. et J. Picard, 1959.

Verrycken, K. "The Development of Philoponus' Thought and Its Chronology." In *Aristotle Transformed: The Ancient Commentators and Their Influence,* 233–74. Edited by R. Sorabji. Ithaca, NY: Cornell University Press, 1990.

Vinogradov, A. "Istochniki, ispolzuemye svyatitelem Grigoriem Palamoj" ["Sources used by saint Gregory Palamas"]. In *Grigorij Palama, svt. Slovo na zhitie prepodobnogo Petra Afonskogo* [*Saint Gregory Palamas Logos on Saint Peter of Athos*], 135-48. Edited by D. A. Pospelov. Athone: Pustyn Novaya Fivaida Afonskogo Russkogo Svyato-Panteleimonova monastyrya [New Thebaid Hermitage of the Athonite Russian Monastery of Saint Panteleimon]. 2007.

Vlad, M. *Damascius et l'ineffable: Récit de l'impossible discours.* Paris: Vrin, 2019.

Walter, D. *Michael Psellos: Christliche Philosophie in Byzanz; Mittelalterliche Philosophie im Verhältnis zu Antike und Spätantike.* Quellen und Studien zur Philosophie 132. Berlin: Walter de Gruyter, 2017.

Watts, E. "Doctrine, Anecdote, and Action: Reconsidering the Social History of the Last Platonists (c. 430–c. 550 C.E.)." *Classical Philology* 106, no. 3 (July 2011): 226–44.

Wehrhahn, H. M. "Spätkarolingische Wandmalerei in Reichenau-Oberzell?" In *Bibliotheca docet: Festgabe für Carl Wehmer*, 335–53. Edited by S. Joost. Amsterdam: Verlag der Erasmus-Buchhandlung, 1963.

Westerink, L. G., trans. *Olympiodorus* (Olymp. *In Phd.*) and *Damascius* (Dam. *In Phd.*). In *The Greek Commentaries on Plato's Phaedo.* Amsterdam: North Holland, 1976–77.

White, D. A. *Myth, Metaphysics and Dialectic in Plato's "Statesman."* Aldershot: Ashgate, 2007.

Whittaker, J. "The Historical Background of Proclus' Doctrine of the Authypostaton." In *De Jamblique à Proclus*, 193–237. Entretiens sur l'antiquité classique 21. Edited by O. Reverdin. Vandoeuvres: Fondation Hardt, 1975.

Wiitala, M. O. "Desire and the Good in Plotinus." *British Journal for the History of Philosophy* 21 (2013): 649–66.

Wiles, M. F. "The Nature of the Early Debate about Christ's Human Soul." *Journal of Ecclesiastical History* 16 (1965): 139–51.

Wilson, N. G. "A List of Plato Manuscripts." *Scriptorium* 16, no. 2 (1962): 386–95.

Wolfson, H. A. *The Philosophy of the Church Fathers.* Cambridge, MA: Harvard University Press, 1964.

Contributors

GEORGE DIAMANTOPOULOS studied philosophy (German studies) and theology in Athens (National and Kapodistrian University). He is a doctor of philosophy (Dr. phil.) of the Ludwig Maximilian University of Munich, where he wrote a dissertation on the hermeneutics of Nicetas Stethatos. He is currently a postdoctoral researcher at the Aristotle University of Thessaloniki (School of Social Theology and Christian Culture, Faculty of Theology) with a project on the hermeneutics in Psellos's *Theologica* and *Allegorica*.

MARK EDWARDS completed his doctoral thesis, "Plotinus and the Gnostics," at Corpus Christi College, Oxford, in 1988. He held a junior research fellowship in classics at New College, Oxford, from 1989 to 1993, and since 1993 has been a university lecturer (now associate professor) in the Faculty of Theology (now Theology and Religion) at the University of Oxford. During this period he has held concomitantly the post of tutor in theology at Christ Church, Oxford. Since 2014 he has also held the title professor of early Christian studies. His books include *Neoplatonic Saints* (2000), *Origen against Plato* (2002), *John through the Centuries* (2003), *Constantine and Christendom* (2004), *Culture and Philosophy in the Age of Plotinus* (2006), *Catholicity and Heresy in the Early Church* (2009), *Image, Word and God in the Early Christian Centuries* (2012), *Religions of the Constantinian Empire* (2015), and *Aristotle and Early Christian Thought* (2019).

JOHN F. FINAMORE is the Roger A. Hornsby Professor of the Classics at the University of Iowa, editor of the *International Journal of the Platonic Tradition*, and president of the US Section of the International Society for Neoplatonic Studies. He has published on all aspects of Platonism and is currently translating Proclus's *Republic* commentary with Dirk Baltzly and Graeme Miles. His recent coedited anthologies include *Studies in Hermias' Commentary on Plato's Phaedrus* with Christina Manolea and Sarah Klitenic Wear (Brill), and *Plato in Late Antiquity, the Middle Ages, and Modern Times: Selected Papers from the Seventeenth Annual Conference of the International Society for Neoplatonic Studies* with Mark Nyvlt (Prometheus Trust).

CHRISTIAN FÖRSTEL is curator in charge of the Greek manuscript collections in the Bibliothèque nationale de France, Paris. His research interests include Greek paleography, late antique and Byzantine philosophy, as well as Renaissance Hellenism. He is currently preparing the edition of Ficino's annotations in his manuscript of Plotinus.

STEPHEN GERSH, during an academic career spanning some forty years, has been the author of numerous books concerning late ancient, medieval, and Renaissance Platonism. His most major work is the two-volume *Middle Platonism and Neoplatonism* (1986), and his most recent is the continuing and partially published multivolume edition and translation of Ficino's *Commentary on Plotinus.* Gersh is a graduate of Cambridge University, from which he holds the degree of doctor of letters (Litt. D.). He is a former fellow of Magdalene College, Cambridge, and emeritus professor of medieval studies at the University of Notre Dame, Indiana. He has also held visiting professorships at the University of Washington, Seattle, and the University of Paris–Sorbonne.

LLOYD P. GERSON is a professor of philosophy in the University of Toronto. He is the author of many books and articles on ancient philosophy. His most recent monograph is *Platonism and Naturalism: The Possibility of Philosophy* (2020). He is the editor and co-translator of *Plotinus: The Enneads* (2018) and the editor of the two-volume *The Cambridge History of Philosophy in Late Antiquity* (2010). He is also a member of the board of directors of the *Journal of the History of Philosophy.*

FILIP IVANOVIĆ is an assistant professor at the University of Donja Gorica and director of the Center for Hellenic Studies (Montenegro). He authored a number of books and papers, including the most recent *Desiring the Beautiful: The Erotic-Aesthetic Dimension of Deification in Dionysius the Areopagite and Maximus the Confessor* (2019).

FREDERICK LAURITZEN is a historian at the Scuola Grande di San Marco, Venice. He studied classics at New College, Oxford, and Columbia University, New York. He has published articles on eleventh-century Neoplatonism, as well as the monograph *The Depiction of Character in the Chronographia of Michael Psellos* (2013).

CARL O'BRIEN is a lecturer in the Department of Philosophy, Ruprecht-Karls-Universität Heidelberg. Publications include *The Demiurge in Ancient Thought* (2015), *Seele und Materie im Neuplatonismus/Soul and Matter in Neoplatonism* (coedited with J. Halfwassen and T. Dangel, 2016), *Platonic Love from Antiquity to the Renaissance* (coedited with J. Dillon, forthcoming), a forthcoming translation of selected writings of J. Halfwassen, *Plotinus, Neoplatonism, and the Transcendence of the One,* and numerous articles on Platonism and early Christian philosophy.

ILARIA RAMELLI, FRHISTS, holds two MAs, a PhD, a doctorate h.c., a postdoctorate, and various Habilitations to Ordinarius. She has been professor of Roman history, senior visiting professor of Greek thought at Harvard and Boston Universities, of Church history at Columbia University, of religion at Erfurt MWK, full professor of theology and endowed chair at the Angelicum, and senior fellow at Durham University (twice), at Princeton (2017–), at Sacred Heart University, and at both Corpus Christi and Christ Church in Oxford. She is also a senior member of the Centre for the Study of Platonism at Cambridge University, a Humboldt Forschungspreis fellow at Erfurt MWK, senior fellow at Bonn University (elect), and professor of theology (Durham University, Hon.) and of patristics and Church history (KUL). Recent books include *The Christian Doctrine of Apokatastasis* (2013), *Evagrius' Kephalaia Gnostika* (2015), *The Role of Religion in Shaping Narrative Forms* (2015), *Social Justice and the Legitimacy of Slavery* (2016), *Evagrius, the Cappadocians, and Neoplatonism* (2017), *A Larger Hope?* (2019), *Bardaisan of Edessa* (2009, 2019), *Lovers of the Soul, Lovers of the Body* (coedited, 2021), *Eriugena's Christian Neoplatonism and His Sources* (2021), and *Patterns of Women's Leadership in Ancient Christianity* (coedited, 2021).

DENIS J.-J. ROBICHAUD earned his PhD from Johns Hopkins University and is associate professor of philosophy in Notre Dame's Program of Liberal Studies, Medieval Institute, and Italian Studies. He is a member of the steering committee of Notre Dame's Workshop on Ancient Philosophy and the History of Philosophy Forum. He won the Rome Prize from the American Academy in Rome and a former Yates fellow at the Warburg Institute. He is presently a fellow at Harvard's Villa I Tatti. He has published articles on ancient, medieval, and Renaissance Platonism and Neoplatonism, traditions of ancient philosophy, the philosophy of religion, Renaissance humanism, the history of scholarship, and manuscript studies. The University of Pennsylvania Press published his book *Plato's Persona: Marsilio Ficino, Renaissance Humanism, and Platonic Traditions* in 2018. He is coeditor of *Marsilio Ficino's Cosmology: Sources and Receptions.*

TIMUR SHCHUKIN graduated from Saint Petersburg Institute of Theology and Philosophy (2004) and Saint Petersburg State University (Philological Department) (2008). At present, he is a postgraduate of Herzen State Pedagogical University (Institute of Philosophy; research associate in Sociological Institute of the Russian Academy of Sciences; editorial board member of *ESSE: Studies in Philosophy and Theology* (Saint Petersburg, Russia); editor in chief of *Living Water: St. Petersburg Church Bulletin.*

DIONYSIOS SKLIRIS holds a PhD from the University of Paris IV-Sorbonne with the title "The Term *Tropos* (Mode) in the Thought of Maximus the Confessor." He is currently a teaching fellow at the Theological Department of the Theological Faculty of the University of Athens and at the Greek Open University. His works include *Healing the World from Evil: Plato–Aristotle–Plotinus-Proclus* (2021), *I Am Loved, Therefore I Think: Chapters of Theological Epistemology and Ontology* (2021, in Greek), *God Chose Those Who Are Not: Chapters of Political Theology* (2021, in Greek), *On the Road to Being: Saint Maximus the Confessor's Syn-odical Ontology* (2018), and *Logos-Mode–Telos: A Study in the Thought of Saint Maximus the Confessor* (2018, in Greek). He is also the editor of the volume *Slavoj Žižek and Christianity* (2018).

MARILENA VLAD is a researcher at the Institute for South-East European Studies of the Romanian Academy and invited professor at the University of Bucharest. She translated into Romanian a first part of Damascius's *De principiis* as well as *The Divine Names* by Pseudo-Dionysius the Areopagite. She recently published *Damascius et l'ineffable: Récit de l'impossible discours* (2019).

DENIS WALTER is lecturer at the Institute for Philosophy at the University of Bonn. His research interests are ancient philosophy, with a focus on Plato's *Parmenides*, and medieval Byzantine philosophy, with a focus on the works of Michael Psellos. He is author of the monograph *Michael Psellos:*

Christliche Philosophie in Byzanz (2017) and coeditor of the collected volume *Körperlichkeit in der Philosophie der Spätantike: Corporeità nella filosofia tardoantica* (2020).

SARAH KLITENIC WEAR is a professor of classics at Franciscan University of Steubenville. She is the author of articles and books on Platonism, including *The Teachings of Syrianus on Plato's Timaeus and Parmenides* (2011), *Despoiling the Hellenes: Pseudo-Dionysius and the Athenian School of Platonism* (with John Dillon, 2007), and *Plotinus on Beauty and Reality (Enn. I.6 and V.1): A Greek Reader* (2017). Most recently, she coedited with John Finamore and Christina Manolea *Studies in Hermias' Commentary on Plato's Phaedrus* (2019). She coedits, with Frederick Lauritzen, the book series *Theandrites: Byzantine Philosophy and Christian Neoplatonism* for Franciscan University Press.

Index

The Byzantine Platonists, 284–1453 was designed in Arno Pro with Mr Eaves display type and composed by Kachergis Book Design of Pittsboro, North Carolina. It was printed on 60-pound House Natural Smooth Web and bound by Sheridan Books of Chelsea, Michigan.